A Quick Guide to Working with Primary Sources

This quick guide provides some basic steps for analyzing the documents and visual sources in this book. For more detailed help in working with primary sources, see pp. xxxiv–xxxviii.

Reading and Analyzing a Written Document

The following questions will help you understand and analyze a written document:

- Who wrote the document?
- When and where was it written?
- What type of document is it (for example, a letter to a friend, a political decree, an exposition of a religious teaching)?
- Why was the document written? Under what circumstances was it composed?
- What point of view does it reflect?
- Who was its intended audience?
- What about the document is believable and what is not?
- What can the document tell us about the individual that produced it and the society from which he or she came?

Viewing and Analyzing a Visual Source

These questions will help you to understand and analyze a visual source:

- When and where was the image or artifact made?
- Who made the image or artifact? How was it made?
- Who paid for or commissioned it?
- Where might the image or artifact have originally been displayed or used?
- For what audience(s) was it intended?
- What message(s) is it trying to convey?
- How could it be interpreted differently depending on who viewed or used it?
- What can this image tell us about the individual that produced it and the society from which he or she came?

Ways of the World

A Brief Global History
with Sources

ROBERT W. STRAYER

California State University, Monterey Bay

Bedford/St. Martin's

Boston • New York

For Gina, Nicole, Alisa, and their generation

For Bedford/St. Martin's

Executive Editor for History:
   Mary Dougherty
Director of Development for History:
   Jane Knetzger
Executive Editor for History:
   Tracy Mueller Crowell
Developmental Editor: Kathryn Abbott
Senior Production Editor: Bridget Leahy
Senior Production Supervisor: Joe Ford
Executive Marketing Manager:
   Jenna Bookin Barry
Editorial Assistant: Robin Soule
Production Assistant: Lidia MacDonald-Carr
Copyeditor: Janet Renard
Editorial Consultant: Eric W. Nelson,
   Missouri State University
Text and Cover Design: Joyce Weston
Photo Research: Carole Frohlich, The Visual
   Connection Image Research, Inc.
Indexer: Leoni Z. McVey

Cover Art: Tomb of Sennedjem (Workmen's
   Tomb), Deir el-Medina, Tombs of the
   Nobles, Thebes, Egypt. Detail showing
   reaping wheat in the mythical fields of
   Iaru. Werner Forman/Art Resources, NY.
Frontispiece: Muslim astronomers. University
   Library, Istanbul, Turkey/The Bridgeman
   Art Library
Cartography: Mapping Specialists Limited
Composition: NK Graphics
Printing and Binding: RR Donnelley
   and Sons

President: Joan E. Feinberg
Editorial Director: Denise B. Wydra
Director of Marketing: Karen R. Soeltz
Director of Editing, Design, and Production:
   Susan W. Brown
*Assistant Director of Editing, Design, and
   Production:* Elise S. Kaiser
Managing Editor: Elizabeth M. Schaaf

Library of Congress Control Number: 2010920404

For information, write: Bedford/St. Martin's, 75 Arlington Street, Boston, MA 02116
(617-399-4000)

ISBN-10: 0-312-48916-1   ISBN-13: 978-0-312-48916-8   (combined edition)
ISBN-10: 0-312-48917-X   ISBN-13: 978-0-312-48917-5   (Vol. 1)
ISBN-10: 0-312-48918-8   ISBN-13: 978-0-312-48918-2   (Vol. 2)
ISBN-10: 0-312-64466-3   ISBN-13: 978-0-312-64466-6   (high school edition)

Preface

WAYS OF THE WORLD FIRST APPEARED in September 2008 and was warmly welcomed by students and teachers, who seemed to like its brevity, clarity, and accessibility. Among the responses that the book provoked, however, was the call for a set of primary sources keyed to its narrative. This version of *Ways of the World* addresses that need in what Bedford/St. Martin's calls a "docutext" format. Each chapter narrative is now followed by a group of related documents and, separately, a collection of visual sources, both of which are organized around particular themes or questions from the chapter. Thus this docutext version of *Ways of the World* presents an integrated package of text and sources that offers instructors a wide range of pedagogical possibilities. For students, it provides a "laboratory" experience, enabling them to engage the evidence directly and to draw conclusions from sources—in short to "do history" rather than simply read history.

The history that students encounter in *Ways of the World* is now widely known as world or global history, a rather new and remarkably ambitious field of study that has come of age during my own career in the academy and particularly during the past quarter of a century. Those of us who practice world history, as teachers or textbook authors, are seldom specialists in the particulars of what we study and teach. Rather we are "specialists of the whole," seeking to find the richest, most suggestive, and most meaningful contexts in which to embed those particulars. We look for the big-picture processes and changes that have marked the human journey; we are alert to the possibilities for comparison across cultural boundaries; and we pay special attention to the multiple interactions among human communities. Our task, fundamentally, is to teach contextual thinking. The documents and visual sources presented here frequently add a personal dimension to these big-picture themes by evoking the words and images of particular historical actors who lived, worked, played, suffered, triumphed, and interacted over the many centuries of the human journey.

What's in a Title?

The title of a book should evoke something of its character and outlook. The main title of *Ways of the World* is intended to suggest at least three dimensions of this text.

The first is **diversity** or **variation**, for the "ways of the world," or the ways of being human in the world, have been many and constantly changing. World history was conceived in part to counteract a Eurocentric perspective on the human past, deriving from several centuries of Western dominance on the world stage. This book seeks to embrace the experience of humankind in its vast diversity, while noticing the changing location of particular centers of innovation and wider influence.

Second, the title *Ways of the World* invokes major **panoramas**, **patterns**, or **pathways** in world history, as opposed to highly detailed narratives. Many world history instructors have found that students often feel overwhelmed by the sheer quantity of data that a course in global history can require of them. In the narrative sections of this book, the larger patterns or the "big pictures" of world history appear in the foreground on center stage, while the still plentiful details, data, and facts occupy the background, serving in supporting roles.

A third implication of the book's title lies in a certain **reflective** or **musing quality** of *Ways of the World*, which appears especially in the Big Picture essays that introduce each part of the book and in a Reflections section at the end of each chapter. This dimension of the text is a product of my own growing appreciation that history of any kind, and world history in particular, offers endless raw material for contemplating large questions. Here are some of the issues that are addressed in this fashion:

- How can we tell when one period of history ends and another begins? What marks off the classical era, for example, or the early modern period of world history? Does the twentieth century deserve to be considered a separate period of time?

- In what ways and why do historians and religious believers sometimes rub each other the wrong way?

- How can we, or should we, make moral judgments in the face of the vast ambiguity of most historical phenomena?

- Are there clear "lessons" to be learned from the past? And does history really repeat itself, as so many students seem to believe?

- How can we avoid Eurocentrism when dealing with recent centuries, in which Europeans were in fact increasingly central to the human story?

- How can we retain a sense of surprise, unexpectedness, contingency, or luck in our telling of the human story, particularly when we know the outcomes of those stories?

None of these questions have clear or easy answers, but the opportunity to contemplate them is among the great gifts that the study of history offers to us all.

Integrating Narrative and Sources: The Docutext Approach

The subtitle of this book, *A Brief Global History with Sources*, refers to its docutext format. Following the narrative portion of each chapter are a set of written primary sources and then another set of visual primary sources. Each collection is organized around a particular theme, issue, or question that derives from the chapter narrative. As the title of these features suggests, they enable students to "consider the evidence" and thus begin to understand the craft of historians as well as their conclusions. All of them are thoroughly cross-referenced with the text, are furnished with brief head-notes providing context for the sources, and are accompanied by a series of probing Using the Evidence questions appropriate for in-class discussion and writing assignments.

Many of these Considering the Evidence features are broadly comparative or cross-cultural. For example, the Documents feature for Chapter 5 invites students to consider the nature of the good life and good society in the thinking of Confucius, the *Bhagavad Gita*, Socrates, and Jesus. Likewise the Visual Sources feature for Chapter 15 raises questions about the display of status derived from items acquired in the transregional commerce of the early modern era, with examples from Europe, the Ottoman Empire, colonial Mexico, and the West African kingdom of Dahomey. Other features are regionally focused, providing a more in-depth look at certain elements of specific societies. In Chapter 7, for example, the Documents feature allows students to explore the history of Axum through a series of texts from the early centuries of the Common Era, while the Visual Sources feature of Chapter 22 examines the communist vision of the future in Mao's China via its poster art.

Achieving Coherence

The great virtue of world history lies in its inclusiveness, for it allows us to see the world and to see it whole. But that virtue is also the source of world history's greatest difficulty—telling a coherent story. How can we meaningfully present the planet's many and distinct peoples and their intersections with one another in the confines of a single book or a single term? What prevents that telling from bogging down in the endless detail of various civilizations or cultures, from losing the forest for the trees, from implying that history is just "one damned thing after another"?

Less Can Be More

Ways of the World seeks to cope with that fundamental conundrum of world history—the tension between inclusion and coherence—in several ways. The first is the relative brevity of the narrative and a corresponding selectivity. This means, of course, leaving some things out or treating them more succinctly than some instructors might expect. But the docutext format allows for exploration of particular topics in greater depth via the Documents and Visual Sources features. The positive side of narrative brevity is that the textbook need not overwhelm students or dominate the pedagogy of the course. It allows for more professorial creativity in constructing individual world history courses and in mixing and matching text and sources.

Narrative brevity also encourages a "themes and cases" rather than a "civilization-by-civilization" approach to the global past. Thus most chapters in this book focus on a broad theme, explored on a global or transregional scale: agricultural revolutions in Chapter 2; classical-era empires in Chapter 4; axial-age religions in Chapter 5; long-distance commerce in Chapters 8 and 15; the colonial experience of the long nineteenth century in Chapter 20; the Communist experiment in Chapter 22; twentieth-century globalization in Chapter 24. Docutext features add substantially to the "themes and cases" dimension of the book.

The Three Cs of World History: Change, Comparison, Connection

As a further aid to achieving coherence on a global scale, *Ways of the World* refers repeatedly to what I call the "**three Cs**" of world history. They represent some of the distinctive perspectives of world history as an academic discipline and are introduced more extensively in the prologue.

The first "C" emphasizes large-scale **changes**, both within and especially across major regions of the world. Change, of course, is a central theme in all historical study and serves to challenge "essentialist" descriptions of particular cultures or peoples. Among the macrochanges highlighted in *Ways of the World* are the peopling of the planet in Chapter 1; the emergence of "civilization" in Chapter 3; the rise of universal religions in Chapter 5; the changing shape of the Islamic world in Chapter 11; the breakthrough of industrialization in Chapter 18; the development of European global dominance in Chapters 19 and 20; the rise and fall of world communism in Chapter 22; the acceleration of globalization in Chapter 24.

The second "C" involves frequent **comparison**. It is a technique of integration through juxtaposition, of bringing several regions or cultures into our field of vision at the same time. It encourages reflection both on the common elements of the human experience and on its many variations. Such comparisons are pervasive throughout the book, informing both the chapter narratives and many of the docutext features. We examine the difference, for example, between the Agricultural Revolution in the Eastern and Western Hemispheres in Chapter 2; between the beginnings of Buddhism and the early period of Christianity in Chapter 5; between patriarchy in Athens and in Sparta in Chapter 6; between European and Asian empires of the early modern era in Chapter 14; between the Chinese and the Japanese response to European intrusion in Chapter 19; between postures toward Islam in twentieth-century Turkey and in Iran in Chapter 23; and many more.

The final "C" emphasizes **connections**, networks of communication and exchange that increasingly shaped the character of those societies that participated in them. For world historians, cross-cultural interaction becomes one of the major motors of historical change. Such connections are addressed in nearly every chapter narrative and many docutext features. For example, Chapter 3 explores the clash of the Greeks and the Persians during the classical era; Chapter 8 highlights the long-distance commercial networks that linked the Afro-Eurasian world, while its Visual Sources feature illustrates Central Asia as a cultural crossroads; Chapter 11 focuses attention on the numerous cross-cultural encounters spawned by the spread of Islam; Chapters 14 and 15 explore various facets of the transhemispheric Columbian exchange of the early modern era; Chapter 17 probes the linkages among the Atlantic revolutions of the late eighteenth and early nineteenth centuries, and its Documents feature displays the interplay of the idea of "rights" across the region; Chapter 24 concludes the book with an examination of globalization, highlighting its economic, feminist, religious, and environmental dimensions.

Organizing World History: Chronology, Theme, and Region

Organizing a world history textbook or a world history course is, to put it mildly, a daunting task. How should we divide up the seamless stream of human experience into manageable and accessible pieces, while recognizing always that such divisions are both artificial and to some extent arbitrary? Historians, of course, debate the issue endlessly. In structuring *Ways of the World*, I have drawn on my own sense of "what works" in the classroom, on a personal penchant for organizational clarity, and on established practice in the field. The outcome has been an effort to balance three principles of organization—chronology, theme, and region—in a flexible format that can accommodate a variety of teaching approaches and organizational strategies.

The chronological principle is expressed most clearly in the overall structure of the book, which divides world history into six major periods. Each of these six "parts" begins with a brief **Big Picture essay** that introduces the general patterns of a particular period and raises questions about the problems historians face in dividing up the human past into meaningful chunks of time.

Part One (to 500 B.C.E.) deals in three separate chapters with beginnings—of human migration and social construction in the Paleolithic era, of agriculture, and of civilization. Each of them pursues an important theme on a global scale and illustrates that theme with regional examples treated comparatively.

Part Two, on the classical era (500 B.C.E. to 500 C.E.), likewise employs the thematic principle in exploring the major civilizations of Eurasia (Chinese, Indian, Persian, and Mediterranean), with separate chapters focusing on their empires (Chapter 4), cultural traditions (Chapter 5), and social organization (Chapter 6). This structure represents a departure from conventional practice, which usually treats the classical era on a civilization-by-civilization basis, but it allows for more effective and pointed comparison. These Eurasian chapters are followed by a single chapter (Chapter 7) that examines regionally the classical era in sub-Saharan Africa and the Americas, while asking whether their histories largely follow Eurasian patterns or depart from them.

Part Three embraces the thousand years between 500 and 1500 C.E., often known simply, and not very helpfully, as the "postclassical" era. The Big Picture essay for Part Three spotlights and seeks to explain a certain vagueness in our descriptions of this period of time, pointing out the various distinctive civilizational patterns of that millennium as well as the accelerating interactions among them. The six chapters of Part Three reflect a mix of thematic and regional principles. Chapter 8 focuses topically on commercial networks, while Chapters 9, 10, and 11 deal regionally with the Chinese, Christian, and Islamic worlds respectively. Chapter 12 treats pastoral societies as a broad theme and the Mongols as the most dramatic illustration of their impact on the larger stage of world history. Chapter 13, which bridges the two volumes of the book, presents an around-the-world tour in the fifteenth century, which serves both to conclude Volume 1 and to open Volume 2.

In considering the early modern era (1450–1750), **Part Four** treats each of its three constituent chapters thematically. Chapter 14 compares European and Asian empires; Chapter 15 lays out the major patterns of global commerce and their consequences (trade in spices, silver, furs, and slaves); and Chapter 16 focuses on cultural patterns, including the globalization of Christianity and the rise of modern science.

Part Five takes up the era of maximum European influence in the world, from 1750 to 1914. Here the Big Picture essay probes how we might avoid Eurocentrism, while describing a period of time in which Europeans were in fact increasingly central to the global story. Part Five, which charts the emergence of a distinctively modern society in Europe, devotes separate chapters to the Atlantic revolutions (Chapter 17) and the Industrial Revolution (Chapter 18). Then it turns to the growing impact of those societies on the rest of humankind—on China, the Ottoman Empire, and Japan, which are treated comparatively in Chapter 19; and on the world of formal colonies in Chapter 20.

The most recent century (1914–2010), which is treated in **Part Six**, is perhaps the most problematic for world historians, given the abundance of data and the absence of time to sort out what is fundamental and what is peripheral. The Big Picture essay that opens Part Six explores this difficulty, asking whether that century deserves the status of a separate period in the human story. Chapters 21, 22, and 23 examine respectively three major regions of the world in that century—the Western or industrial world, the communist world, and the third or developing world—while Chapter 24 explores the multiple processes of globalization, which have both linked and divided the human community in new ways.

Promoting Active Learning

As all instructors know, students can often "do the assignment" or read the required chapter and yet have nearly no understanding of it when they come to class. The problem, frequently, is passive studying—a quick once-over, perhaps some highlighting of the text—but little sustained involvement with the material. A central pedagogical problem in all teaching at every level is how to encourage more active, engaged styles of learning. How can we push students to articulate in their own words the major ideas of a particular chapter or section of the text? How can we encourage them to recognize arguments, even in a textbook, and to identify and evaluate the evidence on which those arguments are based? Active learning seeks to enable students to manipulate the information of the book, using its ideas and data to answer questions, to make comparisons, to draw conclusions, to criticize assumptions, and to infer implications that are not explicitly disclosed in the book itself. This ability to use and rearrange the material of a text, not simply to recall it, lies at the heart of active college-level learning.

This docutext version of *Ways of the World* incorporates a wealth of opportunities to promote active learning, to assist students in reading the book, and to generate livelier classroom exchanges.

- Chief among those opportunities are the docutext **Considering the Evidence features**. Both written and visual sources call for interpretation and imagination, an understanding of context, and consideration of point of view. Working with those sources virtually requires active engagement. A series of prompts for each document or image and the integrative Using the Evidence questions at the end of every feature serve to guide that engagement.

- The part-opening **Big Picture essays** preview for students what follows in the subsequent chapters. In doing so, they provide a larger context for those chapters; they enable students to make comparisons with greater ease; they facilitate making connections across several chapters; and they raise questions about periodization.

- Each Big Picture essay is followed by a **Landmarks timeline**, providing a chronological overview of what follows in that particular part of the book. Each of these Landmarks is organized in a series of parallel regional timelines, allowing students to see at a glance significant developments in various regions of the world during the same time.

- A **contemporary vignette** opens each chapter with a story that links the past and the present. Chapter 1, for example, presents Gudo Mahiya, a twenty-first-century member of a gathering and hunting society in Tanzania, who rejects an opportunity to become a settled farmer or herder. Chapter 15, which describes the Atlantic slave trade, opens with a brief account of an African American woman who in 2002 visits what had been a slave port in Ghana. These vignettes seek to show the continuing resonance of the past in the lives of contemporary people.

- To encourage active learning explicitly, a series of **questions in the margins** provides students with "something to look for" as they read particular sections. Those notations also indicate what kind of question is being asked—about change, comparison, or connection, for example.

- The **Reflections** section at the end of each chapter raises provocative, sometimes quasi-philosophical questions about the craft of the historian and the unfolding of the human story. It provides grist for the mill of vigorous class discussions and personal pondering.

- To further foster active learning, the **Second Thoughts** section at the end of each chapter provides a list of particulars (people, places, events, processes, concepts) under the heading **"What's the Significance?"** inviting students to check their grasp of that chapter's material. The next part of the Second

Thoughts section is a set of **Big Picture Questions**. Unlike the marginal questions, which are keyed specifically to the adjacent material, these Big Picture Questions are not directly addressed in the text. Instead, they provide opportunities for integration, comparison, analysis, and sometimes speculation. Such questions might well become the basis for engaging writing assignments, class discussions, or exam items. Finally, a limited **list of suggested readings**—books, articles, and Web sites-invites further exploration of the material in the chapter.

- **Snapshots** appear in every chapter and present succinct glimpses of particular themes, regions, or time periods, adding some trees to the forest of world history.

- As is always true of books published by Bedford/St. Martin's, a **rich program of maps and images** accompanies the narrative. Because history and geography are so closely related, more than 100 maps have been included in the two volumes of the book. About 150 images, most of them contemporary to the times and places they illustrate, punctuate the narrative text, while dozens of others in the various Visual Sources features provide multiple occasions for students to assess visual sources as historical evidence.

Supplements

A comprehensive collection of print and electronic resources for students and instructors accompanies this book. Developed with my collaboration, they are designed to provide a host of practical learning and teaching aids. You can learn more about the accompanying materials by visiting bedfordstmartins.com/strayersources/catalog.

For Students

Ways of the World: A Brief Global History with Sources **e-Book.** This easy-to-use, searchable e-book integrates the narrative, maps, and images from *Ways of the World* with resources from the Online Study Guide, making it a dynamic learning and study tool. Instructors can share annotations as well as add documents, images, and other materials to customize the text. The e-book can be packaged free with the print text or purchased stand-alone at a discount.

FREE **Student Center at bedfordstmartins.com/strayer.** The Student Center is a free resource to help students master themes and information presented in the textbook and improve their historical skills. **The Online Study Guide** provides students with self-review quizzes and activities for each chapter, including a multiple-choice self-test that focuses on important conceptual ideas; an identification quiz that helps students remember key people, places, and events; a flashcard activity that tests students' knowledge of key terms; and two interactive map activities intended to strengthen students' geography skills. Instructors can monitor students' progress through an online Quiz Gradebook or receive e-mail updates. The Student Center also features **History Research and Writing Help**, which includes *History Research and Reference Sources*, with links to history-related databases, indexes, and journals, plus contact information for state, provincial, local, and professional history organizations; *More Sources and How to Format a History Paper*, with clear advice on how to integrate primary and secondary sources into research papers, how to cite sources correctly, and how to format in MLA, APA, *Chicago*, or CBE style; *Build a Bibliography*, a simple but powerful Web-based tool that addresses the process of collecting sources and generates bibliographies in four commonly used documentation styles; and *Tips on Avoiding Plagiarism*, an online tutorial that reviews the consequences of plagiarism and explains what sources to acknowledge, how to keep good notes, how to organize research, and how to integrate sources appropriately and includes exercises to help students practice integrating sources and recognize acceptable summaries.

For Instructors

HistoryClass for *Ways of the World: A Brief Global History with Sources.* Bedford/St. Martin's online learning space for history gives you the right tools and the rich content to create your course, your way. An interactive e-book enables you to easily assign relevant textbook sections. Additional primary sources supplement the textbook and provide more options for class discussion and assignments. Other resources include guidelines for analyzing primary materials, avoiding plagiarism, and citing sources. Access to the acclaimed content library Make History provides unlimited access to thousands of maps, images, documents, and Web links. Online Study Guide content offers a range of activities to help students assess their progress, study more effectively, and improve their critical thinking skills. Customize the provided content and mix in your own with ease—everything in HistoryClass is integrated to work together in the same space.

Instructor's Resource Manual at bedfordstmartins.com/strayersources/ catalog. This extensive manual by Eric W. Nelson (Missouri State University) and Phyllis G. Jestice (University of Southern Mississippi) offers both experienced and first-time instructors tools for presenting the book's material in exciting and engaging ways. Introductory essays cover teaching with the docutext and analyzing primary written and visual sources. Also included are chapter learning objectives; annotated chapter outlines; lecture strategies; tips for helping students with common misconceptions and difficult topics; a list of key terms and definitions; answer guidelines for in-text chapter questions; and suggestions for in-class activities (including using film, video, and literature), ways to start discussions, topics for debate, and analyzing primary sources. For the Documents and Visual Sources features in each textbook chapter, the instructor's manual includes answers to headnote questions and to the Considering the Evidence comparative questions. The manual also provides suggestions for in-class and out-of-class activities for the Documents and Visual Sources features. Each chapter concludes with a guide to all the chapter-specific supplements available with *Ways of the World*. A guide for first-time teaching assistants, two sample syllabi, a list of useful books for the first-time world history professor, and a list of books that form the basis of a world history reference library are also included.

Instructor's Resource CD-ROM. This disc provides instructors with ready-made and customizable PowerPoint multimedia presentations built around chapter outlines, maps, figures, and all images from the docutext, plus jpeg versions of these maps, figures, and images. Also included are chapter questions formatted in PowerPoint and MS Word for use with i<clicker, a classroom response system, and blank outline maps in PDF format. Many of these resources are also available for download at bedfordstmartins.com/strayersources/catalog.

Computerized Test Bank. Written by Eric W. Nelson (Missouri State University) and Phyllis G. Jestice (University of Southern Mississippi), the test bank provides more than thirty exercises per chapter, including multiple-choice, fill-in-the-blank, short-answer, and full-length essay questions. The answer key includes textbook page numbers, correct answers, and essay outlines. Instructors can customize quizzes, add or edit both questions and answers, and export questions and answers to a variety of formats, including WebCT and Blackboard.

FREE Student Center with Instructor Resources at bedfordstmartins.com/strayer. The Student Center for *Ways of the World* gathers not only all the electronic resources for students but also those for instructors in one easy-to-use site. Instructors can keep track of their students' progress in the Online Study Guide by using the Quiz Gradebook and can also gain access to lecture, assignment, and research materials; PowerPoint chapter outlines and images; and the digital libraries at Make History.

Make History at bedfordstmartins.com/makehistory. Free and open to instructors and students, Make History combines the best Web resources with hundreds of maps and images, to make finding source material simple. Users can browse the collection of thousands of resources by course or by topic, date, and type. Each item has been carefully chosen and helpfully annotated. Instructors can also create collections to share with students or for use in lectures and presentations.

Content for Course Management Systems. A variety of student and instructor resources developed for this textbook is ready for use in course management systems such as Blackboard, WebCT, and other platforms. This e-content includes the book's Online Study Guide, online instructor's resources, and the book's test bank.

Videos and Multimedia. A wide assortment of videos and multimedia CD-ROMs on various topics in world history is available to qualified adopters. Contact your Bedford/St. Martin's representative for more information.

Packaging Opportunities

In addition to using book-specific supplements, instructors have numerous options for packaging other Bedford/St. Martin's titles with *Ways of the World* for free or at a discount. Visit bedfordstmartins.com/strayer/catalog for more information.

Rand McNally Historical Atlas of the World. This collection of almost seventy full-color maps illustrates the eras and civilizations in world history from the emergence of human societies to the present. *Available for $3.00 when packaged with the text.*

The Bedford Glossary for World History. This handy supplement for the survey course gives students historically contextualized definitions for hundreds of terms—from *abolitionism* to *Zoroastrianism*—that students will encounter in lectures, reading, and exams. *Free when packaged with the text.*

World History Matters: A Student Guide to World History Online. Based on the popular World History Matters Web site produced by the Center for History and New Media, this unique resource, edited by Kristin Lehner (The Johns Hopkins University), Kelly Schrum (George Mason University), and T. Mills Kelly (George Mason University), combines reviews of 150 of the most useful and reliable world history Web sites with an introduction that guides students in locating, evaluating, and correctly citing online sources. *Free when packaged with the text.*

The Bedford Series in History and Culture. More than 100 titles in this highly praised series combine first-rate scholarship, historical narrative, and important primary documents for undergraduate courses. Each book is brief, inexpensive, and focused on a specific topic or period. *Package discounts are available.*

Trade Books. Titles published by sister companies Farrar, Straus and Giroux; Henry Holt and Company; Hill and Wang; Picador; St. Martin's Press; and Palgrave Macmillan are *available at a 50 percent discount* when packaged with Bedford/St. Martin's textbooks. For more information, visit bedfordstmartins.com/tradeup.

"It Takes a Village"

In any enterprise of significance, "it takes a village," as they say. Bringing *Ways of the World* to life, it seems, has occupied the energies of several villages.

The largest of these villages consists of those many people who read the manuscript at various stages, and commented on it, sometimes at great length. I continue to be surprised at the power of this kind of collaboration. Frequently, passages I had regarded as polished to a gleaming perfection benefited greatly from the collective wisdom and experience of these thoughtful reviewers. Reviewers in the early phases of this project provided detailed and invaluable advice on the Documents and Visual

Sources features for this docutext. Reviewers commissioned by Bedford/St. Martin's are listed here in alphabetical order, with my great thanks:

Sanjam Ahluwalia, *Northern Arizona University*

Abel Alves, *Ball State University*

Cynthia Bisson, *Belmont University*

Deborah Buffton, *University of Wisconsin–La Crosse*

Brian D. Bunk, *University of Massachusetts–Amherst*

Allen Dieterich-Ward, *Shippensburg University*

Jonathan Dresner, *Pittsburg State University*

Deborah Gerish, *Emporia State University*

Nicholas Germana, *Keene State College*

Terrell Goddard, *Northwest Vista College*

L. Dana Goodrich, *Northwest Vista College*

Andrew Goss, *University of New Orleans*

Candace Gregory-Abbott, *California State University–Sacramento*

Jeanne Harrie, *California State University–Bakersfield*

Stephen Hernon, *Notre Dame Academy (NY)*

Marianne Holdzkom, *Southern Polytechnic State University*

Bryan Jack, *Winston–Salem State University*

Theresa Jordan, *Washington State University*

Jared Brent Krebsbach, *University of Memphis*

John LaValle, *Western New Mexico University*

Otto W. Mandahl Jr., *Skagit Valley College*

Kathryn Mapstone, *Bunker Hill Community College*

John Maunu, *Grosse Ile High School*

Mario D. Mazzarella, *Christopher Newport University*

Mark W. McLeod, *University of Delaware*

Eben Miller, *Southern Maine Community College*

Theodore A. Nitz, *Gonzaga University*

Kenneth Osgood, *Florida Atlantic University*

John Pinheiro, *Aquinas College*

Anthony R. Santoro, *Christopher Newport University*

Alyssa Goldstein Sepinwall, *California State University–San Marcos*

David Simonelli, *Youngstown State University*

Helene Sinnreich, *Youngstown State University*

Steven Stofferahn, *Indiana State University*

Lisa Tran, *California State University–Fullerton*

Wendy Turner, *Augusta State University*

Elaine C. P. Turney, *University of Texas–San Antonio*

Michael Vann, *California State University–Sacramento*

Kurt J. Wertmuller, *Azusa Pacific University*

Nathaniel P. Weston, *Seattle Central Community College*

James Wood, *North Carolina A&T State University*.

Others in the village of reviewers have been friends, family, and colleagues who graciously agreed to read portions of the manuscript and offer helpful counsel: Kabir Helminski, James Horn, Elisabeth Jay, David Northrup, Lynn Parsons, Katherine Poethig, Kevin Reilly, and Julie Shackford–Bradley.

The "Bedford village" has been a second community supporting this enterprise and the one most directly responsible for the book's appearance in print. It would be difficult for any author to imagine a more encouraging and professional publishing team. Developmental editor Kathryn Abbott, herself an experienced professor of history, has been my primary point of contact with the Bedford village as this docutext version of *Ways of the World* unfolded. She has helped to conceptualize the entire project, masterfully summarized and analyzed the numerous reviews of the manuscript, added her own thoughtful suggestions to the mix, and generally kept the project on track—all with grace and courtesy. In a similar role, Jim Strandberg guided the development of the original text with the sensitivity of a fine historian as well as the skill of an outstanding editor. Eric Nelson of Missouri State University has served as a general consultant for the docutext, as well as the co-author of the fine instructor's manual that accompanies the book. A number of the ideas for Considering the Evidence features came from him, and his careful reading of all the features in draft form was extremely helpful. To all of these close collaborators, I acknowledge a debt of gratitude that I am unable to adequately repay.

Publisher Mary Dougherty first broached the idea of my writing a world history text for Bedford and later surprised me with the suggestion for a docutext version of the book. With a manner as lovely as it is professional, she has provided overall editorial leadership and a calming balm to authorial anxieties. More recently these tasks have passed to executive editor Traci Mueller, who has undertaken them with a similar combination of kindness and competence. Jane Knetzger, director of development, has overseen the project from its beginning, bore my many questions with forbearance, and, even better, provided timely answers. Company president Joan Feinberg has, to my surprise and delight, periodically kept her own experienced hand in this pot, while executive editor Beth Welch, though fully engaged in her own projects, has served as counselor from the sidelines. Photo researcher Carole Frohlich identified and acquired the many images that grace *Ways of the World: A Brief Global History with Sources* and did so with amazing efficiency and courtesy. Working with her has been an aesthetic education for me and a personal delight.

Operating more behind the scenes in the Bedford village, a series of highly competent and always supportive people have shepherded this book along its way. Lynn Sternberger and Robin Soule provided invaluable assistance in handling the manuscript, contacting reviewers, and keeping on top of the endless details that such an enterprise demands. Bridget Leahy served as project editor during the book's production and, often under considerable pressure, did so with both grace and efficiency. Copy editor Janet Renard polished the prose and sorted out my inconsistent usages with a seasoned and perceptive eye.

Jenna Bookin Barry and Sally Constable have overseen the marketing process, while history specialist John Hunger and a cadre of humanities specialists and sales representatives have introduced the book to the academic world. Jack Cashman supervised the development of ancillary materials to support the book, and Donna Dennison ably coordinated research for the lovely covers that mark *Ways of the World*.

Yet another "village" that contributed much to *Ways of the World* consists in that group of distinguished scholars and teachers who worked with me on an earlier world history text, *The Making of the Modern World*, published by St. Martin's Press (1988, 1995). They include Sandria Freitag, Edwin Hirschmann, Donald Holsinger, James Horn, Robert Marks, Joe Moore, Lynn Parsons, and Robert Smith. That collective effort resembled participation in an extended seminar, from which I benefited immensely. Their ideas and insights have shaped my own understanding of world history in many ways and greatly enriched *Ways of the World*.

A final and much smaller community sustained this project and its author. It is that most intimate of villages that we know as a marriage. Here I pay wholly inadequate tribute to its other member, my wife, Suzanne Sturn. She knows how I feel, and no one else needs to.

To all my fellow villagers, I offer deep thanks for perhaps the richest intellectual experience of my professional life. I am grateful beyond measure.

Robert Strayer
La Selva Beach, California

Brief Contents

Contents

7. Classical Era Variations: Africa and the Americas, 500 B.C.E.–1200 C.E. *281*

13. The Worlds of the Fifteenth Century   *569*

Maps

Special Features

Landmarks

Snapshots

Working with Primary Sources

Introduction

Historians interpret the past by examining what they refer to as "primary" or "original" sources—documents, images, or objects produced by the very people we are studying and at the time of or soon after the events that they describe or depict. These sources—the "raw material" of the historian's craft—can take many forms: recorded versions of oral traditions, handed down over many centuries; an endless variety of written materials; images and artifacts such as paintings and pottery. Such sources are precious windows into the past. Their survival in large part determines what history can be recovered and what is forever lost. For instance, only the chance survival of the well-preserved agricultural settlement at Çatalhüyük that is among the subjects of Chapter 2's Visual Sources feature allows us to examine what may be the first surviving map in human history.

Using primary sources effectively is no easy task. Unlike textbooks, which are written explicitly for twenty-first-century students, the sources that historians work with were not aimed at you. They were produced in circumstances and with cultural assumptions that are often quite unfamiliar to contemporary readers. And so they require effort: critical reading and observation, systematic analysis, and historical imagination. Working with them is like listening in on conversations from the past, eavesdropping, as it were, on our ancestors. Each source potentially provides a valuable glimpse into the past, but all sources must be analyzed carefully because, like ourselves, our ancestors' understandings of their own lives and time were subject to distortions, fabrications, misunderstandings, and ambiguity.

Working with Written Documents

Written documents are the most common type of primary source that historians use. Typical written sources include personal records, such as diaries, memoirs, business account books, and private correspondence; and public records, including sacred texts, autobiographies, travelers' accounts, newspaper articles, legislation and law codes, court rulings, and wills. Indeed, nearly every written record is potentially a useful primary source depending on the questions that historians are trying to answer. Usually historians are able to draw stronger conclusions when they can locate and examine sources on the same topic from a number of different perspectives. For example, in the Documents feature of Chapter 15, the Atlantic slave trade is explored from the perspective of a slave, a European slave trader, and several African rulers, building up a more complex picture of the trade than any one of these documents could convey on its own. However, even a single source, when analyzed effectively, can provide a window into the past.

Reading a Document

Reading a document requires careful analysis and an understanding of the context in which the document was produced. The following questions provide the basis for understanding and analyzing any primary document:

- Who wrote the document?

- When and where was it written?

- What type of document is it (for example, a letter to a friend, a political decree, an exposition of a religious teaching)?

- Why was the document written? Under what circumstances was it composed? What point of view does it reflect? What other views or opinions is the document arguing against?

- Who was its intended audience?

- What about the document is believable, and what is not?

- What might historians learn from this document?

- What can the document tell us about the individual who produced it and the society from which he or she came from?

Many documents do not answer the first three questions directly. In *Ways of the World: A Brief Global History with Sources*, questions that cannot be answered directly are addressed in the introductory headnote to the document. These headnotes may help you to establish a context for understanding the document and to identify its point of view or potential biases and the larger discourse of which it is a part.

Once these three basic questions are answered, a historian is then likely to consider the next two questions, which often shape what is written and how ideas are presented—why the document was written and who the intended audience was. The document itself and sometimes its headnote will provide information essential for answering these questions. Inspiration and intention are crucial factors that shape the form and content of a source. For instance, one might examine a document differently depending on whether it was intended for a private or a public readership or whether it was intended to be read by a small elite or a wider audience.

Finally, through both establishing the context in which the document was written and carefully reading the document, historians seek to come to some conclusions about the document by asking whether the document is believable, in what ways it sheds light on the past, and what the document tells us about the person who produced it and the time period in which it was generated. In answering these more complex questions, historical imagination is essential. Your imagination, informed by knowledge of the context, enables you to read the document through the eyes of its author and its audience. How might this document have been understood at the time it was written? But in using your imagination, you must take care not to read into the documents your own assumptions and understandings. It is a delicate balance, a kind of dance that historians constantly undertake. Even documents that contain material that historians find unbelievable can be useful, for we seek not only to know the "truth" about what happened in the past but also to grasp the world as our ancestors understood it. Historians sometimes even speak about reading documents "against the grain," seeking understandings that authors certainly did not intend to convey. For example, the Law Code of Hammurabi in Chapter 3's Documents feature depicts an impressive system of justice in ancient Mesopotamia, but it can also be read as an account of the numerous problems or conflicts that that society had to confront.

Reading Documents Together

While each document must be read and understood individually, historians typically draw their strongest conclusions when they analyze a number of documents together. The essays in the Documents features in *Ways of the World* are designed to explore sets of primary sources that address a central theme of the chapter and frequently include several related documents. When considered together, these sources from different perspectives allow the historian to understand the issue or event more fully. A good example of this approach can be found in the Documents feature for Chapter 11, which explores the emergence of Islam through both holy texts such as the Quran and later interpretations of these texts by Sharia legal scholars and Sufi mystics.

The broad theme and approach introduced at the opening of each essay is further defined by the Using the Evidence questions at its conclusion. For instance, Chapter 13's Documents feature, "The Aztecs and Incas through Spanish Eyes," explores the advantages and disadvantages of using sources written by conquerors to reconstruct conquered societies that left few written records of their own.

Working with Visual Sources

Artifacts that derive from the material culture of the past, religious icons or paintings that add to our understanding of belief systems, a family portrait that provides insight into presentations of self in a particular time and place, a building whose layout reveals how power and authority were displayed in a specific empire—all of these visual sources represent another category of primary sources that historians can use to re-create and understand the past. However, visual evidence can be more difficult to interpret than written documents because most people are not trained in visual analysis. Furthermore, it may be more difficult to discern what meanings animated the creators of particular images or artifacts and what understandings they conveyed to those who viewed or used them.

To use visual sources, we must be able to see these pieces of evidence through the eyes of the societies that produced them and to decode the symbols and other features that imbue these visual sources with meaning. The values of past cultures are often far removed from our own; thus the symbols in these images and artifacts are often unfamiliar to our eyes. Nevertheless, interpreting visual sources effectively can provide insights not offered by written documents. Indeed, for some preliterate societies, archeological and artistic evidence is all that remains of their history.

Analyzing an Image or Artifact

Just as with written documents, context is crucial for analyzing visual evidence. Context provides critical information needed to see the visual source through the eyes of its creator and of those for whom it was created. Sometimes the image or artifact will provide this information, but more often in *Ways of the World: A Brief Global History with Sources*, the Visual Sources essay will provide essential context for your interpretation, as in Chapter 16's Visual Sources feature, where the specific contexts in which Christian images were created are critical to their interpretation and analysis.

Once again, a set of fundamental questions, similar to those you would ask a written document, will help you understand and analyze a visual source:

- When and where was the image or artifact made?
- Who made the image or artifact? How was it made?
- Who paid for or commissioned it?
- Where might the image or artifact have originally been displayed or used?
- Where is it now, and how did it get there?
- For what audience(s) was it intended?
- What message(s) is it trying to convey?
- How could it be interpreted differently depending on who viewed or used it?
- What are the meanings of the symbols or other abstract features in the visual source?

While these questions do not always have a single, clear answer, being aware of the possibilities will shape your examination of the source.

Once you have established the context in which the piece of visual evidence was produced, you should then focus on a careful examination of the source itself, asking the following questions:

- If the source is an image, who or what is depicted?
- What information can be gleaned from the positioning of figures, their clothing, hairstyles, and other visual cues?
- What activities are depicted?
- If it is a specifically religious image, what is depicted, and what likely purpose did the image serve?

- If it is an artifact, what function did it serve?
- What can the image tell us about the society that produced it and the time period in which it was created?

Addressing this question can take a historian down many different lines of inquiry. Depending on the visual sources under examination, additional questions arise, such as the following:

- What types of technology or techniques were used to produce the visual source?
- What was the relationship between those who made the visual source and those who used or viewed it?

Considering Visual Evidence Collectively

As with written documents, each piece of visual evidence must be examined and understood in its own right, although historians draw their strongest conclusions when they analyze a number of visual sources together rather than relying on a single source. The Visual Sources essays in *Ways of the World* explore sets of visual sources that address a central theme in the chapter and frequently include several related images that, when considered together, allow the historian to become aware of how multiple perspectives on a single topic can enhance understanding. Moreover, these essays often explore the strengths and weaknesses of a type of visual source for answering questions posed by historians.

The broad theme and approach are introduced at the opening of each essay and are further defined by the Using the Evidence questions at its conclusion. For instance, the Visual Sources feature for Chapter 13, "Sacred Places in the World of the Fifteenth Century," explores the intersections between sacred sites and political authority in fifteenth-century Africa and Eurasia. While each source considered individually speaks to a specific region and has distinctive characteristics, collectively the sources show that these sorts of sites across Africa and Eurasia were frequently set apart from the profane or ordinary world and were linked to a wider sacred geography.

Finally, as you begin to explore the Documents and Visual Sources features in *Ways of the World*, you might think of the experience as a kind of "history laboratory." In working with these materials, you are "doing history," much like lab experiments in chemistry courses represent "doing science." Furthermore, you will probably recognize connections between particular documents and visual sources. When that happens, the work of "doing history" has truly begun, as most historians use visual sources in conjunction with written documents to create an even more complete picture of the past. Enjoy!

Prologue

From Cosmic History to Human History

IN THE BEGINNING, ACCORDING TO THE NAVAHO, the world was created by Holy People, who had long lived underground and were forced to the surface by a great flood, from which they escaped through a hollow reed. First Man and First Woman were later formed from ears of white and yellow corn. To some of the ancient Greeks, an original Cosmic Egg, floating on a formless mixture of air, water, and matter, gave birth to the deities of Earth and Sky, who then created the earth and all its living creatures, as well as the sun, moon, and stars. For the Hebrews of biblical times, God brought order out of a primordial chaos, creating light and darkness, the earth, and all its living creatures. Pronouncing the creation good, God then made the first humans, placing them in the Garden of Eden, where they soon encountered temptation and choice in the form of a serpent.

These are among the multitude of stories, or myths of origin, that seek to answer that fundamentally human question: what happened in the beginning? Such stories seek to anchor particular societies in a larger context, providing their people with a sense of place, purpose, and belonging. Modern scholars, like earlier tellers of creation stories, also seek to puzzle out the beginnings of the cosmos, of the earth, of life, and of humankind. Unlike myths of origin, though, modern creation stories rely largely on those fields of study that emerged from the Scientific Revolution of the sixteenth century and later—astronomy, physics, geology, biology. Such accounts claim to be truer and more certain, at least in a literal sense, for they can be checked and verified rather than simply accepted and believed. They are, however, stronger on *how* things began than on *why*. Although they provide a more factually detailed account of beginnings, they may have less to offer about the meaning of it all. Therefore, many people in the modern world have tried hard to reconcile scientifically derived understandings of "in the beginning" with the meaning-based accounts contained in long-standing religious traditions.

The History of the Universe

World historians, although largely focused on the unfolding of all things human, have recently begun to situate that remarkable story in the larger contexts of both cosmic history and planetary history. The most inclusive of these modern frameworks

Snapshot The History of the Universe as a Cosmic Calendar[1]

Big bang	January 1	13.7 billion years ago
Stars and galaxies begin to form	End of January/ mid-February	12 billion years ago
Milky Way galaxy forms	March/early April	10 billion years ago
Origin of the solar system	September 9	4.7 billion years ago
Formation of the earth	September 15	4.5 billion years ago
Earliest life on earth	Late September/ early October	4 billion years ago
Oxygen forms on earth	December 1	1.3 billion years ago
First worms	December 16	658 million years ago
First fish, first vertebrates	December 19	534 million years ago
First reptiles, first trees	December 23	370 million years ago
Age of dinosaurs	December 24–28	329–164 million years ago
First humanlike creatures	December 31 (late evening)	2.7 million years ago
First agriculture	December 31: 11:59:35	12,000 years ago
Birth of the Buddha/ Greek civilization	December 31: 11:59:55	2,500 years ago
Birth of Jesus	December 31: 11:59:56	2,000 years ago
Aztec and Inca empires	December 31: 11:59:59	500 years ago

■ Change

What have been the major turning points in the prehuman phases of "big history"?

is sometimes called "big history." It is really the "history of everything" from the big bang to the present, and it extends over the enormous, almost unimaginable timescale of some 13.7 billion years, the current rough estimate of the age of the universe.[2]

To make this vast expanse of time even remotely comprehensible, some scholars have depicted the history of the cosmos as if it were a single calendar year (see the Snapshot). On that cosmic calendar, most of the action took place in the first few milliseconds of January 1. As astronomers, physicists, and chemists tell it, the universe that we know began in an eruption of inconceivable power and heat. Out of that explosion of creation emerged matter, energy, gravity, electromagnetism, and the "strong" and "weak" forces that govern the behavior of atomic nuclei. As gravity pulled the rapidly expanding cosmic gases into increasingly dense masses, stars formed, with the first ones lighting up around 1 to 2 billion years after the big bang, or the end of January to mid-February on the cosmic calendar.

Hundreds of billions of stars followed, each with its own history, though following common patterns. They emerge, flourish for a time, and then collapse and die, and in doing so they sometimes generate supernova, black holes, and pulsars—phenomena at least as fantastic as the most exotic of earlier creation stories. Within the stars, enormous nuclear reactions gave rise to the elements that are reflected in the periodic table known to all students of chemistry. Over eons, these stars came together in galaxies, such as our own Milky Way, which probably emerged in March or early April, and in even larger structures called groups, clusters, and superclusters. Adding to the strangeness of our picture of the cosmos is the recent and controversial notion that perhaps 90 percent or more of the total mass of the universe is invisible to us, consisting of a mysterious and mathematically predicted substance known to scholars only as "dark matter."

The contemplation of cosmic history has prompted profound religious or philosophical questions about the meaning of human life. For some, it has engendered a sense of great insignificance in the face of cosmic vastness. In disputing the earth- and human-centered view of the Catholic Church, Voltaire, an eighteenth-century French thinker, wrote: "This little globe, nothing more than a point, rolls in space like so many other globes; we are lost in this immensity."[3] Nonetheless, human awareness of the mystery of this immeasurable universe renders us unique and generates for many people feelings of awe and humility that are almost religious. As tiny but knowing observers of this majestic cosmos, we have found ourselves living in a grander home than ever we knew before.

The History of a Planet

For most of us, one star, our own sun, is far more important than all the others, despite its quite ordinary standing among the billions of stars in the universe and its somewhat remote location on the outer edge of the Milky Way galaxy. Circling that star are a series of planets, formed of leftover materials from the sun's birth. One of those planets, the third from the sun and the fifth largest, is home to all of us. Human history—our history—takes place not only on the earth but also as part of the planet's history.

That history began with the emergence of the entire solar system about two-thirds of the way through cosmic history, some 4.7 billion years ago, or early September on the cosmic calendar. Geologists have learned a great deal about the history of the earth—the formation of its rocks and atmosphere, the movement of its continents, the collision of the tectonic plates that make up its crust, and the constantly changing landscape as mountains formed, volcanoes erupted, and erosion transformed the surface of the planet. All of this has been happening for more than 4 billion years and continues still.

The most remarkable feature of the earth's history—and so far as we know unrepeated elsewhere—was the emergence of life from the chemical soup of the early planet. It happened rather quickly, only about 600 million years after the earth itself took shape, or late September on the cosmic calendar. Then for some 3 billion years, life remained at the level of microscopic single-celled organisms. According to biologists, the many species of larger multicelled creatures—all of the flowers, shrubs, and trees as well as all of the animals of land, sea, and air—have evolved in an explosive proliferation of life-forms, punctuated by massive die-offs as well, over the past 600 million years, or since mid-December on the cosmic calendar.

Each of these species has also had a history as its members struggled to find resources, cope with changing environments, and deal with competitors. The history of dinosaurs, for example, from their rise to their extinction, occupied about 165 million years, or about five days in late December on the cosmic calendar. Ego-centric creatures that we are, however, human beings have usually focused their history books and history courses entirely on a single species—our own, *Homo sapiens*, humankind. On the cosmic calendar, *Homo sapiens* is an upstart primate whose entire history occurred in the last few minutes of December 31. Almost all of what we normally study in history courses—agriculture, writing, civilizations, empires, industrialization—took place in the very last minute of that cosmic year. The entire history of the United States occurred in the last second.

Yet during that brief time, humankind has had a career more remarkable and arguably more consequential for the planet than any other species. At the heart of human uniqueness lies our amazing capacity for accumulating knowledge and skills. Other animals learn, of course, but they learn the same things over and over again. Twenty-first-century chimpanzees in the wild master the same skills as their ancestors did a million years ago, but the exceptional communication abilities provided by human language allow us to learn from one another, to express that learning in abstract symbols, and then to pass it on, cumulatively, to future generations. Thus we have moved from stone-tipped spears to nuclear weapons, from "talking drums" to the Internet, from grass huts to the Taj Mahal and Notre Dame cathedral.

This extraordinary ability has translated into a human impact on the earth that is unprecedented among all living species.[4] Human populations have multiplied far more extensively and have come to occupy a far greater range of environments than has any other large animal. Through our ingenious technologies, we have appropriated for ourselves, according to recent calculations, some 25 to 40 percent of the solar energy that enters the food chain. We have recently gained access to the stored solar energy of coal, gas, and oil, all of which have been many millions of years in the making, and we have the capacity to deplete these resources in a few hundred or a few thousand years. Other forms of life have felt the impact of human activity, as numerous extinct or threatened species testify. Human beings have even affected the atmosphere itself, and global warming is altering the climate of the planet. Thus human history has been, and remains, of great significance not for ourselves alone but also for the earth itself and for the many other living creatures with which we share it.

The History of the Human Species in a Single Paragraph: A Preview

The history of our species has occupied roughly the last 250,000 years, conventionally divided into three major phases, based on the kind of technology that was most widely practiced. The enormously long Paleolithic age, with its gathering and hunting way of life, accounts for 95 percent or more of the time that humans have occupied the planet. People utilizing a Paleolithic technology initially settled every major landmass on the planet and constructed the first human societies (see Chapter 1). Then beginning about 12,000 years ago with the first Agricultural Revolution, the domestication of plants and animals increasingly became the primary means of sustaining human life and societies. In giving rise to farming village societies, to pastoral communities depending on their herds of animals, and to state- and city-based civilizations, this agrarian way of life changed virtually everything and fundamentally shaped the human experience ever since. Finally around 1750, a quite sudden spurt in the rate of technological change, which we know as the Industrial Revolution, took hold. That vast increase in productivity, wealth, and human control over nature once again transformed almost every aspect of human life and gave rise to new kinds of societies that we call "modern."

Here then, in a single paragraph, is the history of humankind—the Paleolithic era, the agricultural era, and, most recently and briefly, the modern industrial era. Clearly this is a world history perspective, based on the notion that the human species as a whole has a history that transcends any of its particular and distinctive cultures. That perspective—known variously as planetary, global, or world history—has become increasingly prominent among those who study the past. Why should this be so?

Why World History?

Not long ago—in the mid-twentieth century, for example—virtually all college-level history courses were organized in terms of particular civilizations or nations. In the United States, courses such as Western Civilization or some version of American History served to introduce students to the study of the past. Since then, however, a set of profound changes has pushed much of the historical profession in a different direction.

The world wars of the twentieth century, revealing as they did the horrendous consequences of unchecked nationalism, persuaded some historians that a broader view of the past might contribute to a sense of global citizenship. Economic and cultural globalization has highlighted both the interdependence of the world's peoples and their very unequal positions within that world. Moreover, we are aware as never before that our problems—whether they involve economic well-being, environmental deterioration, disease, or terrorism—respect no national boundaries. To many thoughtful people, a global present seemed to call for a global past. Furthermore, as

■ **Change**
Why has world history achieved an increasingly prominent place in American education in recent decades?

colonial empires shrank and newly defined third-world peoples asserted themselves on the world stage, these peoples also insisted that their histories be accorded equivalent treatment with those of Europe. An explosion of new knowledge about the histories of Asia, Africa, and pre-Columbian America erupted from the research of scholars around the world. All of this has generated a "world history movement," reflected in college and high school curricula, in numerous conferences and specialized studies, and in a proliferation of textbooks, of which this is one.

This world history movement has attempted to create a global understanding of the human past that highlights broad patterns cutting across particular civilizations and countries, while acknowledging in an inclusive fashion the distinctive histories of its many peoples. This is, to put it mildly, a tall order. How is it possible to encompass within a single book or course the separate stories of the world's various peoples? Surely it must be something more than just recounting the history of one civilization or culture after another. How can we distill a common history of humankind as a whole from the distinct trajectories of particular peoples? Because no world history book or course can cover everything, what criteria should we use for deciding what to include and what to leave out? Such questions have ensured no end of controversy among students, teachers, and scholars of world history, making it one of the most exciting fields of historical inquiry.

Comparison, Connection, and Change: The Three Cs of World History

Despite much debate and argument, one thing is reasonably clear: in world history, nothing stands alone. Every event, every historical figure, every culture, society, or civilization gains significance from its inclusion in some larger context. Most world historians would probably agree on three such contexts that define their field of study. Each of them confronts a particular problem in our understanding of the past.

The first is constant **comparison**. Whatever else it may be, world history is a comparative discipline, seeking to identify similarities and differences in the experience of the world's peoples. What is the difference between the development of agriculture in the Middle East and in Mesoamerica? Was the experience of women largely the same in all patriarchal societies? What did the Roman Empire and Han dynasty China have in common? Why did the Industrial Revolution and a modern way of life evolve first in Western Europe rather than somewhere else? What distinguished the Russian and Chinese revolutions? What different postures toward modernity emerged within the Islamic world? Describing and, if possible, explaining such similarities and differences are among the major tasks of world history. Comparison, then, is a recurring theme in this book, with expressions in every chapter.

Comparison has proven an effective tool in the struggle against Eurocentrism, the notion that Europeans or people of European descent have long been the primary movers and shakers of the historical process. That notion arose in recent centuries when Europeans were in fact the major source of innovation in the world and did for a time exercise something close to world domination. This temporary pre-eminence decisively shaped the way Europeans thought and wrote about their own histories and those of other people. In their own eyes, Europeans alone were progressive people, thanks to some cultural or racial superiority. Everyone else was to some degree stagnant, backward, savage, or barbarian. The unusual power of Europeans allowed them for a time to act on those beliefs and to impose such ways of thinking on much of the world. But comparative world history sets European achievements in a global and historical context, helping us to sort out what was distinctive about its development and what similarities it bore to other major regions of the world. Puncturing the pretensions of Eurocentrism has been high on the agenda of world history.

The art of comparison is a learned skill, entailing several steps. It requires, first of all, asking explicitly comparative questions and determining what particular cases will be involved. If you want to compare revolutions, for example, you would need to decide which ones you are considering—American, French, Russian, Chinese, Cuban. Defining categories of comparison is a further step. Precisely which characteristics of these revolutions will you compare—their origins, their ideologies, the social classes involved, their outcomes? Finally, how will you present your comparison? You might choose a case-by-case analysis in which you would describe, say, the American Revolution first, followed by an account of the Cuban Revolution, which makes explicit comparisons with the former. Or you might choose a thematic approach in which you would consider first the origins of both revolutions, followed by a comparison of their ideologies, and so on. You will find examples of both approaches in this book.

A second context that informs world history involves the interaction, encounters, and **connections** among different and often distant peoples. What happened when people of distinct civilizations or cultures met? Focusing on cross-cultural connections represents an effort to counteract a habit of thinking about particular peoples, states, or cultures as self-contained and isolated communities. Despite the historical emergence of separate and distinct societies, none of them developed alone. Each was embedded in a network of relationships with both near and more distant peoples. Moreover, these cross-cultural connections did not begin with the voyages of Columbus. The Chinese, for example, interacted continuously with the nomadic peoples on their northern border; generated technologies that diffused across all of Eurasia; transmitted elements of their culture to Japan, Korea, and Vietnam; and assimilated a foreign religious tradition, Buddhism, which had originated in India. Though clearly distinctive, China was not a self-contained or isolated civilization. The encounter with strangers, or at least with strange ideas and practices, was everywhere one of the most powerful motors of change in human societies. Thus world history pays attention not only to the internal developments of particular civilizations or peoples but also to the networks, webs, and cross-cultural encounters in which they were enmeshed.

A third context in which the particulars of world history can be situated is found in that perennial question that historians everywhere seek to explore: what changes, what persists, and why. In world history, it is the "big picture" **changes**—those that impact large segments of humankind—that are of greatest interest. How did the transition from a gathering and hunting economy to one based on agriculture take place? How did cities, empires, and civilizations take shape in various parts of the world? What generated the amazing transformations of the "revolution of modernity" in recent centuries? World historians also pay attention to the changes that occur within and between particular civilizations. How can we explain the dramatic collapse of Maya civilization or the fall of the Roman Empire? How did Buddhism change when it entered China? How was Islam transformed when it encountered West African societies? What lay behind the emergence of a new balance of global power after 1500, one that featured the growing prominence of Europe on the world stage?

Both change and comparison provide an antidote to a persistent tendency of human thinking that historians call "essentialism." A more common term is "stereotyping." It refers to our inclination to define particular groups of people with an unchanging or essential set of characteristics. Women are nurturing; peasants are conservative; Americans are aggressive; Hindus are religious. Serious students of history soon become aware that every significant category of people contains endless divisions and conflicts and that human communities are constantly in flux. Peasants may often accept the status quo, except of course when they rebel, as they frequently have. Americans have experienced periods of isolationism and withdrawal from the world as well as times of aggressive engagement with it. Things change.

But some things persist, even if they also change. We should not allow an emphasis on change to blind us to the continuities of human experience. A recognizably Chinese state has operated for more than 2,000 years. Slavery and patriarchy persisted as human institutions for thousands of years until they were challenged in recent centuries, and in various forms they exist still. The teachings of Buddhism, Christianity, and Islam have endured for centuries, though with endless variations and transformations.

Comparisons, connections, and changes—all of them operating on a global scale—represent three contexts or frameworks that can help us bring some coherence to the multiple and complex stories of world history. They will recur repeatedly in the pages that follow.

Second Thoughts

What's the Significance?

myths of origin	big history	the three Cs
cosmic calendar	comparative history	

Big Picture Questions

1. What is the difference between religiously based myths of origin and creation stories derived from scientific accounts?
2. How do you respond personally to modern notions of the immense size and age of the universe?
3. What examples of comparison, connection, and change in world history would you like to explore further as your course unfolds?

Next Steps: For Further Study

David Christian, *Maps of Time* (2004). A brilliant survey of "big history" by a leading world historian.

Ross Dunn, ed., *The New World History* (2000). A collection of articles dealing with the teaching of world history.

Patrick Manning, *Navigating World History* (2003). An up-to-date overview of the growth of world history, the field's achievements, and the debates within it.

J. R. McNeill and William H. McNeill, *The Human Web* (2003). An approach to world history that emphasizes the changing webs of connection among human communities.

David Northrup, "Globalization and the Great Convergence: Rethinking World History in the Long Term," *Journal of World History* (September 2005). A thoughtful essay identifying broad patterns of human history.

"The Cosmic Time-Line," http://visav.phys.uvic.ca/~babul/AstroCourses/P303/BB-slide.htm. A more detailed cosmic calendar.

"World History for Us All," http://worldhistoryforusall.sdsu.edu/dev/default.htm. A model world history curriculum for high school courses.

To assess your mastery of the material in this prologue, see the **Online Study Guide** at bedfordstmartins.com/strayer.

For Web sites and documents related to this prologue, see **Make History** at bedfordstmartins.com/strayer.

Ways of the World

A Brief Global History

with Sources

PART ONE

First Things First

Beginnings in History

TO 500 B.C.E.

Contents

Turning Points in Early World History

Both the ancient sages who developed their societies' creation myths and the grand-parents who still relate the histories of their families have had to decide at what point to begin their stories and what major turning points in those stories to highlight. So too must historians, whether they narrate the tale of a village, a city, a nation, a civilization, or the entire human community. For world historians, concerned with humankind as a whole, four major "beginnings," each of them an extended historical process, have charted the initial stages of the human journey.

The Emergence of Humankind

Ever since Charles Darwin, most scholars have come to view human beginnings in the context of biological change on the planet. In considering this enormous process, we operate on a timescale quite different from the billions of years that mark the history of the universe and of the earth. According to archeologists and anthropologists, the evolutionary line of descent leading to *Homo sapiens* diverged from that leading to chimpanzees, our closest primate relatives, some 5 million to 6 million years ago, and it happened in eastern and southern Africa. There, perhaps twenty or thirty different species emerged, all of them members of the Homininae (or hominid) family of humanlike creatures. What they all shared was bipedalism, the ability to walk upright on two legs. In 1976, the archeologist Mary Leakey uncovered in what is now Tanzania a series of footprints of three such hominid individuals, preserved in cooling volcanic ash about 3.5 million years ago. Two of them walked side by side, perhaps holding hands.

Over time, these hominid species changed. Their brains grew larger, as evidenced by the size of their skulls. About 2.3 million years ago, a hominid creature known as *Homo habilis* began to make and use simple stone tools. Others started to eat meat, at least occasionally. By 1 million years ago, some hominid species, especially *Homo erectus*, began to migrate out of Africa, and their remains have been found in various parts of Eurasia. This species is also associated with the first controlled use of fire.

Eventually all of these earlier hominid species died out, except one: *Homo sapiens*, ourselves. We too emerged first in Africa and quite recently, probably no more than 250,000 years ago, although there is constant debate among specialists about these matters. For a long time, all of the small number of *Homo sapiens* lived in Africa, but sometime after 100,000 years ago, they too began to migrate out of Africa onto the Eurasian landmass, then to Australia, and ultimately into the Western Hemisphere and the Pacific islands. The great experiment of human history had begun.

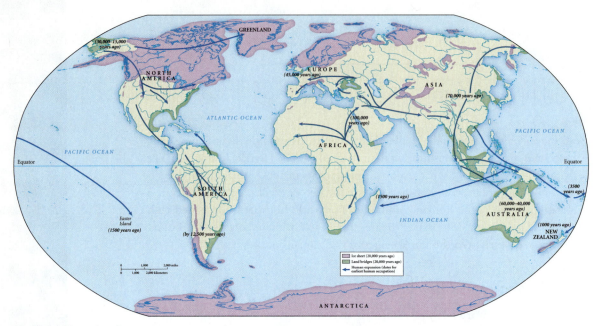

The Global Dispersion of
Humankind (p. 14)

The Globalization of Humankind

Today, every significant landmass on earth is occupied by human beings, but it was not always so. A mere half million years ago our species did not exist, and only 100,000 years ago that species was limited to Africa and numbered, some scholars believe, fewer than 10,000 individuals. These ancient ancestors of ours, rather small in stature and not fast on foot, were armed with a very limited technology of stone tools with which to confront the multiple dangers of the natural world. But then, in perhaps the most amazing tale in all of human history, they moved from this very modest and geographically limited role in the scheme of things to a worldwide and increasingly dominant presence. What kinds of societies, technologies, and understandings of the world accompanied, and perhaps facilitated, this globalization of humankind?

The phase of human history during which these initial migrations took place is known to scholars as the Paleolithic era. The word "Paleolithic" literally means the "old stone age," but it refers more generally to a food-collecting or gathering and hunting way of life, before agriculture allowed people to grow food or raise animals deliberately. Lasting until roughly 11,000 years ago, the Paleolithic era represents over 95 percent of the time that human beings have inhabited the earth, although it accounts for only about 12 percent of the total number of people who have lived on the planet.

It was during this time that *Homo sapiens* colonized the world, making themselves at home in every environmental niche, from the frigid Arctic to the rain forests of Central Africa and Brazil, in mountains, deserts, and plains. It was an amazing achievement, accomplished by no other large species. Accompanying this global migration were slow changes in the technological tool kits of early humankind as well as early attempts to impose meaning on the world through art, ritual, and religion. Although often neglected by historians and history textbooks, this long period of the human experience merits greater attention and is the focus of Chapter 1.

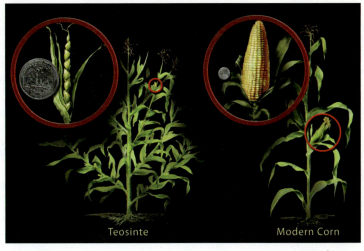

Teosinte   Modern Corn

Teosinte and Maize/Corn (p. 56)

The Revolution of Farming and Herding

In late 2009, almost all of the world's 6.8 billion people lived from the food grown on farms and gardens and from domesticated animals raised for their meat, milk, or eggs, but this was not always so. In fact, before 11,000 years ago, no one survived in this fashion. Then, repeatedly and fairly rapidly, at least in world history terms, human communities in parts of the Middle East, Asia, Africa, and the Americas began the laborious process of domesticating animals and selecting seeds to be planted. This momentous accomplishment represents another "first" in the human story. After countless millennia of relying on the gathering of wild foods and the hunting of wild animals, why and how did human societies begin to practice agriculture and herding? What changes to human life did this new technology bring with it?

This food-producing revolution, considered in Chapter 2, surely marks the single most significant and enduring transformation of the human condition, providing the foundation for virtually everything that followed. The entire period from the beginning of agriculture to the Industrial Revolution around 1750 might be considered a single phase of the human story—the age of agriculture—calculated now on a timescale of millennia or centuries rather than the more extended periods of earlier eras. Although the age of agriculture was far shorter than the immense Paleolithic era that preceded it, farming and herding allowed for a substantial increase in human numbers.

In the various beginnings of food production lay the foundations for some of the most enduring divisions within the larger human community. Much depended on the luck of the draw—on the climate and soils, on the various wild plants and animals that were available for domestication. Many agricultural peoples lived in small settled villages, independent of larger political structures, while drawing their food supply from their own gardens and farms. Some depended on root crops, such as potatoes in the Andes; others relied on tree crops, such as the banana; the most favored areas were those where highly nutritious wild grains such as rice, wheat, or corn could be domesticated. In more arid regions where farming was difficult, some peoples, known as pastoralists, came to depend heavily on their herds of domesticated animals. Because they moved frequently and in regular patterns, in search of pasturelands, they are often referred to as nomads. With regard to animal husbandry, the Americas were at a distinct disadvantage, for there were few large animals that could be tamed—no goats, sheep, pigs, horses, camels, or cattle. In the Afro-Eurasian world, conflicts between settled agricultural peoples and more mobile pastoral peoples represented an enduring pattern of interaction across the region.

The Turning Point of Civilization

The most prominent and powerful human communities to emerge from the Agricultural Revolution were those we often designate as "civilizations," societies that were based in bustling cities and governed by powerful states. Virtually all of the world's people now live in a state with a formal political authority that controls a particular territory, whether it is a single city such as Singapore, a tiny country such as The Gambia, or a huge territory such as Russia. The political, economic, and cultural life of state-based societies everywhere gives prominence to cities. By the early twenty-first century, about half of the world's population lived in urban centers. States and cities have become so common as to seem almost natural.

In world history terms, however, the appearance of states and cities is a rather recent phenomenon. Not until several thousand years *after* the beginning of agriculture did the first cities and states emerge, around 3500 B.C.E. Well after 1000 C.E., substantial numbers of people still lived in communities without any state or urban structures. Nonetheless, people living in state- and city-based societies or civilizations have long constituted the most powerful and innovative human communities on the planet. They gave rise to empires of increasing size, to enduring cultural and religious traditions, to new technologies, to sharp class inequalities, to male domination (patriarchy), and to large-scale warfare.

For all of these reasons, civilizations have featured prominently in accounts of world history, sometimes crowding out the stories of other kinds of human communities. The earliest civilizations, which emerged between 3500 and 500 B.C.E., have long fascinated professional historians and lovers of history everywhere. In at least six separate places—Mesopotamia (present-day Iraq), Egypt, Pakistan and northern India, China, Peru, and Mexico—such state- and city-based societies emerged. What was their relationship to the Agricultural Revolution? What new ways of life did they bring to the experience of humankind? These are the questions that are examined in Chapter 3.

A Note on Dates

Recently it has become standard in the Western world to refer to dates prior to the birth of Christ as B.C.E. (before the Common Era), replacing the earlier B.C. (before Christ) usage. This convention is an effort to become less Christian-centered and

Eurocentric in our use of language, although the chronology remains linked to the birth of Jesus. Similarly, the time following the birth of Christ is referred to as C.E. (the Common Era) rather than A.D. (*Anno Domini*, Latin for "year of the Lord"). Dates in the more distant past are designated in this book simply as so many "years ago." Of course, these conventions are only some of the many ways that human societies have reckoned time. The Chinese frequently dated important events in terms of the reign of particular emperors, while Muslims created a new calendar beginning with Year 1, marking Muhammad's emigration to Medina in 622 C.E. As with so much else, the ways that we measure time reflect the cultures in which we have been born and the historical experience of our societies.

Landmarks of Early World History, to 500 B.C.E.

27,000	26,000	25,000	24,000	23,000	22,000	21,000	20,000	19,000	18,000	17,000	16,000	15,000	14,000

Africa

◀ **250,000 years ago**
Emergence of *Homo sapiens*

◀ **100,000 years ago**
Human migration out of Africa into Eurasia

16,000–9000 B.C.E.
Development of distinctive regional cultures

Eurasia

◀ **60,000 years ago**
Human entry into Australia

◀ **45,000 years ago**
Human entry into Europe

■ **15,000** B.C.E.
Lascaux cave paintings in southern France

The Americas

30,000–15,000 years ago
Human entry into the Americas

13,000	12,000	11,000	10,000	9000	8000	7000	6000	5000	4000	3000	2000	1000	900

3000–2000 B.C.E.
Agricultural breakthroughs
in sub-Saharan Africa

13,000–11,000 B.C.E.
Harvesting of wild grains
in northeastern Africa

9000 B.C.E.
Cattle herding in
Sudanic Africa

3100 B.C.E.
Unification
of Egypt

1000 B.C.E.
Beginning of
ironworking in
sub-Saharan
Africa

3500 B.C.E.
Emergence
of Nubian
civilization

2000 B.C.E. Beginnings
of Bantu migrations

1650 B.C.E. Hyksos
invasion of Egypt

14,000–8000 B.C.E.
End of last Ice Age

9000–7000 B.C.E. First agricultural
breakthrough (Fertile Crescent)

4000 B.C.E.
Domestication
of horses in
Ukraine/south-
ern Russia

2000 B.C.E. Beginnings
of Indus Valley and
Chinese civilizations

1792–1750 B.C.E.
Reign of Hammurabi
in Babylonian Empire

3000–1000 B.C.E.
Indo-European migrations

3500 B.C.E.
Beginning of
Mesopotamian
civilization

1500–1000 B.C.E.
Beginnings of
ironworking in
Anatolia

10,000–9000 B.C.E.
Flourishing of Clovis culture

9000 B.C.E.
Extinction of various large
mammals in North America

3000–2000 B.C.E.
Cultivation of maize, squash, and
beans in Mesoamerica

3000–2000 B.C.E.
Cultivation of potatoes, quinoa,
and manioc in the Andes

3000–1800 B.C.E.
Norte Chico ("mother
civilization" of the Andes)

1000 B.C.E.
Beginnings
of Olmec
civilization

900 B.C.E.
Chavín religious
cult in Peru

First Peoples

Populating the Planet

TO 10,000 B.C.E.

"We do not want cattle, just wild animals to hunt and water that we can drink."[1] That was the view of Gudo Mahiya, a prominent member of the Hadza people of northern Tanzania, when he was questioned in 1997 about his interest in a settled life of farming and cattle raising. With only about 1,000 total members, the Hadza represent one of the very last peoples on earth to continue a way of life that was universal among humankind until 10,000 to 12,000 years ago. At the beginning of the twenty-first century, several hundred Hadza still made a living by hunting game, collecting honey, digging up roots, and gathering berries and fruit. They lived in quickly assembled grass huts located in small mobile camps averaging eighteen people and moved frequently around their remote region. Almost certainly their way of life is doomed, as farmers, governments, missionaries, and now tourists descend on them. The likely disappearance of their culture parallels the experience of many other such societies, which have been on the defensive against more numerous and powerful neighbors for 10,000 years.

NONETHELESS, THAT WAY OF LIFE SUSTAINED HUMANKIND for more than 95 percent of the time that our species has inhabited the earth. During countless centuries, human beings successfully adapted to a wide variety of environments without benefit of deliberate farming or animal husbandry. Instead, our early ancestors wrested a livelihood by gathering wild foods such as berries, nuts, roots, and grain; by scavenging dead animals; by hunting live animals; and

Paleolithic Art: The rock art of gathering and hunting peoples has been found in Africa, Europe, Australia, and elsewhere. This image from the San people of southern Africa represents aspects of their outer life in the form of wild animals and hunters with bows as well as the inner life of their shamans during a trance, reflected in the elongated figures with both human and animal features. (Image courtesy of S.A. Tourism) by fishing. Known to scholars as "gathering and hunting" peoples, they were foragers or food collectors rather than food producers. Instead of requiring the earth to produce what they wanted, they took—or perhaps borrowed—what nature had to offer. Because they used stone rather than metal tools, they also have been labeled "Paleolithic," or "old stone age," peoples.

History courses and history books often neglect this long phase of the human journey and instead choose to begin the story with the coming of agriculture about 12,000 years ago or with the advent of civilizations about 5,000 years ago. Some historians identify "real history" with writing and so dismiss the Paleolithic era as largely unknowable because its people did not write. Others, impressed with the rapid pace of change in human affairs since the coming of agriculture, assume that nothing much of real significance happened in the Paleolithic era—and no change meant no history.

But does it make sense to ignore the first 200,000 years or more of human experience? Although written records are absent, scholars have learned a great deal about Paleolithic peoples through their material remains: stones and bones, fossilized seeds, rock paintings and engravings, and much more. Archeologists, biologists, botanists, demographers, linguists, and anthropologists have contributed much to our growing understanding of gathering and hunting peoples. Furthermore, the achievements of Paleolithic peoples—the initial settlement of the planet, the creation of the earliest human societies, the beginning of reflection on the great questions of life and death—deserve our attention. The changes they wrought, though far slower than those of more recent times, were extraordinarily rapid in comparison to the transformation experienced by any other species. Those changes were almost entirely cultural or learned, rather than the product of biological evolution, and they provided the foundation on which all subsequent human history was constructed. Our grasp of the human past is incomplete—massively so—if we choose to disregard the Paleolithic era.

Out of Africa to the Ends of the Earth: First Migrations

The first 150,000 years or more of human experience was an exclusively African story. Around 250,000 years ago, in the grasslands of eastern and southern Africa, *Homo sapiens* first emerged, following in the footsteps of many other hominid species before it. Time and climate have erased much of the record of these early people, and Africa has witnessed much less archeological research than have other parts of the world, especially Europe. Nonetheless, scholars have turned up evidence of distinctly human behavior in Africa long before its appearance elsewhere. Africa, almost certainly, was the place where the "human revolution" occurred, where "culture," defined as learned or invented ways of living, became more important than biology in shaping behavior.

What kinds of uniquely human activity show up in the early African record?[2] In the first place, human beings began to inhabit new environments within Africa—forests and deserts—where no hominids had lived before. Accompanying these movements of people were technological innovations of various kinds: stone blades

Snapshot   **The Long Road to the Global Presence of Humankind**

(all dates approximate)	**Years Ago**
Earliest bipedal hominids (walking upright on two legs)	7 million to 6 million
Homo habilis (earliest use of stone tools)	2.5 million
Homo erectus (first controlled use of fire and first hominid migrations out of Africa)	1.9 million to 200,000
Earliest *Homo sapiens* in Africa	250,000
Beginnings of human migration out of Africa	100,000–60,000
Human entry into eastern Asia	70,000
Human entry into Australia (first use of boats)	60,000–40,000
Human entry into Europe	45,000
Extinction of large mammals in Australia	30,000
Human entry into the Americas	30,000–15,000
Cave art in Europe	25,000
Extinction of Neanderthals	25,000
End of last Ice Age (global warming)	16,000–10,000
Earliest agricultural revolutions	12,000–10,000
Extinction of large mammals in North America	11,000
Austronesian migration to Pacific islands and Madagascar	3,500–1,000
Human entry into New Zealand (last major region to receive human settlers)	1,000

and points fastened to shafts replaced the earlier hand axes; tools made from bones appeared, and so did grindstones. Evidence of hunting and fishing, not just the scavenging of dead animals, marks a new phase in human food collection. Settlements were planned around the seasonal movement of game and fish. Patterns of exchange over a distance of almost 200 miles indicate larger networks of human communication. The use of body ornaments, beads, and pigments such as ocher as well as possible planned burials suggest the kind of social and symbolic behavior that has characterized human activity ever since. All of this occurred before 100,000 years ago and, based on current evidence, long before such activity surfaced elsewhere in the world.

Then, sometime between 100,000 and 60,000 years ago, human beings began their long trek out of Africa and into Eurasia, Australia, the Americas, and, much later,

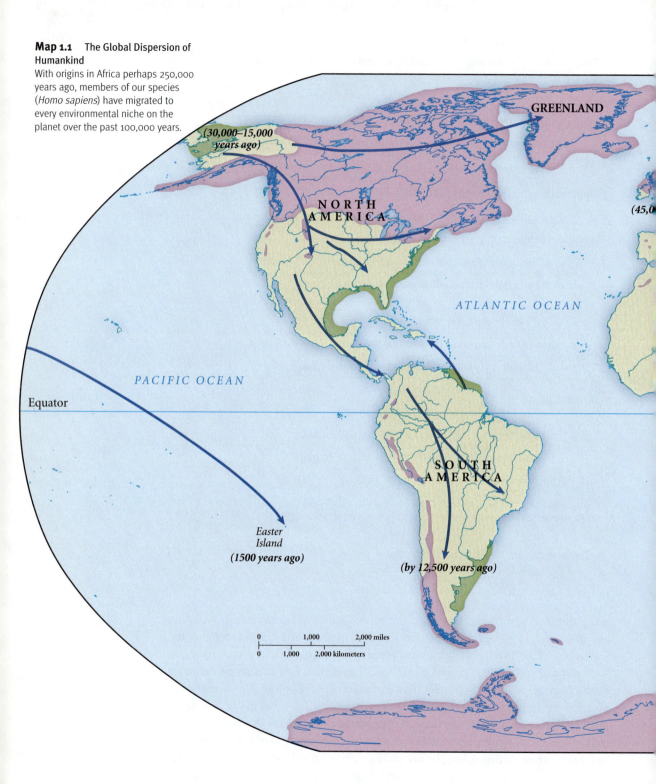

Map 1.1 The Global Dispersion of Humankind
With origins in Africa perhaps 250,000 years ago, members of our species (*Homo sapiens*) have migrated to every environmental niche on the planet over the past 100,000 years.

GREENLAND

(30,000–15,000 years ago)

NORTH AMERICA

(45,0

ATLANTIC OCEAN

PACIFIC OCEAN

Equator

SOUTH AMERICA

Easter Island
(1500 years ago)

(by 12,500 years ago)

0	1,000	2,000 miles

0	1,000	2,000 kilometers

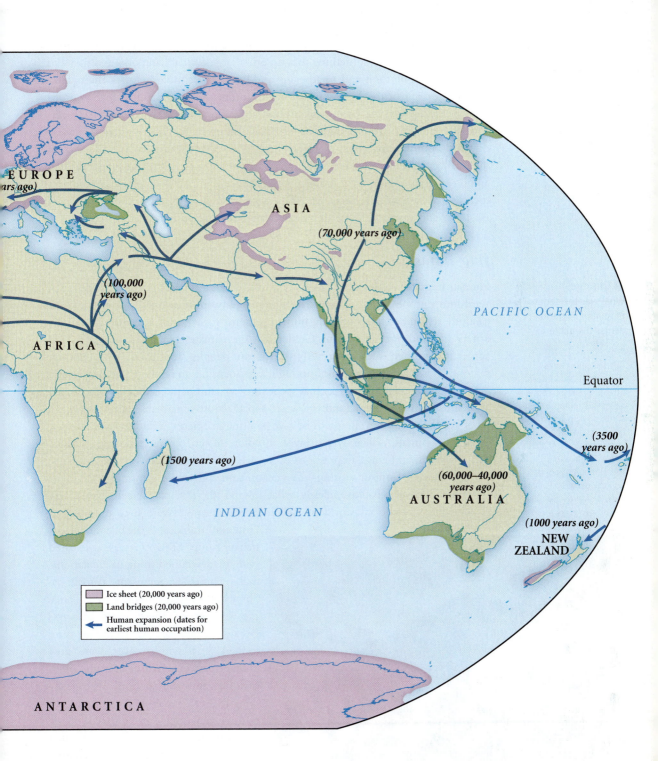

EUROPE
(ars ago)

ASIA

(70,000 years ago)

PACIFIC OCEAN

(100,000 years ago)

AFRICA

Equator

(3500 years ago)

(1500 years ago)

(60,000–40,000 years ago)

AUSTRALIA

INDIAN OCEAN

(1000 years ago)

NEW ZEALAND

Ice sheet (20,000 years ago)
Land bridges (20,000 years ago)
Human expansion (dates for earliest human occupation)

ANTARCTICA

15

the islands of the Pacific (see Map 1.1). In occupying the planet, members of our species accomplished the remarkable feat of learning to live in virtually every environmental niche on earth, something that no other large animal had done; and they did it with only stone tools and a gathering and hunting technology to aid them. Furthermore, much of this long journey occurred during the difficult climatic conditions of the last Ice Age (at its peak around 20,000 years ago), when thick ice sheets covered much of northern Eurasia and North America. The Ice Age did give these outward-bound human beings one advantage, however: the amount of water frozen in northern glaciers lowered sea levels around the planet, creating land bridges among various regions that were separated after the glaciers melted. Britain was then joined to Europe; eastern Siberia was connected to Alaska; and New Guinea, Australia, and Tasmania were all part of a huge supercontinent known as Sahul.

Into Eurasia

■ **Change**
What was the sequence of human migration across the planet?

Human migration out of Africa led first to the Middle East and from there westward into Europe about 45,000 years ago and eastward into Asia. Among the most carefully researched areas of early human settlement in Eurasia are those in southern France and northern Spain. Colder Ice Age climates around 20,000 years ago apparently pushed more northerly European peoples southward into warmer regions. There they altered their hunting habits, focusing on reindeer and horses, and developed new technologies such as spear throwers and perhaps the bow and arrow as well as many different kinds of stone tools.[3] Most remarkably, they also left a record of their world in hundreds of cave paintings, depicting reindeer, bulls, horses, and other animals, brilliantly portrayed in colors of red, yellow, brown, and black. Images of human beings, impressions of human hands, and various abstract designs, perhaps an early form of writing, often accompanied the cave paintings.

The Lascaux Caves
Discovered by four teenage boys in 1940, the Lascaux caves in southern France contain some 2,000 images, dating to perhaps 17,000 years ago. Many of them depict in quite realistic form the wild animals of the region—oxen, bulls, horses, ibex, and birds. (JM Labat/ Photo Researchers, Inc.)

Scholars have debated endlessly what insights these remarkable images might provide into the mental world of Paleolithic Europeans.[4] Were they examples of "totemic" thinking—the belief that particular groups of people were associated with, or descended from, particular animals? Did they represent a form of "hunting magic" intended to enhance the success of these early hunters? Because many of the paintings were located deep within caves, were they perhaps part of religious or ritual practices or rites of passage? Were they designed to pass on information to future generations? Or did they symbolize, as some recent scholars contend, a coded representation of a Paleolithic worldview divided into male and female

realms, both opposed to and balancing each other? We simply do not know. Nonetheless, these images excite our imagination still, 20,000 years or more after they were created. In them we sense a kinship with the humanity of our distant ancestors.

Farther east, archeologists have uncovered still other remarkable Paleolithic adaptations to Ice Age conditions. Across the vast plains of Central Europe, Ukraine, and Russia, new technologies emerged, including bone needles, multilayered clothing, weaving, nets, storage pits, baskets, and pottery. Partially underground dwellings constructed from the bones and tusks of mammoths compensated for the absence of caves and rock shelters. All of this suggests that some of these people had lived in more permanent settlements, at least temporarily abandoning their nomadic journeys. Associated with these Eastern European peoples were numerous female figurines, the earliest of which was uncovered in 2008 in Germany and dated to at least 35,000 years ago. Carved from stone, antlers, mammoth tusks, or, occasionally, baked clay, these so-called Venus figurines depict the female form, often with exaggerated breasts, buttocks, hips, and stomachs (see image, p. 22). They were not limited to a single region but have been found all across Europe, from Spain to Russia, suggesting a network of human communication and cultural diffusion over a wide area.

Into Australia

Early human migration to Australia, currently dated to around 60,000 years ago, came from Indonesia and involved another first in human affairs—the use of boats. Over time, people settled in most regions of this huge continent, though quite sparsely. Scholars estimate the population of Australia at about 300,000 people in 1788, when the first Europeans arrived. Over tens of thousands of years, these people had developed perhaps 250 languages; collected a wide variety of bulbs, tubers, roots, seeds, and cereal grasses; and hunted large and small animals, as well as birds, fish, and other marine life. A relatively simple technology, appropriate to a gathering and hunting economy, sustained Australia's Aboriginal people into modern times. When outsiders arrived in the late eighteenth century, all of the continent's people still practiced that ancient way of life, despite the presence of agriculture in nearby New Guinea.

Accompanying their technological simplicity and traditionalism was the development of an elaborate and complex outlook on the world, known as the Dreamtime. Expressed in endless stories, in extended ceremonies, and in the evocative rock art of the continent's peoples, the Dreamtime recounted the beginning of things: how ancestral beings crisscrossed the land, creating its rivers, hills, rocks, and waterholes; how various peoples came to inhabit the land; and how they related to animals and to one another. In this view of the world, everything in the natural order was a vibration, an echo, a footprint of these ancient happenings, which link the current inhabitants intimately to particular places and to timeless events in the past. (See Document 1.2, pp. 39–41, and Visual Sources: The Aboriginal Rock Painting of Australia, pp. 42–47.)

The journeys of the Dreamtime's ancestral beings reflect in a general way the networks of migration, communication, and exchange that linked the continent's many Paleolithic peoples. Far from isolated groups, they had long exchanged particular stones, pigments, materials for ropes and baskets, wood for spears, feathers and shells for ornaments, and an addictive psychoactive drug known as *pituri* over distances of hundreds of miles.[5] Songs, dances, stories, and rituals likewise circulated. Precisely how far back in time these networks extend is difficult to pinpoint, but it seems clear that Paleolithic Australia, like ancient Europe, was both many separate worlds and, at the same time, one loosely connected world.

Into the Americas

The earliest settlement of the Western Hemisphere occurred much later than that of Australia, for it took some time for human beings to penetrate the frigid lands of eastern Siberia, which was the jumping-off point for the move into the Americas. Experts continue to argue about precisely when the first migrations occurred (somewhere between 30,000 and 15,000 years ago), about the route of migration (by land across the Bering Strait or by sea down the west coast of North America), about how many separate migrations took place, and about how long it took for people to penetrate to the tip of South America.[6] There is, however, good evidence of human activity in southern Chile by 12,500 years ago.

The first clearly defined and widespread cultural tradition in the Americas is associated with people who made a distinctive projectile point, known to archeologists as a Clovis point. Scattered all over North America, Clovis culture flourished around 12,000 to 11,000 years ago. Scattered bands of Clovis people ranged over huge areas, camping along rivers, springs, and waterholes, where large animals congregated. Although they certainly hunted smaller animals and gathered many wild plants, Clovis people show up in the archeological record most dramatically as hunters of very large mammals, such as mammoths and bison. Killing a single mammoth could provide food for many weeks or, in cold weather, for much of the winter. The wide distribution of Clovis point technology suggests yet again a regional pattern of cultural diffusion and at least indirect communication over a large area.

Then, about 10,900 years ago, all trace of the Clovis people disappears from the archeological record at the same time that many species of large animals, including the mammoth and several species of horses and camels, also became extinct. Did the Clovis people hunt these animals to extinction and then vanish themselves as their source of food disappeared? Or did the drier climate that came with the end of the Ice Age cause this megafaunal extinction? Experts disagree, but what happened next was the creation of a much greater diversity of cultures as people adapted to this new situation in various ways. Hunters on the Great Plains continued to pursue bison, which largely avoided the fate of the mammoths. Others learned to live in the desert, taking advantage of seasonal plants and smaller animals, while those who lived near the sea, lakes, or streams drew on local fish and birds. Many peoples retained their gathering and hunting way of life into modern times, while others became farmers and, in a few favored regions, later developed cities and large-scale states.[7]

Into the Pacific

The last phase of the great human migration to the ends of the earth took place in the Pacific Ocean and was distinctive in many ways. In the first place, it occurred quite recently, jumping off only about 3,500 years ago from the Bismarck and Solomon islands near New Guinea as well as from the islands of the Philippines. It was everywhere a waterborne migration, making use of oceangoing canoes and remarkable navigational skills, and it happened very quickly and over a huge area of the planet. Speaking Austronesian languages that trace back to southern China, these oceanic voyagers had settled every habitable piece of land in the Pacific basin within about 2,500 years. Other Austronesians had sailed west from Indonesia across the Indian Ocean to settle the island of Madagascar off the coast of eastern Africa. This extraordinary process of expansion—both rapid and extensive—made the Austronesian family of languages the most widespread in the world. With the occupation of Aotearoa (New Zealand) about 1300 C.E., the initial human settlement of the planet was finally complete (see Map 1.2).

In contrast with all of the other migrations, these Pacific voyages were undertaken by people with an agricultural technology, who carried both domesticated plants and animals in their canoes. Both men and women made these journeys, suggesting a deliberate intention to colonize new lands. Virtually everywhere they went, two developments followed. One was the creation of highly stratified societies or chiefdoms, of which ancient Hawaiian society is a prime example. In Hawaii, an elite class of chiefs with political and military power ruled over a mass of commoners. The other development was the dramatic impact that these migrations had on the environment of previously uninhabited islands. Many species of

■ Comparison

How did Austronesian migrations differ from other early patterns of human movement?

Map 1.2 Migration of Austronesian-Speaking People

People speaking Austronesian languages completed the human settlement of the earth quite recently as they settled the islands of the vast Pacific and penetrated the Indian Ocean to Madagascar, off the coast of southeast Africa.

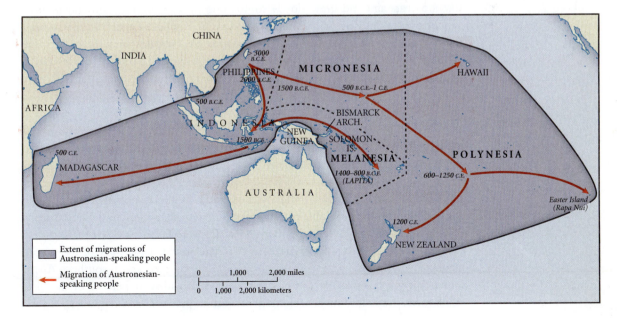

CHINA

INDIA

AFRICA

PHILIPPINES

3000 B.C.E.

2000 B.C.E.

1500 B.C.E.

500 B.C.E.

MICRONESIA

500 B.C.E.–1 C.E.

HAWAII

INDONESIA

500 C.E.

MADAGASCAR

1500 B.C.E.

NEW GUINEA

BISMARCK ARCH.

SOLOMON IS.

MELANESIA

1400–800 B.C.E. (LAPITA)

POLYNESIA

600–1250 C.E.

AUSTRALIA

1200 C.E.

NEW ZEALAND

Easter Island (Rapa Nui)

Extent of migrations of Austronesian-speaking people

Migration of Austronesian-speaking people

0   1,000   2,000 miles

0   1,000   2,000 kilometers

animals quickly became extinct, especially large flightless birds. The destruction of the forests of Rapa Nui (Easter Island) between the fifteenth and seventeenth centuries C.E. brought famine, violent conflict, and a sharp population decline to this small island society, while the absence of large trees ensured that no one could leave the island, for they could no longer build the canoes that had brought them there.[8]

The Ways We Were

During their long journeys across the earth, Paleolithic people created a multitude of separate and distinct societies, each with its own history, culture, language, identity, stories, and rituals, but the limitations of a gathering and hunting technology using stone tools imposed some commonalities on these ancient people. Based on the archeological record and on the example of gathering and hunting societies that still existed in modern times, scholars have sketched out some of the common features of these early societies.

The First Human Societies

■ Change

In what ways did a gathering and hunting economy shape other aspects of Paleolithic societies?

Above all else, these Paleolithic societies were small, consisting of bands of twenty-five to fifty people, in which all relationships were intensely personal and normally understood in terms of kinship. No anonymity or hiding in the crowd was possible in a society of relatives. The available technology permitted only a very low population density and ensured an extremely slow rate of population growth. Scholars estimate that world population may have been as low as 10,000 people around 100,000 years ago and grew slowly to 500,000 by 30,000 years ago and then to 6 million by 10,000 years ago.[9] Paleolithic bands were seasonally mobile or nomadic, moving frequently and in regular patterns to exploit the resources of wild plants and animals on which they depended. The low productivity of a gathering and hunting economy normally did not allow the production of much surplus, and because people were on the move so often, transporting an accumulation of goods was out of the question.

All of this resulted in highly egalitarian societies, lacking the many inequalities of wealth and power that came with later agricultural and urban life. With no formal chiefs, kings, bureaucrats, soldiers, nobles, or priests, Paleolithic people were perhaps freer of tyranny and oppression than any subsequent kind of human society, even if they were more constrained by the forces of nature. Without specialists, most people possessed the same set of skills, although male and female tasks often differed sharply. Relationships between women and men usually were far more equal than in later societies. As the primary food gatherers, women provided the bulk of the family income. One study of a modern gathering and hunting society in southern Africa found that plants, normally gathered by women, provided 70 percent of the diet, while meat, hunted by men, accounted for just 30 percent.[10]

When the British navigator and explorer Captain James Cook first encountered the gathering and hunting peoples of Australia in 1770, he described them, perhaps a little enviously, in this way:

> They live in a Tranquillity which is not disturb'd by the Inequality of Conditions: The Earth and sea of their own accord furnishes them with all things necessary for life, they covet not Magnificent houses, Household-stuff. . . . In short they seem'd to set no value upon any thing we gave them. . . . They think themselves provided with all the necessarys of Life.[11]

Native Australians
A number of Aboriginal Australians maintained their gathering and hunting way of life well into the twentieth century. Here an older woman shows two young boys how to dig for honey ants, a popular food. (Bill Bachman/Alamy)

The Europeans who settled permanently among such people some twenty years later, however, found a society in which physical competition among men was expressed in frequent one-on-one combat and in formalized but bloody battles. It also meant recurrent, public, and quite brutal beatings of wives by their husbands.[12] Although sometimes romanticized by Europeans, the relative social equality of Paleolithic peoples did not always ensure a utopia of social harmony.

Like all other human cultures, Paleolithic societies had rules and structures. A gender-based division of labor usually cast men as hunters and women as gatherers. Values emphasizing reciprocal sharing of goods resulted in clearly defined rules about distributing the meat from an animal kill. Rules about incest and adultery governed sexual behavior, while understandings about who could hunt or gather in particular territories regulated economic activity. Leaders arose as needed to organize a task such as a hunt, but without conferring permanent power on individuals.

Economy and the Environment

For a long time, gathering and hunting peoples were viewed as primitive, impoverished, barely eking out a living from the land. In more recent decades, anthropologists studying contemporary Paleolithic societies—those that survived into the twentieth century—began to paint a different picture. They noted that gathering and hunting people frequently worked fewer hours to meet their material needs than did people in agricultural or industrial societies and so had more leisure time. One scholar referred to them as "the original affluent society," not because they had so much, but because they wanted or needed so little.[13] Nonetheless, life expectancy was low, probably little more than thirty-five years on average. Life in the wild was surely dangerous, and dependency on the vagaries of nature rendered it insecure as well.

But Paleolithic people also acted to alter the natural environment substantially. The use of deliberately set fires to encourage the growth of particular plants certainly changed the landscape and in Australia led to the proliferation of fire-resistant eucalyptus trees at the expense of other plant species. In many parts of the world—Australia, North America, Siberia, Madagascar, Pacific islands—the extinction of various large animals followed fairly quickly after the arrival of human beings, leading scholars to suggest that Paleolithic humankind played a major role, coupled perhaps with changing climates, in the disappearance of these animals. Other hominid, or humanlike, species, such as the Neanderthals in Europe or the recently discovered Flores man in Indonesia, also perished after living side by side with *Homo sapiens* for millennia. Whether their disappearance occurred through massacre, interbreeding, or peaceful competition, they were among the casualties of the rise of humankind. Thus the biological environment inhabited by gathering and hunting peoples was not wholly natural but was shaped in part by their own hands.

The Realm of the Spirit

The religious or spiritual dimension of Paleolithic culture has been hard to pin down because bones and stones tell us little about what people thought, art is subject to many interpretations, and the experience of contemporary gathering and hunting peoples may not reflect the distant past. There is, however, clear evidence for a rich ceremonial life. The presence of rock art deep inside caves and far from living spaces suggests a "ceremonial space" separate from ordinary life. (See Visual Sources: The Aboriginal Rock Painting of Australia, pp. 42–47.) The extended rituals of contemporary Australian Aboriginal people, which sometimes last for weeks, confirm this impression, as do numerous and elaborate burial sites found throughout the world. No full-time religious specialists or priests led these ceremonies, but part-time shamans (people believed to be especially skilled at dealing with the spirit world) emerged as the need arose. Such people often entered an altered state of consciousness or a trance while performing the ceremonies, often with the aid of psychoactive drugs.

Precisely how Paleolithic people understood the nonmaterial world is hard to reconstruct, and speculation abounds. Linguistic evidence from ancient Africa suggests a variety of understandings: some Paleolithic societies were apparently monotheistic; others saw several levels of supernatural beings, including a Creator Deity, various territorial spirits, and the spirits of dead ancestors; still others believed in an impersonal force suffused throughout the natural order that could be accessed by shamans during a trance dance.[14] The prevalence of Venus figurines and other symbols all across Europe has convinced some scholars, but not all, that Paleolithic religious thought had a strongly feminine dimension, embodied in a Great Goddess and concerned with the regeneration and renewal of life.[15] Many gathering and hunting peoples likely developed a cyclical view of time that drew on the changing phases of the moon and on the cycles of female fertility—birth, menstruation,

The Willendorf Venus
Less than four and a half inches in height and dating to about 25,000 years ago, this female figure, which was found near the town of Willendorf in Austria, has become the most famous of the many Venus figurines. Certain features—the absence of both face and feet, the coils of hair around her head, the prominence of her breasts and sexual organs—have prompted much speculation among scholars about the significance of these intriguing carvings. (Naturhistorisches Museum, Vienna, Austria/The Bridgeman Art Library)

Snapshot   **The Paleolithic Era in Perspective**[16]

	Paleolithic Era (from 250,000 to 10,000 years ago)	Agricultural Era (from 10,000 to 200 years ago)	Modern Industrial Era (since 1800)
Duration of each era, as a percentage of 250,000 years	96%	4%	0.08%
Percent of people who lived, out of 80 billion total	12%	68%	20%
Percent of years lived in each era (reflects changing life expectancies)	9%	62%	29%

pregnancy, new birth, and death. Such understandings of the cosmos, which saw endlessly repeated patterns of regeneration and disintegration, differed from later Western views, which saw time moving in a straight line toward some predetermined goal.[17]

Settling Down: The Great Transition

Though glacially slow by contemporary standards, changes in Paleolithic cultures occurred over time as people moved into new environments, as populations grew, as climates altered, and as different human groups interacted with one another. For example, all over the Afro-Eurasian world after 25,000 years ago, a tendency toward the miniaturization of stone tools is evident. Known as micro-blades, these smaller and more refined spear points, arrowheads, knives, and scrapers were carefully struck from larger cores and often mounted in antler, bone, or wooden handles.[18] This ancient and global technological change was similar perhaps to the miniaturization of electronic components in the twentieth century. Another important change in the strategies of Paleolithic people was the collection of wild grains, which represented a major addition to the food supply beyond the use of roots, berries, and nuts. This innovation originated in northeastern Africa around 16,000 years ago.

But the most striking and significant change in the lives of Paleolithic peoples occurred as the last Ice Age came to an end between 16,000 and 10,000 years ago. What followed was a general global warming, though one with periodic fluctuations and cold snaps. Unlike the contemporary global warming, generated by human activity and especially the burning of fossil fuels, this ancient warming phase was a wholly natural phenomenon, part of a long cycle of repeated heating and

■ Change
Why did some Paleolithic peoples abandon earlier, more nomadic ways and begin to live a more settled life?

cooling characteristic of the earth's climatic history. Plants and animals unable to survive in the Ice Age climate now flourished and increased their range, providing a much richer and more diverse environment for many human societies. Under these improved conditions, human populations grew, and some previously nomadic gathering and hunting communities, but not all of them, found it possible to settle down and live in more permanent settlements or villages. These societies were becoming both larger and more complex, and it was less possible to simply move away if trouble struck. Settlement also meant that households could store and accumulate goods to a greater degree than previously. Because some people were more energetic, more talented, or luckier than others, the thin edge of inequality gradually began to wear away the egalitarianism of Paleolithic communities.

Changes along these lines emerged in many places. Paleolithic societies in Japan, known as Jomon, settled down in villages by the sea, where they greatly expanded the number of animals, both land and marine, that they consumed. They also created some of the world's first pottery, along with dugout canoes, paddles, bows, bowls, and tool handles, all made from wood. A similar pattern of permanent settlement, a broader range of food sources, and specialized technologies is evident in parts of Scandinavia, Southeast Asia, North America, and the Middle East between 12,000 and 4,000 years ago. Bows and arrows seem to have been invented separately in Europe, Africa, and the Middle East during this period and spread later to the Americas. In Labrador, longhouses accommodating 100 people appear in the archeological record. Far more elaborate burial sites in many places testify to the growing complexity of human communities and the kinship systems that bound them together. Separate cemeteries for dogs suggest that humankind's best friend was also our first domesticated animal friend.

This process of settling down among gathering and hunting peoples—and the changes that followed from it—marked a major turn in human history, away from countless millennia of nomadic journeys by very small communities. It also provided the setting within which the next great transition would occur. Growing numbers of people, living in settled communities, placed a much greater demand on the environment than did small bands of wandering people. Therefore, it is perhaps not surprising that among the innovations that emerged in these more complex gathering and hunting societies was yet another way for increasing the food supply—agriculture. That epic transition is the subject of the next chapter.

Comparing Paleolithic Societies

Over the 200,000 years or more of the Paleolithic era, human societies naturally differed from one another—in their tool kits, their adaptation to the environment, their beliefs, their social organization, and much more. Here we examine more carefully two such societies, the San of southern Africa and the Chumash of southern California. What they shared was a gathering and hunting way of life and a continuing existence into modern times. Unlike the gathering and hunting peoples who

Jomon Figurines
Female figurines, dating to perhaps 4,000 years ago, have been found among Japan's Paleolithic people, known as the Jomon. Many scholars believe these carvings had a ritual function, associated with fertility. (Tokyo National Museum, Collection of Mrs. Kane Yamazaka)

succumbed to the relentless expansion of agricultural or industrial societies, the San and the Chumash maintained their ancient way of life into the eighteenth, nineteenth, and twentieth centuries. Even though modern gathering and hunting societies studied by anthropologists surely differed in many ways from their ancient counterparts, they do allow us to see the human face of a way of life long vanished from most parts of the earth.

The San of Southern Africa

On the northern fringe of the Kalahari Desert, in an area including Angola, Namibia, and Botswana, lies the country of the San people, who numbered 50,000 to 80,000 at the start of the twenty-first century. Linguistically, they are related to the great Khoisan language family, whose speakers have lived throughout eastern and southern Africa for many millennia. The immediate ancestors of the San have inhabited southern Africa for at least 5,000 years. Economically, Khoisan-speaking peoples practiced a gathering and hunting way of life with a technology of stone tools that was recognizable to their twentieth-century San descendants. Another cultural practice of long standing was the remarkable rock art of southern Africa, depicting people and animals, especially the antelope, in thousands of naturalistic scenes of hunts, battles, and dances. Dating to as far back as 26,000 years ago, this tradition persisted into the nineteenth century, making it the "oldest artistic tradition of humankind."[19] Modern scholars suggest that this art reflected the religious experience of trance healers, who were likely the artists who painted these images. (See chapter opening photo on p. 10.) When a late-nineteenth-century anthropologist showed some of these rock paintings to an elderly San couple, the woman began to sing and dance, while the man became sad, remembering the old songs.[20] In these and other ways, contemporary San people are linked to an ancient cultural tradition that is deeply rooted in the African past.

Most Khoisan gathering and hunting peoples had long ago been absorbed or displaced by the arrival of Bantu-speaking peoples bearing agriculture, domesticated animals, and iron tools, but the San, living in a relatively remote location, endured. Even the colonization of southern Africa by Europeans left the San largely intact until the 1960s and later, but not completely, for they traded with their agricultural neighbors and sometimes worked for them. The San also began to use iron arrowheads, fashioned from metals introduced by the newcomers. Drums, borrowed from their Bantu-speaking neighbors, now supplemented their own stringed instruments and became part of San musical tradition. Despite these borrowings, when anthropologists descended on the San in the 1950s and 1960s and studied every aspect of their culture, they found a people still practicing an ancient way of life. (See Document 1.1, pp. 34–39, for a description of San life from a twentieth-century woman's perspective.) The following account of San culture is drawn largely from the work of Richard Lee, an anthropologist who lived with and was adopted by one of

■ **Description**
What are the most prominent features of San life?

The San of Southern Africa

ANGOLA   ZAMBIA
ZIMBABWE
NAMIBIA   BOTSWANA
KALAHARI
DESERT
SOUTH
AFRICA
ATLANTIC
OCEAN

■ Present area of San habitation

the San groups who called themselves the Ju/'hoansi.[21] The term literally means "real people"; the slash and the apostrophe in the name denote "clicks," which are a distinctive sound in the San language.

In the semidesert conditions of the northern Kalahari, the Ju/'hoansi have drawn a livelihood from a harsh land using some twenty-eight tools for gathering, hunting, and preparing food. The most important implements include an all-purpose wooden digging stick, a large leather garment used for carrying things and also as a blanket, woven ropes, nets, a knife, a spear, a bow, and arrows tipped with a potent poison. The Ju/'hoansi have identified and named some 260 species of wild animals, of which the kudu, wildebeest, and gemsbok are the most commonly hunted, entirely by men. More than 100 species of wild plants, including various nuts, berries, roots, fruits, melons, and greens, were collected, largely by women.

What kind of life did they create for themselves with this modest technology? According to Richard Lee, it was a "happy combination of an adequate diet and a short workweek." He calculated that the Ju/'hoansi consumed 2,355 calories on average every day, about 30 percent from meat and 70 percent from vegetables, well balanced with sufficient protein, vitamins, and minerals—and, he concluded, they "[did] not have to work very hard" to achieve this standard of living. An average workweek involved about seventeen hours of labor in getting food and another twenty-five hours in housework and making and fixing tools, with the total work divided quite equally between men and women. This left plenty of leisure time for resting, visiting, talking, and conducting rituals and ceremonies. Still, it was an uncertain and perpetually anxious life, with fluctuating rainfall, periodic droughts, seasonal depletion of plants, and the unpredictable movement of animals.

What made the Ju/'hoansi way of life possible was a particular kind of society, one characterized by mobility, sharing, and equality. The basic unit of social organization was a band or camp of roughly ten to thirty people, who were connected by ties of exchange and kinship with similar camps across a wide area. The membership of a camp fluctuated over time as many people claimed membership in more than one band. Furthermore, the camps themselves, consisting of quickly built grass huts, were moved frequently, with the Ju/'hoansi seldom staying more than a few months in any one place. The flexibility of this arrangement allowed them to adjust rapidly to the changing seasonal patterns of their desert environment.

At one level, Ju/'hoansi society was extremely simple. No formal leaders, chiefs, headmen, priests, or craft specialists existed, and decisions were made by individual families and camps after much discussion. On another level, social relationships were extremely complex, and it took Richard Lee several years to penetrate them. In addition to common kinship relations of marriage and descent, there were "joking" and "avoidance" relationships that determined the degree of familiarity with which people engaged one another. A further element of complexity lay in a unique "naming" system, which created a deep bond among people with the same name, even though they were not biologically related. For example, a man could not marry any woman who bore the same name as his mother or sister.

At the heart of such a small-scale society of intense personal relationships were values of modesty, cooperation, and equality, which the Ju/'hoansi went to great lengths to inculcate and maintain. One technique, known as "insulting the meat," involved highly negative comments about the size or quality of an animal killed by a hunter and the expectation that a successful hunter would disparage his own kill. As one man put it:

> When a young man kills much meat, he comes to think of himself as a chief or a big man, and he thinks of the rest of us as his servants or inferiors. We can't accept this. We refuse one who boasts, for someday his pride will make him kill someone. So we always speak of his meat as worthless. In this way we cool his heart and make him gentle.

Another practice tending toward equality was the principle that the owner of the arrow that killed an animal, not the successful hunter himself, had the right to distribute the meat from that animal. Because arrows were widely shared, and sometimes owned by women, this custom spread the prestige of meat distribution widely within the society and countered any possibility that the hunter might regard the meat as his private property.

Beyond the sharing of food within a camp was a system of unequal gift exchange among members of different camps. For example, I give you something today, and many months later, you may give me a gift that need not be equivalent in value. When Richard Lee appeared puzzled by the inequality of the exchange, he was told: "We don't trade with things; we trade with people." This system of exchange had more to do with establishing social relations than with accumulating goods. One famous and highly respected hunter named Toma "gave away everything that came into his hands. . . . [I]n exchange for his self-imposed poverty, he won the respect and follow-ing of all the people."[22] It was an economic system that aimed at leveling wealth, not accumulating it, and that defined security in terms of possessing friends or people with obligations to oneself, rather than possessing goods.

Social equality extended also to relations between women and men. Richard Lee noted "relative equality between the sexes with no-one having the upper hand." Teenagers engaged quite freely in sex play, and the concept of female virginity was apparently unknown, as were rape, wife beating, and the sexual double standard. Although polygamy was permitted, most marriages were in fact monogamous because women strongly resisted sharing a husband with another wife. Frequent divorce among very young couples allowed women to leave unsatisfactory marriages easily. Lee found that longer-term marriages seemed to be generally fulfilling and stable. Both men and women expected a satisfying sexual relationship, and both occasionally took lovers, although discreetly.

But not all was sweetness and light among the Ju/'hoansi. Frequent arguments about the distribution of meat or the laziness or stinginess of particular people generated conflict, as did rivalries among men over women. Lee identified twenty-two murders that had occurred between 1920 and 1955 and several cases in which the community came together to conduct an execution of particularly disruptive individuals. Lesser tensions were handled through talk; more serious disputes might result in separation, with some people leaving to join another camp or to start their own.

In confronting the world beyond material and social life, the Ju/'hoansi reflected beliefs and practices that were arguably tens of thousands of years old. Unlike later peoples with their many gods, goddesses, spirits, and powers, the San populated the spiritual universe in a quite limited way. A Creator God, Gao Na, gave rise to the earth, men, women, animals, waterholes, and all other things; but like the Greek gods, Gao Na was a capricious deity who often visited misfortune on humankind, simply because he chose to do so. A lesser god, Gauwa, was even more destructive, spreading disease, conflict, and death, but also on occasion providing assistance to beleaguered humans. The most serious threat to human welfare came from the ghosts of dead ancestors, the *gauwasi,* who were viewed as primarily malevolent. Asked why the ancestral spirits were so destructive, one woman healer replied:

> Longing for the living is what drives the dead to make people sick....They are very very sad....They miss their people on earth. And so they come back to us. They hover near the villages and put sickness into people, saying "Come, come here to me."

The Ju/'hoansi had one powerful resource for countering these evil influences from the world of the gods and ancestors. It was *n/um,* a spiritual potency that lies in the stomach and becomes activated during "curing dances," powerful nightlong rituals held frequently, especially during the dry season when several camps converged on the remaining waterholes. Around a fire, an inner circle of women clapped and sang, while men danced in a circle behind them. Then someone went into a trance and, in that altered state of consciousness, sought to share his or her activated *n/um* with everyone in the camp, pulling the evil out of them. Doing so had the power to heal the sick, to bring harmony to the community, to affect the rainfall and the supply of animals, and to protect everyone from the evil designs of the ancestors.[23]

Recent analysis suggests that the rock art of southern Africa represents the visions achieved by ancient trance dancers as they did battle with the supernatural world. (See chapter opening photo on p. 10.) If so, the Ju/'hoansi of the twentieth century were participating in the longest and most continuous religious tradition in world history.

The trance dance was in many ways a distinctive tradition. It did not seek communion with the supernatural; no gifts or sacrifices were offered to the gods or the ancestors, and few prayers were made for their assistance. Viewing the gods as the source of disease, conflict, and death, the Ju/'hoansi hurled at them words of reproach, abuse, and rejection, seeking to ward them off, to expel them from society. It was, as one scholar put it, a "war with God."[24] The leaders of this war, the trance dancers, were not possessed by any supernatural being but used the trance state to activate their own internal *n/um*. Nor were they a priestly elite. Men and women alike could become healers, although a fearful and extended process of spiritual preparation awaited them. Almost half of the men and one-third of the women whom Lee encountered had entered the trance state. It was a much-sought-after role, but it conveyed no permanent power or authority. Finally, Ju/'hoansi religious thinking located the source of evil and misfortune outside of the community in the activity of the gods and ancestors rather than within society in the form of sorcerers or witches. The curing dances brought the community together, united against the external and supernatural enemy.

The Chumash of Southern California

If the San Ju/'hoansi people provide a window into the life of at least one nomadic and long-established gathering and hunting society, the Chumash are more representative of those later post–Ice Age Paleolithic peoples who settled in permanent villages and constructed more complex societies. Together the San and the Chumash illustrate the immense variation that was possible within the limits of a gathering and hunting way of life.

Located in southern California in the vicinity of present-day Santa Barbara, the Chumash occupied a richer and more varied environment than did the San. Speaking a series of related dialects, they lived along the coast, in the immediate interior, and on a series of offshore islands. Thus they were able to draw on the resources of the sea as well as those of the land to support a much more densely settled population of perhaps 20,000 people when they first encountered the Spanish in the sixteenth century.

Although the area had been sparsely occupied for about 10,000 years, the history of its people comes into sharper focus only in the centuries of the Common Era. The first millennium C.E. witnessed a growing population, the overhunting and depletion of deer herds in the interior, likely food shortages, and consequently increasing levels of violence and warfare among rival groups. Evidence for this violence is found in the large number of skeletons with bashed-in skulls or arrow and spear wounds. Then, in the several centuries after 1150 C.E., the Chumash, according to a noted scholar, "created an entirely new society."[25] Whereas the history of the San is marked by long-term continuities with a distant past, the Chumash experienced an extraordinary transformation.

A major element of that transformation lay in a remarkable technological innovation—the creation of a planked canoe, or *tomol*—an ocean-going vessel some twenty to thirty feet long and with a cargo capacity of two tons. Called "the most technically sophisticated watercraft developed in the New World," the tomol came into general use around 1000 C.E.[26] Building or owning one of these vessels brought immense prestige, wealth, and power, injecting a new element of inequality into Chumash society. The

■ **Comparison**

In what ways, and why, did Chumash culture differ from that of the San?

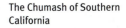

The Chumash of Southern California

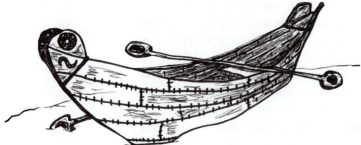

A Chumash Tomol
A technologically sophisticated seagoing canoe, the tomol, shown here in a contemporary drawing, was constructed from redwood or pine planks sewn together and caulked with hard tar and pine pitch. In recent decades, Chumash descendants have built several tomols and paddled them from the California mainland to the Channel Islands, re-creating a voyage that their distant ancestors had made many times. These reenactments were part of an effort to preserve for future generations the culture and traditions of the ancient Chumash. (Gaviota Coast Conservancy/Redrawn by © Elizabeth Leahy)

boatbuilders organized themselves into an elite craft guild, the Brotherhood of the Tomol, which monopolized canoe production and held the tools, knowledge, and sacred medicine associated with these boats. The tomol stimulated a blossoming of trade along the coast and between the coast and the islands as plant food, animal products, tools, and beads now moved regularly among Chumash communities. The boats also made possible deep-sea fishing, with swordfish, central to Chumash religious practice, being the most highly prized and prestigious catch.

In other ways as well, the material life of the Chumash was far more elaborate than that of the San. They lived in round, permanent, substantial houses, covered by grass or reeds, some of them fifty feet in diameter and able to hold up to seventy people. Every village had its own sweathouse, built partially underground and entered through an opening in the roof. Soapstone bowls, wooden plates, beautifully decorated reed baskets, and a variety of items made from bone or shell reflected a pattern of technological innovation far beyond that of the San.

A resource-rich environment, a growing and settled population, flourishing commerce, and technological innovation combined to produce something that scholars not long ago would have considered impossible—a market economy among a gathering and hunting people. Whereas the economic life of the San was regulated almost entirely by custom and tradition, that of the Chumash involved important elements of a market-based system: individuals acting out of a profit motive; the use of money, in the form of stringed beads; regulation of the supply of money to prevent inflation; specialized production of goods such as beads, stone tools, canoes, and baskets; prices attached to various items; payment for services provided by dancers, healers, and buriers; and private ownership of canoes, stores of food, and some tools. This is how an early Spanish observer described the Chumash in 1792:

> All these Indians are fond of traffic and commerce. They trade frequently with those of the mountains, bringing them fish and beadwork which they exchange for seeds and shawls of foxskin and a kind of blanket.... When they trade for profit, beads circulate among them as if they were money, being strung on long threads, according to the greater or smaller wealth of each one.... These strings of beads ... are used by the men to adorn their heads and for collars.... They all make a show of their wealth which they always wear in sight on their heads, whence it is taken for gambling and trafficking.[27]

How different is all this from the life of the Ju/'hoansi! Permanently settled villages, ranging in size from several hundred to a thousand people, would have struck the San as unsustainably large compared to their own mobile camps of twenty-five to fifty people. The specialized skills of the Chumash probably would have surprised the Ju/'hoansi, because all San people possessed pretty much the same set of skills. The San no doubt would have been appalled by the public display of wealth, the impulse toward private accumulation, and the inequalities of Chumash society. A bearskin cape, worn only by the elite of canoe owners and village chiefs, marked the beginnings of class distinctions, as did burials, which were far more elaborate for the wealthy and their children than for commoners. Members of the Brotherhood of the Tomol often were buried with parts of their canoes.

Perhaps most offensive to the egalitarian and independent Ju/'hoansi would have been the emergence of a permanent and hereditary political elite among the Chumash. High-ranking Chumash chiefs, who inherited their positions through the male line, exercised control over a number of communities, but each village also had its own chief, some of whom were women. These political leaders, all of whom were also canoe owners, led their people in war, presided over religious rituals, and regulated the flourishing trade that followed the invention of the tomol. They also named the dates for periodic feasts, during which donations and collections from the wealthy were used to feed the poor and to set aside something for a rainy day. This effort at redistributing wealth might have earned the approval of the Ju/'hoansi, who continually sought to level any social and economic distinctions among themselves.

Whatever the Ju/'hoansi might have thought, these transformations—technological, economic, social, and political—created a more unified and more peaceful life among the Chumash in the several centuries after 1150. Earlier patterns of violence apparently subsided as specialized crafts and enhanced trade evened out the distribution of food, making various Chumash communities dependent on one another. More formal political leadership enabled the peaceful resolution of disputes, which formerly had been resolved in battle. Frequent celebrations served to bring various Chumash villages together, while a society-wide organization of ritual experts provided yet another integrating mechanism. These transformations represent a remarkable achievement, especially because they introduced in a gathering and hunting society many social elements normally associated only with agricultural peoples. However, the coming of the Europeans, with their guns, diseases, and missionaries, largely destroyed Chumash society in the centuries following that epic encounter. The mobile San, in their remote location, were able to preserve their ways of life far longer than the more settled, and therefore vulnerable, Chumash, who were unable to avoid the powerful newcomers.

Reflections: The Uses of the Paleolithic

Even when it is about a past as distant as the Paleolithic era, the study of history is also about those who tell it in the present. We search the past, always, for our own purposes. For a long time, modern people were inclined to view their Paleolithic ancestors as primitive or superstitious, unable to exercise control over nature, and ignorant of its workings. Such a view was, of course, a kind of self-congratulation, designed to highlight the "progress" of modern humankind. It was a way of saying, "Look how far we have come."

In more recent decades, growing numbers of people, disillusioned with modernity, have looked to the Paleolithic era for material with which to criticize, rather than celebrate, contemporary life. Feminists have found in gathering and hunting peoples a much more gender-equal society and religious thinking that featured the divine feminine, qualities that encouragingly suggested that patriarchy was neither inevitable nor eternal. Environmentalists have sometimes identified peoples in the distant past who were uniquely in tune with the natural environment rather than seeking to dominate it. Some nutritionists have advocated a "Paleolithic diet" of wild plants and animals as well suited to our physiology. Critics of modern materialism and competitive capitalism have been delighted to discover societies in which values of sharing and equality predominated over those of accumulation and hierarchy. Still others have asked, in light of the long Paleolithic era, whether the explosive population and economic growth of recent centuries should be considered normal or natural. Perhaps they should be regarded as extraordinary, possibly even pathological. Finally, research about the Paleolithic era has been extremely important in efforts by contemporary gathering and hunting peoples, or their descendants, to maintain or recover their older identities amid the conflicting currents of modern life. All of these uses of the Paleolithic have been a way of asking, "What have we lost in the mad rush to modernity, and how can we recover it?"

Both those who look with disdain on Paleolithic "backwardness" and those who praise, often quite romantically, its simplicity and equality seek to use these ancient people for their own purposes. In our efforts to puzzle out the past, all of us—historians and students of history very much included—stand somewhere. None of us can be entirely detached when we view the past, but this is not necessarily a matter for regret. What we may lose in objectivity, we gain in passionate involvement with the historical record and the many people who inhabit it. Despite its remoteness from us in time and manner of living, the Paleolithic era resonates still in the twenty-first century, reminding us of our kinship with these distant people and the significance of that kinship to finding our own way in a very different world.

Second Thoughts

What's the Significance?

To assess your mastery of the material in this chapter, visit the **Student Center** at bedfordstmartins.com/strayer.

Paleolithic rock art	Austronesian migrations	Paleolithic settling down
Venus figurines	"the original affluent	San culture
Dreamtime	society"	"insulting the meat"
Clovis culture	shamans	Chumash culture
megafaunal extinction	trance dance	Brotherhood of the Tomol

Big Picture Questions

1. What is the significance of the Paleolithic era in world history?
2. In what ways did various Paleolithic societies differ from one another, and how did they change over time?
3. Which statements in this chapter seem to be reliable and solidly based on facts, and which ones are more speculative and uncertain?
4. How might our attitudes toward the modern world influence our assessment of Paleolithic societies?

Next Steps: For Further Study

David Christian, *This Fleeting World: A Short History of Humanity* (2008). A lovely essay by a leading world historian, the first part of which provides a succinct survey of the Paleolithic era.

Brian M. Fagan, *People of the Earth: An Introduction to World Prehistory* (2006). A global account of early human history, written by a leading archeologist.

Clive Gamble, *Timewalkers: The Prehistory of Global Colonization* (2003). A beautifully written account of the initial human settlement of the earth.

Sally McBreatry and Alison S. Brooks, "The Revolution That Wasn't: A New Interpretation of the Origin of Modern Human Behavior," *Journal of Human Evolution* 39 (2000). A long scholarly article laying out the archeological evidence for the emergence of humankind in Africa.

Marjorie Shostak, *Nisa: The Life and Words of an !Kung Woman* (2000). A vivid first-person account of a San woman's life in a twentieth-century gathering and hunting society.

"Prehistoric Art," http://witcombe.sbc.edu/ARTHprehistoric.html#general. An art history Web site with a wealth of links to Paleolithic art around the world.

For Web sites and additional documents related to this chapter, see **Make History** at bedfordstmartins.com/strayer.

Documents

Considering the Evidence:
Glimpses of Paleolithic Life

For historians accustomed to working with documents written during the time period they are studying, the Paleolithic era has often been an exercise in frustration. No such documents exist for the long era of gathering and hunting societies, for writing did not develop until quite late in the history of humankind—around 3500 B.C.E., with the emergence of the first civilizations. Thus historians have been dependent on the slender archeological remains of Paleolithic people—their bones, tools, fossilized seeds, paintings, and sculptures—for understanding the lives of these most distant of our ancestors.

In the twentieth century, anthropologists and other scholars descended on the few remaining gathering and hunting peoples, studying their cultures and collecting their stories, myths, and oral traditions. Historians are often skeptical about the usefulness of such material for understanding the distant past of Paleolithic societies. After all, gatherers and hunters in the modern era have often mixed and mingled with agricultural societies, have come under European colonial rule, or have been in contact with elements of modern civilization. Thus their cultures may well have changed substantially from earlier patterns of Paleolithic life.

While recognizing that twentieth-century accounts may not precisely describe earlier gathering and hunting societies, we are nonetheless fortunate to have these more recent materials. Despite their limitations, they provide us at least a glimpse into ways of living and thinking that have almost completely vanished from the earth. The two documents that follow represent this kind of material.

Document 1.1

A Paleolithic Woman in the Twentieth Century

In 1971 the American anthropologist Marjorie Shostak was conducting research among the San people of the Kalahari Desert on the border of Botswana and South Africa (see map, p. 25). There she became acquainted with a fifty-year-old woman called Nisa. Although Nisa had interacted with neighboring cattle-keeping people and with Europeans, she had lived most of her life "in the bush," fully participating in the gathering and hunting culture of her ancestors. Nisa proved willing to share with Shostak the intimate details of her life, including her memories of childhood, her five marriages, the birth of her children, her relationships with various lovers, and the deaths of loved ones. Those interviews became the basis for the remarkable book from which the following excerpts derive.

- What conflicts in San life does Nisa's account reveal?
- What does her story indicate about San attitudes toward sex and marriage? How might you compare those attitudes with those of contemporary society?
- How does Nisa understand God, or the divine?
- How does she understand the purpose of the curing rituals in which she took part?
- How would you describe Nisa's overall assessment of San life? Do you find it romanticized, realistic, or critical? What evidence from the passages supports your conclusions?
- How does this insider's account of San life support, contradict, or supplement the description of San culture found on pages 25–29?

Nisa
The Life and Words of an !Kung Woman
1969–1976

We are people who live in the bush, and who belong in the bush. We are not village people. I have no goats. I have no cattle. I am a person who owns nothing. That's what people say I am: a poor person....No donkey, either. I still carry things myself, in my kaross when I travel, and that's why I live in the bush....

Family Life

We lived and lived, and as I kept growing, I started to carry my little brother around on my shoulders.

My heart was happy then; I had grown to love him and carried him everywhere. I'd play with him for a while and whenever he would start to cry, I'd take him to Mother so he could nurse. Then I'd take him back with me and we'd play together again.

That was when Kumsa was little. But once he was older and started to talk and then to run around, that's when we were mean to each other and hit and fought all the time. Because that's how children play. One child does mean things and the other children do mean things back. If your father goes out hunting one day, you think, "Won't Daddy bring home meat? Then I can eat it, but I can also *stinge* it!" When your father does come home with meat, you say, "My daddy brought back meat and I won't let you have *any* of it!" The other children say, "How come we play together yet you always treat us so badly?"

Source: Marjorie Shostak, *Nisa: The Life and Words of an !Kung Woman* (Cambridge, Mass.: Harvard University Press, 1981), 41, 69, 87–89, 153–55, 166, 210–11, 226–27, 271, 299, 301–2, 316–17.

When Kumsa was bigger, we were like that all the time. Sometimes we'd hit each other. Other times, I'd grab him and bite him and said, "Oooo…what is this thing that has such a horrible face and no brains and is so mean? How come it is so mean to me when I'm not doing anything to it?" Then he'd say, "I'm going to *hit* you! What's protecting you that I shouldn't?" And I'd say, "You're just a baby! I, *I* am the one who's going to hit *you*! Why are you so miserable to me?" I'd insult him and he'd insult me and I'd insult him back. We'd just stay together and play like that.…

Life in the Bush

We lived in the bush and my father set traps and killed steenbok and duiker and gemsbok and we lived, eating the animals and foods of the bush. We collected food, ground it in a mortar, and ate it. We also ate sweet nin berries and tsin beans. When I was growing up, there were no cows or goats.… I had never seen other peoples and didn't know anything other than life in the bush. That's where we lived and where we grew up.

Whenever my father killed an animal and I saw him coming home with meat draped over a stick, balanced on one shoulder—that's what made me happy. I'd cry out, "Mommy! Daddy's coming and he's bringing *meat*!" My heart would be happy when I greeted him, "Ho, ho, Daddy! We're going to eat meat!"

Or honey. Sometimes he'd go out and come home with honey. I'd be sitting around with my mother and then see something coming from way out in the bush. I'd look hard. Then, "Oooh, Daddy found a beehive! Oh, I'm going to eat honey! Daddy's come back with honey for us to eat!" And I'd thank him and call him wonderful names.

Sometimes my mother would be the one to see the honey. The two of us would be walking around gathering food and she'd find a beehive deep inside a termite mound or in a tree. I remember one time when she found it. I jumped and ran all around and was so excited I couldn't stop moving. We went to the village to get some containers, then went back to the termite mound. I watched as she took the honey out. Then, we went home.…

When we were living in the bush, some people gave and others stinged. But there were always enough people around who shared, people who liked one another, who were happy living together, and who didn't fight. And even if one person did stinge, the other person would just get up and yell about it, whether it was meat or anything else, "What's doing this to you, making you not give us meat?"

When I was growing up, receiving food made my heart happy. There really wasn't anything, other than stingy people, that made me unhappy. I didn't like people who wouldn't give a little of what they had.…

It's the same today. Here I am, long since an adult, yet even now, if a person doesn't give something to me, I won't give anything to that person.…

Marriage

…The day of the wedding, everyone was there. All of Tashay's friends were sitting around, laughing and laughing. His younger brother said, "Tashay, you're too old. Get out of the way so I can marry her. Give her to me." And his nephew said, "Uncle, you're already old. Now, let *me* marry her." They were all sitting around, talking like that. They all wanted me.

I went to my mother's hut and sat there. I was wearing lots of beads and my hair was completely covered and full with ornaments.

That night there was another dance. We danced, and some people fell asleep and others kept dancing.…

The next day they started [to build the marriage hut]. There were lots of people there—Tashay's mother, my mother, and my aunt worked on the hut; everyone else sat around, talking. Late in the day, the young men went and brought Tashay to the finished hut. They set him down beside it and stayed there with him, sitting around the fire.…

They came and brought me back. Then they laid me down inside the hut. I cried and cried. People told me, "A man is not something that kills you; he is someone who marries you, who becomes like your father or your older brother. He kills animals and gives you things to eat. Even tomorrow, while you are crying, Tashay may kill an animal. But when he returns, he won't give you any meat; only he will eat. Beads, too. He will get beads but he won't give them to you. Why are you so afraid of your husband and what are you crying about?"

I listened and was quiet. Later, we went to sleep. Tashay lay down beside the opening of the hut, near the fire, and I lay down inside; he thought I might try and run away again. He covered himself with a blanket and slept....

We began to live together, but I ran away, again and again. A part of my heart kept thinking, "How come I'm a child and have taken another husband?"...

We lived and lived, the two of us, together, and after a while I started to really like him and then, to love him. I had finally grown up and had learned how to love. I thought, "A man has sex with you. Yes, that's what a man does. I had thought that perhaps he didn't."

We lived on and I loved him and he loved me. I loved him the way a young adult knows how to love; I just *loved* him. Whenever he went away and I stayed behind, I'd miss him. I'd think, "Oh, when is my husband ever coming home? How come he's been gone so long?" I'd miss him and want him. When he'd come back my heart would be happy, "Eh, hey! My husband left and once again has come back."

We lived and when he wanted me, I didn't refuse; he just lay with me....

I...gave myself to him, gave and gave. We lay with each other and my breasts were very large. I was becoming a woman.

Loss

It was while we were visiting in the Tswana village and just after Kxau was born that Tashay died....

I lay there and thought, "Why did this happen? The two of us gave so much to each other and lived together so happily. Now I am alone, without a husband. I am already a widow. Why did God

trick me and take my husband? God is stingy! He just takes them from you. God's heart is truly far from people."...

Then I was without my husband and my heart was miserable. Every night I missed him and every night I cried, "I am without the man I married." I thought, "Where will I see the food that will help my children grow? Who is going to help me raise this newborn? My older brother and my younger brother are far away. Who is going to help me now?" Because Kxau had only just been born; he was so small he almost didn't exist. Then I said, "Everyday food will do it. I will start today to gather the food that will bring them up," and I went out and brought back what I could....

In your heart, your child, your mother, and your father are all equal. When any one of them dies, your heart feels pain. When your child dies, you think, "How come this little thing I held beside me and watched all that she did, today has died and left me? She was the only child I had with me; there wasn't another I spent my days with. We two stayed together and talked together. This God...his ways are foul! Why did he give me a little one and then take her away?"...

The death of your parents, husband, or children—they are equal in the amount of pain you feel when you lose them. But when they all die and you have no family left, then you really feel pain. There is no one to take care of you; you are completely alone....

That's the way it is. God is the one who destroys. It isn't people who do it. It is God himself.

Lovers

...Besa [Nisa's fourth husband] and I did argue a lot, usually about sex. He was just like a young man, almost a child, who lies with his wife day after day after day....

Every night Besa wanted me and every night he would make love to me. That Besa, something was wrong with his brain!...

We argued like that all the time....That man, he wanted sex more than anything else! After a while, I realized I didn't like his ways. That's when I thought, "Perhaps I will leave him. Perhaps I'll find another man and see what he is like."

I didn't leave him, not for many years. But I did have lovers and so did he. Because, as I am Nisa, my lovers have been many. At that time, there was Tsaa and Nanau. One day Tsaa would make love to me, another day Nanau. They were jealous of each other, and once Tsaa even went to Besa and told him that Nanau and I were lovers. Besa said, "What can I do about it?" . . .

Because affairs—one married person making love to another not her husband—is something that even people from long ago knew. Even my father's father's father's father knew. There have also always been fights where poison arrows are shot and people are killed because of that. Having affairs is one of the things God gave us.

I have told you about my lovers, but I haven't finished telling you about all of them, because they are as many as my fingers and toes. Some have died and others are still alive. . . . When you are a woman, you don't just sit still and do nothing—you have lovers. You don't just sit with the man of your hut, with just one man. One man can give you very little. One man gives you only one kind of food to eat. But when you have lovers, one brings you something and another brings you something else. One comes at night with meat, another with money, another with beads. Your husband also does things and gives them to you.

But sitting with just one man? We don't do that. Does one man have enough thoughts for you? . . .

A Healing Ritual

. . . N/um—the power to heal—is a very good thing. This is a medicine very much like your medicine because it is strong. As your medicine helps people, our n/um helps people. But to heal with n/um means knowing how to trance. Because, it is in trance that the healing power sitting inside the healer's body—the n/um—starts to work. Both men and women learn how to cure with it, but not everyone wants to. Trance-medicine really hurts! As you begin to trance, the n/um slowly heats inside

you and pulls at you. It rises until it grabs your insides and takes your thoughts away. Your mind and your senses leave and you don't think clearly. Things become strange and start to change. You can't listen to people or understand what they say. You look at them and they suddenly become very tiny. You think, "What's happening? Is God doing this?" All that is inside you is the n/um; that is all you can feel.

You touch people, laying on hands, curing those you touch. When you finish, other people hold you and blow around your head and your face. Suddenly your senses go "Phah!" and come back to you. You think, "Eh hey, there are people here," and you see again as you usually do. . . .

N/um is powerful, but it is also very tricky. Sometimes it helps and sometimes it doesn't, because God doesn't always want a sick person to get better. . . .

I was a young woman when my mother and her younger sister started to teach me about drum-medicine. There is a root that helps you learn to trance, which they dug for me. My mother put it in my little leather pouch and said, "Now you will start learning this, because you are a young woman already." She had me keep it in my pouch for a few days. Then one day, she took it and pounded it along with some bulbs and some beans and cooked them together. It had a horrible taste and made my mouth feel foul. I threw some of it up. If she hadn't pounded it with the other foods, my stomach would have been much more upset and I would have thrown it all up; then it wouldn't have done anything for me. I drank it a number of times and threw up again and again. Finally I started to tremble. People rubbed my body as I sat there, feeling the effect getting stronger and stronger. My body shook harder and I started to cry. I cried while people touched me and helped me with what was happening to me.

Eventually, I learned how to break out of my self and trance. When the drum-medicine songs sounded, that's when I would start. Others would string beads and copper rings into my hair. As I began to trance, the women would say, "She's started to trance, now, so watch her carefully.

Don't let her fall." They would take care of me, touching me and helping. If another woman was also in a trance, she laid on hands and helped me.

They rubbed oil on my face and I stood there—a lovely young woman, trembling—until I was finished.

Document 1.2

Australian Aboriginal Mythology

The Aboriginal, or native, peoples of Australia have lived on their island/continent for probably 60,000 years. Until the arrival of Europeans in the late eighteenth century, they practiced a gathering and hunting way of life. That culture persisted into the twentieth century, and a small number of Aboriginal people practice it still. Over many centuries, an elaborate body of myths, legends, and stories evolved, reflecting Aboriginal understandings of the world. Known collectively as the Dreamtime, such stories served to anchor the landscape and its human and animal inhabitants to distant events and mythical ancestors. A contemporary Aboriginal artist, Semon Deeb, explains:

> Around the beginning the Ancestral Beings rose from the folds of the earth and stretching up to the scorching sun they called, "I am!" As each Ancestor sang out their name, "I am Snake," "I am Honey Ant," they created the most sacred of their songs. Slowly they began to move across the barren land naming all things and thus bringing them into being. Their words forming verses as the Ancestors walked about, they sang mountains, rivers and deserts into existence. Wherever they went, their songs remained, creating a web of Songlines over the Country. As they travelled the Ancestors hunted, ate, made love, sang and danced leaving a trail of Dreaming along the songlines. Finally at the end of their journey the Ancestral Beings sang "back into" the earth where they can be seen as land formations, sleeping.[28]

Transmitted orally and changing over time, numerous Dreamtime stories have been collected and set down in writing over the past two centuries. The tale presented here deals with the relationship of men and women, surely among the great themes of human reflection everywhere.

- What does this story suggest about the relationships between women and men? Does it support or undermine notions of gender equality among Paleolithic peoples? Is it consistent with the story associated with Visual Source 1.2 (see p. 45)?

- How are the familiar features of the known world—rivers, mountains, humans, animals, and male dominance—linked to ancient happenings in the Dreamtime?

- What aspects of a gathering and hunting way of life are reflected in this tale?

Stories from the Dreamtime
Twentieth Century

In the Dreamtime, in the land of the Murinbata people, a great river flowed from the hills through a wide plain to the sea. As it is today, the land then was rich with much fish and game. From the river rose at one place a series of high hills, where lived an old woman named Mutjinga, a woman of power. She it was who called the invisible spirits to her side with secret incantations that none other knew. She was a *kirman*, leader of the ceremonies in which the people sang and danced the exploits of the totemic beings so their spirits would be pleased and would bring food in its season and many children for the people. In those days, all the things in the world had both a physical form that could be touched, seen, and felt, and a spirit form, which was invisible. When living things died, their spirits went to a secret cave where they remained until it was time for them to be born again. Mutjinga was caretaker of this cave. Only she knew where it was. In the cave, she kept the sacred totems to which the spirits returned.

Mutjinga could speak with the spirits. Because she had this power, she could do many things which the men could not. She could send the spirits to frighten away game, to waylay people at night, or to cause a child to be born without life. The men feared the power of Mutjinga and did not consort with her. They called upon her to lead their dances and teach them songs, but none came to sit by her fire.

Mutjinga became lonely and sent for her young granddaughter to keep her company.

Mutjinga and the girl gathered bulbs and nuts and caught small game, but Mutjinga found no satisfaction in this food, for she craved the flesh of men....

[The story then recounts how Mutjinga dug a hole and covered it with branches in order to trap unsuspecting hunters. Magically turning herself into a goanna (a lizard), she

---

Source: Louis A. Allen, *Time Before Morning* (New York: Thomas Y. Crowell, 1975), 145–48.

appeared to hunters, led them to their deaths in the hole, and then ate them. This fate befell even the younger brother of her granddaughter, despite the girl's unsuccessful efforts to save him. He too was killed and partially eaten, while Mutjinga kept the rest of his body in a nearby stream.]

The next morning, the little girl was at her early chores when she saw two men coming up the hillside. As she watched, recognition lit her face and she turned toward Mutjinga.

"It is my father and brother who come. Please do not harm them," she implored.

"I crave their flesh. If you trick me again I shall eat you, as well as your father and brother," Mutjinga warned. "This time I shall wait beside you until the men appear so you cannot deceive me."

The men approached the fire, paid their respects to the old woman, and greeted the child warmly. "Daughter, have you seen your brother who came hunting this way yesterday?" the father asked.

Mutjinga hastened to reply for the child. "No, we have not seen him," she said. "It is too bad, for nearby are many goanna holes. There is a large goanna right there," and she pointed to the hole where she kept the club.

"I thirst. First give me water," said the father.

"There is cold water in the stream," the little girl told him as she pointed down the hill.

The two men walked through the bush to the stream. As the father bent to drink, he saw the leg of his elder son, which Mutjinga had weighted down in the water with a large rock. At once he understood.

"The old woman will kill us unless we kill her first," he said to his younger son, and the two men returned to the fire.

"The goanna went into the tall grass," Mutjinga told them when they appeared. "Leave your spears and light a fire to burn the grass. This will drive the goanna out, and when it runs toward its hole, you can kill it with your spears."

The men went to fire the grass. As soon as they were out of sight, the father said, "Son, climb this tree and watch the old woman closely. She works powerful magic."

This the son did, and he saw Mutjinga speak the magic words. She repeated them twice. He watched as the woman and the girl changed into goannas. From the limb of the tree, he observed the larger goanna chase the smaller one into the bush. Soon great billows of smoke were rising from the burning grass. The small goanna scuttled from the bush, its companion nipping at its heels. They ran past the hunters and disappeared down the hole.

"Get the spears," the father commanded and ran toward the hole. Just as the son returned, spears in hand, the ground beneath the father gave way and he plunged through. Waiting at the bottom was Mutjinga, club raised for the kill. But the son hurled his spear and Mutjinga fell bleeding to the ground.

The father seized her roughly. "Say the magic words that will release my daughter or we shall kill you," he threatened.

Painfully Mutjinga did as she was bidden. The daughter changed into her human form and the two men and the girl climbed from the hole.

"Daughter, show us the secret cave where the spirits are hidden," said the father, "and teach us the magic words you have learned from the old woman. We shall take the spirits to another place, and we shall have the power."

And so it was. The father took the totems from that place and hid them in another cave. He became the *kirman*, the song leader, and he taught the people the sacred dances and ceremonies. To him they brought their problems and he judged between them when they quarreled. And to this day, the men have kept the power.

Using the Evidence: Glimpses of Paleolithic Life

1. **Considering human commonality and diversity:** The study of world history highlights both the common humanity of people from all times and places as well as the vast differences that have separated particular cultures from one another. How might these texts, as well as the paintings in the Visual Sources section (pp. 42–47), serve to illustrate both of these perspectives?

2. **Linking documents and text narrative:** How do these documents and images support or amplify particular statements made about Paleolithic life in this chapter? How might they challenge or contradict that narrative?

3. **Considering the relationship of technology and culture:** How might the gathering and hunting technology of the South African and Australian peoples discussed in this chapter have shaped their cultural understandings as expressed in these documents and images? In what ways might cultural expression, as a product of human imagination, have developed independently of their technology? Does it make sense to evaluate technology as more or less "advanced"? Should culture be assessed in the same way?

Visual Sources

Considering the Evidence:
The Aboriginal Rock Painting of Australia

The rock paintings of the Aboriginal peoples of Australia represent what may be the longest continuously practiced artistic tradition in world history. Scholars have found evidence of these paintings dating to some 40,000 years ago, and the tradition has continued into the twentieth century and beyond as contemporary artists retouched and repainted ancient images and created new ones. A contemporary Aboriginal artist explained what those paintings meant to him:

> When I look at my [dreaming] paintings it makes me feel good—happy in heart, spirit. Everything is there: all there in the caves, not lost. This is my secret side. This is my home—inside me.... Our dreaming, secret side—we must hold on to this, like our fathers, looking after it.... We give to our sons when we die. The sons keep this from their fathers, grandfathers. The sons will remember, they can carry on, not be lost. And it is still there—fathers' country with rock hole, painted cave.... The people keep their ceremony things and pictures—they make them new. They bring young boys for learning to the caves, telling the stories, giving the laws from grandfathers' fathers, learning to do the paintings—[the dreaming] way.[29]

For native peoples of Australia, whose way of life has been so thoroughly disrupted by more than two centuries of European invasion and domination, this continuing artistic tradition provides a link to the past.

Created in caves and protected rock shelters all over this giant island/continent, these paintings were the products of the many distinct peoples of Paleolithic Australia. While they shared a common gathering and hunting way of life, each had its own language, stories, and ceremonies, which found expression in their paintings. Many of them depicted spirit figures or ancestors from the Dreamtime. Such images were often regarded, not as works of art by human artists, but as the actual ancestral beings themselves, able to convey their spiritual energy to their descendants. In this respect, they served something of the same purpose as the much later icons or religious paintings in the Christian world, said to convey the very presence of the divine. (See Visual Sources: Reading Byzantine Icons, pp. 466–71.)

Beyond religious or ceremonial purposes, Aboriginal rock painting also depicted various animals, some of them now extinct; stenciled images of human hands; and abstract designs, believed by scholars to represent coded symbols understood only by those who underwent proper ceremonial initiation. Other paintings portrayed scenes from daily life and were particularly focused on hunting. Still others recorded historical events such as the visits of fishermen from what is now Indonesia to the northern coasts of Australia. Images of European sailing ships, rifles, tools, and animals also found a place in the more recent expressions of Aboriginal rock painting.

The three images shown in this section are from the Kakudu National Park in Australia's Northern Territory, an area inhabited by humans for some 20,000 years. Some of the fading images in the park were repainted in the 1960s by Nayambolmi, one of the last of the traditional rock-art painters. As you examine these images, keep in mind that even the experts do not really know what they meant to the people who created them thousands of years ago. Our task is to appreciate, to imagine, and to speculate about these remarkable paintings rather than to decipher them with any precision.

In Visual Source 1.1, the largest and main figure at the top is Namondjok, a Creation Ancestor, who according to some accounts can be seen in the sky at night as a dark spot in the Milky Way galaxy. Other stories recount that Namondjok violated incest laws by sleeping with a woman from his clan who would have been considered his sister. To the right is Namarrgon, or Lightning Man, who generates the tremendous lightning storms that occur during the rainy season. The arc around his body represents the lightning, while the axes on his head, elbow, and feet are used to split the dark clouds, creating thunder and lightning. The female figure beneath Namondjok is Barrginj, the wife of Lightning Man, while the people below her, elaborately dressed, are perhaps on their way to a ceremony.

- What could an Aboriginal viewer learn about nature from this painting?

- What might he or she understand about the cosmic hierarchy?

- Why do you think the artist positioned people at the bottom of the picture? Might the positioning of Barrginj have meaning as well?

- How might you interpret the relative size of the various images in the painting?

Visual Source 1.1 Namondjok, Namarrgon (Lightning Man), and Barrginj (J. Marshall/Visual Connection Archive)

Visual Source 1.2 depicts Nabulwinjbulwinj, said to be a wicked and dangerous male spirit who kills females by hitting them with a yam and then eating them.

- What message might such a story seek to convey?

- Does this story seem consistent with Document 1.2, which seeks to explain why men have power over women?

Visual Sources 1.1 and 1.2 both reflect a distinctive style of Aboriginal painting known as the X-ray tradition, in which the internal bones and organs of human or animal figures are depicted while also showing their outward appearance.

- What internal structures can you distinguish in these images?

- What purposes or intentions might lay behind such a style?

Visual Source 1.2 Nabulwinjbulwinj (J. Marshall/Visual Connection Archive)

Visual Source 1.3 A Hunting Scene (Oz Outback Internet Services, Queensland, Australia)

Visual Source 1.3 depicts a hunting scene, featuring either people or the thin Mimi spirits, said to inhabit the nooks and crannies of the area's rock formations. Notice the spears that the hunters carry. Various kinds of spears and spear-throwing devices had earlier replaced or supplemented the boomerang, while bows and arrows were unknown to the hunters of Australia before contact with Europeans.

- If the painting depicts real people or actual hunters, what purposes might it serve?

- What different understandings might emerge if the painting is seen as portraying Mimi spirits?

- How might a contemporary Aboriginal artist, such as the one quoted on page 42, understand this painting?

Using the Evidence:
The Aboriginal Rock Painting of Australia

1. **Comparing rock art traditions:** How do these Paleolithic-era paintings compare with those from South Africa and southern France shown on pages 00 and 00?

2. **Considering art and religion:** How do these images reflect the religious understandings of the Dreamtime (see Document 1.2, pp. 39–41)?

3. **Seeking further evidence:** What additional information might help you to understand these images more fully?

4. **Connecting past and present:** In what ways do these paintings retain their ability to speak to people living in industrial societies of the twenty-first century? Or do they have meaning only for those who made them?

CHAPTER TWO

First Farmers

The Revolutions of Agriculture

10,000 B.C.E.–3000 B.C.E.

"After me, I suppose there will be nothing here," remarked seventy-two-year-old Elsie Eiler in 2005. At the time, she was the sole remaining resident of the farm town of Monowi, Nebraska. "There is just no employment for people. Farming is hard and all the small farms have had to merge into bigger ones, and the young people just want to go away to college and a city. Few of them come back." Founded in 1902 by Czech immigrants, Monowi in the early twentieth century boasted a post office, two banks, a high school, a church, and rows of well-built homes. By the early twenty-first century, the church was boarded up, many houses had collapsed, deer and wild elk roamed the town's empty spaces, and flocks of birds nested in thick weeds along what had once been Main Street. With the death of her husband in 2004, Mrs. Eiler became the only living soul in Monowi, where she served as the town's mayor and ran its only business, a tavern whose customers came from passing traffic and nearby settlements.[1]

MRS. EILER'S STORY AND THAT OF HER TOWN were part of a much larger global process taking place over the past several centuries of the industrial age—a dramatic decline in the number of people directly earning their living as farmers. The United States represents an extreme case of this worldwide phenomenon: at the beginning of the twenty-first century, only about 5 percent of Americans lived on farms, and many of them were over the age of sixty-five. Despite the

The Statues of Ain Ghazal: Among the largest of the early agricultural settlements investigated by archeologists is that of Ain Ghazal, located in the modern state of Jordan. Inhabited from about 7200 to 5000 B.C.E., in its prime it was home to some 3,000 people, who lived in multiroomed stone houses; cultivated barley, wheat, peas, and lentils; and herded domesticated goats. These remarkable statues, around three feet tall and made of limestone plaster applied to a core of bundled reeds, were among the most startling finds at that site. Did they represent heroes, gods, goddesses, or ordinary people? No one really knows. (Courtesy, Department of Antiquities of Jordan [DoA]. Photo: Freer Gallery of Art and Arthur M. Sackler Gallery, Washington, DC) small number of American farmers, modern agriculture was so productive that those few people were able to feed the entire country and to export a large amount of food as well. This modern retreat from the farm marked a dramatic reversal of a much more ancient pattern in which growing numbers of people began to farm and agriculture became for the first time the primary occupation for the vast majority of humankind. The beginnings of that epic process represent the central theme of this chapter.

The Agricultural Revolution in World History

The chief feature of the long Paleolithic era—and the first human process to operate on a global scale—was the initial settlement of the earth. Then, beginning around 12,000 years ago, a second global pattern began to unfold—agriculture. The term "Neolithic" (New Stone Age) or "Agricultural Revolution" refers to the deliberate cultivation of particular plants as well as the taming and breeding of particular animals. Thus a whole new way of life gradually replaced the earlier practices of gathering and hunting in most parts of the world. Although it took place over centuries and millennia, the coming of agriculture represented a genuinely revolutionary transformation of human life all across the planet and provided the foundation for almost everything that followed: growing populations, settled villages, animal-borne diseases, horse-drawn chariot warfare, cities, states, empires, civilizations, writing, literature, and much more.

Among the most revolutionary aspects of the age of agriculture was a new relationship between humankind and other living things, for now men and women were not simply using what they found in nature but were actively changing nature as well. They were consciously "directing" the process of evolution. The actions of farmers in the Americas, for example, transformed corn from a plant with a cob of an inch or so to one measuring about six inches by 1500. Later efforts more than doubled that length. Farmers everywhere stamped the landscape with a human imprint in the form of fields with boundaries, terraced hillsides, irrigation ditches, and canals. Animals too were transformed as selective breeding produced sheep that grew more wool, cows that gave more milk, and chickens that laid more eggs than their wild counterparts.

This was "domestication"—the taming, and the changing, of nature for the benefit of humankind—but it created a new kind of mutual dependence. Many domesticated plants and animals could no longer survive in the wild and relied on human action or protection in order to reproduce successfully. Similarly, human beings in the agricultural era lost the skills of their gathering and hunting ancestors, and in any event there were now too many people to live in that older fashion. As a consequence, farmers and herders became dependent on their domesticated plants and animals. From an outside point of view, it might well seem that corn and cows had tamed human beings, using people to ensure their own survival and growth as a species, as much as the other way around.

A further revolutionary aspect of the agricultural age is summed up in the term "intensification." It means getting more for less, in this case more food and resources—far more—from a much smaller area of land than was possible with a gathering and hunting technology. More food meant more people. Growing populations in turn required an even greater need for the intensive exploitation of the environment. And so was launched the continuing human effort to "subdue the earth" and to "have dominion over it," as the biblical story in Genesis recorded God's command to Adam and Eve.

Comparing Agricultural Beginnings

Perhaps the most extraordinary feature of the Neolithic or Agricultural Revolution was that it occurred, separately and independently, in many widely scattered parts of the world: the Fertile Crescent of Southwest Asia, several places in sub-Saharan Africa, China, New Guinea, Mesoamerica, the Andes, and eastern North America (see the Snapshot on p. 52). Even more remarkably, all of this took place at roughly the same time (at least as measured by the 250,000-year span of human history on the planet)—between 12,000 and 4,000 years ago. These facts have generated many questions with which historians and other scholars have long struggled. Why was the Agricultural Revolution so late in the history of humankind? What was unique about the period after 10,000 B.C.E. that may have triggered or facilitated this vast upheaval? In what different ways did the Agricultural Revolution take shape in its various locations? How did it spread from its several points of origin to the rest of the earth? And what impact did it have on the making of human societies?

Common Patterns

It is no accident that the Agricultural Revolution coincided with the end of the last Ice Age, a process of global warming that began some 16,000 years ago. By about 11,000 years ago, the Ice Age was over, and climatic conditions similar to those of our own time generally prevailed. This was but the latest of some twenty-five periods of glaciation and warming that have occurred over the past several million years of the earth's history and which are caused by minor periodic changes in the earth's orbit around the sun. The end of the last Ice Age, however, coincided with the migration of *Homo sapiens* across the planet and created new conditions that made agriculture possible. Combined with active hunting by human societies, climate change in some areas helped to push into extinction various species of large mammals on which Paleolithic people had depended, thus adding to the pressure to find new food sources. The warmer, wetter, and more stable conditions, particularly in the tropical and temperate regions of the earth, also permitted the flourishing of more wild plants, especially cereal grasses, which were the ancestors of many domesticated crops. What climate change took away with one hand, it apparently gave back with the other.

■ Change
What accounts for the emergence of agriculture after countless millennia of human life without it?

$Snapshot$ **Agricultural Breakthroughs**[2]

Location	Dates (B.C.E.)	Plants	Animals
Southwest Asia (Fertile Crescent)	9000–7000	barley, wheat, lentils, figs	goats, sheep, cattle, pigs
China	6500–5000	rice, millet, soybeans	pigs, chickens, water buffalo
Saharan and sub-Saharan Africa	3000–2000	sorghum, millet, yams, teff	cattle (perhaps 8000 B.C.E.)
Highland New Guinea	7000–4000	taro, bananas, yams, sugarcane	—
Andes region	3000–2000	potatoes, quinoa, manioc	llamas, alpaca, guinea pig
Mesoamerica	3000–2000	maize, squash (perhaps 7000 B.C.E.), beans	turkey
Eastern woodlands of North America	2000–1000	sunflower, goosefoot, sumpweed	—

Over their long history, gathering and hunting peoples had already developed a deep knowledge of the natural world and in some cases an ability to manage it actively. They had learned to make use of a large number of plants and to hunt and eat both small and large animals, creating what archeologists call a "broad spectrum diet." In the Middle East, people had developed sickles for cutting newly available wild grain, baskets to carry it, mortars and pestles to remove the husk, and storage pits to preserve it. Peoples of the Amazon and elsewhere had learned to cut back some plants to encourage the growth of their favorites. Native Australians had built elaborate traps in which they could capture, store, and harvest large numbers of eels.

In hindsight, much of this looks like a kind of preparation for agriculture. Because women in particular had long been intimately associated with collecting wild plants, most scholars believe that they were the likely innovators who led the way to deliberate farming, with men perhaps taking the lead in domesticating animals. Clearly the knowledge and technology necessary for agriculture were part of a longer process involving more intense human exploitation of the earth. Nowhere was agriculture an overnight invention.

Using such technologies, and benefiting from the global warming at the end of the last Ice Age, gathering and hunting peoples in various places were able to settle down and establish more permanent villages, abandoning their nomadic ways and more intensively exploiting the local area. This was particularly the case in resource-rich areas close to seas, lakes, marshes, and rivers. In settling down, however, they soon lost some of the skills of their ancestors and found themselves now required to support growing populations. Evidence for increasing human numbers around the world during this period of global warming has persuaded some scholars that agriculture was a response to an impending "food crisis."[3] If the number of people outstripped the local resources, or if sudden fluctuations in climate—prolonged drought or a cold snap, for example—diminished those resources, these newly settled communities were in trouble. It was no longer so easy to simply move away. These vagaries surely motivated people to experiment and to innovate in an effort to increase the food supply. Clearly, many of the breakthroughs to agriculture occurred only *after* gathering and hunting peoples had already grown substantially in numbers and had established a sedentary way of life.

These were some of the common patterns that facilitated the Agricultural Revolution. New opportunities appeared with the improved conditions that came at the end of the Ice Age. New knowledge and technology emerged as human communities explored and exploited that changed environment. The disappearance of many large mammals, growing populations, newly settled ways of life, and fluctuations in the process of global warming—all of these represented pressures or incentives to increase food production and thus to minimize the risks of life in a new era.[4] From some combination of these opportunities and incentives emerged the profoundly transforming process of the Agricultural Revolution.

This new way of life initially operated everywhere with a simple technology—the digging stick or hoe (the plow was developed only later). But the several transitions to this hoe-based agriculture, commonly known as horticulture, varied considerably, depending on what plants and animals were available locally. For example, potatoes were found in the Andes region, but not in Africa or Asia; wheat and wild pigs existed in the Fertile Crescent, but not in the Americas. Furthermore, of the world's 200,000 plant species, only several hundred have been domesticated, and just five of these—wheat, corn, rice, barley, and sorghum—supply more than half of the calories that sustain human life. Only fourteen species of large mammals have been successfully domesticated, of which sheep, pigs, goats, cattle, and horses have been the most important. Because they are stubborn, nervous, solitary, or finicky, many animals simply cannot be readily domesticated.[5] In short, the kind of Agricultural Revolution that unfolded in particular places depended very much on what happened to be available locally, and that in turn depended on sheer luck.

Variations

Among the most favored areas—and the first to experience a full Agricultural Revolution—was the Fertile Crescent, an area sometimes known as Southwest Asia, consisting of present-day Iraq, Syria, Israel/Palestine, and southern Turkey (see Map 2.1). In this region, an extraordinary variety of wild plants and animals capable of domestication provided a rich array of species on which the now largely settled gathering and hunting people could draw. What triggered the transition to agriculture, it seems, was a cold and dry spell between 11,000 and 9500 B.C.E., a temporary

■ **Comparison**
In what different ways did the Agricultural Revolution take shape in various parts of the world?

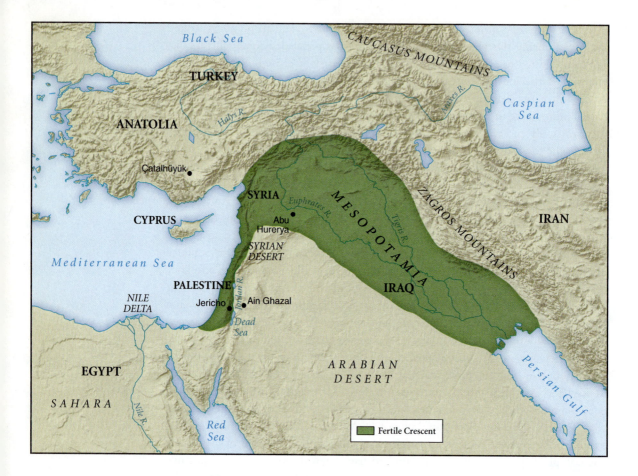

Map 2.1   The Fertile Crescent
Located in what is now called the Middle East, the Fertile Crescent was the site of many significant processes in early world history, including the first breakthrough to agriculture and later the development of some of the First Civilizations.

interruption in the general process of global warming. Larger settled populations were now threatened with the loss of the wild plants and animals on which they had come to depend. Their solution was domestication. In the millennium or so after 9000 B.C.E., figs, wheat, barley, rye, peas, lentils, sheep, goats, pigs, and cattle all came under human control, providing the foundation for the world's first, and most productive, agricultural societies.

Archeological evidence suggests that the transition to a fully agricultural way of life in this region sometimes took place quite quickly, within as few as 500 years. Signs of that transformation included large increases in the size of settlements, which now housed as many as several thousand people. In these agricultural settings, archeologists have found major innovations: the use of sun-dried mud bricks; the appearance of monuments or shrinelike buildings; displays of cattle skulls; more elaborate human burials, including the removal of the skull; and more sophisticated tools, such as sickles, polished axes, and awls.[6] Environmental deterioration in ecologically fragile regions was yet another indication of this new way of life. Numerous settlements in the Jordan River valley and Palestine were abandoned as growing populations of people and goats stripped the area of trees and ground cover, leading to soil erosion and food shortages, which required their human inhabitants to scatter.[7] (See the chapter opening photograph, p. 48, for sculptures from the early agricultural settlement of Ain Ghazal in the Middle East.)

At roughly the same time, perhaps a bit later, another process of domestication was unfolding on the African continent in a most unlikely place—the eastern part of what is now the Sahara in present-day Sudan. Between 10,000 and 5,000 years ago, however, "the Saharan desert . . . effectively did not exist," according to scholars, as the region received more rainfall than currently, had extensive grassland vegetation, and was "relatively hospitable to human life."[8] It seems likely that cattle were domesticated in this region about 1,000 years before they were separately brought under human control in the Middle East and India. At about the same time, the donkey also was domesticated in northeastern Africa near the Red Sea and spread from there into Southwest Asia, even as the practice of raising sheep and goats moved in the other direction. In Africa, animal domestication thus preceded the domestication of plants, while elsewhere in the world it was the other way around.

In terms of farming, the African pattern again was somewhat different. Unlike the Fertile Crescent, where a number of plants were domesticated in a small area, sub-Saharan Africa witnessed the emergence of several widely scattered farming practices. Sorghum, which grows well in arid conditions, was the first grain to be "tamed" in the eastern Sahara region. In the highlands of Ethiopia, teff, a tiny, highly nutritious grain, as well as enset, a relative of the banana, came under cultivation. In the forested region of West Africa, yams, oil palm trees, okra, and the kola nut (still used as a flavoring for Coca-Cola and Pepsi) emerged as important crops. The scattered location of these domestications generated a less productive agriculture than in the more favored and compact Fertile Crescent, but a number of the African domesticates—sorghum, castor beans, gourds, millet, the donkey—subsequently spread to enrich the agricultural practices of Eurasian peoples.

Yet another pattern of agricultural development took shape in the Americas. Like the Agricultural Revolution in Africa, the domestication of plants in the Americas occurred separately in a number of locations—in the coastal Andean regions of western South America, in Mesoamerica, in the Mississippi valley, and perhaps in the Amazon basin—but surely its most distinctive feature lay in the absence of animals that could be domesticated. Of the fourteen major species of large mammals that have been brought under human control, only one, the llama/alpaca, existed in the Western Hemisphere. Without goats, sheep, pigs, cattle, or horses, the peoples of the Americas lacked the sources of protein, manure (for fertilizer), and power (to draw plows or pull carts, for example) that were widely available to societies in the Afro-Eurasian world. Because they could not depend on domesticated animals for meat, agricultural peoples in the Americas relied more on hunting and fishing than did peoples in the Eastern Hemisphere.

Furthermore, the Americas lacked the rich cereal grains that were widely available in Afro-Eurasia. Instead they had maize or corn, first domesticated in southern Mexico by 4000 to 3000 B.C.E. Unlike the cereal grains of the Fertile Crescent, which closely resemble their wild predecessors, the ancestor of corn, a mountain grass

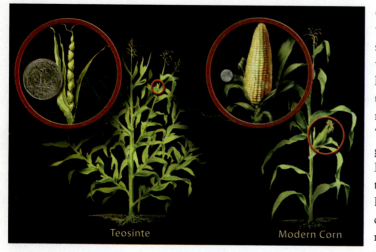

Teosinte   Modern Corn

Teosinte and Maize/Corn
The sharp difference in size between the tiny cobs of teosinte, a wild grass, and usable forms of domesticated maize meant that the Agricultural Revolution took place more slowly in Mesoamerica than it had in Mesopotamia. (Nicolle Rager Fuller, National Science Foundation)

called *teosinte*, looks nothing like what we now know as corn or maize. Thousands of years of selective adaptation were required to develop a sufficiently large cob and number of kernels to sustain a productive agriculture, an achievement that one geneticist has called "arguably man's first, and perhaps his greatest, feat of genetic engineering."[9] Even then, corn was nutritionally poorer than the protein-rich cereals of the Fertile Crescent. To provide sufficient dietary protein, corn had to be supplemented with squash and beans, which were also domesticated in the Americas. Thus while Middle Eastern societies quite rapidly replaced their gathering and hunting economy with agriculture, that process took 3,500 years in Mesoamerica.

Another difference in the progress of the Agricultural Revolution lay in the north/south orientation of the Americas, which required agricultural practices to move through, and adapt to, quite distinct climatic and vegetation zones if they were to spread. The east/west axis of Eurasia meant that agricultural innovations could spread more rapidly because they were entering roughly similar environments. Thus corn, beans, and squash, which were first domesticated in Mesoamerica, took several thousand years to travel the few hundred miles from their Mexican homeland to the southwestern United States and another thousand years or more to arrive in eastern North America. The llama, guinea pig, and potato, which were domesticated in the Andean highlands, never reached Mesoamerica.[10]

The Globalization of Agriculture

■ **Connection**
In what ways did agriculture spread? Where and why was it sometimes resisted?

From the various places where it originated, agriculture spread to much of the rest of the earth, although for a long time it coexisted with gathering and hunting ways of life (see Map 2.2). Broadly speaking, this extension of farming occurred in two ways. The first is called diffusion, which refers to the gradual spread of agricultural techniques, and perhaps of the plants and animals themselves, but without the extensive movement of agricultural people. Neighboring groups exchanged ideas and products in a down-the-line pattern of communication. A second process involved the slow colonization or migration of agricultural peoples as growing populations pushed them outward. Often this meant the conquest, absorption, or displacement of the earlier gatherers and hunters, along with the spread of the languages and cultures of the migrating farmers. In many places, both processes took place.[11] The spread of corn-based agriculture in the Americas, highlighted in the Snapshot on page 57, illustrates the process.

Snapshot   **The History of Maize/Corn**[12]

The earliest domestication of teosinte—a grass from which modern maize/corn subsequently developed in a process of adaptation and "genetic engineering" over thousands of years—occurs in southern Mexico. It may have been used for the sugary syrup found in its stalk as well as the nutritional value of its kernels.	9000–8000 B.C.E.
Maize cultivation spreads to South America (Ecuador, Peru).	2300–1000 B.C.E.
Maize cob reaches length of about six centimeters. There is evidence that corn was ground with stone mortars and baked in flat bread.	by 2000 B.C.E.
Maize becomes the staple of Mesoamerican agriculture. Its cultural importance was reflected in its prominence in various myths of origin. Such stories among the Maya, for example, held that humankind was made first of mud, then of wood, and finally, and most successfully, from maize dough.	1500 B.C.E.
Maize spreads to the southwestern United States as farming people migrate.	1000 B.C.E.
In Peru, the average size of a maize cob doubles. Maize is used for making maize beer.	500 B.C.E.–1 C.E.
Maize cultivation reaches the eastern woodlands of the Mississippi River valley, largely through diffusion, although people of this region had already domesticated several minor crops, such as sunflowers.	500 C.E.
Maize farming is introduced in New England and is widespread by 1300, about 300 years before the arrival of the Pilgrims.	1000 C.E.
Maize spreads to Europe, Africa, and Asia, following European conquest of the Americas.	16th–18th centuries C.E.

Triumph and Resistance

Some combination of diffusion and migration took the original agricultural package of Southwest Asia and spread it widely into Europe, Central Asia, Egypt, and North Africa between 6500 and 4000 B.C.E. Languages originating in the core region accompanied this movement of people and farming practices. Thus Indo-European languages, which originated probably in Turkey and are widely spoken even today from India to Europe, reflect this movement of culture associated with the spread of agriculture. In a similar process, the Chinese farming system moved into Southeast Asia and elsewhere, and with it a number of related language families developed. India received agricultural influences from the Middle East, Africa, and China alike.

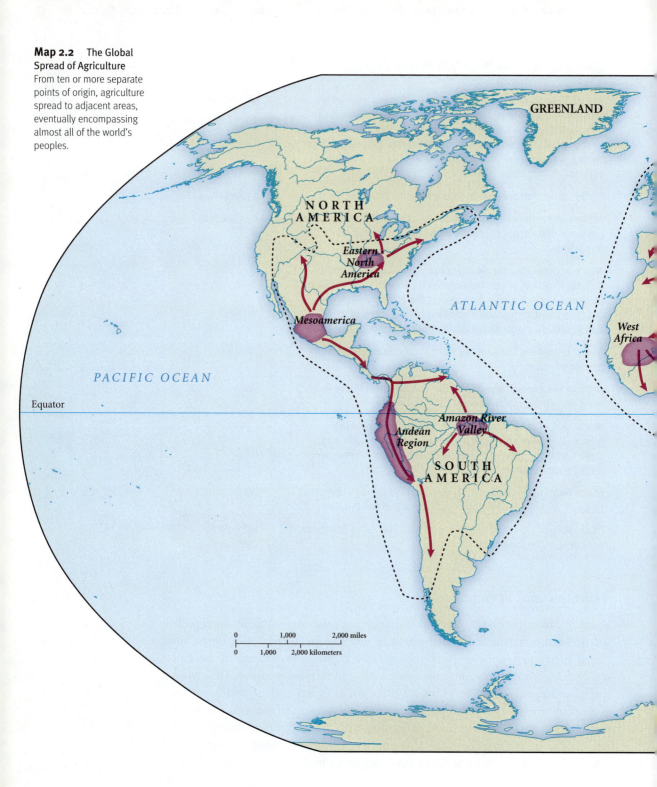

Map 2.2 The Global Spread of Agriculture
From ten or more separate points of origin, agriculture spread to adjacent areas, eventually encompassing almost all of the world's peoples.

GREENLAND

NORTH AMERICA

Eastern North America

ATLANTIC OCEAN

Mesoamerica

West Africa

PACIFIC OCEAN

Equator

Andean Region

Amazon River Valley

SOUTH AMERICA

0   1,000   2,000 miles
0   1,000   2,000 kilometers

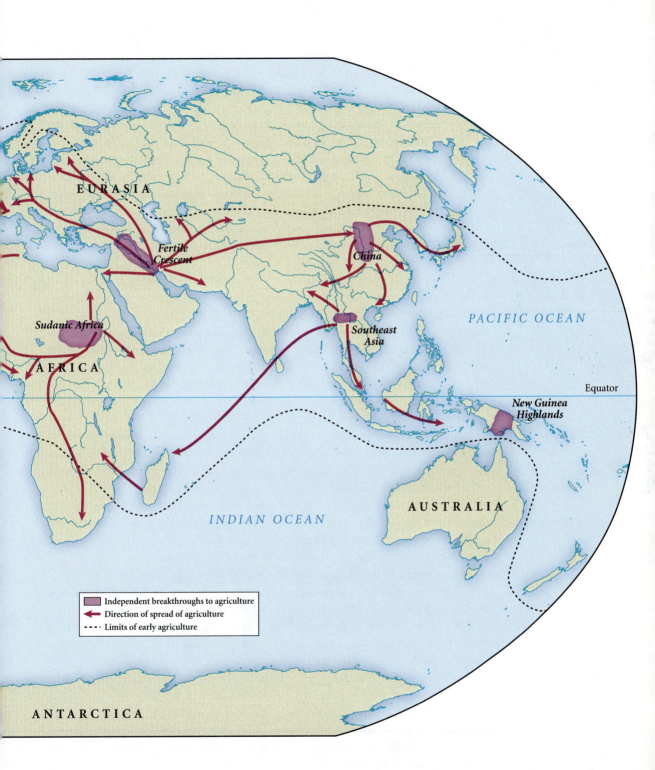

EURASIA

Fertile
Crescent

China

PACIFIC OCEAN

Sudanic Africa

AFRICA

Southeast
Asia

Equator

New Guinea
Highlands

INDIAN OCEAN

AUSTRALIA

Independent breakthroughs to agriculture
Direction of spread of agriculture
Limits of early agriculture

ANTARCTICA

59

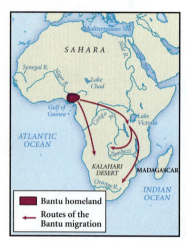

Bantu Migrations

Within Africa, the development of agricultural societies in the southern half of the continent is associated with the migration of peoples speaking one or another of the some 400 Bantu languages. Beginning from what is now southern Nigeria or Cameroon around 3000 B.C.E., Bantu-speaking people moved east and south over the next several millennia, taking with them their agricultural, cattle-raising, and, later, ironworking skills, as well as their languages. The Bantus generally absorbed, killed, or drove away the indigenous Paleolithic peoples or exposed them to animal-borne diseases to which they had no immunities. A similar process brought agricultural Austronesian-speaking people, who originated in southern China, to the Philippine and Indonesian islands, with similar consequences for their earlier inhabitants. Later, Austronesian speakers carried agriculture to the uninhabited islands of the Pacific and to Madagascar off the coast of southeastern Africa (see Map 1.2 on p. 19).

The globalization of agriculture was a prolonged process, lasting 10,000 years or more after its first emergence in the Fertile Crescent, but it did not take hold everywhere. The Agricultural Revolution in New Guinea, for example, did not spread much beyond its core region. In particular, it did not pass to the nearby peoples of Australia, who remained steadfastly committed to gathering and hunting ways of life. The people of the west coast of North America, arctic regions, and southwestern Africa also maintained their gathering and hunting way of life into the modern era. A very few, such as the Hadza, described at the beginning of Chapter 1, practice it still.

Some of those who resisted the swelling tide of agriculture lived in areas unsuitable to farming, such as harsh desert or arctic environments; others lived in regions of particular natural abundance, like the territory of the Chumash, so they felt little need for agriculture. Such societies found it easier to resist agriculture if they were not in the direct line of advance of more powerful agricultural people. But the fact that many of the remaining gathering and hunting peoples knew about agricultural practices from nearby farming neighbors suggests that they quite deliberately chose to resist it, preferring the freer life of their Paleolithic ancestors.

Nonetheless, by the beginning of the Common Era, the global spread of agriculture had reduced gathering and hunting peoples to a small and dwindling minority of humankind. If that process meant "progress" in certain ways, it also claimed many victims as the relentlessly expanding agricultural frontier slowly destroyed gathering and hunting societies. Whether this process occurred through the peaceful diffusion of new technologies, through intermarriage, through disease, or through the violent displacement of earlier peoples, the steady erosion of this ancient way of life has been a persistent thread of the human story over the past 10,000 years. The final chapters of that long story are being written in our own century. After the Agricultural Revolution, the future, almost everywhere, lay with the farmers and herders and with the distinctive societies that they created.

The Culture of Agriculture

What did that future look like? In what ways did societies based on the domestication of plants and animals differ from those rooted in a gathering and hunting economy? In the first place, the Agricultural Revolution led to an increase in human population, as the greater productivity of agriculture was able to support much larger numbers. An early agricultural settlement uncovered near Jericho in present-day Israel probably had 2,000 people, a vast increase in the size of human communities compared to much smaller Paleolithic bands. On a global level, scholars estimate that the world's population was about 6 million around 10,000 years ago, before the Agricultural Revolution got under way, and shot up to some 50 million by 5,000 years ago and 250 million by the beginning of the Common Era. Here was the real beginning of the human dominance over other forms of life on the planet.

> ■ **Change**
>
> What was revolutionary about the Agricultural Revolution?

But larger communities and more people did not necessarily mean an improved life for ordinary people. Farming involved hard work and more of it than in many earlier gathering and hunting societies. The remains of early agricultural people show some deterioration in health—more tooth decay and anemia, a shorter physical stature, and diminished life expectancy. Living close to animals subjected humans to new diseases—smallpox, flu, measles, chicken pox, malaria, tuberculosis, rabies—while living in larger communities generated epidemics for the first time in human history.[13] Furthermore, relying on a small number of plants or animals rendered early agricultural societies vulnerable to famine, in case of crop failure, drought, or other catastrophes. The advent of agriculture bore costs as well as benefits.

Agriculture also imposed constraints on human communities. Some Paleolithic people had settled in permanent villages, but all agricultural people did so, as farming required a settled life. A good example of an early agricultural settlement comes from northern China, one of the original independent sources of agriculture, where rice, millet, pig, and chicken farming gave rise to settled communities by about 7,000 years ago. In 1953, workers digging the foundation for a factory uncovered the remains of an ancient village, now called Banpo, near the present-day city of Xian. Millet, pigs, and dogs had been domesticated, but diets were supplemented with wild plants, animals, and fish. Some forty-five houses covered with thatch laid over wooden beams provided homes to perhaps 500 people. More than 200 storage pits permitted the accumulation of grain, and six kilns and pottery wheels enabled the production of various pots, vases, and dishes, many decorated with geometric designs and human and animal images. A large central space suggests an area for public religious or political activity, and a trench surrounding the village indicates some common effort to defend the community.

Early agricultural villages such as Banpo reveal another feature of the age of agriculture—an explosion of technological innovation. Mobile Paleolithic peoples had little use for pots, but such vessels were essential for settled societies, and their creation and elaboration accompanied agriculture everywhere. So too did the weaving of textiles, made possible by collecting the fibers of domesticated plants (cotton

Women and Weaving
During the Paleolithic era and beyond, the weaving of cloth was widely regarded as women's work. It still is in many places, as this picture from an early twenty-first-century carpet-weaving workshop in Isfahn (Iran) illustrates. (Phil Weymout/Lonely Planet Images/Getty Images)

and flax, for example) and animals such as sheep. Evidence for the invention of looms of several kinds dates back to 7,000 years ago, and textiles, some elaborately decorated, show up in Peru, Switzerland, China, and Egypt. Like agriculture itself, weaving clearly seems to be a technology in which women were the primary innovators. It was a task that was compatible with child-rearing responsibilities, which virtually all human societies assigned primarily to women.[14] Another technology associated with the Agricultural Revolution was metallurgy. The working of gold and copper, then bronze, and, later, iron became part of the jewelry-, tool-, and weapon-making skill set of humankind. The long "stone age" of human technological history was coming to an end, and the age of metals was beginning.

A further set of technological changes, beginning around 4000 B.C.E., has been labeled the "secondary products revolution."[15] These technological innovations involved new uses for domesticated animals, beyond their meat and hides. Agricultural people in parts of Europe, Asia, and Africa learned to milk their animals, to harvest their wool, and to enrich the soil with their manure. Even more important, they learned to ride horses and camels and to hitch various animals to plows and carts. Because these types of animals did not exist in the Americas, this revolutionary new source of power and transportation was available only in the Eastern Hemisphere.

A final feature of early agricultural societies lay in their growing impact on the environment, as farming and herding peoples deliberately altered the natural ecosystem by removing the natural ground cover for their fields, by making use of irrigation, and by grazing their now-domesticated animals. In parts of the Middle East within a thousand years after the beginning of settled agricultural life, some villages were abandoned when soil erosion and deforestation led to declining crop yields, which could not support mounting populations.[16] The advent of more intensive agriculture associated with city-based civilizations only heightened this human impact on the landscape (see Chapter 3).

Social Variation in the Age of Agriculture

■ Comparison
What different kinds of societies emerged out of the Agricultural Revolution?

The resources generated by the Agricultural Revolution opened up vast new possibilities for the construction of human societies, but they led to no single or common outcome. Differences in the natural environment, the encounter with strangers, and sometimes deliberate choices gave rise to several distinct kinds of societies early on in the age of agriculture, all of which have endured into modern times.

Pastoral Societies

One variation of great significance grew out of the difference between the domestication of plants and the domestication of animals. Many societies made use of both, but in regions where farming was difficult or impossible—arctic tundra, some grasslands, and deserts—some people came to depend far more extensively on their animals, such as sheep, goats, cattle, horses, camels, or reindeer. Animal husbandry was a "distinct form of food-producing economy," relying on the milk, meat, and blood of animals.[17] Known as herders, pastoralists, or nomads, such people emerged in Central Asia, the Arabian Peninsula, the Sahara, and in parts of eastern and southern Africa. What they had in common was mobility, for they moved seasonally as they followed the changing patterns of vegetation necessary as pasture for their animals.

The particular animals central to pastoral economies differed from region to region. The domestication of horses by 4000 B.C.E. and the later mastery of horseback-riding skills enabled the growth of pastoral peoples all across the steppes of Central Asia by the first millennium B.C.E. Although organized primarily in kinship-based clans or tribes, these nomads periodically created powerful military confederations, which played a major role in the history of Eurasia for thousands of years. In the Inner Asian, Arabian, and Saharan deserts, domesticated camels made possible the human occupation of forbidding environments. The grasslands south of the Sahara and in parts of eastern Africa supported cattle-raising pastoralists. The absence of large animals capable of domestication meant that no pastoral societies emerged in the Americas.

The relationship between nomadic herders and their farming neighbors has been one of the enduring themes of Afro-Eurasian history. Frequently, it was a relationship of conflict as pastoral peoples, unable to produce their own agricultural products, were attracted to the wealth and sophistication of agrarian societies and sought access to their richer grazing lands as well as their food crops and manufactured products. The biblical story of the deadly rivalry between two brothers—Cain, a "tiller of the ground," and Abel, a "keeper of sheep"—reflects this ancient conflict, which persisted well into modern times. But not all was conflict between pastoral and agricultural peoples. The more peaceful exchange of technologies, ideas, products, and people across the ecological frontier of pastoral and agricultural societies also served to enrich and to change both sides. In the chapters that follow, and especially in Chapter 12, we will encounter pastoral

The Domestication of Animals

Although farming often gets top billing in discussions of the Neolithic Revolution, the raising of animals was equally important, for they provided meat, pulling power, transportation (in the case of horses and camels), and manure. Animal husbandry also made possible pastoral societies, which were largely dependent on their domesticated animals. In this Egyptian carving, dating to about 2380 B.C.E., two workers lead a prime bull to the fields. (G. Dagli Orti/The Art Archive)

societies repeatedly, particularly as they interact with neighboring agricultural and "civilized" peoples. (See Visual Source 2.3, p. 80, for a rock-art painting of an early pastoral community in the Sahara.)

Agricultural Village Societies

The most characteristic early agricultural societies were those of settled village-based farmers, such as those living in Banpo or Jericho. Such societies retained much of the equality and freedom of gathering and hunting communities, as they continued to do without kings, chiefs, bureaucrats, or aristocracies.

An example of this type of social order can be found at Çatalhüyük, a very early agricultural village in southern Turkey. A careful excavation of the site revealed a population of several thousand people who buried their dead under their houses and then filled the houses with dirt and built new ones on top, layer upon layer. No streets divided the houses, which were constructed adjacent to one another. People moved about the village on adjoining rooftops, from which they entered their homes. Despite the presence of many specialized crafts, few signs of inherited social inequality have surfaced. Nor is there any indication of male or female dominance, although men were more closely associated with hunting wild animals and women with plants and agriculture. "Both men and women," concludes one scholar, "could carry out a series of roles and enjoy a range of positions, from making tools to grinding grain and baking to heading a household."[18] (See Visual Sources: Art and Life in the Early Agrarian Era, pp. 76–83, for additional images from Çatalhüyük and for other architectural and artistic expressions of early agricultural settlements.)

Many such village-based agricultural societies flourished well into the modern era, usually organizing themselves in terms of kinship groups or lineages, which incorporated large numbers of people well beyond the immediate or extended family. Such people traced their descent through either the male or the female line to some common ancestor, real or mythical. In many African societies, for example, a lineage system provided the framework within which large numbers of people could make and enforce rules, maintain order, and settle disputes without going to war. In short, the lineage system performed the functions of government, but without the formal apparatus of government, and thus did not require kings or queens, chiefs, or permanent officials associated with a state organization. (See Document 2.2, pp. 71–73 for a description of an East African agricultural village society, the Gikuyu.) The Tiv of central Nigeria organized close to a million people in this fashion at the end of the nineteenth century. Theirs was a system in which power was dispersed

Çatalhüyük
Since the 1960s, archeologists have uncovered the connected homes of Çatalhüyük, shown here in a photo of the excavation, as well as many artifacts, murals, and sculptures from this early agricultural settlement in southern Turkey. (Courtesy, James Mellaart/ Çatalhöyük Research Project)

throughout the society rather than being concentrated in particular people or institutions. In fact, the Tiv had no word for "politics" as a separate aspect of life, for there was no state that specialized in political matters.

Despite their democratic qualities and the absence of centralized authority, village-based lineage societies sometimes developed modest social and economic inequalities. Elders could exploit the labor of junior members of the community and sought particularly to control women's reproductive powers, which were essential for the growth of the lineage. Among the Igbo of southern Nigeria, "title societies" enabled men and women of wealth and character to earn a series of increasingly prestigious "titles" that set them apart from other members of their community, although these honors could not be inherited. Lineages also sought to expand their numbers, and hence their prestige and power, by incorporating war captives or migrants in subordinate positions, sometimes as slaves.

Many agricultural societies, in Africa and elsewhere, conducted their affairs without formal centralized states or full-time rulers, even when they were aware of these institutions and practices from nearby peoples. Given the frequent oppressiveness of organized political power in human history, such experiments with "stateless societies" represent an intriguing alternative to states, kingdoms, and empires, so frequently highlighted in the historical record. These agricultural village societies pioneered the human settlement of vast areas; adapted to a variety of environments; created numerous cultural, artistic, and religious traditions; incorporated new crops, institutions, and people into their cultures; and interacted continuously with their neighbors.

Chiefdoms

In other places, agricultural village societies came to be organized politically as chiefdoms, in which inherited positions of power and privilege introduced a more distinct element of inequality, but unlike later "kings," chiefs could seldom use force to compel the obedience of their subjects. Instead they relied on their generosity or gift giving, their ritual status, or their personal charisma to persuade their followers. The earliest such chiefdoms seem to have emerged in the Tigris-Euphrates river valley called Mesopotamia (present-day Iraq), sometime after 6000 B.C.E., when temple priests organized irrigation systems and controlled trade with nearby societies.

■ **Comparison**
How did chiefdoms differ from stateless agricultural village societies?

Many chiefdoms followed in all parts of the world, and the more recent ones have been much studied by anthropologists. (See Documents 2.1, pp. 68–71, and 2.3, pp. 73–75, for examples of chiefdoms in Europe and the Caribbean.) For example, chiefdoms emerged everywhere in the Pacific islands, which had been colonized by agricultural Polynesian peoples. Chiefs usually derived from a senior lineage, tracing their descent to the first son of an imagined ancestor. With both religious and secular functions, chiefs led important rituals and ceremonies, organized the community for warfare, directed its economic life, and sought to resolve internal conflicts. They collected tribute from commoners in the form of food, manufactured goods, and raw materials. These items in turn were redistributed to warriors, craftsmen, religious specialists, and other subordinates, while the chief kept enough to maintain

Cahokia
Pictured here in an artist's reconstruction, Cahokia (near St. Louis, Missouri) was the center of an important agricultural chiefdom around 1100 C.E. See Chapter 7 for details. (Cahokia Mounds State Historic Site, Illinois. Painting by Lloyd K. Townsend)

his prestigious position and his imposing lifestyle.[19] In North America as well, a remarkable series of chiefdoms emerged in the eastern woodlands, where an extensive array of large earthen mounds testify to the organizational capacity of these early societies. The largest of them, known as Cahokia, flourished around 1100 C.E. In such agricultural chiefdoms—both ancient and more recent—the distinction between elite and commoner, based on birth rather than age or achievement, began to take root. It was a fateful turn in the organization of human societies—one that was replicated, elaborated, and assumed to be natural in all later states and civilizations.

Reflections: The Legacies of Agriculture

Because it is practiced around the world and has achieved virtually universal acceptance, agriculture, or domestication, may seem to be a natural or inevitable feature of the human story. In terms of world history, however, it is a recent development, an adaptation to the unique conditions of the latest interglacial period. Who can say how long those conditions will last or whether agriculture would remain a viable way of life in a renewed Ice Age?

No matter how it turns out in the very long run, during the last 10,000 years or so, the Agricultural Revolution has radically transformed both the trajectory of the human journey and the evolution of life on the planet. This epic transformation granted to one species, *Homo sapiens*, a growing power over many other species of plants and animals. Agriculture made possible an increase in human numbers far beyond what a gathering and hunting economy could support, and it enabled human beings to control and manipulate both plants and animals for their own purposes far more than ever before.

But if agriculture provided humankind with the power to dominate nature, it also, increasingly, enabled some people to dominate others. This was not immediately apparent, and for several thousand years, and much longer in some places, agricultural villages retained much of the social equality that had characterized

Paleolithic life. Slowly, though, many of the resources released by the Agricultural Revolution accumulated in the hands of a few. Rich and poor, chiefs and common- ers, landowners and dependent peasants, rulers and subjects, dominant men and subordinate women, slaves and free people—these distinctions, so common in the record of world history, took shape most extensively in highly productive agricul- tural settings, which generated a substantial economic surplus. There the endless elaboration of such distinctions, for better or worse, became a major feature of those distinctive agricultural societies known to us as "civilizations."

Second Thoughts

What's the Significance?

end of the last Ice Age	Bantu migration	pastoral societies
"broad spectrum diet"	peoples of Australia	Çatalhüyük
Fertile Crescent	Banpo	"stateless societies"
teosinte	"secondary products	chiefdoms
diffusion	revolution"	

To assess your mastery of the material in this chapter, visit the **Student Center** at bedfordstmartins.com/strayer.

Big Picture Questions

1. The Agricultural Revolution marked a decisive turning point in human history. What evidence might you offer to support this claim, and how might you argue against it?
2. How did early agricultural societies differ from those of the Paleolithic era? How does the example of settled gathering and hunting peoples such as the Chumash complicate this comparison?
3. Was the Agricultural Revolution inevitable? Why did it occur so late in the story of humankind?
4. "The Agricultural Revolution provides evidence for 'progress' in human affairs." How would you evaluate this statement?

Next Steps: For Further Study

Elizabeth Wayland Barber, *Women's Work: The First* 20,000 *Years* (1994). Explores the role of women in early technological development, particularly textile making.

Peter Bellwood, *First Farmers* (2005). A recent and up-to-date account of the Agricultural Revolution, considered on a global basis.

Mark Nathan Cohen, *The Food Crisis in Prehistory* (1977). An older work arguing that mounting human population triggered the breakthrough to agriculture.

Jared Diamond, *Guns, Germs, and Steel* (1997). A provocative and much-publicized explanation for regional economic differences, based on variations among early agricultural revolutions.

Steven Mithen, *After the Ice: A Global Human History, 20,000–5000 B.C.* (2004). An imaginative tour of world archeological sites during the Agricultural Revolution.

Neil Roberts, *The Holocene: An Environmental History* (1998). Explores the role of climate change and human activity in shaping the global environment during the age of agriculture.

"The Agricultural Revolution," http://www.wsu.edu/gened/learn-modules/top_agrev/agrev-index .html. A Web-based tutorial from Washington State University.

For Web sites and additional documents related to this chapter, see **Make History** at bedfordstmartins.com/strayer.

Documents

Considering the Evidence:
Agricultural Village Societies

The Agricultural Revolution was arguably the most significant turning point in the larger story of humankind, at least before the Industrial Revolution. And the most celebrated outcome of the agricultural breakthrough was "civilization"—the early city- and state-based societies of Egypt, Mesopotamia, India, China, Peru, and elsewhere (see Chapter 3). Yet the domestication of plants and animals did not everywhere and always lead to civilizations, and certainly not immediately. In the Middle East and Northeastern Africa, for example, thousands of years passed before the transition to agriculture generated a recognizable civilization. Elsewhere, fully agricultural societies without the characteristic features of civilization—cities, empires, written languages, and pronounced social inequalities—persisted well into modern times.

The earliest agricultural village societies, which emerged well before writing had been developed anywhere, have passed into history leaving no documentary record. Therefore, we focus here on three much later examples of such societies—the Germanic neighbors of the Roman Empire during the first century C.E., the Gikuyu people of East Africa in the early twentieth century, and the Taino of the Caribbean islands during the sixteenth century. Since these peoples lacked writing, our documentary evidence about them derives from the descriptions of literate outsiders or from more recent accounts by educated insiders. While varying greatly in their historical and cultural settings, the documents that follow and the peoples they describe nonetheless provide us with some exposure to those agricultural village societies and chiefdoms that were among the major outcomes of the Agricultural Revolution.

Document 2.1

Germanic Peoples of Central Europe

Ancient Germanic-speaking peoples, occupying much of Central Europe north of the Roman Empire, were never a single "nation" but rather a collection of tribes, clans, and chiefdoms, regarded by the Romans as barbarians though admired and feared for their military skills (see Map 4.4, p. 156). They were famously described by Tacitus (56–117 C.E.), a Roman official and well-known historian. Tacitus himself had never visited the lands of the people he describes; rather, he relied on earlier written documents and interviews with merchants and soldiers who had traveled and lived in the region.

- What can we learn from Tacitus's account about the economy, politics, society, and culture of the Germanic peoples of the first century C.E.?

- Which statements of Tacitus might you regard as reliable and which are more suspect? Why?

- Why did Tacitus regard Germanic peoples as distinctly inferior to Romans? How might he have responded to the idea that these people would play a major role in the collapse of the Roman Empire several centuries later?

- Modern scholars have argued that Tacitus used the Germanic peoples to criticize aspects of his own Roman culture. What evidence might support this point of view?

TACITUS

Germania

First Century C.E.

The Germans themselves I should regard as aboriginal, and not mixed at all with other races through immigration or intercourse.... [W]ho would leave Asia, or Africa, or Italy for Germany, with its wild country, its inclement skies, its sullen manners and aspect, unless indeed it were his home? In their ancient songs, their only way of remembering or recording the past, they celebrate an earth-born god, Tuisco, and his son Mannus, as the origin of their race, as their founders....

The tribes of Germany are free from all taint of intermarriages with foreign nations, and they appear as a distinct, unmixed race, like none but themselves. Hence, too, the same physical peculiarities throughout so vast a population. All have fierce blue eyes, red hair, huge frames, fit only for a sudden exertion. They are less able to bear laborious work. Heat and thirst they cannot in the least endure; to cold and hunger their climate and their soil inure them....

They choose their kings by birth, their generals by merit. These kings have not unlimited or arbitrary power, and the generals do more by example than by authority.... But to reprimand, to imprison, even to flog, is permitted to the priests alone, and that not as a punishment, or at the general's bidding, but, as it were, by the mandate of the god whom they believe to inspire the warrior.... And what most stimulates their courage is that their squadrons or battalions, instead of being formed by chance or by a fortuitous gathering, are composed of families and clans. Close by them, too, are those dearest to them, so that they hear the shrieks of women, the cries of infants....

Tradition says that armies already wavering and giving way have been rallied by women who, with earnest entreaties and bosoms laid bare, have vividly represented the horrors of captivity, which the Germans fear with such extreme dread on behalf of their women....They even believe that the sex

Source: Alfred John Church and William Jackson Brodribb, *The Agricola and Germania of Tacitus* (London: Macmillan, 1877), pp. 87ff.

has a certain sanctity and prescience, and they do not despise their counsels, or make light of their answers....

Mercury is the deity whom they chiefly worship, and on certain days they deem it right to sacrifice to him even with human victims....

Augury and divination by lot no people practice more diligently. The use of lots is simple. A little bough is lopped off a fruit-bearing tree, and cut into small pieces; these are distinguished by certain marks, and thrown carelessly and at random over a white garment. In public questions the priest of the particular state, in private the father of the family invokes the gods, and, with his eyes toward heaven, takes up each piece three times, and finds in them a meaning according to the mark previously impression on them....

When they go into battle, it is a disgrace for the chief to be surpassed in valor, a disgrace for his followers not to equal the valor of the chief. And it is an infamy and a reproach for life to have survived the chief, and return from the field. To defend, to protect him, to ascribe one's own brave deeds to his renown, is the height of loyalty. The chief fights for victory; his vassals fight for their chief.... Feasts and entertainments, which though inelegant, are plentifully furnished, are their only pay. The means of this bounty come from war or rapine.° Nor are they as easily persuaded to plough the earth and to wait for the year's produce as to challenge an enemy and earn the honor of wounds. Nay, they actually think it tame and stupid to acquire by the sweat of toil what they might win by their blood.

Whenever they are not fighting, they pass much of their time in the chase, and still more in idleness giving themselves up to sleep and to feasting, the bravest and the most warlike doing nothing, and surrendering the management of the household of the home, and of the land, to the women, the old men, and all the weakest members of the family.... It is the custom of the states to bestow by voluntary and individual contribution on the chief a present of cattle or of grain, which, while accepted as a compliment, supplies their wants. They are particularly delighted by gifts from neighboring tribes...such as choice

steeds, heavy armor, trappings, and neckchains. We have now taught them to accept money also.

It is well known that the nations of Germany have no cities, and that they do not even tolerate closely contiguous dwellings. They live scattered and apart, just as a spring, a meadow, or a wood has attracted them. Their villages they do not arrange in our fashion,...but every person surrounds his dwelling with an open space, either as a precaution against the disasters of fire, or because they do not know how to build. No use is made by them of stone or tile; they employ timber for all purposes, rude masses without ornament or attractiveness....

They all wrap themselves in a cloak which is fastened with a clasp, or, if this is not forthcoming, with a thorn, leaving the rest of their persons bare....They also wear the skins of wild beasts....

Their marriage code, however, is strict, and indeed no part of their manners is more praiseworthy. Almost alone among barbarians they are content with one wife, except a very few among them.... Lest the woman should think herself to stand apart from aspirations after noble deeds and from the perils of war, she is reminded by the ceremony which inaugurates marriage that she is her husband's partner in toil and danger, destined to suffer and to dare with him alike both in peace and in war....

Very rare for so numerous a population is adultery, the punishment of which is prompt, and in the husband's power. Having cut off the hair of the adulteress and stripped her naked, he expels her from the house in the presence of her kinfolk, and then flogs her through the whole village. The loss of chastity meets with no indulgence; neither beauty, youth, nor wealth will procure the culprit a husband. No one in Germany laughs at vice, nor do they call it the fashion to corrupt and to be corrupted....To limit the number of their children or to destroy any of their subsequent offspring is accounted infamous, and good habits are here more effectual than good laws elsewhere....

It is the duty among them to adopt the feuds as well as the friendships of a father or a kinsman. These feuds are not implacable; even homicide is expiated by the payment of a certain number of cattle and of sheep, and the satisfaction is accepted by the entire family, greatly to the advantage of the state, since

---

°**rapine:** a seizure or robbery.

feuds are dangerous in proportion to a people's freedom....

[S]laves are not employed after our manner with distinct domestic duties assigned to them, but each one has the management of a house and home of his own. The master requires from the slave a certain quantity of grain, of cattle, and of clothing, as he would from a tenant, and this is the limit of subjection. All other household functions are discharged by the wife and children....

Of lending money on interest and increasing it by compound interest they know nothing—a more effectual safeguard than if it were prohibited.

Land proportioned to the number of inhabitants is occupied by the whole community in turn, and afterward divided among them according to rank. A wide expanse of plains makes the partition easy. They till fresh fields every year, and they have still more land than enough;... corn [wheat] is the only produce required from the earth.

Document 2.2

Social Organization among the Gikuyu

Occupying the fertile highlands of central Kenya in East Africa, the Gikuyu were an agricultural, iron-working, and Bantu-speaking people who were incorporated into the British Empire during the late nineteenth century (see the map on p. 60). They were among the many "stateless societies" of world history, for they did not organize themselves in a large-scale centralized political authority. Over many centuries, however, they had developed or adapted from their neighbors a mechanism known as age-sets to facilitate social integration and political decision-making. Age-sets were groups of men who were initiated at the same time and then rose collectively through a series of age-grades, or ranks, over the course of their lives. Here, the Gikuyu age-set system, as well as its gendered division of labor, is described by Jomo Kenyatta, a well-known nationalist leader in colonial Kenya and the country's first African president. In his book *Facing Mount Kenya*, published in 1938, Kenyatta described Gikuyu life in a positive (perhaps idealized) fashion, intended to counteract negative British images of African life as primitive, backward, or savage.

■ How does Kenyatta describe the division of labor and marriage practices in Gikuyu families? Does his description suggest gender equality or patriarchy?

■ What were the major stages through which Gikuyu men passed during their lives? What duties were associated with each of the age-grades?

■ How did the age-set system perform some of the functions of states, while avoiding their often oppressive features? How might you define the advantages and disadvantages of a stateless society in comparison to human communities organized around a formal government or state?

■ In light of the colonial setting in which Kenyatta was living, what message was he trying to convey?

Jomo Kenyatta

Facing Mount Kenya

1938

The chief occupations among the Gikuyu are agriculture and the rearing of livestock, such as cattle, sheep, and goats. Each family, i.e., a man, his wife or wives, and their children, constitute an economic unit. This is controlled and strengthened by the system of division of labor according to sex....

In house-building, the heavy work of cutting timbers and putting up the framework falls on men. Carrying and cutting of the grass for thatching and plastering the wall with clay or cow-dung is the work of women.... The entire housework naturally falls within the sphere of women's activities. They cook, bring water from the rivers, wash utensils, and fetch firewood from the forests and bush. They also perform the task of carrying the loads on their backs....

In cultivating the fields, men clear the brush and cut big trees, and also break the virgin soil with digging sticks and hoes. Women come behind them and prepare the ground for sowing seeds. Planting is shared by both sexes....Weeding is done collectively....Harvesting is done chiefly by women....Tending of cattle, sheep, and goats and also slaughtering and distributing the meat and preparing the skins is entirely men's duty. Dress-making, pottery, and weaving of baskets is exclusively women's profession....The brewing of beer is done jointly by both men and women....Trading is done by both sexes....

The Gikuyu customary law of marriage provides that a man may have as many wives as he can support, and that the larger one's family, the better it is for him and the tribe....The custom also provides that all women must be under the protection of men...and that all women must be married in their teens, i.e., fifteen to twenty. Thus there is no term in the Gikuyu language for "unmarried" or "old maids."...

The teaching of social obligations is...emphasized by the classification of age-groups....This binds together those of the same status in ties of closest loyalty and devotion. Men circumcised at the same time stand in the very closest relationship to each other....

The fellowship and unity of these age-groups is rather a remarkable thing. It binds men from all parts of the country, and though they may have been circumcised in places hundreds of miles apart, it is of no consequence. They are like old boys of the same school, though I question whether the Europeans have any association with the same high standards of mutual obligation....Age-groups further emphasize the social grades of junior and senior, inferior and superior....The older group takes precedence over the younger and has rights to service and courtesy which the younger must acknowledge.

...The circumcision ceremony was the only qualification which gave a man the recognition of manhood and the full rights of citizenship....As soon as his circumcision wounds heal, he joins the national council of junior warriors. At this stage his father provides him with necessary weapons, namely spear, shield, and sword; then a sheep or a male goat is given to the senior warriors of the district.... The animal is killed for a ceremony of introducing the young warrior into the general activities and etiquette of the warrior class.

The second stage in warriorhood was celebrated about eighty-two moons or twelve rain seasons following the circumcision ceremony. At this juncture the junior warrior was promoted to the council of the senior warriors....The initiation fee to this rank was two sheep or goats....

The third stage in manhood is marriage. When a man is married and has established his own homestead, he is required to join the council of elders

Source: Jomo Kenyatta, *Facing Mount Kenya* (London: Martin Secker and Warburg, 1938), 53–55, 174, 115–16, 198–205.

(*kiama*); he pays one male goat or sheep and then he is initiated into a first grade of eldership.... [They] act as messengers to the *kiama*, and help to skin animals, to light fires, to bring firewood, to roast meat for the senior elders, and to carry ceremonial articles to and from the *kiama* assemblies. They must not eat kidneys, spleen, or loin, for these are reserved for the senior elders.

Next...comes the council of peace. This stage is reached when a man has a son or daughter older enough to be circumcised.... After this [an elaborate ceremony of induction into this new age-grade], the candidate is invested with his staff of office and a bunch of sacred leaves. This signifies that he is now a peaceful man, that he is no longer a carrier of spear and shield, or a pursuer of the vanity of war and plunder. That he has now attained a stage where he has to take the responsibility of carrying the symbols of peace and to assume the duties of peace-maker in the community....

The last and most honored status in the man's life history is the religious and sacrificial council. This stage is reached when a man has had practically all his children circumcised, and his wife (or wives) has passed the child-bearing age.... The elders of this grade assume a role of "holy men." They are the high priests. All religious and ethical ceremonies are in their hands.

Document 2.3

Religion in a Caribbean Chiefdom

When Christopher Columbus arrived in the Caribbean region in the late fifteenth century, he found a densely settled agricultural people known as the Taino inhabiting the islands now called Hispaniola (modern Haiti and Dominican Republic), Cuba, Jamaica, and Puerto Rico. Organized into substantial village communities governed by a hierarchy of chiefs (*cacique*), Taino society featured modest class distinctions. An elite group of chiefs, warriors, artists, and religious specialists enjoyed a higher status than commoners, who worked the fields, fished, and hunted. Within a half century of Columbus's arrival, almost all of the Taino had perished, victims of Spanish brutality and Old World diseases. Among the witnesses to this catastrophe was the Spanish missionary and Dominican priest Bartolomé de Las Casas (1474–1566). His extensive writings contained a vehement denunciation of Spanish actions in the Americas as well as an informed description of Taino life and culture. Here, Las Casas describes his understanding of Taino religion.

- Based on this account, how might you describe Taino religious practice?

- To what extent does Las Casas's Christian perspective color his account of Taino religion?

- What was the function of the *zemis* in Taino culture?

- What was the relationship between Taino political authorities and the "priests," or *behiques*?

- Which features of Taino religious life did Las Casas appreciate and which did he find offensive or erroneous?

BARTOLOMÉ DE LAS CASAS
Apologetic History of the Indies
1566

The people of this island Hispaniola had a certain faith in and knowledge of a one and true God, who was immortal and invisible, for none can see him, who had no beginning, whose dwelling place and residence is heaven, and they called him Yócahu Vagua Maórocoti....

Into this true and catholic knowledge of the true God these errors intruded, to wit: that God had a mother, whose name was Atabex, and a brother Guaca, and other relatives in like fashion. They must have been like people without a guide on the road of the truth; rather there was one who would lead them astray, clouding the light of their natural reason that could have guided them....

[T]hey had some idols or good-luck statues, and these were generally called *zemis*.... They believed these zemis gave them water and wind and sun when they had need of them, and likewise children and other things they wanted to have. Some of these were made of wood and others of stone....

[P]riests, who are called *behiques* in the language of these islands and who were their theologians, prophets, and soothsayers, practiced some deceptions upon these people, primarily when they acted as physicians, in accordance with what the devil, from the domain allowed to him, dictated to them what they were to say or do. They led the people to believe they spoke with those statues and that the statues revealed their secrets to them, and they find out from those secrets everything they want to know. And it must have been so, because the devil surely spoke in those statues....

They had other idols or images of stone which those priests and physicians made the people believe they took out of the bodies of those who were sick, and these stones were of three kinds. I never saw their form, but they held each one to have its own power: one had the power to favor their sown lands; the second, so that women would have good fortune in childbirth; the power of the third was that they would have water and good rains when they had need of them. Thus they must have been like the gods of the ancients, each one of whom had the responsibility of presiding in his domain, although these peoples sensed this more crudely and simply than the ancients. The kings and lords boasted, and in this the other people must have followed them, about their zemis or gods and considered them more glorious, saying that they had better zemis than the other peoples and lords, and they endeavored to steal them from each other; and although they took great care in guarding these statues or idols or whatever they may have been from other Indians from other kingdoms and dominions, they took incomparably greater care in guarding and concealing them from the Spaniards, and when they suspected their approach, they would take them and hide them in the mountains....

We found that in the season when they gathered the harvest of the fields they had sown and cultivated, which consisted of the bread made from roots, yams, sweet potatoes, and corn, they donated a certain portion as first fruits, almost as if they were giving thanks for benefits received. Since they had no designated temples or houses of religion, as has been said above, they put this portion of first fruits of the crops in the great house of the lords and caciques, which they called *caney*, and they offered and dedicated it to the zemi. They said the zemi sent the water and brought the sun and nurtured all those fruits and gave them children and the other benefits which were there in abundance. All the things offered in this way were left there either until they rotted or the children took them or played with them or until they were spoiled, and thus they were consumed....

Source: Bartolomé de Las Casas, "Apologetic History of the Indies, 1566," in *Taino: Pre-Columbian Art and Culture from the Caribbean*, edited by Fatima Bercht et al., translated by Susan C. Griswold (New York: Monacelli Press, 1997), 175–79.

When I would ask the Indians at times: "Who is this zemi you name?" they answered me: "He who makes it rain and makes the sun shine and gives us children and the other benefits we desire."…

I saw them celebrate their cohoba° a few times, and it was something to see how they took it and what they said. The first to begin was the lord, and while he took it everyone kept silent; when he had taken his cohoba (which is to inhale those powders through the nostrils…), and they took it seated on some low but very well carved benches which they called *duhos*…, he would stay a while with his head turned to one side and his arms placed on his knees, and afterward he would lift his face toward heaven and speak his certain words, which must have been his prayer to the true God, or to the one whom he held to be a god; then everyone would respond almost like when we respond amen, and they would do this with a great clamor of voices or sounds, and then they would give thanks to him, and they must have flattered him with praises, winning his benevolence and begging him to tell what he had seen. He would give them an account of his vision, saying that the zemi had spoken and assured him of good or adverse times, or that there were to be children, or that there was to be a death among them, or that they were to have some contention or war with their neighbors, and other foolishness that came to their imagination, stirred up by that intoxication, or that the devil, perhaps and haplessly, had insinuated to them so as to deceive them and inculcate in them a devotion to him.…

[One particular] zemi brought diseases to men, according to their belief, for which they sought the help of the priests or behiques, who were their prophets and theologians as has been said; these priests would respond that the disease had befallen them because they had been negligent or forgetful in bringing cassava bread and yams and other things to eat to the ministers who swept and cleaned the house or hermitage of Vaybrama, good zemi, and that he had told him so.

°**cohoba:** a hallucinogenic drug used in religious ceremonies.

Using the Evidence:
Agricultural Village Societies

1. **Comparing agricultural societies:** How would you compare the social organization of the three societies described in Documents 2.1, 2.2, and 2.3?

2. **Comparing agricultural and Paleolithic societies:** What features of gathering and hunting societies persisted among agricultural peoples? In what ways did they differ from their Paleolithic ancestors?

3. **Evaluating documents:** Documents 2.1 and 2.3 derive from outsiders to the societies they portray. In what ways did their outsider status influence the authors' understanding of these societies? And how did Kenyatta's position as a modern and Western-educated Gikuyu living in a colonial setting shape his description of his own people in Document 2.2? What assumptions and purposes did each of these writers bring to his task?

4. **Assessing the credibility of sources:** Consider these documents as sources of historical information about the societies they describe. What statements might historians reliably use as evidence and what might they discard or view with skepticism?

Visual Sources

Considering the Evidence:
Art and Life in the Early Agrarian Era

The long period of world history between the beginnings of settled agriculture and the rise of civilizations is known as the early agrarian era or sometimes the Neolithic age. It was a time when the revolutionary implications of the breakthrough to agriculture began to be felt. Since these transformations took place before the advent of writing, historians depend heavily on material remains—art, artifacts, and architecture—for understanding the life of these people. In the absence of written records, scholars are sometimes hard-pressed to know precisely what motivated the creation of these works or what they signified to those who made them. Inference, imagination, and sometimes speculation play an important role in the analysis of this evidence.

Given human creativity and the global scope of the early agrarian era, generalizations about Neolithic art as a whole are difficult to make. But in comparison with the Paleolithic era, the new economy generated by agriculture gave rise to many artistic innovations. Weaving and pottery making became major industries, offering new opportunities for creative expression. Larger-scale stone structures, known as megaliths, appeared in various places, and settled farming communities required more elaborate dwellings, including some substantial stone fortifications. Agrarian societies also produced much larger sculptures than did gathering and hunting societies. Finally, while animals continued to be a focus of Neolithic art, human figures became more prominent and were more realistically depicted than in the cave paintings and Venus figurines of the Paleolithic era.

The art of the early agrarian era sometimes included representations of the distinctive social and economic patterns of this new phase of human history. One example is a remarkable wall painting from Çatalhüyük, an early farming community located in south-central Turkey (see pp. 64–65 and Map 2.1, p. 54). Dated to about 6200 B.C.E., the painting is apparently a stylized portrayal of the village itself, showing some eighty buildings arranged on rising terraces. Behind the town rises an erupting twin-peaked volcano, resembling the nearby actual volcano of Hasan Dag, which was active during the time that Çatalhüyük flourished. In this painting, we have a record of one of the most distinctive outcomes of the Agricultural Revolution—the establishment of settled agricultural villages. It is also perhaps the earliest map and landscape painting

Visual Source 2.1 Çatalhüyük: An Early Map and Landscape Painting (James Mellaart/Çatalhöyuk Research Project)

uncovered to date. Visual Source 2.1 is a reconstruction of that image, which was about ten feet long in its original form.

■ What particular features of the mountain/volcano can you identify? What do you think the dots on the mountain represent? Notice that the volcano is venting from both the top and the base of the mountain, as volcanoes often do.

■ Compare the map with the photograph on page 64 of the uncovered remains of Çatalhüyük. What similar features do you see?

■ Notice that this image contains neither human nor animal figures. What might be the significance of this absence?

■ What do you think the purpose of such an image might have been? Keep in mind that obsidian (black volcanic glass) found at the base of the mountain was a very valuable, and perhaps sacred, item in Çatalhüyük and an important product in regional trading patterns.

Archeological investigation at Çatalhüyük has generated a major debate about the role of women in the religious and social life of this early agricultural village. The first major dig at the site, undertaken by James Mellaart in the 1960s, uncovered a number of small female figurines, the most famous of which is shown here as Visual Source 2.2. It dates to about 5000 B.C.E. and is some eight inches in height. The baked-clay figure depicts a seated female whose arms are resting on two lionesses or leopards. For Mellaart, this was evidence for an ancient and powerful cult of the "mother Goddess," an idea that proved compelling to a number of feminist scholars and goddess worshippers. This understanding also gained support from the absence of similar male figurines. Some goddess devotees have come to view Çatalhüyük as a pilgrimage site.

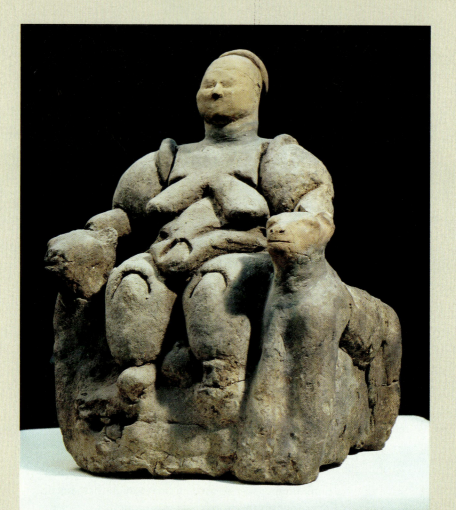

Visual Source 2.2 Women, Men, and Religion in Çatalhüyük (Museum of Anatolian Civilization, Ankara/Gianni Dagli Orti/The Art Archive)

- What features of this statue might support such a view?

- How might the fact that this figurine was discovered in an abandoned grain bin affect your thinking about its significance?

- Why might feminist scholars have been attracted to Mellaart's interpretation of this figure?

- What alternative understandings of this figure can you imagine?

Later archeological research, ongoing since 1993 under the leadership of Ian Hodder, has called some aspects of this "mother Goddess" interpretation into question. Hodder, for example, doubts the existence of an organized cult with an attached priesthood, as Mellaart theorized. Rather, Hodder noted that the image suggests "a close connection between ritual and daily functions." He added:

> I do not think that there was a separate religious elite. I think the religion was an integral part of daily life. It may be wrong to think of the Çatal art as religious or symbolic at all. It may be more that people thought that they had to paint, or make relief sculptures, in order to achieve certain practical ends (such as make the crops grow, or prevent children from dying).[20]

Furthermore, Hodder suggested that while women were certainly prominent in the symbolism of the village, there is little evidence for a "matriarchal society" in which women dominated. Rather, he wrote that "men and women had the same social status. There was a balance of power."[21]

■ Why do you think the life of this small Neolithic village some 7,000 or more years ago continues to provoke such passionate debate? (You might want to do a little research about the controversies surrounding Çatalhüyük.)

The Neolithic or Agricultural Revolution gave rise not only to settled farming communities but also to pastoral nomadic societies, dependent on their herds of domesticated animals (see p. 63). Nowhere has this transformation been more thoroughly documented than in the rock art of the central Sahara region of Africa. There the domestication of cattle actually preceded the development of farming and from perhaps 4500 B.C.E. or earlier, pastoral societies flourished in the area. Later, horses and camels were introduced into the region as well. Visual Source 2.3, a rock-art painting from Tassili-n-Ajjer, in southeastern Algeria, illustrates the early development of such pastoral societies. The multiple colors of the cattle indicate that they were a long-domesticated species.

■ On the left, women and children are attending a line of calves roped together. What might this suggest to historians seeking to understand this society?

■ How would you describe the activities of the other human figures, presumably men? Does this suggest anything about the division of labor in such societies?

■ Notice that the herd of cattle is portrayed in front of some huts, indicated by stylized circles. What might this indicate about the nature of this community?

■ How might you compare the society depicted in this image with that of Çatalhüyük in Visual Source 2.1?

Among the most famous sites of the early agrarian era is Stonehenge, a series of earthworks accompanied by circles of standing stones located in

Visual Source 2.3 An African Pastoral Community (Henri Lhote)

southern England, where the Agricultural Revolution emerged around 4000 B.C.E. Construction of the Stonehenge site began around 3100 B.C.E. and continued intermittently for another 1,500 years.

■ Have a close look at the aerial photograph of Stonehenge in Visual Source 2.4. How would you describe its major features to someone who had never seen it? What questions about the site come to mind?

Almost everything about Stonehenge has been a matter of controversy and speculation among those scholars who have studied it. Prominent among those debates have been the questions of motivation and function. Why was it constructed? What purposes did it serve for those early farming peoples who used it? The discovery of the cremated remains of some 240 individuals, dating to the first five centuries of its existence, has convinced some scholars that it was a burial site, perhaps for members of a single high-ranking family. It was the "domain of the dead" or an abode of the ancestors, remarked one archeologist, linked ritually perhaps to a nearby village of Durrington Walls, a "land of the living" consisting of 300 to 1,000 homes.[22] Others have cast Stonehenge as an astronomical observatory, aligned with the solstices and able to predict eclipses and the movement of heavenly bodies, or perhaps a center of sun worship. Most recently, it has been depicted as "a place of pilgrimage for the sick and injured of the Neolithic world," based on the number of burials in the area that show signs of serious illness, trauma, or deformity as well as the presence of many bluestone rock chips thought to have magical healing properties.[23]

Whatever its purposes, still other controversies surround the manner of its construction. How were those huge slabs of rock, some as heavy as fifty tons and others coming from a location 240 miles away, transported to Stonehenge and put into place? Were they dragged overland or transported partway by boat along the Avon River? Or did the movement of earlier glaciers deposit them in the region?

Visual Source 2.4 The Mystery of Stonehenge (© Skyscan/Corbis)

- ■ What does a structure of the magnitude of Stonehenge suggest about the Neolithic societies that created it?

- ■ What kinds of additional evidence would be most useful to scholars seeking to puzzle out the mysteries of Stonehenge?

The first millennium B.C.E. witnessed the flourishing of an impressive artistic tradition, arising out of the Nok culture, among the agricultural peoples of what is now northern Nigeria. Unlike the earlier Neolithic peoples highlighted in this section, they had learned to make and use iron. Amid the stone axes, iron implements, and pottery found in the region, the material remains of this ancient African culture also yielded a treasure of terra-cotta (fired clay) figures, often life-size, depicting animals and especially people. The highly stylized human figures shared several features: elongated heads often disproportionately large in comparison to their bodies; triangular eyes; pierced noses,

Visual Source 2.5 A Sculpture from the Nok Culture (Musée du Quai Branly/Scala/Art Resource, NY)

pupils, ears, and lips (perhaps to vent the air during the firing process); and elaborate attention to hairstyles, ornamentation, and dress. The artistic sophistication of these pieces has suggested to some scholars that their creators drew on an even earlier, as yet undiscovered, tradition. Some similarities with much later sculptures from Ife and Benin in southern Nigeria suggest the possibility of a long-lasting and widespread artistic tradition in West Africa. Visual Source 2.5 presents one of these Nok sculptures, dating to somewhere between 600 B.C.E. and 600 C.E.

■ What features of Nok sculpture, described above, can you identify in this figure?

■ How might you describe the mood that this figure evokes? Some scholars have dubbed this and many similar Nok sculptures "thinkers." Does it seem more likely that this notion reflects a present-day sensibility or that it might be an insight into the mentality of the ancient artist who created the image? Why?

■ What might you infer about the status of the person represented in this sculpture?

■ No one actually knows the purpose of these works. What possibilities come to mind as you consider Visual Source 2.5?

Using the Evidence:
Art and Life in the Early Agrarian Era

1. **Assessing personal reactions:** How do you respond personally to Visual Sources 2.1–2.5? What do you find surprising or impressive about them? Which of them are most accessible to a person of the early twenty-first century? Which are least accessible? Do you find these images easier to understand than the Paleolithic rock art featured in Chapter 1? Why or why not?

2. **Considering art as evidence:** What insights about early agrarian life might we derive from these images? In what ways do they reflect the technological or economic changes of the Agricultural Revolution?

3. **Reflecting on speculation:** You will notice that our understanding of all of these works is highly uncertain, inviting a considerable amount of speculation, guesswork, or imagination. Why are historians willing to articulate uncertain interpretations of ancient art? Is this an appropriate undertaking for historians, or should scholars remain silent when the evidence does not allow them to speak with certainty and authority?

CHAPTER THREE

First Civilizations

Cities, States, and Unequal Societies

3500 B.C.E.–500 B.C.E.

"Over 100 miles of wilderness, deep exploration into pristine lands, the solitude of backcountry camping, 4×4 trails, and ancient American Indian rock art and ruins. You can't find a better way to escape civilization!"[1] So goes an advertisement for a vacation in Utah's Canyonlands National Park, one of thousands of similar attempts to lure apparently constrained, beleaguered, and "civilized" city-dwellers into the spacious freedom of the wild and the imagined simplicity of earlier times. This urge to "escape from civilization" has long been a central feature in modern life. It is a major theme in Mark Twain's famous novel *The Adventures of Huckleberry Finn*, in which the restless and rebellious Huck resists all efforts to "sivilize" him by fleeing to the freedom of life on the river. It is a large part of the "cowboy" image in American culture, and it permeates environmentalist efforts to protect the remaining wilderness areas of the country. Nor has this impulse been limited to modern societies and the Western world. The ancient Chinese teachers of Daoism likewise urged their followers to abandon the structured and demanding world of urban and civilized life and to immerse themselves in the eternal patterns of the natural order. It is a strange paradox that we count the creation of civilization among the major achievements of humankind and yet people within these civilizations have often sought to escape the constraints, artificiality, hierarchies, and other discontents of city living.

WHAT EXACTLY ARE THESE CIVILIZATIONS that have generated such ambivalent responses among their inhabitants? When, where,

---

Raherka and Mersankh: Writing was among the defining features of civilizations almost everywhere. In ancient Egyptian civilization, the scribes who possessed this skill enjoyed both social prestige and political influence. This famous statue shows Raherka, the chief of the scribes during Egypt's Fifth Dynasty (about 2350 B.C.E.), in an affectionate pose with his wife, Mersankh. (Réunion des Musées Nationaux/Art Resource, NY)

and how did they first arise in human history? What changes did they bring to the people who lived within them? Why might some people criticize or seek to escape from them? These are the issues addressed in this chapter.

As historians commonly use the term, civilization represents a new and particular type of human society, made possible by the immense productivity of the Agricultural Revolution. Such societies encompassed far larger populations than any earlier form of human community and for the first time concentrated some of those people in sizable cities, numbering in the many tens of thousands. In these cities, people were organized and controlled by powerful states whose leaders could use force to compel obedience. Profound differences in economic function, skill, wealth, and status sharply divided the people of civilizations, making them far less equal, and subject to much greater oppression, than had been the case in earlier agricultural villages, pastoral societies, and chiefdoms. Pyramids, temples, palaces, elaborate sculptures, written literature, complex calendars, as well as class, slavery, patriarchy, and large-scale warfare—all of these have been among the cultural products of civilization.

Something New: The Emergence of Civilizations

■ **Change**

When and where did the First Civilizations emerge?

Like agriculture, civilization was a global phenomenon, showing up independently in six major locations scattered around the world during the several millennia after 3500 B.C.E. and in a number of other smaller expressions as well (see Map 3.1). At the time, these breakthroughs to a new way of life were small islands of innovation in a sea of people living in much older ways. In the long run of human history, however, civilizations gradually absorbed, overran, or displaced people practicing other ways of living. Over the next 5,000 years, civilization, as a unique kind of human community, gradually encompassed ever-larger numbers of people and extended over ever-larger territories, even as particular civilizations rose, fell, revived, and changed.

Introducing the First Civilizations

The earliest of these civilizations emerged around 3500 B.C.E. to 3000 B.C.E. in three places. One was the "cradle" of Middle Eastern civilization, expressed in the many and competing city-states of Sumer in southern Mesopotamia (located in present-day Iraq). Much studied by archeologists and historians, Sumerian civilization gave rise to the world's earliest written language, which was used initially by officials to record the goods received by various temples. Almost simultaneously, the Nile River valley in northeastern Africa witnessed the emergence of Egyptian civilization, famous for its pharaohs and pyramids, as well as a separate civilization known as Nubia, farther south along the Nile. Unlike the city-states of Sumer, Egyptian civilization took shape as a unified territorial state in which cities were rather less prominent. Later in this chapter, we will explore these two First Civilizations in greater detail.

Less well known and only recently investigated by scholars was a third early civilization that was developing along the central coast of Peru from roughly 3000 B.C.E. to 1800 B.C.E., at about the same time as the civilizations of Egypt and Sumer. This desert region received very little rainfall, but it was punctuated by dozens of rivers that brought the snowmelt of the adjacent Andes Mountains to the Pacific Ocean. Along a thirty-mile stretch of that coast and in the nearby interior, a series of some twenty-five urban centers emerged in an area known as Norte Chico, the largest of which was Caral, in the Supe River valley. In Norte Chico, archeologists have found monumental architecture in the form of earthen platform mounds, one of them measuring 60 feet tall and 500 feet long, as well as large public ceremonial structures, stone buildings with residential apartments, and other signs of urban life.

Norte Chico was a distinctive civilization in many ways. Its cities were smaller than those of Mesopotamia and show less evidence of economic specialization. The economy was based to an unusual degree on an extremely rich fishing industry in anchovies and sardines along the coast. These items apparently were exchanged for cotton, essential for fishing nets, as well as food crops such as squash, beans, and guava, all of which were grown by inland people in the river valleys using irrigation agriculture. Unlike Egypt and Mesopotamia, Peruvian civilization did not rest upon grain-based farming; the people of Norte Chico did not develop pottery or writing; and few sculptures, carvings, or drawings have been uncovered so far. Archeologists have, however, found a 5,000-year-old *quipu* (a series of knotted cords, later used extensively by the Inca for accounting purposes), which some scholars have suggested may have been an alternative form of writing. Furthermore, the cities of Norte Chico lacked defensive walls, and archeologists have discovered little evidence of warfare, such as burned buildings and mutilated corpses. It was also an unusually self-contained civilization. Whereas Egypt and Mesopotamia had long interacted with each other, the only import from the outside world evident in Norte Chico, or in Andean civilization generally, was maize (corn), which was derived ultimately from Mesoamerica, though without direct contact between the two regions. Norte Chico apparently "lighted a cultural fire" in the Andes and established a pattern for the many Andean civilizations that followed—Chavín, Moche, Nazca, and, much later, the Inca.[2]

Somewhat later, three additional First Civilizations made their appearance. In the Indus and Saraswati river valleys of what is now Pakistan, a remarkable civilization arose during the third millennium B.C.E. By 2000 B.C.E., it embraced a far larger area than Mesopotamia, Egypt, or coastal Peru and was expressed primarily in its elaborately planned cities. All across this huge area, about twice the size of Texas, common patterns prevailed: standardized weights, measures, architectural styles, even the size of bricks. As elsewhere, irrigated agriculture provided the economic foundation for the civilization, and a written language, thus far undeciphered, provides evidence of a literate culture.

Unlike its Middle Eastern counterparts, the Indus Valley civilization apparently generated no palaces, temples, elaborate graves, kings, or warrior classes. In short,

Map 3.1 First Civilizations

Six First Civilizations emerged independently in locations scattered across the planet, all within a few thousand years, from 3500 to 1000 B.C.E.

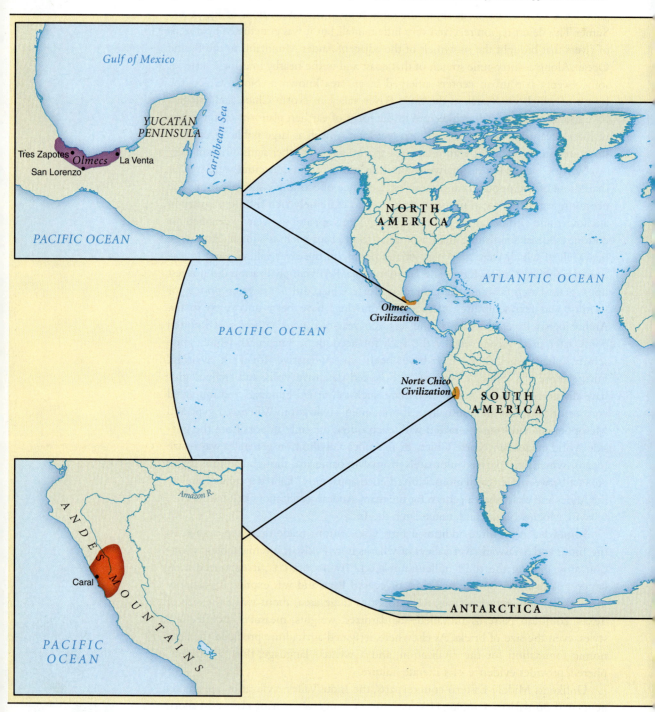

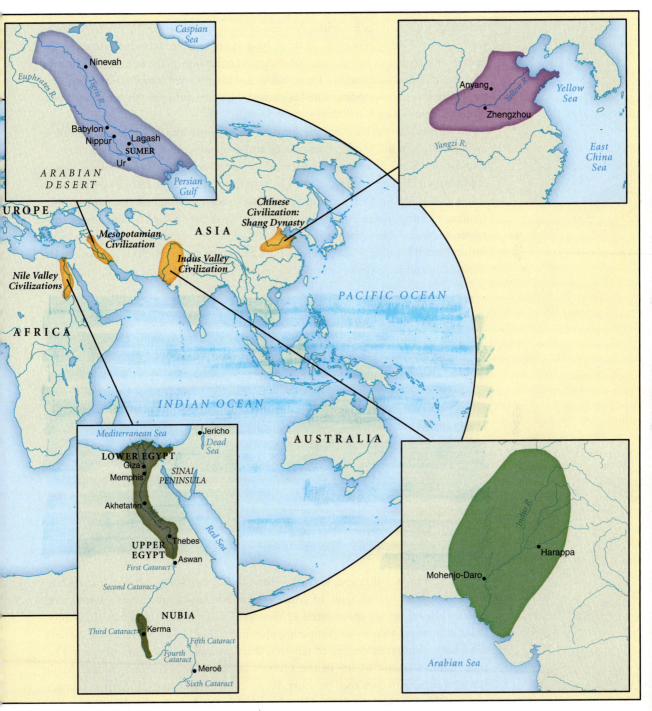

Caspian
Sea

Ninevah

Euphrates R.

Tigris R.

Babylon
Nippur   Lagash
              SUMER
         Ur

ARABIAN
DESERT

Persian
Gulf

Anyang   Yellow R.   Yellow
              Zhengzhou   Sea

Yangzi R.   East
                               China
                               Sea

EUROPE

ASIA   Chinese
                    Civilization:
                    Shang Dynasty

Mesopotamian
Civilization

Indus Valley
Civilization

Nile Valley
Civilizations

AFRICA

PACIFIC OCEAN

INDIAN OCEAN

AUSTRALIA

Jericho
Mediterranean Sea   Dead
                         Sea
LOWER EGYPT
   Giza
Memphis   SINAI
               PENINSULA

Akhetaten   Red Sea

UPPER   Thebes
EGYPT   Aswan
             First Cataract

Second Cataract

NUBIA
Third Cataract   Kerma
                         Fifth Cataract
                 Fourth
                 Cataract
                         Meroë
                 Sixth Cataract

Indus R.

Harappa

Mohenjo-Daro

Arabian Sea

the archeological evidence provides little indication of a political hierarchy or centralized state. This absence of evidence has sent scholars scrambling to provide an explanation for the obvious specialization, coordination, and complexity that the Indus Valley civilization exhibited. A series of small republics, rule by priests, an early form of the caste system—all of these have been suggested as alternative mechanisms of integration in this first South Asian civilization. Although no one knows for sure, the possibility that the Indus Valley may have housed a sophisticated civilization without a corresponding state has excited the imagination of scholars. (See Visual Sources: Indus Valley Civilization, pp. 126–31.)

Whatever its organization, the local environmental impact of the Indus Valley civilization, as in many others, was heavy and eventually undermined its ecological foundations. Repeated irrigation increased the amount of salt in the soil and lowered crop yields. The making of mud bricks, dried in ovens, required an enormous amount of wood for fuel, generating large-scale deforestation and soil erosion. As a result, these magnificent cities were abandoned by about 1700 B.C.E. and largely forgotten thereafter. Nonetheless, many features of this early civilization—ceremonial bathing, ritual burning, yoga positions, bulls and elephants as religious symbols, styles of clothing and jewelry—continued to nourish the later classical civilization of the Indian subcontinent and in fact persist into the present.[3]

The early civilization of China, dating to perhaps 2200 B.C.E., was very different from that of the Indus Valley. The ideal of a centralized state was evident from the days of the Xia dynasty (2200–1766 B.C.E.), whose legendary monarch Wu organized flood control projects that "mastered the waters and made them to flow in great channels." Subsequent dynasties—the Shang (1766–1122 B.C.E.) and the Zhou (1122–256 B.C.E.)—substantially enlarged the Chinese state, erected lavish tombs for their rulers, and buried thousands of human sacrificial victims to accompany them in the world to come. By the Zhou dynasty, a distinctive Chinese political ideology had emerged, featuring a ruler, known as the Son of Heaven. This monarch served as an intermediary between heaven and earth and ruled by the Mandate of Heaven only so long as he governed with benevolence and maintained social harmony among his people. An early form of written Chinese has been discovered on numerous oracle bones, which were intended to predict the future and to assist China's rulers in the task of governing. Chinese civilization, more than any other, has experienced an impressive cultural continuity from its earliest expression into modern times.

A final First Civilization, known as the Olmec, took shape around 1200 B.C.E. along the coast of the Gulf of Mexico near present-day Veracruz in southern Mexico. Based on an agricultural economy of maize, beans, and squash, Olmec cities arose from a series of competing chiefdoms and became ceremonial centers filled with elaborately decorated temples, altars, pyramids, and tombs of rulers. The most famous artistic legacy of the Olmecs lay in some seventeen colossal basalt heads, weighing twenty tons or more. Recent discoveries suggest that the Olmecs may well have created the first written language in the Americas by about 900 B.C.E.

Sometimes regarded as the "mother civilization" of Mesoamerica, Olmec cultural patterns—mound building, artistic styles, urban planning, a game played with a rubber ball, ritual sacrifice, and bloodletting by rulers—spread widely throughout the region and influenced subsequent civilizations, such as the Maya and Teotihuacán.

Beyond these six First Civilizations, other, smaller civilizations also flourished. Lying south of Egypt in the Nile Valley, Nubian civilization was clearly distinctive and independent of its northern neighbor, although Nubia was involved in a long and often contentious relationship with Egypt. Likewise in China, a large city known as Sanxingdui, rich in bronze sculptures

Shang Dynasty Bronze
This bronze tiger, created around 1100 B.C.E., illustrates Chinese skill in working with bronze and the mythological or religious significance of the tiger as a messenger between heaven and the human world. (Jiangxi Provincial Museum, Nanchang/Visual Connection Archive)

and much else, arose separately but at the same time as the more well-known Shang dynasty. As a new way of living and a new form of human society, civilization was beginning its long march toward encompassing almost all of humankind by the twentieth century.

The Question of Origins

The first question that historians ask about almost everything is "How did it get started?" Scholars of all kinds—archeologists, anthropologists, sociologists, and historians—have been arguing about the origins of civilization for a very long time, with no end in sight.[4] Amid all the controversy, one thing seems reasonably clear: civilizations had their roots in the Agricultural Revolution. That is the reason they appeared so late in the human story, for only an agricultural technology permitted human communities to produce sufficient surplus to support large populations and the specialized or elite minorities who did not themselves produce food. Furthermore, all of the First Civilizations emerged from earlier and competing chiefdoms, in which some social ranking and economic specialization had already developed. It was a gradual and evolutionary process. However, not all agricultural societies or chiefdoms developed into civilizations, so something else must have been involved. It is the search for this "something else" that has provoked such great debate among scholars.

Some scholars have emphasized the need to organize large-scale irrigation projects as a stimulus for the earliest civilizations, but archeologists have found that the more complex water control systems appeared long after states and civilizations

■ **Change**
What accounts for the initial breakthroughs to civilization?

had already been established. Others have suggested that powerful states were useful in protecting the privileges of favored groups. Warfare and trade have figured in still other explanations for the rise of civilizations. Anthropologist Robert Carneiro combined several of these factors in a thoughtful approach to the question.[5] He argued that a growing density of population, producing more congested and competitive societies, was a fundamental motor of change, and especially in areas where rich agricultural land was limited, either by geography (oceans, deserts, mountains) or by powerful competing societies. Such settings provided incentives for innovations, such as irrigation or plows that could produce more food, because opportunities for territorial expansion were not readily available. But circumscribed environments with dense populations also generated intense competition among rival groups, which led to repeated warfare. A strong and highly organized state was a decided advantage in such competition. Because losers could not easily flee to new lands, they were absorbed into the winner's society as a lower class. Successful leaders of the winning side emerged as an elite with an enlarged base of land, a class of subordinated workers, and a powerful state at their disposal—in short, a civilization.

Although such a process was relatively rapid by world history standards, it took many generations, centuries, or perhaps millennia to evolve. It was, of course, an unconscious undertaking in which the participants had little sense of the long-term outcome as they coped with the practical problems of survival on a day-to-day basis. What is surprising, though, is the rough similarity of the result in many widely separated places from about 3500 B.C.E. to the beginning of the Common Era.

However they got started (and much about this is still guesswork), the First Civilizations, once established, represented a very different kind of human society than anything that came before. All of them were based on highly productive agricultural economies. Various forms of irrigation, drainage, terracing, and flood control enabled these early civilizations to tap the food-producing potential of their regions. In dry lands with good soil, such as northern China and southern Iraq, water made all the difference and vastly increased the agricultural output. In all these civilizations, pottery likewise enhanced the productivity of farming, as did animal-drawn plows and metalworking in Afro-Eurasia. Ritual sacrifice, often including people, usually accompanied the growth of civilization, and the new rulers normally served as high priests or were seen as divine beings, their right to rule legitimated by association with the sacred.

An Urban Revolution

■ Change
What was the role of cities in the early civilizations?

It was the resources from agriculture that made possible one of the most distinctive features of the First Civilizations—cities. What would an agricultural villager have made of Uruk, ancient Mesopotamia's largest city? Uruk had walls more than twenty feet tall and a population around 50,000 in the third millennium B.C.E. The city's center, visible for miles around, was a stepped pyramid, or ziggurat, topped with a temple (see the photo on p. 100). Inside the city, our village visitor would have found other temples as well, serving as centers of worship and as places for the redistribution of stored food. Numerous craftspeople labored as masons, copper workers, weavers, and in many other specialties, while bureaucrats helped administer the city. It was, surely, a "vibrant, noisy, smelly, sometimes bewildering and dangerous, but also exciting place."[6] Here is how the *Epic of Gilgamesh*, Mesopotamia's ancient epic poem, describes the city:

> Come then, Enkidu, to ramparted Uruk,
> Where fellows are resplendent in holiday clothing,
> Where every day is set for celebration,
> Where harps and drums are played.
> And the harlots too, they are fairest of form,
> Rich in beauty, full of delights,
> Even the great gods are kept from sleeping at night.[7]

Equally impressive to a village visitor would have been the city of Mohenjo Daro, which flourished along the banks of the Indus River around 2000 B.C.E. With a population of perhaps 40,000, Mohenjo Daro and its sister city of Harappa featured large, richly built houses of two or three stories, complete with indoor plumbing, luxurious bathrooms, and private wells. Streets were laid out in a gridlike pattern, and beneath the streets ran a complex sewage system. Workers lived in row upon row of standardized two-room houses. Grand public buildings, including what seems to be a huge public bath, graced the city, while an enormous citadel was surrounded by a brick wall some forty-five feet high (see Visual Source 3.1, p. 127).

Even larger, though considerably later, was the Mesoamerican city of Teotihuacán, located in the central valley of Mexico. It housed perhaps 200,000 people in the middle of the first millennium C.E. Broad avenues, dozens of temples, two huge pyramids, endless stone carvings and many bright frescoes, small apartments for the ordinary, palatial homes for the wealthy—all of this must have seemed another world for a new visitor from a distant village. In shopping for obsidian blades, how was she to decide among the 350 workshops in the city? In seeking relatives, how could she find her way among many different compounds, each surrounded by a wall and housing a different lineage? And what would she make of a neighborhood composed entirely of Mayan merchants from the distant coastal lowlands?

Cities, then, lay at the heart of all of the First Civilizations. They were

Mohenjo Daro
Flourishing around 2000 B.C.E., Mohenjo Daro was by far the largest city of the Indus Valley civilization, covering more than 600 acres. This photograph shows a small part of that city as it has been uncovered by archeologists during the past century. The large watertight tank or pool, shown in the foreground, probably offered bathers an opportunity for ritual purification. In the ruins of Mohenjo Daro, writes archeologist Gregory Possehl, "one can walk down streets well defined by the high walls of homes and other buildings, climb the stairways used in antiquity, peer down ancient wells, and stand in bathing rooms used over 4,000 years ago." (Harappa Images)

political/administrative capitals; they were centers for the production of culture, including art, architecture, literature, ritual, and ceremony; they served as market-places for both local and long-distance exchange; and they housed most manufacturing activity. Everywhere they generated a unique kind of society, compared to earlier agricultural villages. Urban society was impersonal, for it was no longer possible to know everyone. Relationships of class and occupation were at least as important as those of kinship and village loyalty. Most notably, the degree of specialization and inequality far surpassed that of all preceding human communities.

The Erosion of Equality

Among the most novel features of early urban life, at least to our imaginary village visitor, was the amazing specialization of work. In Document 3.5 (pp. 123–25), an Egyptian teacher tries to persuade a reluctant student, preparing to be a scribe (a literate public official), to take his lessons seriously by pointing out the disadvantages of the many other occupations that await him. In ancient Mesopotamia, even scribes were subdivided into many categories: junior and senior scribes, temple scribes and royal scribes, scribes for particular administrative or official functions.[8] None of these people, of course, grew their own food; they were supported by the highly productive agriculture of farmers.

Hierarchies of Class

■ Change
In what ways was social inequality expressed in early civilizations?

Alongside the occupational specialization of the First Civilizations lay their vast inequalities—in wealth, status, and power. Here we confront a remarkable and persistent feature of the human journey. As ingenuity and technology created more-productive economies, the greater wealth now available to societies was everywhere piled up rather than spread out. Early signs of this erosion of equality were evident in the more settled and complex gathering and hunting societies such as the Chumash and in agricultural chiefdoms such as Cahokia, but the advent of urban-based civilizations multiplied and magnified these inequalities many times over, as the egalitarian values of earlier cultures were everywhere displaced. This transition represents one of the major turning points in the social history of humankind.

As the First Civilizations took shape, inequality and hierarchy soon came to be regarded as normal and natural. Upper classes everywhere enjoyed great wealth in land or salaries, were able to avoid physical labor, had the finest of everything, and occupied the top positions in political, military, and religious life. Frequently, they were distinguished by the clothing they wore, the houses they lived in, and the manner of their burial. Early Chinese monarchs bestowed special clothing, banners, chariots, weapons, and ornaments on their regional officials, and all of these items were graded according to the officials' precise location in the hierarchy. In Mesopotamia, the punishments prescribed in the famous Code of Hammurabi depended on social status (see Document 3.2, pp. 118–21). A free-born commoner who struck a person of equal rank had to pay a small fine, but if he struck "a man who is his superior, he shall receive 60 strokes with an oxtail whip in public." Clearly, class had consequences.

In all civilizations, free commoners represented the vast majority of the population and included artisans of all kinds, lower-level officials, soldiers and police, servants, and, most numerous of all, farmers. It was their surplus production—appropriated through a variety of taxes, rents, required labor, and tribute payments—that supported the upper classes. At least some of these people were aware of, and resented, these forced extractions and their position in the social hierarchy. Most Chinese peasants, for example, owned little land of their own and worked on plots granted to them by royal or aristocratic landowners. An ancient poem compared the exploiting landlords to rats and expressed the farmers' vision of a better life:

Large rats! Large rats!
Do not eat our spring grain!
Three years have we had to do with you.
And you have not been willing to think of our toil.
We will leave you,
And go to those happy borders.
Happy borders, happy borders!
Who will there make us always to groan?[9]

At the bottom of social hierarchies everywhere were slaves. Slavery and civilization, in fact, seem to have emerged together. (For early references to slavery, see Document 3.2, pp. 118–21). Female slaves, captured in the many wars among rival Mesopotamian cities, were put to work in large-scale semi-industrial weaving enterprises, while males helped to maintain irrigation canals and construct ziggurats. Others worked as domestic servants in the households of their owners. In all of the First Civilizations, slaves—derived from prisoners of war, criminals, and debtors—were available for sale; for work in the fields, mines, homes, and shops of their owner; or on occasion for sacrifice. From the days of the earliest civilizations until the nineteenth century, the practice of "people owning people" was an enduring feature of state-based societies everywhere.

The practice of slavery in ancient times varied considerably from place to place. Egypt and the Indus Valley civilizations initially had far fewer slaves than did Mesopotamia, which was highly militarized. Later, the Greeks of Athens and the Romans employed slaves far more extensively than did the Chinese or Indians (see Chapter 6). Furthermore, most ancient slavery differed from the type of slavery practiced in the Americas during recent centuries; in the early civilizations, slaves were not a primary agricultural labor force, many children of slaves could become free people, and slavery was not associated primarily with "blackness" or with Africa.

Hierarchies of Gender

■ **Change**

In what ways have historians tried to explain the origins of patriarchy?

Accompanying the hierarchies of class were those of gender, as civilizations everywhere undermined the earlier and more equal relationships between men and women. Most scholars agree that early horticultural societies, those using a hoe or digging stick, continued the relative gender equality that had characterized Paleolithic peoples. In such societies, women were much involved in agricultural labor, which generated most of the food for the village. Women were also engaged in spinning, weaving, and pottery making—activities that were compatible with their role as mothers. Their central economic function, together with their amazing capacity to produce new life, gave women considerable respect and, arguably, a status generally equal to that of men. Some scholars have seen this respect and status reflected, at least in Europe and the Middle East, in a proliferation of figurines, masks, signs, symbols, and myths, all featuring women and feminine themes dealing with birth, growth, death, and regeneration.[10]

But as the First Civilizations took shape, the institutions and values of male dominance, often referred to as patriarchy, gradually emerged. The big question, of course, lies in trying to explain this momentous change. What was it about civilization that seemed to generate patriarchy?

One approach to answering this question highlights the role of a new and more intensive form of agriculture, involving the use of animal-drawn plows and the keeping and milking of large herds of animals. Unlike earlier farming practices that relied on a hoe or digging stick, plow-based agriculture meant heavier work, which men were better able to perform. Taking place at a distance from the village, this new form of agriculture was perhaps less compatible with women's primary responsibility for child rearing. Furthermore, the growing population of civilizations meant that women were more often pregnant and even more deeply involved in child care than before. Thus, in plow-based communities, men took over most of the farming work, and the status of women declined correspondingly, even though their other productive activities—weaving and food preparation, for example—continued. "As women were increasingly relegated to secondary tasks . . . ," writes archeologist Margaret Ehrenberg, "they had fewer personal resources with which to assert their status."[11]

Because patriarchy also developed in civilizations untouched by plow agriculture, such as those of Mesoamerica and the Andes, perhaps something else was at work as well. Historian David Christian suggests that the declining position of women was connected more generally to the growth of social complexity in civilizations as economic, religious, and political "specialists" became more prominent. Because men were less important in the household, they may have been more available to assume the powerful and prestigious specialist roles. From these positions of authority, men were able to shape the values and practices of their societies in ways that benefited themselves at the expense of women. Here, perhaps, lies the origin of an ancient distinction between the realm of the home, defined as the domain of women, and the world of public life, associated with men.[12]

Women have long been identified not only with the home but also with nature, for they are intimately involved in the fundamental natural process of reproduction. But civilization seemed to highlight culture, or the human mastery of nature, through agriculture, monumental art and architecture, and the creation of large-scale cities and states. Did this mean, as some scholars have suggested, that women were now associated with an inferior dimension of human life (nature), while men assumed responsibility for the higher order of culture?[13]

A further aspect of civilization that may well have contributed to patriarchy was warfare. Large-scale military conflict with professionally led armies was a feature of almost all of the First Civilizations, and female prisoners of war often were the first slaves. With military service largely restricted to men, its growing prominence in the affairs of civilizations served to enhance the power and prestige of a male warrior class. So too, perhaps, did private property and commerce, central elements of the First Civilizations. Without sharp restrictions on women's sexual activity, how could a father be certain that family property would be inherited by his offspring? In addition, the buying and selling associated with commerce were soon applied to male rights over women, as female slaves, concubines, and wives were exchanged among men.

Patriarchy in Practice

Whatever the precise origins of patriarchy, male dominance permeated the First Civilizations, marking a gradual change from the more equal relationships of men and women within agricultural villages or Paleolithic bands. Historian Gerda Lerner documented this transition in ancient Mesopotamian civilization. By the second millennium B.C.E., various written laws codified and sought to enforce a patriarchal family life that offered women a measure of paternalistic protection while insisting on their submission to the unquestioned authority of men. Central to these laws was the regulation of female sexuality. A wife caught sleeping with another man might be drowned at her husband's discretion, whereas he was permitted to enjoy sexual relations with his female servants, though not with another man's wife. Divorce was far easier for the husband than for the wife. Rape was a serious offense, but the injured party was primarily the father or the husband of the victim, rather than the violated woman herself. Even elite women, who were often allowed to act on behalf of their powerful husbands, saw themselves as dependent. "Let all be well with [my husband]," prayed one such wife, "that I may prosper under his protection."[14]

■ **Comparison**

How did Mesopotamian and Egyptian patriarchy differ from each other?

Furthermore, women in Mesopotamian civilization were sometimes divided into two sharply distinguished categories. Respectable women, those under the protection and sexual control of one man, were required to be veiled when outside the home, whereas nonrespectable women, such as slaves and prostitutes, were forbidden to wear veils and were subject to severe punishment if they presumed to cover their heads.

Finally, the powerful goddesses of earlier times were gradually relegated to the home and hearth. They were replaced in the public arena by dominant male deities, who now were credited with the power of creation and fertility and viewed as the patrons of wisdom and learning. The culmination of this "demotion of the goddess," argues Gerda Lerner, lies in the Hebrew Scriptures, in which a single male deity, Yahweh, alone undertakes the act of creation without any participation of a female goddess.

Patriarchy was not everywhere the same, however. Egypt, while clearly patriarchal, afforded its women greater opportunities than did most other First Civilizations. In Egypt, women were recognized as legal equals to men, able to own property and slaves, to administer and sell land, to make their own wills, to sign their own marriage contracts, and to initiate divorce. Royal women occasionally exercised significant political power, acting as regents for their young sons or, more rarely, as queens in their own right. Clearly, though, this was seen as abnormal, for Egypt's most famous queen, Hatshepsut (reigned 1472–1457 B.C.E.), was sometimes portrayed in statues as a man, dressed in male clothing and sporting the traditional false beard of the pharaoh. Moreover, married women in Egypt were not veiled as in Mesopotamia. Statues and paintings often showed men and women in affectionate poses and as equal partners, as can be seen in the photo (p. 84) at the beginning of this chapter. Although marriages were clearly arranged by parents, the love poetry of New Kingdom Egypt (1550–1064 B.C.E.) suggests an element of romance and longing. One lovesick boy lamented the absence of his beloved, referred to as a "sister":

> Seven days since I saw my sister,
> and sickness invaded me; . . .
> The sight of her makes me well . . .
> Her speaking makes me strong;
> Embracing her expels my malady. . . .

And a young woman exults at the sight of her love:

> I passed before his house,
> I found his door ajar;
> My brother stood by his mother; . . .
> He looked at me as I passed by, . . .
> How my heart exulted in gladness,
> My brother, at your sight.[15]

The Rise of the State

What, we might reasonably ask, held ancient civilizations together despite the many tensions and complexities of urban living and the vast inequalities of civilized societies? Why did they not fly apart amid the resentments born of class and gender hierarchies? The answer, in large part, lay in yet another distinctive feature of the First Civilizations—states. Organized around particular cities or larger territories, early states were headed almost everywhere by kings, who employed a variety of ranked officials, exercised a measure of control over society, and defended the state against external enemies. To modern people, the state is such a familiar reality that we find it difficult to imagine life without it. Nonetheless, it is a quite recent invention in human history, with the state replacing, or at least supplementing, kinship as the basic organizing principle of society and exercising far greater authority than earlier chiefdoms.

Coercion and Consent

Early states in Mesopotamia, Egypt, China, Mesoamerica, and elsewhere drew their power from various sources, all of which assisted in providing cohesion for the First Civilizations. One basis of power was the recognition that the complexity of life in cities or densely populated territories required some authority to coordinate and regulate the community. Someone had to organize the irrigation systems of river valley civilizations. Someone had to adjudicate conflicts among the many different peoples, unrelated to one another, who rubbed elbows in the early cities. Someone had to direct efforts to defend the city or territory against aggressive outsiders. The state, in short, solved certain widely shared problems and therefore had a measure of voluntary support among the population. For many people, it was surely useful.

■ **Change**
What were the sources of state authority in the First Civilizations?

The state, however, was more useful for some people than for others, for it also served to protect the privileges of the upper classes, to require farmers to give up a portion of their product to support city-dwellers, and to demand work on large public projects such as pyramids and fortifications. If necessary, state authorities had the ability, and the willingness, to use force to compel obedience. The Egyptian teacher mentioned earlier described to his reluctant student what happens to a peasant unable to pay his tax in grain:

> Now the scribe lands on the shore. He surveys the harvest. Attendants are behind him with staffs, Nubians with clubs. One says [to the peasant], "Give grain." There is none. He is beaten savagely. He is bound, thrown into a well, submerged head down. His wife is bound in his presence. His children are in fetters. His neighbors abandon them and flee.[16]

Such was the power of the state, as rulers accumulated the resources to pay for officials, soldiers, police, and attendants. This capacity for violence and coercion marked

A Mesopotamian Ziggurat
This massive ziggurat/temple to the Mesopotamian moon god Nanna was built around 2100 B.C.E. in the city of Ur. The solitary figure standing atop the staircase illustrates the size of this huge structure. (Richard Ashworth/Robert Harding World Imagery/Corbis)

off the states of the First Civilizations from earlier chiefdoms, whose leaders had only persuasion, prestige, and gifts to back up their authority.

Force, however, was not always necessary, for the First Civilizations soon generated ideas suggesting that state authority and class and gender inequalities were normal, natural, and ordained by the gods. Kingship everywhere was associated with the sacred. Ancient Chinese kings were known as the Son of Heaven, and they alone could perform the rituals and sacrifices necessary to keep the cosmos in balance. Mesopotamian rulers were thought to be the stewards of their city's patron gods. Their symbols of kingship—crown, throne, scepter, mace—were said to be of divine origin, sent to earth when the gods established monarchy. Egyptians, most of all, invested their pharaohs with divine qualities. Rulers claimed to embody all the major gods of Egypt, and their supernatural power ensured the regular flooding of the Nile and the defeat of the country's enemies.

But if religion served most often to justify unequal power and privilege, it might also on occasion be used to restrain, or even undermine, the established order. Hammurabi claimed that his law code was inspired by Marduk, the chief god of Babylon, and was intended to "bring about the rule of righteousness in the land, to destroy the wicked and the evil-doers; so that the strong should not harm the weak."[17] Another Mesopotamian monarch, Urukagina from the city of Lagash, claimed authority from the city's patron god for reforms aimed at ending the corruption and tyranny of a previous ruler. In China during the Zhou dynasty (1122–256 B.C.E.), emperors ruled by the Mandate of Heaven, but their bad behavior could result in the removal of that mandate and their overthrow.

Writing and Accounting

A further support for state authority lay in the remarkable invention of writing. It was a powerful and transforming innovation, regarded almost everywhere as a gift from the gods, while people without writing often saw it as something magical or supernatural. Distinctive forms of writing emerged in all of the First Civilizations

Snapshot   Writing in Ancient Civilizations

Most of the early writing systems were "logophonetic," using symbols to designate both whole words and particular sounds or syllables. Chinese characters, which indicated only words, were an exception. None of the early writing systems employed alphabets.

Location	Type	Initial Use	Example	Comment
Sumer	Cuneiform: wedge-shaped symbols on clay tablets representing objects, abstract ideas, sounds, and syllables	Records of economic transactions, such as temple payments and taxes	bird	Regarded as the world's first written language; other languages such as Babylonian and Assryian were written with Sumerian script
Egypt	Hieroglyphs ("sacred carvings"): a series of signs that denote words and consonants (but not vowels or syllables)	Business and administrative purposes; later used for religious inscriptions, stories, poetry, hymns, and mathematics	rain, dew, storm	For everyday use, less formal systems of cursive writing (known as "hieratic" and "demotic") were developed
Andes	Quipu: a complex system of knotted cords in which the color, length, type, and location of knots conveyed mostly numerical meaning	Various accounting functions; perhaps also used to express words	numerical data (possibly in codes), words, and ideas	Widely used in the Inca Empire; recent discoveries place quipus in Caral some 5,000 years ago
Indus River Valley	Some 400 pictographic symbols representing sounds and words, probably expressing a Dravidian language currently spoken in southern India	Found on thousands of clay seals and pottery; probably used to mark merchandise	6 fish	As yet undeciphered
China	Oracle bone script: pictographs (stylized drawings) with no phonetic meaning	Inscribed on turtle shells or animal bones; used for divination (predicting the future) in the royal court of Shang dynasty rulers	horse	Direct ancestor of contemporary Chinese characters
Olmec	Signs that represent sounds (syllables) and words; numbering system using bars and dots	Used to record the names and deeds of rulers and shamans, as well as battles and astronomical data	jaguar	Structurally similar to later Mayan script; Olmec calendars were highly accurate and the basis for later Mesoamerican calendars

except the Andes, although some scholars now regard their knotted strings, or quipus, as a kind of writing.[18]

Writing sustained the First Civilizations and their successors in many ways. Literacy defined elite status and conveyed enormous prestige to those who possessed it. (See Document 3.5, pp. 123–25, for a celebration of writing.) Because it can be learned, writing also provided a means for some commoners to join the charmed circle of the literate. Writing as propaganda, celebrating the great deeds of the kings, was prominent, especially among the Egyptians and later among the Maya. A hymn to the pharaoh, dating to about 1850 B.C.E., extravagantly praised the ruler:

> He has come unto us . . . and has given peace to the two Riverbanks
> . . . and has made Egypt to live; he hath banished its suffering;
> . . . he has caused the throat of the subjects to breathe
> . . . and has trodden down foreign countries
> . . . he has delivered them that were robbed
> . . . he has come unto us, that we may [nurture up?] our children and
> bury our aged ones.[19]

In Mesopotamia and elsewhere, writing served an accounting function, recording who had paid their taxes, who owed what to the temple, and how much workers had earned. Thus it immensely strengthened bureaucracy. Complex calendars indicated precisely when certain rituals should be performed. Writing also gave weight and specificity to orders, regulations, and laws. Hammurabi's famous law code (see Document 3.2, pp. 118–21), while correcting certain abuses, made crystal clear that fundamental distinctions divided men and women and separated slaves, commoners, and people of higher rank.

Once it had been developed, writing, like religion, proved hard to control and operated as a wild card in human affairs. It gave rise to literature and philosophy, to astronomy and mathematics, and, in some places, to history. On occasion, the written word proved threatening, rather than supportive, to rulers. China's so-called First Emperor, Qin Shihuangdi (reigned 221–210 B.C.E.), allegedly buried alive some 460 scholars and burned their books when they challenged his brutal efforts to unify China's many warring states, or so his later critics claimed (see Chapter 4). Thus writing became a major arena for social and political conflict, and rulers always have sought to control it.

The Grandeur of Kings

Yet another source of state authority derived from the lavish lifestyle of elites, the impressive rituals they arranged, and the imposing structures they created. Everywhere, kings, high officials, and their families lived in luxurious palaces, dressed in splendid clothing, bedecked themselves with the loveliest jewelry, and were attended by endless servants. Their deaths triggered elaborate burials, of which the pyramids of the Egyptian pharaohs were perhaps the most ostentatious. Almost all of the First

Civilizations accompanied high-status funerals with the human sacrifice of numerous retainers, who would nourish the souls or serve the needs of their rulers in the afterlife. Monumental palaces, temples, ziggurats, pyramids, and statues conveyed the immense power of the state and its elite rulers. The Olmec civilization of Mesoamerica (1200–400 B.C.E.) erected enormous human heads, more than ten feet tall and weighing at least twenty tons, carved from blocks of basalt and probably representing particular rulers. Somewhat later the Maya Temple of the Giant Jaguar, towering 154 feet tall, was the most impressive among many temples, pyramids, and palaces that graced the city of Tikal. All of this must have seemed overwhelming to common people in the cities and villages of the First Civilizations.

Olmec Head

This colossal statue, some six feet high and five feet wide, is one of seventeen such carvings, dating to the first millennium B.C.E., that were discovered in the territory of the ancient Olmec civilization. Thought to represent individual rulers, each of the statues has a distinct and realistically portrayed face. (Danny Lehman/Corbis)

Comparing Mesopotamia and Egypt

A productive agricultural technology, city living, immense class inequalities, patriarchy, the emerging power of states—all of these were common features of First Civilizations across the world and also of those that followed. Still, these civilizations were not everywhere the same, for differences in political organization, religious beliefs and practices, the role of women, and much more gave rise to distinctive traditions. Nor were they static. Like all human communities, they changed over the centuries. Finally, these civilizations did not exist in isolation, for they participated in networks of interactions with near and sometimes more distant neighbors. In looking more closely at two of these First Civilizations—Mesopotamia and Egypt—we can catch a glimpse of the differences, changes, and connections that characterized early civilizations.

■ **Comparison**

In what ways did Mesopotamian and Egyptian civilizations differ from each other?

Environment and Culture

The civilizations of both Mesopotamia and Egypt grew up in river valleys and depended on their rivers to sustain a productive agriculture in otherwise arid lands. Those rivers, however, were radically different. At the heart of Egyptian life was the Nile, "that green gash of teeming life," which rose predictably every year to bring the soil and water that nurtured a rich Egyptian agriculture. The Tigris and Euphrates rivers, which gave life to Mesopotamian civilization, also rose annually, but "unpredictably and fitfully, breaking man's dikes and submerging his crops."[20]

Snapshot   **Key Moments in Mesopotamian History**

Beginning of irrigated agriculture	6000 B.C.E.
Period of independent Sumerian city-states	3200–2350 B.C.E.
Earliest cuneiform texts	3000 B.C.E.
First Sumerian law codes	2500 B.C.E.
First Mesopotamian empire: conquest of Sumer by Sargon of Akkad	2350 B.C.E.
Epic of Gilgamesh compiled	after 2000 B.C.E.
Babylonian empire	1900–1500 B.C.E.
Reign of Hammurabi	1792–1750 B.C.E.
Assyrian rule in Mesopotamia	900–612 B.C.E.
Assyrian conquest of Israel	722 B.C.E.
Babylonian conquest of Judah by King Nebuchadnezzar	586 B.C.E.
Mesopotamia incorporated into Persian empire	by 500 B.C.E.

(See Map 3.2.) Furthermore, an open environment without serious obstacles to travel made Mesopotamia far more vulnerable to invasion than the much more protected space of Egypt, which was surrounded by deserts, mountains, seas, and cataracts. For long periods of its history, Egypt enjoyed a kind of "free security" from external attack that Mesopotamians could only have envied.

Does the physical environment shape the human cultures that develop within it? Most historians are reluctant to endorse any kind of determinism, especially one suggesting that "geography is destiny," but in the case of Mesopotamia and Egypt, many scholars have seen some relationship between the physical setting and culture.

In at least some of its literature, the Mesopotamian outlook on life, which developed within a precarious, unpredictable, and often violent environment, viewed humankind as caught in an inherently disorderly world, subject to the whims of capricious and quarreling gods, and facing death without much hope of a pleasant life beyond. A Mesopotamian poet complained: "I have prayed to the gods and sacrificed, but who can understand the gods in heaven? Who knows what they plan for us? Who has ever been able to understand a god's conduct?"[21] The famous Mesopotamian *Epic of Gilgamesh*, excerpted in Document 3.1, pages 115–18, likewise depicted a rather pessimistic view of the gods and of the possibility for eternal life.

By contrast, elite literate culture in Egypt, developing in a more stable, predictable, and beneficent environment, produced a rather more cheerful and hopeful outlook on the world. The rebirth of the sun every day and of the river every year seemed to assure Egyptians that life would prevail over death. The amazing

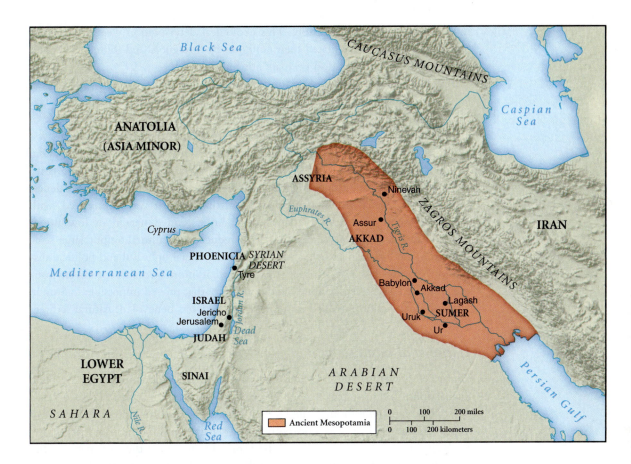

Map 3.2 Mesopotamia

After about 1,000 years of independent and competitive existence, the city-states of Sumer were incorporated into a number of larger imperial states based in Akkad, Babylon, and then Assyria.

pyramids, constructed during Egypt's Old Kingdom (2663–2195 B.C.E.), reflected the firm belief that at least the pharaohs and other high-ranking people could successfully make the journey to eternal life in the Land of the West. Incantations for the dead, such as those illustrated in Document 3.3, describe an afterlife that Gilgamesh could only have envied. Over time, larger groups of people, beyond the pharaoh and his entourage, came to believe that they could gain access to the afterlife if they followed proper procedures and lived a morally upright life (see Documents 3.3 and 3.4, pp. 121–23). Thus Egyptian civilization not only affirmed the possibility of eternal life but also expanded access to it.

If the different environments of Mesopotamia and Egypt shaped their societies and cultures, those civilizations, with their mounting populations and growing demand for resources, likewise had an impact on the environment.[22] In Sumer (southern Mesopotamia), deforestation and soil erosion decreased crop yields by some 65 percent between 2400 and 1700 B.C.E. Also contributing to this disaster was the increasing salinization of the soil, a long-term outcome of intensive irrigation. By 2000 B.C.E., there were reports that "the earth turned white" as salt accumulated in the soil. As a result, wheat was largely replaced by barley, which is far more tolerant of salty conditions. This ecological deterioration clearly weakened Sumerian city-states, facilitated their conquest by foreigners, and shifted the center of Mesopotamian civilization permanently to the north.

Egypt, by contrast, created a more sustainable agricultural system, which lasted for thousands of years and contributed to the remarkable continuity of its civilization. Whereas Sumerian irrigation involved a complex and artificial network of canals and dikes that led to the salinization of the soil, its Egyptian counterpart was much less intrusive, simply regulating the natural flow of the Nile. Such a system avoided the problem of salty soils, allowing Egyptian agriculture to emphasize wheat production, but it depended on the general regularity and relative gentleness of the Nile's annual flooding. On occasion, that pattern was interrupted, with serious consequences for Egyptian society. An extended period of low floods between 2250 and 1950 B.C.E. led to sharply reduced agricultural output, large-scale starvation, the loss of livestock, and, consequently, social upheaval and political disruption. Nonetheless, Egypt's ability to work *with* its more favorable natural environment enabled a degree of stability and continuity that proved impossible in Sumer, where human action intruded more heavily into a less benevolent natural setting.

Cities and States

Politically as well as culturally and environmentally, Mesopotamian and Egyptian civilizations differed sharply. For its first thousand years (3200–2350 B.C.E.), Mesopotamian civilization, located in the southern Tigris-Euphrates region known as Sumer, was organized in a dozen or more separate and independent city-states. Each city-state was ruled by a king, who claimed to represent the city's patron deity and who controlled the affairs of the walled city and surrounding rural area. Quite remarkably, some 80 percent of the population of Sumer lived in one or another of these city-states, making Mesopotamia the most thoroughly urbanized society of ancient times. The chief reason for this massive urbanization, however, lay in the great flaw of this system, for frequent warfare among these Sumerian city-states caused people living in rural areas to flee to the walled cities for protection. With no overarching authority, rivalry over land and water often led to violent conflict. After one such conflict destroyed the city of Ur and desecrated its temple, a poet lamented the city's sad fate:

> After your city had been destroyed, how now can you exist!
> After your house had been destroyed, how has your heart led you on!
> Your city has become a strange city...
> Your house has become a house of tears.[23]

These conflicts, together with environmental devastation, eventually left Sumerian cities vulnerable to outside forces, and after about 2350 B.C.E., stronger peoples from northern Mesopotamia conquered Sumer's warring cities, bringing an end to the Sumerian phase of Mesopotamian civilization. First the Akkadians (2350–2000 B.C.E.) and later the Babylonians (1900–1500 B.C.E.) and the Assyrians (900–612

B.C.E.) created larger territorial states or bureaucratic empires that encompassed all or most of Mesopotamia. Periods of political unity now descended upon this First Civilization, but it was unity imposed from outside. Much later, a similar process befell the Greek city-states, whose endemic warfare invited Macedonian invasion and their subsequent incorporation into the empires of Alexander the Great and then of the Romans (see Chapter 4).

Egyptian civilization, by contrast, began its history around 3100 B.C.E., with the merger of several earlier states or chiefdoms into a unified territory that stretched some 1,000 miles along the Nile. For an amazing 3,000 years, Egypt maintained that unity and independence, though with occasional interruptions. A combination of wind patterns that made it easy to sail south along the Nile and a current flowing north facilitated communication, exchange, unity, and stability within the Nile Valley. Here was a record of political longevity and continuity that the Mesopotamians and many other ancient peoples might well have envied.

Cities in Egypt were less important than in Mesopotamia, although political capitals, market centers, and major burial sites gave Egypt an urban presence as well. Most people lived in agricultural villages along the river rather than in urban centers, perhaps because Egypt's greater security made it less necessary for people to

Snapshot   Key Moments in Nile Valley Civilizations

Small-scale states in Sudanic Africa	5000 B.C.E.
Nubian kingdom of Ta-Seti	3400–3200 B.C.E.
Unification of Egypt as a single state	3100 B.C.E.
Frequent warfare between Egypt and Nubian states	3100–2600 B.C.E.
Old Kingdom Egypt (high point of pharaohs' power and pyramid building)	2663–2195 B.C.E.
Nubian kingdom of Kush established	2500 B.C.E.
Egyptian commercial expeditions to Nubia	2300 B.C.E.
Hyksos invasion and rule of Egypt	1650–1550 B.C.E.
New Kingdom Egypt	1550–1064 B.C.E.
Emergence of Egyptian empire	1500 B.C.E.
Queen Hatshepsut launches expeditions to Land of Punt, probably along the East African coast	1473–1458 B.C.E.
Kush conquest of Egypt	760–660 B.C.E.
Assyrian conquest of Egypt	671–651 B.C.E.
Persian rule in Egypt	525–404 B.C.E.
Roman conquest of Egypt	30 B.C.E.

gather in fortified towns. The focus of the Egyptian state resided in the pharaoh, believed to be a god in human form. He alone ensured the daily rising of the sun and the annual flooding of the Nile. All of the country's many officials served at his pleasure; the law of the land was simply the pharaoh's edict; and access to the afterlife lay in proximity to him and burial in or near his towering pyramids.

This image of the pharaoh and his role as an enduring symbol of Egyptian civilization persisted over the course of three millennia, but the realities of Egyptian political life changed over time. By 2400 B.C.E., the power of the pharaoh had diminished, as local officials and nobles, who had been awarded their own land and were able to pass their positions on to their sons, assumed greater authority. When changes in the weather resulted in the Nile's repeated failure to flood properly around 2200 B.C.E., the authority of the pharaoh was severely discredited, and Egypt dissolved for several centuries into a series of local principalities.

Even when centralized rule was restored around 2000 B.C.E., the pharaohs never regained their old power and prestige. Kings were now warned that they too would have to account for their actions at the Day of Judgment. Nobles no longer sought to be buried near the pharaoh's pyramid but instead created their own more modest tombs in their own areas. Osiris, the god of the dead, became increasingly prominent, and "all men who were worthy . . . not merely those who had known the pharaoh in life" could aspire to immortality in his realm.[24]

Interaction and Exchange

■ Connection

In what ways were Mesopotamian and Egyptian civilizations shaped by their interactions with near and distant neighbors?

Although Mesopotamia and Egypt represented separate and distinct civilizations, they interacted frequently with each other and with both near and more distant neighbors. Even in these ancient times, the First Civilizations were embedded in larger networks of commerce, culture, and power. None of them stood alone.

The early beginnings of Egyptian civilization illustrate the point. Its agriculture drew upon wheat and barley, which reached Egypt from Mesopotamia, as well as gourds, watermelon, domesticated donkeys, and cattle, which derived from Sudan. Some scholars argue that Egypt's step pyramids and its system of writing were stimulated by Mesopotamian models. The practice of "divine kingship" seems to have derived from the central or eastern Sudan, where small-scale agricultural communities had long viewed their rulers as sacred and buried them with various servants and officials. From this complex of influences, the Egyptians created something distinct and unique, but that civilization had roots in both Africa and Southwest Asia.[25]

Furthermore, once they were established, both Mesopotamia and Egypt carried on extensive long-distance trade. Sumerian merchants had established seaborne contact with the Indus Valley civilization as early as 2300 B.C.E. Other trade routes connected it to Anatolia (present-day Turkey), Egypt, Iran, and Afghanistan. During Akkadian rule over Mesopotamia, a Sumerian poet described its capital of Agade:

> In those days the dwellings of Agade were filled with gold,
> its bright-shining houses were filled with silver,
> into its granaries were brought copper, tin, slabs of
> lapis lazuli [a blue gemstone], its silos bulged at the sides . . .
> its quay where the boats docked were all bustle. . . .[26]

All of this and more came from far away.

Egyptian trade likewise extended far afield. Beyond its involvement with the Mediterranean and the Middle East, Egyptian trading journeys extended deep into Africa, including Nubia, south of Egypt in the Nile Valley, and Punt, along the East African coast of Ethiopia and Somalia. One Egyptian official described his return from an expedition to Nubia: "I came down with three hundred donkeys laden with incense, ebony, . . . panther skins, elephant tusks, throw sticks, and all sorts of good products."[27] What most intrigued the very young pharaoh who sent him, however, was a dancing dwarf that accompanied the expedition back to Egypt.

Along with trade goods went cultural influence from the civilizations of Mesopotamia and Egypt. Among the smaller societies of the region to feel this influence were the Hebrews, who had migrated from Mesopotamia to Palestine and Egypt early in their history. Their sacred writings, recorded in the Old Testament, showed the influence of Mesopotamia in the "eye for an eye" principle of their legal system and in the story of a flood that destroyed the world. Unique to the Hebrews, however, was their emerging awareness of a merciful and single deity, Yahweh, who demanded an ethical life from his people. This conception subsequently achieved global significance when it was taken over by Christianity and Islam.

The Phoenicians, who were commercially active in the Mediterranean basin from their homeland in present-day Lebanon, also were influenced by Mesopotamian civilization. They adopted the Mesopotamian fertility goddess Ishtar, renaming her Astarte. They also adapted the Sumerian cuneiform method of writing to a much easier alphabetic system, which later became the basis for Greek and Latin writing. Various Indo-European peoples, dispersing probably from north-central Anatolia, also

Egypt and Nubia
By the fourteenth century B.C.E., Nubia was a part of an Egyptian empire. This wall painting shows Nubian princes bringing gifts or tribute, including rings and bags of gold, to Huy, the Egyptian viceroy of Nubia. The mural comes from Huy's tomb. (Courtesy of the Trustees of the British Museum)

Map 3.3 An Egyptian Empire
During the New Kingdom period after 1550 B.C.E., Egypt became for several centuries an empire, extending its political control southward into Nubia and northward into Palestine.

Black Sea

ANATOLIA
(ASIA MINOR)

Tigris R.

SYRIA

Euphrates R.

Aegean Sea

Crete

Cyprus

PALESTINE

Mediterranean Sea

Jericho

Dead Sea

LOWER EGYPT

Giza
Memphis

SINAI PENINSULA

ARABIA

Akhetaten
(Tell el-Amarna)

Nile R.

Thebes

UPPER EGYPT

Aswan

Red Sea

S A H A R A

First Cataract

PUNT

Second Cataract

NUBIA

Third Cataract Kerma

Fourth Cataract

Fifth Cataract

Napata

Hittite empire

Egyptian empire,
ca. 1450 B.C.E.

| 0 | 100 | 200 miles |
| 0 | 100 | 200 kilometers |

Meroë

Sixth Cataract

incorporated Sumerian deities into their own religions as well as bronze metallurgy and the wheel into their economies. When their widespread migrations carried them across much of Eurasia, they took these Sumerian cultural artifacts with them.

Egyptian cultural influence likewise spread in several directions. Nubia, located to the south of Egypt in the Nile Valley, not only traded with its more powerful neighbor but also was subject to periodic military intervention and political control from Egypt. Skilled Nubian archers were actively recruited for service as mercenaries in Egyptian armies. They often married Egyptian women and were buried in Egyptian style. All of this led to the diffusion of Egyptian culture in Nubia, expressed in building Egyptian-style pyramids, worshipping Egyptian gods and goddesses, and making use of Egyptian hieroglyphic writing. Despite this cultural borrowing, Nubia remained a distinct civilization, developing its own alphabetic script, retaining many of its own gods, developing a major ironworking industry by 500 B.C.E., and asserting its political independence whenever possible. The Nubian kingdom of Kush, in fact, invaded Egypt in 760 B.C.E. and ruled it for about 100 years.

In the Mediterranean basin, clear Egyptian influence is visible in the art of the Minoan civilization, which emerged on the island of Crete about 2500 B.C.E. More controversial has been the claim by historian Martin Bernal in a much-publicized book, *Black Athena* (1987), that ancient Greek culture—its art, religion, philosophy, and language—drew heavily upon Egyptian as well as Mesopotamian precedents. His book lit up a passionate debate among scholars. To some of his critics, Bernal seemed to undermine the originality of Greek civilization by suggesting that it had Afro-Asian origins. His supporters accused the critics of Eurocentrism. Whatever its outcome, the controversy surrounding Bernal's book served to focus attention on Egypt's relationship to black Africa and to the world of the Mediterranean basin.

Influence was not a one-way street, however, as Egypt and Mesopotamia likewise felt the impact of neighboring peoples. Pastoral peoples, speaking Indo-European languages and living in what is now southern Russia, had domesticated the horse by perhaps 4000 B.C.E. and later learned to tie that powerful animal to wheeled carts and chariots. This new technology provided a fearsome military potential that enabled various chariot-driving peoples to temporarily overwhelm ancient civilizations. Based in Anatolia, the Hittites overran the powerful Babylonian empire of Mesopotamia in 1595 B.C.E. About the same time, another pastoral group with chariots, the Hyksos, invaded Egypt and ruled it for more than a century (1650–1535 B.C.E.). But chariot technology was portable, and soon both the Egyptians and the Mesopotamians incorporated it into their own military forces. In fact, this powerful military innovation, together with the knowledge of bronze metallurgy, spread quickly and widely, reaching China by 1200 B.C.E. There it enabled the creation of a strong Chinese state ruled by the Shang dynasty. All of these developments provide evidence of at least indirect connections across the entire Eurasian landmass in ancient times. Even then, no civilization was wholly isolated from larger patterns of interaction.

In Egypt, the intrusion of the chariot-driving Hyksos shattered the sense of security that this Nile Valley civilization had long enjoyed. It also stimulated the normally complacent Egyptians to adopt a number of technologies pioneered earlier in Asia, including the horse-drawn chariot; new kinds of armor, bows, daggers, and swords; improved methods of spinning and weaving; new musical instruments; and olive and pomegranate trees. Absorbing these foreign innovations, Egyptians expelled the Hyksos and went on to create their own empire, both in Nubia and in the eastern Mediterranean regions of Syria and Palestine. By 1500 B.C.E., the previously self-contained Egypt became for several centuries an imperial state bridging Africa and Asia, ruling over substantial numbers of non-Egyptian peoples (see Map 3.3). It also became part of an international political system that included the Babylonian and later Assyrian empires of Mesopotamia as well as many other peoples of the region. Egyptian and Babylonian rulers engaged in regular diplomatic correspondence, referred to one another as "brother," exchanged gifts, and married their daughters into one another's families. One Babylonian king complained to an Egyptian pharaoh that the delegation that had come to take his daughter to Egypt contained only five carriages. What would his courtiers say about the daughter of a great ruler traveling with such a paltry escort?[28]

Reflections: "Civilization": What's in a Word?

In examining the cultures of ancient Mesopotamia and Egypt, we are worlds away from life in agricultural villages or Paleolithic camps. Much the same holds for those of the Indus Valley, China, Mesoamerica, and the Andes. Strangely enough, historians have been somewhat uncertain as to how to refer to these new forms of human community. Following common practice, I have called them "civilizations," but scholars have reservations about the term for two reasons. The first is its implication of superiority. In popular usage, "civilization" suggests refined behavior, a "higher" form of society, something unreservedly positive. The opposite of "civilized"— "barbarian," "savage," or "uncivilized"—is normally understood as an insult implying inferiority. That, of course, is precisely how the inhabitants of many civilizations have viewed those outside their own societies, particularly those neighboring peoples living without the alleged benefit of cities and states.

Modern assessments of the First Civilizations reveal a profound ambiguity about these new, larger, and more complex societies. On the one hand, these civilizations have given us inspiring art, profound reflections on the meaning of life, more productive technologies, increased control over nature, and the art of writing—all of which have been cause for celebration. On the other hand, as anthropologist Marvin Harris noted, "[H]uman beings learned for the first time how to bow, grovel, kneel, and kowtow."[29] Massive inequalities, state oppression, slavery, large-scale warfare, the subordination of women, and epidemic disease also accompanied the rise of civilization, generating discontent, rebellion, and sometimes the urge to escape. This ambiguity about the character of civilizations has led some historians to avoid the word, referring to early Egypt, Mesopotamia, and other regions instead as complex societies, urban-based societies, state-organized societies, or some more neutral term.

A second reservation about using the term "civilization" derives from its implication of solidity—the idea that civilizations represent distinct and widely shared identities with clear boundaries that mark them off from other such units. It is unlikely, however, that many people living in Mesopotamia, Norte Chico, or ancient China felt themselves part of a shared culture. Local identities defined by occupation, clan affiliation, village, city, or region were surely more important for most people than those of some larger civilization. At best, members of an educated upper class who shared a common literary tradition may have felt themselves part of some more inclusive civilization, but that left out most of the population. Moreover, unlike modern nations, none of the earlier civilizations had definite borders. Any identification with that civilization surely faded as distance from its core region increased. Finally, the line between civilizations and other kinds of societies is not always clear. Just when does a village or town become a city? At what point does a chiefdom become a state? Scholars continue to argue about these distinctions.

Given these reservations, should historians discard the notion of civilization? Maybe so, but this book continues to use it both because it is so deeply embedded in our way of thinking about the world and because no alternative concept has achieved widespread usage for making distinctions among different kinds of human communities. When the term appears in the text, try to keep in mind two points. First, as used by historians, "civilization" is a purely descriptive term, designating a particular type of human society—one with cities and states—and does not imply any judgment or assessment, any sense of superiority or inferiority. Second, it is used to define broad cultural patterns in particular geographic regions—Mesopotamia, the Peruvian coast, or China, for example—even though many people living in those regions may have been more aware of differences and conflicts than of those commonalities.

Second Thoughts

What's the Significance?

Norte Chico/Caral	Mohenjo Daro/Harappa	*Epic of Gilgamesh*
Indus Valley civilization	Code of Hammurabi	Egypt: "the gift of the Nile"
Olmec civilization	patriarchy	Nubia
Uruk	rise of the state	Hyksos

To assess your mastery of the material in this chapter, visit the **Student Center** at bedfordstmartins.com/strayer.

Big Picture Questions

1. What distinguished civilizations from other forms of human community?
2. How does the use of the term "civilization" by historians differ from that of popular usage? How do you use the term?
3. "Civilizations were held together largely by force." Do you agree with this assessment, or were there other mechanisms of integration as well?
4. In the development of the First Civilizations, what was gained for humankind, and what was lost?

Next Steps: For Further Study

For Web sites and additional documents related to this chapter, see **Make History** at bedfordstmartins.com/strayer.

Cyril Aldred, *The Egyptians* (1998). A brief and up-to-date account from a widely recognized expert.

Samuel Noah Kramer, *History Begins at Sumer* (1981). A classic account of Sumerian civilization, filled with wonderful stories and anecdotes.

David B. O'Connor, *Ancient Nubia: Egypt's Rival in Africa* (1994). An overview of this ancient African civilization, with lovely illustrations based on a museum exhibit.

Christopher A. Pool, *Olmec Archeology and Early Mesoamerica* (2007). A scholarly and up-to-date account of the earliest civilization in Mesoamerica.

Lauren Ristvet, *In the Beginning* (2007). A sweeping examination of the early phases of world history, from human evolution to the First Civilizations.

"The Ancient Indus Civilization," http://www.harappa.com/har/haro.html. Hundreds of vivid pictures and several brief essays on the Indus Valley civilization.

The British Museum, "Ancient Egypt," http://www.ancientegypt.co.uk/menu.html. An interactive exploration of Egyptian civilization.

Documents

Considering the Evidence:
Life and Afterlife in Mesopotamia and Egypt

The advent of writing was not only a central feature of the First Civilizations but also a great boon to later historians. Access to early written records from these civilizations allows us some insight, in their own words, as to how these ancient peoples thought about their societies and their place in the larger scheme of things. Such documents, of course, tell only a small part of the story, for they most often reflect the thinking of the literate few—usually male, upper-class, powerful, and well-to-do—rather than the outlook of the vast majority who lacked such privileged positions. Nonetheless, historians have been grateful for even this limited window on the life of at least some of our ancient ancestors.

Among the First Civilizations, accessible written records are most widely available for Mesopotamia and Egypt. Those excerpted here disclose something about those peoples' beliefs regarding life in this world—class and gender, crime and justice, occupation and kingship—as well as about what awaits in the life beyond. Such reflections about life and afterlife allow us to catch a glimpse of the social organization and cultural outlook of these First Civilizations.

Document 3.1

In Search of Eternal Life

The most well-known of the writings from the world of the First Civilizations is surely the *Epic of Gilgamesh*. Inscribed on clay tablets in various versions, the Gilgamesh epic has been pieced together by scholars over the past century or so. Its origins no doubt go back to stories and legends circulating during the life of the historical Gilgamesh, the powerful ruler of the Sumerian city of Uruk around 2700 B.C.E., although the earliest written version of the epic dates to around 2000 B.C.E. (see Map 3.2, p. 105).

The epic poem itself recounts the adventures of Gilgamesh, said to be part human and part divine. As the story opens, he is the energetic and yet oppressive ruler of Uruk. The pleas of his people persuade the gods to send Enkidu, an uncivilized man from the wilderness, to counteract this oppression. But before he can confront the erring monarch, Enkidu must become civilized, a process that occurs at the hands of a seductive harlot. When the two men finally meet, they engage in a titanic wrestling match from which Gilgamesh emerges victorious. Thereafter they bond in a deep friendship and undertake a series of adventures together. In the course of these adventures, they offend the gods, who then determine that Enkidu must die. Devastated by the loss of his friend and the realization of his own mortality, Gilgamesh undertakes an extended search for eternal life. During this search, he meets a tavern owner, a wise woman named Siduri, as well as Utnapishtim, the only human being ever granted immortality by the gods. In the end, however, Gilgamesh learns that eternal life is not available to mere mortals and thus his quest proves futile.

The excerpts that follow illustrate something of Mesopotamian views of kingship, of the gods, and of the possibilities of life and afterlife.

- How would you define the Mesopotamian ideal of kingship? What is the basis of the monarch's legitimacy?

- What understanding of the afterlife does the epic suggest?

- What philosophy of life comes across in the Gilgamesh story?

- How does the *Epic of Gilgamesh* portray the gods and their relationship to humankind?

The Epic of Gilgamesh
ca. 2700 B.C.E.–2500 B.C.E.

On Kingship

[These first selections deal with the nature of kingship. They tell of the great deeds of Gilgamesh and his oppression of the people as well as recounting the instructions about kingship from Enlil, the chief Sumerian god, who is responsible for determining the destinies of humankind.]

I will proclaim to the world the deeds of Gilgamesh. This was the man to whom all things were known; this was the king who knew the countries of the world. He was wise, he saw mysteries and knew secret things, he brought us a tale of the days before the flood. He went on a long journey, was weary, worn-out with labor, returning he rested, he engraved on a stone the whole story.

When the gods created Gilgamesh they gave him a perfect body. Shamash the glorious sun endowed him with beauty, Adad the god of the storm endowed him with courage, the great gods made his beauty perfect, surpassing all others, terrifying like a great wild bull. Two-thirds they made him god and one-third man.

In Uruk he built walls, a great rampart, and the temple of blessed Eanna for the god of the firmament Anu, and for Ishtar the goddess of love. Look at it still today: the outer wall where the cornice runs, it shines with the brilliance of copper; and the inner wall, it has no equal. Touch the threshold, it is ancient. Approach Eanna the dwelling of Ishtar, our lady of love and war, the like of which no latter-day king, no man alive can equal. Climb upon the wall of Uruk; walk along it, I say; regard the foundation terrace and examine the masonry: is it not burnt brick and good? The seven sages laid the foundations.

Gilgamesh went abroad in the world, but he met with none who could withstand his arms till he

Source: *The Epic of Gilgamesh*, translated by N. K. Sanders (London: Penguin, 1972), 61–62; 70; 92–93; 101–2; 106–11.

came to Uruk. But the men of Uruk muttered in their houses, "Gilgamesh sounds the tocsin for his amusement, his arrogance has no bounds by day or night. No son is left with his father, for Gilgamesh takes them all, even the children; yet the king should be a shepherd to his people. His lust leaves no virgin to her lover, neither the warrior's daughter nor the wife of the noble; yet this is the shepherd of the city, wise, comely, and resolute."

Enlil of the mountain, the father of the gods, had decreed the destiny of Gilgamesh. So Gilgamesh dreamed and Enkidu said, "The meaning of the dream is this. The father of the gods has given you kingship, such is your destiny; everlasting life is not your destiny. Because of this do not be sad at heart, do not be grieved or oppressed. He has given you power to bind and to loose, to be the darkness and the light of mankind. He has given you unexampled supremacy over the people, victory in battle from which no fugitive returns, in forays and assaults from which there is no going back. But do not abuse this power, deal justly with your servants in the palace, deal justly before Shamash.

On the Search for Immortality

[As Enkidu lies dying, he tells Gilgamesh of a dream he had about the afterlife.]

"[T]his is the dream I dreamed last night. The heavens roared, and earth rumbled back an answer; between them stood I before an awful being, the somber-faced man-bird; he had directed on me his purpose. His was a vampire face, his foot was a lion's foot, his hand was an eagle's talon. He fell on me and his claws were in my hair, he held me fast and I smothered; then he transformed me so that my arms became wings covered with feathers. He turned his stare toward me, and he led me away to the palace of Irkalla, the Queen of Darkness, to the house from which none who enters ever returns, down the road from which there is no coming back.

"There is the house whose people sit in darkness; dust is their food and clay their meat. They are clothed like birds with wings for covering, they see no light, they sit in darkness. I entered the house of dust and I saw the kings of the earth, their crowns put away for ever; rulers and princes, all those who once wore kingly crowns and ruled the world in the days of old. They who had stood in the place of the gods like Anu and Enlil, stood now like servants to fetch baked meats in the house of dust, to carry cooked meat and cold water from the water-skin. In the house of dust which I entered were high priests and acolytes, priests of the incantation and of ecstasy.... Then I awoke like a man drained of blood who wanders alone in a waste of rushes."

[When Gilgamesh in his quest for immortality meets Siduri, the tavern keeper, he confesses to her his fear and anguish, and receives some wise counsel in return.]

"[M]y friend who was very dear to me and who endured dangers beside me, Enkidu my brother, whom I loved, the end of mortality has overtaken him. I wept for him seven days and nights till the worm fastened to him. Because of my brother I am afraid of death, because of my brother I stray through the wilderness and cannot rest. But now, young woman, maker of wine, since I have seen your face do not let me see the face of death which I dread so much."

She answered, "Gilgamesh, where are you hurrying to? You will never find that life for which you are looking. When the gods created man they allotted to him death, but life they retained in their own keeping. As for you, Gilgamesh, fill your belly with good things; day and night, night and day, dance and be merry, feast and rejoice. Let your clothes be fresh, bathe yourself in water, cherish the little child that holds your hand, and make your wife happy in your embrace; for this too is the lot of man."

[Later, when Gilgamesh reaches Utnapishtim, the only man to survive the great flood and receive eternal life from the gods, he hears a similar message.]

Utnapishtim said, "There is no permanence. Do we build a house to stand forever, do we seal a contract to hold for all time? Do brothers divide an inheritance to keep forever, does the flood-time of rivers endure?... From the days of old there is no permanence. The sleeping and the dead, how alike they are, they are like a painted death. What is there between the master and the servant when both have fulfilled their doom? When the Anunnaki, the judges, come together, and Mammetun the mother of destinies, together they decree the fates of men. Life and death they allot but the day of death they do not disclose."

On the Gods

[In his conversation with Utnapishtim, Gilgamesh learns something about the nature of Mesopotamian gods and the origins of the great flood, which ages ago had destroyed humankind.]

"You know the city Shurrupak, it stands on the banks of the Euphrates? That city grew old and the gods that were in it were old. There was Anu, lord of the firmament, their father, and warrior Enlil their counselor, Ninurta the helper, and Ennugi watcher over canals; and with them also was Ea. In those days the world teemed, the people multiplied, the world bellowed like a wild bull, and the great god was aroused by the clamor. Enlil heard the clamor and he said to the gods in council, 'The uproar of mankind is intolerable and sleep is no longer possible by reason of the babel.' So the gods agreed to exterminate mankind...

"With the first light of dawn a black cloud came from the horizon; it thundered within where Adad, lord of the storm, was riding. In front over hill and plain Shullat and Hanish, heralds of the storm, led on. Then the gods of the abyss rose up; Nergal pulled out the dams of the nether waters, Ninurta the war-lord threw down the dykes, and the seven judges of hell, the Annunaki, raised their torches, lighting the land with their livid flame. A stupor of despair went up to heaven when the god of the storm turned daylight to darkness, when he smashed the land like a cup. One whole day the tempest raged, gathering fury as it went, it poured over the people like the tides of battle; a man could not see his brother nor the people be seen from heaven. Even the gods were terrified at the flood, they fled to the highest heaven, the firmament of Anu; they crouched against the walls, cowering like curs. Then Ishtar the sweet-voiced Queen of Heaven cried out like a woman in travail: 'Alas the days of old are turned to dust because I commanded evil; why did I command this evil in the council of all the gods? I commanded wars to destroy the people, but are they not my people, for I brought them forth? Now like the spawn of fish they float in the ocean.' The great gods of heaven and of hell wept, they covered their mouths."

Document 3.2

Law and Justice in Ancient Mesopotamia

If the *Epic of Gilgamesh* affords us some insight into Mesopotamian cultural and religious thinking, the so-called Code of Hammurabi provides a glimpse of this First Civilization's social and economic life. Hammurabi (reigned ca. 1795–1750 B.C.E.) was the ruler of the Babylonian Empire, which for a time gave a measure of political unity to the rival cities and kingdoms of Mesopotamia. Sometime during his reign he ordered inscribed on a large stone pillar a number of laws, judgments, or decrees. They were intended, in Hammurabi's words, "to bring about the rule of righteousness in the land, to destroy the wicked and the evil-doers; so that the strong should not harm the weak..., to further the well-being of mankind."

■ If you knew nothing else about ancient Mesopotamia, what could you conclude from the Code of Hammurabi about the economy and society of this civilization in the eighteenth century B.C.E.? How might you describe the economy of the region? What distinct social groups are mentioned in the code? What rights did women enjoy and to what restrictions were they subject?

■ What can you infer from the code about the kind of social problems that afflicted ancient Mesopotamia?

■ How would you define the principles of justice that underlay Hammurabi's code? In what different ways might twenty-first-century observers and those living at the time of Hammurabi assess that system of justice?

■ How did the code seek to realize the aims of Hammurabi as described above?

The Law Code of Hammurabi
ca. 1800 B.C.E.

On Crime, Punishment, and Justice

2. If any one bring an accusation against a man, and the accused go to the river and leap into the river, if he sink in the river his accuser shall take possession of his house. But if the river prove that the accused is not guilty, and he escape unhurt, then he who had brought the accusation shall be put to death, while he who leaped into the river shall take possession of the house that had belonged to his accuser....

3. If any one bring an accusation of any crime before the elders, and does not prove what he has charged, he shall, if it be a capital offense charged, be put to death....

5. If a judge try a case, reach a decision, and present his judgment in writing; if later error shall appear in his decision, and it be through his own fault, then he shall pay twelve times the fine set by him in the case, and he shall be publicly removed from the judge's bench, and never again shall he sit there to render judgment....

22. If any one is committing a robbery and is caught, then he shall be put to death....

196. If a man put out the eye of another man, his eye shall be put out.

197. If he break another man's bone, his bone shall be broken....

On the Economy

26. If a chieftain or a man [common soldier], who has been ordered to go upon the king's highway for war does not go, but hires a mercenary, if he withholds the compensation, then shall this officer or man be put to death, and he who represented him shall take possession of his house....

30. If a chieftain or a man leave his house, garden, and field and hires it out, and some one else takes possession of his house, garden, and field and uses it for three years: if the first owner return and claims his house, garden, and field, it shall not be given to him, but he who has taken possession of it and used it shall continue to use it....

Source: *The Code of Hammurabi*, translated by L. W. King, 1915.

53. If any one be too lazy to keep his dam in proper condition, and does not so keep it; if then the dam break and all the fields be flooded, then shall he in whose dam the break occurred be sold for money, and the money shall replace the corn which he has caused to be ruined....

104. If a merchant give an agent corn, wool, oil, or any other goods to transport, the agent shall give a receipt for the amount, and compensate the merchant therefore. Then he shall obtain a receipt from the merchant for the money that he gives the merchant....

122. If any one give another silver, gold, or anything else to keep, he shall show everything to some witness, draw up a contract, and then hand it over for safe keeping....

229. If a builder build a house for some one, and does not construct it properly, and the house which he built fall in and kill its owner, then that builder shall be put to death....

253. If any one agree with another to tend his field, give him seed, entrust a yoke of oxen to him, and bind him to cultivate the field, if he steal the corn or plants, and take them for himself, his hands shall be hewn off....

271. If any one hire oxen, cart, and driver, he shall pay one hundred and eighty ka of corn per day....

On Class and Slavery

8. If any one steal cattle or sheep, or an ass, or a pig or a goat, if it belong to a god or to the court, the thief shall pay thirtyfold therefore; if they belonged to a freed man of the king he shall pay tenfold; if the thief has nothing with which to pay, he shall be put to death....

15. If any one take a male or female slave of the court, or a male or female slave of a freed man, outside the city gates, he shall be put to death....

17. If any one find runaway male or female slaves in the open country and bring them to their masters, the master of the slaves shall pay him two shekels of silver....

117. If any one fail to meet a claim for debt, and sell himself, his wife, his son, and daughter for money or give them away to forced labor: they shall work for three years in the house of the man who bought them, or the proprietor, and in the fourth year they shall be set free....

198. If he put out the eye of a freed man, or break the bone of a freed man, he shall pay one gold mina.

199. If he put out the eye of a man's slave, or break the bone of a man's slave, he shall pay one-half of its value....

202. If any one strike the body of a man higher in rank than he, he shall receive sixty blows with an ox-whip in public....

215. If a physician make a large incision with an operating knife and cure it, or if he open a tumor [over the eye] with an operating knife, and saves the eye, he shall receive ten shekels in money.

216. If the patient be a freed man, he receives five shekels.

217. If he be the slave of some one, his owner shall give the physician two shekels....

On Men and Women

110. If a "sister of a god" [a woman formally dedicated to the temple of a god] open a tavern, or enter a tavern to drink, then shall this woman be burned to death....

128. If a man take a woman to wife, but have no intercourse with her, this woman is no wife to him.

129. If a man's wife be surprised with another man, both shall be tied and thrown into the water, but the husband may pardon his wife and the king his slaves.

130. If a man violate the wife [betrothed wife or child-wife] of another man, who has never known a man, and still lives in her father's house, and sleep with her and be surprised, this man shall be put to death, but the wife is blameless.

131. If a man bring a charge against one's wife, but she is not surprised with another man, she must take an oath and then may return to her house.

132. If the "finger is pointed" at a man's wife about another man, but she is not caught sleeping with the other man, she shall jump into the river for her husband....

136. If any one leave his house, run away, and then his wife go to another house, if then he return, and wishes to take his wife back: because he fled from his home and ran away, the wife of this runaway shall not return to her husband.

137. If a man wish to separate from a woman who has borne him children, or from his wife who has borne him children: then he shall give that wife her dowry, and a part of the usufruct [the right to use] of field, garden, and property, so that she can rear her children. When she has brought up her children... she may then marry the man of her heart....

142. If a woman quarrel with her husband, and say: "You are not congenial to me," the reasons for her prejudice must be presented. If she is guiltless, and there is no fault on her part, but he leaves and neglects her, then no guilt attaches to this woman, she shall take her dowry and go back to her father's house.

143. If she is not innocent, but leaves her husband, and ruins her house, neglecting her husband, this woman shall be cast into the water....

148. If a man take a wife, and she be seized by disease, if he then desire to take a second wife, he shall not put away his wife who has been attacked by disease, but he shall keep her in the house which he has built and support her so long as she lives.

Document 3.3

The Afterlife of a Pharaoh

Egyptian thinking about life, death, and afterlife bears comparison with that of Mesopotamia. In the selections that follow, we catch a glimpse of several Egyptian ways of understanding these fundamental human concerns. The first excerpt comes from a group of so-called pyramid texts, inscribed on the walls of a royal tomb as spells, incantations, or prayers to assist the pharaoh in entering the realm of eternal life among the gods in the Land of the West. This one was discovered in the tomb of the Egyptian king Teti, who ruled between roughly 2345 and 2333 B.C.E. Such texts represent the oldest religious writings in world history.

- How is the afterlife of the pharaoh represented in this text?

- How does it compare with depictions of the afterlife in the *Epic of Gilgamesh*?

A Pyramid Text

2333 B.C.E.

Oho! Oho! Rise up, O Teti!
Take your head, collect your bones,

Gather your limbs, shake the earth from your flesh!
Take your bread that rots not, your beer that sours not,
Stand at the gates that bar the common people!
The gatekeeper comes out to you, he grasps your hand,

Source: Miriam Lichtheim, *Ancient Egyptian Literature* (Berkeley: University of California Press, 1975), 1:41–42.

Takes you into heaven, to you father Geb.
He rejoices at your coming, gives you his hands,
Kisses you, caresses you,
Sets you before the spirits, the imperishable
   stars....
The hidden ones worship you,
The great ones surround you,
The watchers wait on you,

Barley is threshed for you,
Emmer° is reaped for you,
Your monthly feasts are made with it,
Your half-month feasts are made with it,
As ordered done for you by Geb, your father,
Rise up, O Teti, you shall not die!

_____

°**Emmer:** a variety of wheat

Document 3.4

A New Basis for Egyptian Immortality

Much later, during the New Kingdom period of ancient Egyptian history (1550–1064 B.C.E.), the *Book of the Dead* was compiled, gathering together a number of magical spells designed to ensure a smooth passage to eternal life. Written on papyrus, the spells could be purchased by anyone who could afford them. The owner then inscribed his own name and title and had the document placed in his tomb. The most famous of these texts is the so-called Negative Confession, which portrays the deceased person appearing before the gods in a place of judgment to demonstrate his moral life and his fitness for a place in the Land of the West. Such practices extended to people other than just the pharaoh the possibility of magical assistance in gaining eternal life with the gods.

- What changes in Egyptian religious thinking does the Negative Confession mark?

- On what basis are the users of the Negative Confession making their claim for eternal life?

- What does the Negative Confession suggest about the sources of conflict and discord in New Kingdom Egypt? How do these compare with the social problems revealed in the Code of Hammurabi?

Book of the Dead
ca. 1550–1064 B.C.E.

When the deceased enters the hall of the goddesses of Truth, he says:

Homage to thee, O great god, thou Lord of Truth. I have come to thee, my Lord, and I have brought myself hither that I may see thy beauties. I know thee, I know thy name. I know the names of the Two-and-Forty gods who live with thee in this Hall of Maati. In truth I have come to thee. I have brought Truth to thee. I have destroyed wickedness for thee.

I have not sinned against men.
I have not oppressed (or wronged) [my] kinsfolk.

Source: E. A. Wallis Budge, *Osiris, the Egyptian Religion of Resurrection* (London: P. L. Warner; New York: G. P. Putnam's Sons, 1911), 1:337–39.

I have not committed evil in the place
    of truth.°

I have not known worthless men.

I have not committed acts of abomination.

I have not caused my name to appear for honors.

I have not domineered over slaves.

I have not thought scorn of the god.

I have not defrauded the poor man of his goods.

I have not caused harm to be done to the slave by
    his master.

I have caused no man to suffer.

I have allowed no man to go hungry.

I have made no man weep. I have slain no man.

I have not given the order for any man to be
    slain.

I have not caused pain to the multitude.

I have not filched the offerings in the temples.

I have not purloined the cakes of the gods.

I have not stolen the offerings of the spirits.

°**place of truth:** a temple or burial place.

I have not defiled myself in the pure places of the
    god of my city.

I have not cheated in measuring of grain.

I have not filched land or added thereto.

I have not encroached upon the fields of others.

I have not added to the weight of the balance.

I have not cheated with the pointer of the scales.

I have not taken away the milk from the mouths
    of the babes.

I have not driven away the beasts from their
    pastures.

I have not netted the geese of the preserves of
    the gods.

I have not obstructed water when it should run.

I have not cut a cutting in a canal of rating water.

I have not extinguished a flame when it ought to
    burn.

I have not abrogated the days of offering the
    chosen offerings.

I have not turned off cattle from the property of
    the gods.

I am pure. I am pure. I am pure. I am pure.

Document 3.5

The Occupations of Old Egypt

Compared to small Paleolithic communities and later agricultural village societies, civilizations developed a far more complex division of labor and a much
greater sense of social hierarchy. Such features of the First Civilizations are on
display in the Egyptian text commonly known as "Be a Scribe." Dating from
the Middle Kingdom period (2066–1650 B.C.E.), it was a school text that students training for administrative positions would copy in an effort to improve
their writing. It also conveyed to them the exalted position of a scribe in contrast to many other occupations. One such text suggested that writing granted
a kind of immortality to the scribe: "Man decays; his corpse is dust; all his kin
have perished. But a book makes him remembered through the mouth of its
reciter."[30]

■ What might historians learn from this text about the occupational and
   social structure of Middle Kingdom Egypt?

■ What does learning to write offer to a young Egyptian? What advantages of a scribal position are suggested in the document?

■ What timeless frustrations of a teacher are evident in this text?

Be a Scribe

ca. 2066–1650 B.C.E.

Apply yourself to [this] noble profession....You will find it useful....You will be advanced by your superiors. You will be sent on a mission....Love writing, shun dancing; then you become a worthy official....By day write with your fingers; recite by night. Befriend the scroll, the palette. It pleases more than wine. Writing for him who knows it is better than all other professions. It pleases more than bread and beer, more than clothing and ointment. It is worth more than an inheritance in Egypt, than a tomb in the west.

Young fellow, how conceited you are!...But though I beat you with every kind of stick, you do not listen....You are a person fit for writing, though you have not yet known a woman. Your heart discerns, your fingers are skilled, your mouth is apt for reciting....

But though I spend the day telling you "Write," it seems like a plague to you....

See for yourself with your own eye. The occupations lie before you.

The washerman's day is going up, going down. All his limbs are weak, [from] whitening his neighbor's clothes every day, from washing their linen.

The maker of pots is smeared with soil.... [H]e is like one who lives in the bog.

The cobbler mingles with vats. His odor is penetrating. His hands are red..., like one who is smeared with blood....

The watchman prepares garlands and polishes vase-stands. He spends a night of toil just as one on whom the sun shines.

The merchants travel downstream and upstream. They are as busy as can be, carrying goods from one town to another. They supply him who has wants. But the tax collectors carry off the gold, that most precious of metals.

The ships' crews from every house [of commerce], they receive their loads. They depart from Egypt for Syria, and each man's god is with him. [But] not one of them says: "We shall see Egypt again!"

[The] outworker who is in the fields, his is the toughest of all the jobs. He spends the day loaded with his tools, tied to his toolbox. When he returns home at night, he is loaded with the toolbox and the timbers, his drinking mug, and his whetstones....

Let me also expound to you the situation of the peasant, that other tough occupation. [Comes] the inundation and soaks him..., he attends to his equipment. By day he cuts his farming tools; by night he twists rope. Even his midday hour he spends on farm labor. He equips himself to go to the field as if he were a warrior....When he reaches his field he finds [it?] broken up. He spends time cultivating, and the snake is after him. It finishes off the seed as it is cast to the ground. He does not see a green blade. He does three plowings with borrowed grain. His wife has gone down to the merchants and found nothing for barter....

If you have any sense, be a scribe. If you have learned about the peasant, you will not be able to be one....Look, I instruct you to...make you become one whom the king trusts; to make you gain entrance to treasury and granary. To make you receive the shipload at the gate of the granary. To make you issue the offerings on feast days. You are dressed in fine clothes; you own horses. Your boat is on the river; you are supplied with attendants. You stride about inspecting. A mansion is built in your town. You have a powerful office, given you by the king. Male and female slaves are about you. Those who are in the fields grasp your hand, on plots that you have made....Put the writings in your heart, and you will be protected from all kinds of toil. You will become a worthy official.

Do you not recall the [fate of] the unskilled man? His name is not known. He is ever burdened

---

Source: Miriam Lichtheim, *Ancient Egyptian Literature* (Berkeley: University of California Press, 1975), 2:168–72.

[like an ass carrying things] in front of the scribe who knows what he is about.

Come, [let me tell] you the woes of the soldier, and how many are his superiors: the general, the troop-commander, the officer who leads, the standard-bearer, the lieutenant, the scribe, the commander of fifty, and the garrison-captain. They go in and out in the halls of the palace, saying: "Get laborers!" He is awakened at any hour. One is after him as [after] a donkey. He toils until the Aten sets in his darkness of night. He is hungry, his belly hurts; he is dead while yet alive. When he receives the grain-ration, having been released from duty, it is not good for grinding.

He is called up for Syria. He may not rest. There are no clothes, no sandals....His march is uphill through mountains. He drinks water every third day; it is smelly and tastes of salt. His body is ravaged by illness. The enemy comes, surrounds him with missiles, and life recedes from him. He is told: "Quick, forward, valiant soldier! Win for yourself a good name!" He does not know what he is about. His body is weak, his legs fail him. When victory is won, the captives are handed over to his majesty, to be taken to Egypt....His wife and children are in their village; he dies and does not reach it. If he comes out alive, he is worn out from marching....

Be a scribe, and be spared from soldiering! You call and one says: "Here I am." You are safe from torments. Every man seeks to raise himself up. Take note of it!

Using the Evidence:
Life and Afterlife in Mesopotamia and Egypt

1. **Defining civilization:** What features of civilization, described in Chapter 3, do these documents illustrate?

2. **Making comparisons:** What similarities and differences between ancient Mesopotamian and Egyptian civilizations can you infer from these documents? How might you account for the differences?

3. **Considering past and present:** What elements of thought and practice from these early pieces of written literature resonate still in the twenty-first century? What elements remain strange or unfamiliar to modern sensibilities?

4. **Seeking further evidence:** What dimensions of these civilizations' social life and religious thinking are not addressed in these documents? What other perspectives might you want to seek out?

5. **Reading between the lines:** Historians often use documents to obtain insights or information that the authors did not intend to convey. How might these documents be used in this fashion? What are the advantages and dangers in this use of ancient texts?

Visual Sources

Considering the Evidence:
Indus Valley Civilization

⊔

In most accounts of the First Civilizations, Egypt and Mesopotamia hold center stage. And yet the civilization of the Indus River valley was much larger, and its archeological treasures have been equally impressive, though clearly distinctive (see pp. 86–91). This civilization arose around 2600 B.C.E., about a thousand years later than its better-known counterparts in the Middle East and North Africa. By 1500 B.C.E. Indus Valley civilization was in decline, as the center of Indian or South Asian civilization shifted gradually eastward to the plains of the Ganges River. In the process, all distinct memory of the earlier Indus Valley civilization vanished, to be rediscovered only in the early twentieth century as archeologists uncovered its remarkable remains. Here is yet another contrast with Egypt and Mesopotamia, where a memory of earlier achievements persisted long after those civilizations had passed into history. The images that follow are drawn from archeological investigations of the Indus Valley civilization and offer us a glimpse of its many achievements and unique features. Since its written language was limited in extent and has not yet been deciphered, scholars have been highly dependent on its physical remains for understanding this First Civilization.

Among the most distinctive elements of Indus Valley civilization were its cities, of which Mohenjo Daro and Harappa were the largest and are the most thoroughly investigated. Laid out systematically on a grid pattern and clearly planned, they were surrounded by substantial walls made from mud bricks of a standardized size and interrupted by imposing gateways. Inside the walls, public buildings, market areas, large and small houses, and craft workshops stood in each of the cities' various neighborhoods. Many houses had indoor latrines, while wide main streets and narrow side lanes had drains to carry away polluted water and sewage. Visual Source 3.1 is a modern drawing of ancient Harappa by one of the leading archeologists of the city, Jonathan M. Kenoyer. Also see the photo on page 93, which shows a section of the excavated city of Mohenjo Daro.

- Based on these images, how would you describe an Indus Valley city to someone who had never seen it?

- Compare these images of Indus Valley cities with those of the early agrarian village of Çatalhüyük (see the photo on p. 64 and Visual

Visual Source 3.1 Ancient Harappa (J. Mark Kenoyer/Harappa Images)

Source 2.1 on p. 77). What differences can you identify between these two types of settlements? What had changed in the intervening centuries?

In many ancient and more recent societies, seals have been used for imprinting an image on a document or a product. Such seals have been among the most numerous artifacts found in the Indus Valley cities. They generally carried the image of an animal—a bull, an elephant, a crocodile, a buffalo, or even a mythic creature such as a unicorn—as well as a title or inscription in the still undeciphered script of this civilization. Thus the seals were accessible to an illiterate worker loading goods on a boat as well as to literate merchants or officials. Particular seals may well have represented a specific clan, a high official, or a prominent individual. Unicorn seals have been the most numerous finds and were often used to make impressions on clay tags attached to bundled goods, suggesting that their owners were involved in trade or commerce. Because bull seals, such as that shown in Visual Source 3.2, were rarer, their owners may have been high-ranking officials or members of a particularly powerful clan. The bull, speculates archeologist Jonathan Kenoyer, "may symbolize the leader of the herd, whose strength and virility protects the herd and ensures the procreation of the species, or it may stand for a sacrificial animal."[31] Indus Valley seals, as well as pottery, have been found in Mesopotamia, indicating a well-developed trade between these two First Civilizations.

■ How might a prominent landowner, a leading official, a clan head, or a merchant make use of such a seal?

■ What meaning might you attach to the use of animals as totems or symbols of a particular group or individual?

Visual Source 3.2 A Seal from the Indus Valley (J. Mark Kenoyer/Harappa Images)

■ Notice the five characters of the Indus Valley script at the top of the
   seal. Do a little research on the script with an eye to understanding why
   it has proved so difficult to decipher.

The most intriguing features of Indus Valley civilization involve what is
missing, at least in comparison with ancient Egypt and Mesopotamia. No
grand temples or palaces; no elite burial places filled with great wealth; no
images of warfare, conquest, or the seizing of captives; no monuments to celebrate powerful rulers. These absences have left scholars guessing about the
social and political organization of this civilization. Kenoyer has suggested that
the great cities were likely controlled not by a single ruler, but by "a small
group of elites, comprised of merchants, landowners, and ritual specialists."[32]
Visual Source 3.3, a statue seven inches tall and found in Mohenjo Daro, likely
depicts one of these elite men.

■ What specific features of the statue can you point out?

■ What possible indication of elite status can you identify?

■ What overall impression does the statue convey?

Visual Source 3.3 Man from Mohenjo Daro (Department of Archaeology and Museums, Karachi, Pakistan)

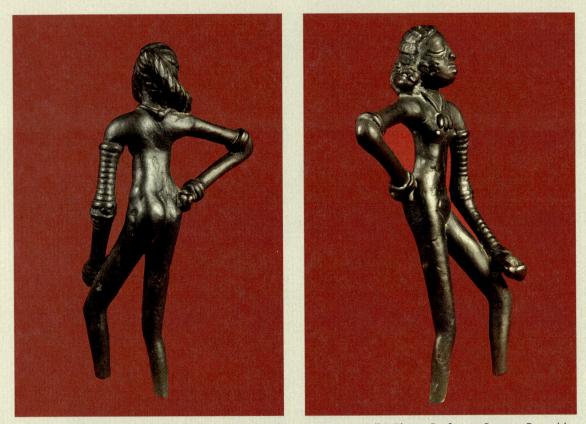

Visual Source 3.4 Dancing Girl (Courtesy, National Museum, New Delhi. Photo: Professor Gregory Possehl, Curator, Asian Department, University of Pennsylvania Museum)

Limited archeological evidence suggests that at least some urban women played important social and religious roles in the Indus Valley civilization. Figurines of women or goddesses are more common than those of men. Women, apparently, were buried near their mothers and grandmothers, while men were not interred with their male relatives. The great variety of clothing, hairstyles, and decorations displayed on female figurines indicates considerable class, ethnic, and perhaps individual variation.

Among the most delightful discoveries in the Indus Valley cities is the evocative statue shown in Visual Source 3.4. It is about four inches tall and dated to around 2500 B.C.E. This young female nude is known generally as the "dancing girl." Cast in bronze using a sophisticated "lost wax" method, this statue provides evidence for a well-developed copper/bronze industry. The figure herself was portrayed in a dancer's pose, her hair gathered in a bun and her left arm covered with bangles and holding a small bowl. Both her arms and legs seem disproportionately long. She has been described variously as a queen, a high-status woman, a sacred temple dancer, and a tribal girl.

Although no one really knows her precise identity, she has evoked wide admiration and appreciation. Mortimer Wheeler, a famous British archeologist, described her as "a girl perfectly, for the moment, perfectly confident of herself and the world." American archeologist Gregory Possehl, also active in the archeology of the Indus Valley civilization, commented: "We may not be certain that she was a dancer, but she was good at what she did and she knew it."[33]

■ What features of this statue may have provoked such observations?

■ How do you react to this statue? What qualities does she evoke?

■ What does Visual Source 3.4 suggest about views of women, images of female beauty, and attitudes about sexuality and the body?

Using the Evidence:
Indus Valley Civilization

1. **Using art as evidence:** What can we learn about Indus Valley civilization from these visual sources? How does our level of understanding of this civilization differ from that of Egypt and Mesopotamia where plentiful written records are available?

2. **Considering art without writing:** Based on these visual sources and those in Chapters 1 and 2, consider the problem of interpreting history through art, artifacts, or archeological sites in the absence of writing. What can we know with some certainty? What can we only guess at?

3. **Comparing art across time:** How would you compare the rock art of Australian Paleolithic peoples (Chapter 1), the art of early agricultural and pastoral peoples (Chapter 2), and the art from the Indus Valley? Consider issues of style, content, and accessibility to people of the twenty-first century. Is it possible to speak of artistic "progress" or "development," or should we be content with simply noticing differences?

4. **Comparing representations of people:** Notice the various ways that human figures were portrayed in the visual sources shown in Chapters 1–3. How might you define those differences? What variations in the depiction of men and women can you identify?

5. **Seeking further evidence:** What additional kinds of archeological discoveries would be helpful in furthering our understanding of Indus Valley civilization?

PART TWO

The Classical Era in World History

500 B.C.E.–500 C.E.

Contents

After the First Civilizations: What Changed and What Didn't?

Studying world history has much in common with using the zoom lens of a camera. Sometimes, we pull the lens back in order to get a picture of the broadest possible panorama. At other times, we zoom in a bit for a middle-range shot, or even farther for a close-up of some particular feature of the historical landscape. Students of world history soon become comfortable with moving back and forth among these several perspectives.

As we bid farewell to the First Civilizations, we will take the opportunity to pull back the lens and look broadly, and briefly, at the entire age of agricultural civilizations, a period from about 3500 B.C.E., when the earliest of the First Civilizations arose, to about 1750 C.E., when the first Industrial Revolution launched a new and distinctively modern phase of world history. During these more than 5,000 years, the most prominent large-scale trend was the globalization of civilization as this new form of human community increasingly spread across the planet, encompassing more people and larger territories.

The first wave of that process, addressed in Chapter 3, was already global in scope, with expressions in Asia, Africa, and the Americas. Those First Civilizations generated the most impressive and powerful human societies created thus far, but they proved fragile and vulnerable as well. The always-quarreling city-states of ancient Mesopotamia had long ago been absorbed into the larger empires of Babylon and Assyria. During the first millennium B.C.E., Egypt too fell victim to a series of foreign invaders, including the forces of Nubia, Assyria, Alexander the Great, and the Roman Empire. The Indus Valley civilization likewise declined sharply, as deforestation, topsoil erosion, and decreased rainfall led to desertification and political collapse by 1500 B.C.E. Norte Chico civilization seems to have faded away by 1800 B.C.E. The end of Olmec civilization around 400 B.C.E. has long puzzled historians, for it seems that the Olmecs themselves razed and then abandoned their major cities even as their civilizational style spread to neighboring peoples. About the same time, China's unified political system fragmented into a series of warring states.

Even if particular First Civilizations broke down, there was no going back. Civilization as a form of human community proved durable and resilient as well as periodically fragile. Thus, in the thousand years between 500 B.C.E. and 500 C.E., new or enlarged urban-centered and state-based societies emerged to replace the First Civilizations in the Mediterranean basin, the Middle East, India, China, Mesoamerica, and the Andes. Furthermore, smaller expressions of civilization began to take shape elsewhere—in Ethiopia and West Africa, in Japan and Indonesia, in Vietnam and Cambodia. In short, the development of civilization was becoming a global process.

Many of these "second wave" civilizations likewise perished, as the collapses of the Roman Empire, Han dynasty China, and the Mayan cities remind us. They were followed by yet a "third wave" of civilizations (roughly 500 to 1500 C.E.; see Part Three). Some of them represented the persistence or renewal of older patterns, as in the case of China, for example, while elsewhere—such as in Western Europe, Russia, Japan, and West Africa—new civilizations emerged, all of which borrowed heavily from their more-established neighbors. The largest of these, Islamic civilization, incorporated a number of older centers of civilization, Egypt and Mesopotamia for example, under the umbrella of a new religion. The globalization of civilization continued apace.

The size and prominence of these civilizations sometimes lead historians and history textbooks to ignore those cultures that did not embrace the city- and state-centered characteristic of civilizations. World history, as a field of study, has often been slanted in the direction of civilizations at the expense of other forms of human community. To counteract that tendency, the following chapters will, on occasion, point out the continuing historical development of gathering and hunting peoples, agricultural societies organized around kinship principles and village life, emerging chiefdoms, and pastoral peoples.

Continuities in Civilization

The renewal and expansion of civilization, however, remains the leading story. As this account of the human journey moves into the second and third waves of civilization, the question arises as to how they differed from the first ones. From a panoramic perspective, the answer is "not much." States and empires rose, expanded, and collapsed with a tiresome regularity, requiring history students to remember who was up and who was down at various times. It is arguable, however, that little fundamental change occurred amid these constant fluctuations. Monarchs continued to rule most of the new civilizations; men continued to dominate women; a sharp divide between the elite and everyone else persisted almost everywhere, as did the practice of slavery.[1]

Furthermore, no technological or economic breakthrough occurred to create new kinds of human societies as the Agricultural Revolution had done earlier or as the Industrial Revolution would do in later centuries. Landowning elites had little incentive to innovate, for they benefited enormously from simply expropriating the surplus that peasant farmers produced. Nor would peasants have any reason to invest much effort in creating new forms of production when they knew full well that any gains they might generate would be seized by their social superiors. Merchants, who often were risk takers, might have spawned innovations, but they usually were dominated by powerful states and were viewed with suspicion and condescension by more prestigious social groups.

Many fluctuations, repetitive cycles, and minor changes characterize this long era of agricultural civilization, but no fundamental or revolutionary transformation of social or economic life took place. The major turning points in human history had occurred earlier with the emergence of agriculture and the birth of the First Civilizations and would occur later with the breakthrough of industrialization.

Changes in Civilization

While this panoramic perspective allows us to see the broadest outlines of the human journey, it also obscures much of great importance that took place during the second and third waves of the age of agrarian civilization. If we zoom in a bit more closely, significant changes emerge, even if they did not result in a thorough transformation of human life. Population, for example, grew more rapidly than ever before during this period, as the Snapshot illustrates. Even though the overall trend was up, important fluctuations interrupted the pattern, especially during the first millennium C.E., when no overall growth took place. Moreover, the rate of growth, though rapid in comparison with Paleolithic times, was quite slow if we measure it against the explosive expansion of recent centuries, when human numbers quadrupled in the twentieth century alone. This modest and interrupted pattern of population growth during the age of agrarian civilization reflected the absence of any fundamental economic breakthrough, which could have supported much larger numbers.

Snapshot   **World Population during the Age of Agricultural Civilization**[2]

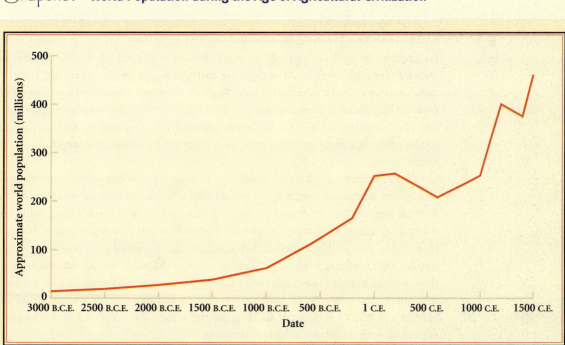

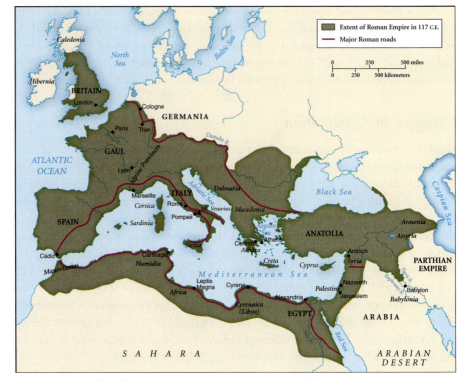

The Roman Empire (p. 156)

Another change lies in the growing size of the states or empires that structured civilizations. The Roman, Persian, Indian, and Chinese empires of second-wave civilizations, as well as the Arab, Mongol, and Inca empires of the third wave, all dwarfed the city-states of Mesopotamia and the Egypt of the pharaohs. Each of these empires brought together in a single political system a vast diversity of peoples. Even so, just to keep things in perspective, as late as the seventeenth century C.E., only one-third of the world's landmass was under the control of any state-based system, although these societies now encompassed a considerable majority of the world's people.

The rise and fall of these empires likewise represented very consequential changes to the people who experienced them. In the course of its growth, the Roman Empire utterly destroyed the city of Carthage in North Africa, with the conquerors allegedly sowing the ground with salt so that nothing would ever grow there again. Similar bloodshed and destruction accompanied the creation of other much-celebrated states. Their collapse also had a dramatic impact on the lives of their people. Scholars have estimated that the large population of Mayan civilization shrank by some 85 percent in less than a century as that society dissolved around 840 C.E. It is difficult to imagine the sense of trauma and bewilderment associated with a collapse of this magnitude.

Second- and third-wave civilizations also generated important innovations in many spheres. Those in the cultural realm have been perhaps the most widespread and enduring. Distinctive "wisdom traditions"—the great philosophical/religious systems of Confucianism and Daoism in China; Hinduism and Buddhism in India; Greek rationalism in the Mediterranean; and Judaism, Zoroastrianism, Christianity, and Islam in the Middle East—have provided the moral and spiritual framework within which most of the world's peoples have sought to order their lives and define their relationship to the mysteries of life and death. All of these philosophical and religious systems are the product of second- and third-wave civilizations.

Although no technological breakthrough equivalent to the Agricultural or Industrial Revolution took place during the second and third waves of agrarian civilizations, more modest innovations considerably enhanced human potential for manipulating the environment. China was a primary source of such technological change, though by no means the only one. "Chinese inventions and discoveries," wrote one prominent historian, "passed in a continuous flood from East to West for twenty centuries before the scientific revolution."[3] They included piston bellows, the draw-loom, silk-handling machinery, the wheelbarrow, a better harness for draft animals, the crossbow, iron casting, the iron-chain suspension bridge, gunpowder, firearms, the magnetic compass, paper, printing, and porcelain. India pioneered the crystallization of sugar and techniques for the manufacture of cotton textiles. Roman technological achievements were particularly apparent in construction and civil engineering—the building of roads, bridges, aqueducts, and fortifications—and in the art of glassblowing.

A further process of change following the end of the First Civilizations lay in the emergence of far more elaborate, widespread, and dense networks of communication and exchange that connected many of the world's peoples to one another. Many of the technologies mentioned here diffused widely across large areas. Sugar production provides a telling example. The syrup from sugarcane, which was initially domesticated in New Guinea early in the age of agriculture, was first processed into crystallized sugar in India by 500 C.E. During the early centuries of the Islamic era, Arab traders brought this technology from India to the Middle East and the Mediterranean, where Europeans learned about it during the Crusades. Europeans then transferred the practice of making sugar to the Atlantic islands and finally to the Americas, where it played a major role in stimulating a plantation economy and the Atlantic slave trade.[4]

Long-distance trade routes represented another form of transregional interaction. Caravan trade across northern Eurasia, seaborne commerce within the Indian Ocean basin, the exchange of goods across the Sahara, river-based commerce in the eastern woodlands of North America, various trading networks radiating from Mesoamerica—all of these carried goods, and sometimes culture as well. Buddhism, Hinduism, Christianity, and especially Islam spread widely beyond their places of origin, often carried on the camels and ships of merchants, creating ties of culture and religion among distant peoples within the Afro-Eurasian zone. Disease also increasingly linked distant human communities. According to the famous Greek historian Thucydides, a mysterious plague "from parts of Ethiopia above Egypt" descended on Athens in 430 B.C.E. and decimated the city, "inflicting a blow on Athenian society from which it never entirely recovered."[5]

Thus the second and third waves of civilization gave rise to much larger empires, new and distinctive cultural/religious traditions, any number of technological innovations, and novel patterns of interaction among far-flung societies. In these ways, the world became quite different from what it had been in the age of the First Civilizations, even though fundamental economic and social patterns had not substantially changed.

Classical Civilizations

At this point, and in the four chapters that follow, our historical lens zooms in to a middle-range focus on the major second-wave civilizations during the thousand years between 500 B.C.E. and 500 C.E. Historians frequently refer to this period of time as the "classical era" of world history, a term that highlights enduring traditions that have lasted into modern times and persist still in the twenty-first century. Confucianism, Hinduism, Buddhism, Judaism, and Christianity all took shape during this era of second-wave civilizations, and all of them remain very much alive at the dawn of the third millennium C.E. Despite the many and profound transformations of modernity, billions of people in the contemporary world still guide their lives, or at least claim to, according to teachings that first appeared 2,000 or more years ago.

Beyond the practices of individuals, the current identities of entire countries, regions, and civilizations are still linked to the achievements of the classical era. In 1971, a largely Muslim Iran mounted a lavish and much-criticized celebration of the 2,500th anniversary of the ancient Persian Empire. In 2004, a still communist China permitted public celebrations to mark the 2,555th birthday of its ancient sage Confucius. Students in Western schools and universities continue to read the works of Plato and Aristotle, produce the plays of Aeschylus and Sophocles, and admire the accomplishments of Athens. Many Indians still embrace the ancient religious texts called the Vedas and the Upanishads and continue to deal with the realities of caste. These are the continuities and enduring legacies that are reflected in the notion of "classical civilizations."

Designating the millennium between 500 B.C.E. and 500 C.E. as a "classical era" in world history is derived largely from the experience of Eurasian peoples, for it was on the outer rim of that huge continent that the largest and most influential civilizations took shape—in China, India, Persia, and the Mediterranean basin. Furthermore, that continent housed the vast majority of the world's people, some 80 percent or more.[6] Thus the first three chapters of Part Two focus exclusively on these Eurasian civilizations. Chapter 4 introduces them by examining and comparing their political frameworks and especially the empires (great or terrible, depending on your point of view) in which most of them were expressed. Chapter 5 looks at the cultural or religious traditions that each of them generated, while Chapter 6 probes their social organization—class, caste, slavery, and gender. Chapter 7 turns the spotlight on Africa and the Americas, asking whether their histories during the classical era paralleled Eurasian patterns or explored alternative possibilities.

In recalling the classical era, we will have occasion to compare the experiences of its various peoples, to note their remarkable achievements, to lament the tragedies that befell them and the suffering to which they gave rise, and to ponder their continuing power to fascinate us still.

Landmarks of the Classical Era, 500 B.C.E.–500 C.E.

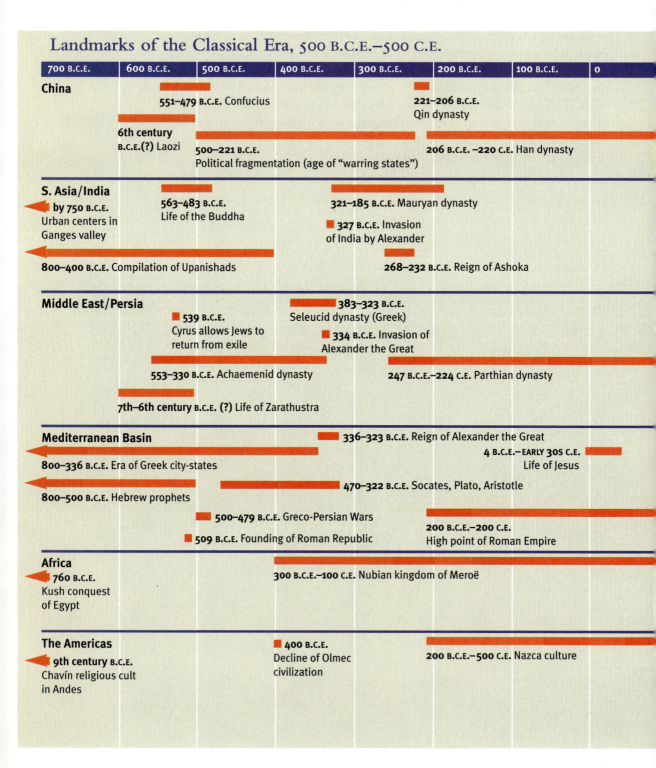

700 B.C.E.	600 B.C.E.	500 B.C.E.	400 B.C.E.	300 B.C.E.	200 B.C.E.	100 B.C.E.	0

China

551–479 B.C.E. Confucius

221–206 B.C.E. Qin dynasty

6th century B.C.E.(?) Laozi

500–221 B.C.E. Political fragmentation (age of "warring states")

206 B.C.E.–220 C.E. Han dynasty

S. Asia/India

by 750 B.C.E. Urban centers in Ganges valley

563–483 B.C.E. Life of the Buddha

321–185 B.C.E. Mauryan dynasty

327 B.C.E. Invasion of India by Alexander

800–400 B.C.E. Compilation of Upanishads

268–232 B.C.E. Reign of Ashoka

Middle East/Persia

383–323 B.C.E. Seleucid dynasty (Greek)

539 B.C.E. Cyrus allows Jews to return from exile

334 B.C.E. Invasion of Alexander the Great

553–330 B.C.E. Achaemenid dynasty

247 B.C.E.–224 C.E. Parthian dynasty

7th–6th century B.C.E. (?) Life of Zarathustra

Mediterranean Basin

336–323 B.C.E. Reign of Alexander the Great

800–336 B.C.E. Era of Greek city-states

4 B.C.E.–EARLY 30S C.E. Life of Jesus

800–500 B.C.E. Hebrew prophets

470–322 B.C.E. Socates, Plato, Aristotle

500–479 B.C.E. Greco-Persian Wars

509 B.C.E. Founding of Roman Republic

200 B.C.E.–200 C.E. High point of Roman Empire

Africa

760 B.C.E. Kush conquest of Egypt

300 B.C.E.–100 C.E. Nubian kingdom of Meroë

The Americas

400 B.C.E. Decline of Olmec civilization

200 B.C.E.–500 C.E. Nazca culture

9th century B.C.E. Chavín religious cult in Andes

| 100 C.E. | 200 C.E. | 300 C.E. | 400 C.E. | 500 C.E. | 600 C.E. |

3rd century C.E. Spread of Buddhism begins

589–618 C.E. Sui dynasty reunites China

184 C.E. Yellow Turban Rebellion

320–550 C.E. Gupta dynasty

224–651 C.E. Sassanid dynasty

380 C.E. Christianity as official state religion of the Roman Empire

476 C.E. Collapse of western Roman Empire

100 C.E. Rise of Axum

3rd–5th centuries C.E. Early cities/states in West Africa

by 500 C.E. Arrival of banana in Africa

300 C.E. Beginning of trans-Saharan trade

4th century C.E. Introduction of Christianity in Axum

300–700 C.E. Moche civilization (Peru)

300–800 C.E. Mayan civilization

400–600 C.E. High point of Teotihuacán

Eurasian Empires

500 B.C.E. – 500 C.E.

Are We Rome? It was the title of a thoughtful book, published in 2007, asking what had become a familiar question in the early twenty-first century: "Is the United States the new Roman Empire?"[1] With the collapse of the Soviet Union by 1991 and the subsequent U.S. invasions of Afghanistan and Iraq, some commentators began to make the comparison. The United States' enormous multicultural society, its technological achievements, its economically draining and overstretched armed forces, its sense of itself as unique and endowed with a global mission, its concern about foreigners penetrating its borders, its apparent determination to maintain military superiority — all of this invited comparison with the Roman Empire. Supporters of a dominant role for the United States argue that Americans must face up to their responsibilities as "the undisputed master of the world" as the Romans did in their time. Critics warn that the Roman Empire became overextended abroad and corrupt and dictatorial at home and then collapsed, suggesting that a similar fate may await the American empire. Either way, the point of reference was an empire that had passed into history some 1,500 years earlier, a continuing reminder of the relevance of the distant past to our contemporary world. In fact, for at least several centuries, that empire has been a source of metaphors and "lessons" about personal morality, corruption, political life, military expansion, and much more.

Even in a world largely critical of empires, they still excite the imagination of historians and readers of history. The earliest ones

Statue of Augustus: Likely dating from about 20 B.C.E., this statue has become symbolic of the emerging Roman Empire. Commemorating a major Roman military victory, it shows Augustus as imperator, or military commander, with his right arm extended as if he were addressing his troops. According to some scholars, his barefoot posture suggests divinity. So does the small figure of Cupid riding a dolphin at the base, for Cupid was the son of the Roman goddess Venus and serves to link Augustus to this much beloved deity. (Scala/Art Resource, NY) show up in the era of the First Civilizations when Akkadian, Babylonian, and Assyrian empires encompassed the city-states of Mesopotamia and established an enduring imperial tradition in the Middle East. Egypt became an imperial state when it temporarily ruled Nubia and the lands of the eastern Mediterranean. Following in their wake were many more empires, whose rise and fall have been central features of world history for the past 4,000 years.

BUT WHAT EXACTLY IS AN EMPIRE? At one level, empires are simply states, political systems that exercise coercive power. The term, however, is normally reserved for larger and more aggressive states, those that conquer, rule, and extract resources from other states and peoples. Thus empires have generally encompassed a considerable variety of peoples and cultures within a single political system, and they have often been associated with political and cultural oppression. No clear line divides empires and small multiethnic states, and the distinction between them is arbitrary and subjective. Frequently, empires have given political expression to a civilization or culture, as in the Chinese and Persian empires. Civilizations have also flourished without a single all-encompassing state or empire, as in the competing city-states of Mesopotamia, Greece, and the Maya or the many rival states of post-Roman Europe. In such cases, civilizations were expressed in elements of a common culture rather than in a unified political system.

The Eurasian empires of the classical era—those of Persia, Greece under Alexander the Great, Rome, China during the Qin and Han dynasties, India during the Mauryan and Gupta dynasties—shared a set of common problems. Would they seek to impose the culture of the imperial heartland on their varied subjects? Would they rule conquered people directly or through established local authorities? How could they extract the wealth of empire in the form of taxes, tribute, and labor while maintaining order in conquered territories? And, no matter how impressive they were at their peak, they all sooner or later collapsed, providing a useful reminder to their descendants of the fleeting nature of all human creation.

Why have these and other empires been of such lasting fascination to both ancient and modern people? Perhaps in part because they were so big, creating a looming presence in their respective regions. Their armies and their tax collectors were hard to avoid. Maybe also because they were so bloody. Conquest and the violence that accompanies it easily grab our attention, and certainly, all of these empires were founded and sustained at a great cost in human life. The collapse of these once-powerful states is likewise intriguing, for the fall of the mighty seems somehow satisfying, perhaps even a delayed form of justice. The study of empires also sets off by contrast those times and places in which civilizations have prospered without an enduring imperial state.

But empires have also commanded attention simply because they were important. Very large numbers of people—probably the majority of humankind before the twentieth century—have lived out their lives in empires, where they were often governed by rulers culturally different from themselves. These imperial states brought together people of quite different traditions and religions and so stimulated the exchange of ideas, cultures, and values. The Roman Empire, for example, provided the arena within which Christianity was transformed from a small Jewish sect into a world religion. Despite their violence, exploitation, and oppression, empires also imposed substantial periods of peace and security, which fostered economic and artistic development, commercial exchange, and cultural mixing.

Empires and Civilizations in Collision: The Persians and the Greeks

The classical era in Eurasia witnessed the flowering of second-wave civilizations in the Mediterranean world, the Middle East, India, and China. For the most part, these distant civilizations did not directly encounter one another, as each established its own political system, cultural values, and ways of organizing society. A great exception to that rule lay in the Mediterranean world and in the Middle East, where the emerging Persian Empire and Greek civilization, physically adjacent to each other, experienced a centuries-long interaction and clash. It was one of the most consequential cultural encounters of the classical world.

The Persian Empire

In 500 B.C.E., the largest and most impressive of the world's empires was that of the Persians, an Indo-European people whose homeland lay on the Iranian plateau just north of the Persian Gulf. Living on the margins of the earlier Mesopotamian civilization, the Persians constructed an imperial system that drew upon previous examples, such as the Babylonian and Assyrian empires, but far surpassed them all in size and splendor. Under the leadership of the famous monarchs Cyrus (reigned 557–530 B.C.E.) and Darius (reigned 522–486 B.C.E.), Persian conquests quickly reached from Egypt to India, encompassing in a single state some 35 million people, an immensely diverse realm containing dozens of peoples, states, languages, and cultural traditions (see Map 4.1).

The Persian Empire centered on an elaborate cult of kingship in which the monarch, secluded in royal magnificence, could be approached only through an elaborate ritual. When the king died, sacred fires all across the land were extinguished, Persians were expected to shave their hair in mourning, and the manes of horses were cut short. Ruling by the will of the great Persian god Ahura Mazda, kings were absolute monarchs, more than willing to crush rebellious regions or officials. Interrupted on one occasion while he was with his wife, Darius ordered the offender, a high-ranking nobleman, killed, along with his entire clan. In the eyes of many, Persian monarchs fully deserved their effusive title—"Great king, King of kings, King of countries containing all kinds of men, King in this great earth far and wide." Darius himself best expressed the authority of the Persian ruler when he observed: "what was said to them by me, night and day, it was done."[2]

■ **Comparison**

How did Persian and Greek civilizations differ in their political organization and values?

Map 4.1   The Persian Empire
At its height, the Persian Empire was the largest in the world. It dominated the lands of the First Civilizations in the Middle East and was commercially connected to neighboring regions.

But more than conquest and royal decree held the empire together. An effective administrative system placed Persian governors, called *satraps*, in each of the empire's twenty-three provinces, while lower-level officials were drawn from local authorities. A system of imperial spies, known as the "eyes and ears of the King," represented a further imperial presence in the far reaches of the empire. A general policy of respect for the empire's many non-Persian cultural traditions also cemented the state's authority. Cyrus won the gratitude of the Jews when in 539 B.C.E. he allowed those exiled in Babylon to return to their homeland and rebuild their temple in Jerusalem. In Egypt and Babylon, Persian kings took care to uphold local religious cults in an effort to gain the support of their followers and officials. The Greek historian Herodotus commented that "there is no nation which so readily adopts foreign customs. They have taken the dress of the Medes and in war they wear the Egyptian breastplate. As soon as they hear of any luxury, they instantly make it their own."[3] For the next 1,000 years or more, Persian imperial bureaucracy and court life, replete with administrators, tax collectors, record keepers, and translators, provided a model for all subsequent regimes in the region, including, later, those of the Islamic world.

The infrastructure of empire included a system of standardized coinage, predictable taxes levied on each province, and a newly dug canal linking the Nile with the Red Sea, which greatly expanded commerce and enriched Egypt. A "royal road," some 1,700 miles in length, facilitated communication and commerce across this vast empire. Caravans of merchants could traverse this highway in three months, but agents of the imperial courier service, using a fresh supply of horses every twenty-five to thirty miles, could carry a message from one end of the road to another in a week or two. Herodotus was impressed. "Neither snow, nor rain, nor heat, nor darkness of night," he wrote, "prevents them from accomplishing the task proposed to them with utmost speed." That description of the imperial Persian postal system was much later adopted as the unofficial motto for its counterpart in the United States Postal Service.

The immense wealth and power of the Persian Empire were reflected in the construction of elaborate imperial centers, particularly Susa and Persepolis. Palaces, audience halls, quarters for the harem, monuments, and carvings made these cities into powerful symbols of imperial authority. Materials and workers alike were drawn from all corners of the empire and beyond. Inscribed in the foundation of Persepolis was Darius's commentary on what he had set in motion: "And Ahura Mazda was of such a mind, together with all the other gods, that this fortress [should] be built. And [so] I built it. And I built it secure and beautiful and adequate, just as I was intending to."[4]

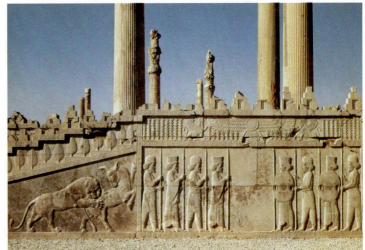

Persepolis
The largest palace in Persepolis, the Persian Empire's ancient capital, was the Audience Hall. The emperor officially greeted visiting dignitaries at this palace, which was constructed around 500 B.C.E. This relief, which shows a lion attacking a bull and Persian guards at attention, adorns a staircase leading to the Audience Hall. (Gianni Dagli Orti/Corbis)

The Greeks

It would be hard to imagine a sharper contrast than that between the huge and centralized Persian Empire, governed by an absolute and almost unapproachable monarch, and the small competing city-states of classical Greece, which allowed varying degrees of popular participation in political life. Like the Persians, the Greeks were an Indo-European people whose early history drew on the legacy of the First Civilizations. The classical Greece of historical fame emerged around 750 B.C.E. as a new civilization and flourished for about 400 years before it was incorporated into a succession of foreign empires. During that relatively short period, the civilization of Athens and Sparta, of Plato and Aristotle, of Zeus and Apollo took shape and collided with its giant neighbor to the east.

Calling themselves Hellenes, the Greeks created a civilization that was distinctive in many ways, particularly in comparison with the Persians. The total population of

■ **Change**
Why did semidemocratic governments emerge in some of the Greek city-states?

Greece and the Aegean basin was just 2 million to 3 million, a fraction of that of the Persian Empire. Furthermore, Greek civilization took shape on a small peninsula, deeply divided by steep mountains and valleys. Its geography certainly contributed to the political shape of that civilization, which found expression not in a Persian-style empire, but in hundreds of city-states or small settlements (see Map 4.2). Most were quite modest in size, with between 500 and 5,000 male citizens. Each of these city-states was fiercely independent and in frequent conflict with its neighbors, yet they had much in common, speaking the same language and worshipping the same gods. Every four years they temporarily suspended their persisting rivalries to participate together in the Olympic Games, which had begun in 776 B.C.E. Despite this emerging sense of Greek cultural identity, it did

Map 4.2   Classical Greece
The classical civilization of Greece was centered on a small peninsula of southeastern Europe, but Greek settlers spread that civilization along the coasts of the Mediterranean and Black seas.

little to overcome the endemic political rivalries of the larger city-states—Athens, Sparta, Thebes, Corinth, and many others.

Like the Persians, the Greeks were an expansive people, but their expansion took the form of settlement in distant places rather than conquest and empire. Pushed by a growing population, Greek traders in search of iron and impoverished Greek farmers in search of land stimulated a remarkable emigration. Between 750 and 500 B.C.E., Greek settlements were established all around the Mediterranean basin and the rim of the Black Sea. Settlers brought Greek culture, language, and building styles to these new lands, even as they fought, traded, and intermarried with their non-Greek neighbors.

The most distinctive feature of Greek civilization, and the greatest contrast with Persia, lay in the extent of popular participation in political life that occurred within at least some of the city-states. It was the idea of "citizenship," of free people running the affairs of state, of equality for all citizens before the law, that was so unique. A foreign king, observing the operation of the public assembly in Athens, was amazed that male citizens as a whole actually voted on matters of policy: "I find it astonishing," he noted, "that here wise men speak on public affairs, while fools decide them."[5] Compared to the rigid hierarchies, inequalities, and absolute monarchies of Persia and other ancient civilizations, the Athenian experiment was remarkable. This is how one modern scholar defined it:

> Among the Greeks the question of who should reign arose in a new way. Previously the most that had been asked was whether one man or another should govern and whether one alone or several together. But now the question was whether all the citizens, including the poor, might govern and whether it would be possible for them to govern as citizens, without specializing in politics. In other words, should the governed themselves actively participate in politics on a regular basis?[6]

The extent of participation and the role of "citizens" varied considerably, both over time and from city to city. Early in Greek history, only the wealthy and well-born had the rights of full citizenship, such as speaking and voting in the assembly, holding public office, and fighting in the army. Gradually, middle- and lower-class men, mostly small-scale farmers, also obtained these rights. At least in part, this broadening of political rights was associated with the growing number of men able to afford the armor and weapons that would allow them to serve as *hoplites*, or infantrymen, in the armies of the city-states. In many places, strong but benevolent rulers known as *tyrants* emerged for a time, usually with the support of the poorer classes, to challenge the prerogatives of the wealthy. Sparta—famous for its extreme forms of military discipline and its large population of *helots*, conquered people who lived in slavelike conditions—vested most political authority in its Council of Elders. The council was composed of twenty-eight men over the age of sixty, derived from the wealthier and more influential segment of society, who served for life and provided political leadership for Sparta.

Snapshot   Key Moments in Classical Greek History

Traditional date for first Olympic Games	776 B.C.E.
Emergence of Greek city-states and overseas colonization	750–700 B.C.E.
Evolution of hoplite military tactics	700–650 B.C.E.
Tyrants rule in many city-states	670–500 B.C.E.
Sparta dominant in Peloponnesus	550 B.C.E.
Cleisthenes' political reforms in Athens	507 B.C.E.
Greco-Persian Wars	490–479 B.C.E.
Golden Age of Athens (building of Parthenon; Athenian democracy, rule of Pericles)	479–429 B.C.E.
Helot rebellion in Sparta	463 B.C.E.
Peloponnesian War	431–404 B.C.E.
Macedonian conquest of Greece	338 B.C.E.
Conquests of Alexander the Great	333–323 B.C.E.
Hellenistic era	323–30 B.C.E.
Greece comes under Roman control	2nd century B.C.E.

It was in Athens that the Greek experiment in political participation achieved its most distinctive expression. Early steps in this direction were the product of intense class conflict, leading almost to civil war. A reforming leader named Solon emerged in 594 B.C.E. to push Athenian politics in a more democratic direction, breaking the hold of a small group of aristocratic families. Debt slavery was abolished, access to public office was opened to a wider group of men, and all citizens were allowed to take part in the Assembly. Later reformers such as Cleisthenes and Pericles extended the rights of citizens even further. By 450 B.C.E., all holders of public office were chosen by lot and were paid, so that even the poorest could serve. The Assembly, where all citizens could participate, became the center of political life.

Athenian democracy, however, was different from modern democracy. It was direct, rather than representative, democracy, and it was distinctly limited. Women, slaves, and foreigners, together far more than half of the population, were wholly excluded from political participation. Nonetheless, political life in Athens was a world away from that of the Persian Empire and even from that of many other Greek cities.

■ **Connection**
What were the consequences for both sides of the encounter between the Persians and the Greeks?

Collision: The Greco-Persian Wars

If ever there was an unequal conflict between civilizations, surely it was the collision of the Greeks and the Persians. The confrontation between the small and divided

Greek cities and Persia, the world's largest empire, grew out of their respective patterns of expansion. A number of Greek settlements on the Anatolian seacoast, known to the Greeks as Ionia, came under Persian control as that empire extended its domination to the west. In 499 B.C.E., some of these Ionian Greek cities revolted against Persian domination and found support from Athens on the Greek mainland. Outraged by this assault from the remote and upstart Greeks, the Persians twice in ten years (490 and 480 B.C.E.) launched major military expeditions to punish the Greeks in general and Athens in particular. Against all odds and all expectations, the Greeks held them off, defeating the Persians on both land and sea.

Though no doubt embarrassing, this defeat on the far western fringes of its empire had little effect on the Persians, but it had a profound impact on the Greeks and especially on Athens, whose forces had led the way to victory. Beating the Persians in battle was a source of enormous pride for Greece. Years later, elderly Athenian men asked one another how old they had been when the Greeks triumphed in the momentous Battle of Marathon in 490 B.C.E. In their view, this victory was the product of Greek freedoms, because those freedoms had motivated men to fight with extraordinary courage for what they valued so highly. It led to a worldview in which Persia represented Asia and despotism, whereas Greece signified Europe and freedom. Thus was born the notion of an East / West divide, which has shaped European and American thinking about the world into the twenty-first century.

The Greeks' victory also radicalized Athenian democracy, for it had been men of the poorer classes who had rowed their ships to victory, and now they were in a position to insist on full citizenship. The fifty years or so after the Greco-Persian Wars were not only the high point of Athenian democracy but also the Golden Age of Greek culture. During this period, the Parthenon, that marvelous temple to the Greek goddess Athena, was built; Greek theater was born from the work of Aeschylus, Sophocles, and Euripides; and Socrates was beginning his career as a philosopher and an irritant in Athens. The great Athenian statesman Pericles celebrated the uniqueness of Athens in a famous speech, excerpted in Document 4.1 (pp. 170–72).

But Athens's Golden Age was also an era of incipient empire. In the Greco-Persian Wars, Athens had led a coalition of more than thirty Greek city-states on the basis of its naval power, but Athenian leadership in the struggle against Persian aggression had spawned an imperialism of its own. After the war, Athenian efforts to solidify Athens's dominant position among the allies led to intense resentment and finally to a bitter civil war (431–404 B.C.E.), with Sparta taking the lead in defending the traditional independence of Greek city-states. In this bloody conflict, known as the Peloponnesian War, Athens was defeated, while the Greeks exhausted themselves and magnified their distrust of one another. Thus the way was open to their eventual takeover by the growing forces of Macedonia, a frontier region on the northern fringes of the Greek world. The glory days of the Greek experiment were over, but the spread of Greek culture was just beginning.

Collision: Alexander and the Hellenistic Era

■ **Connection**
What changes did
Alexander's conquests
bring in their wake?

The Macedonian takeover of Greece, led by Philip II, finally accomplished by
338 B.C.E. what the Greeks themselves had been unable to achieve—the political
unification of Greece, but at the cost of much of the prized independence of its
various city-states. It also set in motion a second round in the collision of Greece
and Persia as Philip's son, Alexander, prepared to lead a massive Greek expedition
against the Persian Empire. Such a project appealed to those who sought vengeance
for the earlier Persian assault on Greece, but it also served to unify the fractious
Greeks in a war against their common enemy.

Map 4.3   Alexander's
Empire and Successor
States
Alexander's conquests,
though enormous, did not
long remain within a single
empire, for his generals
divided them into three
successor states shortly
after his death. This was the
Hellenistic world within
which Greek culture spread.

The story of this ten-year expedition (333–323 B.C.E.), accomplished while
Alexander was still in his twenties, has become the stuff of legend (see Map 4.3).
Surely it was among the greatest military feats of the classical world in that it created a Greek empire from Egypt and Anatolia in the west to Afghanistan and India
in the east. In the process, the great Persian Empire was thoroughly defeated; its
capital, Persepolis, was looted and burned; and Alexander was hailed as the "king of
Asia." In Egypt, Alexander, then just twenty-four years old, was celebrated as a lib-
erator from Persian domination, was anointed as pharaoh, and was declared by
Egyptian priests to be the "son of the gods." Arrian, a later Greek historian,
described Alexander in this way:

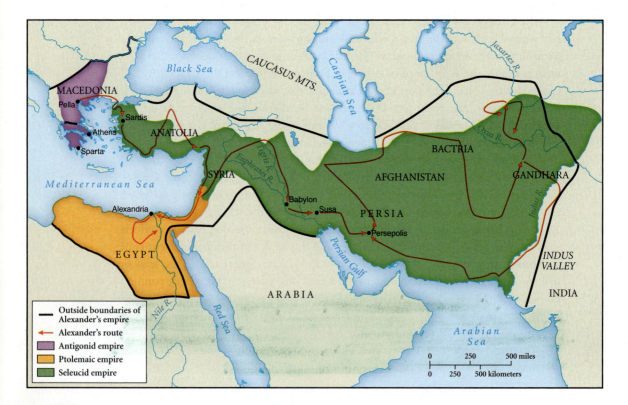

His passion was for glory only, and in that he was insatiable.... Noble indeed was his power of inspiring his men, of filling them with confidence, and in the moment of danger, of sweeping away their fear by the spectacle of his own fearlessness.[7]

Alexander died in 323 B.C.E., without returning to Greece, and his empire was soon divided into three kingdoms, ruled by leading Macedonian generals.

From the viewpoint of world history, the chief significance of Alexander's amazing conquests lay in the widespread dissemination of Greek culture during what historians call the Hellenistic era (323–30 B.C.E.). Elements of that culture, generated in a small and remote Mediterranean peninsula, now penetrated the lands of the First Civilizations—Egypt, Mesopotamia, and India—resulting in one of the great cultural encounters of the classical world.

The major avenue for the spread of Greek culture lay in the many cities that Alexander and later Hellenistic rulers established throughout the empire. Complete with Greek monuments and sculptures, Greek theaters and markets, Greek councils and assemblies, these cities attracted many thousands of Greek settlers serving as state officials, soldiers, or traders. Alexandria in Egypt—the largest of these cities, with half a million people—was an enormous cosmopolitan center where Egyptians, Greeks, Jews, Babylonians, Syrians, Persians, and many others rubbed elbows. A harbor with space for 1,200 ships facilitated long-distance commerce. Greek learning flourished thanks to a library of some 700,000 volumes and the Museum, which sponsored scholars and writers of all kinds.

From cities such as these, Greek culture spread. A simplified form of the Greek language was widely spoken from the Mediterranean to India. The Indian monarch Ashoka published some of his decrees in Greek, while an independent Greek state was established in Bactria in what is now northern Afghanistan. The attraction of many young Jews to Greek culture prompted the Pharisees to develop their own school system, as this highly conservative Jewish sect feared for the very survival of Judaism.

Cities such as Alexandria were very different from the original city-states of Greece, both in their cultural diversity and in the absence of the independence so valued by Athens and Sparta. Now they were part of large conquest states ruled by Greeks: the Ptolemaic empire in Egypt and the Seleucid empire in Persia. These were imperial states, which, in their determination to preserve order, raise taxes, and maintain the

Alexander the Great
This mosaic of Alexander on horseback comes from the Roman city of Pompeii. It depicts the Battle of Issus (333 B.C.E.), in which Greek forces, although considerably outnumbered, defeated the Persian army, led personally by Emperor Darius III. (Scala/Art Resource, NY)

authority of the monarch, resembled the much older empires of Mesopotamia, Egypt, Assyria, and Persia. Macedonians and Greeks, representing perhaps 10 percent of the population in these Hellenistic kingdoms, were clearly the elite and sought to keep themselves separate. In Egypt, different legal systems for Greeks and native Egyptians maintained this separation. An Egyptian agricultural worker complained that his supervisors despised him and refused to pay him, he said, "because I am an Egyptian."[8] Periodic rebellions expressed resentment at Greek arrogance, condescension, and exploitation.

But the separation between the Greeks and native populations was by no means complete, and a fair amount of cultural interaction and blending occurred. Alexander himself had taken several Persian princesses as his wives and actively encouraged intermarriage between his troops and Asian women. In both Egypt and Mesopotamia, Greek rulers patronized the building of temples to local gods and actively supported their priests. A growing number of native peoples were able to become Greek citizens by getting a Greek education, speaking the language, dressing appropriately, and assuming a Greek name. In India, Greeks were assimilated into the hierarchy of the caste system as members of the Kshatriya (warrior) caste, while in Bactria a substantial number of Greeks converted to Buddhism, including one of their kings, Menander. A school of Buddhist art that emerged in the early centuries of the Common Era depicted the Buddha in human form for the first time, but in Greek-like garb with a face resembling the god Apollo. Clearly, not all was conflict between the Greeks and the peoples of the East.

In the long run, much of this Greek cultural influence faded as the Hellenistic kingdoms that had promoted it weakened and vanished by the first century B.C.E. While it lasted, however, it represented a remarkable cultural encounter, born of the collision of two empires and two classical civilizations. In the western part of that Hellenistic world, Greek rule was replaced by that of the Romans, whose empire, like Alexander's, also served as a vehicle for the continued spread of Greek culture and ideas.

Comparing Empires: Roman and Chinese

While the adjacent civilizations of the Greeks and the Persians collided, two other classical empires were taking shape—the Roman Empire on the far western side of Eurasia and China's imperial state on the far eastern end. They flourished at roughly the same time (200 B.C.E.–200 C.E.); they occupied a similar area (about 1.5 million square miles); and they encompassed populations of a similar size (50 to 60 million). They were the giant empires of their time, shaping the lives of close to half of the world's population. Unlike the Greeks and the Persians, the Romans and the Chinese were only dimly aware of each other and had almost no direct contact. Historians, however, have seen them as fascinating variations on an imperial theme and have long explored their similarities and differences.

Rome: From City-State to Empire

How do empires arise? This is one of the perennial questions that historians tackle. Like the Persian Empire, that of the Romans took shape initially on the margins of the civilized world and was an unlikely rags-to-riches story. Rome began as a small and impoverished city-state on the western side of central Italy in the eighth century B.C.E., so weak, according to legend, that Romans were reduced to kidnapping neighboring women in order to reproduce. In a transformation of epic proportions, Rome became the center of an enormous imperial state that encompassed the Mediterranean basin and included parts of continental Europe, Britain, North Africa, and the Middle East.

Originally ruled by a king, Roman aristocrats around 509 B.C.E. threw off the monarchy and established a republic in which the wealthy class, known as *patricians*, dominated. Executive authority was exercised by two consuls, who were advised by a patrician assembly, the Senate. Deepening conflict with the poorer classes, called *plebeians*, led to important changes in Roman political life. A written code of law offered plebeians some protection from abuse; a system of public assemblies provided an opportunity for lower classes to shape public policy; and a new office of *tribune*, who represented plebeians, allowed them to block unfavorable legislation. Romans took great pride in this political system, believing that they enjoyed greater freedom than did many of their more autocratic neighbors. The values of the republic—rule of law, the rights of citizens, the absence of pretension, upright moral behavior, keeping one's word—were later idealized as "the way of the ancestors."

With this political system and these values, the Romans launched their empire-building enterprise, a prolonged process that took more than 500 years (see Map 4.4). It began in the 490s B.C.E. with Roman control over its Latin neighbors in central Italy and over the next several hundred years encompassed most of the Italian peninsula. Between 264 and 146 B.C.E., victory in the Punic Wars with Carthage, a powerful empire with its capital in North Africa, extended Roman control over the western Mediterranean and made Rome a naval power. Subsequent expansion in the eastern Mediterranean brought the ancient civilizations of Greece, Egypt, and Mesopotamia under Roman domination. Rome also expanded into territories in Southern and Western Europe, including present-day Spain, France, and Britain. By early in the second century C.E., the Roman Empire had reached its maximum extent.

No overall design or blueprint drove the building of empire, nor were there any precedents to guide the Romans. What they created was something wholly new—an empire that encompassed the entire Mediterranean basin and beyond. It was a piecemeal process, which the Romans invariably saw as defensive. Each addition of territory created new vulnerabilities, which could be assuaged only by more conquests. For some, the growth of empire represented opportunity. Poor soldiers hoped for land, loot, or salaries that might lift their families out of poverty. The well-to-do or well-connected gained great estates, earned promotion, and sometimes achieved

■ Change

How did Rome grow from a single city to the center of a huge empire?

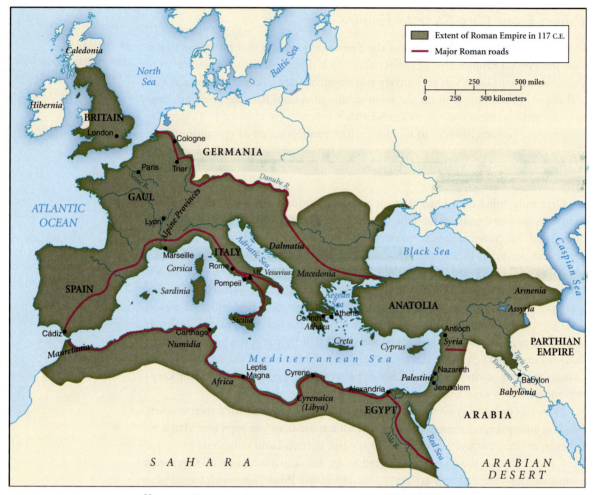

Map 4.4   The Roman Empire

At its height in the second century C.E., the Roman Empire incorporated the entire Mediterranean basin, including the lands of the Carthaginian Empire, the less developed region of Western Europe, the heartland of Greek civilization, and the ancient civilizations of Egypt and Mesopotamia.

public acclaim and high political office. The wealth of long-established societies in the eastern Mediterranean (Greece and Egypt, for example) beckoned, as did the resources and food supplies of the less developed western regions, such as Carthage and Spain. There was no shortage of motivation for the creation of the Roman Empire.

Although Rome's central location in the Mediterranean basin provided a convenient launching pad for empire, it was the army, "well-trained, well-fed, and well-rewarded," that built the empire.[9] Drawing on the growing population of Italy, that army was often brutal in war. Carthage, for example, was utterly destroyed; the city

$\mathcal{S}$napshot   **Key Moments in the History of the Roman Empire**

Traditional date of Rome's founding as a monarchy	753 B.C.E.
Establishment of Roman Republic	509 B.C.E.
Turmoil between patricians and plebeians ("struggle of the orders")	509–287 B.C.E.
Twelve Tables (Rome's first written law code)	450 B.C.E.
Punic Wars	264–146 B.C.E.
Civil war; Julius Caesar appointed dictator and then assassinated	49–44 B.C.E.
Reign of Caesar Augustus	27 B.C.E.–14 C.E.
Great fire in Rome; Emperor Nero blames Christians	64 C.E.
Roman citizenship extended to almost all free subjects	212 C.E.
Constantine converts to Christianity	312 C.E.
Founding of Constantinople as the "New Rome"	324 C.E.
Roman Empire split into eastern and western halves	395 C.E.
"Barbarian" invasions	4th–5th centuries C.E.
Collapse of western Roman Empire	476 C.E.

was razed to the ground, and its inhabitants were either killed or sold into slavery. Nonetheless, Roman authorities could be generous to former enemies. Some were granted Roman citizenship; others were treated as allies and allowed to maintain their local rulers. As the empire grew, so too did political forces in Rome that favored its continued expansion and were willing to commit the necessary manpower and resources.

The relentless expansion of empire raised a profound question for Rome: could republican government and values survive the acquisition of a huge empire? The wealth of empire enriched a few, enabling them to acquire large estates and slaves to work those estates, while pushing growing numbers of free farmers into the cities and poverty. Imperial riches also empowered a small group of military leaders—Marius, Sulla, Pompey, Julius Caesar—who recruited their troops directly from the ranks of the poor and whose fierce rivalries brought civil war to Rome during the first century B.C.E. Traditionalists lamented the apparent decline of republican values—simplicity, service, free farmers as the backbone of the army, the authority of the Senate—amid the self-seeking ambition of the newly rich and powerful. When the dust settled from the civil war, Rome was clearly changing, for authority was now vested primarily in an emperor, the first of whom was Octavian, later granted the title

Queen Boudica
This statue in London commemorates the resistance of the Celtic people of eastern Britain against Roman rule during a revolt in 60–61 C.E., led by Queen Boudica. A later Roman historian lamented that "all this ruin was brought upon the Romans by a woman, a fact which in itself caused them the greatest shame." (Daniel Boulet, photographer)

■ **Comparison**

How and why did the making of the Chinese empire differ from that of the Roman Empire?

of Augustus (reigned 27 B.C.E.–14 C.E.), which implied a divine status for the ruler. The republic was history; Rome was becoming an empire.

But it was an empire with an uneasy conscience, for many felt that in acquiring an empire, Rome had betrayed and abandoned its republican origins. Augustus was careful to maintain the forms of the republic—the Senate, consuls, public assemblies—and referred to himself as "first man" rather than "king" or "emperor" even as he accumulated enormous personal power. And in a bow to republican values, he spoke of the empire's conquests as reflecting the "power of the Roman people" rather than of the Roman state. Despite this rhetoric, he was emperor in practice, if not in name, for he was able to exercise sole authority, backed up by his command of a professional army. Later emperors were less reluctant to flaunt their imperial prerogatives. During the first two centuries C.E., this empire in disguise provided security, grandeur, and relative prosperity for the Mediterranean world. This was the *pax Romana*, the Roman peace, the era of imperial Rome's greatest extent and greatest authority. (See Document 4.2, pp. 172–74, for a Greek celebration of the Roman Empire.)

China: From Warring States to Empire

About the same time, on the other side of Eurasia, another huge imperial state was in the making—China. Here, however, the task was understood differently. It was not a matter of creating something new, as in the case of the Roman Empire, but of restoring something old. As one of the First Civilizations, a Chinese state had emerged as early as 2200 B.C.E. and under the Xia, Shang, and Zhou dynasties had grown progressively larger, but by 500 B.C.E. this Chinese state was in shambles. Any earlier unity vanished in an age of warring states, featuring the endless rivalries of seven competing kingdoms.

To many Chinese, this was a wholly unnatural and unacceptable condition, and rulers in various states vied to reunify China. One of them, known to history as Qin Shihuangdi (i.e., Shihuangdi from the state of Qin), succeeded brilliantly. The state of Qin had already developed an effective bureaucracy, had subordinated its aristocracy, had equipped its army with iron weapons, and enjoyed rapidly rising agricultural output and a growing population. It also had adopted a political philosophy called Legalism, which advocated clear rules and harsh punishments as a means of enforcing the authority of the state. (See Document 4.3, pp. 174–75, for a sample of Legalist thinking.) With these resources, Shihuangdi (ruled 221–210 B.C.E.) launched a military campaign to reunify China and in just ten years soundly defeated the other warring states. Believing that he had created a universal and eternal empire, he grandly named himself Shihuangdi, which means the "first emperor." Unlike Augustus, he showed little ambivalence about empire. Subsequent conquests extended China's boundaries far to the south into the northern part of Vietnam, to the northeast into Korea, and to the northwest, where the Chinese pushed back the nomadic pastoral people of the steppes. Although the boundaries fluctuated over time, Shihuangdi laid the foundations for a unified Chinese state, which has endured, with periodic interruptions, to the present (see Map 4.5).

Building on earlier precedents, the Chinese process of empire formation was far more compressed than the centuries-long Roman effort, but it was no less dependent on military force and no less brutal. Scholars who opposed Shihuangdi's policies

Map 4.5 Classical China
The brief Qin dynasty brought unity to the heartland of Chinese civilization, and the much longer Han dynasty extended its territorial reach south toward Vietnam, east to Korea, and west into Central Asia. To the north lay the military confederacy of the nomadic Xiongnu.

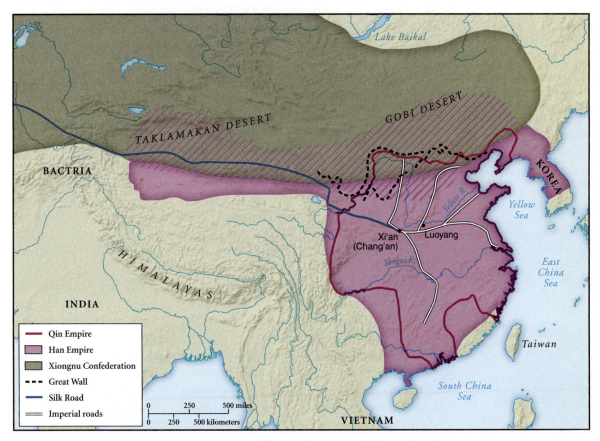

were executed and their books burned. (See Visual Source 4.1, p. 181.) Aristocrats who might oppose his centralizing policies were moved physically to the capital. Hundreds of thousands of laborers were recruited to construct the Great Wall of China, designed to keep out northern "barbarians," and to erect a monumental mausoleum as the emperor's final resting place. That enormous tomb complex is described and illustrated in Visual Sources: Qin Shihuangdi and China's Eternal Empire, pages 180–86. More positively, Shihuangdi imposed a uniform system of weights, measures, and currency and standardized the length of axles for carts and the written form of the Chinese language.

As in Rome, the creation of the Chinese empire had domestic repercussions, but they were brief and superficial compared to Rome's transition from republic to empire. The speed and brutality of Shihuangdi's policies ensured that his own Qin dynasty did not last long, and it collapsed unmourned in 206 B.C.E. The Han dynasty that followed (206 B.C.E.–220 C.E.) retained the centralized features of Shihuangdi's creation, although it moderated the harshness of his policies, adopting a milder and moralistic Confucianism in place of Legalism as the governing philosophy of the states. (See Document 5.1, pp. 217–19, for a sample of Confucius's thinking.) It was Han dynasty rulers who consolidated China's imperial state and established the political patterns that lasted into the twentieth century.

Consolidating the Roman and Chinese Empires

■ **Comparison**

In comparing the Roman and Chinese empires, which do you find more striking—their similarities or their differences?

Once established, these two huge imperial systems shared a number of common features. Both, for example, defined themselves in universal terms. The Roman writer Polybius spoke of bringing "almost the entire world" under the control of Rome,[10] while the Chinese state was said to encompass "all under heaven." Both of them invested heavily in public works—roads, bridges, aqueducts, canals, protective walls—all designed to integrate their respective domains militarily and commercially.

Furthermore, Roman and Chinese authorities both invoked supernatural sanctions to support their rule. By the first century C.E., Romans began to regard their deceased emperors as gods and established a religious cult to bolster the authority of living emperors. It was the refusal of early Christians to take part in this cult that provoked their periodic persecution by Roman authorities.

In China, a much older tradition had long linked events on earth with affairs in heaven. In this conception, heaven was neither a place nor a supreme being, but rather an impersonal moral force that regulated the universe. Emperors were called the Son of Heaven and were said to govern by the Mandate of Heaven so long as they ruled morally and with benevolence. Peasant rebellions, "barbarian" invasions, or disastrous floods were viewed as signs that the emperor had ruled badly and thus had lost the Mandate of Heaven. Among the chief duties of the emperor was the performance of various rituals thought to maintain the appropriate relationship between heaven and earth. What moral government meant in practice was spelled out in the writings of Confucius and his followers, which became the official ideology of the empire (see Chapter 5).

Both of these classical civilizations also absorbed a foreign religious tradition—Christianity in the Roman Empire and Buddhism in China—although the process unfolded somewhat differently. In the case of Rome, Christianity was born as a small sect of a small province in a remote corner of the empire. Aided by the *pax Romana* and Roman roads, the new faith spread slowly for several centuries, particularly among the poor and lower classes. Women were prominent in the leadership of the early church, as were a number of more well-to-do individuals from urban families. After suffering intermittent persecution, Christianity in the fourth century C.E. obtained state support from emperors who hoped to shore up a tottering empire with a common religion, and thereafter the religion spread quite rapidly.

In the case of China, by contrast, Buddhism came from India, far beyond the Chinese world. It was introduced to China by Central Asian traders and received little support from Han dynasty rulers. In fact, the religion spread only modestly among Chinese until after the Han dynasty collapsed (220 C.E.), when it appealed to people who felt bewildered by the loss of a predictable and stable society. Not until the Sui dynasty emperor Wendi (581–604 C.E.) reunified China did the new religion gain state support, and then only temporarily. Buddhism thus became one of several alternative cultural traditions in a complex Chinese mix, while Christianity, though divided internally, ultimately became the dominant religious tradition throughout Europe.

The Roman and Chinese empires also had a different relationship to the societies they governed. Rome's beginnings as a small city-state meant that Romans, and even Italians, were always a distinct minority within the empire. The Chinese empire, by contrast, grew out of a much larger cultural heartland, already ethnically Chinese. Furthermore, as the Chinese state expanded, especially to the south, it actively assimilated the non-Chinese or "barbarian" people. In short, they became Chinese, culturally, linguistically, through intermarriage, and in physical appearance as well. Many Chinese in modern times are in fact descended from people who at one point or another were not Chinese at all.

The Roman Empire also offered a kind of assimilation to its subject peoples. Gradually and somewhat reluctantly, the empire granted Roman citizenship to various individuals, families, or whole communities for their service to the empire or in recognition of their adoption of Roman culture. In 212 C.E., Roman citizenship was bestowed on almost all free people of the empire. Citizenship offered clear advantages—the right to hold public office, to serve in the Roman military units known as legions, to wear a toga, and more—but it conveyed a legal status, rather than cultural assimilation, and certainly did not erase other identities, such as being Greek, Egyptian, or a citizen of a particular city.

Various elements of Roman culture—its public buildings, its religious rituals, its Latin language, its style of city life—were attractive, especially in Western Europe, where urban civilization was something new. In the eastern half of the empire, however, things Greek retained tremendous prestige. Many elite Romans in fact regarded Greek culture—its literature, philosophy, and art—as superior to their own and proudly sent their sons to Athens for a Greek education. To some extent, the two blended into a mixed Greco-Roman tradition, which the empire served to disseminate throughout the realm. Other non-Roman cultural traditions—such as the cult of the Persian god Mithra or the compassionate Egyptian goddess Isis, and, most extensively, the Jewish-derived religion of Christianity—also spread throughout the empire. Nothing similar occurred in Han dynasty China, except for Buddhism, which established a modest presence, largely among foreigners. Chinese culture, widely recognized as the model to which others should conform, experienced little competition from older, venerated, or foreign traditions.

Language served these two empires in important but contrasting ways. Latin, an alphabetic language depicting sounds, gave rise to various distinct languages—Spanish, Portuguese, French, Italian, Romanian—whereas Chinese did not. Chinese characters, which represented words or ideas more than sounds, were not easily transferable to other languages, but written Chinese could be understood by all literate people, no matter which spoken dialect of the language they used. Thus Chinese, more than Latin, served as an instrument of elite assimilation. For all of these reasons, the various peoples of the Roman Empire were able to maintain their separate cultural identities far more than was the case in China.

Politically, both empires established effective centralized control over vast regions and huge populations, but the Chinese, far more than the Romans, developed an elaborate bureaucracy to hold the empire together. The Han emperor Wudi (reigned 141–87 B.C.E.) established an imperial academy for training officials for an emerging bureaucracy with a curriculum based on the writings of Confucius. This was the beginning of a civil service system, complete with examinations and selection by merit, which did much to integrate the Chinese empire and lasted into the early twentieth century. Roman administration was a somewhat ramshackle affair, rely-

Snapshot   Key Moments in Classical Chinese History

Political fragmentation ("warring states" period)	500–221 B.C.E.
Unification of China: Shihuangdi and Qin dynasty	221–206 B.C.E.
Beginning of Han dynasty, with Liu Bang as its first emperor	206–195 B.C.E.
Reign of Emperor Wudi, who established Confucian Academy for training imperial bureaucrats	141–87 B.C.E.
Emperor Wang Mang attempts land reform, without success	9–23 C.E.
Yellow Turban peasant revolt	184 C.E.
Collapse of Han dynasty	220 C.E.
Renewed political fragmentation	220–581 C.E.
China's unity is restored (Sui dynasty)	589–618 C.E.
Tang dynasty	618–907 C.E.

ing more on regional aristocratic elites and the army to provide cohesion. Unlike the Chinese, however, the Romans developed an elaborate body of law, applicable equally to all people of the realm, dealing with matters of justice, property, commerce, and family life. Chinese and Roman political development thus generated different answers to the question of what made for good government. For those who inherited the Roman tradition, it was good laws, whereas for those in the Chinese tradition, it was good men.

The Collapse of Empires

Empires rise, and then, with some apparent regularity, they fall, and in doing so, they provide historians with one of their most intriguing questions: What causes the collapse of these once-mighty structures? In China, the Han dynasty empire came to an end in 220 C.E.; the traditional date for the final disintegration of the Roman Empire is 476 C.E., although a process of decline had been under way for several centuries. In the Roman case, however, only the western half of the empire collapsed, while the eastern part, subsequently known as the Byzantine Empire, maintained the tradition of imperial Rome for another thousand years.

■ **Comparison**

How did the collapse of empire play out differently in the Roman world and in China?

Despite this difference, a number of common factors have been associated with the end of these imperial states. At one level, they simply got too big, too overextended, and too expensive to be sustained by the available resources, and no fundamental technological breakthrough was available to enlarge these resources. Furthermore, the growth of large landowning families with huge estates enabled them to avoid paying taxes, turned free peasants into impoverished tenant farmers, and diminished the authority of the central government. In China, such conditions led to a major peasant revolt, known as the Yellow Turban Rebellion, in 184 C.E.

Rivalry among elite factions created instability in both empires and eroded imperial authority. In China, persistent tension between castrated court officials (*eunuchs*) loyal to the emperor and Confucian-educated scholar-bureaucrats weakened the state. In the Roman Empire between 235 and 284 C.E., some twenty-six individuals claimed the title of Roman emperor, only one of whom died of natural causes. In addition, epidemic disease ravaged both societies. The population of the Roman Empire declined by 25 percent in the two centuries following 250 C.E., a demographic disaster that meant diminished production, less revenue for the state, and fewer men available for the defense of the empire's long frontiers.

To these mounting internal problems was added a growing threat from nomadic or semi-agricultural peoples occupying the frontier regions of both empires. The Chinese had long developed various ways of dealing with the Xiongnu and other nomadic people to the north—building the Great Wall to keep them out, offering them trading opportunities at border markets, buying them off with lavish gifts, contracting marriage alliances with nomadic leaders, and conducting periodic military campaigns against them. But as the Han dynasty weakened in the second and third centuries C.E., such peoples more easily breached the frontier defenses and set

Meeting of Attila and Pope Leo I
Among the "barbarian" invaders of the Roman Empire, none were more feared than the Huns, led by the infamous Attila. In a celebrated meeting in 452 C.E., Pope Leo I persuaded Attila to spare the city of Rome and to withdraw from Italy. This painting from about 1360 C.E. records that remarkable meeting. (National Szechenyi Library, Budapest)

up a succession of "barbarian states" in north China. Culturally, however, many of these foreign rulers gradually became Chinese, encouraging intermarriage, adopting Chinese dress, and setting up their courts in Chinese fashion.

A weakening Roman Empire likewise faced serious problems from Germanic-speaking peoples living on its northern frontier. Growing numbers of these people began to enter the empire in the fourth century C.E.—some as mercenaries in Roman armies and others as refugees fleeing the invasions of the ferocious Huns, who were penetrating Europe from Central Asia. Once inside the declining empire, various Germanic groups established their own kingdoms, at first controlling Roman emperors and then displacing them altogether by 476 C.E. Unlike the nomadic groups in China, who largely assimilated Chinese culture, Germanic kingdoms in Europe developed their own ethnic identity—Visigoths, Franks, Anglo-Saxons, and others—even as they drew on Roman law and adopted Roman Christianity. Far more than in China, the fall of the Roman Empire produced a new culture, blending Latin and Germanic elements, which provided the foundation for the hybrid civilization that would arise in Western Europe.

The collapse of empire meant more than the disappearance of centralized government and endemic conflict. In both China and post-Roman Europe, it also meant the decline of urban life, a contracting population, less area under cultivation, diminishing international trade, and vast insecurity for ordinary people. It must have seemed that civilization itself was unraveling.

The most significant difference between the collapse of empire in China and that in the Mediterranean basin lay in what happened next. In China, after about 350 years of disunion, disorder, frequent warfare, and political chaos, a Chinese imperial state, similar to that of the Han dynasty, was reassembled under the Sui (589–618 C.E.), Tang (618–907), and Song (960–1279) dynasties. Once again, a single emperor ruled; a bureaucracy selected by examinations governed; and the ideas of Confucius informed the political system. Such a Chinese empire persisted into the early twentieth century, establishing one of the most continuous political traditions of any civilization in world history.

The story line of European history following the end of the Roman Empire was very different indeed. No large-scale, centralized, imperial authority encompassing all of Western Europe has ever been successfully reestablished there for any length of time. The memory of Roman imperial unity certainly persisted, and many subsequently tried unsuccessfully to re-create it. But most of Western Europe dissolved into a highly decentralized political system involving kings with little authority, nobles, knights and vassals, various city-states in Italy, and small territories ruled by princes, bishops, or the pope. From this point on, Europe would be a civilization without an encompassing imperial state.

From a Chinese point of view, Western Europe's post-Roman history must seem an enormous failure. Why were Europeans unable to reconstruct something of the unity of their classical empire, while the Chinese clearly did? Surely the greater cultural homogeneity of Chinese civilization made that task easier than it was amid the vast ethnic and linguistic diversity of Europe. The absence in the Roman legacy of a strong bureaucratic tradition also contributed to European difficulties, whereas in China the bureaucracy provided stability even as dynasties came and went. The Chinese also had in Confucianism a largely secular ideology that placed great value on political matters in the here and now. The Roman Catholic Church in Europe, however, was frequently at odds with state authorities, and its "otherworldliness" did little to support the creation of large-scale empires. Finally, Chinese agriculture was much more productive than that of Europe, and for a long time its metallurgy was more advanced.[11] These conditions gave Chinese state-builders more resources to work with than were available to their European counterparts.

Intermittent Empire: The Case of India

Among the classical civilizations of Eurasia, empire loomed large in Persian, Mediterranean, and Chinese history, but it played a rather less prominent role in India. In the Indus River valley flourished the largest of the First Civilizations, embodied in exquisitely planned cities such as Harappa but with little evidence of any central political authority. The demise of this early civilization by 1500 B.C.E. was followed over the next thousand years by the creation of a new civilization based farther east, along the Ganges River on India's northern plain. That process has occasioned considerable scholarly debate, which has focused on the role of the Aryans, a pastoral Indo-European people long thought to have invaded and destroyed the Indus Valley civilization and created the new one along the Ganges. More recent research has called this view into question. Did the Aryans invade suddenly, or did they migrate slowly into the Indus River valley, or were they already there as a part of the Indus Valley population? Was the new civilization largely the work of Aryans, or did it evolve gradually from Indus Valley culture? About all of this, scholars have yet to reach agreement.[12]

However it occurred, by 600 B.C.E. what would become the classical civilization of South Asia had begun to take shape across northern India. Politically, that civilization emerged as a fragmented collection of towns and cities, some small republics governed by public assemblies, and a number of regional states ruled by kings. An astonishing range of ethnic, cultural, and linguistic diversity also characterized this civilization, as an endless variety of peoples migrated into India from Central Asia across the mountain passes in the northwest. These features of Indian civilization — political fragmentation and vast cultural diversity — have informed much of South

■ **Comparison**

Why were centralized empires so much less prominent in India than in China?

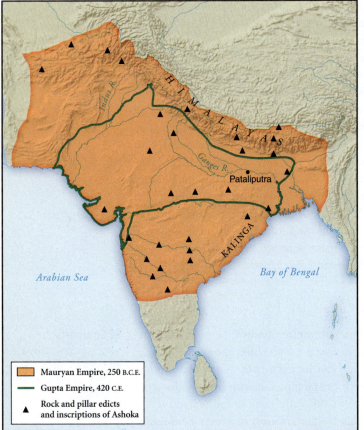

Mauryan Empire, 250 B.C.E.

Gupta Empire, 420 C.E.

▲ Rock and pillar edicts
and inscriptions of Ashoka

Map 4.6 Empire in South Asia

Large-scale empires in the Indian subcontinent were less frequent and less enduring than in China. Two of the largest efforts were those of the Mauryan and Gupta dynasties.

Asian history throughout many centuries, offering a sharp contrast to the pattern of development in China. What gave Indian civilization a recognizable identity and character was neither an imperial tradition nor ethnolinguistic commonality, but rather a distinctive religious tradition, known later to outsiders as Hinduism, and a unique social organization, the caste system. These features of Indian life are explored further in Chapters 5 and 6.

Nonetheless, empires and emperors were not entirely unknown in India's long history. Northwestern India had been briefly ruled by the Persian Empire and then conquered by Alexander the Great. These Persian and Greek influences helped stimulate the first and largest of India's short experiments with a large-scale political system, the Mauryan Empire (326–184 B.C.E.), which encompassed all but the southern tip of the subcontinent (see Map 4.6).

The Mauryan Empire was an impressive political structure, equivalent to the Persian, Chinese, and Roman empires, though not nearly as long-lasting. With a population of perhaps 50 million, the Mauryan Empire boasted a large military force, reported to include 600,000 infantry soldiers, 30,000 cavalry, 8,000 chariots, and 9,000 elephants. A civilian bureaucracy featured various ministries and a large contingent of spies to provide the rulers with local information. A famous treatise called the *Arthashastra* (*The Science of Worldly Wealth*) articulated a pragmatic, even amoral, political philosophy for Mauryan rulers. It was, according to one scholar, a book that showed "how the political world does work and not very often stating how it ought to work, a book that frequently discloses to a king what calculating and sometimes brutal measures he must carry out to preserve the state and the common good."[13] The state also operated many industries—spinning, weaving, mining, shipbuilding, and armaments. This complex apparatus was financed by taxes on trade, on herds of animals, and especially on land, from which the monarch claimed a quarter or more of the crop.[14]

Mauryan India is perhaps best known for one of its emperors, Ashoka (reigned 268–232 B.C.E.), who left a record of his activities and his thinking in a series of edicts carved on rocks and pillars throughout the kingdom. A sample of those edicts is contained in Document 4.4 on pp. 176–78. Ashoka's conversion to Buddhism and his moralistic approach to governance gave his reign a different tone than that of China's Shihuangdi or of Alexander the Great, who, according to legend, wept because he had no more worlds to conquer. His legacy to modern India has been that of an enlightened ruler, who sought to govern in accord with the religious values and moral teachings of Hinduism and Buddhism.

Despite their good intentions, these policies did not long preserve the empire, which broke apart soon after Ashoka's death. Several other short-lived imperial experiments, such as the Gupta Empire (320–550 C.E.), also marked India's history, but none lasted long. India's political history thus resembled that of Western Europe after the collapse of the Roman Empire far more than that of China or Persia. Neither imperial nor regional states commanded the kind of loyalty or exercised the degree of influence that they did in other classical civilizations. India's unparalleled cultural diversity surely was one reason, as was the frequency of invasions from Central Asia, which repeatedly smashed states that might have provided the nucleus for an all-India empire. Finally, India's social structure, embodied in a caste system linked to occupational groups, made for intensely local loyalties at the expense of wider identities (see Chapter 6).

Ashoka of India
This twelfth-century stone relief provides a visual image of the Mauryan dynasty's best-known ruler. (Philip Baird/ www.anthroarcheart.org)

Nonetheless, a frequently vibrant economy fostered a lively internal commerce and made India the focal point of an extensive network of trade in the Indian Ocean basin. In particular, its cotton textile industry long supplied cloth throughout the Afro-Eurasian world. Strong guilds of merchants and artisans provided political leadership in major towns and cities, and their wealth patronized lavish temples, public buildings, and religious festivals. Great creativity in religious matters generated Hindu and Buddhist traditions that later penetrated much of Asia. Indian mathematics and science, especially astronomy, also were impressive; Indian scientists plotted the movements of stars and planets and recognized quite early that the earth was round. Clearly, the absence of consistent imperial unity did not prevent the evolution of an enduring civilization.

Reflections: Classical Empires and the Twentieth Century

The classical empires discussed in this chapter have long ago passed into history, but their descendants have kept them alive in memory, for they have proved useful, even in the twentieth and early-twenty-first centuries. Those empires have provided legitimacy for contemporary states, inspiration for new imperial ventures, and abundant warnings and cautions for those seeking to criticize more recent empires. For example, in bringing communism to China in the twentieth century, the Chinese leader Mao Zedong compared himself to Shihuangdi, the unifier of China and the brutal founder of its Qin dynasty. Reflecting on his campaign against intellectuals in general and Confucianism in particular, Mao declared to a Communist Party conference: "Emperor Qin Shihuang was not that outstanding. He only buried alive 460 Confucian scholars. We buried 460 thousand Confucian scholars.... To the charge of being like Emperor Qin, of being a dictator, we plead guilty."[15]

In contrast, modern-day Indians, who have sought to present their country as a model of cultural tolerance and nonviolence, have been quick to link themselves to Ashoka and his policies of inclusiveness. When the country became independent from British colonial rule in 1947, India soon placed an image of Ashoka's Pillar on the new nation's currency.

In the West, it has been the Roman Empire that has provided a template for thinking about political life. Many in Great Britain celebrated their own global empire as a modern version of the Roman Empire. In the early twentieth century, African students in a mission school in British-ruled Kenya were asked on a history exam to list the benefits that Roman occupation brought to Britain. The implication was obvious. If the British had been "civilized" by Roman rule, then surely Africans would benefit from falling under the control of the "superior" British. Likewise, to the Italian fascist dictator Benito Mussolini, his country's territorial expansion during the 1930s and World War II represented the creation of a new Roman Empire. Most recently, of course, America's dominant role in the world has prompted the question: Are the Americans the new Romans?

Historians frequently cringe as politicians and students use (and perhaps misuse) historical analogies to make their case for particular points of view in the present. But we have little else to go on except history in making our way through the complexities of contemporary life, and historians themselves seldom agree on the "lessons" of the past. Lively debate about the continuing relevance of classical empires shows that although the past may be gone, it surely is not dead.

Second Thoughts

What's the Significance?

To assess your mastery of the material in this chapter, visit the **Student Center** at bedfordstmartins.com/strayer.

Persian Empire	Alexander the Great	Qin Shihuangdi
Athenian democracy	Hellenistic era	Han dynasty
Greco-Persian Wars	Caesar Augustus	Mauryan Empire
	pax Romana	Ashoka

Big Picture Questions

1. What common features can you identify in the empires described in this chapter?
2. In what ways did these empires differ from one another? What accounts for those differences?
3. Are you more impressed with the "greatness" of empires or with their destructive and oppressive features? Why?
4. Do you think that the classical empires hold "lessons" for the present, or are contemporary circumstances sufficiently unique as to render the distant past irrelevant?

Next Steps: For Further Study

Arthur Cotterell, *The First Emperor of China* (1988). A biography of Shihuangdi.

Christopher Kelley, *The Roman Empire: A Very Short Introduction* (2006). A brief, up-to-date, and accessible account of the Roman achievement.

Cullen Murphy, *Are We Rome? The Fall of an Empire and the Fate of America* (2007). A reflection on the usefulness and the dangers of comparing the Roman Empire to the present-day United States.

Sarah Pomeroy et al., *Ancient Greece* (1999). A highly readable survey of Greek history by a team of distinguished scholars.

Walter Scheidel, ed. *Rome and China: Comparative Perspectives on Ancient World Empires* (2009). A series of scholarly essays that systematically compare these two empires.

Romila Thapar, *Ashoka and the Decline of the Mauryas* (1961). A classic study of India's early empire builder.

Illustrated History of the Roman Empire. http://www.roman-empire.net. An interactive Web site with maps, pictures, and much information about the Roman Empire.

For Web sites and additional documents related to this chapter, see **Make History** at bedfordstmartins.com/strayer.

Documents

Considering the Evidence:
Political Authority in Classical Civilizations

States, empires, and their rulers are surely not the whole story of the human past, although historians have sometimes treated them as though they were. But they are important, because their actions shaped the lives of many millions of people. The city-states of ancient Greece, the Roman Empire, the emerging Chinese empire of the Qin dynasty, and the Indian Empire of the Mauryan dynasty—these were among the impressive political structures of the classical era in Eurasia. Rulers seeking to establish or maintain their authority mobilized a variety of ideas to give legitimacy to their regimes. Reflection on political authority was a central issue in the discourse of educated people all across classical Eurasia. In the documents that follow, four contemporary observers—two rulers and two scholars—describe some of the political institutions and ideas that operated within Mediterranean, Chinese, and Indian civilizations.

Document 4.1

In Praise of Athenian Democracy

The Greeks of Athens generated political ideas that have long been celebrated in the West, although they were exceptional even in the small world of classical Greece. (See pp. 147–50 and Map 4.2, p. 148.) The most well-known expression of praise for Athenian democracy comes from Pericles, the most prominent Athenian leader during the fifth century B.C.E. Sometimes called the "first citizen of Athens," Pericles initiated the grand building projects that still grace the Acropolis and led his city in its military struggles with archrival Sparta. To his critics, he was a populist, manipulating the masses to enhance his own power, and an Athenian imperialist whose aggressive policies ultimately ruined the city. His famous speech in praise of Athens was delivered around 431–430 B.C.E. at the end of the first year of the Peloponnesian War against Sparta. The setting was a public funeral service for Athenian citizens who had died in that conflict. Pericles' oration was recorded by the Greek historian Thucydides, who was probably present at that event.

- How does Pericles describe Athenian democracy?

- Does his argument for democracy derive from fundamental principles, such as human equality, or from the practical benefits that derive from such a system of government?

- What kind of citizens does he believe democracy produces? Keep in mind that not everyone shared this idealized view of Athenian democracy. How might critics have responded to Pericles' arguments?

- Although Pericles praised Athenian military prowess, his city lost the Peloponnesian War. In what ways does this affect your assessment of his arguments?

PERICLES

Funeral Oration

431–430 B.C.E.

Our form of government does not enter into rivalry with the institutions of others. We do not copy our neighbors, but are an example to them. It is true that we are called a democracy, for the administration is in the hands of the many and not of the few. But while the law secures equal justice to all alike in their private disputes, the claim of excellence is also recognized; and when a citizen is in any way distinguished, he is preferred to the public service, not as a matter of privilege, but as the reward of merit. Neither is poverty a bar, but a man may benefit his country whatever be the obscurity of his condition. There is no exclusiveness in our public life, and in our private intercourse we are not suspicious of one another, nor angry with our neighbor if he does what he likes.... While we are thus unconstrained in our private intercourse, a spirit of reverence pervades our public acts; we are prevented from doing wrong by respect for the authorities and for the laws....

And we have not forgotten to provide for our weary spirits many relaxations from toil; we have regular games and sacrifices throughout the year; our homes are beautiful and elegant; and the delight which we daily feel in all these things helps to banish melancholy. Because of the greatness of our city the fruits of the whole earth flow in upon us; so that we enjoy the goods of other countries as freely as of our own.

Then, again, our military training is in many respects superior to that of our adversaries. Our city is thrown open to the world, and we never expel a foreigner or prevent him from seeing or learning anything of which the secret if revealed to an enemy might profit him. We rely not upon management or trickery, but upon our own hearts and hands. And in the matter of education, whereas they from early youth are always undergoing laborious exercises which are to make them brave, we live at ease, and yet are equally ready to face the perils which they face....

For we are lovers of the beautiful, yet simple in our tastes, and we cultivate the mind without loss of manliness....To avow poverty with us is no disgrace; the true disgrace is in doing nothing to avoid

Source: Benjamin Jowett, *Thucydides, translated into English, to which is prefixed an essay on inscriptions and a note on the geography of Thucydides*, 2nd ed. (Oxford: Clarendon Press, 1900), Book 2, para. 37–41.

it. An Athenian citizen does not neglect the state because he takes care of his own household; and even those of us who are engaged in business have a very fair idea of politics. We alone regard a man who takes no interest in public affairs, not as a harmless; but as a useless character; and if few of us are originators, we are all sound judges of a policy. The great impediment to action is, in our opinion, not discussion, but the want of that knowledge which is gained by discussion preparatory to action. For we have a peculiar power of thinking before we act and of acting too, whereas other men are courageous from ignorance but hesitate upon reflection. And they are surely to be esteemed the bravest spirits who, having the clearest sense both of the pains and pleasures of life, do not on that account shrink from danger....

To sum up: I say that Athens is the school of Hellas, and that the individual Athenian in his own person seems to have the power of adapting himself to the most varied forms of action with the utmost versatility and grace....

For we have compelled every land and every sea to open a path for our valor, and have everywhere planted eternal memorials of our friendship and of our enmity. Such is the city for whose sake these men nobly fought and died; they could not bear the thought that she might be taken from them; and every one of us who survive should gladly toil on her behalf.

Document 4.2

In Praise of the Roman Empire

By the second century C.E. the Roman Empire, now encompassing the Mediterranean basin and beyond, was in its glory days. With conquest largely completed, the *pax Romana* (Roman peace) generally prevailed and commerce flourished, as did the arts and literature. The empire enjoyed a century (96–180 C.E.) of autocratic but generally benevolent rule. In 155 C.E. a well-known scholar and orator from the city of Smyrna on the west coast of Anatolia (present-day Turkey) arrived for a visit to the imperial capital of Rome. He was Aelius Aristides (ca. 117–181 C.E.), a widely traveled Greek-speaking member of a wealthy landowning family whose members had been granted Roman citizenship several decades earlier. While in Rome, Aristides delivered to the imperial court and in front of the emperor, Antonius, a formal speech of praise and gratitude, known as a panegyric, celebrating the virtues and achievements of the Roman Empire.

■ What did Aristides identify as the unique features of the Roman Empire? Which of these features in particular may have given the empire a measure of legitimacy in the eyes of its many subject peoples? What other factors, unmentioned by Aristides, may have contributed to the maintenance of Roman authority?

■ What does Aristides mean by referring to the empire as a "common democracy of the world"?

■ Why might Aristides, a Greek-speaking resident of a land well outside the Roman heartland, be so enamored of the empire?

■ To what extent does Aristides' oration provide evidence for the development of a composite Greco-Roman culture and sensibility within the Roman Empire?

■ How does this speech compare, in both style and content, with that of Pericles in Document 4.1?

AELIUS ARISTIDES

The Roman Oration

155 C.E.

A certain prose writer said about Asia that one man "rules all as far as is the course of the sun," untruly, since he excluded all Africa and Europe from the sun's rising and setting. [This refers to the Persian Empire.] But now it has turned out to be true that the course of the sun and your possessions are equal.... [N]or do you rule within fixed boundaries, nor does another prescribe the limits of your power....

About the [Mediterranean] sea the continents [Africa, Asia, and Europe] lie... ever supplying you with products from those regions. Here is brought from every land and sea all the crops of the seasons and the produce of each land, river and lake, as well as the arts of the Greeks and barbarians.... So many merchant ships arrive here... that the city is like a factory common to the whole earth. It is possible to see so many cargoes from India and even from [southern] Arabia.... Your farmlands are Egypt, Sicily, and all of [North] Africa which is cultivated. The arrival and departure of ships never stops....

Although your empire is so large and so great, it is much greater in its good order than in its circumference.... [Nor] are satraps° fighting against one another, as if they had no king; nor do some cities side with these and others with those.... But like the enclosure of a courtyard, cleansed of every disturbance, a circle encompasses your empire.... All everywhere are equally subjects....

°**satraps:** local authorities.

Source: Aelius Aristides, *The Complete Works*, vol. 2, translated by P. Charles A. Behr (Leiden: E. J. Brill, 1986), 73–97.

You are the only ones ever to rule over free men....[Y]ou govern throughout the whole inhabited world as if in a single city....You appoint governors... for the protection and care of their subjects, not to be their masters....And here there is a great and fair equality between weak and powerful, obscure and famous, poor and rich and noble....To excel the barbarians in wealth and power, while surpassing the Greeks in knowledge and moderation, seems to me to be an important matter....

You have divided into two parts all the men of your empire... and everywhere you have made citizens all those who are the more accomplished, noble, and powerful people, even if they retain their native affinities, while the remainder you have made subjects and the governed. And neither does the sea nor a great expanse of intervening land keep one from being a citizen, nor here are Asia and Europe distinguished. But all lies open to all men....There has been established a common democracy of the world, under one man, the best ruler and director....

You have divided people into Romans [citizens] and non-Romans [subjects]... [M]any in each city are citizens of yours... and some of them have not even seen this city....There is no need of garrisons..., but the most important and powerful people in each place guard their countries for you....Yet no envy walks in your empire.... [T]here has arisen a single harmonious government which has embraced all men.

[Y]ou have established a form of government such as no one else of mankind has done....Your government is like a mixture of all the constitutions [democracy, aristocracy, monarchy] without the inferior side of each....Therefore whenever one considers the power of the people and how easily they attain all their wishes and requests, he will believe that it is a democracy....But when he considers the Senate deliberating and holding office, he will believe there is no more perfect aristocracy than this. But when he has considered the overseer and president of all these [the emperor], he sees in this man the possessor of the most perfect monarchy, free of the evils of the tyrant and greater than the dignity of the king....

And the whole inhabited world, as it were attending a national festival, has laid aside...the carrying of weapons and has turned...to adornments and all kinds of pleasures....Everything is full of gymnasiums, fountains, gateways, temples, handicrafts, and schools...and a boundless number of games....Now it possible for both Greek and barbarian...to travel easily wherever he wishes....[I]t is enough for his safety that he is a Roman or rather one of those under you.

Document 4.3

Governing a Chinese Empire

As the Roman Empire was taking shape in the Mediterranean basin, a powerful Chinese empire emerged in East Asia. More than in the Roman world, the political ideas and practices of classical China drew on the past. The notion of China as a unified state ruled by a single sage/emperor who mediated between heaven and the human realm had an ancient pedigree. After a long period of political fragmentation, known as the era of warring states, such a unified Chinese state took shape once again during the short-lived Qin dynasty (221–206 B.C.E.), led by its formidable ruler Shihuangdi (see pp. 158–60). That state operated under a version of Legalism (see Chapter 5, pp. 192–93), a political philosophy that found expression in the writings of Han Fei (280–233 B.C.E.) and that in large measure guided the practices of Shihuangdi and the Qin dynasty. Han Fei's Legalist thinking was discredited by the brutality and excesses of Shihuangdi's reign, and the Han dynasty that followed was sharply critical of his ideas, favoring instead the "government by morality" approach of Confucianism. Nonetheless, Han Fei's emphasis on the importance of laws and the need to enforce them influenced all succeeding Chinese dynasties.

- Why is Han Fei's approach to governing China referred to as Legalism? According to him, what is required for effective government?

- What are the "two handles"?

- To whom does Han Fei believe his measures should apply?

- What view of human nature underpins Han Fei's argument?

The Writings of Master Han Fei
Third Century B.C.E.

No country is permanently strong. Nor is any country permanently weak. If conformers to law are strong, the country is strong; if conformers to law are weak, the country is weak....

Any ruler able to expel private crookedness and uphold public law, finds the people safe and the state in order; and any ruler able to expunge private action and act on public law, finds his army strong and his enemy weak. So, find out men following the discipline of laws and regulations, and place them above the body of officials. Then the sovereign cannot be deceived by anybody with fraud and falsehood....

Therefore, the intelligent sovereign makes the law select men and makes no arbitrary promotion himself. He makes the law measure merits and makes no arbitrary regulation himself. In consequence, able men cannot be obscured, bad characters cannot be disguised; falsely praised fellows cannot be advanced, wrongly defamed people cannot be degraded. To govern the state by law is to praise the right and blame the wrong.

The law does not fawn on the noble....Whatever the law applies to, the wise cannot reject nor can the brave defy. Punishment for fault never skips ministers, reward for good never misses commoners. Therefore, to correct the faults of the high, to rebuke the vices of the low, to suppress disorders, to decide against mistakes, to subdue the arrogant, to straighten the crooked, and to unify the folkways of the masses, nothing could match the law. To warn the officials and overawe the people, to rebuke obscenity and danger, and to forbid falsehood and deceit, nothing could match penalty. If penalty is severe, the noble cannot discriminate against the humble. If law is definite, the superiors are esteemed and not violated. If the superiors are not violated, the sovereign will become strong and able to maintain the proper course of government. Such was the reason why the early kings esteemed Legalism and handed it down to posterity. Should the lord of men discard law and practice selfishness, high and low would have no distinction.

The means whereby the intelligent ruler controls his ministers are two handles only. The two handles are chastisement and commendation. What are meant by chastisement and commendation? To inflict death or torture upon culprits is called chastisement; to bestow encouragements or rewards on men of merit is called commendation.

Ministers are afraid of censure and punishment but fond of encouragement and reward. Therefore, if the lord of men uses the handles of chastisement and commendation, all ministers will dread his severity and turn to his liberality. The villainous ministers of the age are different. To men they hate they would, by securing the handle of chastisement from the sovereign, ascribe crimes; on men they love they would, by securing the handle of commendation from the sovereign, bestow rewards. Now supposing the lord of men placed the authority of punishment and the profit of reward not in his hands but let the ministers administer the affairs of reward and punishment instead; then everybody in the country would fear the ministers and slight the ruler, and turn to the ministers and away from the ruler. This is the calamity of the ruler's loss of the handles of chastisement and commendation.

Source: *The Complete Works of Han Fei Tzu*, vol. 1, translated by W. L. Liano (London: Arthur Probsthain, 1939), 40, 45–47.

Document 4.4

Governing an Indian Empire

Among the rulers of the classical era, Ashoka, of India's Mauryan dynasty (reigned 268–232 B.C.E.), surely stands out, both for the personal transformation he experienced and for the benevolent philosophy of government that he subsequently articulated (see pp. 165–67). Ashoka's career as emperor began in a familiar fashion—ruthless consolidation of his own power and vigorous expansion of the state's frontiers. A particularly bloody battle against the state of Kalinga marked a turning point in his reign. Apparently repulsed by the destruction, Ashoka converted to Buddhism and turned his attention to more peaceful and tolerant ways of governing his huge empire. His edicts and advice, inscribed on rocks and pillars throughout his realm, outlined this distinctive approach to imperial governance.

The following document provides samples of instructions from Ashoka, who is referred to as King Piyadasi, or the Beloved of the Gods. The term *dhamma*, used frequently in edicts of Ashoka, refers to the "way" or the "truth" that is embodied in religious teachings.

- How would you describe Ashoka's philosophy of state?

- How might Han Fei have responded to Ashoka's ideas?

- What specific changes did Ashoka make in state policies and practices?

- Can you think of practical reasons why he might have adopted these policies? Did he entirely abandon the use of harsher measures?

Although Ashoka's reputation as an enlightened ruler has persisted to this day, his policies ultimately were not very successful. Shortly after Ashoka's death, the Mauryan Empire broke apart into a more common Indian pattern of competing regional states that rose and fell with some regularity. Of course Shihuangdi's much harsher Legalist policies were also unsuccessful, at least in maintaining his dynasty, which lasted a mere fifteen years.

- How might this outcome affect your assessment of Ashoka?

- What does this suggest about the relationship between political philosophies and the success or longevity of political systems?

ASHOKA

The Rock Edicts

ca. 268–232 B.C.E.

Beloved-of-the-Gods, King Piyadasi, conquered the Kalingas eight years after his coronation. One hundred and fifty thousand were deported, one hundred thousand were killed, and many more died [from other causes]. After the Kalingas had been conquered, Beloved-of-the-Gods came to feel a strong inclination towards the Dhamma, a love for the Dhamma and for instruction in Dhamma. Now Beloved-of-the-Gods feels deep remorse for having conquered the Kalingas....

Now Beloved-of-the-Gods thinks that even those who do wrong should be forgiven where forgiveness is possible.

Even the forest people, who live in Beloved-of-the-Gods' domain, are entreated and reasoned with to act properly. They are told that despite his remorse Beloved-of-the-Gods has the power to punish them if necessary, so that they should be ashamed of their wrong and not be killed. Truly, Beloved-of-the-Gods desires non-injury, restraint, and impartiality to all beings, even where wrong has been done.

Now it is conquest by Dhamma that Beloved-of-the-Gods considers to be the best conquest....

I have had this Dhamma edict written so that my sons and great-grandsons may not consider making new conquests, or that if military conquests are made, that they be done with forbearance and light punishment, or better still, that they consider making conquest by Dhamma only, for that bears fruit in this world and the next. May all their intense devotion be given to this which has a result in this world and the next.

1. Here (in my domain) no living beings are to be slaughtered or offered in sacrifice.... Formerly, in the kitchen of Beloved-of-the-Gods, King Piyadasi, hundreds of thousands of animals were killed every day to make curry. But now with the writing of this Dhamma edict only three creatures, two peacocks and a deer are killed, and the deer not always. And in time, not even these three creatures will be killed.

2.... [E]verywhere has Beloved-of-the-Gods... made provision for two types of medical treatment: medical treatment for humans and medical treatment for animals. Wherever medical herbs suitable for humans or animals are not available, I have had them imported and grown.... Along roads I have had wells dug and trees planted for the benefit of humans and animals.

3. Everywhere in my domain the [royal officers] shall go on inspection tours every five years for the purpose of Dhamma instruction and also to conduct other business. Respect for mother and father is good, generosity to friends, acquaintances, relatives, Brahmans and ascetics is good, not killing living beings is good, moderation in spending and moderation in saving is good.

4. In the past, for many hundreds of years, killing or harming living beings and improper behavior toward relatives, and improper behavior toward Brahmans and ascetics has increased. But now due to Beloved-of-the-Gods' Dhamma practice, the sound of the drum [for announcing the punishment of criminals] has been replaced by the sound of the Dhamma. The sighting of heavenly cars, auspicious elephants, bodies of fire, and other divine sightings has not happened for many hundreds of years. But now because Beloved-of-the-Gods, King Piyadasi, promotes restraint in the killing and harming of living beings, proper behavior towards relatives, Brahmans and ascetics, and respect for mother, father and elders, such sightings have increased.

5. In the past there were no [officers of the Dhamma] but such officers were appointed by me

Source: *The Edicts of King Ashoka*, translated by Ven S. Dhammika (Kandy, Sri Lanka: Buddhist Publication Society, 1993).

thirteen years after my coronation. Now they work among all religions for the establishment of Dhamma....They work among soldiers, chiefs, Brahmans, householders, the poor, the aged and those devoted to Dhamma—for their welfare and happiness—so that they may be free from harassment. They...work for the proper treatment of prisoners, towards their unfettering....They are occupied everywhere....

7. Beloved-of-the-Gods, King Piyadasi, desires that all religions should reside everywhere, for all of them desire self-control and purity of heart.

8. In the past kings used to go out on pleasure tours during which there was hunting and other entertainment. But ten years after Beloved-of-the-Gods had been coronated, he went on a tour to Sambodhi° and thus instituted Dhamma tours. During these tours, the following things took place: visits and gifts to Brahmans and ascetics, visits and gifts of gold to the aged, visits to people in the countryside, instructing them in Dhamma....

12. Beloved-of-the-Gods, King Piyadasi, honors both ascetics and the householders of all religions, and he honors them with gifts and honors of various kinds....Whoever praises his own religion, due to excessive devotion, and condemns others with the thought "Let me glorify my own religion," only harms his own religion. Therefore contact [between religions] is good. One should listen to and respect the doctrines professed by others.

––––––––––

°**Sambodhi:** the site of the Buddha's enlightenment.

Using the Evidence:
Political Authority in Classical Civilizations

1. **Making comparisons:** How would you describe the range of political thinking and practice expressed in these documents? What, if any, common elements do these writings share? Another approach to such a comparison is to take the ideas of one writer and ask how they might be viewed by several of the others. For example, how might Pericles, Aristides, and Han Fei have responded to Ashoka?

2. **Considering variation within civilizations:** You will notice that none of these civilizations practiced a single philosophy of government. Athens was governed very differently from Sparta, the practices of the Roman Empire differed substantially from those of the Republic, Legalism and Confucianism represented alternative approaches to Chinese political life, and Ashoka's ideas broke sharply with prevailing practice of Indian rulers. How can you account for these internal differences? How might you imagine an internal dialogue between each of these writers and their likely domestic critics?

3. **Comparing ancient and modern politics:** What enduring issues of political life do these documents raise? What elements of political thinking and practice during the classical era differ most sharply from those of the modern world of the last century or two? What are the points of similarity?

4. **Distinguishing "power" and "authority":** Some scholars have made a distinction between "power," the ability of rulers to coerce their subjects into some required behavior, and "authority," the ability of those rulers to persuade their subjects to obey voluntarily by convincing them that it is proper, right, or natural to do so. What appeals to "power" and "authority" can you find in these documents? How does the balance between them differ among these documents?

5. **Noticing point of view:** From what position and with what motivation did these writers compose their documents? How did this affect what they had to say?

Visual Sources

Considering the Evidence:
Qin Shihuangdi and China's Eternal Empire

In the vast saga of empire building in world history, few rulers have surpassed China's so-called First Emperor, Qin Shihuangdi (reigned 221–210 B.C.E.), in terms of imperial ambition. During his life, Shihuangdi forcefully and violently brought unity to the warring states of China with policies that were as brutal as they were effective (see pp. 158–60). That achievement gained him the respect of many Chinese in the centuries that followed. No less a figure than Mao Zedong, the twentieth-century communist revolutionary, proudly compared himself to the First Emperor. But Shihuangdi was widely hated in his own time and subject to numerous attempts at assassination, while Confucian scholars in the centuries that followed his death were also highly critical of his brutal methods of governing China.

No artistic images of Shihuangdi survive from the time of his reign, but he was the subject of many paintings in later centuries. Visual Source 4.1, dating from the eighteenth century, depicts a famous scene from his reign, when he allegedly ordered the burning of books critical of his policies and the execution of respected Confucian scholars by burying hundreds of them alive.

- ■ What signs of imperial authority are apparent in the painting?

- ■ What impression of the First Emperor does this painting convey? Do you think the artist sought to celebrate or criticize Shihuangdi?

- ■ What accusations against Shihuangdi might arise from the action depicted at the bottom of Visual Source 4.1?

However his reign may have been evaluated, Shihuangdi's conception of the empire he created was grand indeed. It was to be a universal or cosmic empire. In tours throughout his vast realm, he offered sacrifices to the various spirits, bringing them, as well as the rival kingdoms of China, into a state of unity and harmony. One of the inscriptions he left behind suggested the scope of his reign: "He universally promulgated the shining laws, gave warp and woof to all under heaven."[16] Shihuangdi saw himself in the line of ancient sage kings, who had originally given order to the world.

In Shihuangdi's thinking, that empire was not only universal, encompassing the entire world known to him, but also eternal. The emperor vigorously pursued personal immortality, seeking out pills, herbs, and potions

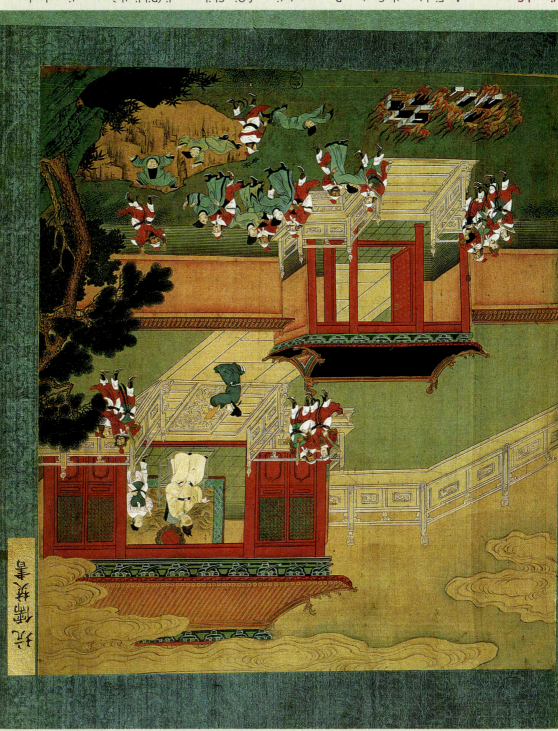

believed to convey eternal life and sending expeditions to the mythical Isles of the Immortals, thought to lie off the east coast of China. But the most spectacular expression of the eternal character of his empire lay in a vast tomb complex constructed during his lifetime near the modern city of Xian (see Map 4.5, p. 159).

In early 1974, some Chinese peasants digging a well stumbled across a small corner of that complex, leading to what has become perhaps the most cele-brated archeological discovery of the twentieth century. In subsequent and con-tinuing excavations, archeologists have uncovered thousands of life-size ceramic statues of soldiers of various ranks, arrayed for battle and equipped with real weapons. Other statues portrayed officials, acrobats, musicians, wrestlers, horses, bronze chariots, birds, and more—all designed to accompany Shihuangdi into the afterlife.

This amazing discovery, however, was only a very small part of an immense tomb complex covering some fifty-six square kilometers and centered on the still-unexcavated burial mound of Shihuangdi. Begun in 246 B.C.E. and still incomplete when Shihuangdi died in 210 B.C.E., the construction of this gigan-tic complex was described by the great Chinese historian Sima Qian about a century later:

As soon as the First Emperor became king of Qin, excavations and building had been started at Mount Li, while after he won the empire, more than 700,000 conscripts from all parts of the country worked there. They dug through three subterranean streams and poured molten copper for the outer coffin, and the tomb was filled with…palaces, pavilions, and offices as well as fine vessels, precious stones, and rarities. Artisans were ordered to fix up crossbows so that any thief breaking in would be shot. All the country's streams, the Yellow River and the Yangtze were reproduced in quicksilver [mercury] and by some mechan-ical means made to flow into a miniature ocean. The heavenly con-stellations were above and the regions of the earth below. The candles were made of whale oil to insure the burning for the longest possible time.[17]

Buried with Shihuangdi were many of the workers who had died or were killed during construction as well as sacrificed aristocrats and concubines.

This massive project was no mere monument to a deceased ruler. In a culture that believed the living and the dead formed a single community, Shihuangdi's tomb complex was a parallel society, complete with walls, palaces, cemeteries, demons, spirits, soldiers, administrators, entertainers, calendars, texts, divination records, and the luxurious objects appropriate to royalty. The tomb mound itself was like a mountain, a geographic feature that in Chinese think-ing was home to gods, spirits, and immortals. From this mound, Shihuangdi would rule forever over his vast domain, although invisible to the living.

The visual sources that follow provide a small sample of the terra-cotta army that protected that underground world, as it has emerged from the exca-vations of the past several decades. The largest pit (Visual Source 4.2) is now covered with a canopy and conveys something of the massive size of this undertaking. Located about a mile east of Shihuangdi's burial mound, this ceramic army, replete with horses and chariots, faced the pass in the mountains from which enemies might be expected. Some six thousand terra-cotta fig-ures have been uncovered and painstakingly pieced together in this pit alone.

■ How do you suppose Shihuangdi thought about the function of this "army" in the larger context of his tomb complex?

■ What kind of organizational effort would be required to produce such a ceramic army?

Visual Source 4.2 The Terra-Cotta Army of Shihuangdi (Dennis Cox/China Stock)

Visual Source 4.3 Terra-Cotta Infantry (Keren Su/China Span/Alamy)

Scholars have long been impressed with the apparent individuality of these terra-cotta figures, and some have argued that they were actually modeled on particular living soldiers. More recent research suggests, however, that they were "an early feat of mass production."[18] Well-organized workshops produced a limited variety of face shapes, body parts, hairstyles, and uniforms, which were then assembled in various combinations and slightly reworked to convey an impression of individuality. Visual Source 4.3 shows a group of infantry-men, located at the front of the formation, while Visual Source 4.4 represents a kneeling archer.

- What similarities and differences can you identify between the infantry-men and the archer? Which of them do you imagine had a higher status?
- What impressions do their postures and facial expressions convey?
- What details help to convey a highly realistic image of these figures?

Visual Source 4.4 Terra-Cotta Archer (Museum of the Terra Cotta Army, Xian/Visual Connection Archive)

Visual Source 4.5   A Bronze Horse-Drawn Chariot (Private Collection/The Bridgeman Art Library)

Among the most delightful finds in Shihuangdi's funerary complex were two exquisitely detailed bronze carriages, each portrayed as half-sized models and pulled by four horses. Coachmen with swords provided protection on both sides. Some seven kilograms of gold and silver served to decorate the carriage and horses, which consisted of more than 3,000 separate pieces. These finds, however, were not part of the terra-cotta army and its military machine. Rather, they were found some distance away, quite close to the actual burial place of the emperor. Visual Source 4.5 shows the larger of the two carriages and features a team of horses, a driver, three windows, and a rear door. The compartment is decorated inside and out with geometric and cloud patterns, while the round roof, perhaps, represents the sun, the sky, or the heavens above.

■ Scholars differ as to the precise purpose of this carriage. Perhaps it was intended to allow the emperor to tour his realm in the afterlife much as he had done while alive. Or did it serve a one-time purpose to transport the emperor's soul into the afterlife? What line of reasoning might support either of these interpretations?

■ The carriages were found deliberately buried in a wooden coffin and facing west. What significance might you attach to these facts?

Using the Evidence:
Qin Shihuangdi and China's Eternal Empire

1. **Describing Shihuangdi:** Based on these visual sources and what you have learned about Shihuangdi's tomb complex, how would you characterize him as a ruler and as a man? In what ways did his reign reflect the views of Han Fei in Document 4.3?

2. **Evaluating Shihuangdi:** What aspects of Shihuangdi's reign might have provoked praise or criticism both during his life and later?

3. **Making comparisons:** In what ways were Shihuangdi's reign and his funerary arrangements unique, and in what respects did they fit into a larger pattern of other early rulers? Consider him in relationship to Egyptian pharaohs, Persian rulers, Alexander the Great, Augustus, or Ashoka.

Eurasian Cultural Traditions

500 B.C.E.–500 C.E.

In 2004, some 180 married couples in Beijing, China, stood before a picture of their country's ancient sage, Confucius, and took an oath, pledging fidelity to each other and promising never to divorce. This was a small part of a nationwide celebration of the 2,555th anniversary of the birth of Confucius. A public memorial service was held in his hometown of Qufu, while high government officials warmly welcomed delegates attending an international symposium devoted to his teaching. What made this celebration remarkable was that it took place in a country still ruled by the Communist Party, which had long devoted enormous efforts to discrediting Confucius and his teachings. In the view of communist China's revolutionary leader, Mao Zedong, Confucianism was associated with class inequality, patriarchy, feudalism, superstition, and all things old and backward, but the country's ancient teacher and philosopher had apparently outlasted its revolutionary hero. High-ranking political leaders, all officially communist, have begun to invoke Confucius and to urge "social harmony," rather than class conflict, as China rapidly modernizes. Many anxious parents offer prayers at Confucian temples when their children are taking the national college entrance exams.

Buddhism also has experienced something of a revival in China, as thousands of temples, destroyed during the heyday of communism, have been repaired and reopened. Christianity too has grown rapidly since the death of Mao in 1976, with professing Christians numbering some 7 percent of China's huge population by the early twenty-first century. Here are reminders, in a Chinese context, of the continuing appeal of cultural traditions forged during the clas-

China's Cultural Traditions: In this idealized painting, attributed to the Chinese artist Wang Shugu (1649–1730), the Chinese teacher Confucius presents a baby Buddha to the Daoist master Laozi. The image illustrates the assimilation of a major Indian religion into China as well as the generally peaceful coexistence of these three traditions. (British Museum/The Art Archive)

sical era. Those traditions are among the most enduring legacies that second-wave civilizations have bequeathed to the modern world.

IN THE SEVERAL CENTURIES SURROUNDING 500 B.C.E., something quite remarkable happened all across Eurasia. More or less simultaneously, in China, India, the Middle East, and Greece, there emerged cultural traditions that spread widely, have persisted in various forms into the twenty-first century, and have shaped the values and outlooks of most people who have inhabited the planet over the past 2,500 years.

In China, it was the time of Kong Fuzi (Confucius) and Laozi, whose teachings gave rise to Confucianism and Daoism, respectively. In India, a series of religious writings known as the *Upanishads* gave expression to the classical philosophy of Hinduism, while a religious reformer, Siddhartha Gautama, set in motion a separate religion known later as Buddhism. In the Middle East, a distinctively monotheistic religious tradition appeared. It was expressed in Zoroastrianism, derived from the teachings of the Persian prophet Zarathustra, and in Judaism, articulated in Israel by a number of Jewish prophets such as Amos, Jeremiah, and Isaiah. Finally, in Greece, a rational and humanistic tradition found expression in the writings of Socrates, Plato, Aristotle, and many others.

These cultural traditions differed greatly. Chinese and Greek thinkers focused more on the affairs of this world and credited human rationality with the power to understand that reality. Indian, Persian, and Jewish intellectuals, who explored the realm of the divine and its relationship to human life, were much more religious. All of these traditions sought an alternative to an earlier polytheism, in which the activities of various gods and spirits explained what happened in this world. These gods and spirits had generally been seen as similar to human beings, though much more powerful. Through ritual and sacrifice, men and women might placate the gods or persuade them to do human bidding. In contrast, the new cultural traditions of the classical era sought to define a single source of order and meaning in the universe, some moral or religious realm, sharply different from and higher than the sphere of human life. The task of humankind, according to these new ways of thinking, was personal moral or spiritual transformation—often expressed as the development of compassion—by aligning ourselves with that higher order.[1] These enormously rich and varied traditions have collectively posed the great questions of human life and society that have haunted and inspired much of humankind ever since. They also defined the distinctive cultures that distinguished the various classical civilizations from one another.

Why did these traditions all emerge at roughly the same time? Here we encounter an enduring issue of historical analysis: What is the relationship between ideas and the circumstances in which they arise? Are ideas generated by particular political, social, and economic conditions? Or are they the product of creative human imagination independent of the material environment? Or do they derive from some combination of the two? In the case of the classical cultural traditions, many historians have

Snapshot   Thinkers and Philosophies of the Classical Era

Person	Date	Location	Religion/Philosophy	Key Ideas
Zoroaster	7th century B.C.E. (?)	Persia (present-day Iran)	Zoroastrianism	Single High God; cosmic conflict of good and evil
Hebrew prophets (Isaiah, Amos, Jeremiah)	9th–6th centuries B.C.E.	Eastern Mediterranean/ Palestine/Israel	Judaism	Transcendent High God; covenant with chosen people; social justice
Anonymous writers of Upanishads	800–400 B.C.E.	India	Brahmanism/ Hinduism	Brahma (the single impersonal divine reality); karma; rebirth; goal of liberation (moksha)
Confucius	6th century B.C.E.	China	Confucianism	Social harmony through moral example; secular outlook; importance of education; family as model of the state
Mahavira	6th century B.C.E.	India	Jainism	All creatures have souls; purification through nonviolence; opposed to caste
Siddhartha Gautama	6th century B.C.E.	India	Buddhism	Suffering caused by desire/ attachment; end of suffering through modest and moral living and meditation practice
Laozi, Zhuangzi	6th–3rd centuries B.C.E.	China	Daoism	Withdrawal from the world into contemplation of nature; simple living; end of striving
Socrates, Plato, Aristotle	5th–4th centuries B.C.E.	Greece	Greek rationalism	Style of persistent questioning; secular explanation of nature and human life
Jesus	early 1st century C.E.	Palestine/Israel	Christianity	Supreme importance of love based on intimate relationship with God; at odds with established authorities
Saint Paul	1st century C.E.	Palestine/Israel/ eastern Roman Empire	Christianity	Christianity as a religion for all; salvation through faith in Jesus Christ

noted the tumultuous social changes that accompanied the emergence of these new teachings. An iron-age technology, available since roughly 1000 B.C.E., made possible more productive economies and more deadly warfare. Growing cities, increased trade, the prominence of merchant classes, the emergence of new states and empires, new contacts among civilizations—all of these disruptions, occurring in already-literate societies, led thinkers to question older outlooks and to come up with new solutions to fundamental questions: What is the purpose of life? How should human society be ordered? What is the relationship between human life in this world and the moral or spiritual realms that lie beyond? But precisely why various societies developed their own distinctive answers to these questions remains elusive—a tribute, perhaps, to the unpredictable genius of the human imagination.

China and the Search for Order

As one of the First Civilizations, China had a tradition of state building that historians have traced back to around 2000 B.C.E. or before. By the time the Zhou dynasty took power in 1122 B.C.E., the notion of the Mandate of Heaven had taken root, as had the idea that the normal and appropriate condition of China was one of political unity. By the eighth century B.C.E., the authority of the Zhou dynasty and its royal court had substantially weakened, and by 500 B.C.E. any unity that China had earlier enjoyed was long gone. What followed was a period (403–221 B.C.E.) of chaos, growing violence, and disharmony that became known as the "age of warring states" (see pp. 158–60). During these dreadful centuries of disorder and turmoil, a number of Chinese thinkers began to consider how order might be restored, how the apparent tranquillity of an earlier time could be realized again. From their reflections emerged classical cultural traditions of Chinese civilization.

The Legalist Answer

■ **Comparison**

What different answers to the problem of disorder arose in classical China?

One answer to the problem of disorder—though not the first to emerge—was a hardheaded and practical philosophy known as Legalism. To Legalist thinkers, the solution to China's problems lay in rules or laws, clearly spelled out and strictly enforced through a system of rewards and punishments. "If rewards are high," wrote Han Fei, one of the most prominent Legalist philosophers, "then what the ruler wants will be quickly effected; if punishments are heavy, what he does not want will be swiftly prevented."[2] (See Document 4.3, pp. 174–75, for an extract from the writing of Han Fei.) Legalists generally entertained a rather pessimistic view of human nature. Most people were stupid and shortsighted. Only the state and its rulers could act in their long-term interests. Doing so meant promoting farmers and soldiers, the only two groups in society who performed essential functions, while suppressing artisans, merchants, aristocrats, scholars, and other classes regarded as useless.

Legalist thinking provided inspiration and methods for the harsh reunification of China under Shihuangdi and the Qin dynasty (221–206 B.C.E.), but the brutality of that short dynasty thoroughly discredited Legalism. Although its techniques and practices played a role in subsequent Chinese statecraft, no philosopher or ruler ever again openly advocated its ideas. The Han and all subsequent dynasties drew instead on the teachings of China's greatest sage—Confucius.

The Confucian Answer

Born to an aristocratic family in the state of Lu in northern China, Confucius (551–479 B.C.E.) was both learned and ambitious. Believing that he had found the key to solving China's problem of disorder, he spent much of his adult life seeking a political position from which he might put his ideas into action. But no such opportunity came his way. Perhaps it was just as well, for it was as a thinker and a teacher that Confucius left a profound imprint on Chinese history and culture and also on other East Asian societies, such as Korea and Japan. After his death, his students collected his teachings in a short book called the *Analects*, and later scholars elaborated and commented endlessly on his ideas, creating a body of thought known as Confucianism (see Document 5.1, pp. 217–19).

The Confucian answer to the problem of China's disorder was very different from that of the Legalists. Not laws and punishments, but the moral example of superiors was the Confucian key to a restored social harmony. For Confucius, human society consisted primarily of unequal relationships: the father was superior to the son; the husband to the wife; the older brother to the younger brother; and, of course, the ruler to the subject. If the superior party in each of these relationships behaved with sincerity, benevolence, and genuine concern for others, then the inferior party would be motivated to respond with deference and obedience. Harmony then would prevail. As Confucius put it, "The relation between superiors and inferiors is like that between the wind and the grass. The grass must bend when the wind blows across it." Thus, in both family life and in political life, the cultivation of *ren*—translated as humanheartedness, benevolence, goodness, nobility of heart—was the essential ingredient of a tranquil society.

But how are these humane virtues to be nurtured? Believing that people have a capacity for improvement, Confucius emphasized education as the key to moral betterment. He prescribed a broad liberal arts education emphasizing language, literature, history, philosophy, and ethics, all applied to the practical problems of government. Ritual and ceremonies were also important, for they conveyed the rules of appropriate

■ **Description**
Why has Confucianism been defined as a "humanistic philosophy" rather than a supernatural religion?

Filial Piety
This Song dynasty painting served as an illustration of an ancient Chinese text in the Confucian tradition called the "Classic of Filial Piety," originally composed sometime around the fourth century B.C.E. and subsequently reissued many times. Here, a son kneels submissively in front of his parents. The long-enduring social order that Confucius advocated began at home with unquestioning obedience and the utmost respect for parents and other senior members of the family. (National Palace Museum, Taipei, Taiwan, Republic of China)

behavior in the many and varying circumstances of life. For the "superior person," or "gentleman" in Confucian terms, this process of improvement involved serious personal reflection and a willingness to strive continuously to perfect his moral character.

Such ideas left a deep mark on Chinese culture. The discrediting of Legalism during the Qin dynasty opened the door to the adoption of Confucianism as the official ideology of the Chinese state, to such an extent that Confucianism became almost synonymous with Chinese culture. As China's bureaucracy took shape during the Han dynasty and after, Confucianism became the central element of the educational system, which prepared students for the series of examinations required to gain official positions. In those examinations, candidates were required to apply the principles of Confucianism to specific situations that they might encounter once in office. Thus generation after generation of China's male elite was steeped in the ideas and values of Confucianism.

Family life had long been central to Chinese popular culture, expressed in the practice of ancestor veneration, including visiting the graves of the deceased, presenting them with offerings, and erecting commemorative tablets and shrines in their honor. In Confucian thinking, the family became a model for political life, a kind of miniature state. Filial piety, the honoring of one's ancestors and parents, was both an end in itself and a training ground for the reverence due to the emperor and state officials. Confucianism also set the tone for defining the lives of women. A somewhat later woman writer, Ban Zhao (45–116 C.E.), penned a famous work called *Lessons for Women*, which spelled out the implication of Confucian thinking for women:

> Let a woman modestly yield to others. . . . Always let her seem to tremble and to fear. . . . Then she may be said to humble herself before others. . . . To guard carefully her chastity . . . to choose her words with care . . . , to wash and scrub filth away . . . , with whole-hearted devotion to sew and to weave, to love not gossip and silly laughter, in cleanliness and order to prepare the wine and food for serving guests: [These] may be called the characteristics of womanly work.[3]

Ban Zhao called for greater attention to education for young girls, not because they were equal to boys, but so that a young woman might be better prepared to serve her husband. (See Document 6.2, pp. 263–66, for a longer selection from Ban Zhao.)

Confucianism also placed great importance on history, for the ideal good society lay in the past. Confucian ideas were reformist, perhaps even revolutionary, but they were consistently presented as an effort to restore a past golden age. Those ideas also injected a certain democratic element into Chinese elite culture, for the great sage had emphasized that "superior men" and potential government officials were those of outstanding moral character and intellectual achievement, not simply those of aristocratic background. Usually only young men from wealthy families could afford the education necessary for passing examinations, but on occasion villagers could find the resources to sponsor one of their bright sons. Thus the Confucian-based examination system provided a modest element of social mobility in an otherwise hierarchical society. Confucian values clearly justified the many inequalities of Chinese society, but they also established certain expectations for government. Emperors should keep taxes low, administer justice, and provide for the material needs of the people. Those who failed to govern by the moral norms of Confucian values forfeited the Mandate of Heaven and invited upheaval and their replacement by another dynasty.

Finally, Confucianism marked Chinese elite culture by its secular, or nonreligious, character. Confucius did not deny the reality of gods and spirits. In fact, he advised people to participate in family and state rituals "as if the spirits were present," and he believed that the universe had a moral character with which human beings should align themselves. But the thrust of Confucian teaching was distinctly this-worldly and practical, concerned with human relationships, effective government, and social harmony. Asked on one occasion about his view of death and the spirits, Confucius replied that because we do not fully understand this life, we cannot possibly know anything about the life beyond. Although members of the Chinese elite generally acknowledged that magic, the gods, and spirits were perhaps necessary for the lower orders of society, they felt that educated people would find them of little help in striving for moral improvement and in establishing a harmonious society.

The Daoist Answer

No civilization has ever painted its cultural outlook in a single color. As Confucian thinking became generally known in China, a quite different school of thought also took shape. Known as Daoism, it was associated with the legendary figure Laozi, who, according to tradition, was a sixth-century B.C.E. archivist. He is said to have penned a short poetic volume, the *Daodejing* (*The Way and Its Power*), before vanishing in the wilderness to the west of China on his water buffalo. Daoist ideas were later expressed in a more explicit fashion by the philosopher Zhuangzi (369–286 B.C.E.).

In many ways, Daoist thinking ran counter to that of Confucius, who had emphasized the importance of education and earnest striving for moral improvement and good government. The Daoists ridiculed such efforts as artificial and useless, generally making things worse. In the face of China's disorder and chaos,

Chinese Landscape Paintings
Focused largely on mountains and water, Chinese landscape paintings were much influenced by the Daoist search for harmony with nature. Thus human figures and buildings were usually eclipsed by towering peaks, waterfalls, clouds, and trees. This seventeenth-century painting entitled *Temple on a Mountain Ledge* shows a Buddhist monastery in such a setting, while the poem in the upper right refers to the artist's earlier wanderings, a metaphor for the Buddhist quest for enlightenment. (Mr. and Mrs. John D. Rockefeller 3rd Collection of Asian Art/Asia Society 179.124)

■ **Comparison**
How did the Daoist outlook differ from that of Confucianism?

they urged withdrawal into the world of nature and encouraged behavior that was spontaneous, individualistic, and natural. Whereas Confucius focused on the world of human relationships, the Daoists turned the spotlight on the immense realm of nature and its mysterious unfolding patterns. "Confucius roams within society," the Chinese have often said. "Laozi wanders beyond."

The central concept of Daoist thinking is *dao*, an elusive notion that refers to the way of nature, the underlying and unchanging principle that governs all natural phenomena. According to the *Daodejing*, the dao "moves around and around, but does not on this account suffer. All life comes from it. It wraps everything with its love as in a garment, and yet it claims no honor, for it does not demand to be lord. I do not know its name and so I call it the Dao, the Way, and I rejoice in its power."[4]

Applied to human life, Daoism invited people to withdraw from the world of political and social activism, to disengage from the public life so important to Confucius, and to align themselves with the way of nature. It meant simplicity in living, small self-sufficient communities, limited government, and the abandonment of education and active efforts at self-improvement. "Give up learning," declares the *Daodejing*, "and put an end to your troubles." The flavor of the Daoist approach to life is evident in this passage from the *Daodejing*:

> A small country has few people.
> Though there are machines that can work ten to a hundred times faster
> than man, they are not needed. . . .
> Though they have boats and carriages, no one uses them. . . .
> Men return to the knotting of ropes in place of writing.
> Their food is plain and good, their clothes fine but simple. . . .
> They are happy in their ways.
> Though they live within sight of their neighbors,
> And crowing cocks and barking dogs are heard across the way,
> Yet they leave each other in peace while they grow old and die.[5]

The Yin Yang Symbol

Despite its sharp differences with the ideas of Confucianism, the Daoist perspective was widely regarded by elite Chinese as complementing rather than contradicting Confucian values (see the chapter-opening image on p. 188). Such an outlook was facilitated by the ancient Chinese concept of *yin* and *yang*, which expressed a belief in the unity of opposites.

Thus a scholar-official might pursue the Confucian project of "government by goodness" during the day, but upon returning home in the evening or following his retirement, he might well behave in a more Daoist fashion—pursuing the simple life, reading Daoist philosophy, practicing Daoist meditation and breathing exercises, or enjoying landscape paintings in which tiny human figures are dwarfed by the vast peaks and valleys of the natural world (see image on p. 195). Daoism also shaped the culture of ordinary people as it entered popular religion. This kind of Daoism sought to tap the power of the dao for practical uses and came to include magic, fortune-telling, and the search for immortality. It also on occasion provided an ideology for peasant uprisings, such as the Yellow Turban Rebellion (184–204 C.E.), which imagined a utopian society without the oppression of governments and landlords (see Chapter 6). In its many and varied forms, Daoism, like Confucianism, became an enduring element of the Chinese cultural tradition.

Cultural Traditions of Classical India

The cultural development of Indian civilization was far different from that of China. Whereas Confucianism paid little attention to the gods, spirits, and speculation about religious matters, Indian elite culture embraced the divine and all things spiritual with enthusiasm and generated elaborate philosophical visions about the nature of ultimate reality. Still, the Indian religious tradition, known to us as Hinduism, differed from other world religions. Unlike Buddhism, Christianity, or Islam, Hinduism had no historical founder; rather, it grew up over many centuries along with Indian civilization. Although it later spread into Southeast Asia, Hinduism was not a missionary religion seeking converts, but was, like Judaism, associated with a particular people and territory.

In fact, "Hinduism" was never a single tradition at all, and the term itself derived from outsiders — Greeks, Muslims, and later the British — who sought to reduce the infinite variety of Indian cultural patterns into a recognizable system. From the inside, however, Hinduism dissolved into a vast diversity of gods, spirits, beliefs, practices, rituals, and philosophies. This endlessly variegated Hinduism served to incorporate into Indian civilization the many diverse peoples who migrated into or invaded the South Asian peninsula over many centuries and several millennia. Its ability to accommodate this diversity gave India's cultural development a distinctive quality.

South Asian Religion: From Ritual Sacrifice to Philosophical Speculation

Despite the fragmentation and variety of Indian cultural and religious patterns, an evolving set of widely recognized sacred texts provided some commonality. The earliest of these texts, known as the *Vedas*, were collections of poems, hymns, prayers, and rituals. Compiled by priests called *Brahmins*, the Vedas were for centuries transmitted orally and were reduced to writing in Sanskrit around 600 B.C.E. In the Vedas, historians have caught fleeting glimpses of classical Indian civilization in its formative centuries (1500–600 B.C.E.). Those sacred writings tell of small competing chiefdoms or kingdoms, of sacred sounds and fires, of numerous gods, rising and falling in importance over the centuries, and of the elaborate ritual sacrifices that they required. Performing these sacrifices and rituals with great precision enabled the Brahmins to acquire enormous power and wealth, sometimes exceeding even that of kings and warriors. But Brahmins also generated growing criticism, as ritual became mechanical and formal and as Brahmins required heavy fees to perform them.

From this dissatisfaction arose another body of sacred texts, the Upanishads. Composed by largely anonymous thinkers between 800 and 400 B.C.E., these were

■ **Change**

In what ways did the religious traditions of South Asia change over the centuries?

Hindu Ascetics
Hinduism called for men in the final stage of life to leave ordinary ways of living and withdraw into the forests to seek spiritual liberation, or moksha. Here, in an illustration from an early thirteenth-century Indian manuscript, a holy man explores a text with three disciples in a secluded rural setting. (Réunion des Musées Nationaux/Art Resource, NY)

mystical and highly philosophical works that sought to probe the inner meaning of the sacrifices prescribed in the Vedas. In the Upanishads, external ritual gave way to introspective thinking, which expressed in many and varied formulations the central concepts of philosophical Hinduism that have persisted into modern times. Chief among them was the idea of Brahman, the World Soul, the final and ultimate reality. Beyond the multiplicity of material objects and individual persons and beyond even the various gods themselves lay this primal unitary energy or divine reality infusing all things, similar in some ways to the Chinese notion of the dao. This alone was real; the immense diversity of existence that human beings perceived with their senses was but an illusion.

The fundamental assertion of philosophical Hinduism was that the individual human soul, or *atman*, was in fact a part of Brahman. Beyond the quest for pleasure, wealth, power, and social position, all of which were perfectly normal and quite legitimate, lay the effort to achieve the final goal of humankind—union with Brahman, an end to our illusory perception of a separate existence. This was *moksha*, or liberation, compared sometimes to a bubble in a glass of water breaking through the surface and becoming one with the surrounding atmosphere.

Achieving this exalted state was held to involve many lifetimes, as the notion of *samsara*, or rebirth/reincarnation, became a central feature of Hindu thinking. Human souls migrated from body to body over many lifetimes, depending on one's actions. This was the law of *karma*. Pure actions, appropriate to one's station in life, resulted in rebirth in a higher social position or caste. Thus the caste system of distinct and ranked groups, each with its own duties, became a register of spiritual progress. Birth in a higher caste was evidence of "good karma," based on actions in a previous life, and offered a better chance to achieve moksha, which brought with it an end to the painful cycle of rebirth.

Various ways to this final release, appropriate to people of different temperaments, were spelled out in Hindu teachings. Some might achieve moksha through knowledge or study; others by means of detached action in the world, doing one's work without regard to consequences; still others through passionate devotion to some deity or through extended meditation practice. Such ideas—carried by Brahmin priests and even more by wandering ascetics, who had withdrawn from ordinary life to pursue their spiritual development—became widely known throughout India. (See Document 5.2, pp. 219–21.)

The Buddhist Challenge

About the same time as philosophical Hinduism was taking shape, there emerged another movement that soon became a distinct and separate religious tradition— Buddhism. Unlike Hinduism, this new faith had a historical founder, Siddhartha Gautama (ca. 566–ca. 486 B.C.E.), a prince from a small north Indian state. According to Buddhist tradition, the prince had enjoyed a sheltered and delightful youth but was shocked to his core upon encountering old age, sickness, and death. Leaving family and fortune behind, he then set out on a six-year spiritual quest, finally achieving insight, or "enlightenment," at the age of thirty-five. For the rest of his life, he taught what he had learned and gathered a small but growing community whose members came to see him as the Buddha, the Enlightened One.

"I teach but one thing," the Buddha said, "suffering and the end of suffering." To the Buddha, suffering or sorrow—experiencing life as imperfect, impermanent, and unsatisfactory—was the central and universal feature of human life. Its cause was desire or craving for individual fulfillment and particularly attachment to the notion of a core self or ego that is uniquely and solidly "me." The cure for this "dis-ease" lay in living a modest and moral life combined with meditation practice. Those who followed the Buddhist path most fully could expect to achieve enlightenment, or *nirvana*, a virtually indescribable state in which individual identity would be "extinguished" along with all greed, hatred, and delusion. With the pain of unnecessary suffering finally ended, the enlightened person would experience an overwhelming serenity, even in the midst of difficulty, as well as an immense loving-kindness, or compassion, for all beings. It was a simple message, elaborated endlessly and in various forms by those who followed him.

Much of the Buddha's teaching reflected the Hindu traditions from which it sprang. The idea that ordinary life is an illusion, the concepts of karma and rebirth, the goal of overcoming the incessant demands of the ego, the practice of meditation, the hope for final release from the cycle of rebirth—all of these Hindu elements found their way into Buddhist teaching. In this respect, Buddhism was a simplified and more accessible version of Hinduism.

Other elements of Buddhist teaching, however, sharply challenged prevailing Hindu thinking. Rejecting the religious authority of the Brahmins, the Buddha ridiculed their rituals and sacrifices as irrelevant to the hard work of dealing with one's

Comparison

In what ways did Buddhism reflect Hindu traditions, and in what ways did it challenge them?

The Mahabodhi Temple
Constructed on the traditional site of the Buddha's enlightenment in northern India, the Mahabodhi temple became a major pilgrimage site and was lavishly patronized by local rulers. (Alison Wright/Robert Harding World Imagery/Getty Images)

suffering. Nor was he much interested in abstract speculation about the creation of the world or the existence of God, for such questions, he declared, "are not useful in the quest for holiness; they do not lead to peace and to the direct knowledge of *nirvana*." Individuals had to take responsibility for their own spiritual development with no help from human authorities or supernatural beings. It was a religion of intense self-effort, based on personal experience. The Buddha also challenged the inequalities of a Hindu-based caste system, arguing that neither caste position nor gender was a barrier to enlightenment. The possibility of "awakening" was available to all.

When it came to establishing a formal organization of the Buddha's most devoted followers, though, the prevailing patriarchy of Indian society made itself felt. Buddhist texts recount that the Buddha's foster mother, Prajapati Gotami, sought to enter the newly created order of monks but was repeatedly refused admission by the Buddha himself. Only after the intervention of the Buddha's attendant, Ananda, did he relent and allow women to join a separate order of nuns. Even then, these nuns were subjected to a series of rules that clearly subordinated them to men. Male monks, for example, could officially admonish the nuns, but the reverse was forbidden.

Nonetheless, thousands of women flocked to join the Buddhist order of nuns, where they found a degree of freedom and independence unavailable elsewhere in Indian society. The classic Hindu text, *The Laws of Manu*, had clearly defined the position of women: "In childhood a female must be subject to her father; in youth to her husband; when her lord is dead to her sons; a woman must never be independent."[6] But Buddhist nuns delighted in the relative freedom of their order, where they largely ran their own affairs, were forbidden to do household chores, and devoted themselves wholly to the search for "awakening," which many apparently achieved. A nun named Mutta declared: "I am free from the three crooked things: mortar, pestle, and my crooked husband. I am free from birth and death and all that dragged me back."[7] (See Document 5.3, pp. 221–23, for further examples of early poetry by Indian Buddhist women.)

Gradually, Buddhist teachings found an audience in India. Buddhism's egalitarian message appealed especially to lower-caste groups and to women. The availability of its teaching in the local language of Pali, rather than the classical Sanskrit, made it accessible. Establishing monasteries and stupas containing relics of the Buddha on the site of neighborhood shrines to earth spirits or near a sacred tree linked the new religion to local traditions. The most dedicated followers joined monasteries, devoting their lives to religious practice and spreading the message among nearby people. State support during the reign of Ashoka (268–232 B.C.E.) likewise helped the new religion gain a foothold in India as a distinct tradition separate from Hinduism.

As Buddhism spread, both within and beyond India, differences in understanding soon emerged, particularly as to how nirvana could be achieved or, in a common Buddhist metaphor, how to cross the river to the far shore of enlightenment.

■ **Comparison**

What is the difference between the Theravada and Mahayana expressions of Buddhism?

The Buddha had taught a rather austere doctrine of intense self-effort, undertaken most actively by monks and nuns who withdrew from society to devote themselves fully to the quest. This early version of the new religion, known as Theravada (Teaching of the Elders), portrayed the Buddha as an immensely wise teacher and model, but certainly not divine. It was more psychological than religious, a set of practices rather than a set of beliefs. The gods, though never completely denied, played little role in assisting believers in their search for enlightenment. In short, individuals were on their own in crossing the river. Clearly this was not for everyone.

By the early centuries of the Common Era, a modified form of Buddhism called Mahayana (Great Vehicle) had taken root in parts of India, proclaiming that help was available for the strenuous voyage. Buddhist thinkers developed the idea of *bodhisattvas*, spiritually developed people who postponed their own entry into nirvana in order to assist those who were still suffering. The Buddha himself became something of a god, and both earlier and future Buddhas were available to offer help. Elaborate descriptions of these supernatural beings, together with various levels of heavens and hells, transformed Buddhism into a popular religion of salvation. Furthermore, religious merit, leading to salvation, might now be earned by acts of piety and devotion, such as contributing to the support of a monastery, and that merit might be transferred to others. This was the Great Vehicle, allowing far more people to make the voyage across the river. (See the Visual Sources: Representations of the Buddha, pp. 227–35, for the evolution of Buddhism reflected in images.)

Hinduism as a Religion of Duty and Devotion

Strangely enough, Buddhism as a distinct religious practice ultimately died out in the land of its birth as it was reincorporated into a broader Hindu tradition, but it spread widely and flourished, particularly in its Mahayana form, in other parts of Asia. Buddhism declined in India perhaps in part because the mounting wealth of monasteries and the economic interests of their leading figures separated them from ordinary people. Competition from Islam after 1000 C.E. also may have played a role. The most important reason for Buddhism's decline in India, however, was the growth during the first millennium C.E. of a new kind of popular Hinduism, which the masses found more accessible than the elaborate sacrifices of the Brahmins or the philosophical speculations of intellectuals. Some scholars have seen this phase of Hinduism as a response to the challenge of Buddhism. Expressed in the widely known epic poems known as the *Mahabharata* and the *Ramayana*, this revived Hinduism indicated more clearly that action in the world and the detached performance of caste duties might also provide a path to liberation.

In the much-beloved Hindu text known as the *Bhagavad Gita* (see Document 5.2, pp. 219–21), the troubled warrior-hero Arjuna is in anguish over the necessity of killing his kinsmen as a decisive battle approaches. But he is assured by his charioteer Lord Krishna, an incarnation of the god Vishnu, that performing his duty as a warrior, and doing so selflessly without regard to consequences, is an act of devotion

■ **Change**
What new emphases characterized Hinduism as it responded to the challenge of Buddhism?

that would lead to "release from the shackles of repeated rebirth." This was not an invitation to militarism, but rather an affirmation that ordinary people, not just Brahmins, could also make spiritual progress by selflessly performing the ordinary duties of their lives: "The man who, casting off all desires, lives free from attachments, who is free from egoism, and from the feeling that this or that is mine, obtains tranquillity." Withdrawal and asceticism were not the only ways to moksha.

Also becoming increasingly prominent was yet another religious path—the way of devotion to one or another of India's many gods and goddesses. Beginning in south India and moving northward, this *bhakti* (worship) movement involved the intense adoration of and identification with a particular deity through songs, prayers, and rituals associated with the many cults that emerged throughout India. By far the most popular deities were Vishnu, the protector and preserver of creation and associated with mercy and goodness, and Shiva, representing the divine in its destructive aspect, but many others also had their followers. This proliferation of gods and goddesses, and of their *bhakti* cults, occasioned very little friction or serious religious conflict. "Hinduism," writes a leading scholar, "is essentially tolerant, and would rather assimilate than rigidly exclude."[8] This capacity for assimilation extended to an already-declining Buddhism, which for many people had become yet another cult worshipping yet another god. The Buddha in fact was incorporated into the Hindu pantheon as the ninth incarnation of Vishnu. By 1000 C.E., Buddhism had largely disappeared as a separate religious tradition within India.

Thus a constantly evolving and enormously varied South Asian religious tradition had been substantially transformed. An early emphasis on ritual sacrifice gave way to that of philosophical speculation, devotional worship, and detached action in the world. In the process, that tradition had generated Buddhism, which became the first of the great universal religions of world history, and then had absorbed that new religion back into the fold of an emerging popular Hinduism.

Moving toward Monotheism: The Search for God in the Middle East

Paralleling the evolution of Chinese and Indian cultural traditions was the movement toward a distinctive monotheistic religious tradition in the Middle East, which found expression in Persian Zoroastrianism and in Judaism. Neither of these religions themselves spread very widely, but the monotheism that they nurtured became the basis for both Christianity and Islam, which have shaped so much of world history over the past 2,000 years. Amid the proliferation of gods and spirits that had long characterized religious life throughout the ancient world, monotheism—the idea of a single supreme deity, the sole source of all creation and goodness—was a radical cultural innovation. That conception created the possibility of a universal religion, open to all of humankind, but it could also mean an exclusive and intolerant faith.

Zoroastrianism

During the glory years of the powerful Persian Empire, a new religion arose to challenge the polytheism of earlier times. Tradition dates its Persian prophet, Zarathustra (Zoroaster to the Greeks), to the sixth or seventh century B.C.E., although some scholars place him hundreds of years earlier. Whenever he actually lived, his ideas took hold in Persia and received a degree of state support during the Achaemenid dynasty (558–330 B.C.E.). Appalled by the endemic violence of recurring cattle raids, Zarathustra recast the traditional Persian polytheism into a vision of a single unique god, Ahura Mazda, who ruled the world and was the source of all truth, light, and goodness. This benevolent deity was engaged in a cosmic struggle with the forces of evil, embodied in an equivalent supernatural figure, Angra Mainyu. Ultimately this struggle would be decided in favor of Ahura Mazda, aided by the arrival of a final savior who would restore the world to its earlier purity and peace. At a day of judgment, those who had aligned with Ahura Mazda would be granted new resurrected bodies and rewarded with eternal life in Paradise. Those who had sided with evil and the "Lie" were condemned to everlasting punishment. Zoroastrian teaching thus placed great emphasis on the free will of humankind and the necessity for each individual to choose between good and evil.

The Zoroastrian faith achieved widespread support within the Persian heartland, although it also found adherents in other parts of the empire, such as Egypt, Mesopotamia, and Anatolia. Because it never became an active missionary religion, it did not spread widely beyond the region. Alexander the Great's invasion of the Persian Empire and the subsequent Greek-ruled Seleucid dynasty (330–155 B.C.E.) were disastrous for Zoroastrianism, as temples were plundered, priests slaughtered, and sacred writings burned. But the new faith managed to survive this onslaught and flourished again during the Parthian (247 B.C.E.–224 C.E.) and Sassanid (224–651 C.E.) dynasties. It was the arrival of Islam and an Arab empire that occasioned the final decline of Zoroastrianism in Persia, although a few believers fled to India, where they became known as Parsis ("Persians"). The Parsis have continued their faith into present times.

Like Buddhism, the Zoroastrian faith vanished from its place of origin, but unlike Buddhism, it did not spread beyond Persia in a recognizable form. Some elements of the Zoroastrian belief system, however, did become incorporated into other religious traditions. The presence of many Jews in the Persian Empire meant that they surely became aware of Zoroastrian ideas. Many of those ideas— including the conflict of God and an evil counterpart (Satan); the notion of a last judgment and resurrected bodies; and a belief in the final defeat of evil, the arrival of a savior (Messiah), and the remaking of the world at the end of time—found a place in an evolving Judaism. Some of these teachings, especially the concepts of heaven and hell, later became prominent in those enormously

■ **Connection**
What aspects of Zoroastrianism and Judaism subsequently found a place in Christianity and Islam?

Zoroastrian Fire Altar
Representing the energy of the Creator God Ahura Mazda, the fire altar became an important symbol of Zoroastrianism and was often depicted on Persian coins in association with images of Persian rulers. This particular coin dates from the third century C.E. (©AAAC/Topham/The Image Works)

influential successors to Judaism—Christianity and Islam.[9] Thus the Persian tradition of Zoroastrianism continued to echo well beyond its disappearance in the land of its birth.

Judaism

■ **Description**
What was distinctive about the Jewish religious tradition?

While Zoroastrianism emerged in the greatest empire of its time, Judaism, the Middle East's other ancient monotheistic tradition, was born among one of the region's smaller and, at the time, less significant peoples—the Hebrews. Their traditions, recorded in the Old Testament, tell of an early migration from Mesopotamia to Palestine under the leadership of Abraham. Those same traditions report that a portion of these people later fled to Egypt, where they were first enslaved and then miraculously escaped to rejoin their kinfolk in Palestine. There, around 1000 B.C.E., they established a small state, which soon split into two parts—a northern kingdom called Israel and a southern state called Judah.

In a region politically dominated by the large empires of Assyria, Babylon, and Persia, these tiny Hebrew communities lived a precarious existence. Israel was conquered by Assyria in 722 B.C.E., and many of its inhabitants were deported to distant regions, where they assimilated into the local culture. In 586 B.C.E., the kingdom of Judah likewise came under Babylonian control, and its elite class was shipped off to exile. In Babylon, these people, now calling themselves Jews, retained their cultural identity and later were able to return to their homeland. A large part of that identity lay in their unique religious ideas. It was in creating that religious tradition, rather than in building a powerful empire, that this small people cast a long shadow in world history.

From their unique historical experience of exodus from Egypt and exile in Babylon, the Jews evolved over many centuries a distinctive conception of God. Unlike the peoples of Mesopotamia, India, Greece, and elsewhere—all of whom populated the invisible realm with numerous gods and goddesses—the Jews found in their God, whom they called Yahweh, a powerful and jealous deity, who demanded their exclusive loyalty. "Thou shalt have no other gods before me"—this was the first of the Ten Commandments. It was a difficult requirement, for as the Jews turned from a pastoral life to agriculture, many of them were continually attracted by the fertility gods of neighboring peoples. Their neighbors' goddesses also were attractive, offering a kind of spiritual support that the primarily masculine Yahweh could not. This was not quite monotheism, for the repeated demands of the Hebrew prophets to turn away from other gods show that those deities remained real for many Jews. Over time, however, Yahweh triumphed. The Jews came to understand their relationship to him as a contract or a covenant. In return for their sole devotion and obedience, Yahweh would consider the Jews his chosen people, favoring them in battle, causing them to grow in numbers, and bringing them prosperity and blessing.

Ancient Israel

Unlike the bickering, arbitrary, polytheistic gods of Mesopotamia or ancient Greece, which were associated with the forces of nature and behaved in quite human fashion, Yahweh was increasingly seen as a lofty, transcendent deity of utter holiness and purity, set far above the world of nature, which he had created. But unlike the impersonal conceptions of ultimate reality found in Daoism and Hinduism, Yahweh was encountered as a divine person with whom people could actively communicate. He also acted within the historical process, bringing the Jews out of Egypt or using foreign empires to punish them for their disobedience.

Furthermore, Yahweh was transformed from a god of war, who ordered his people to "utterly destroy" the original inhabitants of the Promised Land, to a god of social justice and compassion for the poor and the marginalized, especially in the passionate pronouncements of Jewish prophets such as Amos and Isaiah. The prophet Isaiah describes Yahweh as rejecting the empty rituals of his chosen but sinful people: "What to me is the multitude of your sacrifices, says the Lord. . . . Wash yourselves, make yourselves clean, . . . cease to do evil, learn to do good; seek justice; correct oppression; defend the fatherless; plead for the widow."[10]

Here was a distinctive conception of the divine—singular, transcendent, personal, separate from nature, engaged in history, and demanding social justice and moral righteousness above sacrifices and rituals. This set of ideas sustained a separate Jewish identity in both ancient and modern times, and it was this understanding of God that provided the foundation on which both Christianity and Islam were built.

The Cultural Tradition of Classical Greece: The Search for a Rational Order

Unlike the Jews, the Persians, or the civilization of India, Greek thinkers of the classical era generated no lasting religious tradition of world historical importance. The religion of these city-states brought together the unpredictable, quarreling, and lustful gods of Mount Olympus, secret fertility cults, oracles predicting the future, and the ecstatic worship of Dionysus, the god of wine. The distinctive feature of the classical Greek cultural tradition was the willingness of many Greek intellectuals to abandon this mythological framework, to affirm that the world was a physical reality governed by natural laws, and to assert that human rationality could both understand these laws and work out a system of moral and ethical life. In separating science and philosophy from conventional religion, the Greeks developed a way of thinking that bore some similarity to the secularism of Confucian thought in China.

Precisely why Greek thought evolved in this direction is hard to say. Perhaps the diversity and incoherence of Greek religious mythology presented its intellectuals with a challenge to bring some order to their understanding of the world. Greece's geographic position on the margins of the great civilizations of Mesopotamia,

■ **Description**

What are the distinctive features of the Greek intellectual tradition?

Egypt, and Persia certainly provided intellectual stimulation. Furthermore, the growing role of law in the political life of Athens possibly suggested that a similar regularity also underlay the natural order.

The Greek Way of Knowing

The Death of Socrates
Condemned to death by an Athenian jury, Socrates declined to go into exile, voluntarily drank a cup of poison hemlock, and died in 399 B.C.E. in the presence of his friends. The dramatic scene was famously described by Plato and much later was immortalized on canvas by the French painter Jacques-Louis David in 1787. (Image copyright © The Metropolitan Museum of Art/Art Resource, NY)

The foundations of this Greek rationalism emerged in the three centuries between 600 and 300 B.C.E., coinciding with the flourishing of Greek city-states, especially Athens, and with the growth of its artistic, literary, and theatrical traditions. The enduring significance of Greek thinking lay not so much in the answers it provided to life's great issues, for the Greeks seldom agreed with one another, but rather in its way of asking questions. Its emphasis on argument, logic, and the relentless questioning of received wisdom; its confidence in human reason; its enthusiasm for puzzling out the world without much reference to the gods—these were the defining characteristics of the Greek cultural tradition.

The great exemplar of this approach to knowledge was Socrates (469–399 B.C.E.), an Athenian philosopher who walked about the city engaging others in conversation about the good life. He wrote nothing, and his preferred manner of teaching was not the lecture or exposition of his own ideas but rather a constant questioning of the

assumptions and logic of his students' thinking. Concerned always to puncture the pretentious, he challenged conventional ideas about the importance of wealth and power in living well, urging instead the pursuit of wisdom and virtue. He was critical of Athenian democracy and on occasion had positive things to say about Sparta, the great enemy of his own city. Such behavior brought him into conflict with city authorities, who accused him of corrupting the youth of Athens and sentenced him to death. At his trial, he defended himself as the "gadfly" of Athens, stinging its citizens into awareness. To any and all, he declared, "I shall question, and examine and cross-examine him, and if I find that he does not possess virtue, but says he does, I shall rebuke him for scorning the things that are most important and caring more for what is of less worth."[11] (See Document 5.3, pp. 221–23, for a more extensive excerpt from this famous speech.)

The earliest of the classical Greek thinkers, many of them living on the Ionian coast of Anatolia, applied this rational and questioning way of knowing to the world of nature. For example, Thales, drawing on Babylonian astronomy, predicted an eclipse of the sun and argued that the moon simply reflected the sun's light. He also was one of the first Greeks to ask about the fundamental nature of the universe and came up with the idea that water was the basic stuff from which all else derived, for it existed as solid, liquid, and gas. Others argued in favor of air or fire or some combination. Democritus suggested that atoms, tiny "uncuttable" particles, collided in various configurations to form visible matter. Pythagoras believed that beneath the chaos and complexity of the visible world lay a simple, unchanging mathematical order. What these thinkers had in common was a commitment to a rational and nonreligious explanation for the material world.

Such thinking also served to explain the functioning of the human body and its diseases. Hippocrates and his followers came to believe that the body was composed of four fluids, or "humors," which, when out of proper balance, caused various ailments. He also traced the origins of epilepsy, known to the Greeks as "the sacred disease," to simple heredity: "It is thus with regard to the disease called sacred: it appears to me to be nowise more divine nor more sacred than other diseases, but has a natural cause . . . like other afflictions."[12] The Hippocratic Oath taken by all new doctors is named for this ancient Greek scientist.

A similar approach informed Greek thinking about the ways of humankind. Herodotus, who wrote about the Greco-Persian Wars, explained his project as an effort to discover "the reason why they fought one another." This assumption that human reasons lay behind the conflict, not simply the whims of the gods, was what made Herodotus a historian in the modern sense of that word. Ethics and government also figured importantly in Greek thinking. Plato (429–348 B.C.E.) famously sketched out in *The Republic* a design for a good society. It would be ruled by a class of highly educated "guardians" led by a "philosopher-king." Such people would be able to penetrate the many illusions of the material world and to grasp the "world of forms," in which ideas such as goodness, beauty, and justice lived a real and unchanging existence. Only such people, he argued, were fit to rule.

Aristotle (384–322 B.C.E.), a student of Plato and a teacher of Alexander the Great, was perhaps the most complete expression of the Greek way of knowing, for he wrote or commented on practically everything. With an emphasis on empirical observation, he cataloged the constitutions of 158 Greek city-states, identified hundreds of species of animals, and wrote about logic, physics, astronomy, the weather, and much else besides. Famous for his reflections on ethics, he argued that "virtue" was a product of rational training and cultivated habit and could be learned. As to government, he urged a mixed system, combining the principles of monarchy, aristocracy, and democracy.

The Greek Legacy

The rationalism of the Greek tradition was clearly not the whole of Greek culture. The gods of Mount Olympus continued to be a reality for many people, and the ecstatic songs and dances that celebrated Dionysus, the god of wine, were anything but rational and reflective. The death of Socrates at the hands of an Athenian jury showed that philosophy could be a threat as well as an engaging pastime. Nonetheless, Greek rationalism, together with Greek art, literature, and theater, persisted long after the glory days of Athens were over. The Roman Empire facilitated the spread of Greek culture within the Mediterranean basin, and not a few leading Roman figures sent their children to be educated in Athens at the Academy, which Plato had founded. An emerging Christian theology was expressed in terms of Greek philosophical concepts, especially those of Plato. Even after the western Roman Empire collapsed, classical Greek texts were preserved in the eastern half, known as Byzantium (see Chapter 10).

In the West, however, direct access to Greek texts was far more difficult in the chaotic conditions of post-Roman Europe, and for centuries classical scholarship was neglected in favor of Christian writers. Much of that legacy was subsequently rediscovered after the twelfth century C.E. as European scholars gained access to classical Greek texts. From that point on, the Greek legacy has been viewed as a central element of an emerging "Western" civilization. It played a role in formulating an updated Christian theology, in fostering Europe's Scientific Revolution, and in providing a point of departure for much of European philosophy.

Long before this European rediscovery, the Greek legacy had also entered Islamic culture. Systematic translations of Greek works of science and philosophy into Arabic, together with Indian and Persian learning, stimulated Muslim thinkers and scientists, especially in the fields of medicine, astronomy, mathematics, geography, and chemistry. It was in fact largely from Arabic translations of Greek writers that Europeans became reacquainted with the legacy of classical Greece, especially during the twelfth and thirteenth centuries. Despite the many centuries that have passed since the flourishing of classical Greek culture, that tradition has remained, especially in the West, an inspiration for those who celebrate the powers of the human mind to probe the mysteries of the universe and to explore the equally challenging domain of human life.

Snapshot   **Reflections on Human Love from Mediterranean Civilization**

From the Jews: The Song of Solomon

My beloved speaks and says to me: "Arise my love, my fair one, and come away; for lo, the winter is past; the rain is over and gone. The flowers appear on the earth; the time of singing has come, and the voice of the turtle dove is heard in our land. The fig tree puts forth its figs; and the vines are in blossom; they give fragrance. Arise my love, my fair one, and come away."

From the Greeks: Fragments from Sappho of Lesbos

If you will come, I shall put out new pillows for you to rest on.
I was so happy. Believe me, I prayed that that night might be doubled for us.
Now I know why Eros, of all the progeny of Earth and Heaven, has been most dearly loved.

From the Romans: Ovid Giving Advice to a Young Man on the Art of Love

Add gifts of mind to bodily advantage. A frail advantage is beauty, that grows less as time draws on and is devoured by its own years. . . . O handsome youth, will soon come hoary hairs; soon will come furrows to make wrinkles in your body. Now make thee a soul that will abide, and add to it thy beauty; only that endures to the ultimate pyre. Nor let it be a slight care to cultivate your mind in the liberal arts, or to learn the two languages well. Ulysses was not comely, but he was eloquent; yet he fired two goddesses of the sea with love.

From the Christians: Saint Paul on Love: 1 Corinthians 13

Love is patient and kind; love is not jealous or boastful; it is not arrogant or rude. Love does not insist on its own way; it is not irritable or resentful; it does not rejoice at wrong, but rejoices in the right. Love bears all things, believes all things, hopes all things, endures all things. Love never ends. . . . So faith, hope and love abide, these three, but the greatest of these is love.

Comparing Jesus and the Buddha

About 500 years after the time of Confucius, the Buddha, Zarathustra, and Socrates, a young Jewish peasant/carpenter in the remote province of Judaea in the Roman Empire began a brief three-year career of teaching and miracle-working before he got in trouble with local authorities and was executed. In one of history's most unlikely stories, the teachings of that obscure man, barely noted in the historical records of the time, became the basis of the world's second great universal religion. This man, Jesus of Nazareth, and the religion of Christianity, which grew out of his life and teaching, had a dramatic impact on world history, similar to and often compared with that of India's Siddhartha Gautama, the Buddha.

■ **Comparison**

How would you compare the lives and teachings of Jesus and the Buddha? In what different ways did the two religions evolve after the deaths of their founders?

The Lives of the Founders

The family background of the two teachers could hardly have been more different. Gautama was born to royalty and luxury, whereas Jesus was a rural or small-town worker from a distinctly lower-class family. But both became spiritual seekers, mystics in their respective traditions, who claimed to have personally experienced another level of reality. Those powerful religious experiences provided the motivation for their life's work and the personal authenticity that attracted their growing band of followers.

Both were "wisdom teachers," challenging the conventional values of their time, urging the renunciation of wealth, and emphasizing the supreme importance of love or compassion as the basis for a moral life. The Buddha had instructed his followers in the practice of *metta*, or loving-kindness: "Just as a mother would protect her only child at the risk of her own life, even so, let [my followers] cultivate a boundless heart towards all beings."[13] In a similar vein during his famous Sermon on the Mount, Jesus told his followers: "You have heard that it was said 'Love your neighbor and hate your enemy,' but I tell you 'Love your enemies and pray for those who persecute you.'"[14] Both Jesus and the Buddha called for the personal transformation of their followers, through "letting go" of the grasping that causes suffering, in the Buddha's teaching, or "losing one's life in order to save it," in the language of Jesus.[15]

Despite these similarities, there were also some differences in their teachings and their life stories. Jesus inherited from his Jewish tradition an intense devotion to a single personal deity with whom he was on intimate terms, referring to him as *Abba* ("papa" or "daddy"). According to the New Testament, the miracles he performed reflected the power of God available to him as a result of that relationship. The Buddha's original message, by contrast, largely ignored the supernatural, involved no miracles, and taught a path of intense self-effort aimed at ethical living and mindfulness as a means of ending suffering. Furthermore, Jesus' teachings had a sharper social and political edge than did those of the Buddha. Jesus spoke more clearly on behalf of the poor and the oppressed, directly criticized the hypocrisies of the powerful, and deliberately associated with lepers, adulterous women, and tax collectors, all of whom were regarded as "impure." In doing so, Jesus reflected his own lower-class background, the Jewish tradition of social criticism, and the reality of Roman imperial rule over his people, none of which corresponded to the Buddha's experience. Finally, Jesus' public life was very brief, probably less than three years, compared to more than forty years for the Buddha. His teachings had so antagonized both Jewish and Roman authorities that he was crucified as a common criminal. The Buddha's message was apparently less threatening to the politically powerful, and he died a natural death at age eighty.

■ **Change**
In what ways was Christianity transformed in the five centuries following the death of Jesus?

Establishing New Religions

It seems likely that neither Jesus nor the Buddha had any intention of founding a new religion; rather, they sought to reform the traditions from which they had come. Nonetheless, Christianity and Buddhism soon emerged as separate religions, distinct from Judaism and Hinduism, proclaiming their messages to a much wider and more inclusive audience. In the process, both teachers were transformed by their followers into gods. According to many scholars, Jesus never claimed divine status, seeing himself as a teacher or a prophet, whose close relationship to God could be imitated by anyone.[16] The Buddha likewise viewed himself as an enlightened but fully human person, an example of what was possible for anyone who followed the path. But in Mahayana Buddhism, the Buddha became a supernatural being who could be worshipped and prayed to and was spiritually available to his followers. Jesus too soon became divine in the eyes of his followers, "the Son of God, Very God of Very God," according to one of the creeds of the early Church, while his death and resurrection made possible the forgiveness of sins and the eternal salvation of those who believed.

The transformation of Christianity from a small Jewish sect to a world religion began with Saint Paul (10–65 C.E.), an early convert whose missionary journeys in the eastern Roman Empire led to the founding of small Christian communities that included non-Jews. The Good News of Jesus, Paul argued, was for everyone, and Gentile (non-Jewish) converts need not follow Jewish laws or rituals such as circumcision. In one of his many letters to these new communities, later collected as part of the New Testament, Paul wrote, "There is neither Jew nor Greek . . . neither slave nor free . . . neither male nor female, for you are all one in Christ Jesus."[17] Despite Paul's egalitarian pronouncement, early Christianity, like Buddhism, reflected prevailing patriarchal values, even as they both offered women new opportunities. Although women apparently played leadership roles in the "house churches" of the first century C.E., Paul counseled women to "be subject to your husbands" and declared that "it is shameful for a woman to speak in church."[18]

Nonetheless, the inclusive message of early Christianity was one of the attractions of the new faith as it spread very gradually within the Roman Empire during the several centuries after Jesus' death. The earliest converts were usually lower-stratum people—artisans, traders, and a considerable number of women—mostly from towns and cities, while a scattering of wealthier, more prominent, and better-educated people subsequently joined the ranks of Christians.[19] The spread of the faith was often accompanied by reports of miracles, healings, and the casting out of demons—all of which were impressive to people thoroughly accustomed to seeing the supernatural behind the

Women in the Early Church
This third-century C.E. fresco from a Roman catacomb is called the *Fractio Panis,* "the breaking of the bread" or Holy Communion. Some scholars argue that the figures are those of women, suggesting that women held priestly office in the early Church and were only later excluded from it. (Scala/Art Resource, NY)

events of ordinary life.[20] Christian communities also attracted converts by the way their members cared for one another. In the middle of the third century C.E., the church in Rome supported 154 priests (of whom 52 were exorcists) and some 1,500 widows, orphans, and destitute people.[21] By 300 C.E., perhaps 10 percent of the Roman Empire's population (some 5 million people) identified themselves as Christians.

In the Roman world, the strangest and most offensive feature of the new faith was its exclusive monotheism and its antagonism to all other supernatural powers, particularly the cult of the emperors. Christians' denial of these other gods caused them to be tagged as "atheists" and was one reason behind the empire's intermittent persecution of Christians during the first three centuries of the Common Era. All of that ended with Emperor Constantine's conversion in the early fourth century C.E. and with growing levels of state support for the new religion in the decades that followed.

Roman rulers sought to use an increasingly popular Christianity as glue to hold together a very diverse population in a weakening imperial state. Constantine and his successors thus provided Christians with newfound security and opportunities. The emperor Theodosius (reigned 379–395 C.E.) enforced a ban on all polytheistic ritual sacrifices and ordered their temples closed. Christians by contrast received patronage for their buildings, official approval for their doctrines, suppression of their rivals, prestige from imperial recognition, and, during the late fourth century, the proclamation of Christianity as the official state religion. All of this set in motion a process by which the Roman Empire, and later all of Europe, became overwhelmingly Christian. Beyond the Roman world, the new religion also found a home in various parts of Africa, the Middle East, and Asia (see Map 5.1).

The situation in India was quite different. Even though Ashoka's support gave Buddhism a considerable boost, it was never promoted to the exclusion of other faiths. Ashoka sought harmony among India's diverse population through religious tolerance rather than uniformity. The kind of monotheistic intolerance that Christianity exhibited was quite foreign to Indian patterns of religious practice. Although Buddhism subsequently died out in India as it was absorbed into a reviving Hinduism, no renewal of Roman polytheism occurred, and Christianity became an enduring element of European civilization. Nonetheless, Christianity did adopt some elements of religious practice from the Roman world, including perhaps the cult of saints and the dating of the birth of Jesus to the winter solstice. In both cases, however, these new religions spread widely beyond their places of origin. Buddhism provided a network of cultural connections in much of Asia, and Christianity did the same for western Eurasia and parts of Africa.

Creating Institutions

As Christianity spread within the Roman Empire and beyond, it developed a hierarchical organization, with patriarchs, bishops, and priests—all men—replacing

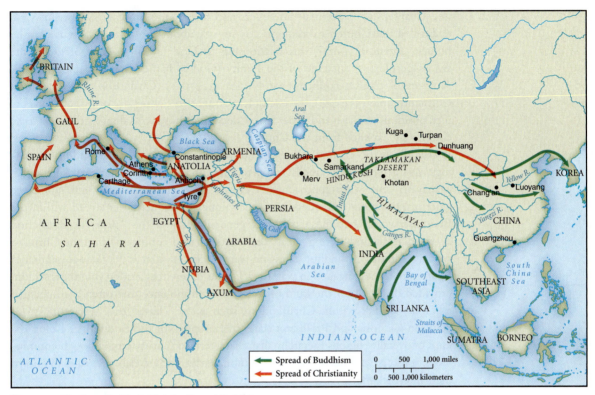

Map 5.1   The Spread of Early Christianity and Buddhism
In the five centuries after the birth of Jesus, Christianity found converts from Spain to northeast Africa, Central Asia, and India. In the Roman Empire, Axum, and Armenia, the new religion enjoyed state support as well. Subsequently Christianity took root solidly in Europe and after 1000 C.E. in Russia as well. Meanwhile, Buddhism was spreading from its South Asian homeland to various parts of Asia, even as it was weakening in India itself.

the house churches of the early years, in which women played a more prominent part. At least in some places, however, women continued to exercise leadership and even priestly roles, prompting Pope Gelasius in 494 to speak out sharply against those who encouraged women "to officiate at the sacred altars, and to take part in all matters imputed to the offices of the male sex, to which they do not belong."[22] In general, though, the exclusion of women from the priesthood established a male-dominated clergy and a patriarchal church, which has lasted into the twenty-first century.

This emerging hierarchical structure of the Church, together with its monotheistic faith, also generated a great concern for unity in matters of doctrine and practice. The bishop of Rome gradually emerged as the dominant leader, or pope, of the Church in the western half of the empire, but this role was not recognized in the east. This division contributed to the later split between Roman Catholic and Eastern Orthodox branches of Christendom, a schism that continues to the present (see Chapter 10). Doctrinal differences also tore at the unity of Christianity and embroiled the Church in frequent controversy about the nature of Jesus (was he human, divine, or both?), his relationship to God (equal or inferior?), and the always-perplexing doctrine of the Trinity (God as Father, Son, and Holy Spirit). A series of church councils—at Nicaea (325 C.E.), Chalcedon (451 C.E.), and Constantinople (553 C.E.), for example—sought to define an "orthodox," or correct, position on these and other issues, declaring those who disagreed as *anathema*, completely expelled from the Church.

Buddhists too clashed over their various interpretations of the Buddha's teachings, and a series of councils failed to prevent the division between Theravada, Mahayana, and other approaches. A considerable proliferation of different sects, practices, teachings, and meditation techniques subsequently emerged within the Buddhist world, but these divisions generally lacked the "clear-cut distinction between 'right' and 'wrong' ideas" that characterized conflicts within the Christian world.[23] Although Buddhist states and warrior classes (such as the famous samurai of Japan) sometimes engaged in warfare, religious differences among Buddhists seldom provided the basis for the kind of bitterness and violence that often accompanied religious conflict within Christendom, such as the Thirty Years' War (1618–1648) between Catholic and Protestant states in Europe. Nor did Buddhists develop the kind of overall religious hierarchy that characterized Christianity, although communities of monks and nuns, organized in monasteries, created elaborate rules to govern their internal affairs.

Reflections: Religion and Historians

To put it mildly, religion has always been a sensitive subject, and no less so for historians than for anyone else. For believers or followers of particular traditions, religion partakes of another world—that of the sacred or the divine—which is not accessible to historians or other scholars, who depend on evidence available in this world. This situation has generated various tensions or misunderstandings between historians and religious practitioners.

One of these tensions involves the question of change. Most religions present themselves as timeless, partaking of eternity or at least reflecting ancient practice. In the eyes of historians, however, the religious aspect of human life changes as much as any other. The Hindu tradition changed from a religion of ritual and sacrifice to one of devotion and worship. Buddhism became more conventionally religious, with an emphasis on the supernatural, as it evolved from Theravada to Mahayana forms. A male-dominated hierarchical Christian Church, with its pope, bishops, priests, and state support, was very different from the small house churches that suffered persecution by imperial authorities in the early Christian centuries. The implication—that religions are at least in part a human phenomenon—has been troublesome to some believers.

Historians, on the other hand, have sometimes been uncomfortable in the face of claims by believers that they have actually experienced a divine reality. Some secular scholars have been inclined to dismiss such claims as unprovable at best. Even the biographical details of the lives of the Buddha and Jesus are difficult to prove by the standards of historians. Certainly, modern historians are in no position to validate or refute the spiritual claims of these teachers, but we need to take them seriously. Although we will never know precisely what happened to the Buddha as he sat in meditation in northern India or what transpired when Jesus spent forty days in the wilderness, clearly those experiences changed the two men and motivated their subsequent actions. Later, Muhammad likewise claimed to have received revelations from God in the caves outside Mecca. Millions of the followers of these religious leaders have also acted on the basis of what they perceived to be an encounter with the divine or other levels of reality. This interior dimension of human experience, though difficult to grasp with any precision, has been a significant mover and shaper of the historical process.

Yet a third problem arises from debates within particular religious traditions about which group most accurately represents the "real" or authentic version of the faith. Historians usually refuse to take sides in such disputes. They simply notice with interest that most human cultural traditions generate conflicting views, some of which become the basis for serious conflict in their societies.

Reconciling personal religious convictions with the perspectives of modern historical scholarship is no easy task. At the very least, all of us can appreciate the immense human effort that has gone into the making of classical religious traditions, and we can acknowledge the enormous significance of these traditions in the unfolding of the human story. They have shaped the meanings that billions of people over thousands of years have attached to the world they inhabit. These religious traditions have justified the vast social inequalities and oppressive states of human civilizations, but they also have enabled human beings to endure those difficulties and on occasion have stimulated reform and rebellion. And they have guided much of humankind in our endless efforts to penetrate the mysteries of the world beyond and of the world within.

Second Thoughts

What's the Significance?

Legalism

Confucianism

Ban Zhao

Daoism

Vedas

Upanishads

Siddhartha Gautama (the
    Buddha)

Theravada/Mahayana

Bhagavad Gita

Zoroastrianism

Judaism

Greek rationalism

Socrates, Plato, Aristotle

Jesus of Nazareth

Saint Paul

To assess your mastery of the material in this chapter, visit the **Student Center** at bedfordstmartins.com/strayer.

Big Picture Questions

1. "Religions are fundamentally alike." Does the material in this chapter support or undermine this idea?
2. Is a secular outlook on the world an essentially modern phenomenon, or does it have precedents in the classical era?
3. "Religion is a double-edged sword, both supporting and undermining political authority and social elites." How would you support both sides of this statement?
4. How would you define the appeal of the religious/cultural traditions discussed in this chapter? To what groups were they attractive, and why?

Next Steps: For Further Study

For Web sites and additional documents related to this chapter, see **Make History** at bedfordstmartins.com/strayer.

Karen Armstrong, *The Great Transformation* (2006). A comparative and historical study of the major classical-era religions by a well-known scholar.

Peter Brown, *The Rise of Western Christendom* (2003). A history of the first 1,000 years of Christianity, cast in a global framework.

Don Johnson and Jean Johnson, *Universal Religions in World History* (2007). A comparative study of the historical development of Buddhism, Christianity, and Islam.

Huston Smith, *An Illustrated World's Religions* (1994). A sympathetic account of major world religions, beautifully illustrated, by a prominent scholar of comparative religion.

Arthur Waley, *Three Ways of Thought in Ancient China* (1983). A classic work, first published more than half a century ago, about the major philosophies of old China.

Jonathan S. Walters, *Finding Buddhists in Global History* (1998). A brief account that situates Buddhism in a world history framework.

"Religions of the World," http://www.mnsu.edu/emuseum/cultural/religion. A succinct and attractively illustrated introduction to six major world religious traditions.

Documents

Considering the Evidence:
The Good Life in Classical Eurasia

What constitutes a good life for an individual person? How can people live together in communities most effectively? These are among the central questions that have occupied human beings since the beginning of conscious thought. And they certainly played a major role in the emerging cultural traditions of the classical era all across Eurasia. The documents that follow present a sample of this thinking drawn from Confucian, Hindu, Greek, and Christian traditions.

Document 5.1

Reflections from Confucius

No one was more central to the making of classical Chinese culture than Confucius (551–479 B.C.E.). In the several generations following their master's death, his disciples recalled his teachings and his conversations, recording them in a small book called *The Analects*. This text became a touchstone for all educated people in China and across much of East Asia as well. Over the centuries, extensive commentaries and interpretations of Confucius's teachings gave rise to a body of literature known generally as Confucianism, though these ideas encompassed the thinking of many others as well.

In the translation that follows, the word "virtue" refers to the qualities of a complete or realized human being, sometimes referred to in Confucian literature as a "gentleman" or a "virtuous man."

- How would Confucius define such a person?

- How might one become this kind of person?

The terms "propriety" and "rites of propriety" point to an elaborate set of rituals or expectations that defined appropriate behavior in virtually every circumstance of life, depending on one's gender, age, or class.

- What role does propriety or ritual play in the making of a virtuous man?

- What understanding of "learning" or education comes through in this text?

- What is "filial piety" and why is it so important in Confucius's understanding of a good society?

- How do "virtue," "filial piety," and "learning" relate to the larger task of creating good government or a harmonious society?

- How does Confucius understand the role of the supernatural—gods, spirits, and ancestors for example?

CONFUCIUS

The Analects

ca. 479–221 B.C.E.

The philosopher Yu said, "They are few who, being filial and fraternal, are fond of offending against their superiors. There have been none, who, not liking to offend against their superiors, have been fond of stirring up confusion...."

The Master said, "To rule a country of a thousand chariots, there must be reverent attention to business, and sincerity; economy in expenditure, and love for men; and the employment of the people at the proper seasons."

The Master said, "A youth, when at home, should be filial, and, abroad, respectful to his elders. He should be earnest and truthful. He should overflow in love to all, and cultivate the friendship of the good. When he has time and opportunity, after the performance of these things, he should employ them in polite studies."

Tsze-hsia said, "If a man withdraws his mind from the love of [beautiful women], and applies it as sincerely to the love of the virtuous; if, in serving his parents, he can exert his utmost strength; if, in serving his prince, he can devote his life; if, in his intercourse with his friends, his words are sincere: although men say that he has not learned, I will certainly say that he has."

The philosopher Tsang said, "Let there be a careful attention to perform the funeral rites to parents, and let them be followed when long gone

with the ceremonies of sacrifice; then the virtue of the people will resume its proper excellence."

The Master said, "He who exercises government by means of his virtue may be compared to the north polar star, which keeps its place and all the stars turn toward it."

The Master said, "If the people be led by laws, and uniformity sought to be given them by punishments, they will try to avoid the punishment, but have no sense of shame. If they be led by virtue, and uniformity sought to be given them by the rules of propriety, they will have the sense of shame, and moreover will become good."

The Duke Ai asked, saying, "What should be done in order to secure the submission of the people?" Confucius replied, "Advance the upright and set aside the crooked, then the people will submit. Advance the crooked and set aside the upright, then the people will not submit."

Chi K'ang asked how to cause the people to reverence their ruler, to be faithful to him, and to go on to nerve themselves to virtue. The Master said, "Let him preside over them with gravity; then they will reverence him. Let him be final and kind to all; then they will be faithful to him. Let him advance the good and teach the incompetent; then they will eagerly seek to be virtuous."

The Master said, "If the will be set on virtue, there will be no practice of wickedness."

The Master said, "Riches and honors are what men desire. If they cannot be obtained in the proper way, they should not be held. Poverty and mean-

Source: Confucius, *The Analects*, translated by James Legge (1893).

ness are what men dislike. If they cannot be avoided in the proper way, they should not be avoided."

The Master said, "In serving his parents, a son may remonstrate with them, but gently; when he sees that they do not incline to follow his advice, he shows an increased degree of reverence, but does not abandon his purpose; and should they punish him, he does not allow himself to murmur."

Fan Ch'ih asked what constituted wisdom. The Master said, "To give one's self earnestly to the duties due to men, and, while respecting spiritual beings, to keep aloof from them, may be called wisdom."

The Master said, "The superior man, extensively studying all learning, and keeping himself under the restraint of the rules of propriety, may thus likewise not overstep what is right."

The Master's frequent themes of discourse were the Odes, the History, and the maintenance of the Rules of Propriety. On all these he frequently discoursed.

The Master was wishing to go and live among the nine wild tribes of the east. Some one said, "They are rude. How can you do such a thing?" The Master said, "If a superior man dwelt among them, what rudeness would there be?"

Chi Lu asked about serving the spirits of the dead. The Master said, "While you are not able to serve men, how can you serve their spirits?" Chi Lu added, "I venture to ask about death?" He was answered, "While you do not know life, how can you know about death?"

Yen Yuan asked about perfect virtue. The Master said, "To subdue one's self and return to propriety, is perfect virtue. If a man can for one day subdue himself and return to propriety, all under heaven will ascribe perfect virtue to him."

Chung-kung asked about perfect virtue. The Master said, "It is, when you go abroad, to behave to every one as if you were receiving a great guest; to employ the people as if you were assisting at a great sacrifice; not to do to others as you would not wish done to yourself; to have no murmuring against you in the country, and none in the family."

Chi K'ang asked Confucius about government. Confucius replied, "To govern means to rectify. If you lead on the people with correctness, who will dare not to be correct?"

Truly, if the ruler is not a ruler, the subject not a subject, the father not a father, the son not a son, then even if there be grain, would I get to eat it?

The Master said, "Of all people, girls and servants are the most difficult to behave to. If you are familiar with them, they lose their humility. If you maintain a reserve toward them, they are discontented."

Document 5.2

Reflections from the Hindu Scriptures

The flavor of Indian thinking about the good life and the good society is quite different from that of China. This distinctive outlook is reflected in these selections from the *Bhagavad Gita (The Song of the Lord)*, perhaps the most treasured of classical Hindu writings. Its dating is highly uncertain, although most scholars put it somewhere between the fifth and second centuries B.C.E. The *Bhagavad Gita* itself is an episode within the *Mahabharata*, one of the huge epic poems of India's classical tradition, which describes the struggle for power between two branches of the same family. The setting of the *Bhagavad Gita* takes places on the eve of a great battle in which the fearless warrior Arjuna is overcome with the realization that in this battle he will be required to kill some of his own kinsmen. In his distress he turns for advice to his charioteer, Lord Krishna, who is an incarnation of the great god Vishnu. Krishna's response to Arjuna's anguished questions, a part of which is reproduced here, conveys the essence of Hindu thinking about life and action in this world. A central question in the *Bhagavad Gita* is how a person can achieve spiritual fulfillment while remaining active in the world.

■ What is Krishna's answer to this dilemma?

■ What reasons does Krishna give for urging Arjuna to perform his duty as a warrior?

■ How does Krishna describe the good society?

■ What major themes of Hindu teaching can you find in this passage?

■ How does this text differ from that of *The Analects*? Are they asking the same questions? What similarities in outlook, if any, can you identify in these two texts?

Bhagavad Gita
ca. Fifth to Second Century B.C.E.

The deity said, you have grieved for those who deserve no grief.... Learned men grieve not for the living nor the dead. Never did I not exist, nor you, nor these rulers of men; nor will any one of us ever hereafter cease to be. As in this body, infancy and youth and old age come to the embodied self, so does the acquisition of another body; a sensible man is not deceived about that. The contacts of the senses...which produce cold and heat, pleasure and pain, are not permanent, they are ever coming and going. Bear them, O descendant of Bharata!

He who thinks it [a person's soul, or *atman*] to be the killer and he who thinks it to be killed, both know nothing. It kills not, [and] is not killed. It is not born, nor does it ever die, nor, having existed, does it exist no more. Unborn, everlasting, unchangeable, and primeval, it is not killed when the body is killed.... As a man, casting off old clothes, puts on others and new ones, so the embodied self, casting off old bodies, goes to others and new ones.... It is everlasting, all-pervading, stable, firm, and eternal.

It is said to be unperceived, to be unthinkable, to be unchangeable. Therefore, knowing it to be such, you ought not to grieve.... For to one that is born, death is certain; and to one that dies, birth is certain....

Having regard to your own duty also, you ought not to falter, for there is nothing better for a Kshatriya° than a righteous battle. Happy those Kshatriyas, O son of Pritha! who can find such a battle...an open door to heaven! But if you will not fight this righteous battle, then you will have abandoned your own duty and your fame, and you will incur sin....

Your business is with action alone, not by any means with fruit. Let not the fruit of action be your motive to action. Let not your attachment be fixed on inaction. Having recourse to devotion...perform actions, casting off all attachment, and being equable in success or ill-success; such equability is called devotion.... The wise who have obtained devotion cast off the fruit of action, and released from the shackles of repeated births, repair to that seat where there is no unhappiness....

The man who, casting off all desires, lives free from attachments, who is free from egoism and from

Source: Tashinath Trimbak Teland, trans., *The Bhagavad Gita*, in Max Mueller, ed., *The Sacred Books of the East*, 50 vols. (Oxford; Clarendon Press, 1879–1910), 8:43–46, 48–49, 51–52, 126–28.

°**Kshatriya:** a member of the warrior/ruler caste.

the feeling that this or that is mine, obtains tranquility. This, O son of Pritha! is the Brahmic state. Attaining to this, one is never deluded, and remaining in it in one's last moments, one attains the Brahmic bliss [*nirvana*, or merging with the divine]....

I have passed through many births, O Arjuna! and you also. I know them all, but you...do not know them....Whensoever, O descendant of Bharata! piety languishes, and impiety is in the ascendant, I create myself. I am born age after age, for the protection of the good, for the destruction of evil-doers, and the establishment of piety....

The fourfold division of castes was created by me according to the appointment of qualities and duties....The duties of Brahmins, Kshatriyas, and Vaisyas, and of Sudras, too...are distinguished according to the qualities born of nature. Tranquillity, restraint of the senses, penance, purity, forgiveness, straightforwardness, also knowledge, experience, and belief in a future world, this is the natural duty of Brahmins. Valor, glory, courage, dexterity, not slinking away from battle, gifts, exercise of lordly power, this is the natural duty of Kshatriyas. Agriculture, tending cattle, trade, this is the natural duty of Vaisyas. And the natural duty of Sudras, too, consists in service.

Every man intent on his own respective duties obtains perfection. Listen, now, how one intent on one's own duty obtains perfection. Worshipping, by the performance of his own duty, him from whom all things proceed, and by whom all this is permeated, a man obtains perfection. One's duty, though defective, is better than another's duty well performed. Performing the duty prescribed by nature, one does not incur sin. O son of Kunti! one should not abandon a natural duty though tainted with evil; for all actions are enveloped by evil, as fire by smoke.

One who is self-restrained, whose understanding is unattached everywhere, from whom affections have departed, obtains the supreme perfection of freedom from action by renunciation. Learn from me, only in brief, O son of Kunti! how one who has obtained perfection attains the Brahman, which is the highest culmination of knowledge. A man possessed of a pure understanding, controlling his self by courage, discarding sound and other objects of sense, casting off affection and aversion, who frequents clean places, who eats little, whose speech, body, and mind are restrained, who is always intent on meditation and mental abstraction, and has recourse to unconcern, who, abandoning egoism, stubbornness, arrogance, desire, anger, and all belongings, has no thought that this or that is mine, and who is tranquil, becomes fit for assimilation with the Brahman.

Document 5.3

Reflections from Socrates

Document 5.3 comes from the tradition of Greek rationalism. The excerpt is from Socrates' famous defense of himself before a jury of 501 fellow Athenians in 399 B.C.E., as recorded by Plato, Socrates' student and disciple. Charged with impiety and corrupting the youth of the city, Socrates was narrowly condemned to death by that jury. His speech at the trial has come to be viewed as a powerful defense of intellectual freedom and the unfettered life of the mind.

■ How does Socrates respond to the charges laid against him?

■ How might Socrates define "the good life"? How does he understand "wisdom" and "virtue"? Do you think that Confucius and Socrates would agree about the nature of "virtue"?

- Why does Socrates believe he has been useful to Athens?

- What do his frequent references to God reveal about his understanding of the supernatural and its relevance to social life?

- Why did he accept the death penalty and refuse to consider a lesser sentence? (See the photo on p. 206.)

PLATO

Apology

ca. 399 B.C.E.

I will begin at the beginning, and ask what the accusation is which has given rise to this slander of me.... What do the slanderers say?... "Socrates is an evil-doer, and a curious person, who searches into things under the earth and in heaven, and he makes the worse appear the better cause; and he teaches the aforesaid doctrines to others...."

I found that the men most in repute were all but the most foolish; and that some inferior men were really wiser and better....

O men of Athens,... God only is wise;... the wisdom of men is little or nothing;... And so I go my way, obedient to the god, and make inquisition into the wisdom of anyone, whether citizen or stranger, who appears to be wise; and if he is not wise, then... I show him that he is not wise; and this occupation quite absorbs me....

There is another thing: young men of the richer classes, who have not much to do, come about me of their own accord; they like to hear the pretenders examined, and they often imitate me, and examine others themselves; there are plenty of persons, as they soon enough discover, who think that they know something, but really know little or nothing: and then those who are examined by them instead of being angry with themselves are angry with me: This confounded Socrates, they say; this villainous misleader of youth!... [T]hey repeat the ready-made charges which are used against all philosophers about teaching things up in the clouds and under the earth, and having no gods, and making the worse appear the better cause; for they do not like to confess that their pretence of knowledge has been detected....

Someone will say: And are you not ashamed, Socrates, of a course of life which is likely to bring you to an untimely end? To him I may fairly answer: There you are mistaken: a man who is good for anything ought not to calculate the chance of living or dying; he ought only to consider whether in doing anything he is doing right or wrong, acting the part of a good man or of a bad.... Had Achilles° any thought of death and danger? For wherever a man's place is, whether the place which he has chosen or that in which he has been placed by a commander, there he ought to remain in the hour of danger; he should not think of death or of anything, but of disgrace....

And therefore if you let me go now, and... if you say to me, Socrates, this time we will... let you off, but upon one condition, that you are not to inquire and speculate in this way any more, and that if you are caught doing this again you shall die; if this was the condition on which you let me go, I should reply: Men of Athens, I honor and love you; but I shall obey God rather than you, and while I have life and strength I shall never cease from the practice and teaching of philoso-

---

Source: Plato, *Apology*, translated by Benjamin Jowett (1891).

°**Achilles:** the great warrior-hero of *The Illiad*.

phy, exhorting anyone whom I meet after my manner....I interrogate and examine and cross-examine him, and if I think that he has no virtue, but only says that he has, I reproach him with undervaluing the greater, and overvaluing the less....For I do nothing but go about persuading you all, old and young alike, not to take thought for your persons and your properties, but first and chiefly to care about the greatest improvement of the soul....Wherefore, O men of Athens, I say to you...either acquit me or not; but whatever you do, know that I shall never alter my ways, not even if I have to die many times....

[I]f you kill such a one as I am, you will injure yourselves more than you will injure me....For if you kill me you will not easily find another like me, who, if I may use such a ludicrous figure of speech, am a sort of gadfly, given to the state by the God; and the state is like a great and noble steed who is tardy in his motions owing to his very size, and requires to be stirred into life. I am that gadfly which God has given the state and all day long and in all places am always fastening upon you, arousing and persuading and reproaching you....I dare say that you may feel irritated at being suddenly awakened when you are caught napping; and you may think that if you were to strike me dead..., which you easily might, then you would sleep on for the remainder of your lives....

[After the jury finds Socrates guilty, he accepts the sentence of death, rejecting the alternative punishments of prison or exile.]

There are many reasons why I am not grieved, O men of Athens, at the vote of condemnation. The difficulty, my friends, is not in avoiding death, but in avoiding unrighteousness....

I am not angry with my accusers, or my condemners....Still I have a favor to ask of them. When my sons are grown up, I would ask you, O my friends, to punish them...if they seem to care about riches, or anything, more than about virtue; or if they pretend to be something when they are really nothing, then reprove them, as I have reproved you, for not caring about that for which they ought to care, and thinking that they are something when they are really nothing. And if you do this, I and my sons will have received justice at your hands.

The hour of departure has arrived, and we go our ways—I to die, and you to live. Which is better, God only knows.

Document 5.4

Reflections from Jesus

Like Confucius, Jesus apparently never wrote anything himself. His sayings and his actions were recorded in the Gospels by his followers. The Gospel of Matthew, from which this selection is taken, was composed during the second half of the first century C.E. For Christian people, this passage, known as the Sermon on the Mount, has long been among the most beloved of biblical texts, regarded as a guide for effective living and the core of Jesus' ethical and moral teachings. In this selection, Jesus contrasts the "broad road" of conventional understanding and values with the "narrow road that leads to life."

■ In what ways does his teaching challenge or contradict the conventional outlook of his time?

■ What criticisms does he make of those referred to as hypocrites, Pharisees, and the teachers of the law?

- How would you summarize "the good life" as Jesus might have defined it?

- How might Jesus and Confucius have responded to each other's teachings?

- What is Jesus' posture toward Jewish law?

- Beyond its use as a guide for personal behavior, what are the larger social implications of the Sermon on the Mount?

The Gospel of Matthew
ca. 70–100 C.E.

Now when he [Jesus] saw the crowds, he went up on a mountainside and sat down. His disciples came to him, and he began to teach them saying:

"Blessed are the poor in spirit, for theirs is the kingdom of heaven.

"Blessed are those who mourn, for they will be comforted.

"Blessed are the meek, for they will inherit the earth.

"Blessed are those who hunger and thirst for righteousness, for they will be filled.

"Blessed are the merciful, for they will be shown mercy.

"Blessed are the pure in heart, for they will see God.

"Blessed are the peacemakers, for they will be called sons of God.

"Blessed are those who are persecuted because of righteousness, for theirs is the kingdom of heaven.

"You are the salt of the earth. But if the salt loses its saltiness, how can it be made salty again? It is no longer good for anything, except to be thrown out and trampled by men.

"You are the light of the world. A city on a hill cannot be hidden. Neither do people light a lamp and put it under a bowl. Instead they put it on its stand, and it gives light to everyone in the house. In the same way, let your light shine before men, that they may see your good deeds and praise your Father in heaven.

"Do not think that I have come to abolish the Law or the Prophets; I have not come to abolish them but to fulfill them. I tell you the truth, until heaven and earth disappear, not the smallest letter, not the least stroke of a pen, will by any means disappear from the Law until everything is accomplished. Anyone who breaks one of the least of these commandments and teaches others to do the same will be called least in the kingdom of heaven, but whoever practices and teaches these commands will be called great in the kingdom of heaven. For I tell you that unless your righteousness surpasses that of the Pharisees and the teachers of the law, you will certainly not enter the kingdom of heaven.

"You have heard that it was said to the people long ago, 'Do not murder, and anyone who murders will be subject to judgment.' But I tell you that anyone who is angry with his brother will be subject to judgment....

"Therefore, if you are offering your gift at the altar and there remember that your brother has something against you, leave your gift there in front of the altar. First go and be reconciled to your brother; then come and offer your gift.

"Settle matters quickly with your adversary who is taking you to court. Do it while you are still with him on the way, or he may hand you over to

Source: Matthew 5–7 (New International Version).

the judge, and the judge may hand you over to the officer, and you may be thrown into prison. I tell you the truth, you will not get out until you have paid the last penny.

"You have heard that it was said, 'Do not commit adultery.' But I tell you that anyone who looks at a woman lustfully has already committed adultery with her in his heart....

"You have heard that it was said, 'Eye for eye, and tooth for tooth.' But I tell you, Do not resist an evil person. If someone strikes you on the right cheek, turn to him the other also. And if someone wants to sue you and take your tunic, let him have your cloak as well. If someone forces you to go one mile, go with him two miles. Give to the one who asks you, and do not turn away from the one who wants to borrow from you.

"You have heard that it was said, 'Love your neighbor and hate your enemy.' But I tell you: Love your enemies and pray for those who persecute you, that you may be sons of your Father in heaven. He causes his sun to rise on the evil and the good, and sends rain on the righteous and the unrighteous. If you love those who love you, what reward will you get? Are not even the tax collectors doing that? And if you greet only your brothers, what are you doing more than others? Do not even pagans do that? Be perfect, therefore, as your heavenly Father is perfect.

"Be careful not to do your 'acts of righteousness' before men, to be seen by them.... So when you give to the needy, do not announce it with trumpets, as the hypocrites do in the synagogues and on the streets, to be honored by men....But when you give to the needy, do not let your left hand know what your right hand is doing, so that your giving may be in secret. Then your Father, who sees what is done in secret, will reward you.

"And when you pray, do not be like the hypocrites, for they love to pray standing in the synagogues and on the street corners to be seen by men....But when you pray, go into your room, close the door and pray to your Father, who is unseen. Then your Father, who sees what is done in secret, will reward you. And when you pray, do not keep on babbling like pagans, for they think

they will be heard because of their many words. Do not be like them, for your Father knows what you need before you ask him....

"Do not store up for yourselves treasures on earth, where moth and rust destroy, and where thieves break in and steal. But store up for yourselves treasures in heaven, where moth and rust do not destroy, and where thieves do not break in and steal. For where your treasure is, there your heart will be also....

"So do not worry, saying, 'What shall we eat?' or 'What shall we drink?' or 'What shall we wear?' For the pagans run after all these things, and your heavenly Father knows that you need them. But seek first his kingdom and his righteousness, and all these things will be given to you as well. Therefore do not worry about tomorrow, for tomorrow will worry about itself. Each day has enough trouble of its own.

"Do not judge, or you too will be judged. For in the same way you judge others, you will be judged, and with the measure you use, it will be measured to you.

"Why do you look at the speck of sawdust in your brother's eye and pay no attention to the plank in your own eye? How can you say to your brother, 'Let me take the speck out of your eye,' when all the time there is a plank in your own eye? You hypocrite, first take the plank out of your own eye, and then you will see clearly to remove the speck from your brother's eye....

"Ask and it will be given to you; seek and you will find; knock and the door will be opened to you. For everyone who asks receives; he who seeks finds; and to him who knocks, the door will be opened.

"Enter through the narrow gate. For wide is the gate and broad is the road that leads to destruction, and many enter through it. But small is the gate and narrow the road that leads to life, and only a few find it...."

When Jesus had finished saying these things, the crowds were amazed at his teaching, because he taught as one who had authority, and not as their teachers of the law.

Using the Evidence:
The Good Life in Classical Eurasia

1. **Making comparisons:** In describing the "good life" or the "good society," what commonalities do you see among these four documents? What differences are apparent? How might the authors of each text respond to the ideas of the others?

2. **Placing texts in context:** In what ways was each of these texts reacting *against* the conventional wisdom of their times? How was each shaped by the social and political circumstances in which they were composed?

3. **Relating spirituality and behavior:** What is the relationship between religion (the transcendent realm of the gods or the divine) and moral behavior on earth in each of these documents? How does the "good life" relate to politics?

4. **Defining the "good person":** How do each of these texts characterize the superior person or the fully realized human being? How do they define personal virtue?

Visual Sources

Considering the Evidence:
Representations of the Buddha

Buddhism derived from a single individual, Siddhartha Gautama, born in northern India between the sixth and fourth centuries B.C.E. Legendary accounts of his life often begin with his miraculous conception and birth, as a sacred white elephant pierced his mother's side with its trunk. The son of royalty, the young Siddhartha enjoyed a splendid but sheltered upbringing encased in luxury, and his father spared no effort to protect the child from anything painful or difficult. At the age of sixteen, he was married to a beautiful cousin, Yasodhara, who bore him a son thirteen years later. But while riding beyond the palace grounds, this curious and lively young man encountered human suffering in the form of an old man, a sick person, and a corpse. Shattered by these revelations of aging, illness, and death, Siddhartha determined to find the cause of such sufferings and a remedy for them. And so, at the age of twenty-nine and on the very day his son was born, the young prince left his luxurious life as well as his wife and child, shed his royal jewels, cut off his hair, and set off on a quest for enlightenment. This act of severing his ties to the attachments of ordinary life is known in Buddhist teaching as the Great Renunciation.

What followed were six years of spiritual experimentation that finally led Siddhartha to a particular tree in northern India, where, legend tells us, he began a forty-nine-day period of intensive meditation. There he was assailed by that figure of temptation and illusion known as Mara, who sent demons, wild beasts, and his beautiful daughters to frighten or seduce Siddhartha from his quest. But his persistence was finally rewarded with the almost indescribable experience of full enlightenment. Now he was the Buddha, the man who had awakened.

For the next forty years, he taught what he had learned, setting in motion the cultural tradition we know as Buddhism. Over many centuries, the religion evolved, as it attracted growing numbers of converts and as it intersected with various cultures throughout Asia, including China, Japan, Tibet, Korea, and Vietnam. Those changes affected not only matters of doctrine and practice but also the images that expressed the core teachings of Buddhism.

For almost five centuries after his death, which likely took place in the early fifth century B.C.E., artists represented the Buddha as an empty throne, a horse with no rider, a tree, a wheel, or in some other symbolic way, while largely shunning any depiction of him in human form. No one knows precisely why. Regarding the Buddha as a fully human teacher and guide, perhaps they sought to prevent his being perceived as a divine figure that might be worshipped. On his deathbed, after all, he had counseled his followers: "Be a lamp unto yourselves. Work out your own salvation." But it was hardly a unique form of religious representation, for some Christians and almost all Muslims likewise declined to portray their prophetic figures in human terms.

Among the most widespread of these early symbolic representations of the Buddha were images of his footprints. Found throughout Buddhist Asia, such footprints indicated the Buddha's spiritual presence and served as a focus for devotion or contemplation. They also reminded his followers that since he had passed into *nirvana*, he could not be physically present. One Buddhist text declared that those who looked upon those footprints "shall be freed from the bonds of error, and conducted upon the Way of Enlightenment."[24]

Visual Source 5.1 shows a footprint image from northwestern India dating probably from the second century C.E. and containing a number of Buddhist symbols. In the center of each footprint is a *dharmachakra*, a wheel-like structure that had long symbolized the Buddha's teaching. Here, it surrounds a lotus flower, representing the Buddha's purity. Near the heel is a three-pronged emblem known as a *triratna*. It symbolizes the three things in which Buddhists can take refuge: the Buddha himself, his teaching, and the *sangha* (the Buddhist community). This particular footprint image also includes in the bottom corners two *yakshis*, Indian female earth spirits suggesting fertility. The position of their hands conveys a respectful greeting.

■ Why might the wheel serve as an effective symbol of the Buddha's message?

■ What does the inclusion of the *yakshis* add to the message of this image?

■ What overall religious message might this footprint convey to those who gazed upon it?

By the first century C.E., the impulse to depict the Buddha in human form had surfaced, with some of the earliest examples coming from the region of South Asia known as Gandhara in what is now northern Pakistan and eastern Afghanistan (see Map 4.3, p. 152). That area had been a part of the empire of Alexander the Great and his Hellenistic successors from about 322 B.C.E. to 50 B.C.E. and had developed commercial ties to the Roman Empire as well. These early images of the Buddha reflect this Greco-Roman influence, depicting him with a face similar to that of the Greek god Apollo, dressed in a Roman-style toga, and with curly hair characteristic of the Mediterranean region.

Visual Source 5.1 Footprints of the Buddha (Courtesy, John Eskanazi Ltd, London. Photo: A. C. Cooper N & P Ltd, London)

By the time of India's Gupta dynasty (320–550 C.E.), the Greco-Roman influence of the Gandhara style was fading, replaced by more completely Indian images of the Buddha, which became the "classic" model that spread widely across Asia. Visual Source 5.2 represents one such image, deriving from Bihar in eastern India during the sixth century C.E. Notice here the hand gestures known as *mudras*. The Buddha's right hand, for example, with palm facing the viewer, indicates reassurance, or "have no fear." The partially webbed fingers are among the *lakshanas*, or signs of a Buddha image, that denote the Buddha's unique status. So too is the knot on the top of his head, symbolizing enlightenment.

- What might account for the emergence of human images of the Buddha?

- What overall impression or religious meaning is this statue intended to convey?

Visual Source 5.2 A Classic Indian Buddha (Image copyright © The Metropolitan Museum of Art/Art Resource, NY)

■ The elongated earlobes remind the viewer that, earlier in his life, the prince Siddhartha had worn heavy and luxurious earrings. What does their absence suggest about his transformation as the Buddha?

■ Notice the partially closed and downcast eyes of the Buddha as well as his bare feet. What might these features of the image suggest?

Among the conditions favoring the proliferation of Buddha images in the early centuries of the Common Era was the growth of a new form of Buddhist belief and practice known as Mahayana (Great Vehicle). As the message of the Buddha gained a mass following in the several centuries after his death, some of its early features—rigorous and time-consuming meditation practice, a focus on monks and nuns withdrawn from ordinary life, the absence of accessible supernatural figures able to provide help and comfort—proved difficult for or beyond the reach of many converts. Expressed in various sects, practices, and schools of thought, Mahayana Buddhism offered a more accessible version of the faith, a spiritual path available to a much wider range of people beyond the monks and ascetics, who were the core group in early Buddhism.

In most expressions of Mahayana Buddhism, enlightenment (or becoming a Buddha), was available to everyone; it was possible within the context of ordinary life, rather than a monastery; and it might occur within a single life-time rather than over the course of many lives. While Buddhism had originally put a premium on spiritual wisdom, leading to liberation from rebirth and the achievement of nirvana, Mahayana expressions of the faith emphasized compassion—the ability to feel the sorrows of other people as if they were one's own. This compassionate religious ideal found expression in the notion of *bodhisattvas*, fully enlightened beings who postponed their own final liber-ation in order to assist a suffering humanity. They were spiritual beings, inter-mediaries between mortal humans and the Buddhas, whose countless images in sculpture or painting became objects of worship and sources of comfort and assistance to many Buddhists.

Across the world of Asian Mahayana Buddhism, the most widely popular of the many bodhisattva figures was that of Avalokitesvara, known in China as Guanyin and in Japan as Kannon. This Bodhisattva of Compassion, often portrayed as a woman or with distinctly feminine characteristics, was known as the "the one who hears the cries of the world." Calling upon him/her for assistance, devotees could be rescued from all kinds of danger and distress. Women might petition for a healthy child. Moral transformation too was pos-sible. According to the *Lotus Sutra*, a major Mahayana text, "Those who act under the impulse of hatred will, after adoring the Bodhisattva Avalokitesvara, be freed from hatred."

Among the most striking of the many representation of this bodhisattva are those that portray him/her with numerous heads, with which to hear the many cries of a suffering humanity, and with multiple arms to aid them.

Visual Source 5.3 A Bodhisattva of Compassion: Kannon of 1,000 Arms (From *The Concise History of Japanese Buddhist Sculpture*, Bijutu Shuppan-sha. Photo: Lightstream)

Visual Source 5.3 provides one illustration of such a figure, the Senju Kannon, from Japan of the eighth century C.E.

- What elements of Buddhist imagery can you identify in this statue?

- To whom might such an image appeal? And why?

- Notice the lotus flower, for centuries a rich Buddhist symbol, on which the bodhisattva is resting. With its roots in the mud, the lotus emerges on the surface of the water as a pure, beautiful, and fragrant flower. Why would the artist choose to place the bodhisattva atop such a flower?

■ Some scholars have identified similarities between the Bodhisattva of Compassion and the Virgin Mary in the Christian tradition. What common elements and what differences can you identify?

Beyond numerous bodhisattvas, Mahayana Buddhism also populated the spiritual universe with various Buddhas in addition to the historical Buddha. One of these is the Maitreya Buddha or the Buddha of the future, predicted to appear when the teachings of the historical Buddha have been lost or forgotten. In China, this Buddha of the future was sometimes portrayed as the "laughing Buddha," a fat, smiling, contented figure, said to be modeled on a tenth-century monk named Budai, who wandered the country merrily spreading happiness and good cheer, while evoking contentment and abundance. Visual Source 5.4 illustrates this Chinese Maitreya Buddha together with some of his disciples in a carving, dating to the tenth through fourteenth centuries, in China's Feilai Feng caves.

Visual Source 5.4 The Chinese Maitreya Buddha (Nazima Kowail/Corbis)

■ How does this Buddha image differ, both physically and in its religious implications, from the Buddhas in Visual Sources 5.2 and 5.3?

■ Why might this image be appealing to some Buddhists, and why might others take exception to it?

■ In what ways does this figure represent an adaptation of Buddhist imagery to Chinese culture? Consider what you know about Confucian and Daoist postures to the world.

Visual Source 5.5 The Amitabha Buddha (The State Hermitage Museum, St. Petersburg. Photograph © The State Hermitage Museum)

Yet another Buddha figure within the Mahayana tradition is that of Amitabha, or Amida, the Buddha of Infinite Light, associated with the Pure Land school of China and other parts of East Asia. In this version of Buddhism, worship of the Amitabha Buddha, by sincerely chanting his name, for example, would earn devotees rebirth in the Western Paradise, or the Pure Land. Often imagined as a place of constant light, fragrant breezes, luxuriant vegetation, and abundant water, the Western Paradise was as accessible to commoners, even criminals and outcasts, as it was to monks and nuns.

Visual Source 5.5, dating from somewhere between the twelfth and the fourteenth centuries, depicts Amitabha in bright robes, accompanied by several bodhisattvas. They are shown welcoming a deceased person, represented as a naked boy in the stream of light that comes from the Amitabha's forehead, into the Pure Land, where he will be installed on the golden lotus throne, carried by the bodhisattvas. There he can continuously hear the teachings of the Buddha, while working off any remaining negative karma, before achieving complete liberation in nirvana.

- Why do you think the practice of Pure Land Buddhism became so widely popular in China by the mid-seventh century? What features of this image might help to explain its appeal?

- What details from this painting support the sacred character of the Buddha and bodhisattva figures?

- What is the significance of the small figure sitting in meditation under a tree at the bottom left of the painting?

Using the Evidence:
Representations of the Buddha

1. **Tracing change:** What transformations in Buddhist belief and practice are disclosed in these images?

2. **Identifying cultural adaptation:** What evidence do these images provide about the blending of Buddhism into a variety of cultural settings?

3. **Understanding the growth of Buddhism:** What do these images suggest about the appeal of Buddhism to growing numbers of people across Asia?

4. **Considering cultural boundaries:** To what extent are these images meaningful to people outside of the Buddhist tradition? In what ways do they speak to universal human needs or desires? What is specifically Buddhist or Asian about them?

CHAPTER SIX

Eurasian Social Hierarchies

500 B.C.E–500 C.E.

She is a twenty-six-year-old Hindu woman from Goa, on India's west coast. She speaks the Marathi language, has a high school education, is not currently employed, neither smokes nor drinks, but occasionally eats meat. Like millions of other Indians, she is seeking a partner by placing a personal ad in the newspaper or on the Internet. In addition to the personal and professional data found everywhere in such ads, in India they almost always contain another piece of information—the caste of the seeker. The young woman from Goa lists herself as a member of a "scheduled caste" known as Chambar, formerly called "untouchables," the lowest category in the hierarchy of India's ranked society. That personal ads in twenty-first-century India still refer to caste points out how deeply entrenched and enduring ancient patterns of social life can be.

THE MOST RECENT 250 YEARS OF WORLD HISTORY have called into question social structures long assumed to be natural and permanent. The French, Russian, and Chinese revolutions challenged and destroyed ancient monarchies and class hierarchies; the abolitionist movement of the nineteenth century attacked slavery, largely unquestioned for millennia; the women's movement confronted long and deeply held patriarchal assumptions about the proper relationship between women and men; and Mahatma Gandhi, during India's struggle for independence in the twentieth century, sought to raise the status of "untouchables," referring to them as Harijan, or "children of God." Nevertheless, caste, class, patriarchy, and even slavery have certainly not vanished from human society, even now.

Indian Society: A fresco from the time of India's Gupta dynasty (320–600 C.E.) shows townspeople in a royal procession. (© Benoy K. Behl)

During the era of "second-wave" civilizations in Eurasia, these patterns of inequality found expressions and generated social tensions that remain recognizable to the contemporary descendants of these classical societies.

Millions of individual people, inhabiting the classical civilizations of Eurasia, lived within a political framework of states or empires. They occupied as well a world of ideas, religions, and values that derived both from local folkways and from the teaching of the great religious or cultural traditions of their civilizations. They also lived within established societies that defined relationships between rich and poor, powerful and powerless, slaves and free people, and men and women. Those social relationships shaped the daily lives and the life chances of everyone; they provided the foundation for political authority as well as challenges to it; they were both justified and challenged by the religious and cultural traditions of these civilizations.

Like the First Civilizations, those of the classical era were sharply divided along class lines, and they too were patriarchal, with women clearly subordinated to men in most domains of life. In constructing their societies, however, the classical civilizations differed substantially from one another. Chinese, Indian, and Mediterranean civilizations provide numerous illustrations of the many and varied ways in which peoples of the classical era organized their social life. The assumptions, tensions, and conflicts accompanying these social patterns provided much of the distinctive character and texture that distinguished these diverse civilizations from one another.

Society and the State in Classical China

Chinese society was unique in the ancient world in the extent to which it was shaped by the actions of the state. Nowhere was this more apparent than in the political power and immense social prestige of Chinese state officials. For more than 2,000 years, these officials, bureaucrats acting in the name of the emperor both in the capital and in the provinces, represented the cultural and social elite of Chinese civilization. This class had its origins in the efforts of early Chinese rulers to find administrators loyal to the central state rather than to their own families or regions. Philosophers such as Confucius had long advocated selecting such officials on the basis of merit and personal morality rather than birth or wealth. As the Han dynasty established its authority in China around 200 B.C.E., its rulers required each province to send men of promise to the capital, where they were examined and chosen for official positions on the basis of their performance.

An Elite of Officials

■ **Description**
How would you characterize the social hierarchy of classical China?

Over time, this system of selecting administrators evolved into the world's first professional civil service. In 124 B.C.E., Emperor Wu Di established an imperial academy where potential officials were trained as scholars and immersed in Chinese classical texts dealing with history, literature, art, and mathematics, with an emphasis on Confucian teachings. By the end of the Han dynasty, it enrolled some 30,000 students, who were by then subjected to a series of written examinations to select officials of various grades. Private schools in the provinces funneled still more aspiring candidates into this examination system, which persisted until the early twentieth century. In theory open to all men, this system in practice favored those whose families were wealthy enough to provide the years of education required to pass even the lower-level exams. Proximity to the capital and family connections to the imperial court also helped in gaining a position in this highest of Chinese elites. Nonetheless, village communities or a local landowner might sponsor the education of a bright young man from a commoner family, enabling him to enter the charmed circle of officialdom. One rags-to-riches story told of a pig farmer who became an adviser to the emperor himself. Thus the examination system provided a modest measure of social mobility in an otherwise quite hierarchical society.

In later dynasties, that system grew to be even more elaborate and became an enduring and distinguishing feature of Chinese civilization. During the Tang dynasty, the famous poet and official Po Chu-I (772–846 C.E.) wrote a poem entitled "After Passing the Examination," which shows something of the fame and fortune that awaited an accomplished student as well as the continuing loyalty to family and home that ideally marked those who succeeded:

> For ten years I never left my books,
> I went up . . . and won unmerited praise.
> My high place I do not much prize;
> The joy of my parents will first make me proud.
> Fellow students, six or seven men,
> See me off as I leave the City gate.
> My covered coach is ready to drive away;
> Flutes and strings blend their parting tune.
> Hopes achieved dull the pains of parting;
> Fumes of wine shorten the long road. . . .
> Shod with wings is the horse of him who rides
> On a Spring day the road that leads to home.[1]

Those who made it into the bureaucracy entered a realm of high privilege and enormous prestige. Senior officials moved about in carriages and were bedecked with robes, ribbons, seals, and headdresses appropriate to their rank. Even lower officials who served in the provinces rather than the capital were distinguished by their polished speech, their cultural sophistication, and their urban manners as well as their political authority. Proud of their learning, they were the bearers, and often the makers, of Chinese culture. "Officials are the leaders of the populace," stated an imperial edict of 144 B.C.E., "and it is right and proper that the carriages they ride in and the robes that they wear should correspond to the degrees of their dignity."[2]

The Landlord Class

Most officials came from wealthy families, and in China wealth meant land. When the Qin dynasty unified China by 210 B.C.E., most land was held by small-scale peasant farmers. But by the first century B.C.E., the pressures of population growth, taxation, and indebtedness had generated a class of large landowners as impoverished peasants found it necessary to sell their lands to more prosperous neighbors. This accumulation of land in large estates was a persistent theme in Chinese history, and one that was persistently, though not very successfully, opposed by state authorities. Landlords of large estates often were able to avoid paying taxes, thus decreasing state revenues and increasing the tax burden for the remaining peasants. In some cases, they could also mount their own military forces that might challenge the authority of the emperor.

One of the most dramatic state efforts to counteract the growing power of large landowners is associated with Wang Mang, a high court official of the Han dynasty who usurped the emperor's throne in 8 C.E. and immediately launched a series of startling reforms. A firm believer in Confucian good government, Wang Mang saw his reforms as re-creating a golden age of long ago in which small-scale peasant farmers represented the backbone of Chinese society. Accordingly, he ordered the great private estates to be nationalized and divided up among the landless. Government loans to peasant families, limits on the amount of land a family might own, and an end to private slavery were all part of his reform program, but these measures proved impossible to enforce. Opposition from wealthy landowners, nomadic invasions, poor harvests, floods, and famines led to the collapse of Wang Mang's reforms and his assassination in 23 C.E.

Large landowning families, therefore, remained a central feature of Chinese society, although the fate of individual families rose and fell as the wheel of fortune raised them to great prominence or plunged them into poverty and disgrace. As a class, they benefited both from the wealth that their estates generated and from the power and prestige that accompanied their education and their membership in the official elite. The term "scholar-gentry" reflected their twin sources of privilege. With homes in both urban and rural areas, members of the scholar-gentry class lived luxuriously. Multistoried houses, the finest of silk clothing, gleaming carriages, private orchestras, high-stakes gambling—all of this was part of the life of China's scholar-gentry class.

Peasants

■ **Change**
What class conflicts disrupted Chinese society?

Throughout the history of China's civilization, the vast majority of its population has been peasants, living in small households representing two or three generations. Some owned enough land to support their families and perhaps even sell something on the local market. Many others could barely survive. Nature, the state, and landlords combined to make the life of most peasants extremely vulnerable. Famines, floods, droughts, hail, and pests could wreak havoc without warning. State authorities required the payment of taxes, demanded about a month's labor every year on various public projects, and conscripted young men for two years of military service. During the Han dynasty, growing numbers of impoverished and desperate peasants had to sell out to large landlords and work as tenants or sharecroppers on their estates, where rents could run as high as one-half to two-thirds of the crop. Other peasants fled, taking to a life of begging or joining a gang of bandits in a remote area.

An eighth-century C.E. Chinese poem by Li Shen reflects poignantly on the enduring hardships of peasant life:

Chinese Peasants

For many centuries, the normal activities of Chinese peasant farmers included plowing, planting, and threshing grain, as shown in this painting from China's Song dynasty (960–1279 C.E.). (*Farmers at Work,* Northern Song Dynasty, 960–1279 [wall painting]/ Mogao Caves, Dunhuang/The Bridgeman Art Library)

> The cob of corn in springtime sown
> In autumn yields a hundredfold.
> No fields are seen that fallow lie:
> And yet of hunger peasants die.
>
> As at noontide they hoe their crops,
> Sweat on the grain to earth down drops.
> How many tears, how many a groan,
> Each morsel on thy dish did mold![3]

Such conditions provoked periodic peasant rebellions, which punctuated Chinese history over the past 2,000 years. Toward the end of the second century C.E., wandering bands of peasants began to join together as floods along the Yellow River and resulting epidemics compounded the misery of landlessness and poverty. What emerged was a massive peasant uprising known as the Yellow Turban Rebellion because of the yellow scarves the peasants wore around their heads. That movement, which swelled to about 360,000 armed followers by 184 C.E., found leaders, organization, and a unifying ideology in a popular form of Daoism. Featuring supernatural healings, collective trances, and public confessions of sin, the Yellow Turban movement looked forward to the "Great Peace"—a golden age of complete equality, social harmony, and common ownership of property. Although the rebellion was suppressed by the military forces of the Han dynasty, the Yellow Turban and other peasant upheavals devastated the economy, weakened the state, and contributed to the overthrow of the dynasty a few decades later. Repeatedly in Chinese history, such peasant movements, often expressed in religious terms, registered

Yellow Turban Rebellion

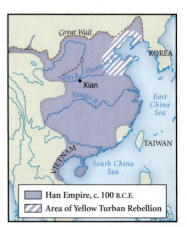

Great Wall
KOREA
Hei R.
Huang He R.
Xian
Yangzi R.
East China Sea
TAIWAN
VIETNAM
South China Sea

Han Empire, c. 100 B.C.E.
Area of Yellow Turban Rebellion

the sharp class antagonisms of Chinese society and led to the collapse of more than one ruling dynasty.

Merchants

Peasants were oppressed in China and certainly exploited, but they were also honored and celebrated in the official ideology of the state. In the eyes of the scholar-gentry, peasants were the solid productive backbone of the country, and their hard work and endurance in the face of difficulties were worthy of praise. Merchants, however, did not enjoy such a favorable reputation in the eyes of China's cultural elite. They were widely viewed as unproductive, making a shameful profit from selling the work of others. Stereotyped as greedy, luxury-loving, and materialistic, merchants stood in contrast to the alleged frugality, altruism, and cultured tastes of the scholar-gentry. They were also seen as a social threat, as their ill-gained wealth impoverished others, deprived the state of needed revenues, and fostered resentments.

Such views lay behind periodic efforts by state authorities to rein in merchant activity and to keep them under control. Early in the Han dynasty, merchants were forbidden to wear silk clothing, ride horses, or carry arms. Nor were they permitted to sit for civil service examinations or hold public office. State monopolies on profitable industries such as salt, iron, and alcohol served to limit merchant opportunities. Later dynasties sometimes forced merchants to loan large sums of money to the state. Despite this active discrimination, merchants frequently became quite wealthy. Some tried to achieve a more respectable elite status by purchasing landed estates or educating their sons for the civil service examinations. Many had backdoor relationships with state officials and landlords who found them useful and were not averse to profiting from business connections with merchants, despite their unsavory reputation.

Class and Caste in India

India's social organization shared certain broad features with that of China. In both civilizations, birth determined social status for most people; little social mobility was available for the vast majority; sharp distinctions and great inequalities characterized social life; and religious or cultural traditions defined these inequalities as natural, eternal, and ordained by the gods. Despite these similarities, the organization, flavor, and texture of ancient Indian society were distinctive compared to almost all other classical civilizations. These unique aspects of Indian society have long been embodied in what we now call the caste system, a term that comes from the Portuguese word *casta*, which means "race" or "purity of blood." That social organization emerged over thousands of years and in some respects has endured into modern times.

■ **Description**

What set of ideas underlies India's caste-based society?

Caste as Varna

The origins of the caste system are at best hazy. An earlier theory—that caste evolved from a racially defined encounter between light-skinned Aryan invaders and the darker-hued native peoples—has been challenged in recent years, but no clear alternative has emerged. Perhaps the best we can say at this point is that the distinctive social system of classical India grew out of the interaction of many culturally different peoples on the South Asian peninsula together with the development of economic and social differences among these peoples as the inequalities of "civilization" spread in the Ganges River valley and beyond. Notions of race, however, seem less central to the growth of the caste system than those of economic specialization and of culture.

By the beginning of the classical era, around 500 B.C.E., the idea that society was forever divided into four ranked classes known as *varna* was deeply embedded in Indian thinking. Everyone was born into and remained within one of these classes for life. At the top of this hierarchical system were the Brahmins, priests whose rituals and sacrifices alone could ensure the proper functioning of the world. They were followed by the Kshatriya class, warriors and rulers charged with protecting and governing society. Next was the Vaisya class, originally commoners who cultivated the land. These three classes came to be regarded as pure Aryans and were called the "twice-born," for they experienced not only a physical birth but also formal initiation into their respective varnas and status as people of Aryan descent. Far below these twice-born in the hierarchy of varna groups were the Sudras, native peoples incorporated into the margins of Aryan society in very subordinate positions. Regarded as servants of their social betters, they were not allowed to hear or repeat the Vedas or to take part in Aryan rituals. So little were they valued that a Brahmin who killed a Sudra was penalized as if he had killed a cat or a dog.

According to varna theory, these four classes were formed from the body of the god Purusha and were therefore eternal and changeless. Although these divisions are widely recognized in India even today, historians have noted considerable social flux in ancient Indian history. Members of the Brahmin and Kshatriya groups, for example, were frequently in conflict over which ranked highest in the varna hierarchy, and only slowly did the Brahmins emerge clearly in the top position. Both of them, although theoretically purely Aryan, absorbed various tribal peoples as classical Indian civilization expanded. Tribal medicine men or sorcerers found a place as Brahmins, while warrior groups entered the Kshatriya varna. The Vaisya varna, originally defined as cultivators, evolved into a business class with a prominent place for

India's Untouchables
Although the Indian constitution of 1950 legally abolished "untouchability," active discrimination persists against this lowest group in the caste hierarchy, now known as Dalits, or the oppressed. Sweeping is just one of many Dalit occupations; here several sweepers perform their tasks in front of an upper-caste home. (Lindsay Hebberd/Corbis)

merchants, while the Sudra varna became the domain of peasant farmers. Finally a whole new category, ranking lower even than the Sudras, emerged in the so-called untouchables, people who did the work considered most unclean and polluting, such as cremating corpses, dealing with the skins of dead animals, and serving as executioners.

Snapshot Social Life and Duty in Classical India

Much personal behavior in classical India, at least ideally, was regulated according to caste. Each caste was associated with a particular color, with a part of the body of the god Purusha, and with a set of duties.

Caste (Varna)	Color/Symbolism	Part of Purusha	Duties
Brahmin	white/spirituality	head	priests, teachers
Kshatriya	red/courage	shoulders	warriors, rulers
Vaisya	yellow/wealth	thighs	farmers, merchants, artisans
Sudra	black/ignorance	feet	labor
Untouchables (outside of the varna system; thus no color and not associated with Purusha)	—	—	polluted labor

Beyond caste, behavior was ideally defined in terms of four stages of life, at least for the first three varna groups. Each new stage was marked by a *samskara*, a ritual initiating the person into this new phase of life.

Stage of Life	Duties
Student	Boys live with a teacher (guru); learn Sanskrit, rituals, Vedas; practice obedience, respect, celibacy, nonviolence.
Householder	Marriage and family; men practice caste-based career/occupation; women serve as wives and mothers, perform household rituals and sacrifices, actively support children and elders.
Retirement	Both husband and wife withdraw to the forests following birth of grandchildren; diminished household duties; greater focus on spiritual practice; sex permitted once a month.
Wandering ascetic	Only for men (women return to household); total rejection of ordinary existence; life as wandering hermit without shelter or possessions; caste becomes irrelevant; focus on achieving *moksha* and avoiding future rebirth.

Caste as Jati

As the varna system took shape in India, another set of social distinctions also arose, deriving largely from specific occupations. In India as elsewhere, urban-based civilization gave rise to specialized occupations, many organized in guilds that regulated their own affairs in a particular region. Over time, these occupationally based groups, known as *jatis*, blended with the varna system to create classical India's unique caste-based society.

The many thousands of jatis became the primary cell of India's social life beyond the family or household, but each of them was associated with one of the great classes (varnas). Thus Brahmins were divided into many separate jatis, or subcastes, as were each of the other varnas as well as the untouchables. In a particular region or village, each jati was ranked in a hierarchy known to all, from the highest of the Brahmins to the lowest of the untouchables. Marriage and eating together were permitted only within an individual's own jati. Each jati was associated with a particular set of duties, rules, and obligations, which defined its members' unique and separate place in the larger society. Brahmins, for example, were forbidden to eat meat, while Kshatriyas were permitted to do so. Upper-caste women, of course, covered their breasts, while some lower-caste women were forbidden to do so as a sign of their lower ranking. "It is better to do one's own duty badly than another's well"—this frequently quoted saying summed up the underlying idea of Indian society.[4]

With its many separate, distinct, and hierarchically ranked social groups, Indian society was quite different from that of China or the Greco-Roman world. It was also unique in the set of ideas that explained and justified that social system. Foremost among them was the notion of ritual purity and pollution applied to caste groups. Brahmins or other high-caste people who came in contact with members of lower castes, especially those who cleaned latrines, handled corpses, or butchered and skinned dead animals, were in great danger of being polluted, or made ritually unclean. Thus untouchables were forbidden to use the same wells or to enter the temples designated for higher-caste people. Sometimes they were required to wear a wooden clapper to warn others of their approach. A great body of Indian religious writing defined various forms of impurity and the ritual means of purification.

A further support for this idea of inherent inequality and permanent difference derived from emerging Hindu notions of *karma, dharma*, and rebirth. Being born into a particular caste was generally regarded as reflecting the good or bad deeds (karma) of a previous life. Thus an individual's own prior actions were responsible for his or her current status. Any hope for rebirth in a higher caste rested on the faithful and selfless performance of one's present caste duties (dharma) in this life. Doing so contributed to spiritual progress by subduing the relentless demands of the ego. Such teachings, like that of permanent impurity, provided powerful ideological support for the inequalities of Indian society. So too did the threat of social

■ **Comparison**

What is the difference between varna and jati as expressions of classical India's caste system?

ostracism, because each jati had the authority to expel members who violated its rules. No greater catastrophe could befall a person than this, for it meant the end of any recognized social life and the loss of all social support.

As caste restrictions tightened, it became increasingly difficult—virtually impossible—for individuals to raise their social status during their lifetimes, but another kind of upward mobility enabled entire jatis, over several generations, to raise their standing in the local hierarchy of caste groups. By acquiring land or wealth, by adopting the behaviors of higher-caste groups, by finding some previously overlooked "ancestor" of a higher caste, a particular jati might slowly be redefined in a higher category. Thus India's caste system was in practice rather more fluid and changing than the theory of caste might suggest.

■ **Comparison**

How did India's caste system differ from China's class system?

India's social system thus differed from that of China in several ways. It gave priority to religious status and ritual purity (the Brahmins), whereas China elevated political officials to the highest of elite positions. The caste system divided Indian society into vast numbers of distinct social groups; China had fewer, but broader, categories of society—scholar-gentry, landlords, peasants, merchants. Finally, India's caste society defined these social groups far more rigidly and with even less opportunity for social mobility than in China.

The Functions of Caste

A caste-based social structure shaped India's classical civilization in various ways. Because caste (jati) was a very local phenomenon, rooted in particular regions or villages, it focused the loyalties of most people on a quite restricted territory and weakened the appeal or authority of larger all-Indian states. This localization is one reason that India, unlike China, seldom experienced an empire that encompassed the entire subcontinent (see Chapter 4). Caste, together with the shared culture of Hinduism, provided a substitute for the state as an integrative mechanism for Indian civilization. It offered a distinct and socially recognized place for almost everyone. In looking after widows, orphans, and the destitute, jatis provided a modest measure of social security and support. Even the lowest-ranking jatis had the right to certain payments from the social superiors whom they served.

Furthermore, caste represented a means of accommodating the many migrating or invading peoples who entered the subcontinent. The cellular, or honeycomb, structure of caste society allowed various peoples, cultures, and traditions to find a place within a larger Indian civilization while retaining something of their unique identity. The process of assimilation was quite different in China, however; incorporation into Chinese civilization meant becoming Chinese ethnically, linguistically, and culturally. Finally, India's caste system facilitated the exploitation of the poor by the wealthy and powerful. The multitude of separate groups into which it divided the impoverished and oppressed majority of the population made class consciousness and organized resistance across caste lines much more difficult to achieve.

Slavery in the Classical Era: The Case of the Roman Empire

Beyond the inequalities of class and caste lay those of slavery, a social institution with deep roots in human history. One scholar has suggested that the early domestication of animals provided the model for enslaving people.[5] Certainly slave owners have everywhere compared their slaves to tamed animals. Aristotle, for example, observed that the ox is "the poor man's slave." War, patriarchy, and the notion of private property, all of which accompanied the First Civilizations, also contributed to the growth of slavery. Large-scale warfare generated numerous prisoners, and everywhere in the ancient world capture in war meant the possibility of enslavement. Early records suggest that women captives were the first slaves, usually raped and then enslaved as concubines, whereas male captives were killed. Patriarchal societies, in which men sharply controlled and perhaps even "owned" women, may have suggested the possibility of using other people, men as well as women, as slaves. The class inequalities of early civilizations, which were based on great differences in privately owned property, also made it possible to imagine people owning other people.

Slavery and Civilization

Whatever its precise origins, slavery generally meant ownership by a master, the possibility of being sold, working without pay, and the status of an "outsider" at the bottom of the social hierarchy. For most, it was a kind of "social death,"[6] for slaves usually lacked any rights or independent personal identity recognized by the larger society. By the time Hammurabi's law code casually referred to Mesopotamian slavery (around 1750 B.C.E.), it was already a long-established tradition in the region and in all of the First Civilizations. Likewise, virtually all subsequent civilizations—in the Americas, Africa, and Eurasia—practiced some form of slavery.

■ **Comparison**

How did the inequalities of slavery differ from those of caste?

Slave systems throughout history have varied considerably. In some times and places, such as classical Greece and Rome, a fair number of slaves might be emancipated in their own lifetimes, through the generosity or religious convictions of their owners, or to avoid caring for them in old age, or by allowing slaves to purchase their freedom with their own funds. In some societies, the children of slaves inherited the status of their parents, while in others, such as the Aztec Empire, they were considered free people. Slaves likewise varied considerably in the labor they were required to do, with some working for the state in high positions, others performing domestic duties in their owner's household, and still others toiling in fields or mines in large work gangs.

The classical civilizations of Eurasia differed considerably in the prominence and extent of slavery in their societies. In China, it was a minor element, amounting to perhaps 1 percent of the population. Convicted criminals and their families, confiscated by the government and sometimes sold to wealthy private individuals, were among the earliest slaves in Han dynasty China. In desperate circumstances, impoverished or indebted peasants might sell their children into slavery. In southern China, teenage boys of poor families could be purchased by the wealthy, for whom they served as status symbols. Chinese slavery, however, was never very widespread and did not become a major source of labor for agriculture or manufacturing.

In India as well, people could fall into slavery as criminals, debtors, or prisoners of war and served their masters largely in domestic settings, but religious writings and secular law offered, at least in theory, some protection for slaves. Owners were required to provide adequately for their slaves and were forbidden to abandon them in old age. According to one ancient text, "a man may go short himself or stint his

Snapshot   Comparing Greco-Roman and American Slavery

	Greco-Roman Slavery (500 B.C.E.–500 C.E.)	Slavery in the Americas (1500–1888)
Source of slaves	Majority were prisoners from Roman wars of conquest; victims of pirate kidnapping; obtained through networks of long-distance trade; result of natural reproduction; abandoned children	Derived almost entirely from transatlantic slave trade; many were prisoners of African wars, debtors, or criminals in African societies
Race	Not a major factor	Came to be associated with Africa and "blackness"
Manumission (granting legal freedom to slaves)	Quite common; freed slaves received citizenship in Roman Empire but not in Greece	Much less common, especially in North America; freed slaves were long feared and discriminated against in North America, but less so in Latin America
Roles/Work	No distinction between slave and wage labor; slaves worked at wide variety of jobs, from poets, physicians, scholars, and teachers to field hands and mine laborers	Majority worked as agricultural laborers on plantations producing for export; few held elite occupations
Fate of slavery	Gradual transformation from slavery to serfdom as Roman Empire collapsed; no abolitionist movements; Christianity provided general support for slavery, though some encouragement for manumission	Ended in nineteenth century as a result of slave rebellions, industrialization, and abolitionist movements, some based in Christian teaching; replaced by sharecropping or indentured labor

wife and children, but never his slave who does his dirty work for him."[7] Slaves in India could inherit and own property and earn money in their spare time. A master who raped a slave woman was required to set her free and pay compensation. The law encouraged owners to free their slaves and allowed slaves to buy their freedom. All of this suggests that Indian slavery was more restrained than that of other ancient civilizations. Nor did Indian civilization depend economically on slavery, for most work was performed by lower-caste, though free, people.

The Making of a Slave Society: The Case of Rome

In sharp contrast to other classical civilizations, slavery played an immense role in the Mediterranean, or Western, world. Although slavery was practiced in Chinese, Indian, and Persian civilizations, the Greco-Roman world can be described as a slave society. By a conservative estimate, classical Athens alone was home to perhaps 60,000 slaves, or about one-third of the total population. In Athens, ironically, the growth of democracy and status as a free person were defined and accompanied by the simultaneous growth of slavery on a mass scale. The greatest of the Greek philosophers, Aristotle, developed the notion that some people were "slaves by nature" and should be enslaved for their own good and for that of the larger society.

"The ancient Greek attitude toward slavery was simple," writes one modern scholar. "It was a terrible thing to become a slave, but a good thing to own a slave."[8] Even poor households usually had at least one or two female slaves, providing domestic work and sexual services for their owners. Although substantial numbers of Greek slaves were granted freedom by their owners, they usually did not become citizens or gain political rights. Nor could they own land or marry citizens, and particularly in Athens they had to pay a special tax. Their status remained "halfway between slavery and freedom."[9]

Practiced on an even larger scale, slavery was a defining element of Roman society. By the time of Christ, the Italian heartland of the Roman Empire had some 2 to 3 million slaves, representing 33 to 40 percent of the population.[10] Not until the modern slave societies of the Caribbean, Brazil, and the southern United States was slavery practiced again on such an enormous scale. Wealthy Romans could own many hundreds or even thousands of slaves. One woman in the fifth century C.E. freed 8,000 slaves when she withdrew into a life of Christian monastic practice.

■ **Comparison**

How did Greco-Roman slavery differ from that of other classical civilizations?

Roman Slavery
This Roman mosaic from the third century C.E. shows the slave Myro serving a drink to his master, Fructus. (Bardo Museum Tunis/Gianni Dagli Orti/The Art Archive)

Even people of modest means frequently owned two or three slaves. In doing so, they confirmed their own position as free people, demonstrated their social status, and expressed their ability to exercise power. Slaves and former slaves also might be slave owners. One freedman during the reign of Augustus owned 4,116 slaves at the time of his death. (For the role of slaves in Roman Pompeii, see Visual Sources: Pompeii as a Window on the Roman World, pp. 272–79.)

The vast majority of Roman slaves had been prisoners captured in the many wars that accompanied the creation of the empire. In 146 B.C.E., following the destruction of the North African city of Carthage, some 55,000 people were enslaved en masse. From all over the Mediterranean basin, such people were funneled into the major slave-owning regions of Italy and Sicily. Pirates also furnished slaves, kidnapping tens of thousands of people and selling them to Roman slave traders on the island of Delos. Roman merchants purchased still other slaves through networks of long-distance commerce extending to the Black Sea, the East African coast, and northwestern Europe. The supply of slaves also occurred through natural reproduction, as the children of slave mothers were regarded as slaves themselves. Such "home-born" slaves had a certain prestige and were thought to be less troublesome than those who had known freedom earlier in their lives. Finally, abandoned or exposed children could legally become the slave of anyone who rescued them.

Unlike New World slavery of later times, Roman slavery was not identified with a particular racial or ethnic group. Egyptians, Syrians, Jews, Greeks, Gauls, North Africans, and many other people found themselves alike enslaved. From within the empire and its adjacent regions, an enormous diversity of people were bought and sold at Roman slave markets.

Like slave owners everywhere, Romans regarded their slaves as "barbarians"— lazy, unreliable, immoral, prone to thieving—and came to think of certain peoples, such as Asiatic Greeks, Syrians, and Jews, as slaves by nature. Nor was there any serious criticism of slavery in principle, although on occasion owners were urged to treat their slaves in a more benevolent way. Even the triumph of Christianity within the Roman Empire did little to undermine slavery, for Christian teaching held that slaves should be "submissive to [their] masters with all fear, not only to the good and gentle, but also to the harsh."[11] In fact, Saint Paul used the metaphor of slavery to describe the relationship of believers to God, styling them as "slaves of Christ," while Saint Augustine (354–430 C.E.) described slavery as God's punishment for sin. Thus slavery was deeply embedded in the religious thinking and social outlook of elite Romans.

Similarly, slavery was entrenched throughout the Roman economy. No occupation was off-limits to slaves except military service, and no distinction existed between jobs for slaves and those for free people. Frequently they labored side by side. In rural areas, slaves provided much of the labor force on the huge estates, or *latifundia*, which produced grain, olive oil, and wine, mostly for export, much like the later plantations in the Americas. There they often worked chained together. In the cities, slaves worked in their owners' households, but also as skilled artisans, teachers, doctors, business agents, entertainers, and actors. In the empire's many mines and quarries, slaves and criminals labored under brutal conditions. Slaves in the service of the emperor provided manpower for the state bureaucracy, maintained temples and shrines, and kept Rome's water supply system functioning. Trained in special schools, they also served as gladiators in the violent spectacles of Roman public life. Thus slaves were represented among the highest and most prestigious occupations and in the lowest and most degraded.

Slave owners in the Roman Empire were supposed to provide the necessities of life to their slaves. When this occurred, slaves may have had a more secure life than was available to impoverished free people, who had to fend for themselves, but the price of this security was absolute subjection to the will of the master. Beatings, sexual abuse, and sale to another owner were constant possibilities. Lacking all rights in the law, slaves could not legally marry, although many contracted unofficial unions. Slaves often accumulated money or possessions, but such property legally belonged to their masters and could be seized at any time. If a slave murdered his master, Roman law demanded the lives of all of the victim's slaves. When one Roman official was killed by a slave in 61 C.E., every one of his 400 slaves was condemned to death. For an individual slave, the quality of life depended almost entirely on the character of the master. Brutal owners made it a living hell. Benevolent owners made life tolerable and might even grant favored slaves their freedom or permit them to buy that freedom. As in Greece, manumission of slaves was a widespread practice, and in the Roman Empire, unlike Greece, freedom was accompanied by citizenship.

Resistance and Rebellion

Roman slaves, like their counterparts in other societies, responded to enslavement in many ways. Most, no doubt, did what they had to simply to survive, but there are recorded cases of Roman prisoners of war who chose to commit mass suicide rather than face the horrors of slavery. Others, once enslaved, resorted to the "weapons of the weak"—small-scale theft, sabotage, pretending illness, working poorly, and placing curses on their masters. Fleeing to the anonymous crowds of the city or to remote rural areas prompted owners to post notices in public places, asking for information about their runaways. Catching runaway slaves became an organized private business. Occasional murders of slave owners made masters conscious of the dangers they faced. "Every slave we own is an enemy we harbor" ran one Roman saying.[12]

On several notable occasions, the slaves themselves rose in rebellion. The most famous uprising occurred in 73 B.C.E. when a slave gladiator named Spartacus led seventy other slaves from a school for gladiators in a desperate bid for freedom. The surprising initial success of their revolt attracted a growing following of rebellious slaves, numbering perhaps 120,000 at the height of the uprising. For two years, they set Italy ablaze. In a dramatic reversal of roles, they crucified some captured slave owners and set others to fighting one another in the style of gladiators. Following a series of remarkable military victories, the movement split and eventually succumbed

The Rebellion of Spartacus

to the vastly superior numbers of the Roman legions. A terrible vengeance followed as some 6,000 rebel slaves were nailed to crosses along the Appian Way from Rome to Capua, where the revolt had begun.

Nothing on the scale of the Spartacus rebellion occurred again in the Western world of slavery until the Haitian Revolution of the 1790s. But Haitian rebels sought the creation of a new society free of slavery altogether. None of the Roman slave rebellions, including that of Spartacus, had any such overall plan or goal. They simply wanted to escape Roman slavery themselves. Although rebellions created a perpetual fear in the minds of slave owners, the slave system itself was hardly affected.

Comparing Patriarchies of the Classical Era

No division of human society has held greater significance for the lives of individuals than that between male and female. Every human community has elaborated that basic biological difference into a gender system that sought to define masculinity and femininity and to determine the appropriate roles and positions of men and women in the larger society. At least since the emergence of the First Civilizations, those gender systems have been everywhere patriarchal, featuring the dominance of men over women in the family and in society generally. More widespread than slavery, these inequalities of gender, like those of class or caste, shaped the character of the classical civilizations.

In all of them, men were regarded as superior to women, and sons were generally preferred over daughters. Men had legal and property rights unknown to most women. Public life in general was a male domain, while women's roles—both productive and reproductive—took place mostly in domestic settings. Frequently men could marry more than one woman and claimed the right to regulate the social and sexual lives of the wives, daughters, and sisters in their families. Widely seen as weak and feared as potentially disruptive, women required the protection and control of men.

These common elements of patriarchy have been so widespread and pervasive that historians have been slow to recognize that gender systems evolved, changing over time. New agricultural technologies, the rise or decline of powerful states, the incorporation of world religions, interaction with culturally different peoples—all of these developments and more generated significant change in gender systems. Nor has patriarchy been everywhere the same. Restrictions on women were far sharper in classical civilizations than in those pastoral or agricultural societies that lay beyond the reach of urban centers and powerful empires. The degree and expression of patriarchy also varied from one civilization to another, as the discussion of Mesopotamia and Egypt in Chapter 3 illustrated. (See the Documents: Patriarchy and Women's Voices in the Classical Era, pp. 262–71, for various expressions of and reactions to patriarchy across classical Eurasia.)

Within particular civilizations, gender interacted with class to generate usually a more restricted life for upper-class women, who were largely limited to the home and the management of servants. In contrast, lower-class women often had a somewhat freer but more burdensome life, for economic necessity required them to work in the fields, to shop in the streets, or to serve in the homes of their social superiors. China provides a fascinating example of how patriarchy changed over time, while the contrasting patriarchies of Athens and Sparta illustrate clear variations even within the limited world of Greek civilization.

A Changing Patriarchy: The Case of China

As Chinese civilization took shape during the Han dynasty, elite thinking about gender issues became more explicitly patriarchal, more clearly defined, and linked to an emerging Confucian ideology (see Document 6.1, pp. 262–63,

Chinese Women Musicians
This tenth-century rendering by the painter Gu Hongzhong shows these upper-class women serving as musicians for a high official of a Tang dynasty emperor. It was titled *The Night Revels of Han Xizai*. The painter was apparently sent by the emperor to spy on the suspicious behavior of the minister, who in various tellings was suspected of either rebellion or undignified activity. (Werner Forman/Art Resource, NY)

and Document 6.2, pp. 263–66). Long-established patterns of thinking in terms of pairs of opposites were now described in gendered and unequal terms. The superior principle of *yang* was viewed as masculine and related to heaven, rulers, strength, rationality, and light, whereas *yin*, the lower feminine principle, was associated with the earth, subjects, weakness, emotion, and darkness. Thus female inferiority was permanent and embedded in the workings of the universe.

■ **Change**
In what ways did the expression of Chinese patriarchy change over time, and why did it change?

What this meant more practically was spelled out repeatedly over the centuries in various Confucian texts. Two notions in particular summarized the ideal position of women, at least in the eyes of elite male writers. The adage "Men go out, women stay in" emphasized the public and political roles of men in contrast to the domestic and private domain of women. A second idea, known as the "three obediences," emphasized a woman's subordination first to her father, then to her husband, and finally to her son. "Why is it," asked one text, "that according to the rites the man takes his wife, whereas the woman leaves her house [to join her husband's family]? It is because the *yin* is lowly, and should not have the initiative; it proceeds to the *yang* in order to be completed."[13]

The Chinese woman writer and court official Ban Zhao (45–116 C.E.), whose *Lessons for Women* is excerpted in Document 6.2, pages 263–66, observed that the ancients had practiced three customs when a baby girl was born. She was placed below the bed to show that she was "lowly and weak," required always to "humble herself before others." Then she was given a piece of broken pottery to play with, signifying that "her primary duty [was] to be industrious." Finally, her birth was announced to the ancestors with an offering to indicate that she was responsible for "the continuation of [ancestor] worship in the home."[14]

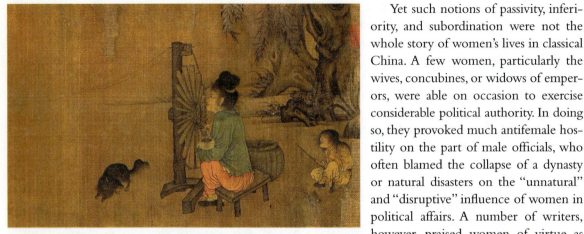

Chinese Women at Work
For a long time, the spinning and weaving of cloth were part of women's domestic work in China. So too was fishing, as illustrated by the woman at the bottom right of this Chinese painting. (Palace Museum, Beijing)

Yet such notions of passivity, inferiority, and subordination were not the whole story of women's lives in classical China. A few women, particularly the wives, concubines, or widows of emperors, were able on occasion to exercise considerable political authority. In doing so, they provoked much antifemale hostility on the part of male officials, who often blamed the collapse of a dynasty or natural disasters on the "unnatural" and "disruptive" influence of women in political affairs. A number of writers, however, praised women of virtue as wise counselors to their fathers, husbands, and rulers and depicted them positively as active agents.[15]

Within her husband's family, a young woman was clearly subordinate as a wife and daughter-in-law, but as a mother of sons, she was accorded considerable honor for her role in producing the next generation of male heirs to carry on her husband's lineage. When her sons married, she was able to exercise the significant authority of a mother-in-law. Furthermore, a woman, at least in the upper classes, often brought with her a considerable dowry, which was regarded as her own property and gave her some leverage within her marriage. Women's roles in the production of textiles, often used to pay taxes or to sell commercially, made her labor quite valuable to the family economy. And a man's wife was sharply distinguished from his concubines, for the wife alone produced the legitimate heirs who could carry on the family tradition. Thus women's lives were more complex and varied than the prescriptions of Confucian orthodoxy might suggest.

Much changed in China following the collapse of the Han dynasty in the third century C.E. Centralized government vanished amid much political fragmentation and conflict. Confucianism, the main ideology of Han China, was discredited, while Daoism and Buddhism attracted a growing following. Pastoral and nomadic people invaded northern China and ruled a number of the small states that had replaced the Han government. These new conditions resulted in some loosening of the strict patriarchy of classical China over the next five or six centuries.

The cultural influence of nomadic peoples, whose women were far less restricted than those of China, was noticed, and criticized, by more Confucian-minded male observers. One of them lamented the sad deterioration of gender roles under the influence of nomadic peoples:

In the north of the Yellow river it is usually the wife who runs the household. She will not dispense with good clothing or expensive jewelry. The husband has to settle for old horses and sickly servants. The traditional niceties between husband and wife are seldom observed, and from time to time he even has to put up with her insults.[16]

Others criticized the adoption of nomadic styles of dress, makeup, and music. By the time of the Tang dynasty (618–907), writers and artists depicted elite women as capable of handling legal and business affairs on their own and on occasion riding horses and playing polo, bareheaded and wearing men's clothing. Tang legal codes even recognized a married daughter's right to inherit property from her family of birth. Such images of women were quite different from those of Han dynasty China.

A further sign of a weakening patriarchy and the cause of great distress to advocates of Confucian orthodoxy lay in the unusual reign of Empress Wu (reigned 690–705 C.E.), a former high-ranking concubine in the imperial court, who came to power amid much palace intrigue and was the only woman ever to rule China with the title of emperor. With the support of China's growing Buddhist establishment, Empress Wu governed despotically, but she also consolidated China's civil service examination system for the selection of public officials and actively patronized scholarship and the arts. Some of her actions seem deliberately designed to elevate the position of women. She commissioned the biographies of famous women, decreed that the mourning period for mothers be made equal to that for fathers, and ordered the creation of a Chinese character for "human being" that suggested the process of birth flowing from one woman without a prominent male role. Her reign was brief and unrepeated.

The growing popularity of Daoism provided new images of the feminine and new roles for women. Daoist texts referred to the *dao* as "mother" and urged the traditionally feminine virtues of yielding and passive acceptance rather than the male-oriented striving of Confucianism. Daoist sects often featured women as priests, nuns, or reclusive meditators, able to receive cosmic truth and to use it for the benefit of others. A variety of female deities from Daoist or Buddhist traditions found a place in Chinese village religion,[17] while growing numbers of women found an alternative to family life in Buddhist monasteries. None of this meant an end to patriarchy, but it does suggest some change in the tone and expression of that patriarchy.

Contrasting Patriarchies in Athens and Sparta

The patriarchies of the classical era not only fluctuated over time but also varied considerably from place to place. Nowhere is this variation more apparent than in the contrasting cases of Athens and Sparta, two of the leading city-states of classical Greek civilization (see Map 4.2, p. 148). Even within the small area of classical Greece, the opportunities available to women and the restrictions imposed on them differed substantially. Although Athens has been celebrated as a major source of Western democracy and rationalism, its posture toward women was far more negative and restrictive

■ **Comparison**
How did the patriarchies of Athens and Sparta differ from each other?

Women of Athens
This painting on a seventh-century B.C.E. ceramic vase shows Athenian women gathering water at a fountain. (Museo di Villa Giulia Rome/ Gianni Dagli Orti/The Art Archive)

than that of the highly militaristic and much less democratic Sparta.

In the several centuries between about 700 and 400 B.C.E., as the men of Athens moved toward unprecedented freedom and participation in political life, the city's women experienced growing limitations. They had no role whatsoever in the assembly, the councils, or the juries of Athens, which were increasingly the focus of life for free men. In legal matters, women had to be represented by a guardian, and court proceedings did not even refer to them by name, but only as someone's wife or mother.

Greek thinkers, especially Aristotle, provided a set of ideas that justified women's exclusion from public life and their general subordination to men. According to Aristotle, "a woman is, as it were, an infertile male. She is female in fact on account of a kind of inadequacy." That inadequacy lay in her inability to generate sperm, which contained the "form" or the "soul" of a new human being. Her role in the reproductive process was passive, providing a receptacle for the vital male contribution. Compared often to children or domesticated animals, women were associated with instinct and passion and lacked the rationality to take part in public life. "It is the best for all tame animals to be ruled by human beings," wrote Aristotle. "For this is how they are kept alive. In the same way, the relationship between the male and the female is by nature such that the male is higher, the female lower, that the male rules and the female is ruled."[18]

As in China, proper Greek women were expected to remain inside the home, except perhaps for religious festivals or funerals. Even within the home, women's space was quite separate from that of men. Although poorer women, courtesans, and prostitutes had to leave their homes to earn money, collect water, or shop, ideal behavior for upper-class women assigned these tasks to slaves or to men and involved a radical segregation of male and female space. "What causes women a bad reputation," wrote the Greek playwright Euripides in *The Trojan Women*, "is not remaining inside."

Within the domestic realm, Athenian women were generally married in their mid-teens to men ten to fifteen years older than themselves. Their main function was the management of domestic affairs and the production of sons who would become citizens. These sons were expected to become literate, while their sisters were normally limited to learning spinning, weaving, and other household tasks. The Greek writer Menander exclaimed: "Teaching a woman to read and write? What a terrible thing to do! Like feeding a vile snake on more poison." Nor did women have much economic power. Although they could own personal property obtained through dowry, gifts, or inheritance, land was passed through male heirs, with a few exceptions. By law, women were forbidden to buy or sell land and could negotiate contracts only if the sum involved was valued at less than a bushel of barley.

There were exceptions, although rare, to the restricted lives of Athenian women, the most notable of which was Aspasia (ca. 470–400 B.C.E.). She was born in the Greek city of Miletus, on the western coast of Anatolia, to a wealthy family that believed in educating its daughters. As a young woman, Aspasia found her way to Athens, where her foreign birth gave her somewhat more freedom than was normally available to the women of that city. She soon attracted the attention of Pericles, Athens's leading political figure. The two lived together as husband and wife until Pericles' death in 429 B.C.E., although they were not officially married. Treated as an equal partner by Pericles, Aspasia proved to be a learned and witty conversationalist who moved freely in the cultured circles of Athens. Her foreign birth and her apparent influence on Pericles provoked critics to suggest that she was a *hetaera,* a professional, educated, high-class entertainer and sexual companion, similar to a Japanese geisha. Although little is known about her, a number of major Athenian writers commented about her, both positively and negatively. She was, by all accounts, a rare and remarkable woman in a city that offered little opportunity for individuality or achievement to its female population.

The evolution of Sparta differed in many ways from that of Athens. Early on, Sparta solved the problem of feeding a growing population, not by creating overseas colonies as did many Greek city-states, but by conquering their immediate neighbors and reducing them to a status of permanent servitude, not far removed from slavery. Called *helots,* these dependents far outnumbered the free citizens of Sparta and represented a permanent threat of rebellion. Solving this problem shaped Spartan society decisively. Sparta's answer was a militaristic regime, constantly ready for war to keep the helots in their place. To maintain such a system, all boys were removed from their families at the age of seven to be trained by the state in military camps, where they learned the ways of war. There they remained until the age of thirty. The ideal Spartan male was a warrior, skilled in battle, able to endure hardship, and willing to die for his city. Mothers are said to have told their sons departing for battle to "come back with your shield . . . or on it." Although economic equality for men was the ideal, it was never completely realized in practice. And unlike Athens, political power was exercised primarily by a small group of wealthy men.

This militaristic and far-from-democratic system had implications for women that, strangely enough, offered them greater freedoms and fewer restrictions. Their central task was reproduction—bearing warrior sons for Sparta. To strengthen their bodies for childbearing, girls were encouraged to take part in sporting events—running, wrestling, throwing the discus and javelin, even driving chariots. At times, they competed in the nude before mixed audiences. Their education, like that of boys, was prescribed by the state, which also insisted that newly married women cut their hair short, unlike adult Greek women elsewhere. Thus Spartan women were not secluded or segregated, as were their Athenian counterparts. Furthermore,

A Girl of Sparta

This figurine portrays a young female Spartan athlete or runner. Compare her clothing with that worn by the Athenian women depicted on the vase (shown on page 256. (National Archaeological Museum, Athens/Archaeological Receipts Fund)

Spartan young women, unlike those of Athens, usually married men of their own age, about eighteen years old, thus putting the new couple on a more equal basis. Marriage often began with a trial period to make sure the new couple could produce children, with divorce and remarriage readily available if they could not. Because men were so often away at war or preparing for it, women exercised much more authority in the household than was the case in Athens.

It is little wonder that the freedom of Spartan women appalled other Greeks, who believed that it undermined good order and state authority. Aristotle complained that the more egalitarian inheritance practices of Spartans led to their women controlling some 40 percent of landed estates. In Sparta, he declared, women "live in every sort of intemperance and luxury" and "the [male] rulers are ruled by women." Plutarch, a Greek writer during the heyday of the Roman Empire, observed critically that "the men of Sparta always obeyed their wives." The clothing worn by Spartan women to give them greater freedom of movement seemed immodest to other Greeks.

Nonetheless, in another way, Sparta may have been more restrictive than Athens and other Greek city-states, particularly in its apparent prohibition of homosexuality. At least this was the assertion of the Athenian writer Xenophon (427–355 B.C.E.), who stated that Sparta's legendary founder Lycurgus "caused lovers to abstain from sexual intercourse with boys."[19] Elsewhere, however, homoerotic relationships were culturally approved and fairly common for both men and women, although this did not prevent their participants from entering heterosexual marriages as well. The ideal homosexual relationship—between an older man and a young adolescent boy—was viewed as limited in time, for it was supposed to end when the boy's beard began to grow. Unlike contemporary Western societies where sexuality is largely seen as an identity, the ancient Greeks viewed sexual choice more casually and as a matter of taste.

Sparta clearly was a patriarchy, with women serving as breeding machines for its military system and lacking any formal role in public life, but it was a lighter patriarchy than that of Athens. The joint efforts of men and women seemed necessary to maintain a huge class of helots in permanent subjugation. Death in childbirth was considered the equivalent of death in battle, for both contributed to the defense of Sparta, and both were honored alike. In Athens, on the other hand, growing freedom and democracy were associated with the strengthening of the male-dominated, property-owning household, and within that household men, the cornerstone of Athenian society, were expected to exercise authority. Doing so required increasingly severe limitations and restrictions on the lives of women. Together, the cases of Athens and Sparta illustrate how the historical record appears different when viewed through the lens of gender. Athens, so celebrated for its democracy and philosophical rationalism, offered little to its women, whereas Sparta, often condemned for its militarism and virtual enslavement of the helots, provided a somewhat wider scope for the free women of the city.

Reflections: Arguing with Solomon and the Buddha

"What has been will be again; what has been done will be done again; there is nothing new under the sun." Recorded in the Old Testament book of Ecclesiastes and generally attributed to King Solomon, this was a despairing view about the essential changelessness and futility of human life. In contrast, central to Buddhist teachings has been the concept of "impermanence"—the notion that "everything changes; nothing remains without change." These observations from classical-era thinkers were intended to point to other levels of reality that lay beyond the dreary constancy or the endless changeability of this world. For students of history, however, these comments from Solomon and the Buddha serve to focus attention on issues of change and continuity in the historical record of classical Eurasian civilizations. What is more impressive—the innovations and changes or the enduring patterns and lasting features of these civilizations?

Clearly there were some new things under the sun, even if they had roots in earlier times. The Greek conquest of the Persian Empire under the leadership of Alexander the Great was both novel and unexpected. The Roman Empire encompassed the entire Mediterranean basin in a single political system for the first time. Buddhism and Christianity emerged as new, distinct, and universal religious traditions, although both bore the marks of their origin in Hindu and Jewish religious thinking respectively. The collapse of dynasties, empires, and civilizations long thought to be solidly entrenched—the Chinese and Roman, for example—must surely have seemed to people of the time as something new under the sun. Historians therefore might take issue with Solomon's dictum, should we seek to apply it to the history of the classical era.

Students of the past might also argue a little with the Buddha and his insistence on the "impermanence" of everything. Much that was created in the classical era—particularly its social and cultural patterns—has demonstrated an impressive continuity over many centuries, even if it also changed in particular ways over time. China's scholar-gentry class retained its prominence throughout the ups and downs of changing dynasties and into the twentieth century. India's caste-based social structure still endures as a way of thinking and behaving for hundreds of millions of people on the South Asian peninsula. Although slavery gave way to serfdom in the post-Roman world, it was massively revived in Europe's American colonies after 1500 and remained an important and largely unquestioned feature of all civilizations until the nineteenth century. Patriarchy, with its assumptions of male superiority and dominance, has surely been the most fundamental, long-lasting, and taken-for-granted feature of all civilizations. Not until the twentieth century were those assumptions effectively challenged, but even then patriarchy has continued to shape the lives and the thinking of the vast majority of humankind. And many hundreds of millions of people in the twenty-first century still honor or practice religious and cultural traditions begun during the classical era.

Neither the insight of Solomon nor that of the Buddha, taken alone, offers an effective guide to the study of history, for continuity and change alike have long provided the inextricable warp and woof of historical analysis. Untangling their elusive relationship has figured prominently in the task of historians and has contributed much to the enduring fascination of historical study.

Second Thoughts

What's the Significance?

To assess your mastery of the material in this chapter, visit the **Student Center** at bedfordstmartins.com/strayer.

Wang Mang	"ritual purity" in Indian social	the "three obediences"
China's scholar-gentry class	practice	Empress Wu
Yellow Turban Rebellion	Greek and Roman slavery	Aspasia and Pericles
caste as varna and jati	Spartacus	helots

Big Picture Questions

1. What is the difference between class and caste?
2. Why was slavery so much more prominent in Greco-Roman civilization than in India or China?
3. What philosophical, religious, or cultural ideas served to legitimate the class and gender inequalities of classical civilizations?
4. "Social inequality was both accepted and resisted in classical civilizations." What evidence might support this statement?
5. What changes in the patterns of social life of the classical era can you identify? What accounts for these changes?
6. "Cultural and social patterns of civilizations seem to endure longer than the political framework of states and empires." Based on Chapters 4, 5, and 6, would you agree with this statement?

Next Steps: For Further Study

For Web sites and additional documents related to this chapter, see **Make History** at bedfordstmartins.com/strayer.

Jeannine Auboyer, *Daily Life in Ancient India* (2002). A social history of classical India, with a focus on caste, ritual, religion, and art.

Sue Blundell, *Women in Ancient Greece* (1999). A well-written academic study, with occasional humorous stories and anecdotes.

Keith Bradley, *Slavery and Society at Rome* (1994). A scholarly but very readable account of slavery in the Roman Empire.

Michael Lowe, *Everyday Life in Early Imperial China* (1968). A vivid description of social life during the Han dynasty.

Bonnie Smith, ed., *Women's History in Global Perspective*, 3 volumes (2004). A collection of thoughtful essays by major scholars covering world history from ancient times to the twentieth century.

"Women in World History," http://chnm.gmu.edu/wwh/index.html. Documents, reviews, and lesson plans for learning and teaching about women's history in a global context.

Documents

Considering the Evidence:
Patriarchy and Women's Voices in the Classical Era

In American colleges and universities, courses in world history as well as those in women's history and gender history entered the curriculum at about the same time, both of them growing rapidly in the last decades of the twentieth century. During that time, world historians have increasingly sought to address on a global level the issues about gender raised by other historians within a national or local setting:

■ How did patriarchy emerge? How was it expressed and experienced? How did it change over time?

■ What mix of opportunities and limitations did women encounter in various societies and at various times?

■ To what extent were women able to act in the arena of public life and in domestic settings?

■ How did different cultural traditions define appropriate gender roles and gender identities, both feminine and masculine?

In exploring such questions, historians face a major problem: the scarcity of sources written by women themselves, especially in the pre-modern era. Furthermore, most of the female-authored sources we do have derive from elite women. As a result, scholars must sometimes make careful use of documents written by men, often "reading between the lines" to discern the perspectives of women. The documents that follow explore various expressions of patriarchy and the women's voices that emerged within them in several of the classical civilizations.

Document 6.1

A Male View of Chinese Women's Lives

In the third century C.E., Fu Xuan, a male poet, described the life of a Chinese woman. Raised as an impoverished orphan, Fu Xuan only later gained fame and wealth owing to his literary talents. Perhaps it was this early experience that allowed him to sympathize with the plight of women.

- What differences between the lives of women and men does the poem highlight?

- What is Fu Xuan's own attitude toward the women he describes?

- In what ways does this portrayal of women's lives reflect or contradict Confucian values? (See pp. 193–95 and Document 5.1, pp. 217–19.)

FU XUAN

How Sad It Is to Be a Woman

Third Century C.E.

How sad it is to be a woman!
Nothing on earth is held so cheap.
Boys stand leaning at the door
Like Gods fallen out of Heaven.
Their hearts brave the Four Oceans,
The wind and dust of a thousand miles.
No one is glad when a girl is born:
By her the family sets no store.
Then she grows up, she hides in her room
Afraid to look a man in the face.
No one cries when she leaves her home—
Sudden as clouds when the rain stops.
She bows her head and composes her face,

Her teeth are pressed on her red lips:
She bows and kneels countless times.
She must humble herself even to the servants.
His love is distant as the stars in Heaven,
Yet the sunflower bends toward the sun.
Their hearts more sundered than water and fire—
A hundred evils are heaped upon her.
Her face will follow the years' changes:
Her lord will find new pleasures.
They that were once like substance and shadow
Are now as far as Hu from Ch'in.°
Yet Hu and Ch'in shall sooner meet
Than they whose parting is like Ts'an and Ch'en.°

Source: Fu Xuan, "How Sad It Is to Be a Woman," in Arthur Waley, *Translations from the Chinese* (New York: Alfred A. Knopf, 1941), 72–73.

°**Hu from Ch'in:** two distant places.

°**Ts'an and Ch'en:** two distant stars.

Document 6.2

A Chinese Woman's Instructions to Her Daughters

Confucius himself apparently said little about women, perhaps reflecting his assumptions about their limited importance in Chinese society. Nonetheless, Confucianism as a social philosophy, formulated by the sage's later followers, had profound implications for the lives of women. Those sentiments found expression in the work of Ban Zhao (45–116 C.E.), a remarkable woman born into an elite family with connections to the imperial court. Although she received a fine literary education, she was married at the age of fourteen, gave birth to several children, and was widowed early in life. Although she never remarried, Ban Zhao had a significant career as a court historian and as an adviser to the empress-dowager (the widow of a deceased emperor). Her most famous work, *Lessons for Women*, was an effort to apply the principles of Confucianism to the lives and behavior of women.

- Why do you think Ban Zhao began her work in such a self-deprecating manner?

- In what ways does *Lessons for Women* reflect Confucian attitudes (see Document 5.1, pp. 217–19)? Why do you think *The Analects* itself seldom referred directly to women?

- How would Ban Zhao define an ideal woman? An ideal man? An ideal marriage?

- In what ways is she critical of existing attitudes and practices regarding women?

- How does she understand the purposes of education for boys and for girls?

- Does *Lessons for Women* support or undermine the view of women's lives that appears in Fu Xuan's poem?

BAN ZHAO

Lessons for Women

Late First Century C.E.

I, the unworthy writer, am unsophisticated, unenlightened, and by nature unintelligent, but I am fortunate both to have received not a little favor from my scholarly Father, and to have had a cultured mother and instructresses upon whom to rely for a literary education as well as for training in good manners. More than forty years have passed since at the age of fourteen I took up the dustpan and the broom in the Cao family [the family into which she married]. During this time with trembling heart I feared constantly that I might disgrace my parents, and that I might multiply difficulties for both the women and the men of my husband's family. Day and night I was distressed in heart, but I labored without confessing weariness. Now and

hereafter, however, I know how to escape from such fears.

Being careless, and by nature stupid, I taught and trained my children without system....I do grieve that you, my daughters, just now at the age for marriage, have not...learned the proper customs for married women. I fear that by failure in good manners in other families you will humiliate both your ancestors and your clan....At hours of leisure I have composed...these instructions under the title, *Lessons for Women*.

Humility

On the third day after the birth of a girl the ancients observed three customs: first to place the baby below the bed; second to give her a potsherd° with which to play; and third to announce her birth

Source: Nancy Lee Swann, trans., *Pan Chao: Foremost Woman Scholar of China*, (New York: Century, 1932), 82–90.

°**potsherd:** a piece of a broken pot.

to her ancestors by an offering. Now to lay the baby below the bed plainly indicated that she is lowly and weak, and should regard it as her primary duty to humble herself before others. To give her potsherds with which to play indubitably signified that she should practice labor and consider it her primary duty to be industrious. To announce her birth before her ancestors clearly meant that she ought to esteem as her primary duty the continuation of the observance of worship in the home.

These three ancient customs epitomize woman's ordinary way of life and the teachings of the traditional ceremonial rites and regulations. Let a woman modestly yield to others; let her respect others; let her put others first, herself last.... Always let her seem to tremble and to fear. When a woman follows such maxims as these then she may be said to humble herself before others....

Let a woman retire late to bed, but rise early to duties; let her nor dread tasks by day or by night.... When a woman follows such rules as these, then she may be said to be industrious.

Let a woman be correct in manner and upright in character in order to serve her husband.... Let her love not gossip and silly laughter. Let her cleanse and purify and arrange in order the wine and the food for the offerings to the ancestors. When a woman observes such principles as these, then she may be said to continue ancestral worship.

No woman who observes these three fundamentals of life has ever had a bad reputation or has fallen into disgrace. If a woman fails to observe them, how can her name be honored; how can she but bring disgrace upon herself?

Husband and Wife

The Way of husband and wife is intimately connected with Yin and Yang and relates the individual to gods and ancestors. Truly it is the great principle of Heaven and Earth, and the great basis of human relationships....

If a husband be unworthy, then he possesses nothing by which to control his wife. If a wife be unworthy, then she possesses nothing with which to serve her husband. If a husband does not control his wife, then the rules of conduct manifesting his authority are abandoned and broken. If a wife does not serve her husband, then the proper relationship between men and women and the natural order of things are neglected and destroyed. As a matter of fact the purpose of these two is the same.

Now examine the gentlemen of the present age. They only know that wives must be controlled, and that the husband's rules of conduct manifesting his authority must be established. They therefore teach their boys to read books and study histories. But they do not in the least understand that husbands and masters must also be served, and that the proper relationship and the rites should be maintained. Yet only to teach men and not to teach women—is that not ignoring the essential relation between them? According to the "Rites" [a classic text], it is the rule to begin to teach children to read at the age of eight years, and by the age of fifteen years they ought then to be ready for cultural training. Only why should it not be that girls' education as well as boys' be according to this principle?

Respect and Caution

As Yin and Yang are not of the same nature, so man and woman have different characteristics. The distinctive quality of the Yang is rigidity; the function of the Yin is yielding. Man is honored for strength; a woman is beautiful on account of her gentleness. Hence there arose the common saying: "A man though born like a wolf may, it is feared, become a weak monstrosity; a woman though born like a mouse may, it is feared, become a tiger."

Now for self-culture nothing equals respect for others.... Consequently it can be said that the Way of respect and acquiescence is woman's most important principle of conduct.... Those who are steadfast in devotion know that they should stay in their proper places....

If husband and wife have the habit of staying together, never leaving one another, and following each other around within the limited space of their own rooms, then they will lust after and take liberties with one another. From such action improper language will arise between the two. This kind of discussion may lead to licentiousness. But of licentiousness will be born a heart of disrespect to the husband. Such a result comes from not knowing that one should stay in one's proper place....

If wives suppress not contempt for husbands, then it follows that such wives rebuke and scold their husbands. If husbands stop not short of anger, then they are certain to beat their wives. The correct relationship between husband and wife is based upon harmony and intimacy, and conjugal love is grounded in proper union. Should actual blows be dealt, how could matrimonial relationship be preserved? Should sharp words be spoken, how could conjugal love exist? If love and proper relationship both be destroyed, then husband and wife are divided.

Womanly Qualifications

A woman ought to have four qualifications: (1) womanly virtue; (2) womanly words; (3) womanly bearing; and (4) womanly work. Now what is called womanly virtue need not be brilliant ability, exceptionally different from others. Womanly words need be neither clever in debate nor keen in conversation. Womanly appearance requires neither a pretty nor a perfect face and form. Womanly work need not be work done more skillfully than that of others.

To guard carefully her chastity; to control circumspectly her behavior; in every motion to exhibit modesty; and to model each act on the best usage, this is womanly virtue.

To choose her words with care; to avoid vulgar language; to speak at appropriate times; and nor to weary others with much conversation, may be called the characteristics of womanly words.

To wash and scrub filth away; to keep clothes and ornaments fresh and clean; to wash the head and bathe the body regularly, and to keep the person free from disgraceful filth, may be called the characteristics of womanly bearing.

With whole-hearted devotion to sew and to weave; to love not gossip and silly laughter; in cleanliness and order to prepare the wine and food for serving guests, may be called the characteristics of womanly work....

Implicit Obedience

Whenever the mother-in-law says, "Do not do that," and if what she says is right, unquestionably the daughter-in-law obeys. Whenever the mother-in-law says, "Do that," even if what she says is wrong, still the daughter-in-law submits unfailingly to the command. Let a woman not act contrary to the wishes and the opinions of parents-in-law about right and wrong; let her not dispute with them what is straight and what is crooked. Such docility may be called obedience which sacrifices personal opinion. Therefore the ancient book, *A Pattern for Women*, says: "If a daughter-in-law who follows the wishes of her parents-in-law is like an echo and shadow, how could she not be praised?"

Document 6.3

An Alternative to Patriarchy in India

About the same time that Ban Zhao was applying the principles of Confucianism to women in China, *The Laws of Manu* was being compiled in India. A core text of classical Indian civilization, those laws defined and sharply circumscribed the behavioral expectations appropriate for women. According to one passage, "In childhood a female must be subject to her father, in youth to her husband, when her lord is dead to her sons; a woman must never be independent."

One path of release for women from such conditions of Indian patriarchy lay in becoming a Buddhist nun and entering a monastery where women were relatively less restricted and could exercise more authority than in ordinary life. Known as *bikkhunis*, such women composed hundreds of poems in the early centuries of Indian Buddhism. They were long recited and transmitted in an oral form and brought together in a collection known as the *Psalms of the Sisters*, which was set to writing probably during the first century B.C.E. These poems became part of the officially recognized Buddhist scriptures, known as the Pali Canon. As such, they represent the only early text in any of the world's major religions that was written by women and about the religious experience of women. A selection of those poems follows here.

- What kinds of women were attracted to Buddhist monastic life? What aspects of life as a *bikkhuni* appealed to them?

- What views of the world, of sensuality, and of human fulfillment are apparent in these poems?

- In what ways might these poems represent a criticism of Hindu patriarchy?

- What criticism of these women would you anticipate? How might advocates of Hindu patriarchy view the renunciation that these nuns practiced?

- How do these poems reflect core Buddhist teachings?

Psalms of the Sisters
First Century B.C.E.

Sumangala's Mother

O woman well set free! how free am I,
How throughly free from kitchen drudgery!
Me stained and squalid 'mong my cooking-pots
My brutal husband ranked as even less
Than the sunshades he sits and weaves alway.
Purged now of all my former lust and hate,
I dwell, musing at ease beneath the shade
Of spreading boughs—O, but 'tis well with me!

A Former Courtesan

How was I once puff'd up, incens'd with the
    bloom of my beauty,

Vain of my perfect form, my fame and success
    'midst the people,
Fill'd with the pride of my youth, unknowing the
    Truth and unheeding!
Lo! I made my body, bravely arrayed, deftly
    painted,
Speak for me to the lads, whilst I at the door of
    the harlot
Stood, like a crafty hunter, weaving his snares,
    ever watchful.
Yea, I bared without shame my body and wealth
    of adorning;
Manifold wiles I wrought, devouring the virtue
    of many.
To-day with shaven head, wrapt in my robe,
I go forth on my daily round for food;...
Now all the evil bonds that fetter gods
And men are wholly rent and cut away....
Calm and content I know Nibbana's
    Peace.

Source: *Psalms of the Sisters*, Vol. I, in *Psalms of the Early Buddhists*, translated by Mrs. Rhys Davids (London: Henry Frowde, Oxford University Press Warehouse, Amen Corner, E.C., 1909), poems 21, 39, 49, 54, 70.

The Daughter of a Poor Brahmin

Fallen on evil days was I of yore.
No husband had I, nor no child, no friends
Or kin—whence could I food or raiment find?
As beggars go, I took my bowl and staff,
And sought me alms, begging from house to
    house,
Sunburnt, frost-bitten, seven weary years.
Then came I where a woman Mendicant
Shared with me food, and drink, and welcomed me,
And said: "Come forth into our homeless life!"...
I heard her and I marked, and did her will.

The Daughter of a Wealthy Treasurer

Daughter of Treas'rer Majjha's famous house,
Rich, beautiful and prosperous, I was born
To vast possessions and to lofty rank.
Nor lacked I suitors—many came and wooed;
The sons of Kings and merchant princes came
With costly gifts, all eager for my hand....
But I had seen th' Enlightened, Chief o' the
    World, The One Supreme. [the Buddha]
And [I] knew this world should see me ne'er
    return.

Then cutting off the glory of my hair,
I entered on the homeless ways of life.
'Tis now the seventh night since first all sense
Of craving drièd up within my heart.

The Goldsmith's Daughter

A maiden I, all clad in white, once heard
The Norm,° and hearkened eager, earnestly,
So in me rose discernment of the Truths.
Thereat all worldly pleasures irked me sore,
For I could see the perils that beset
This reborn compound, 'personality,'
And to renounce it was my sole desire.
So I forsook my world—my kinsfolk all,
My slaves, my hirelings, and my villages,
And the rich fields and meadows spread around,
Things fair and making for the joy of life—
All these I left, and sought the Sisterhood,
Turning my back upon no mean estate....
See now this Subhā, standing on the Norm,
Child of a craftsman in the art of gold!
Behold! she hath attained to utter calm....

––––––––––––––
°**Norm:** Buddhist teaching.

Document 6.4

Roman Women in Protest

On occasion women not only wrote but also acted in the public arena. A particularly well-known example of such action took place in Rome in the wake of the Second Punic War with Carthage in North Africa. In 218 B.C.E. the Carthaginian commander Hannibal had invaded the Italian peninsula and threatened Rome itself. In those desperate circumstances Roman authorities passed the Oppian Laws (215 B.C.E.), which restricted women's use of luxury goods so as to preserve resources for the war effort. Twenty years later (195 B.C.E.), with Rome now secure and prosperous, Roman women demanded the repeal of those laws and in the process triggered a major debate among Roman officials. That debate and the women's protest that accompanied it were chronicled early in the first century C.E. by Livy, a famous Roman historian.

■ How did Roman women make their views known? Do you think the protesters represented all Roman women or those of a particular class?

- How might you summarize the arguments against repeal (Cato) and those favoring repeal (Lucius Valerius)? To what extent did the two men actually differ in their views of women?

- How might one of the Roman women involved in the protest have made her own case?

- What can we learn from Livy's account about the social position of Roman women and the attitudes of Roman men?

- This document was written by a male historian and records the speeches of two other male officials. How might this affect the ability of historians to use it for understanding Roman women?

LIVY

History of Rome

Late First Century B.C.E. to Early First Century C.E.

The law said that no woman might own more than half an ounce of gold nor wear a multi-colored dress nor ride in a carriage in the city or in a town within a mile of it, unless there was a religious festival.... [A] crowd of men, both supporters and opponents [of repeal], filled the Capitoline Hill. The matrons, whom neither counsel nor shame nor their husbands' orders could keep at home, blockaded every street in the city and every entrance to the Forum. As the men came down to the Forum, the matrons besought them to let them, too, have back the luxuries they had enjoyed before, giving as their reason that the republic was thriving and that everyone's private wealth was increasing with every day. This crowd of women was growing daily, for now they were even gathering from the towns and villages. Before long they dared go up and solicit the consuls, praetors, and other magistrates; but one of the consuls could not be moved in the least, Marcus Porcius Cato, who spoke in favor of the law:

"If each man of us, fellow citizens, had established that the right and authority of the husband should be held over the mother of his own family,

we should have less difficulty with women in general; now, at home our freedom is conquered by female fury, here in the Forum it is bruised and trampled upon, and, because we have not contained the individuals, we fear the lot....

"Indeed, I blushed when, a short while ago, I walked through the midst of a band of women. Had not respect for the dignity and modesty of certain ones (not them all!) restrained me....I should have said, 'What kind of behavior is this? Running around in public, blocking streets, and speaking to other women's husbands! Could you not have asked your own husbands the same thing at home? Are you more charming in public with others' husbands than at home with your own? And yet, it is not fitting even at home... for you to concern yourselves with what laws are passed or repealed here.' Our ancestors did not want women to conduct any— not even private—business without a guardian; they wanted them to be under the authority of parents, brothers, or husbands; we (the gods help us!) even now let them snatch at the government and meddle in the Forum and our assemblies. What are they doing now on the streets and crossroads, if they are not persuading the tribunes to vote for repeal? Give the reins to their unbridled nature and this unmastered creature....They want freedom, nay license... in all things. If they are victorious now, what will

Source: Livy, "History of Rome" in *Women's Life in Greece and Rome*, 2nd ed., edited by Mary R. Lefkowitz and translated by Maureen B. Fant (Baltimore: Johns Hopkins Press, 1982), 143–47.

they not attempt?... As soon as they begin to be your equals, they will have become your superiors....

"What honest excuse is offered, pray, for this womanish rebellion? 'That we might shine with gold and purple,' says one of them, 'that we might ride through the city in coaches on holidays and working-days.'...

"The woman who can spend her own money will do so; the one who cannot will ask her husband. Pity that husband—the one who gives in and the one who stands firm! What he refuses, he will see given by another man. Now they publicly solicit other women's husbands, and, what is worse, they ask for a law and votes, and certain men give them what they want.... Fellow citizens, do not imagine that the state which existed before the law was passed will return..., as when wild animals are first chafed by their chains and then released."

After this... Lucius Valerius spoke on behalf of the motion....

"[Cato]... has called this assemblage 'secession' and sometimes 'womanish rebellion,' because the matrons have publicly asked you, in peacetime when the state is happy and prosperous, to repeal a law passed against them during the straits of war....

'What, may I ask, are the women doing that is new, having gathered and come forth publicly in a case which concerns them directly? Have they never appeared in public before this?... Listen to how often they have done so—always for the public good. From the very beginning—the reign of Romulus— when the Capitoline had been taken by the Sabines and there was fighting in the middle of the Forum, was not the battle halted by the women's intervention between the two lines?... When Rome was in the hands of the Gauls, who ransomed it? Indeed the matrons agreed unanimously to turn their gold over to the public need.... Indeed, as no one is amazed that they acted in situations affecting men and women alike, why should we wonder that they have taken action in a case which concerns themselves?... We have proud ears indeed, if, while masters do not scorn the appeals of slaves, we are angry when honorable women ask something of us....

"Who then does not know that this is a recent law, passed twenty years ago? Since our matrons lived for so long by the highest standards of behavior without any law, what risk is there that, once it is repealed, they will yield to luxury?...

"Shall it be our wives alone to whom the fruits of peace and tranquility of the state do not come?... Shall we forbid only women to wear purple? When you, a man, may use purple on your clothes, will you not allow the mother of your family to have a purple cloak, and will your horse be more beautifully saddled than your wife is garbed?...

"[Cato] has said that, if none of them had anything, there would be no rivalry among individual women. By Hercules! All are unhappy and indignant when they see the finery denied them permitted to the wives of the Latin allies, when they see them adorned with gold and purple, when those other women ride through the city and they follow on foot, as though the power belonged to the other women's cities, not to their own. This could wound the spirits of men; what do you think it could do the spirits of women, whom even little things disturb? They cannot partake of magistracies, priesthoods, triumphs, badges of office, gifts, or spoils of war; elegance, finery, and beautiful clothes are women's badges, in these they find joy and take pride, this our forebears called the women's world. When they are in mourning, what, other than purple and gold, do they take off? What do they put on again when they have completed the period of mourning? What do they add for public prayer and thanksgiving other than still greater ornament? Of course, if you repeal the Oppian law, you will not have the power to prohibit that which the law now forbids; daughters, wives, even some men's sisters will be less under your authority—never, while her men are well, is a woman's slavery cast off; and even they hate the freedom created by widowhood and orphanage. They prefer their adornment to be subject to your judgment, not the law's; and you ought to hold them in marital power and guardianship, not slavery; you should prefer to be called fathers and husbands to masters. The consul just now used odious terms when he said 'womanish rebellion' and 'secession'. For there is danger—he would have us believe— that they will seize the Sacred Hill as once the angry plebeians did.... It is for the weaker sex to submit to whatever you advise. The more power you possess, all the more moderately should you exercise your authority."

When these speeches for and against the law had been made, a considerably larger crowd of women poured forth in public the next day; as a single body they besieged the doors of the Brutuses, who were vetoing their colleagues' motion, and they did not stop until the tribunes took back their veto.... Twenty years after it was passed, the law was repealed.

Using the Evidence:
Patriarchy and Women's Voices in the Classical Era

1. **Comparing gender systems:** Based on these documents, how might you compare the gender systems of China, India, and the Roman Empire? What common features of patriarchy did they share? In what ways did they differ?

2. **Evaluating the possibilities of action for women:** In what ways were women able to challenge at least some elements of their classical-era patriarchal societies? Is there evidence in these documents of anything similar to the feminist thinking or action of our own times?

3. **Internalizing social values:** To what extent did women in the classical era civilizations internalize or accept the patriarchal values of their societies? Why might they have done so?

4. **Making judgments:** If you were a woman living in the classical era, which of these civilizations would you prefer to live in and why? Do you think this kind of question—judging the past by the standards of the present—is a valid approach to historical inquiry?

Visual Sources

Considering the Evidence:
Pompeii as a Window on the Roman World

You could hear the shrieks of women, the wailing of infants, and the shouting of men; some were calling their parents, others their children or their wives, trying to recognize them by their voices. People bewailed their own fate or that of their relatives, and there were some who prayed for death in their terror of dying. Many besought the aid of the gods, but still more imagined there were no gods left, and that the universe was plunged into eternal darkness for evermore."[20]

Written by a prominent Roman known as Pliny the Younger, this eyewitness account details reactions to the volcanic eruption of Mount Vesuvius, located on the southwestern side of the Italian peninsula, on August 24, 79 C.E. That eruption buried the nearby Roman city of Pompeii, but it also preserved the city, frozen in time, until archaeologists began to uncover it in the mid-eighteenth century (see Map 4.4, p. 156). Now substantially excavated, Pompeii is an archaeological and historical treasure, offering a unique window into life in the Roman Empire during the first century C.E.

As this city of perhaps 20,000 people emerged from layers of ash, it stood revealed as a small but prosperous center of commerce and agriculture, serving as a point of entry for goods coming to the southern Italian peninsula by sea. Pompeii also hosted numerous vineyards, production facilities for wine and olive oil, and a fisheries industry. In addition, the city was a tourist destination for well-to-do Romans. The houses of the wealthy were elegant structures, often built around a central courtyard, and decorated with lovely murals displaying still-life images, landscapes, and scenes from Greek and Roman mythology. An inscription found on the threshold of one house expressed the entrepreneurial spirit of the town: "Gain is pure joy."[21]

Laid out in a grid pattern with straight streets, the city's numerous public facilities included a central bathing/swimming pool, some twenty-five street fountains, various public bathhouses, and a large food market as well as many bars and small restaurants. More than thirty brothels, often featuring explicit erotic art, offered sexual services at relatively inexpensive prices. One inscription, apparently aimed at local tourists, declared: "If anyone is looking for some tender love in this town, keep in mind that here all the girls are very

Visual Source 6.1 Terentius Neo and His Wife (Scala/Art Resource, NY)

Visual Source 6.2 A Pompeii Banquet (Museo Archeologico Nazionale, Naples/Roger-Viollet/The Bridgeman Art Library)

friendly." Graffiti too abounded, much of it clearly sexual. Here are three of the milder examples: "Atimetus got me pregnant"; "Sarra, you are not being very nice, leaving me all alone like this"; and "If anyone does not believe in Venus, they should gaze at my girlfriend."[22]

The preserved art of Pompeii, especially the wall paintings, provides a glimpse into the social life of that city. Most of that art, of course, catered to and reflected the life of the more prosperous classes. Visual Source 6.1 shows a portrait of Terentius Neo, a prominent businessman and magistrate (an elected public official), and his wife. He is wearing a toga and holding a papyrus scroll, while she wears a tunic and is holding to her lips a stylus, used for writing on the wax-covered wooden tablet that she carries. Her hair is styled in a fashion popular in the mid-first century.

- What do you think the artist is trying to convey by highlighting the literacy of both people?

- What overall impression of these two people and their relationship to each other does this painting suggest?

Terentius Neo and his wife were no doubt served by slaves in their home, as slave owning was common in the Roman world, particularly among the upper classes. In the streets and homes of urban areas, slaves and free people mingled quite openly. Roman slavery was not distinguished by race, and the outward signs of urban slavery were few, especially for those practicing professions. Such a couple no doubt gave and attended banquets similar to the one depicted in Visual Source 6.2, where well-to-do guests reclined on padded couches while slaves served them food and drink. Dancers, acrobats, and singers often provided entertainment at such events, which provided an occasion for elites to impress others with their lavish display of wealth and generosity.

- What signs of social status are evident in this painting?

- How are slaves, shown here in the foreground, portrayed?

The lives of the less exalted appear infrequently in the art of Pompeii, but the images in Visual Source 6.3 provide some entrée into their world. These are frescoes painted on the wall of a *caupona*, an inn or tavern catering to the lower classes. This particular caupona was located at the intersection of two busy streets where it might easily attract customers. The first image shows Myrtale, a prostitute, kissing a man, while the caption above reads: "I don't want to, with Myrtale." In the second image a female barmaid serves two

Visual Source 6.3 Scenes in a Pompeii Tavern (©Ministero per I Beni e le Attivita Culturali—Soprintendenza archeologica di Napoli)

customers with a large jug and a cup, while they compete for her attention. In the third image, two men playing dice are arguing.

- Why do you think a tavern owner might have such paintings in his place of business?

- What might we learn about tavern life from these images?

- What roles did women play in the tavern?

- What differences do you notice between these paintings and those depicting the lives of the upper classes?

The excavated ruins of Pompeii have much to tell us about the religious as well as the social life of the Roman world in the first century C.E., before Christianity had spread widely. Based on ritual observance rather than doctrine or theology, Roman religious practice sought to obtain the favor of the gods as a way of promoting success, prosperity, and good fortune. A core expression of the diverse and eclectic world of Roman religion was the imperial cult. In Pompeii, a number of temples were dedicated to one or another of the deified emperors, employing together a large cadre of priests and priestesses. Linked to the imperial cult were temples devoted to the traditional Greco-Roman gods such as Apollo, Venus, and Jupiter.

Probably more important to ordinary people were their *lararia* (household shrines), often a niche in the wall that housed paintings or sculptures of *lares* (guardian spirits or deities believed to provide protection within the home). Families offered gifts of fruit, cakes, and wine to these spirits, and the lararia were the focal point for various sacrifices and rituals associated with birth, marriage, and death. Visual Source 6.4 shows one of these shrines, uncovered in the home of a well-to-do freedman (former slave) named Vetti. Protecting the family from external danger were two lares, standing on either side of the lararium and holding their drinking horns. In the center was the *genius*, the spirit of the male head of household. Dressed in a toga and offering a sacrifice, this spirit embodied the character of the man, especially his procreative powers, and so guaranteed many children for the household. The snake at the bottom represented still other benevolent guardian spirits of the family in a fashion very different from Christian symbolism of the snake.

- Why might such a shrine and the spirits it accommodated be more meaningful for many people than the state-approved cults?

- What significance might you find in the temple-like shape of the lararium?

Visual Source 6.4 A Domestic Shrine (Alinari/Art Resource, NY)

In addition to the official cults and the worship of household gods, by the first century C.E. a number of newer traditions, often called "mystery religions," were spreading widely in the Roman Empire. Deriving from the eastern realm of the empire and beyond (Greece, Egypt, and Persia, for example), these mystery religions illustrate the kinds of cultural exchange that took place within the Empire. They offered an alternative to the official cults, for they were more personal, emotional, and intimate, usually featuring a ritual initiation into sacred mysteries, codes of moral behavior, and the promise of an afterlife. Among the most popular of these mystery cults in Pompeii was that of Isis, an Egyptian goddess who restored her husband/brother, Osiris, to life and was worshipped as a compassionate protector of the downtrodden.

Visual Source 6.5 Mystery Religions: The Cult of Dionysus (Werner Forman/Corbis)

Another mystery cult, this one of Greek origin, was associated with Dionysus, a god of wine, ecstasy, and poetic inspiration and especially popular with women. Often associated with drunkenness, trance states, wild dancing, and unrestrained sexuality, the cult of Dionysus encouraged at least the temporary abandonment of conventional inhibitions and social restrictions as initiates sought union with Dionysus. A series of wall paintings on a Pompeii building known as the Villa of Mysteries depicts the process of initiation into the cult of Dionysus, perhaps in preparation for marriage. Visual Source 6.5 shows a particularly dramatic phase of that initiation in which a woman is ritually whipped, while a naked devotee dances ecstatically with a pair of cymbals above her head and a companion holds a rod of phallic symbolism that is sacred to Dionysus. In any such process of religious initiation, the initiate undergoes a series of trials or purifications in which he or she "dies" symbolically, achieves mystical union with the god, and is "reborn" into the new community of the cult.

- What aspects of the initiation process are visible in this image?

- How might you understand the role of whipping in the initiation process? How would you interpret the relationship of the initiate and the woman on whose lap she is resting her head?

- In what way is sexual union, symbolized by the rod, significant in the initiation?

- Why do you think Roman authorities took action against these mystery religions, even as they did against Christianity?

- What did the mystery cults of Isis or Dionysus provide that neither the state cults nor household gods might offer?

Using the Evidence:
Pompeii as a Window on the Roman World

1. **Characterizing Pompeii:** What does the art of Pompeii, as reflected in these visual sources, tell us about the social and religious life of this small Roman city in the first century C.E.? To what extent, if at all, should historians generalize from Pompeii to the Roman Empire as a whole?

2. **Noticing class differences:** What class or social distinctions are apparent in these visual sources?

3. **Identifying gender roles:** What do these visual sources suggest about the varied lives and social roles of women and men in Pompeii?

CHAPTER SEVEN

Classical Era Variations

Africa and the Americas

500 B.C.E.—1200 C.E.

"In a [Maya] community called Xolep, there was no paper or pencils where I taught. I started by drawing figures in the dirt. We then taught letters by forming them with sticks. One day students brought flower petals to shape the letters. . . . When we were able to gather enough money for notebooks, we gave them to the students and asked them to report the next day to the tree where we were holding school. . . . They proudly filed under the teaching tree, notebooks tucked under their arms, feeling that they were now officially students."[1]

This incident, reported in 1999 by a participant in an independent schools movement among the Maya of southern Mexico, was a tiny part of an ongoing revival of Maya culture. Despite the collapse of their famous classical civilization more than a thousand years ago, Maya language and folkways have persisted among some 6 million people currently living in Mexico, Belize, Guatemala, and Honduras. And despite five centuries of repression, exploitation, and neglect at the hands of Spanish colonizers and the independent governments that followed, they were now in the midst of what one writer called "a new time of the Maya."[2] They were writing their own histories, celebrating their own culture, creating their own organizations, and teaching their children to read. The most dramatic expression of this recent Maya revival was an armed uprising, begun in early 1994 and led by the Zapatista Army of National Liberation. Growing out of long-term social and economic grievances against local landowners and an unresponsive government, that rebellion stunned Mexico and focused global attention on the poverty and misery of the country's indigenous Maya people. Once

The Maya Temple of the Great Jaguar in Tikal: Located in the Maya city of Tikal in present-day Guatemala, this temple was constructed in the eighth century C.E. and excavated by archeologists in the late nineteenth century. It served as the tomb of the Tikal ruler Jasaw Chan K'awiil I (682–734). Some 144 feet tall, it was topped by a three-room temple complex and a huge roofcomb showing the ruler on his throne. Carved on a wooden beam inside the temple is an image of the ruler protected by a huge jaguar along with illustrations of his military victories. (Peter M. Wilson/Alamy) again, some 1,500 years after the high point of their classical civilization, the Maya were making history.

FOR MANY PEOPLE, THE CLASSICAL ERA EVOKES most vividly the civilizations of Eurasia—especially the Greeks and the Romans, the Persians and the Chinese, and the Indians of South Asia—yet those were not the only classical-era civilizations. During this period, the Mesoamerican Maya and the Peruvian Moche thrived, as did several civilizations in Africa, including Meroë, Axum, and the Niger River valley. Furthermore, those peoples who did not organize themselves around cities or states likewise had histories of note and alternative ways of constructing their societies, although they are often neglected in favor of civilizations. This chapter explores the histories of the varied peoples of Africa and the Americas during the classical era. On occasion, those histories will extend some centuries beyond the chronological boundaries of the classical age in Eurasia, because patterns of historical development around the world did not always coincide precisely.

At the broadest level, however, human cultures evolved in quite similar fashion around the world. All, of course, were part of that grand process of human migration that initially peopled the planet. Beginning in Africa, that vast movement of human-kind subsequently encompassed Eurasia, Australia, the Americas, and Oceania. Almost everywhere, gathering and hunting long remained the sole basis for sustaining life and society. Then, on the three supercontinents—Eurasia, Africa, and the Americas—the momentous turn of the Agricultural Revolution took place independently and in several distinct areas of each landmass. That revolutionary transformation of human life subsequently generated, in particularly rich agricultural environments of all three regions, those more complex societies that we know as civilizations, which featured cities, states, monumental architecture, and great social inequality. In these ways, the historical trajectory of the human journey on the earth has a certain unity and sim-ilarity across quite distinct continental regions. At the beginning of the Common Era, that trajectory had generated a total world population of about 250 million people, substantially less than the current population of the United States alone. By contemporary standards, it was still a sparsely populated planet.

The world's human population was distributed very unevenly across the three giant continents, as the Snapshot indicates. If these estimates are even reasonably accurate, then during the classical era Eurasia was home to more than 80 percent of the world's people, Africa about 11 percent, and the Americas between 5 and 7 percent. That unevenness in population distribution is part of the reason why world historians focus more attention on Eurasia than on Africa or the Americas. Here lies one of the major differences among the continents.

There were other differences as well. The absence of most animals capable of domestication meant that no pastoral societies developed in the Americas, and no draft animals were available to pull plows or carts or to carry heavy loads for long dis-tances. Africa lacked wild sheep, goats, chickens, horses, and camels, but its proxim-ity to Eurasia meant that these animals, once domesticated, became widely available

Snapshot   Continental Population in the Classical Era[3]

(Note: Population figures for such early times are merely estimates and are often controversial among scholars. Percentages do not always total 100 percent due to rounding.)

	Eurasia	Africa	North America	Central/South America	Australia/ Oceania	Total World
Area (in square miles and as percentage of world total)						
	21,049,000 (41%)	11,608,000 (22%)	9,365,000 (18%)	6,880,000 (13%)	2,968,000 (6%)	51,870,000
Population (in millions and as percentage of world total)						
400 B.C.E.	127 (83%)	17 (11%)	1 (0.7%)	7 (5%)	1 (0.7%)	153
10 C.E.	213 (85%)	26 (10%)	2 (0.8%)	10 (4%)	1 (0.4%)	252
200 C.E.	215 (84%)	30 (12%)	2 (0.8%)	9 (4%)	1 (0.4%)	257
600 C.E.	167 (80%)	24 (12%)	2 (1%)	14 (7%)	1 (0.5%)	208
1000 C.E.	195 (77%)	39 (15%)	2 (0.8%)	16 (6%)	1 (0.4%)	253

to African peoples. Metallurgy in the Americas was likewise far less developed than in the Eastern Hemisphere, where iron tools and weapons played such an important role in economic and military life. In the Americas, writing was limited to the Mesoamerican region and was most highly developed among the Maya, whereas in Africa it was confined to the northern and northeastern parts of the continent during the classical era. In Eurasia, by contrast, writing emerged elaborately in many regions. Classical-era civilizations in Africa and the Americas were fewer in number and generally smaller than those of Eurasia, and larger numbers of their people lived in communities that did not feature cities and states.

To illustrate the historical developments of the classical era beyond Eurasia, this chapter focuses on three regions in Africa and three in the Americas. To what extent did these histories parallel those of Eurasia? In what ways did they forge new or different paths?

The African Northeast

When historians refer to Africa during the classical era, they are speaking generally of a geographic concept, a continental landmass, and not a cultural identity. Certainly no one living on the continent at that time thought of himself or herself as an African. Like Eurasia or the Americas, Africa hosted numerous separate societies, cultures, and civilizations with vast differences among them as well as some interaction between them.

Many of these differences grew out of the continent's environmental variations. Small regions of Mediterranean climate in the northern and southern extremes, large deserts (the Sahara and the Kalahari), even larger regions of savanna grasslands, tropical rain forest in the continent's center, highlands and mountains in eastern Africa — all of these features, combined with the continent's enormous size, ensured variation and difference among Africa's many peoples. Africa did, however, have one distinctive environmental feature: bisected by the equator, it was the most tropical of the world's three supercontinents. Persistent warm temperatures caused the rapid decomposition of vegetable matter called humus, resulting in poorer and less fertile soils and a less productive agriculture than in the more temperate Eurasia. Those climatic conditions also spawned numerous disease-carrying insects and parasites, which have long created serious health problems in many parts of the continent. It was within these environmental constraints that African peoples made their histories.

A further geographic feature shaped African history — its proximity to Eurasia, which allowed parts of Africa to interact with Eurasian civilizations. During the classical era, North Africa was incorporated into the Roman Empire and used to produce wheat and olives on large estates with slave labor. Christianity spread widely, giving rise to some of the early Church's most famous martyrs and to one of its most important theologians, Saint Augustine (354–430 C.E.). The Christian faith found an even more permanent foothold in the lands now known as Ethiopia.

Arabia was another point of contact with the larger world for African peoples. The arrival of the domesticated camel, probably from Arabia, generated a nomadic pastoral way of life among some of the Berber peoples of the western Sahara during the first three centuries C.E. A little later, camels also made possible trans-Saharan commerce, which linked interior West Africa to the world of Mediterranean civilization. Over many centuries, the East African coast was a port of call for Egyptian, Roman, and Arab merchants, and that region subsequently became an integral part of Indian Ocean trading networks.

Both the external connections and, more important, the internal development of African societies generated various patterns of historical change during the classical era. Three regions — northeastern Africa, the Niger River basin in West Africa, and the vast world of Bantu-speaking Africa south of the equator — serve to illustrate these differences and the many social and cultural experiments spawned by the peoples of this continent.

Meroë: Continuing a Nile Valley Civilization

■ Connection
How did the history of Meroë and Axum reflect interaction with neighboring civilizations?

In the Nile Valley south of Egypt lay the lands of Nubian civilization, almost as old as Egypt itself. Over many centuries, Nubians both traded and fought with Egypt, alternately conquering and being conquered by their northern neighbor. While borrowing heavily from Egypt, Nubia remained a distinct and separate civilization

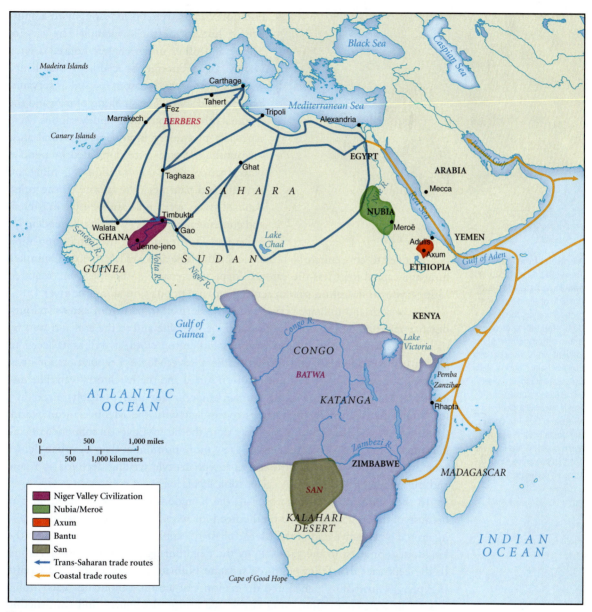

Map 7.1 Africa in the Classical Era

During the classical era, older African civilizations such as Egypt and Nubia persisted and changed, while new civilizations emerged in Axum and the Niger River valley. South of the equator, Bantu-speaking peoples spread rapidly, creating many new societies and identities.

(see Chapter 3). By the classical era, as Egypt fell under foreign control, Nubian civilization came to center on the southern city of Meroë, where it flourished between 300 B.C.E. and 100 C.E. (see Map 7.1).

Politically, the Kingdom of Meroë was governed by an all-powerful and sacred monarch, a position occasionally conferred on women. In accordance with ancient

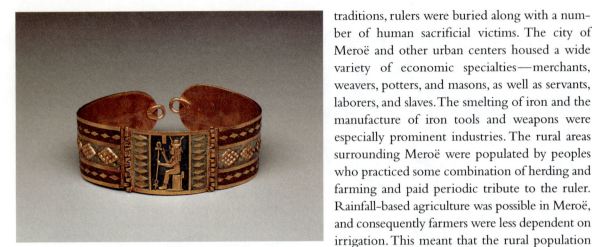

A Bracelet from Meroë

This gold bracelet, dating to about 100 B.C.E., illustrates the skill of Meroë's craftsmen as well as the kingdom's reputation as one of the wealthiest states of the ancient world. (Bracelet with image of Hathor, Nubian, Meroitic Period, about 100 B.C.E. Object Place: Sudan, Nubia, Gebel Barkal, Pyramid 8, Gold, enamel. Museum of Fine Arts, Boston, Harvard University–Boston Museum of Fine Arts Expedition, 20.333. Photograph © 2008 Museum of Fine Arts, Boston)

traditions, rulers were buried along with a number of human sacrificial victims. The city of Meroë and other urban centers housed a wide variety of economic specialties—merchants, weavers, potters, and masons, as well as servants, laborers, and slaves. The smelting of iron and the manufacture of iron tools and weapons were especially prominent industries. The rural areas surrounding Meroë were populated by peoples who practiced some combination of herding and farming and paid periodic tribute to the ruler. Rainfall-based agriculture was possible in Meroë, and consequently farmers were less dependent on irrigation. This meant that the rural population did not need to concentrate so heavily along the Nile and was less directly controlled from the capital than was the case in Egypt, where state authorities were required to supervise an irrigation system serving a dense population along the river.

The wealth and military power of Meroë derived in part from extensive long-distance trading connections, to the north via the Nile and to the east and west by means of camel caravans. Its iron weapons and cotton cloth, as well as its access to gold, ivory, tortoiseshells, and ostrich feathers, gave Meroë a reputation for great riches in the classical world of northeastern Africa and the Mediterranean. The discovery in Meroë of a statue of the Roman emperor Augustus, probably seized during a raid on Roman Egypt, testifies to contact with the Mediterranean world. Culturally, Meroë seemed to move away from the heavy Egyptian influence of earlier times. A local lion god, Apedemek, grew more prominent than Egyptian deities such as Isis and Osiris, while the use of Egyptian-style writing declined as a new and still undeciphered Meroitic script took its place.

In the centuries following 100 C.E., the Kingdom of Meroë declined, in part because of deforestation caused by the need for wood to make charcoal for smelting iron. The effective end of the Meroë phase of Nubian civilization came with the kingdom's conquest in the 340s C.E. by the neighboring and rising state of Axum. In the centuries that followed, three separate Nubian states emerged, and Coptic (Egyptian) Christianity penetrated the region. For almost a thousand years, Nubia was a Christian civilization, using Greek as a liturgical language and constructing churches in Coptic or Byzantine fashion. After 1300 or so, political division, Arab immigration, and the penetration of Islam eroded this Christian civilization, and Nubia became part of the growing world of Islam.

Axum: The Making of a Christian Kingdom

If Meroë and Nubia represented the continuation of an old African civilization, Axum marked the emergence of a new one. (For various accounts about or from

Axum, see Documents: Axum and the World, pp. 307–15.) Axum lay in the Horn of Africa, in what is now Eritrea and northern Ethiopia (see Map 7.1). Its economic foundation was a highly productive agriculture that used a plow-based farming system, unlike most of the rest of Africa, which relied on the hoe or digging stick. Axum's agriculture generated substantial amounts of wheat, barley, millet, and teff, a highly nutritious grain unique to that region. By 50 C.E. or so, a substantial state had emerged, stimulated by its participation in Red Sea and Indian Ocean commerce. At Adulis, then the largest port on the East African coast, a wide range of merchants sought the products of the African interior—animal hides, rhinoceros horn, ivory, obsidian, tortoiseshells, and slaves. Taxes on this trade provided a major source of revenue for the Axumite state and the complex society that grew up within it.

The interior capital city, also known as Axum, was a center of monumental building and royal patronage for the arts. The most famous buildings were huge stone obelisks, which most likely marked royal graves. Some of them were more than 100 feet tall and at the time were the largest structures in the world hewn from a single piece of rock. The language used at court, in the towns, and for commerce was Geez, written in a script derived from South Arabia. The Axumite state exercised a measure of control over the mostly Agaw-speaking people of the country through a loose administrative structure focusing on the collection of tribute payments. To the Romans, Axum was the third major empire within the world they knew, following their own and the Persian Empire.

Through its connections to Red Sea trade and the Roman world, particularly Egypt, Axum was introduced to Christianity in the fourth century C.E. Its monarch at the time, King Ezana, adopted the new religion about the same time as Constantine did in the Roman Empire. Supported by royal authority, Christianity took root in Axum, linking that kingdom religiously to Egypt, where a distinctive Christian church known as Coptic was already well established. Although Egypt subsequently became largely Islamic, reducing its Christian community to a small minority, Christianity maintained a dominant position in the mountainous terrain of highland Ethiopia and in the early twenty-first century still represents the faith of perhaps half of the country's population.

During the fourth through the sixth century C.E., Axum mounted a campaign of imperial expansion that took its forces into the Kingdom of Meroë and across the Red Sea into Yemen in South Arabia. By 571, the traditional date for the birth of Muhammad, an Axumite army, including a number of African war elephants, had reached the gates of Mecca, but it was a fairly short-lived imperial

The Columns of Axum
Dating to the time when Axum first encountered Christianity (300–500 C.E.), this column, measuring some seventy-nine feet tall, probably served as a funeral monument for the kingdom's ancient rulers. (Antonello Langellotto/TIPS Images)

venture. The next several centuries were ones of decline for the Axumite state, owing partly to environmental changes, such as soil exhaustion, erosion, and deforestation, brought about by intensive farming. Equally important was the rise of Islam, which altered trade routes and diminished the revenue available to the Axumite state. Its last coins were struck in the early seventh century. When the state revived several centuries later, it was centered farther south on the Ethiopian plateau. There emerged the Christian church and the state that present-day Ethiopia has inherited, but the link to ancient Axum was long remembered and revered.

With their long-distance trading connections, urban centers, centralized states, complex societies, monumental architecture, written languages, and imperial ambitions, both Meroë and Axum paralleled on a smaller scale the major features of the classical civilizations of Eurasia. Furthermore, both were in direct contact with the world of Mediterranean civilizations. Elsewhere in Africa during the classical era, quite different histories unfolded.

Along the Niger River: Cities without States

In the middle stretches of the Niger River in West Africa, the classical era witnessed the emergence of a remarkable urbanization (see Map 7.1). A prolonged dry period during the five centuries after 500 B.C.E. brought growing numbers of people from the southern Sahara into the fertile floodplain of the middle Niger in search of more reliable access to water. Accompanying them were their domesticated cattle, sheep, and goats; their agricultural skills; and their ironworking technology. Over the centuries of the classical era and beyond (roughly 300 B.C.E.–900 C.E.), the peoples of this region created a distinctive city-based civilization. The most fully studied of the urban clusters that grew up along the middle Niger was the city of Jenne-jeno, which at its high point probably housed more than 40,000 people.

■ **Description**
How does the experience of the Niger Valley challenge conventional notions of "civilization"?

Among the most distinctive features of the Niger Valley civilization was the apparent absence of a corresponding state structure. Unlike the cities of Egypt, China, the Roman Empire, or Axum, these middle Niger urban centers were not encompassed within some larger imperial system. Nor were they like the city-states of ancient Mesopotamia, in which each city had its own centralized political structure, embodied in a monarch and his accompanying bureaucracy. According to a leading historian of the region, they were "cities without citadels," complex urban centers that apparently operated without the coercive authority of a state, for archeologists have found in their remains few signs of despotic power, widespread warfare, or deep social inequalities.[4] In this respect, these urban centers resemble the early cities of the Indus Valley civilization, where likewise little archeological evidence of centralized state structures has been found (see Chapter 3).

In place of such hierarchical organization, Jenne-jeno and other cities of the region emerged as clusters of economically specialized settlements surrounding a larger central town. The earliest and most prestigious of these specialized occupations was iron smithing. Working with fire and earth (ore) to produce this highly useful metal, the smiths of the Niger Valley were both feared and revered. Archeologist Roderick McIntosh, a leading figure in the excavation of Jenne-jeno, argued that "their knowledge of the transforming arts—earth to metal, insubstantial fire to the mass of iron—was the key to a secret, occult realm of immense power and immense danger."[5]

Other specializations followed. Villages of cotton weavers, potters, leather workers, and griots (praise-singers who preserved and recited the oral traditions of their societies) grew up around the central towns. Gradually these urban artisan communities became occupational castes, whose members passed their jobs and skills to their children and could marry only within their own group. In the surrounding rural areas, as in all urban-based civilizations, farmers tilled the soil and raised their animals, but specialization also occurred in farming as various ethnic groups focused on fishing, rice cultivation, or some other agricultural pursuit. At least for a time, these middle Niger cities represented an African alternative to an oppressive state, which in many parts of the world accompanied an increasingly complex urban economy and society. A series of distinct and specialized economic groups shared authority and voluntarily used the services of one another, while maintaining their own identities through physical separation.

Accompanying this unique urbanization, and no doubt stimulating it, was a growing network of indigenous West African commerce. The middle Niger floodplain supported a rich agriculture and had clay for pottery, but it lacked stone, iron ore, salt, and fuel. This scarcity of resources was the basis for long-distance commerce, which operated by boat along the Niger River and overland by donkey to the north and south. Iron ore from more than 50 miles away, copper from mines 200 miles distant, gold from even more distant sources, stones and salt from the Sahara—all of these items have been found in Jenne-jeno, in return no doubt for grain, fish, smoked meats, iron implements, and other staples. Jenne-jeno itself was an important transshipment point in this commerce, in which goods were transferred from boat to donkey or vice versa. By the 500s C.E., there is evidence of an even wider commerce and at least indirect contact, from Mauritania in the west to present-day Mali and Burkina-Faso in the east.

In the second millennium C.E., new historical patterns developed in West Africa (see Chapter 8). A number of large-scale states or empires emerged in the region— Ghana, Mali, and Songhay, among the most well known. At least partially responsible for this development was the flourishing of a camel-borne trans-Saharan commerce, previously but a trickle across the great desert. As West Africa became more firmly connected to North Africa and the Mediterranean, Islam penetrated the region, marking a gradual but major cultural transformation. All of this awaited West Africa in the postclassical era, submerging, but not completely eliminating, the decentralized city life of the Niger Valley.

South of the Equator: The World of Bantu Africa

Farther south on the African continent, patterns of historical change differed from those that gave rise to the small civilizations of Nubia/Meroë, Axum, and the Niger River valley. In this vast region, and particularly south of the equator, the most significant development of the classical era involved the accelerating movement of Bantu-speaking peoples into the enormous subcontinent. It was a process that had begun many centuries earlier from a homeland region in what is now southeastern Nigeria and the Cameroons. In the long run, that movement of peoples generated some 400 distinct but closely related languages, known collectively as Bantu. By the first century C.E., agricultural peoples speaking Bantu languages had largely occupied the forest regions of equatorial Africa, and at least a few of them had probably reached the East African coast. In the several centuries that followed, they established themselves quite rapidly in most of eastern and southern Africa (see Map 7.1), introducing immense economic and cultural changes to a huge region of the continent.

Bantu expansion was not a conquest or invasion such as that of Alexander the Great; nor was it a massive and self-conscious migration like that of Europeans to the Americas. Rather, it was a slow movement of peoples, perhaps a few extended families at a time, but taken as a whole, it brought to Africa south of the equator a measure of cultural and linguistic commonality, marking it as a distinct region of the continent.

Cultural Encounters

■ Connection

In what ways did the arrival of Bantu-speaking peoples stimulate cross-cultural interaction?

That movement of peoples also generated numerous cross-cultural encounters, as the Bantu-speaking newcomers interacted with already-established societies, changing both of them in the process. Among those encounters, none was more significant than that between the agricultural Bantu and the gathering and hunting peoples who earlier occupied Africa south of the equator. This was part of a long-term global phenomenon in which farmers largely replaced foragers as the dominant people on the planet (see Chapter 2).

In this encounter, Bantu-speaking farmers had various advantages. One was numerical, as agriculture generated a more productive economy, enabling larger numbers to live in a smaller area than was possible with a gathering and hunting way of life. Another advantage was disease, for the farmers brought with them both parasitic and infectious diseases—malaria, for example—to which foraging people had little immunity. A third advantage was iron, so useful for tools and weapons, which Bantu migrants brought to many of their interactions with peoples still operating with stone-age technology. Thus, during the classical era, gathering and hunting peoples were displaced, absorbed, or largely eliminated in most parts of Africa south of the equator—but not everywhere.

In the Kalahari region of southwestern Africa and a few places in East Africa, gathering and hunting peoples such as the San (see Chapter 1) survived into modern times. Furthermore, many of the Bantu languages of southern Africa retain to this day the distinctive "clicks" that they borrowed from the now-vanished gathering and hunting peoples who long preceded them in the region.

In the rain forest region of Central Africa, the foraging Batwa (Pygmy) people, at least some of them, became "forest specialists" who produced honey, wild game, elephant products, animal skins, and medicinal barks and plants, all of which entered regional trading networks in exchange for the agricultural products of their Bantu neighbors. They also adopted Bantu languages, while maintaining a nonagricultural lifestyle and a separate identity. For their part, the Bantu farmers regarded their Batwa

Khoikhoi of South Africa
The Khoikhoi people of South Africa, several of whom are shown here in an 1886 photograph, were originally gatherers and hunters who adopted cattle and sheep raising from outsiders, perhaps from early Bantu-speaking immigrants to the region, but did not practice agriculture. Living in southern Africa for most of the last two millennia, they illustrate the interaction and selective cultural borrowing that took place among the various peoples of the region. (Hulton-Deutsch Collection/Corbis)

neighbors as first-comers to the region and therefore closest to the ancestral and territorial spirits that determined the fertility of the land and people. Thus, as forest-dwelling and Bantu-speaking farmers grew in numbers and created chiefdoms, those chiefs appropriated the Batwa title of "owners of the land" for themselves, claimed Batwa ancestry, and portrayed the Batwa as the original "civilizers" of the earth.[6]

In other ways as well, Bantu cultures changed as they encountered different peoples. In the drier environment of East Africa, the yam-based agriculture of the West African Bantu homeland was unable to support their growing numbers, so Bantu farmers increasingly adopted grains as well as domesticated sheep and cattle from the already-established people of the region. Their agriculture also was enriched by acquiring a variety of food crops from Southeast Asia—coconuts, sugarcane, and especially bananas—which were brought to East Africa by Indonesian sailors and immigrants early in the first millennium C.E. Bantu farmers then spread this agricultural package and their acquired ironworking technology throughout the vast area of eastern and southern Africa, probably reaching present-day South Africa by 400 C.E. They also brought a common set of cultural and social practices, which diffused widely across Bantu Africa. One prominent historian described these practices as encompassing,

> in religion, the centrality of ancestor observances; in philosophy, the problem of evil understood as the consequence of individual malice or of the failure to honor one's ancestors; in music, an emphasis on polyrhythmic performance with drums as the key instrument; in dance, a new form of expression in which a variety of prescribed body movements took preference over footwork; and in agriculture, the pre-eminence of women as the workers and innovators.[7]

All of this became part of the common culture of Bantu-speaking Africa.

Society and Religion

In the thousand years or so (500–1500 C.E.) that followed their initial colonization of Africa south of the equator, agricultural Bantu-speaking peoples also created a wide variety of quite distinct societies and cultures. Some—in present-day Kenya, for example—organized themselves without any formal political specialists at all. Instead they made decisions, resolved conflicts, and maintained order by using kinship structures or lineage principles supplemented by age grades, which joined men of a particular generation together across various lineages (see Document 2.2, pp. 309–10). Elsewhere, lineage heads who acquired a measure of personal wealth or who proved skillful at mediating between the local spirits and the people might evolve into chiefs with a modest political authority. In several areas, such as the region around Lake Victoria or present-day Zimbabwe, larger and more substantial kingdoms evolved. Along the East African coast after 1000 C.E., dozens of rival city-states linked the African interior with the commerce of the Indian Ocean basin (see Chapter 8). The kind of society that developed in any particular area depended on a host of local factors, including population density, trading opportunities, and interaction among culturally different peoples.

In terms of religion, Bantu practice in general placed less emphasis on a High or Creator God, who was viewed as remote and largely uninvolved in ordinary life, and focused instead on ancestral or nature spirits. The power of dead ancestors might be accessed through rituals of sacrifice, especially that of cattle. Supernatural power deriving from ancient heroes, ancestors, or nature spirits also resided in charms, which could be activated by proper rituals and used to control the rains, defend the village, achieve success in hunting, or identify witches. Belief in witches was widespread, reflecting the idea that evil or misfortune was the work of malicious people. Diviners, skilled in penetrating the world of the supernatural, used dreams, visions, charms, or trances to identify the source of misfortune and to prescribe remedies. Was a particular illness the product of broken taboos, a dishonored ancestor, an unhappy nature spirit, or a witch? Was a remedy to be found in a cleansing ceremony, a sacrifice to an ancestor, the activation of a charm, or the elimination of a witch?[8] Such issues constantly confronted the people of Bantu Africa.

Unlike the major monotheistic religions, with their "once and for all" revelations from God through the Christian Bible or the Muslim Quran, Bantu religious practice was predicated on the notion of "continuous revelation"—the possibility of constantly receiving new messages from the world beyond. Moreover, unlike Buddhism, Christianity, or Islam, Bantu religions were geographically confined, intended to explain, predict, and control local affairs, with no missionary impulse or inclination toward universality.

Civilizations of Mesoamerica

Westward across the Atlantic Ocean lay the altogether separate world of the Americas. Although geography permitted some interaction between African and Eurasian peoples, the Atlantic and Pacific oceans ensured that the cultures and societies of the Western Hemisphere had long operated in a world apart from their Afro-Eurasian counterparts. Nor were the cultures of the Americas stimulated by the kind of fruitful interaction among their own peoples that played such an important role in the Eastern Hemisphere. Nothing similar to the contact between Egypt and Mesopotamia, or Persia and the Greeks, or the extensive communication along the Silk Road trading network enriched the two major centers of civilization in the Americas—Mesoamerica and the Andes—which had little if any direct contact with each other. Furthermore, the remarkable achievements of early American civilizations and cultures occurred without the large domesticated animals or ironworking technologies that were so important throughout the Eastern Hemisphere.

Accounts of pre-Columbian American societies often focus primarily on the Aztec and Inca empires (see Chapter 13), yet these impressive creations, flourishing in the fifteenth and early sixteenth centuries, were but the latest in a long line of civilizations that preceded them in Mesoamerica and the Andes respectively. Although these two regions housed the vast majority of the population of the Americas, the peoples of North America, the Amazon River basin, and elsewhere were the centers of their own worlds and made their own histories. It is the period preceding the Aztecs and Incas that represents the classical era in the history of the Americas.

Stretching from central Mexico to northern Central America, the area known as Mesoamerica was, geographically speaking, one of "extraordinary diversity compressed into a relatively small space."[9] That environment ranged from steamy lowland rain forests to cold and windy highland plateaus, cut by numerous mountains and valleys and generating many microclimates. Such conditions contributed to substantial linguistic and ethnic diversity and to many distinct and competing cities, chiefdoms, and states.

Despite this diversity, Mesoamerica, like Bantu Africa, was also a distinct region, bound together by elements of a common culture. Its many peoples shared an intensive agricultural technology devoted to raising maize, beans, chili peppers, and squash; they prepared maize in a distinctive and highly nutritious fashion; they based their economies on market exchange; they practiced religions featuring a similar pantheon of deities, belief in a cosmic cycle of creation and destruction, human sacrifice, and monumental ceremonial centers; they employed a common ritual calendar of 260 days and hieroglyphic writing; and they interacted frequently among themselves. During the first millennium B.C.E., for example, the various small states and chiefdoms of the region, particularly the Olmec, exchanged a number of luxury goods used to display social status and for ritual purposes—jade, serpentine, obsidian tools, ceramic pottery, shell ornaments, stingray spines, and turtle shells. As a result, aspects of Olmec culture, such as artistic styles, temple pyramids, the calendar system, and rituals involving human sacrifice, spread widely throughout Mesoamerica and influenced many of the civilizations that followed.

Classical Civilizations of Mesoamerica

The Maya: Writing and Warfare

■ Comparison
With what Eurasian
civilizations might the
Maya be compared?

Among the Mesoamerican civilizations, none has attracted more attention than that of the Maya, the major classical civilization of Mesoamerica. Scholars have traced the beginnings of the Maya people to ceremonial centers constructed as early as 2000 B.C.E. in present-day Guatemala and the Yucatán region of Mexico, but it was during the classical phase of Maya civilization, between 250 and 900 C.E., that their most notable cultural achievements emerged. Their intellectuals, probably priests, developed a mathematical system that included the concept of zero and place notation and was capable of complex calculations. They combined this mathematical ability with careful observation of the night skies to plot the cycles of planets, to predict eclipses of the sun and the moon, to construct elaborate calendars, and to calculate accurately the length of the solar year. The distinctive art of the Maya elite, featured in Visual Sources: Art and the Maya Elite, pages 216–23, was likewise impressive to later observers.

Accompanying these intellectual and artistic achievements was the creation of the most elaborate writing system in the Americas, which used both pictographs and phonetic or syllabic elements. Carved on stone and written on bark paper or deerskin books, Mayan writing recorded historical events, masses of astronomical data, and religious or mythological texts. Temples, pyramids, palaces, and public plazas abounded, graced with painted murals and endless stone carving. It is not surprising that early scholars viewed Maya civilization as a peaceful society led by gentle stargazing priest-kings devoted to temple building and intellectual pursuits.

The economic foundations for these cultural achievements were embedded in an "almost totally engineered landscape."[10] The Maya drained swamps, terraced hillsides, flattened ridgetops, and constructed an elaborate water management system. Much of this underpinned a flourishing agriculture, which supported a very rapidly growing and dense population by 750 C.E. This agriculture sustained substantial elite classes of nobles, priests, merchants, architects, and sculptors, as well as specialized artisans producing pottery, tools, and cotton textiles. And it was sufficiently productive to free a large labor force for work on the many public structures that continue to amaze contemporary visitors.

We now know that these many achievements took place within a highly fragmented political system of city-states, local lords, and regional kingdoms with no central authority, with frequent warfare, and with the extensive capture and sacrifice of prisoners (see Visual Source 7.2, p. 319). The larger political units of Maya civilization were densely populated urban and ceremonial centers, ruled by powerful kings, who were divine rulers or "state shamans" able to mediate between humankind and the supernatural. One of these cities, Tikal, contained perhaps 50,000 people, with another 50,000 or so in the surrounding countryside, by 750 C.E.[11] (See the chapter opening photo, p. 280, of a temple from Tikal.) Some of these city-states were clearly imperialistic, but none succeeded in creating a unified Maya empire. Various centers of Maya civilization rose and fell; fluctuating alliances among them alternated with periods of sporadic warfare; ruling families intermarried; the elite classes sought luxury goods from far away—jade, gold, shells, feathers from exotic birds, cacao—to bolster their authority and status. In its political dimensions, classical Maya civilization more closely resembled the competing city-states of ancient Mesopotamia or classical Greece than the imperial structures of Rome, Persia, or China.

But that imposing civilization collapsed with a completeness and rapidity rare in world history. In less than a century following the onset of a long-term drought in 840, the population of the low-lying southern heartland of the Maya dropped by 85 percent or more as famine, epidemic, and fratricidal warfare reaped a horrific toll. It was a catastrophe from which there was no recovery. Elements of Maya culture survived in scattered settlements, but the great cities were deserted, and large-scale construction and artistic work ceased. The last date inscribed in stone corresponds to 909 C.E. As a complex civilization, the Maya had passed into history.

Explaining this remarkable demise has long kept scholars guessing. It seems clear that neither foreign invasion nor internal rebellion played a major role, as they had in the collapse of the Roman and Chinese empires. One recent account focuses on ecological and political factors.[12] Extremely rapid population growth after 600 C.E. pushed total Maya numbers to perhaps 5 million or more and soon outstripped available resources, resulting in deforestation and the erosion of hillsides. Under such conditions, climate change in the form of prolonged droughts in the 800s may well have triggered the collapse, while political disunity and endemic rivalries prevented a coordinated and effective response to the emerging catastrophe. Maya warfare in fact became more frequent as competition for increasingly scarce land for cultivation became sharper. Whatever the precise explanation, the Maya collapse, like that of the Romans and others, illustrates the fragility of civilizations, whether they are embodied in large empires or organized in a more decentralized fashion.

Teotihuacán: The Americas' Greatest City

At roughly the same time as the Maya flourished in the southern regions of Mesoamerica, the giant city of Teotihuacán, to the north in the Valley of Mexico, was also thriving. Begun around 150 B.C.E. and apparently built to a plan rather than evolving haphazardly, the city came to occupy about eight square miles and by 550 C.E. had a population variously estimated between 100,000 and 200,000. It was by far the largest urban complex in the Americas at the time and one of the six largest in the world. Beyond this, much about Teotihuacán is unknown, such as its original name, the language of its people, the kind of government that ordered its life, and the precise function of its many deities.

Physically, the city was enormously impressive, replete with broad avenues, spacious plazas, huge marketplaces, temples, palaces, apartment complexes, slums, waterways, reservoirs, drainage systems, and colorful murals. Along the main north/south boulevard, now known as the Street of the Dead, were the grand homes of the elite, the headquarters of state authorities, many temples, and two giant pyramids. One of them, the Pyramid of the Sun, had been constructed over an ancient tunnel leading to a cave and may well have been regarded as the site of creation itself, the birthplace

■ **Connection**
In what ways did Teotihuacán shape the history of Mesoamerica?

of the sun and the moon. At the Temple of the Feathered Serpent, archeologists have found the remains of some 200 people, their hands and arms tied behind them; they were the apparently unwilling sacrificial victims meant to accompany into the afterlife the high-ranking persons buried there.

Off the main avenues in a gridlike pattern of streets lay thousands of residential apartment compounds, home to the city's commoners, each with its own kitchen area, sleeping quarters, courtyards, and shrines. In these compounds, perhaps in groups of related families or lineages, lived many of the farmers who tilled the lands outside the city. Thousands of Maya specialists—masons, leather workers, potters, construction laborers, merchants, civil servants—also made their homes in these apartments. So too did skilled makers of obsidian blades, who plied their trade in hundreds of separate workshops, generating products that were in great demand throughout Mesoamerica. At least two small sections of the city were reserved exclusively for foreigners.

Buildings, both public and private, were decorated with mural paintings, sculptures, and carvings. Many of these works of art display abstract geometric and stylized images. Others depict gods and goddesses, arrayed in various forms—feathered serpents, starfish, jaguars, flowers, and warriors. One set of murals shows happy people cavorting in a paradise of irrigated fields, playing games, singing, and chasing butterflies, which were thought to represent the souls of the dead. Another portrays dancing warriors carrying elaborate curved knives, to which were attached bleeding human hearts.

The art of Teotihuacán, unlike that of the Maya, has revealed few images of self-glorifying rulers or individuals. Nor did the city have a tradition of written public inscriptions as the Maya did, although a number of glyphs or characters suggest at least a limited form of writing. One scholar has suggested that "the rulers of Teotihuacán might have intentionally avoided the personality cult of the dynastic art and writing" so characteristic of the Maya.[13] Some have argued that those rulers may have constituted an oligarchy or council of high-ranking elites rather than a single monarch.

However it was governed, Teotihuacán cast a huge shadow over Mesoamerica, particularly from 300 to 600 C.E., although scholars disagree as to precisely how its power and influence were exercised. A core region of perhaps 10,000 square miles was administered directly from the city itself, while

A Mural of Teotihuacán
This mural depicts the paradise of Tlaloc, the god of the rain, which was available only to those who had died through drowning, storms, or lightning. Fish and human figures swim and play in the river, while others cavort on the land in what seems to be a fertile and happy place. The dating of such murals is uncertain, but most were apparently created between 450 and 650 C.E. (Richard Seaman)

tribute was no doubt exacted from other areas within its broader sphere of influence. At a greater distance, the power of Teotihuacán's armies gave it a presence in the Maya heartland more than 600 miles to the east. At least one Maya city, Kaminalijuyu in the southern highlands, was completely taken over by the Teotihuacán military and organized as a colony. In Tikal, a major lowland Maya city, in the year 378 C.E., agents of Teotihuacán apparently engineered a coup that placed a collaborator on the throne and turned the city for a time into an ally or a satellite. Elsewhere—in the Zapotec capital of Monte Alban, for example—murals show unarmed persons from Teotihuacán engaged in what seems to be more equal diplomatic relationships.

At least some of this political and military activity was no doubt designed to obtain, either by trade or by tribute, valued commodities from afar—food products, cacao beans, tropical bird feathers, honey, salt, medicinal herbs. The presence in Teotihuacán of foreigners, perhaps merchants, from the Gulf Coast and Maya lowlands, as well as much pottery from those regions, provides further evidence of long-distance trade. Moreover, the sheer size and prestige of Teotihuacán surely persuaded many, all across Mesoamerica, to imitate the architectural and artistic styles of the city. Thus, according to a leading scholar, "Teotihuacán meant something of surpassing importance far beyond its core area."[14] Almost a thousand years after its still-mysterious collapse around 650 C.E., the peoples of the Aztec Empire dubbed the great metropolis as Teotihuacán, the "city of the gods."

Civilizations of the Andes

Yet another center of civilization in the Americas lay in the dramatic landscape of the Andes. Bleak deserts along the coast supported human habitation only because they were cut by dozens of rivers flowing down from the mountains, offering the possibility of irrigation and cultivation. The offshore waters of the Pacific Ocean also provided an enormously rich marine environment with an endless supply of seabirds and fish. The Andes themselves, a towering mountain chain with many highland valleys, afforded numerous distinct ecological niches, depending on altitude. On its steep slopes, people carved out huge staircase terrace systems, which remain impressive in the twenty-first century.

The most well known of the civilizations to take shape in this environment was that of the Incas, which encompassed practically the entire region, some 2,500 miles in length, in the fifteenth century. Yet the Incas represented only the most recent and the largest in a long history of civilizations in the area.

The coastal region of central Peru had in fact generated one of the world's First Civilizations, known as Norte Chico, dating back to around 3000 B.C.E. (see Chapter 3). The classical era in Andean civilization, roughly 1000 B.C.E. to 1000 C.E., provides an opportunity to look briefly at several of the cultures that followed Norte Chico and preceded the Inca civilization. Because none of them had developed writing, historians are largely dependent on archeology for an understanding of these civilizations.

Classical Civilizations of the Andes

Chavín: A Pan-Andean Religious Movement

■ **Connection**

What kind of influence did Chavín exert in the Andes region?

In both the coastal and highland regions of Peru, archeologists have uncovered numerous local ceremonial centers or temple complexes, dating to between 2000 and 1000 B.C.E. Often constructed in a characteristic U shape, they were associated with small-scale irrigation projects and suggest the growing authority of religious leaders. Human trophy heads indicate raiding, warfare, and violence among these local centers. Then around 900 B.C.E., one of them, located in the Andean highlands at a village called Chavín de Huántar, became the focus of a religious movement that soon swept through both coastal and highland Peru.

Chavín de Huántar enjoyed a strategic location, high in the Andes and situated on trade routes to both the coastal region to the west and the Amazon rain forest to the east. By perhaps 750 B.C.E., it had become a small town of 2,000 to 3,000 people, with clear distinctions between an elite class, who lived in stone houses, and ordinary people, with adobe dwellings. An elaborate temple complex included numerous galleries, hidden passageways, staircases, ventilation shafts, drainage canals, and distinctive carvings. Little is known about the rituals or beliefs that animated Chavín's religious practice, but the artwork suggests that it drew on ideas from both the desert coastal region and the rain forests. Major deities were represented as jaguars, crocodiles, and snakes, all of them native to the Amazon basin. Shamans or priests likely made use of the San Pedro cactus, native to the Andes Mountains, employing its hallucinogenic properties to penetrate the supernatural world. Some of the fantastic artwork of this civilization—its jaguar-human images, for example—may well reflect the visions of these religious leaders.

Over the next several centuries, this blended religious movement proved attractive across much of Peru and beyond, as Chavín-style architecture, sculpture, pottery, religious images, and painted textiles were widely imitated within the region. Chavín itself became a pilgrimage site and perhaps a training center for initiates from distant centers. At locations three weeks or more away by llama caravan, temples were remodeled to resemble that of Chavín, although in many cases with locally inspired variations.[15] Much of the spread of Chavín religious imagery and practice paralleled the trade routes that linked highland and coastal Peru. Although there is some evidence for violence and warfare, no Chavín "empire" emerged. Instead, a widespread religious cult, traveling on the back of a trading network, provided for the first time and for several centuries a measure of economic and cultural integration to much of the Peruvian Andes.

Moche: A Regional Andean Civilization

■ **Description**

What features of Moche life characterize it as a civilization?

By 200 B.C.E., the pan-Andes Chavín cult had faded, replaced by a number of regional civilizations. Among them, the Moche civilization clearly stands out. Dominating a 250-mile stretch of Peru's northern coast and incorporating thirteen river valleys, the Moche people flourished between about 100 and 800 C.E. Their economy was rooted in a complex irrigation system, requiring constant maintenance, which funneled runoff from the Andes into fields of maize, beans, and squash and acres of cotton, all fertilized by rich bird droppings called guano. Moche fishermen also harvested millions of anchovies from the bountiful Pacific.

Politically, Moche was governed by warrior-priests, some of whom lived atop huge pyramids. The largest of these structures, dubbed the Pyramid of the Sun, had been constructed from 143 million sun-dried bricks. There shaman-rulers, often under the influence of hallucinogenic drugs, conducted ancient rituals that mediated between the world of humankind and that of the gods. They also presided over the ritual sacrifice of human victims, drawn from their many prisoners of war, which became central to the politico-religious life of the Moche. Images on Moche pottery show a ruler attired in a magnificent feather headdress and seated on a pyramid, while a parade of naked prisoners marches past him. Other scenes of decapitation and dismemberment indicate the fate that awaited those destined for sacrifice. For these rulers, the Moche world was apparently one of war, ritual, and diplomacy.

The immense wealth of this warrior-priest elite and the exquisite artistry of Moche craftsmen are reflected in the elaborate burials accorded the rulers. At one site, Peruvian archeologists uncovered the final resting place of three such individuals, whom they named the Lords of Sipan. Laid in adobe burial chambers, one above the other, each was decked out in his ceremonial regalia—elaborate gold masks, necklaces, and headdresses; turquoise and gold bead bracelets; cotton tunics covered with copper plates; a gold rattle showing a Moche warrior smashing a prisoner with his war club; and a copper knife. In 2005, in another remarkable discovery dating to about 450 C.E., archeologists found the burial place of a very high-status woman, who was in her late twenties and heavily tattooed. She had been laid to rest with hundreds of funeral objects, including gold sewing needles; weaving tools; much gold, silver, and copper jewelry; and a female sacrificial victim lying beside her. Even more suggestive were two elaborate war clubs and twenty-three spear throwers. Was she perhaps a warrior, a priest, or a ruler?

The most accessible aspect of Moche life and much of what scholars know about the Moche world derive from the superb skill of their craftspeople, such as metalworkers, potters, weavers, and painters. Face masks, figures of animals, small earrings, and other jewelry items, many plated in gold, display amazing technical abilities and a striking artistic sensibility. On their ceramic pottery are naturalistic portraits of noble lords and rulers and images from the life of common people, including the blind and the sick. Battle scenes show warriors confronting their enemies with raised clubs. Erotic encounters between men and women and gods making love to humans likewise represent common themes, as do grotesque images of their many gods and goddesses. Much of this, of course, reflects the culture of the Moche elite. We know much less about the daily life of the farmers, fishermen, weavers, traders, construction workers, and servants whose labor made that elite culture possible.

These cultural achievements, however, rested on fragile environmental foundations, for the region was subject to drought, earthquakes, and occasional torrential

The Lord of Sipan

The Moche ruler in the center of the grave, dating to about 290 C.E., was about forty years old when he died and, at five feet five inches, was quite tall for the time. Except for early signs of arthritis, he was in good health and seems to have performed little physical labor during his life. Accompanying him in death were the four individuals shown here, plus three young women, a priest, a guard, a dog, and considerable food and drink. (Kevin Schafter/Corbis)

rains associated with El Niño episodes (dramatic changes in weather patterns caused by periodic warming of Pacific Ocean currents). Scholars believe that during the sixth century C.E. some combination of these forces caused extended ecological disruption, which seriously undermined Moche civilization. In these circumstances, the Moche were vulnerable to aggressive neighbors and possibly to internal social tensions as well. By the end of the eighth century C.E., that civilization had passed into history.[16]

The Chavín and Moche civilizations were but two of the many that grew up in the Andes region before the Incas consolidated the entire area into a single empire. The Nazca, for example, on the arid southern coast of Peru, have become famous for their underground irrigation canals, polychrome pottery, and textiles, but especially for their gigantic and mysterious lines in the desert in the form of monkeys, birds, spiders, whales, and various abstract designs. In the interior, a series of larger states emerged. One of them was centered on Tiwanaku, a city of monumental buildings and perhaps 40,000 to 50,000 people that flourished during much of the first millennium C.E. The Huari and Chimu kingdoms were further examples of this Andean civilization, to which the Incas gave a final and spectacular expression before all of the Americas was swallowed up in European empires from across the sea.

North America in the Classical Era: From Chaco to Cahokia

The peoples of the Americas in the pre-Columbian era might be divided into three large groupings. The most prominent and well known are those of the Mesoamerican and Andean regions, where cities, states, and dense populations created civilizations broadly similar to those of classical Eurasia. Elsewhere, gathering and hunting peoples carried on the most ancient of human adaptations to the environment. Arctic and subarctic cultures; the bison hunters of the Great Plains; the complex and settled communities of the Pacific coast, such as the Chumash (see Chapter 1); nomadic bands living in the arid regions of southern South America—all of these represent the persistence of gathering and hunting peoples in substantial regions of the Americas.

North America in the Classical Era

Even larger areas—the eastern woodlands of the United States, Central America, the Amazon basin, the Caribbean islands—were populated by peoples sometimes defined as "semi-sedentary."[17] These were agricultural societies, although less intensive and productive than those of Mesoamerica or the Andes and supporting usually much smaller populations. Nor did they generate large urban centers or inclusive empires.

These peoples who lived beyond the direct reach of the major civilizations also made their own histories, changing in response to their unique environments, their interactions with outsiders, and their own visions of the world. The Anasazi of the southwestern United States, now called the Ancestral Pueblo, and the mound-building cultures of the eastern woodlands provide two illustrations from North America during the classical era.

Pit Houses and Great Houses: The Ancestral Pueblo

The southwestern region of North America, an arid land cut by mountain ranges and large basins, first acquired maize from its place of origin in Mesoamerica during the second millennium B.C.E., but it took roughly 2,000 years for that crop, later supplemented by beans and squash, to become the basis of a settled agricultural way of living. In a desert region, farming was risky, and maize had to be gradually adapted to the local environment. Not until around 600 to 800 C.E. did permanent village life take hold widely. People then lived in pit houses with floors sunk several feet below ground level. Some settlements had only a few such homes, whereas others contained twenty-five or more. By 900 C.E., many of these villages also included kivas, much larger pit structures used for ceremonial purposes, which symbolized the widespread belief that humankind emerged into this world from another world below. Individual settlements were linked to one another in local trading networks and sometimes in wider webs of exchange that brought them buffalo hides, copper, turquoise, seashells, macaw feathers, and coiled baskets from quite distant locations.

■ **Comparison**

In what ways were the histories of the Ancestral Pueblo and the Mound Builders similar to each other, and how did they differ?

Pueblo Bonito
Called Pueblo Bonito ("pretty village") by the Spanish, this great house of the Ancestral Pueblo people was at its high point in the eleventh century C.E. The circular structures, known as kivas, were probably ceremonial sites. Their prominence, and the absence of major trash collections, have persuaded some scholars that Pueblo Bonito was more of a ritual center than a residential town. (Courtesy, Chaco Canyon National Historic Park)

These processes of change—growing dependence on agriculture, increasing population, more intensive patterns of exchange—gave rise to larger settlements and adjacent aboveground structures known as pueblos. The most spectacular of these took shape in Chaco canyon in what is now northwestern New Mexico. There, between 860 and 1130 C.E., five major pueblos emerged. This Chaco Phenomenon encompassed 25,000 square miles and linked some seventy outlying settlements to the main centers. The population was not large, perhaps as few as 5,000 people, although experts continue to debate the issue. The largest of these towns, or "great houses," Pueblo Bonito, stood five stories high and contained more than 600 rooms and many kivas. Hundreds of miles of roads, up to forty feet wide, radiated out from Chaco, likewise prompting much debate among scholars. Without wheeled carts or large domesticated animals, such an elaborate road system seems unnecessary for ordinary trade or travel. Did the roads represent, as some scholars speculate, a "sacred landscape which gave order to the world," joining its outlying communities to a "Middle Place," an entrance perhaps to the underworld?[18]

Among the Chaco elite were highly skilled astronomers, who constructed an observatory of three large rock slabs situated so as to throw a beam of light across a spiral rock carving behind it at the summer solstice. By the eleventh century, Chaco also had become a dominant center for the production of turquoise ornaments, which became a major item of regional commerce, extending as far south as Mesoamerica. Not all was sweetness and light, however. Warfare, internal conflict, and occasional cannibalism (a matter of much controversy among scholars) apparently increased in frequency as an extended period of drought in the half century following 1130 brought this flourishing culture to a rather abrupt end. By 1200, the great houses had been abandoned and their inhabitants scattered in small communities that later became the Pueblo peoples of more recent times.

The Mound Builders of the Eastern Woodlands

Unlike the Chaco region in the southwest, the eastern woodlands of North America and especially the Mississippi River valley hosted an independent Agricultural Revolution. By 2000 B.C.E., many of its peoples had domesticated local plant species, including sunflowers, sumpweed, goosefoot, some gourds and squashes, and a form of artichoke. These few plants, however, were not sufficient to support a fully settled agricultural village life; rather they supplemented diets derived from gathering and hunting without fundamentally changing that ancient way of life. Such peoples created societies distinguished by arrays of large earthen mounds, found all over the United States east of the Mississippi, prompting archeologists to dub them the Mound Builders.[19] The earliest of them date to around 2000 B.C.E., but the most elaborate and widespread of these mound-building cultures took shape between 200 B.C.E. and 400 C.E. and is known to scholars as the Hopewell culture, after an archeological site in Ohio.

Several features of the Hopewell culture have intrigued archeologists. Particularly significant are the striking burial mounds and geometric earthworks, sometimes covering areas equivalent to several city blocks, and the wide variety of artifacts found within them—smoking pipes, human figurines, mica mirrors, flint blades, fabrics, and jewelry of all kinds. The mounds themselves were no doubt the focus of elaborate burial rituals, but some of them were aligned with the moon with such precision as to allow the prediction of lunar eclipses. Developed most elaborately in the Ohio River valley, Hopewell-style earthworks, artifacts, and ceremonial pottery have also been found throughout the eastern woodlands region of North America. Hopewell centers in Ohio contained mica from the Appalachian Mountains, volcanic glass from Yellowstone, conch shells and sharks' teeth from the Gulf of Mexico, and copper from the Great Lakes. All of this suggests an enormous "Hopewell Interaction Sphere," linking this huge region in a loose network of exchange, as well as a measure of cultural borrowing of religious ideas and practices within this immense area.[20]

The next and most spectacular phase in the history of these mound-building peoples took shape as corn-based agriculture, derived ultimately but indirectly from Mexico, gained ground in the Mississippi valley after 800 C.E., allowing larger populations and more complex societies to emerge. The dominant center was Cahokia, near present-day St. Louis, Missouri, which flourished from about 900 to 1250 C.E. Its central mound, a terraced pyramid of four levels, measured 1,000 feet long by 700 feet wide, rose more than 100 feet above the ground, and occupied fifteen acres. It was the largest structure north of Mexico, the focal point of a community numbering 10,000 or more people, and the center of a widespread trading network (see an artist's reconstruction of Cahokia on p. 66).

Cahokia emerged and flourished at about the same time as did the great houses of Chaco canyon, but its urban presence was far larger than that of its southwestern counterpart. Both were made possible by the arrival of corn-based agriculture, originating in Mesoamerica, though direct contact with Mexico is much more apparent in Chaco. Finally, Cahokia emerged as the climax of a long history of mound-building cultures in the eastern woodlands, whereas Chaco was more of a "start-up" culture, emerging quite quickly "with a relatively shallow history."[21]

Evidence from burials and from later Spanish observers suggests that Cahokia and other centers of this Mississippi culture were stratified societies with a clear elite and with rulers able to mobilize the labor required to build such enormous structures. One high-status male was buried on a platform of 20,000 shell beads, accompanied by 800 arrowheads, sheets of copper and mica, and a number of sacrificed men and women nearby.[22] Well after Cahokia had declined and was abandoned, sixteenth-century Spanish and French explorers encountered another such chiefdom among the Natchez people, located in southwestern Mississippi. Paramount chiefs, known as Great Suns, dressed in knee-length fur coats and lived luxuriously in deerskin-covered homes. An elite class of "principal men" or "honored peoples" clearly occupied a different status from commoners, sometimes referred to as "stinkards." These sharp class distinctions were blunted by the requirement that upper-class people, including the Great Suns, had to marry "stinkards."

The military capacity of these Mississippi chiefdoms greatly impressed European observers, as this Spanish account indicates:

> The next day the cacique [paramount chief] arrived with 200 canoes filled with men, having weapons... the warriors standing erect from bow to stern, holding bows and arrows.... [F]rom under the canopy where the chief man was, the course was directed and orders issued to the rest.... [W]hat with the awnings, the plumes, the shields, the pennons, and the number of people in the fleet, it appeared like a famous armada of galleys.[23]

Here then in the eastern woodlands of North America were peoples who independently generated a modest Agricultural Revolution, assimilated corn and beans from distant sources, developed increasingly complex societies, and created monumental structures, new technologies, and artistic traditions. In doing so, they gave rise to a regional cultural complex that enveloped much of the United States east of the Mississippi in a network of ceremonial, economic, and cultural exchange.

Reflections: Deciding What's Important: Balance in World History

Among the perennial problems that teachers and writers of world history confront is sorting through the vast record of times past and choosing what to include and what to leave out. A related issue involves the extent to which particular peoples or civilizations will be treated. Should the Persians get as much space as the Greeks? Does Africa merit equal treatment with Eurasia? Where do the Americas fit in the larger human story? What, in short, are the criteria for deciding what is important in telling the story of the human venture?

One standard might be duration. Should ways of living that have endured for longer periods of time receive greater attention than those of lesser length? If historians followed only this criterion, then the Paleolithic era of gathering and hunting should occupy 90 percent or more of any world history text. On the other hand, perhaps change is more important than continuity. If so, then something new merits more space than something old. Thus we pay attention to both agriculture and civilizations because they represent significant turning points in human experience. Population provides yet another principle for determining inclusion. That, of course, is the reason that Eurasia, with about 80 percent of the world's population during the classical era, is addressed in three chapters of this book, whereas Africa and the Americas together receive only one chapter. There is also the related issue of influence. Buddhism, Christianity, and Islam spread more widely and shaped the lives of more people than did the religions of the Maya or the Bantu-speaking peoples of Africa. Do the major religions therefore deserve more extended treatment? Still another factor involves the availability of evidence. In this respect, classical-era Eurasia generated far more written records than either Africa or the Americas did, and therefore its history has been investigated far more thoroughly.

A final possible criterion involves the location of the historian and his or her audience. The recent development of world history as a field of study has sought vigorously to counteract a Eurocentric telling of the human story. Still, is there anything inherently wrong with an account of world history that is centered on one's own people? When I taught history in an Ethiopian high school in the mid-1960s, I was guided by an Afrocentric curriculum, which focused first on Ethiopian history, then on Africa as a whole, and finally on the larger world. Might a world historian from the Middle East, for example, legitimately strike a somewhat different balance in the treatment of various civilizations than someone writing for a largely Western audience or for Chinese readers?

Any account of the world's past will mix and match these criteria in various and contested ways. Among scholars, there exists neither a consensus about this question nor any formula to ensure a "proper" balance. You may want to consider whether the balance struck in this chapter, this section, and the book as a whole is appropriate or somehow out of line.

Second Thoughts

What's the Significance?

To assess your mastery of the material in this chapter, visit the **Student Center** at bedfordstmartins.com/strayer.

Meroë	Maya civilization	Chaco Phenomenon
Axum	Teotihuacán	Mound Builders/Cahokia
Niger Valley civilization	Chavín	
Bantu expansion	Moche	

Big Picture Questions

1. "The histories of Africa and the Americas during the classical era largely resemble those of Eurasia." Do you agree with this statement? Explain why or why not.

2. "The particular cultures and societies of Africa and of the Americas discussed in this chapter developed largely in isolation from one another." What evidence would support this statement, and what might challenge it?

3. What generated change in the histories of Africa and the Americas during the classical era?

Next Steps: For Further Study

For Web sites and additional documents related to this chapter, see **Make History** at bedfordstmartins.com/strayer.

Richard E. W. Adams, *Ancient Civilizations of the New World* (1997). A broad survey based on current scholarship of the Americas before Columbus.

Christopher Ehret, *The Civilizations of Africa* (2002). A recent overview of African history before 1800 by a prominent scholar.

Brian M. Fagan, *Ancient North America* (2005). A prominent archeologist's account of North American history.

Eric Gilbert and Jonathan T. Reynolds, *Africa in World History* (2004). An accessible account of African history set in a global context.

Guy Gugliotta, "The Maya: Glory and Ruin," *National Geographic* (August 2007). A beautifully illustrated account of the rise and fall of Maya civilization.

Kairn A. Klieman, *"The Pygmies Were Our Compass": Bantu and Batwa in the History of West Central Africa, Early Times to c. 1900 C.E.* (2003). A scholarly examination of the Pygmies (Batwa) of the Congo River basin and their interaction with Bantu-speaking peoples.

Charles Mann, *1491* (2005). A thoughtful journalist's account, delightfully written, of the controversies surrounding the history of the Americas before 1492.

"Ancient Africa's Black Kingdoms," http://www.homestead.com/wysinger/ancientafrica.html. A Web site exploring the history of Nubia.

"Maya Adventures," http://www.smm.org/sln/ma. A collection of text and pictures about the Maya, past and present.

Documents

Considering the Evidence:
Axum and the World

In the world of ancient African history, Axum has occupied a unique position in several ways. (See Map 7.1, p. 285, and pp. 286–88.) It is one of the few places in Africa, outside of Egypt, for which considerable documentary evidence exists. Some of the written sources—royal inscriptions and coins, for example—derive from within Axum itself, while others come from Greco-Roman and Christian visitors. Furthermore, after the rise of Islam, Axum—and its Ethiopian successor state—was the major surviving outpost of a Christian tradition, which had earlier spread widely across north and northeast Africa. Finally, Axum demonstrated an impressive cultural and religious continuity. Even after the decline of the Axumite empire by the eighth century C.E., the city of Axum remained a major pilgrimage site for Christians, while Ethiopian kings into the twentieth century were crowned there.[24] The documents that follow offer a series of windows on this classical-era African kingdom.

Document 7.1

A Guidebook to
the World of Indian Ocean Commerce

The earliest documentary reference to Axum was composed during the first century C.E. in an anonymous text known as *The Periplus of the Erythraean Sea.* Likely written by a sea captain from Roman-controlled Egypt, the *Periplus* offers a guide to the places and conditions that merchants might encounter as they traversed the Red Sea and the East African coast while on their way to India.

■ According to this text, why is the Axumite port of Adulis significant?

■ What evidence does the *Periplus* provide about Axum's cultural and economic ties to the larger world?

■ Based on the list of imports and exports, how would you describe Axum's role in the international commerce of the first century C.E.?

■ How might Axum's participation in long-distance trade have stimulated and sustained its growth as an empire?

The Periplus of the Erythraean Sea
First Century C.E.

Below Ptolemais of the Hunts°...there is Adulis, a port established by law, lying at the inner end of a bay that runs in toward the south. Before the harbor lies the so-called Mountain Island, about two hundred stadia° sea-ward from the very head of the bay, with the shores of the mainland close to it on both sides. Ships bound for this port now anchor here because of attacks from the land. They used formerly to anchor at the very head of the bay, by an island called Diodorus, close to the shore, which could be reached on foot from the land; by which means the barbarous natives attacked the island. Opposite Mountain Island, on the mainland twenty stadia from shore, lies Adulis, a fair-sized village, from which there is a three-days' journey to Coloe, an inland town and the first market for ivory. From that place to the city of the people called Axumites there is a five days' journey more; to that place all the ivory is brought from the country beyond the Nile through the district called Cyeneum, and thence to Adulis. Practically the whole number of elephants and rhinoceros that are killed live in the places inland, although at rare intervals they are hunted on the seacoast even near Adulis. Before the harbor of that market-town, out at sea on the right hand, there lie a great many little sandy islands called Alalaei, yielding tortoise-shell, which is brought to market there by the Fish-Eaters.

And about eight hundred stadia beyond there is another very deep bay, with a great mound of sand piled up at the right of the entrance; at the bottom of which the opsian° stone is found, and this is the only place where it is produced. These places...are governed by Zoscales,° who is miserly in his ways and always striving for more, but otherwise upright, and acquainted with Greek literature.

There are imported into these places undressed cloth made in Egypt for the Berbers; robes from Arsinoe; cloaks of poor quality dyed in colors; double-fringed linen mantles; many articles of flint glass, and others of murrhine, made in Diospolis;° and brass, which is used for ornament and in cut pieces instead of coin; sheets of soft copper, used for cooking utensils and cut up for bracelets and anklets for the women; iron, which is made into spears used against the elephants and other wild beasts, and in their wars. Besides these, small axes are imported, and adzes and swords; copper drinking-cups, round and large; a little coin° for those coming to the market [probably foreign merchants living in Adulis]; wine of Laodicea and Italy, not much; olive oil, not much; for the king, gold and silver plate made after the fashion of the country, and for clothing, military cloaks, and thin coats of skin, of no great value. Likewise from the district of Ariaca° across this sea, there are imported Indian iron, and steel, and Indian cotton cloth; the broad cloth called *monache* and that called *sagimtogene*, and girdles, and coats of skin and mallow-colored cloth, and a few muslins, and colored lac.° There are exported from these places ivory, and tortoise-shell and rhinoceros-horn. The most from Egypt is brought to this market from the month of January, to September, that is, from Tybi to Thoth; but seasonably they put to sea about the month of September.

°**Ptolemais of the Hunts:** near modern Port Sudan on the Red Sea.

°**stadia:** 1 stadium = ⅛ mile.

°**opsian:** obsidian.

Source: Wilfred H. Schoff, *The Periplus of the Erythraean Sea* (New York: Longman, Green and Co., 1912), Sections 4–6.

°**Zoscales:** an Axumite ruler.

°**Diospolis:** Thebes.

°**coin:** Roman money.

°**Ariaca:** an area in western India.

°**lac:** a resinous secretion of an insect, used in the form of shellac.

Document 7.2

The Making of an Axumite Empire

At its high point in the mid-fourth century C.E., Axum ruled an empire stretching from Meroë in the upper Nile Valley, across most of what is now Eritrea and Ethiopia, and incorporating parts of southern Arabia on the opposite side of the Red Sea. Document 7.2 comes from an Axumite inscription written in Greek on a stone throne adorned with figures of the Greek gods Hercules and Mercury. Commissioned by an unknown Axumite monarch, the inscription dates probably from the second or third century C.E. It was copied and then published in the sixth century by Cosmas, a Greek merchant born in Alexandria, Egypt, who had become a monk. This text describes some of the conquests that generated the Axumite Empire.

- What internal evidence from the document itself dates it prior to Axum's acceptance of Christianity?

- How would you describe the point of view from which the document was written?

- What techniques of imperial control does the document reveal?

- How might you account for the obvious Greek influence that is apparent in the inscription?

- How would you describe the religious or ideological underpinnings of this empire? Why might the Axumite ruler who commissioned this inscription single out Ares, Zeus, and Poseidon for special attention?

Inscription on a Stone Throne
Second or Third Century C.E.

Having after this with a strong hand compelled the nations bordering on my kingdom to live in peace, I made war upon the following nations, and by force of arms reduced them to subjection. I warred first with the nation of Gaze [Axum, probably in an internal struggle for power], then with Agame and Sigye, and having conquered them, I exacted the half of all that they possessed. I next reduced Aua and Tiamo, called Tziam, and the Gambela, and the tribes near them, and Zingabene and Angabe and Tiama and Athagaus and Kalaa, and the Semenoi—a people who lived beyond the Nile on mountains difficult of access and covered with snow, where the year is all winter with hailstorms, frosts and snows into which a man sinks knee-deep. I passed the river to attack these nations, and reduced them. I next subdued Lazine and Zaa and Gabala, tribes which inhabit mountains with steep declivities abounding with hot springs, the Atalmo and Bega, and all the tribes in the same quarter along with them.°

Source: J. W. McCrindle, trans. and ed., *The Christian Topography of Cosmas, an Egyptian Monk* (London: The Hakluyt Society, 1897), 59–66.

°(Note that scholars are often unable to precisely locate the people or places mentioned in the text.)

I proceeded next against the Tangaltae, who adjoin the borders of Egypt; and having reduced them I made a footpath giving access by land into Egypt from that part of my dominions. Next I reduced Annine and Metine—tribes inhabiting precipitous mountains. My arms were next directed against the Sesea nation. These had retired to a high mountain difficult of access; but I blockaded the mountain on every side, and compelled them to come down and surrender. I then selected for myself the best of their young men and their women, with their sons and daughters and all besides that they possessed. The tribes of Rhausi I next brought to submission: a barbarous race spread over wide waterless plains in the interior of the frankincense country. [Advancing thence toward the sea,] I encountered the Solate, whom I subdued, and left with instructions to guard the coast.

All these nations, protected though they were by mountains all but impregnable, I conquered, after engagements in which I was myself present. Upon their submission I restored their territories to them, subject to the payment of tribute. Many other tribes besides these submitted of their own accord, and became likewise tributary. And I sent a fleet and land forces against the Arabitae and Cinaedocolpitae who dwelt on the other side of the Red Sea [southern Arabia], and having reduced the sovereigns of both, I imposed on them a land tribute and charged them to make traveling safe both by sea and by land. I thus subdued the whole coast from Leuce Come to the country of the Sabaeans.

I first and alone of the kings of my race made these conquests. For this success I now offer my thanks to my mighty god, Ares,° who begat me, and by whose aid I reduced all the nations bordering on my own country, on the east to the country of frankincense, and on the west to Ethiopia and Sasu. Of these expeditions, some were conducted by myself in person, and ended in victory, and the others I entrusted to my officers. Having thus brought all the world under my authority to peace, I came down to Adulis and offered sacrifice to Zeus,° and to Ares, and to Poseidon,° whom I entreated to befriend all who go down to the sea in ships.° Here also I reunited all my forces, and setting down this Chair [throne] in this place, I consecrated it to Ares in the twenty-seventh year of my reign.

_____

°**Ares:** the Greek god of warfare and slaughter.

°**Zeus:** the chief god of the Greek pantheon.

°**Poseidon:** the Greek god of the sea.

°(Note that many Axumite deities derived from southern Arabia but came to be identified with the gods of the Greek pantheon.)

Document 7.3

The Coming of Christianity to Axum

The introduction of Christianity in the mid-fourth century represented a major change in the cultural history of Axum. It meant that Axum would be more closely aligned to Christian Egypt and Byzantium than to South Arabia, from which many of its earlier cultural traditions had derived. Document 7.3 relates the story of the coming of Christianity to Axum. It was written by Rufinus (345–410 C.E.), a Christian monk and writer who was born in Italy but spent much of his life in Jerusalem, where he heard this story from those who had taken part in it. Note that Greco-Roman writers of this time used "India" to refer vaguely to East Africa and Southern Arabia as well as the south Asian peninsula.

- According to this document, by what means was Christianity introduced to Axum? What do you think was the relative importance of Frumentius and Aedesius, as opposed to Roman merchants living in Axum?

- Why do you think the Axumite royal family was so receptive to this foreign religion? How might the story differ if told from the ruling family's perspective?

- How does the fact that this document was written by outsiders shape the emphasis of the story?

RUFINUS

On the Evangelization of Abyssinia
Late Fourth Century C.E.

One Metrodorus, a philosopher, is said to have penetrated to further India [the Red Sea area including Axum] in order to view places and see the world. Inspired by his example, one Meropius, a philosopher [and a Christian merchant] of Tyre,° wished to visit India with a similar object, taking with him two small boys who were related to him and whom he was educating in humane studies. The younger of these was called Aedesius, the other Frumentius. When, having seen and taken note of what his soul fed upon, the philosopher had begun to return, the ship on which he traveled put in for water or some other necessary at a certain port. It is the custom of the barbarians of these parts that, if ever the neighboring tribes report that their treaty with the Romans is broken, all Romans found among them should be massacred. The philosopher's ship was boarded; all with himself were put to the sword.

The boys were found studying under a tree and preparing their lessons, and, preserved by the mercy of the barbarians, were taken to the king [of Axum]. He made one of them, Aedesius, his cupbearer.

Frumentius, whom he had perceived to be sagacious and prudent, he made his treasurer and secretary. Thereafter they were held in great honor and affection by the king. The king died, leaving his wife with an infant son [Ezana] as heir of the bereaved kingdom. He gave the young men liberty to do what they pleased but the queen besought them with tears, since she had no more faithful subjects in the whole kingdom, to share with her the cares of governing the kingdom until her son should grow up, especially Frumentius, whose ability was equal to guiding the kingdom, for the other, though loyal and honest of heart, was simple.

While they lived there and Frumentius held the reins of government in his hands, God stirred up his heart and he began to search out with care those of the Roman merchants who were Christians and to give them great influence and to urge them to establish in various places conventicles to which they might resort for prayer in the Roman manner. He himself, moreover, did the same and so encouraged the others, attracting them with his favor and his benefits, providing them with whatever was needed, supplying sites for buildings and other necessaries, and in every way promoting the growth of the seed of Christianity in the country. When the prince [Ezana] for whom they exercised the regency had grown up, they completed and faithfully delivered over their trust, and, though the queen and her son

---

°**Tyre:** a city in Lebanon.

Source: Quoted in A. H. M. Jones and Elizabeth Monroe, *A History of Abyssinia* (Oxford: Oxford University Press, 1935), 26–27.

sought greatly to detain them and begged them to remain, returned to the Roman Empire.

Aedesius hastened to Tyre to revisit his parents and relatives. Frumentius went to Alexandria, saying that it was not right to hide the work of God. He laid the whole affair before the bishop and urged him to look for some worthy man to send as bishop over the many Christians already congregated and the churches built on barbarian soil. Then Athanasius (for he had recently assumed the episcopate), having carefully weighed and considered Frumentius' words and deeds, declared in a council of the priests: "What other man shall we find in whom the Spirit of God is as in thee, who can accomplish these things?" And he consecrated him and bade him return in the grace of God whence he had come. And when he had arrived in India [Axum] as bishop, such grace is said to have been given to him by God that apostolic miracles were wrought by him and a countless number of barbarians were converted by him to the faith. From which time Christian peoples and churches have been created in the parts of India, and the priesthood has begun. These facts I know not from vulgar report but from the mouth of Aedesius himself, who had been Frumentius' companion and was later made a priest in Tyre.

Document 7.4

A Byzantine View of an Axumite Monarch

In the sixth century, Axum became embroiled in the larger conflict between the Byzantine and Persian empires, then the superpowers of the region. In this epic struggle the Persians found an ally in the Himyarite kingdom of Arabia, several of whose leaders had converted to Judaism and were actively persecuting Christians. In 530–531, the Byzantine emperor Justinian sent an emissary to King Kaleb of Axum, appealing for his aid in attacking this threat to their common Christian faith. That emissary, named Julian, subsequently made a report to Justinian that contained a description of the court of the Axumite ruler and his now Christian court.

- ■ Why do you think King Kaleb was so eager join Byzantium in its struggle against Persia and its Arab Himyarite ally? Consider both religious and strategic reasons.

- ■ What evidence in the document suggests that the Byzantine authorities considered King Kaleb an equal? What evidence might suggest that they saw him as a subordinate?

- ■ What did Julian find especially striking about King Kaleb's appearance and behavior?

JULIAN

Report to the Byzantine Emperor on Axum

530–531

In the same year, the Romans and Persians broke their peace. The Persian war was renewed because of the embassy of the...Himyarite Arabs to the Romans. The Romans sent the Magistrianos Julian from Alexandria down the Nile River and through the Indian Ocean with sacral letters to [Kaleb], the king of the Ethiopans. King [Kaleb] received him with great joy, since [Kaleb] longed after the Roman Emperor's friendship.

On his return (to Constantinople), this same Julian reported that King [Kaleb] was naked when he received him but had round his kidneys a loin-cloth of linen and gold thread. On his belly he wore linen with precious pearls; his bracelets had five spikes, and he wore gold armlets by his hands. He had a linen-and-gold cloth turban round his head, with four cords hanging down from both its straps.

He stood on (a carriage drawn by) four standing elephants which had a yoke and four wheels. Like

---

Source: Theophanes, *Chronographia*, Annus mundi 6064. Unpublished translation by Dr. Harry Turtledove. In *Ancient African Civilizations: Kush and Axum*, edited by Stanley Burstein (Princeton: Markus Weiner, 1998), 125–26.

any stately carriage, it was ornamented with golden petals, just as are the carriages of provincial governors. While he stood upon it, he held in his hands a small gilded shield and two gold javelins. His counselors were all armed, and sang musical tunes.

When the Roman ambassador was brought in and had performed the prostration, he was ordered to rise by the king and was led before him. [Kaleb] accepted the Emperor's sacral letters and tenderly kissed the seal which had the Emperor's image. He also accepted Julian's gifts and greatly rejoiced.

When he read the letter, he found that it was urgent for him to arm himself against the Persian king, devastate Persian territory near him [in South Arabia], and in the future no longer make covenants with the Persian. Rather, the letter arranged that the land of the [Himyarites] would conduct its business with Egyptian Alexandria by way of the Nile River.

In the sight of the envoy, King [Kaleb] immediately began to campaign: he set war in motion against the Persians and sent out his Saracens [Arabs]. He himself also went off against Persian territory and pillaged all of it in that area. After conquering, King [Kaleb] gave Julian a kiss of peace on the head and sent him off with a large retinue and many gifts.

Document 7.5

Axum and the Gold Trade

The foundations of the Axumite state lay not only in its military conquests and its adoption of a new religion but also in its economic ties to the larger world. Among these ties was its reputation as a major source of gold for the Roman Empire. Document 7.5 describes the distinctive fashion in which Axumite traders obtained the gold from the African peoples living on the margins of the Axumite state. The author, Cosmas (see Document 7.2, pp. 309–10), was involved in this trade.

■ How would you define the pattern of exchange described in this document? Was it state-directed trade, private enterprise, or both? To what problems of cross-cultural interaction was it a response?

- Who, if anyone, had the upper hand in this trade? Was it conducted between politically equal parties?

- What purposes did this trade serve for the people who mined and "sold" the gold?

- Beyond the peaceful trade for gold described here, what other purposes did this region serve for Axum?

COSMAS
The Christian Topography
Sixth Century C.E.

The country known as that of Sasu is itself near the ocean, just as the ocean is near the frankincense country,° in which there are many gold mines. The King of the Axumites accordingly, every other year, through the governor of Agau, sends thither special agents to bargain for the gold, and these are accompanied by many other traders—upwards, say, of five hundred—bound on the same errand as themselves. They take along with them to the mining district oxen, lumps of salt, and iron, and when they reach its neighborhood, they make a halt at a certain spot and form an encampment, which they fence round with a great hedge of thorns. Within this they live, and having slaughtered the oxen, cut them in pieces, and lay the pieces on the top of the thorns, along with the lumps of salt and the iron. Then come the natives bringing gold in nuggets like peas, and lay one or two or more of these upon what pleases them—the pieces of flesh or the salt or the iron, and then they retire to some distance off. Then the owner of the meat approaches, and if he is satisfied he takes the gold away, and upon seeing this, its owner comes and takes the flesh or the salt or the iron. If, however, he is not satisfied, he leaves the gold, when the native, seeing that he has not taken it, comes and either puts down more gold, or takes up what he had laid down, and goes away. Such is the mode in which business is transacted with the people of that country, because their language is different and interpreters are hardly to be found.

The time they stay in that country is five days more or less, according as the natives, more or less readily coming forward, buy up all their wares. On the journey homeward they all agree to travel well-armed, since some of the tribes through whose country they must pass might threaten to attack them from a desire to rob them of their gold. The space of six months is taken up with this trading expedition, including both the going and the returning. In going they march very slowly, chiefly because of the cattle, but in returning they quicken their pace lest on the way they should be overtaken by winter and its rains. For the sources of the river Nile lie somewhere in these parts, and in winter, on account of the heavy rains, the numerous rivers which they generate obstruct the path of the traveler. The people there have their winter at the time we have our summer... and during the three months the rain falls in torrents, and makes a multitude of rivers all of which flow into the Nile.

The facts which I have just recorded fell partly under my own observation and partly were told me by traders who had been to those parts....

For most of the slaves which are now found in the hands of merchants who resort to these parts are taken from the tribes of which we speak. As for the Semenai, where...there are snows and ice, it is to that country the King of the Axumites expatriates anyone whom he has sentenced to be banished.

°**frankincense country:** probably what is now Somalia.

Source: J. W. McCrindle, trans. and ed., *The Christian Topography of Cosmas, an Egyptian Monk* (London: The Hakluyt Society, 1897), 52–54, 67.

Using the Evidence:
Axum and the World

1. **Assessing sources:** How does each of these documents reflect the distinctive perspective of its author? What different perspectives can you notice between those documents written from within Axum and those written by outsiders? How did the particular social role that each author represents (missionary, monarch, merchant) affect his view of Axum?

2. **Considering external influences:** Based on these documents, how would you describe Axum's various relationships with the world beyond its borders? How did its geographical location shape those relationships? (See Map 7.1, p. 285.) In what ways did those external connections influence Axum's historical development? From another perspective, how did Axum actively assimilate foreign influences or deliberately take advantage of opportunities that came from outside?

3. **Explaining the rise and significance of Axum:** How might you account for the flourishing of Axum during its classical era? What was the religious and military significance of Axum within the region?

4. **Comparing civilizations:** In what ways might Axum be viewed as a smaller-scale version of the classical civilizations of Eurasia? In what ways did it differ from them?

5. **Seeking further evidence:** What else would you like to know about Axum? If you could uncover one additional document, what would you want it to reveal?

Visual Sources

Considering the Evidence:
Art and the Maya Elite

The ancient Maya world," writes a major scholar of the region, "was a world of Maya art."[25] In magnificent architecture, carvings, pottery, ceramic figures, wall paintings, and illustrated books, Maya culture was suffused by a distinctive style of artistic expression, more complex, subtle, extensive, and innovative than any other in the Americas. Commissioned by Maya rulers, that art centered on life at court, depicting kings, nobles, warriors, and wealthy merchants together with the women, musicians, and artists who served them as well as the many deities who populated the Maya universe. Far more than in China, India, or Europe, historians rely on art and archeology for their insights into Maya civilization. While the Maya had writing, their literature was less extensive than that of classical-era Eurasian cultures and much of it was tragically destroyed during the early decades of Spanish rule. The images that follow provide a window into the life of the Maya elite during its classical era (see the map on p. 293).

Visual Source 7.1 shows a royal couple from the Maya city of Yaxchilan in the year 724 C.E. with the king Shield Jaguar, on the left, and his primary wife, Lady Xok, on the right. In helping him dress for a war-related ceremony or sacrifice, Lady Xok offers her husband his helmet, the head of a jaguar, an animal that was widely associated with strength, bravery, aggression, warfare, and high social status. The T-shaped frame at the center top, which contains a number of Maya glyphs (written symbols), indicates a doorway and thus sets the action in an interior space. The king is wearing cotton body armor and carrying a knife, while his wife is clad in a *huipil*, a blouse similar to those still worn by Maya women in southern Mexico.

- What elements of their dress and decoration serve to mark their high status?

- What aspects of the physical appearance of this couple might represent ideal male and female characteristics in Maya culture? Pay attention to their hair, foreheads, and noses, as well as to the attitude suggested by their faces.

- What might you infer about the relationship of Shield Jaguar and Lady Xok from this carving? Notice the relatively equal size of the two figures and the gesture that Shield Jaguar makes with his left hand. Keep in mind that the carving comes from a temple in Yaxchilan dedicated to Lady Xok.

Visual Source 7.1 Shield Jaguar and Lady Xok: A Royal Couple of Yaxchilan (Museo Nacional de Antropologia—INAH, Mexico)

Warfare was frequent among Maya cities and thus a common theme in their court art. Fought with spear throwers, lances, clubs, axes, swords, and shields, Maya wars were depicted as chaotic affairs aimed at the capture of individual prisoners, who were destined for sacrifice or slavery. Those prisoners were often named in the glyphs that accompanied the portrayal of battles along with the inscription "He is seized/roped."

Visual Source 7.2, a reconstructed image, comes from a Maya archeological site in southern Mexico called Bonampak, well known for its vivid murals. Depicting events that took place in 792 C.E., this mural shows King Chan Muwan of Bonampak (in the center) holding a staff and receiving nine prisoners of war from his victorious noble warriors. To the king's right are two allies from the nearby city of Yaxchilan, followed by the king's wife, his mother, and a servant-musician playing a conch. To the king's left are six more high-ranking warriors from Bonampak, while lower-level warriors guard each side of the door at the bottom.

The prisoners hold center stage in the mural. Notice in particular the dead captive sprawling below the king's staff as a severed head lies on a bed of leaves below him. The four small images at the top indicate constellations, showing the favorable position of the sky for this occasion. The turtle on the far right, for example, depicts the constellation Gemini, while the three stars on its back represent what we know as Orion's belt.

- What can you infer about Maya warfare and court practice from this mural?

- What do the various postures of the captives suggest?

- Notice that a number of the captives have blood dripping from their fingers. What does this indicate? What might be happening to the prisoner at the far left?

- What status distinctions can you observe among the figures in the mural? Notice the jaguar skins worn by the king and three other warriors.

- What meaning might you attach to the presence of the king's wife and mother at this event?

The bleeding and ultimately the sacrifice of the captives in Visual Source 7.2 was only part of a more pervasive practice of bloodletting that permeated Maya religious and court life. Significant occasions—giving birth, getting married, dying, planting crops, dedicating buildings, and many more—were sanctified with human blood, the most valued and holy substance in the world. Behind this practice lay the Maya belief in the mutual relationship of humans and their gods. Two of the major scholars in this field explain: "The earth and its creatures were created through a sacrificial act of the gods, and human beings, in turn, were required to strengthen and nourish the gods."[26] The means of

Visual Source 7.2 The Presentation of Captives (Peabody Museum, Harvard University, Cambridge, MA, USA/The Bridgeman Art Library)

doing so was blood. The massive loss of blood often triggered a trancelike state that the Maya experienced as mystical union with their gods or ancestors. The lancets used to draw blood—usually from the tongue in women and often from the penis in men—were invested with sacred power.

Kings and their wives were central to this bloodletting ritual, as Visual Source 7.3 so vividly shows. Here we meet again Shield Jaguar and Lady Xok, depicted also in Visual Source 7.1. The date of this carving is October 28,

Visual Source 7.3 A Bloodletting Ritual
(© Justin Kerr, K2887)

709 C.E. The king is holding a large torch, suggesting that the ritual occurs at night, while his kneeling wife draws a thorn-studded rope through her perforated tongue. The rope falls into a basket of bloody paper, which will later be burned with the resulting smoke nourishing the gods. Shield Jaguar too will soon let his own blood flow, for the glyphs accompanying this carving declare that "he is letting blood" and "she is letting blood."

- What details can you notice in the exquisitely carved work?

- What significance might you attribute to the fact that the couple is performing this ritual together?

- Why do you think Lady Xok is kneeling?

- Notice the shrunken head in Shield Jaguar's headdress. How would you assess its significance? How might it enhance his status?

- To what extent is this pervasive bloodletting a uniquely mesoamerican religious practice? What roles do blood and sacrifice play in other religious traditions?

Among the most well-known and intriguing features of Maya life was a ball game in which teams of players, often two on a side, sought to control a rubber ball, using only their thighs, torsos, and upper arms to make it hit a marker or ring. Deeply rooted in Maya mythology, the game was played both before and after the classical Maya era on ball courts found throughout the Maya territory as well as elsewhere in Mesoamerica. On one level, the game was sport, often played simply for entertainment and recreation. But it also reflected and symbolized the prevalence of warfare among Maya cities. As one recent account put it: "[T]he game re-enacted the paradigms for war and sacrifice, where the skillful and blessed triumph and the weak and undeserving are vanquished."[27] The ball game was yet another occasion for the shedding of blood, as losing players, often war captives, were killed, sometimes bound in ball-like fashion and rolled down the steps of the court to their death. Thus the larger mythic context of the ball game was the eternal struggle of life and death, so central to Maya religious thinking.

Visual Source 7.4, a rollout of a vase dating from the seventh or eighth century C.E., depicts the ball game in action. The two players on each side echo the Hero Twins of Maya mythology, famous ball players who triumphed over the lords of the underworld in an extended game and who were later transformed triumphantly into the sun and moon. The glyphs accompanying this image named two kings of adjacent cities, suggesting that the game may have been played on occasion as a substitute for warfare between rival cities.

■ What might the elaborate dress of the players suggest about the function of the game and the status of its players?

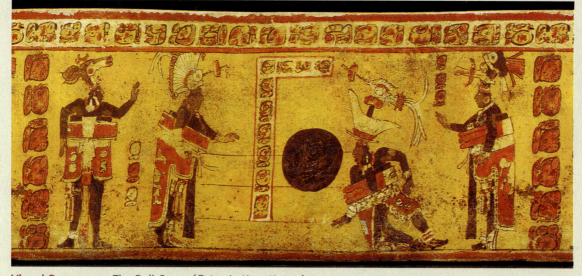

Visual Source 7.4 The Ball Game (© Justin Kerr, K2803)

■ Notice the deer headdress on the player at the far left and the vulture
image on the corresponding player at the far right. What do the headdresses suggest about the larger mythic context in which the game was
understood?

■ Notice the heavy protective padding around the waist as well as the
wrappings around one knee, foot, and upper arm of the two lead players.
What was the purpose of such padding? Keep in mind that the rubber
ball, shown here in an exaggerated form, was roughly the size of a modern
volleyball but weighed perhaps seven or eight pounds.

Visual Source 7.5 An Embracing Couple (© Dumbarton Oaks,
Pre-Columbian Collection, Washington, D.C.)

■ How might you compare this ancient Maya ball game to contemporary athletic contests? Consider the larger social meaning of the game as well as its more obvious features.

Certainly not all was war, sacrifice, and bloodletting among the Maya. Visual Source 7.5, a ceramic figurine from the late classical era, illustrates a more playful and explicitly sexual side to Maya art.

■ How might you describe what is transpiring between this older man and the much younger woman? Notice the position of their hands, the woman's knee, and the expression of their faces.

As was frequently the case among the Maya, artistic expression had a mythic significance. Here the young woman probably represents the moon goddess, associated with sexuality, fertility, night, death, and frequent change of lovers, reflecting the changing cycles of the moon. In an effort to spy out her infidelities, her husband/lover, the aged sun god in Maya mythology, took on the form of a deer as represented in his headdress.

■ What might this image and its mythological context tell us about Maya views of sexuality?

Using the Evidence:
Art and the Maya Elite

1. **Considering art as evidence:** What can you learn from these visual sources about the values, preoccupations, and outlook of the Maya elite? What are the strengths and limitations of art as a source of evidence? What other kinds of evidence would you want to discover to further your understanding of the Maya elite?

2. **Assessing gender roles:** In what ways are women and men depicted in these visual sources? What might this suggest about their respective roles in the elite circles of Maya society?

3. **Making comparisons:** How might you compare the life of the Maya elite depicted in these visual sources with that of the Roman elite of Pompeii shown in the Visual Sources section of Chapter 6 (pp. 272–79)? For a second comparison, consider the similarities and differences of Maya and Axumite civilizations.

4. **Considering the values of the historian:** What feelings or judgments do these visual sources evoke in you? Which of your values might get in the way of a sympathetic understanding of the Maya elite?

PART THREE

An Age
of Accelerating
Connections

500–1500

Contents

Defining a Millennium

History seldom turns sharp corners, and historians often have difficulty deciding just when one phase of the human story ends and another begins. Between roughly 200 and 850 C.E., many of the classical states and civilizations of the world (Han dynasty China, the Roman Empire, Gupta India, Meroë, Axum, Maya, Teotihuacán, Moche) experienced severe disruption, decline, or collapse. For many historians, this marks the end of the classical era and the start of some new period of world history. Furthermore, almost everyone agrees that the transatlantic voyages of Columbus around 1500 represent yet another new departure in world history. This coupling of the Eastern and Western hemispheres set in motion historical processes that transformed most of the world and signaled the beginning of the modern era.

But how are we to understand the thousand years (roughly 500 to 1500) between the end of the classical era and the beginning of modern world history? Historians, frankly, have had some difficulty in defining a distinct identity for this millennium, and this problem is reflected in the vague terms used to describe it. Many textbooks, including this one on occasion, refer to this 1,000-year period simply as the "postclassical" age, but that, of course, merely indicates that it came after the classical era. Others have termed it "medieval," a middle or intermediate age, something in between the classical and modern eras. Many historians feel uncomfortable with this term because it derives specifically from European history and thus runs the risk of appearing Eurocentric. It also seems to suggest that this millennium was merely a run-up to modernity, rather than something of significance in its own right. This book sometimes uses the concept of "third-wave civilizations," distinguishing, at least chronologically, those that emerged after 500 C.E. from both the First Civilizations and those of the classical era (the second-wave civilizations). At best, these terms indicate where this period falls in the larger time frame of world history, but none of them are very descriptive.

Third-Wave Civilizations: Something New, Something Old, Something Blended

A large part of the problem lies in the rather different trajectories of various regions of the world during this postclassical era. It is not easy to identify clearly defined features that encompass all the major civilizations during this period and distinguish them from what went before, but we can point to several distinct patterns of development among these third-wave societies of the postclassical era.

In some areas, for example, wholly new but smaller civilizations arose where none had existed before. Along the East African coast, Swahili civilization emerged in a string of thirty or more city-states, very much engaged in the commercial life of the Indian Ocean basin. In the area now encompassed by Ukraine and western Russia, another new civilization, known as Kievan Rus, likewise took shape with a good deal of cultural borrowing from Mediterranean civilization. East and Southeast Asia also witnessed new centers of civilization. Those in Japan, Korea, and Vietnam were strongly influenced by China, while Srivijaya on the Indonesian island of Sumatra and later the Angkor kingdom, centered in present-day Cambodia, drew on the Hindu and Buddhist traditions of India.

All of these represent a continuation of a well-established pattern in world history—the globalization of civilization. It began with the First Civilizations of Mesopotamia, Egypt, and elsewhere about 3000 B.C.E. and then took new and larger forms in the classical era (500 B.C.E.–500 C.E.), when Greco-Roman, Persian, Indian, and Chinese civilizations flourished across Eurasia. Each of the new third-wave civilizations was, of course, culturally unique, but like their predecessors, they too featured states, cities, specialized economic roles, sharp class and gender inequalities, and other elements of "civilized" life. They were certainly distinctive, but not fundamentally different from earlier civilizations. As newcomers to the growing number of civilizations, all of them borrowed heavily from larger or more established centers.

The largest, most expansive, and most widely influential of the new third-wave civilizations was surely that of Islam. It began in Arabia in the seventh century C.E., projecting the Arab peoples into a prominent role as builders of an enormous empire while offering a new, vigorous, and attractive religion. Viewed as a new civilization defined by its religion, the world of Islam came to encompass many other centers of civilization, including Egypt, Mesopotamia, Persia, India, the interior of West Africa and the coast of East Africa, Spain, southeastern Europe, and more. Here was a uniquely cosmopolitan or "umbrella" civilization that, according to one leading scholar, "came closer than any had ever come to uniting all mankind under its ideals."[1]

Yet another, and quite different, historical pattern during the postclassical millennium involved older or classical civilizations that persisted or were reconstructed. The Byzantine Empire, embracing the eastern half of the old Roman Empire, continued the patterns of Mediterranean Christian civilization and persisted until 1453, when it was overrun by the Ottoman Turks. In China, following almost four centuries of fragmentation, the Sui, Tang, and Song dynasties (589–1279) restored China's imperial unity and reasserted its Confucian tradition. Indian civilization retained its ancient patterns of caste and Hinduism amid vast cultural diversity, even as parts of India fell under the control of Muslim rulers. The West African savanna kingdoms of Ghana, Mali, and Songhay, stimulated and sustained by long-distance trade across the Sahara, built upon the earlier Niger Valley civilization.

Variations on this theme of continuing or renewing older traditions took shape in the Western Hemisphere, where two centers of civilization—in Mesoamerica and in the Andes—had been long established. In Mesoamerica, the collapse of classical Maya civilization and of the great city-state of Teotihuacán by about 900 C.E. opened the way for other peoples to give new shape to this ancient civilization. The most well known of these efforts was associated with the Mexica or Aztec people, who created a powerful and impressive state in the fifteenth century. About the same time, on the western rim of South America, a Quechua-speaking people, now known as the Inca, incorporated various centers of Andean civilization into a huge bureaucratic empire. Both the Aztecs and the Incas gave a new political expression to much older patterns of civilized life.

Yet another pattern took shape in Western Europe following the collapse of the Roman Empire. There would-be kings and church leaders alike sought to maintain links with the older Greco-Roman-Christian traditions of classical Mediterranean civilization. In the absence of empire, though, new and far more decentralized societies emerged, led now by Germanic peoples and centered in Northern and Western Europe, considerably removed from the older centers of Rome and Athens. It was a hybrid civilization, combining old and new, classical and Germanic elements, in a unique blending. For five centuries or more, this region was a relative backwater, compared to the more vibrant, prosperous, and powerful civilizations of the Islamic world and of China. During the centuries after 1000 C.E., however, Western European civilization emerged as a rapidly growing and expansive set of competitive states, willing, like other new civilizations, to borrow quite extensively from their more developed neighbors.

The Ties That Bind: Transregional Interaction in the Postclassical Era

These quite different patterns of development within particular civilizations of the postclassical millennium have made it difficult to define that era in a single, all-encompassing fashion. In another way, though, a common theme emerges, for during this time, the world's various regions, cultures, and peoples interacted with one another far more extensively. More than before, change in human societies was the product of contact with strangers, or at least with their ideas, armies, goods, or diseases. In a variety of places—island Southeast Asia, coastal East Africa, Central Asian cities, parts of Western Europe, the Islamic Middle East, and the Inca Empire—local cosmopolitan regions emerged in which trade, migration, or empire had brought peoples of different cultures together in a restricted space. These "mini-globalizations," both larger and more common than in the classical era, became a distinctive feature of third-wave civilizations.

"No man is an island, entire of itself," wrote the seventeenth-century English poet John Donne. "Every man is a piece of the continent, a part of the main." Much the same might be said of every civilization, culture, or region. None of them were wholly isolated or separate from their neighbors, although the range and intensity of cross-cultural interaction certainly varied over time. In limited ways, that was the case for the First Civilizations as well as their classical successors. Both Egyptian and Mesopotamian cultural influence spread well beyond the core regions of those civilizations. Horseback-riding skills and chariot technology diffused widely across Eurasia. The encounter of the Greeks and Persians changed both of those classical civilizations. Cross-cultural mixing in northern India gave rise to the caste system, while the Silk Road trading networks across Eurasia provided some modest contact among the distant empires of Rome, China, and India.

The scale and pace of such interaction accelerated considerably during the era of third-wave, or postclassical, civilizations. Much of Part Three highlights these intersections and spells out their many and varied consequences. Three major mechanisms of cross-cultural interaction, which we will meet in the chapters that follow, were of particular significance for transforming the lives and societies of those who took part in them.

One such mechanism was trade. The exchange of goods has been everywhere one of the primary means of cross-cultural interaction, and virtually every human society has engaged in it at some level. Although most trade in the premodern world occurred locally among nearby communities, world historians have focused attention especially on long-distance trade, commercial relationships that linked distant human communities. This kind of commerce grew considerably during the postclassical era—along the Silk Roads of Eurasia, within the Indian Ocean basin, across the Sahara, and along the Mississippi and other rivers. Everywhere it acted as an agent of change for all of its participants. In places where long-distance trade was practiced extensively, it required that more people devote their energies to producing for a distant market rather than for the consumption of their own communities. Those who controlled this kind of trade often became extremely wealthy, exciting envy or outrage among those less fortunate. Many societies learned about new products via these trade routes. Europe's knowledge of pepper and other spices, for example, derived from Roman seaborne trade with India beginning in the first century C.E. Many centuries later, Europeans' desire for Asian spices played a part in propelling Western commercial and military expansion into the Indian Ocean.

Such trade also had political consequences as many new states or empires were established on the basis of resources derived from long-distance commerce. The West African kingdoms of Ghana and Mali, the Swahili cities of the East African coast, the early eastern Slavic state known as Rus, and the Indonesian state of Srivijaya are four such examples. Furthermore, far more than goods traveled the trade routes that linked various third-wave civilizations with one another. Religious ideas, technologies, and germs also made their ways along those paths of commerce, bringing significant change to their participants.

Yet another mechanism of cross-cultural interaction lay in large empires. Not only did they incorporate many distinct cultures within a single political system, but their size and stability also provided the security that encouraged travelers and traders to journey long distances from their homelands. Empires, of course, were nothing new in world history, but many of those associated with third-wave civilizations were distinctive. In the first place, they were larger. The Arab Empire, which accompanied the initial spread of Islam, stretched from Spain to India. Even more extensive was the Mongol Empire of the thirteenth and fourteenth centuries. In the Western Hemisphere, the Inca Empire encompassed dozens of distinct peoples in a huge state that ran some 2,500 miles along the spine of the Andes Mountains.

Furthermore, the largest of these empires were the creation of nomadic or pastoral peoples. Classical empires in the Mediterranean basin, China, India, and Persia had been the work of settled farming societies. But now, in the thousand years between

500 and 1500, peoples with a recent history of a nomadic or herding way of life entered the stage of world history as empire builders—Arabs, Turks, Mongols, Aztecs—ruling over agricultural peoples and established civilizations. These empires changed those who created them as well as those who were forcibly incorporated within them. They also did much to foster cross-cultural interaction. Marco Polo, for example, made his way from Italy to China and back in the thirteenth century, thanks largely to the security provided by the Mongol Empire.

Together, large-scale empires and long-distance trade facilitated the spread of ideas, technologies, food crops, and germs far beyond their points of origin. Buddhism spread from India to much of Asia; Christianity encompassed Europe and took root in distant Russia as well as in northeastern Africa, southern India, and western China. Hinduism attracted followers in Southeast Asia; and more than any of the other world religions, Islam became an Afro-Eurasian phenomenon with an enormous reach. Beyond the connections born of commerce and conquest, those of culture and religion generated lasting ties among many peoples of the Eastern Hemisphere.

Technologies, too, were diffused widely. Until the sixth century C.E., China maintained a monopoly on the manufacture of raw silk. Then this technology spread beyond East Asia, allowing the development of a silk industry in the eastern Mediterranean and later in Italy. India too contributed much to the larger world—crystallized sugar, a system of numerals and the concept of zero, techniques for making cotton textiles, and many food crops. Arabs, who were responsible for spreading many of these Indian innovations, found India a "place of marvels."[2] In the Americas, corn gradually diffused from Mesoamerica, where it was initially domesticated, to North America, where it stimulated population growth and the development of more complex societies. Disease also linked distant communities. The plague, or Black Death, decimated many parts of Eurasia and North Africa as it made its deadly way from east to west in the fourteenth century.

A focus on these accelerating connections across cultural boundaries puts the historical spotlight on merchants, travelers, missionaries, migrants, soldiers, and administrators—people who traveled abroad rather than those who stayed at home. Frequently, they stimulated cultural change in the lands they visited, and of course they themselves often were changed by the experience. More than a few of the Christian Crusaders who invaded the Middle East to rescue the holy places from Islamic control wound up as Muslims themselves.

This cross-cultural emphasis in world history also raises provocative questions about what happens when cultures interact or when strangers meet. How did external stimuli operate to produce change within particular societies? How did individuals or societies decide what to accept and what to reject when confronted with new ideas or practices? Were they free to decide such questions, or were they acting under pressure or constraints that limited the possibilities of real choice? In what ways did they alter foreign customs or traditions to better meet their own needs and correspond to their own values? These are some of the questions that will arise as we consider the accelerating connections associated with third-wave civilizations.

Landmarks in the Era of Accelerating Connections, 500–1500

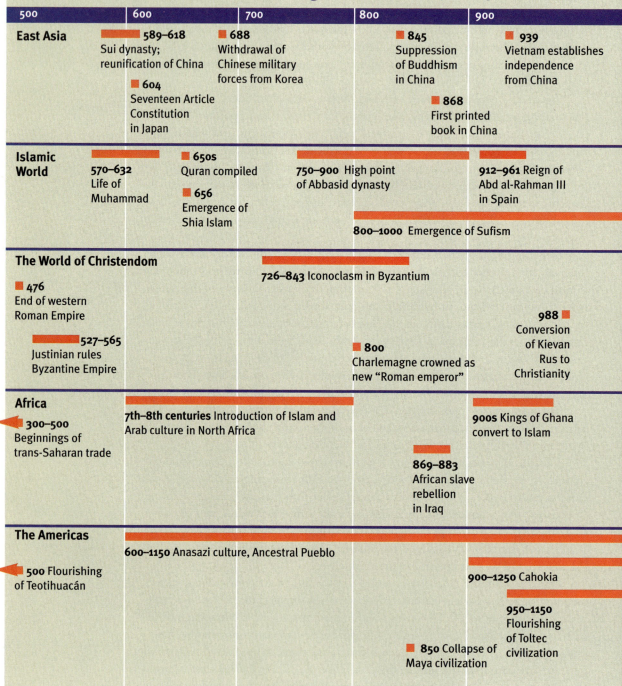

	500	600	700	800	900
East Asia		**589–618** Sui dynasty; reunification of China	**688** Withdrawal of Chinese military forces from Korea	**845** Suppression of Buddhism in China	**939** Vietnam establishes independence from China
		604 Seventeen Article Constitution in Japan		**868** First printed book in China	
Islamic World	**570–632** Life of Muhammad	**650s** Quran compiled	**750–900** High point of Abbasid dynasty		**912–961** Reign of Abd al-Rahman III in Spain
		656 Emergence of Shia Islam	**800–1000** Emergence of Sufism		
The World of Christendom	**476** End of western Roman Empire		**726–843** Iconoclasm in Byzantium		**988** Conversion of Kievan Rus to Christianity
	527–565 Justinian rules Byzantine Empire			**800** Charlemagne crowned as new "Roman emperor"	
Africa	**300–500** Beginnings of trans-Saharan trade	**7th–8th centuries** Introduction of Islam and Arab culture in North Africa		**869–883** African slave rebellion in Iraq	**900s** Kings of Ghana convert to Islam
The Americas	**500** Flourishing of Teotihuacán	**600–1150** Anasazi culture, Ancestral Pueblo		**850** Collapse of Maya civilization	**900–1250** Cahokia
					950–1150 Flourishing of Toltec civilization

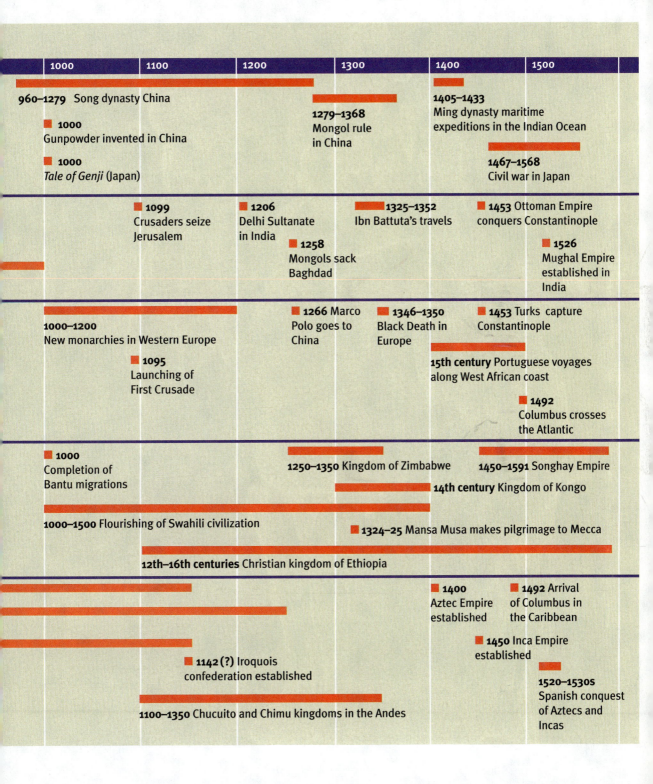

| 1000 | 1100 | 1200 | 1300 | 1400 | 1500 |

960–1279 Song dynasty China

■ **1000**
Gunpowder invented in China

■ **1000**
Tale of Genji (Japan)

1279–1368
Mongol rule
in China

1405–1433
Ming dynasty maritime
expeditions in the Indian Ocean

1467–1568
Civil war in Japan

■ **1099**
Crusaders seize
Jerusalem

■ **1206**
Delhi Sultanate
in India

■ **1325–1352**
Ibn Battuta's travels

■ **1453** Ottoman Empire
conquers Constantinople

■ **1258**
Mongols sack
Baghdad

■ **1526**
Mughal Empire
established in
India

1000–1200
New monarchies in Western Europe

■ **1266** Marco
Polo goes to
China

■ **1346–1350**
Black Death in
Europe

■ **1453** Turks capture
Constantinople

■ **1095**
Launching of
First Crusade

15th century Portuguese voyages
along West African coast

■ **1492**
Columbus crosses
the Atlantic

■ **1000**
Completion of
Bantu migrations

1250–1350 Kingdom of Zimbabwe

1450–1591 Songhay Empire

14th century Kingdom of Kongo

1000–1500 Flourishing of Swahili civilization

■ **1324–25** Mansa Musa makes pilgrimage to Mecca

12th–16th centuries Christian kingdom of Ethiopia

■ **1400**
Aztec Empire
established

■ **1492** Arrival
of Columbus in
the Caribbean

■ **1450** Inca Empire
established

■ **1142 (?)** Iroquois
confederation established

1520–1530s
Spanish conquest
of Aztecs and
Incas

1100–1350 Chucuito and Chimu kingdoms in the Andes

Commerce and Culture

500–1500

"Forget compass readings, camel caravans, and disorienting, potentially deadly Jeep journeys through the world's most fabled and forbidding desert. Soon it will be possible to take a leisurely drive along a paved two-lane highway from the spot where Europe kisses the tip of this continent into the heart of sub-Saharan Africa. That's the idea, anyway."[1] So wrote a journalist for the *New York Times* in late 2003, describing international plans for a modern highway across the Sahara, linking Europe and North Africa with the vast interior of West Africa. Such a road, its advocates hoped, would not only promote tourism, trade, and economic growth but also provide an alternative route for West African Muslims making the pilgrimage to Mecca. At the same time, in early 2004, some twenty-three nations signed an agreement to build a network of highways all across Asia, ultimately linking Tokyo with Istanbul and enabling a number of landlocked countries of Central Asia to participate more fully in the world economy.

THESE TWO AMBITIOUS PROJECTS OF THE EARLY TWENTY-FIRST CENTURY were part of the accumulating infrastructure of contemporary globalization. But they also evoked much older patterns of global commerce, the famous Silk Road network across Eurasia and the trans-Saharan trade routes, both of which flourished in the postclassical era. Here is a reminder, from the viewpoint of world history, that exchange among distant peoples is not altogether new and that the roots of economic globalization lie deep in the past.

Travels on the Silk Road: This Chinese ceramic figurine from the Tang dynasty (618–907 C.E.) shows a group of musicians riding on a camel along the famous Silk Road commercial network that long linked the civilizations of western and eastern Eurasia. The bearded figures represent Central Asian merchants, while the others depict Chinese. (©Asian Art & Archaeology, Inc./Corbis)

The exchange of goods among communities occupying different ecological zones has long been a prominent feature of human history. Coastlands and highlands, steppes and farmlands, islands and mainlands, valleys and mountains, deserts and forests—each generates different products desired by others. Furthermore, some societies have been able to monopolize, at least temporarily, the production of particular products, such as silk in China or certain spices in Southeast Asia, which others have found valuable. This uneven distribution of goods and resources, whether natural or resulting from human activity, has long motivated exchange, not only within particular civilizations or regions but among them as well. In the world of 500–1500, long-distance trade became more important than ever before in linking and shaping distant societies and peoples. For the most part, it was indirect, a chain of separate transactions in which goods traveled farther than individual merchants. Nonetheless, a network of exchange and communication extending all across the Afro-Eurasian world, and separately in parts of the Americas as well, slowly came into being.

In what ways was trade significant? How did it generate change within the societies that it connected? Economically speaking, it often altered consumption, enabling West Africans, for example, to import scarce salt, necessary for human diets and useful for seasoning and preserving food, from distant mines in the Sahara in exchange for the gold of their region. Trade also affected the day-to-day working lives of many people, encouraging them to specialize in producing particular products for sale in distant markets rather than for use in their own communities. Trade, in short, diminished the economic self-sufficiency of local societies.

Trade shaped the structure of those societies as well. Traders often became a distinct social group, viewed with suspicion by others because of their impulse to accumulate wealth without actually producing anything themselves. In some societies, trade became a means of social mobility, as Chinese merchants, for example, were able to purchase landed estates and establish themselves within the gentry class. Long-distance trade also enabled elite groups in society to distinguish themselves from commoners by acquiring prestigious goods from a distance—silk, tortoiseshells, rhinoceros horn, or particular feathers, for example. The association with faraway or powerful societies, signaled by the possession of their luxury goods, often conveyed status in communities more remote from major civilizations.

Political life also was sometimes transformed by trade. The wealth available from controlling and taxing trade motivated the creation of states in various parts of the world and sustained those states once they had been constructed. Furthermore, commerce posed a set of problems to governments everywhere. Should trade be left in private hands, as in the Aztec Empire, or should it be controlled by the state, as in the Inca Empire? How should state authorities deal with men of commerce, who were both economically useful and potentially disruptive?

Moreover, the saddlebags of camel caravans or the cargo holds of merchant vessels carried more than goods. Trade became the vehicle for the spread of religious ideas, technological innovations, disease-bearing germs, and plants and animals to regions far from their places of origin. In just this fashion, Buddhism made its way from India to Central and East Asia, and Islam crossed the Sahara into West Africa. So did the pathogens that devastated much of Eurasia during the Black Death. These immense cultural and biological transformations were among the most significant outcomes of the increasingly dense network of long-distance commerce during the era of third-wave civilizations.

Silk Roads: Exchange across Eurasia

The Eurasian landmass has long been home to the majority of humankind as well as to the world's most productive agriculture, largest civilizations, and greatest concentration of pastoral peoples. Beyond its many separate societies and cultures, Eurasia also gave rise to one of the world's most extensive and sustained networks of exchange among its diverse peoples. Known to scholars as the Silk Roads, a reference to their most famous product, these land-based trade routes linked pastoral and agricultural peoples as well as the large civilizations on the continent's outer rim (see Map 8.1). None of its numerous participants knew the full extent of this network's reach, for it was largely a "relay trade" in which goods were passed down the line, changing hands many times before reaching their final destination. Nonetheless, the Silk Roads provide a certain unity and coherence to Eurasian history alongside the distinct stories of its separate civilizations and peoples.

Map 8.1 The Silk Roads For 2,000 years, goods, ideas, technologies, and diseases made their way across Eurasia on the several routes of the Silk Roads.

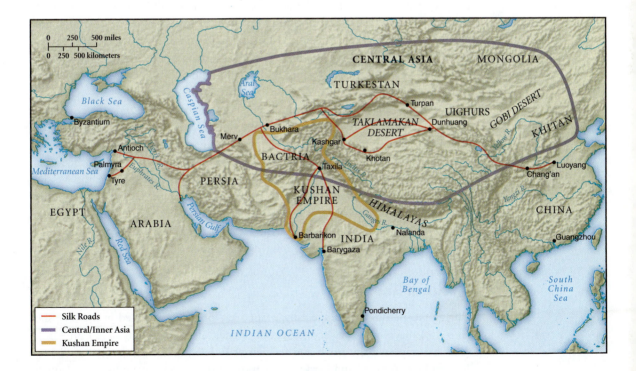

Legend:
— Silk Roads
— Central/Inner Asia
— Kushan Empire

The Growth of the Silk Roads

■ Change
What lay behind the emergence of Silk Road commerce, and what kept it going for so many centuries?

The beginnings of the Silk Roads lay in both geography and history. As a geographic unit, Eurasia is often divided into inner and outer zones that represent quite different environments. Outer Eurasia consists of relatively warm, well-watered areas, suitable for agriculture, which provided the setting for the great civilizations of China, India, the Middle East, and the Mediterranean. Inner Eurasia—the lands of eastern Russia and Central Asia—lies farther north and has a harsher and drier climate, much of it not conducive to agriculture. Herding their animals from horseback, the pastoral people of this region had for centuries traded with and raided their agricultural neighbors to the south. Products of the forest and of semi-arid northern grasslands known as the steppes—such as hides, furs, livestock, wool, and amber—were exchanged for the agricultural products and manufactured goods of adjacent civilizations. The movement of pastoral peoples for thousands of years also served to diffuse Indo-European languages, bronze metallurgy, horse-based technologies, and more all across Eurasia.

The construction of the classical civilizations and their imperial states during the last five centuries B.C.E. added another element to these earlier Eurasian connections. From the south, the Persian Empire invaded the territory of pastoral peoples in present-day Turkmenistan and Uzbekistan. From the west, Alexander the Great's empire stretched well into Central Asia. From the east, China's Han dynasty extended its authority westward, seeking to control the nomadic Xiongnu and to gain access to the powerful "heavenly horses" that were so important to Chinese military forces. By the early centuries of the Common Era, indirect trading connections, often brokered by pastoral peoples, linked the classical civilizations in a network of transcontinental exchange. (For the role of Central Asian pastoral peoples in the exchange of the Silk Roads, see Visual Sources: Art, Religion, and Cultural Exchange in Central Asia, pp. 367–77.)

Silk Road trading networks prospered most when large and powerful states provided security for merchants and travelers. Such conditions prevailed during the classical era when the Roman and Chinese empires anchored long-distance commerce at the western and eastern ends of Eurasia. Silk Road trade flourished again during the seventh and eighth centuries C.E. as the Byzantine Empire, the Muslim Abbasid dynasty, and Tang dynasty China created an almost continuous belt of strong states across Eurasia. In the thirteenth and fourteenth centuries, the Mongol Empire briefly encompassed almost the entire route of the Silk Roads in a single state, giving a renewed vitality to long-distance trade.

Goods in Transit

During prosperous times especially, a vast array of goods (detailed in the Snapshot on p. 337) made their way across the Silk Roads, often carried in large camel caravans that traversed the harsh and dangerous steppes, deserts, and oases of Central Asia. In high demand and hard to find, most of these goods were luxury products,

$\mathcal{S}$napshot   **Economic Exchange along the Silk Roads**

Region	Products Contributed to Silk Road Commerce
China	silk, bamboo, mirrors, gunpowder, paper, rhubarb, ginger, lacquerware, chrysanthemums
Forest lands of Siberia and grasslands of Central Asia	furs, walrus tusks, amber, livestock, horses, falcons, hides, copper vessels, tents, saddles, slaves
India	cotton textiles, herbal medicine, precious stones, spices
Middle East	dates, nuts, almonds, dried fruit, dyes, lapis lazuli, swords
Mediterranean basin	gold coins, glassware, glazes, grapevines, jewelry, artworks, perfume, wool and linen textiles, olive oil

destined for an elite and wealthy market, rather than staple goods, for only readily moved commodities of great value could compensate for the high costs of transportation across such long and forbidding distances.

Of all these luxury goods, it was silk that came to symbolize this Eurasian exchange system. When China held a monopoly on silk-producing technology, this precious fabric moved generally from east to west. The demand for silk as well as cotton textiles from India was so great in the Roman Empire that various Roman writers were appalled at the drain of resources that it represented. They also were outraged at the moral impact of wearing revealing silk garments. "I can see clothes of silk," lamented Seneca the Younger in the first century C.E., "if materials that do not hide the body, nor even one's decency, can be called clothes. . . . Wretched flocks of maids labour so that the adulteress may be visible through her thin dress, so that her husband has no more acquaintance than any outsider or foreigner with his wife's body."[2]

By the sixth century C.E., however, the knowledge and technology for producing raw silk had spread beyond China. An old Chinese story attributes it to a Chinese princess who smuggled out silkworms in her turban when she was married off to a Central Asian ruler. In a European version of the tale, Christian monks living in China did the deed by hiding some silkworms in a bamboo cane, an act of industrial espionage that allowed an independent silk-producing and silk-weaving industry to take hold in the Byzantine Empire. However it happened, Koreans, Japanese, Indians, and Persians likewise learned how to produce this precious fabric.

As the supply of silk increased, its many varieties circulated even more extensively across Eurasian trade routes. In Central Asia, silk was used as currency and as a means of accumulating wealth. In both China and the Byzantine Empire, silk became a symbol of high status, and governments passed laws that restricted silk clothing to members of the elite. Furthermore, silk became associated with the sacred in the expanding world religions of Buddhism and Christianity. Chinese Buddhist pilgrims who made their way to India seeking religious texts and relics took with them large quantities of silk as gifts to the monasteries they visited (see

■ **Significance**
What made silk such a highly desired commodity across Eurasia?

Visual Source 8.2, p. 370). Buddhist monks in China received purple silk robes from Tang dynasty emperors as a sign of high honor. In the world of Christendom, silk wall hangings, altar covers, and vestments became highly prestigious signs of devotion and piety. Because no independent silk industry developed in Western Europe until the twelfth century C.E., a considerable market developed for silks imported from the Islamic world. Ironically, the splendor of Christian churches depended in part on Islamic trading networks and on silks manufactured in the Muslim world. Some of those silks were even inscribed with passages in Arabic from the Quran, unbeknownst to their European buyers.[3]

■ **Connection**

What were the major economic, social, and cultural consequences of Silk Road commerce?

Compared to contemporary global commerce, the volume of trade on the Silk Roads was small, and its focus on luxury goods limited its direct impact on most people. Nonetheless, it had important economic and social consequences. Peasants in the Yangzi River delta of southern China sometimes gave up the cultivation of food crops, choosing to focus instead on producing silk, paper, porcelain, lacquerware, or iron tools, much of which was destined for the markets of the Silk Roads. In this way, the impact of long-distance trade trickled down to affect the lives of ordinary farmers. Furthermore, favorably placed individuals could benefit immensely from long-distance trade. The twelfth-century Persian merchant Ramisht made a personal fortune from his long-distance trading business and with his profits purchased an enormously expensive silk covering for the Kaaba, the central shrine of Islam in Mecca.[4]

Cultures in Transit

■ **Change**

What accounted for the spread of Buddhism along the Silk Roads?

More important even than the economic impact of the Silk Roads was their role as a conduit of culture. Buddhism in particular, a cultural product of Indian civilization, spread widely throughout Central and East Asia, owing much to the activities of merchants along the Silk Roads. From its beginnings in India during the sixth century B.C.E., Buddhism had appealed to merchants, who preferred its universal message to that of a Brahmin-dominated Hinduism that privileged the higher castes. Indian traders and Buddhist monks, sometimes supported by rulers such as Ashoka, brought the new religion to the trans-Eurasian trade routes. To the west, Persian Zoroastrianism largely blocked the spread of Buddhism, but in the oasis cities of Central Asia, such as Merv, Samarkand, Khotan, and Dunhuang, Buddhism quickly took hold. By the first century B.C.E., many of the inhabitants of these towns had converted to Buddhism, and foreign merchant communities soon introduced it to northern China as well.[5] (See Visual Sources 8.1 and 8.2, pp. 369 and 370, as well as Document 8.1, pp. 356–59.)

Conversion to Buddhism in the oasis cities was a voluntary process, without the pressure of conquest or foreign rule. Dependent on long-distance trade, the inhabitants and rulers of those sophisticated and prosperous cities found in Buddhism a link to the larger, wealthy, and prestigious civilization of India. Well-to-do Buddhist merchants could earn religious merit by building monasteries and supporting monks. The monasteries in turn provided convenient and culturally familiar places of rest and resupply for merchants making the long and arduous trek across Central Asia. Many of these cities became cosmopolitan centers of learning and commerce. Scholars have found thousands of Buddhist texts in the city of Dunhuang, where several branches of the Silk Roads joined to enter western China, together with hundreds of cave temples, lavishly decorated with murals and statues.

Outside of the oasis communities, Buddhism progressed only slowly among pastoral peoples of Central Asia. The absence of a written language was an obstacle to the penetration of a highly literate religion, and their nomadic ways made the founding of monasteries, so important to Buddhism, quite difficult. But as pastoralists became involved in long-distance trade or came to rule settled agricultural peoples, Buddhism seemed more attractive. The nomadic Jie people, who controlled much of northern China after the collapse of the Han dynasty, are a case in point. Their ruler in the early fourth century C.E., Shi Le, became acquainted with a Buddhist monk called Fotudeng, who had traveled widely on the Silk Roads. The monk's reputation as a miracle worker, a rain-maker, and a fortune-teller and his skills as a military strategist cemented a personal relationship with Shi Le and led to the conversions of thousands and the construction of hundreds of Buddhist temples. In China itself, Buddhism remained for many centuries a religion of foreign merchants or foreign rulers. Only slowly did it become popular among the Chinese themselves, a process examined more closely in Chapter 9.

As Buddhism spread across the Silk Roads from India to Central Asia, China, and beyond, it also changed. The original faith had shunned the material world, but Buddhist monasteries in the rich oasis towns of the Silk Roads found themselves very much involved in secular affairs. Some of them became quite wealthy, receiving gifts from well-to-do merchants, artisans, and local rulers. The begging bowls of the monks became a symbol rather than a daily activity. Sculptures and murals in the monasteries depicted musicians and acrobats, women applying makeup, and even drinking parties.[6]

Doctrines changed as well. It was the more devotional Mahayana form of Buddhism (see Chapter 5)—featuring the Buddha as a deity, numerous bodhisattvas, an emphasis on compassion, and the possibility of earning merit—that flourished on the Silk Roads, rather than the more austere psychological teachings of the original Buddha. Moreover, Buddhism picked up elements of other cultures while in transit on the Silk Roads. In the area northwest of India that had been

Dunhuang
Located in western China at a critical junction of the Silk Road trading network, Dunhuang was also a center of Buddhist learning, painting, and sculpture as that religion made its way from India to China and beyond. In some 492 caves, a remarkable gallery of Buddhist art has been preserved. These images of Buddhist deities and heavenly beings date from the sixth century C.E. (© Benoy K. Behl)

influenced by the invasions of Alexander the Great, statues of the Buddha reveal distinctly Greek influences. The Greco-Roman mythological figure of Herakles, the son of Zeus and associated with great strength, courage, masculinity, and sexual prowess, was used to represent Vajrapani, one of the divine protectors of the Buddha (see Visual Source 8.1, p. 369). In a similar way, the gods of many peoples along the Silk Roads were incorporated into Buddhist practice as bodhisattvas.

Disease in Transit

■ Connection

What was the impact of disease along the Silk Roads?

Beyond goods and cultures, diseases too traveled the trade routes of Eurasia, and with devastating consequences.[7] Each of the major population centers of the Afro-Eurasian world had developed characteristic disease patterns, mechanisms for dealing with them, and in some cases immunity to them. But when contact among human communities occurred, people were exposed to unfamiliar diseases for which they had little immunity or few effective methods of coping. An early example involved Athens, which in 430–429 B.C.E. was suddenly afflicted by a new and still unidentified infectious disease that had entered Greece via seaborne trade from Egypt, killing perhaps 25 percent of its army and permanently weakening the city-state.

Even more widespread diseases affected the Roman Empire and Han dynasty China during the classical era as the Silk Roads promoted contact all across Eurasia. Smallpox and measles devastated the populations of both empires, contributing to their political collapse. Paradoxically, these disasters may well have strengthened the appeal of Christianity in Europe and Buddhism in China, for both of them offered compassion in the face of immense suffering.

Again in the period between 534 and 750 C.E., intermittent outbreaks of bubonic plague ravaged the coastal areas of the Mediterranean Sea as the black rats that carried the disease arrived via the seaborne trade with India, where they originally lived. What followed was catastrophic. Constantinople, the capital city of the Byzantine Empire, lost some 10,000 people per day during a forty-day period in 534 C.E., according to a contemporary historian. Disease played an important role in preventing Byzantium from reintegrating Italy into its version of a renewed Roman Empire encompassing the Mediterranean basin. The repeated recurrence of the disease over the next several centuries also weakened the ability of Christendom to resist the Muslim armies that poured out of Arabia in the seventh century C.E.

The most well-known dissemination of disease was associated with the Mongol Empire, which briefly unified much of the Eurasian landmass during the thirteenth and fourteenth centuries C.E. (see Chapter 12). That era of intensified interaction facilitated the spread of the Black Death—identified variously with the bubonic plague, anthrax, or a package of epidemic diseases—from China to Europe. Its consequences were enormous. Between 1346 and 1350, one-third or more of the population of Europe perished from the plague. "A dead man," wrote the Italian writer Boccaccio, "was then of no more account than a dead goat."[8] Despite the terrible human toll, some among the living benefited. Tenant farmers and urban workers, now in short supply, could demand higher wages or better terms. Some landowning nobles, on the other hand, were badly hurt as the price of their grains dropped and the demands of their dependents grew.

A similar death toll afflicted China and parts of the Islamic world. The Central Asian steppes, home to many nomadic peoples including the Mongols, also suffered terribly, undermining Mongol rule and permanently altering the balance between pastoral and agricultural peoples to the advantage of settled farmers. In these and many other ways, disease carried by long-distance trade shaped the lives of millions and altered their historical development.

In the long run of world history, the exchange of diseases gave Europeans a certain advantage when they confronted the peoples of the Western Hemisphere after 1500. Exposure over time had provided them with some degree of immunity to Eurasian diseases. In the Americas, however, the absence of domesticated animals, the less intense interaction among major centers of population, and their isolation from the Eastern Hemisphere ensured that native peoples had little defense against the diseases of Europe and Africa. Thus, when their societies were suddenly confronted by Europeans and Africans from across the Atlantic, they perished in appalling numbers. Such was the long-term outcome of the very different histories of the two hemispheres.

Sea Roads: Exchange across the Indian Ocean

If the Silk Roads linked Eurasian societies by land, sea-based trade routes likewise connected distant peoples all across the Eastern Hemisphere. Since the days of the Phoenicians, Greeks, and Romans, the Mediterranean Sea had been an avenue of maritime commerce throughout the region, a pattern that continued during the postclassical era. The Italian city of Venice, for example, emerged by 1000 C.E. as a major center of commerce, with its ships and merchants active in the Mediterranean and Black seas as well as on the Atlantic coast. Much of its wealth derived from control of expensive and profitable imported goods from Asia, many of which came up the Red Sea through the Egyptian port of Alexandria. There Venetian merchants picked up those goods and resold them throughout the Mediterranean basin. This type of transregional exchange linked the maritime commerce of the Mediterranean Sea to the much larger and more extensive network of seaborne trade in the Indian Ocean basin.

Until the creation of a genuinely global oceanic system of trade after 1500, the Indian Ocean represented the world's largest sea-based system of communication and exchange, stretching from southern China to eastern Africa (see Map 8.2). Like the Silk Roads, oceanic trade also grew out of the vast environmental and cultural diversities of the region. The desire for various goods not available at home—such as porcelain from China, spices from the islands of Southeast Asia, cotton goods and pepper from India, ivory and gold from the African coast—provided incentives for Indian Ocean commerce. Transportation costs were lower on the Sea

■ **Comparison**

How did the operation of the Indian Ocean trading network differ from that of the Silk Roads?

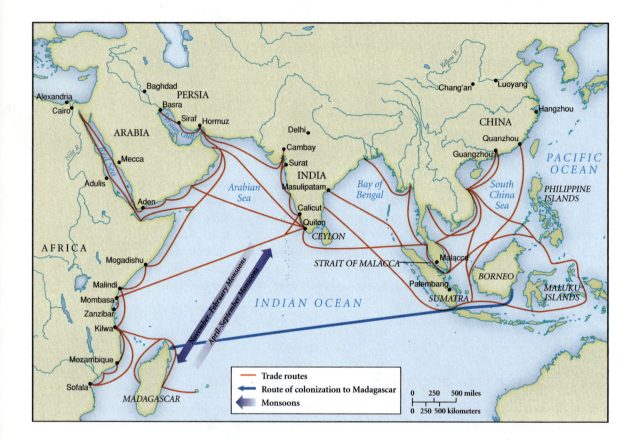

Map 8.2 **The Sea Roads** Paralleling the Silk Road trading network, a sea-based commerce in the Indian Ocean basin connected the many peoples between China and East Africa.

Roads than on the Silk Roads, because ships could accommodate larger and heavier cargoes than camels. This meant that the Sea Roads could eventually carry more bulk goods and products destined for a mass market—textiles, pepper, timber, rice, sugar, wheat—whereas the Silk Roads were limited largely to luxury goods for the few.

What made Indian Ocean commerce possible were the monsoons, alternating wind currents that blew predictably eastward during the summer months and westward during the winter. An understanding of monsoons and a gradually accumulating technology of shipbuilding and oceanic navigation drew on the ingenuity of many peoples—Chinese, Malays, Indians, Arabs, Swahilis, and others. Collectively they made "an interlocked human world joined by the common highway of the Indian Ocean."[9]

But this world of Indian Ocean commerce did not occur between entire regions and certainly not between "countries," even though historians sometimes write about India, Indonesia, Southeast Asia, or East Africa as a matter of shorthand or convenience. It operated rather across an "archipelago of towns" whose merchants often had more in common with one another than with the people of their own hinterlands.[10] It was these urban centers, strung out around the entire Indian Ocean basin, that provided the nodes of this widespread commercial network.

Weaving the Web of an Indian Ocean World

The world of Indian Ocean commerce was long in the making, dating back to the time of the First Civilizations. Seaborne trade via the Persian Gulf between ancient Mesopotamia and the Indus Valley civilization is reflected in archeological finds in both places. Some scholars believe that the still-undeciphered Indian writing system may have been stimulated by Sumerian cuneiform. The ancient Egyptians, and later the Phoenicians, likewise traded down the Red Sea, exchanging their manufactured goods for gold, ivory, frankincense, and slaves from the coasts of Ethiopia, Somalia, and southern Arabia. These ventures mostly hugged the coast and took place over short distances. An exception was Malay sailors; speaking Austronesian languages, they jumped off from the islands of present-day Indonesia during the first millennium B.C.E. and made their way in double-outrigger canoes across thousands of miles of open ocean to the East African island of Madagascar. There they introduced their language and their crops. Those food crops—bananas, coconuts, and cocoyams—soon spread to the mainland, where they greatly enriched the diets of African peoples. Also spread to the mainland was a Malayo-Polynesian xylophone, which is still played in parts of Africa today.

The tempo of Indian Ocean commerce picked up in the era of classical civilizations during the early centuries of the Common Era, as mariners learned how to ride the monsoons. Merchants from the Roman Empire, mostly Greeks, Syrians, and Jews, established settlements in southern India and along the East African coast. The introduction of Christianity into both Ethiopia and Kerala (in southern India) testifies to the long-term cultural impact of that trade. In the eastern Indian Ocean and the South China Sea, Chinese and Southeast Asian merchants likewise generated a growing commerce, and by 100 C.E. Chinese traders had reached India.

The fulcrum of this growing commercial network lay in India itself. Its ports bulged with goods from both west and east, as illustrated in the Snapshot. Its merchants were in touch with Southeast Asia by the first century C.E., and settled communities of Indian traders appeared throughout the Indian Ocean basin and as far away as

Snapshot   **Economic Exchange in the Indian Ocean Basin**

Region	Products Contributed to Indian Ocean Commerce
Mediterranean basin	ceramics, glassware, wine, gold, olive oil
East Africa	ivory, gold, iron goods, slaves, tortoiseshells, quartz, leopard skins
Arabia	frankincense, myrrh, perfumes
India	grain, ivory, precious stones, cotton textiles, spices, timber, tortoiseshells
Southeast Asia	tin, sandalwood, cloves, nutmeg, mace
China	silks, porcelain, tea

Alexandria in Egypt. Indian cultural practices, such as Hinduism and Buddhism, as well as South Asian political ideas began to take root in Southeast Asia.

■ Change
What lay behind the flourishing of Indian Ocean commerce in the postclassical millennium?

In the era of third-wave civilizations between 500 and 1500, two major processes changed the landscape of the Afro-Eurasian world and wove the web of Indian Ocean exchange even more densely than before. One was the economic and political revival of China, some four centuries after the collapse of the Han dynasty. Especially during the Tang and Song dynasties (618–1279), China reestablished an effective and unified state, which actively encouraged maritime trade. Furthermore, the impressive growth of the Chinese economy sent Chinese products pouring into the circuits of Indian Ocean commerce, while providing a vast and attractive market for Indian and Southeast Asian goods. Chinese technological innovations, such as larger ships and the magnetic compass, likewise added to the momentum of commercial growth.

A second transformation in the world of Indian Ocean commerce involved the sudden rise of Islam in the seventh century C.E. and its subsequent spread across much of the Afro-Eurasian world (see Chapter 11). Unlike Confucian culture, which was quite suspicious of merchants, Islam was friendly to commercial life; the Prophet Muhammad himself had been a trader. The creation of an Arab Empire, stretching from the Atlantic Ocean through the Mediterranean basin and all the way to India, brought together in a single political system an immense range of economies and cultural traditions and provided a vast arena for the energies of Muslim traders.

Those energies greatly intensified commercial activity in the Indian Ocean basin in many ways. Middle Eastern gold and silver flowed into southern India to purchase pepper, pearls, textiles, and gemstones. Muslim merchants and sailors, as well as Jews and Christians living within the Islamic world, established communities of traders from East Africa to the southern China coast. Efforts to reclaim wasteland in Mesopotamia to produce sugar and dates for export stimulated a slave trade from East Africa, which landed thousands of Africans in southern Iraq to work on plantations and in salt mines under horrendous conditions. A massive fifteen-year revolt (868–883) among these slaves badly disrupted the Islamic Abbasid Empire before it was brutally crushed.[11]

Beyond these specific outcomes, the expansion of Islam gave rise to an international maritime culture by 1000, shared by individuals living in the widely separated port cities around the Indian Ocean. The immense prestige, power, and prosperity of the Islamic world stimulated widespread conversion, which in turn facilitated commercial transactions. Even those who did not convert to Islam, such as Buddhist rulers in Burma, nonetheless regarded it as commercially useful to assume Muslim names.[12] Thus was created "a maritime Silk Road . . . a commercial and informational network of unparalleled proportions."[13] After 1000, the culture of this network was increasingly Islamic.

Sea Roads as a Catalyst for Change: Southeast Asia and Srivijaya

■ Connection
What is the relationship between the rise of Srivijaya and the world of Indian Ocean commerce?

Oceanic commerce transformed all of its participants in one way or another, but nowhere more so than in Southeast Asia and East Africa, at opposite ends of the Indian Ocean network. In both regions, trade stimulated political change as ambitious or aspiring rulers used the wealth derived from commerce to construct larger and more centrally governed states or cities. Both areas likewise experienced cultural change as local people were attracted to foreign religious ideas from Hindu, Buddhist, or Islamic sources. As on the Silk Roads, trade was a conduit for culture.

Located between the major civilizations of China and India, Southeast Asia was situated by geography to play an important role in the evolving world of Indian Ocean commerce. When Malay sailors, long active in the waters around Southeast Asia, opened an all-sea route between India and China through the Straits of Malacca around 350 C.E., the many small ports along the Malay Peninsula and the coast of Sumatra began to compete intensely to attract the growing number of traders and travelers making their way through the straits. From this competition emerged the Malay kingdom of Srivijaya, which dominated this critical choke point of Indian Ocean trade from 670 to 1025. A number of factors—Srivijaya's plentiful supply of gold; its access to the source of highly sought-after spices, such as cloves, nutmeg, and mace; and the taxes levied on passing ships—provided resources to attract supporters, to fund an embryonic bureaucracy, and to create the military and naval forces that brought some security to the area.

Srivijaya monarchs drew upon local beliefs that chiefs possessed magical powers and were responsible for the prosperity of their people, but they also made use of imported Indian political ideas and Buddhist religious concepts, which had been brought to the area by a multitude of Indian merchants and teachers. Some Indians were employed as advisers, clerks, or officials to Srivijaya rulers, who began to assign Sanskrit titles to their subordinates. The capital city of Palembang was a cosmopolitan place, where even the parrots were said to speak four languages. Buddhism in particular provided a "higher level of magic" for rulers as well as the prestige of association with Indian civilization.[14] These rulers sponsored the creation of images of the Buddha and various bodhisattvas whose faces resembled those of deceased kings and were inscribed with traditional curses against anyone who would destroy them. Srivijaya grew into a major center of Buddhist observance and teaching, attracting thousands of monks and students from throughout the Buddhist world. The seventh-century Chinese monk Yi Jing was so impressed that he advised Buddhist monks headed for India to study first in Srivijaya for several years.[15]

Srivijaya was not the only part of Southeast Asia to be influenced by Indian culture. The Sailendra kingdom in central Java, an agriculturally rich region closely allied with Srivijaya, mounted a massive building program between the eighth and tenth centuries featuring Hindu temples and Buddhist monuments. The most famous, known as Borobudur, is an enormous mountain-shaped structure of ten levels, with a three-mile walkway and elaborate carvings illustrating the spiritual journey from ignorance and illusion to full enlightenment. The largest Buddhist monument anywhere in the world, it is nonetheless a distinctly Javanese creation, whose carved figures have Javanese features and whose scenes are clearly set in Java, not India. Its shape resonated with an ancient Southeast Asian veneration of mountains as

Southeast Asia ca. 1200 C.E.

Borobudur

This huge Buddhist monument, constructed probably in the ninth century C.E., was subsequently abandoned and covered with layers of volcanic ash and vegetation as Java came under Islamic influence. It was rediscovered by British colonial authorities in the early nineteenth century and has undergone several restorations over the past two centuries. Although Indonesia is a largely Muslim country, its Buddhist minority (about 1 percent of the country's population) still celebrates the Buddha's birthday at Borobudur. (Robert Harding World Imagery/Alamy)

sacred places and the abode of ancestral spirits. Borobudur represents the process of Buddhism becoming culturally grounded in a new place.

Temple complexes such as Borobudur and others constructed in Burma, in the Khmer state of Angkor, and elsewhere illustrate vividly the penetration of Indian culture—in both Hindu and Buddhist forms—throughout mainland and island Southeast Asia. Some scholars have spoken of the "Indianization" of the region, similar perhaps to the earlier spread of Greek culture within the empires of Alexander the Great and Rome. In the case of Southeast Asia, however, no imperial control accompanied Indian cultural influence. It was a matter of voluntary borrowing by independent societies that found Hindu or Buddhist ideas useful and were free to adapt those ideas to their own needs and cultures. Somewhat later, but in much the same way, Islam too began to penetrate Southeast Asia, as the world of Indian Ocean commerce brought yet another religious tradition to the region.

■ Connection

What was the role of Swahili civilization in the world of Indian Ocean commerce?

Sea Roads as a Catalyst for Change: East Africa and Swahili Civilization

On the other side of the Indian Ocean, the transformative processes of long-distance trade were likewise at work, giving rise to an East African civilization known as

Swahili. Emerging in the eighth century C.E., this civilization took shape as a set of commercial city-states stretching all along the East African coast, from present-day Somalia to Mozambique.

The earlier ancestors of the Swahili lived in small farming and fishing communities, spoke Bantu languages, and traded with the Arabian, Greek, and Roman merchants who occasionally visited the coast during the classical era. But what stimulated the growth of Swahili cities was the far more extensive commercial life of the western Indian Ocean following the rise of Islam. As in Southeast Asia, local people and aspiring rulers found opportunity for wealth and power in the growing demand for East African products associated with an expanding Indian Ocean commerce. Gold, ivory, quartz, leopard skins, and sometimes slaves acquired from interior societies, as well as iron and processed timber manufactured along the coast, found a ready market in Arabia, Persia, India, and beyond. In response to such opportunities, an African merchant class developed, villages turned into sizable towns, and clan chiefs became kings. A new civilization was in the making.

Between 1000 and 1500, that civilization flourished along the coast, and it was a very different kind of society than the farming and pastoral cultures of the East African interior. It was thoroughly urban, centered in cities of 15,000 to 18,000 people, such as Lamu, Mombasa, Kilwa, Sofala, and many others. Like the city-states of ancient Greece, each Swahili city was politically independent, generally governed by its own king, and in sharp competition with other cities. No imperial system or larger territorial states unified the world of Swahili civilization. Nor did any of them control a critical choke point of trade, as Srivijaya did for the Straits of Malacca. Swahili cities were commercial centers that accumulated goods from the interior and exchanged them for the products of distant civilizations, such as Chinese porcelain and silk, Persian rugs, and Indian cottons. While the transoceanic journeys occurred largely in Arab vessels, Swahili craft navigated the coastal waterways, concentrating goods for shipment abroad. Swahili cities were class-stratified societies with sharp distinctions between a mercantile elite and commoners.

Culturally as well as economically, Swahili civilization participated in the larger Indian Ocean world. Arab, Indian, and perhaps Persian merchants were welcome visitors, and some settled permanently. Many ruling families of Swahili cities claimed Arab or Persian origins as a way of bolstering their prestige, even while they dined off Chinese porcelain and dressed in Indian cottons. The Swahili language, widely spoken in East Africa today, was grammatically an African tongue within the larger Bantu family of languages, but it was written in Arabic script and contained a number of Arabic loan words. A small bronze lion found in the Swahili city of Shanga and dating to about 1100 illustrates the distinctly cosmopolitan character of Swahili culture. It depicted a clearly African lion, but it was created in a distinctly Indian artistic style and was made from melted-down Chinese copper coins.[16]

Most important, however, Swahili civilization rapidly became Islamic. Introduced by Arab traders, Islam was voluntarily and widely adopted within

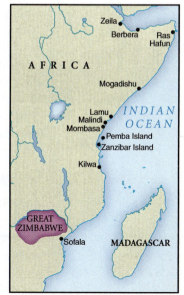

The Swahili Coast of East Africa

the Swahili world. Like Buddhism in Southeast Asia, Islam linked Swahili cities to the larger Indian Ocean world. These East African cities were soon dotted with substantial mosques. When Ibn Battuta, a widely traveled Arab scholar, merchant, and public official, visited the Swahili coast in the early fourteenth century, he found altogether Muslim societies in which religious leaders often spoke Arabic, and all were eager to welcome a learned visitor from the heartland of Islam. But these were African Muslims, not colonies of transplanted Arabs. "The rulers, scholars, officials, and big merchants as well as the port workers, farmers, craftsmen, and slaves, were dark-skinned people speaking African tongues in everyday life."[17]

Islam sharply divided the Swahili cities from their African neighbors to the west, for neither the new religion nor Swahili culture penetrated much beyond the coast until the nineteenth century. Economically, however, the coastal cities acted as intermediaries between the interior producers of valued goods and the Arab merchants who carried them to distant markets. Particularly in the southern reaches of the Swahili world, this relationship extended the impact of Indian Ocean trade well into the African interior. Hundreds of miles inland, between the Zambezi and Limpopo rivers, lay rich sources of gold, much in demand on the Swahili coast. The emergence of a powerful state, known as Great Zimbabwe, seems clearly connected to the growing trade in gold to the coast as well as to the wealth embodied in its large herds of cattle. At its peak between 1250 and 1350, Great Zimbabwe had the resources and the labor power to construct huge stone enclosures entirely without mortar, with walls sixteen feet thick and thirty-two feet tall. "[It] must have been an astonishing sight," writes a recent scholar, "for the subordinate chiefs and kings who would have come there to seek favors at court."[18] Here in the interior of southeastern Africa lay yet another example of the reach and transforming power of Indian Ocean commerce.

Sand Roads: Exchange across the Sahara

In addition to the Silk Roads and the Sea Roads, another important pattern of long-distance trade—this one across the vast reaches of the Sahara—linked North Africa and the Mediterranean world with the land and peoples of interior West Africa. Like the others, these Sand Road commercial networks had a transforming impact, stimulating and enriching West African civilization and connecting it to larger patterns of world history during the postclassical era.

Commercial Beginnings in West Africa

Trans-African trade, like the commerce of the Silk Roads and the Sea Roads, was rooted in environmental variation. The North African coastal regions, long part of Roman or later Arab empires, generated cloth, glassware, weapons, books, and other manufactured goods. The great Sahara held deposits of copper and especially salt, while its oases produced sweet and nutritious dates. Although the sparse populations of the desert were largely pastoral and nomadic, farther south lived agricultural peoples who grew a variety of crops, produced their own textiles and metal products, and mined a considerable amount of gold. The agricultural regions of sub-Saharan Africa are normally divided into two ecological zones: the savanna grasslands immediately south of the Sahara, which produced grain crops such as millet and sorghum; and the forest areas farther south, where root and tree crops such as yams and kola nuts predominated. These quite varied environments provided the economic incentive for the exchange of goods.

The earliest long-distance trade within this huge region was not across the Sahara at all, but largely among the agricultural peoples themselves in the area later known to Arabs as the Sudan, or "the land of black people." During the first millennium B.C.E., the peoples of Sudanic West Africa began to exchange metal goods, cotton textiles, gold, and various food products across considerable distances using boats along the Niger River and donkeys overland. On the basis of this trade, a number of independent urban clusters emerged by the early centuries of the Common Era. The most well known was Jenne-jeno, which was located at a crucial point on the Niger River where goods were transshipped from boat to donkey or vice versa.[19] This was the Niger Valley civilization, described in Chapter 7.

Gold, Salt, and Slaves: Trade and Empire in West Africa

A major turning point in African commercial life occurred with the introduction of the camel to North Africa and the Sahara in the early centuries of the Common Era. This remarkable animal, which could go for ten days without water, finally made possible the long trek across the Sahara. It was camel-owning dwellers of desert oases who initiated regular trans-Saharan commerce by 300 to 400 C.E. Several centuries later, North African Arabs, now bearing the new religion of Islam, also organized caravans across the desert.

■ **Connections**
What changes did trans-Saharan trade bring to West Africa?

What they sought, above all else, was gold, which was found in some abundance in the border areas straddling the grasslands and the forests of West Africa. From its source, it was transported by donkey to transshipment points on the southern edge of the Sahara and then transferred to camels for the long journey north across the desert. African ivory, kola nuts, and slaves were likewise in considerable demand in the desert, the Mediterranean basin, and beyond. In return, the peoples of the Sudan received horses, cloth, dates, various manufactured goods, and especially salt from the rich deposits in the Sahara.

Thus the Sahara was no longer simply a barrier to commerce and cross-cultural interaction; it quickly became a major international trade route that fostered new relationships among distant peoples. The caravans that made the desert crossing could be huge, with as many as 5,000 camels and hundreds of people. Traveling mostly at night to avoid the daytime heat, the journey might take up to seventy days, covering fifteen to twenty-five miles per day. For well over 1,000 years, such caravans traversed the desert, linking the interior of West Africa with lands and people far to the north.

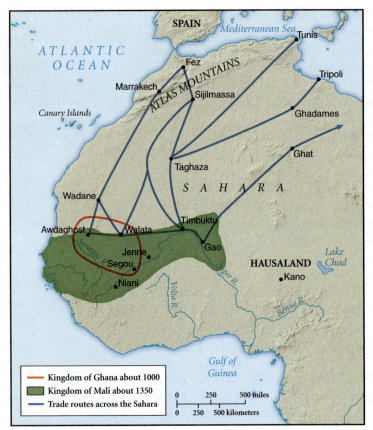

Map 8.3   The Sand Roads
For a thousand years or more, the Sahara was an ocean of sand that linked the interior of West Africa with the world of North Africa and the Mediterranean but separated them as well.

As in Southeast Asia and East Africa, long-distance trade across the Sahara provided both incentive and resources for the construction of new and larger political structures. It was the peoples of the western and central Sudan, living between the forests and the desert, who were in the best position to take advantage of these new opportunities. Between roughly 500 and 1600, they constructed a series of states, empires, and city-states that reached from the Atlantic coast to Lake Chad, including Ghana, Mali, Songhay, Kanem, and the city-states of the Hausa people (see Map 8.3).

All of them were monarchies with elaborate court life and varying degrees of administrative complexity and military forces at their disposal. All drew upon the wealth of trans-Saharan trade, taxing the merchants who conducted it. In the wider world, these states soon acquired a reputation for great riches. An Arab traveler in the tenth century C.E. described the ruler of Ghana as "the wealthiest king on the face of the earth because of his treasures and stocks of gold."[20] At its high point in the fourteenth century, Mali's rulers monopolized the import of strategic goods such as horses and metals; levied duties on salt, copper, and other merchandise; and reserved large nuggets of gold for themselves while permitting the free export of gold dust.

As in all civilizations, slavery found a place in West Africa. Early on, most slaves had been women, working as domestic servants and concubines. As West African civilization crystallized, however, male slaves were put to work as state officials, porters, craftsmen, miners harvesting salt from desert deposits, and especially agricultural laborers producing for the royal granaries on large estates or plantations. Most came from non-Islamic and stateless societies farther south, which were raided during the dry season by cavalry-based forces of West African states, though some white slave women from the eastern Mediterranean also made an appearance in Mali. A song in honor of one eleventh-century ruler of Kanem boasted of his slave-raiding achievements.

> The best you took (and sent home) as the first fruits of battle. The children crying on their mothers you snatched away from their mothers. You took the slave wife from a slave, and set them in lands far removed from one another.[21]

Most of these slaves were used within this emerging West African civilization, but a trade in slaves also developed across the Sahara. Between 1100 and 1400, perhaps 5,500 slaves per year made the perilous trek across the desert. When the famous Muslim traveler Ibn Battuta visited Mali in the fourteenth century, he returned home to Morocco with a caravan that included 600 female slaves, who walked across the burning desert, while he rode a camel. Most such slaves were put to work in the homes of the wealthy in Islamic North Africa, but a small number were sold in Europe. Those who arrived in Ireland, for example, were termed "blue men." Far more significant in Europe were slaves from the Slavic-speaking regions along the northern coast of the Black Sea. They were so numerous that the word "slave" in many European languages derives from the term "Slav." Not until the Atlantic slave trade developed after the 1440s did Africans become the major source of slaves for Europeans.

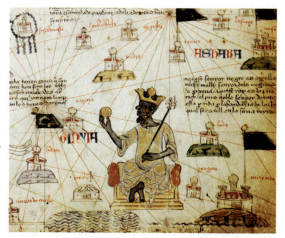

The Gold of Mali
This detail from the *Catalan Atlas*, a series of maps issued in Spain in 1375, illustrates Mali's reputation in Europe for its great wealth in gold. This reputation later propelled Portuguese voyages down the west coast of Africa in search of direct access to that wealth. (Bibliothèque nationale de France)

These states of Sudanic Africa developed substantial urban and commercial centers—such as Koumbi-Saleh, Jenne, Timbuktu, Gao, Gobir, and Kano—where traders congregated and goods were exchanged. Some of these cities also became centers of manufacturing, creating finely wrought beads, iron tools, or cotton textiles, some of which entered the circuits of commerce. Visitors described them as cosmopolitan places where court officials, artisans, scholars, students, and local and foreign merchants all rubbed elbows. As in East Africa, Islam accompanied trade and became an important element in the urban culture of West Africa (see Document 8.3, pp. 362–65). The growth of long-distance trade had stimulated the development of an African civilization, which was linked to the wider networks of exchange in the Eastern Hemisphere.

An American Network: Commerce and Connection in the Western Hemisphere

Before the voyages of Columbus, the world of the Americas developed quite separately from that of the Eastern Hemisphere. Despite intriguing hints of occasional contacts, no sustained interaction between the peoples of these two great landmasses took place. But if the Silk, Sea, and Sand Roads linked the diverse peoples of the Afro-Eurasian world, did a similar network of interaction join and transform the various societies of the Western Hemisphere?

Clearly, direct connections among the various civilizations and cultures of the Americas were less densely woven than in the Afro-Eurasian region. The llama and the potato, both domesticated in the Andes, never reached Mesoamerica; nor did the writing system of the Maya diffuse to Andean civilizations. The Aztecs and the Incas, contemporary civilizations in the fifteenth century, had little if any direct contact with each other. The limits of these interactions owed something to the

■ **Comparison**

In what ways did networks of interaction in the Western Hemisphere differ from those in the Eastern Hemisphere?

absence of horses, donkeys, camels, wheeled vehicles, and large oceangoing vessels, all of which facilitated long-distance trade and travel in Afro-Eurasia.

Geographic or environmental differences added further obstacles. The narrow bottleneck of Panama, largely covered by dense rain forests, surely inhibited contact between South and North America. Furthermore, the north/south orientation of the Americas—which required agricultural practices to move through, and adapt to, quite distinct climatic and vegetation zones—slowed the spread of agricultural products. By contrast, the east/west axis of Eurasia meant that agricultural innovations could diffuse more rapidly because they were entering roughly similar environments. Thus nothing equivalent to the long-distance trade of the Silk, Sea, or Sand Roads of the Eastern Hemisphere arose in the Americas, even though local and regional commerce flourished in many places. Nor did distinct cultural traditions such as Buddhism, Christianity, and Islam spread so widely to integrate distant peoples.

Nonetheless, scholars have discerned "a loosely interactive web stretching from the North American Great Lakes and upper Mississippi south to the Andes."[22] (See Map 8.4.) Partly, it was a matter of slowly spreading cultural elements, such as the gradual diffusion of maize from its Mesoamerican place of origin to the southwestern United States and then on to much of eastern North America as well as to much of South America in the other direction. A game played with rubber balls on an outdoor court has left traces in the Caribbean, Mexico, and northern South America. Construction in the Tantoc region of northeastern Mexico resembled the earlier building styles of Cahokia, suggesting the possibility of some interaction between the two regions.[23] The spread of particular pottery styles and architectural conventions likewise suggests at least indirect contact over wide distances.

Commerce too played an important role in the making of this "American web." A major North American chief-

Map 8.4   The American Web
Transcontinental interactions within the American web were more modest than those of the Afro-Eurasian hemisphere. The most intense areas of exchange and communication occurred within the Mississippi valley, Mesoamerican, and Andean regions.

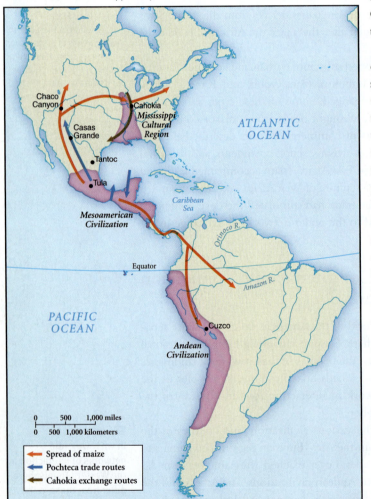

dom at Cahokia, near present-day St. Louis, flourished from about 900 to 1250 at the confluence of the Mississippi, Illinois, and Missouri rivers (see pp. 303–04). Cahokia lay at the center of a widespread trading network that brought it shells from the Atlantic coast, copper from the Lake Superior region, buffalo hides from the Great Plains, obsidian from the Rocky Mountains, and mica from the southern Appalachian Mountains. Sturdy dugout canoes plied the rivers of the eastern woodlands, connecting their diverse but related societies. Early European explorers and travelers along the Amazon and Orinoco rivers of South America reported active networks of exchange that may well have operated for many centuries. Caribbean peoples using large oceangoing canoes had long conducted an inter-island trade, and the Chincha people undertook ocean-based exchange in copper, beads, and shells along the Pacific coasts of Peru and Ecuador in large seagoing rafts.[24] Another regional commercial network, centered in Mesoamerica, extended north to what is now the southwestern United States and south to Ecuador and Colombia. Many items from Mesoamerica—copper bells, macaw feathers, tons of shells—have been found in the Chaco region of New Mexico. Residents of Chaco also drank liquid chocolate, using jars of Mayan origin and cacao beans imported from Mesoamerica, where the practice began.[25] Turquoise, mined and worked among the Ancestral Pueblo (see pp. 301–03) flowed in the other direction.

But the most active and dense networks of communication and exchange in the Americas lay within, rather than between, the regions that housed the two great civilizations of the Western Hemisphere—Mesoamerica and the Andes. During the classical era of Mesoamerican civilization (200–900 C.E.), both the Maya cities in the Yucatán area of Mexico and Guatemala and the huge city-state of Teotihuacán in central Mexico maintained commercial relationships with one another and throughout the region. In addition to this land-based trade, the Maya conducted a seaborne commerce, using large dugout canoes holding forty to fifty people, along both the Atlantic and Pacific coasts.[26] Although most of this trade was in luxury goods rather than basic necessities, it was critical to upholding the position and privileges of royal and noble families. Items such as cotton clothing, precious jewels, and feathers from particular birds marked the status of elite groups and served to attract followers. Controlling access to such high-prestige goods was an important motive for war among Mesoamerican states.[27] Among the Aztecs of the fifteenth century, professional merchants, known as *pochteca*, undertook large-scale trading expeditions both within and well beyond the borders of

Inca Roads
Used for transporting goods by pack animal or sending messages by foot, the Inca road network included some 2,000 inns where travelers might find food and shelter. Messengers, operating in relay, could cover as many as 150 miles a day. Here a modern-day citizen of Peru walks along an old Inca trail road. (Loren McIntyre/lorenmcintyre.com)

their empire, sometimes as agents for the state or for members of the nobility, but more often acting on their own as private businessmen.

Unlike the Aztec Empire, in which private traders largely handled the distribution of goods, economic exchange in the Andean Inca Empire during the fifteenth century was a state-run operation, and no merchant group similar to the Aztec *pochteca* emerged there. Instead, great state storehouses bulged with immense quantities of food, clothing, military supplies, blankets, construction materials, and more, all carefully recorded on *quipus* (knotted cords used to record numerical data) by a highly trained class of accountants. From these state centers, goods were transported as needed by caravans of human porters and llamas across the numerous roads and bridges of the empire. Totaling some 20,000 miles, Inca roads traversed the coastal plain and the high Andes in a north/south direction, while lateral roads linked these diverse environments and extended into the eastern rain forests and plains as well. Despite the general absence of private trade, local exchange took place at highland fairs and along the borders of the empire with groups outside the Inca state.

Reflections: Economic Globalization— Ancient and Modern

The densely connected world of the modern era, linked by ties of commerce and culture around the planet, certainly has roots in much earlier patterns. Particularly in the era of third-wave civilizations from 500 to 1500, the Silk, Sea, and Sand roads of the Afro-Eurasian world and the looser networks of the American web linked distant peoples both economically and culturally, prompted the emergence of new states, and sustained elite privileges in many ancient civilizations. In those ways, they resembled the globalized world of modern times.

In other respects, though, the networks and webs of the premodern millennium differed sharply from those of more recent centuries. Most people still produced primarily for their own consumption rather than for the market, and a much smaller range of goods was exchanged in the marketplaces of the world. Far fewer people then were required to sell their own labor for wages, an almost universal practice in modern economies. Because of transportation costs and technological limitations, most trade was in luxury goods rather than in necessities. In addition, the circuits of commerce were rather more limited than the truly global patterns of exchange that emerged after 1500.

Furthermore, the world economy of the modern era increasingly had a single center—industrialized Western European countries—which came to dominate much of the world both economically and politically during the nineteenth century. Though never completely equal, the economic relationships of earlier times occurred among much more equivalent units. For example, no one region dominated the complex pattern of Indian Ocean exchange, although India and China generally offered manufactured goods, while Southeast Asia and East Africa contributed agricultural products or raw materials. And with the exception of the brief Mongol control of the Silk Roads and the Inca domination of the Andes for a century, no single power exercised political control over the other major networks of world commerce.

The world of third-wave civilizations, in short, was a more balanced, multicentered world than that of the modern era. Although massive inequalities occurred within particular regions or societies, relationships among the major civilizations operated on a rather more equal basis than in the globalized world of the past several centuries. With the rise of China and India as major players in the world economy of the twenty-first century, are we perhaps returning to that earlier pattern?

Second Thoughts

What's the Significance?

Silk Roads	Srivijaya	Sand Roads
Black Death	Borobudur	Ghana, Mali, Songhay
Indian Ocean trading network	Swahili civilization	trans-Saharan slave trade
	Great Zimbabwe	American web

To assess your mastery of the material in this chapter, visit the **Student Center** at bedfordstmartins.com/strayer.

Big Picture Questions

1. What motivated and sustained the long-distance commerce of the Silk Roads, Sea Roads, and Sand Roads?
2. Why did the Eastern Hemisphere develop long-distance trade more extensively than did the societies of the Western Hemisphere?
3. In what ways did commercial exchange foster other changes?
4. In what ways was Afro-Eurasia a single interacting zone, and in what respects was it a vast region of separate cultures and civilizations?

Next Steps: For Further Study

Jerry Bentley, *Old World Encounters* (1993). A wonderfully succinct and engaging history of cross-cultural interaction all across Afro-Eurasia before 1500.

E. W. Bovill, *The Golden Trade of the Moors* (1970). A classic account of the trans-Saharan trade.

Rainer Buschmann, *Oceans in World History* (2007). A brief study of communication and exchange across the world's oceans.

K. N. Chaudhuri, *Trade and Civilization in the Indian Ocean* (1985). A well-regarded study that treats the Indian Ocean basin as a single region linked by both commerce and culture during the postclassical era.

Philip Curtin, *Cross-Cultural Trade in World History* (1984). Explores long-distance trade as a generator of social change on a global level.

Liu Xinru and Lynda Shaffer, *Connections across Eurasia* (2007). A brief, accessible, and up-to-date account by two major scholars of the Silk Road trading network.

Bridging World History, http://www.learner.org/channel/courses/worldhistory. Units 9 and 10 of this Web-based guide to world history provide an illustrated examination of global trade in the postclassical millennium.

For Web sites and additional documents related to this chapter, see **Make History** at bedfordstmartins.com/strayer.

Documents

Considering the Evidence: Travelers' Tales and Observations

Historians generally prefer to rely on "insiders" for understanding the societies and cultures they study. Documents, artifacts, and images created by people actually living in those times and places have an authenticity that accounts by foreigners may lack. Nonetheless, scholars often find it helpful—even necessary—to make use of records written by outsiders as well. During the postclassical millennium, as long-distance trade flourished and large transregional empires grew, opportunities for individuals to travel far beyond their homelands increased. Their accounts have provided historians with invaluable information about particular regions and cultures, as well as about interactions among disparate peoples. The authors of these accounts, perhaps inadvertently, also reveal much about themselves and about the perceptions and misperceptions generated by cross-cultural encounters. The selections that follow provide three examples of intrepid long-distance travelers and their impressions of the societies they encountered on their arduous journeys.

Document 8.1

A Chinese Buddhist in India

During the seventh century, Xuanzang (600–664 C.E.), a highly educated Buddhist monk from China, made a long and difficult journey to India through some of the world's most daunting deserts and mountain ranges, returning home in 645 C.E. after sixteen years abroad (see Visual Source 8.2, p. 370). His motives, like those of many other Buddhist travelers to India, were essentially religious. "I regretted that the teachings of [Buddhism] were not complete and the scriptures deficient in my own country," he wrote. "I have doubts and have puzzled in my mind, but I could find no one to solve them. That was why I decided to travel to the West...."[28] In India, the homeland of Buddhism, he hoped to find the teachers and the sacred texts that would answer his questions, enrich Buddhist practice in China, and resolve the many disputes that had created serious divisions within the Buddhist community of his own country.

During a ten-year stay in India, Xuanzang visited many of the holy sites associated with the Buddha's life and studied with leading Buddhist teachers, particularly those at Nalanda University, a huge monastic complex dedicated to Buddhist scholarship (see Map 8.1, p. 335). He traveled widely within India and established a personal relationship with Harsha, the ruler of the state which then encompassed much of northern India. On his return journey to China, he carried hundreds of manuscripts, at least seven statues of the Buddha, and even some relics. Warmly greeted by the Chinese emperor, Xuanzang spent the last two decades of his life translating the texts he had collected into Chinese. He also wrote an account of his travels, known as the *Record of the Western Regions,* and shared his recollections with a fellow monk and translator named Huili, who subsequently wrote a biography of Xuanzang.[29] The selections that follow derive from these two accounts and convey something of Xuanzang's impressions of Indian civilization in the seventh century C.E.

- What do you think surprised or impressed Xuanzang on his visit to India? What features of Indian life might seem most strange to a Chinese visitor?

- How might these selections serve to illustrate or to contradict the descriptions of classical Indian civilization in Chapters 4–6?

- What can this document contribute to our understanding of Buddhist practice in India?

Huili

A Biography of the Tripitaka Master
Seventh Century C.E.

[Certainly the emotional highlight of Xuanzang's travels in India was his visit to the site of the Buddha's enlightenment under the famous Bodhi tree. The great traveler's biographer, Huili, recorded his Master's response.]

Upon his arrival there, the Master worshipped the Bodhi tree and the image of the Buddha attaining enlightenment made by Maitreya Bodhisattva. After having looked at the image with deep sincerity, he prostrated himself before it and deplored sadly, saying with self-reproach, "I do not know where I was born in the course of transmigration at the time

when the Buddha attained enlightenment. I could only come here at this time.... It makes me think that my karmic hindrances must have been very heavy!" While he was saying so, his eyes brimmed with sorrowful tears. As that was the time when the monks dismissed the summer retreat, several thousand people forgathered from far and near. Those who saw the Master were choked by sobs in sympathy with him.

[The great Buddhist monastery/university at Nalanda was likewise a major destination of Xuanzang's journey. It must have been a place of wonder and delight to the Chinese monk, as he described it to Huili.]

Ten thousand monks always lived there, both hosts and guests. They studied Mahayana teachings and the doctrines of the eighteen schools, as well as

Source: Li Rongxi (trans.), *A Biography of the Tripitaka Master of the Great Ci'en Monastery of the Great Tang Dynasty* (Berkeley: Numata Center for Buddhist Translation, 1995), 89–90, 94–95.

wordly books such as the Vedas. They also learned about works on logic, grammar, medicine, and divination.... Lectures were given at more than a hundred places in the monastery every day, and the students studied diligently without wasting a single moment. As all the monks who lived there were men of virtue, the atmosphere in the monastery was naturally solemn and dignified. For more than seven hundred years since its establishment, none of the monks had committed any offence. Out of respect for them, the king gave more than a hundred villages for their sustenance. Each village had two hundred families, who daily provided several hundred *shi* of polished nonglutinous rice, butter, and milk. Thus the students could enjoy sufficient supplies of the four requisites without the trouble of going to beg for them. It was because of this effort of their supporters that the scholars could gain achievements in learning.

Xuanzang

Record of the Western Region
Seventh Century C.E.

[Selections from Xuanzang's more general description of Indian civilization follow here drawn from his own account.]

On Towns and Villages

The towns and villages have inner gates; the walls are wide and high; the streets and lanes are tortuous, and the roads winding. The thoroughfares are dirty and the stalls arranged on both sides of the road with appropriate signs. Butchers, fishers, dancers, executioners, and scavengers, and so on [untouchables], have their abodes without [outside] the city. In coming and going these persons are bound to keep on the left side of the road till they arrive at their homes. Their houses are surrounded by low walls and form the suburbs. The earth being soft and muddy, the walls of the towns are mostly built of brick or tiles....

On Buddhist Studies

The different schools are constantly at variance, and their contending utterances rise like the angry waves of the sea. The different sects have their separate masters....

There are eighteen schools, each claiming pre-eminence. The partisans of the Great and Little Vehicle are content to dwell apart. There are some who give themselves up to quiet contemplation, and devote themselves, whether walking or standing still or sitting down, to the acquirement of wisdom and insight; others, on the contrary, differ from these in raising noisy contentions about their faith. According to their fraternity, they are governed by distinctive rules and regulations....

The *Vinaya* discourses [rules governing monastic life] are equally Buddhist books. He who can entirely explain one class of these books is exempted from the control of the *karmadâna*°. If he can explain two classes, he receives in addition the equipments of an upper seat (*room*); he who can explain three classes has allotted to him different servants to attend to and obey him; he who can explain four classes has "pure men" allotted to him as attendants; he who can explain five classes of books is then allowed an elephant carriage; he who can explain six classes of books is allowed a surrounding escort. When a man's renown has reached to a high distinction, then at different times he convokes an assembly for discussion. He judges of the superior or inferior talent of those who take part in it; he distinguishes their good or bad points; he praises the clever and reproves the faulty; if one of the assembly distinguishes himself by refined language, subtle

Source: Samuel Beal (trans.), *Su-Yu-Ki: Buddhist Records of the Western World* (London: K. Paul, Trench, Trubner & Co., 1906), vol. I, book 2, 73–74, 77, 79–84.

°*karmadâna*: a high monastic official.

investigation, deep penetration, and severe logic, then he is mounted on an elephant covered with precious ornaments, and conducted by a numerous suite to the gates of the convent.

If, on the contrary, one of the members breaks down in his argument, or uses poor and inelegant phrases, or if he violates a rule in logic and adapts his words accordingly, they proceed to disfigure his face with red and white, and cover his body with dirt and dust, and then carry him off to some deserted spot or leave him in a ditch. Thus they distinguish between the meritorious and the worthless, between the wise and the foolish.

On Caste and Marriage

With respect to the division of families, there are four classifications. The first is called the Brâhman, men of pure conduct. They guard themselves in religion, live purely, and observe the most correct principles. The second is called Kshattriya, the royal caste. For ages they have been the governing class: they apply themselves to virtue and kindness. The third is called Vaiśyas, the merchant class: they engage in commercial exchange, and they follow profit at home and abroad. The fourth is called Sûdra, the agricultural class: they labor in plowing and tillage. In these four classes purity or impurity of caste assigns to every one his place. When they marry they rise or fall in position according to their new relationship. They do not allow promiscuous marriages between relations. A woman once married can never take another husband. Besides these there are other classes of many kinds that intermarry according to their several callings.

On Manners and Justice

With respect to the ordinary people, although they are naturally light-minded, yet they are upright and honorable. In money matters they are without craft, and in administering justice they are considerate. They dread the retribution of another state of existence, and make light of the things of the present world. They are not deceitful or treacherous in their conduct, and are faithful to their oaths and promises. In their rules of government there is remarkable rectitude, whilst in their behavior there is much gentleness and sweetness. With respect to criminals or rebels, these are few in number, and only occasionally troublesome. When the laws are broken or the power of the ruler violated, then the matter is clearly sifted and the offenders imprisoned. There is no infliction of corporal punishment; they are simply left to live or die, and are not counted among men. When the rules of propriety or justice are violated, or when a man fails in fidelity or filial piety, then they cut his nose or his ears off, or his hands and feet, or expel him from the country or drive him out into the desert wilds. For other faults, except these, a small payment of money will redeem the punishment. In the investigation of criminal cases there is no use of rod or staff to obtain proofs (*of guilt*).

Document 8.2

A European Christian in China

Of all the travelers along the Silk Road network, the most well-known and celebrated, at least in the West, was Marco Polo (1254–1324). Born and raised in the prosperous commercial city-state of Venice in what is now northern Italy, Marco Polo was a member of a family prominent in the long-distance trade of the Mediterranean and Black sea regions. At the age of seventeen, Marco accompanied his father and an uncle on an immense journey across Eurasia which by 1275 brought the Polos to China, recently conquered by the Mongols. It was, in fact, the relative peace which the Mongols had created in their huge transcontinental empire that facilitated the Polos' journey (see Map 12.1, p. 530). For the next seventeen years, they lived in China, where they were employed in minor administrative positions by Khublai Khan, the country's Mongol ruler. During these years, Marco Polo apparently traveled widely within China where he gathered material for the book about his travels, which he dictated to a friend after returning home in 1295.

Marco Polo's journey and the book that described it, generally known as *The Travels of Marco Polo*, were important elements of the larger process by which an emerging West European civilization reached out to and became aware of the older civilizations of the East. Christopher Columbus carried a marked-up copy of the book on his transatlantic journeys, believing that he was seeking by sea the places Marco Polo had visited by land. Some modern scholars are skeptical about parts of Marco Polo's report, and a few even question whether he ever got to China at all, largely because he omitted any mention of certain prominent features of Chinese life, for example, foot binding, the Great Wall, and tea drinking. Most historians, however, accept the basic outlines of Marco Polo's account, even as they notice exaggerations as well as an inflated perception of his own role within China. The selection that follows conveys Marco Polo's description of the city of Hangzhou, which he referred to as Kinsay. At the time of Marco Polo's visit, it was among the largest cities in the world.

■ How would you describe Marco Polo's impressions of the city? What did he notice? What surprised him?

■ Why did Marco Polo describe the city as "the finest and the noblest in the world"?

■ What marks his account of the city as that of a foreigner and a Christian?

■ What evidence of China's engagement with a wider world does this account offer?

MARCO POLO

The Travels of Marco Polo

1299

The city is beyond dispute the finest and the noblest in the world. In this we shall speak

Source: *The Book of Sir Marco Polo the Venetian Concerning the Kingdoms and Marvels of the East*, 3rd ed., translated and edited by Henry Yule, revised by Henri Cordier (London: John Murray, 1903), vol. 2:185–206.

according to the written statement which the Queen of this Realm sent to Bayan, the [Mongol] conqueror of the country for transmission to the Great Kaan, in order that he might be aware of the surpassing grandeur of the city and might be moved to save it from destruction or injury. I will tell you all the truth as it was set down in that document. For truth it was, as the said Messer Marco Polo at a later date was able to witness with his own eyes....

First and foremost, then, the document stated the city of Kinsay to be so great that it hath an hundred miles of compass. And there are in it 12,000 bridges of stone.... [Most scholars consider these figures a considerable exaggeration.] And though the bridges be so high, the approaches are so well contrived that carts and horses do cross them.

The document aforesaid also went on to state that there were in this city twelve guilds of the different crafts, and that each guild had 12,000 houses in the occupation of its workmen. Each of these houses contains at least twelve men, whilst some contain twenty and some forty.... And yet all these craftsmen had full occupation, for many other cities of the kingdom are supplied from this city with what they require.

The document aforesaid also stated that the number and wealth of the merchants, and the amount of goods that passed through their hands, were so enormous that no man could form a just estimate thereof. And I should have told you with regard to those masters of the different crafts who are at the head of such houses as I have mentioned, that neither they nor their wives ever touch a piece of work with their own hands, but live as nicely and delicately as if they were kings and queens. The wives indeed are most dainty and angelical creatures! Moreover it was an ordinance laid down by the King that every man should follow his father's business and no other, no matter if he possessed 100,000 bezants.°

Inside the city there is a Lake... and all round it are erected beautiful palaces and mansions, of the richest and most exquisite structure that you can imagine, belonging to the nobles of the city. There are also on its shores many abbeys and churches of the Idolaters [Buddhists]. In the middle of the Lake are two Islands, on each of which stands a rich, beautiful, and spacious edifice, furnished in such style as to seem fit for the palace of an Emperor. And when any one of the citizens desired to hold a marriage feast, or to give any other entertainment, it used to

be done at one of these palaces. And everything would be found there ready to order, such as silver plate, trenchers, and dishes, napkins and table-cloths, and whatever else was needful.... Sometimes there would be at these palaces an hundred different parties; some holding a banquet, others celebrating a wedding... in so well-ordered a manner that one party was never in the way of another....

Both men and women are fair and comely, and for the most part clothe themselves in silk, so vast is the supply of that material, both from the whole district of Kinsay, and from the imports by traders from other provinces. And you must know they eat every kind of flesh, even that of dogs and other unclean beasts, which nothing would induce a Christian to eat....

You must know also that the city of Kinsay has some 3,000 baths, the water of which is supplied by springs. They are hot baths, and the people take great delight in them, frequenting them several times a month, for they are very cleanly in their persons. They are the finest and largest baths in the world....

And the Ocean Sea comes within twenty-five miles of the city at a place called Ganfu, where there is a town and an excellent haven, with a vast amount of shipping which is engaged in the traffic to and from India and other foreign parts, exporting and importing many kinds of wares, by which the city benefits....

I repeat that everything appertaining to this city is on so vast a scale, and the Great Kaan's yearly revenues therefrom are so immense, that it is not easy even to put it in writing....

In this part are the ten principal markets, though besides these there are a vast number of others in the different parts of the town.... [T]oward the [market] squares are built great houses of stone, in which the merchants from India and other foreign parts store their wares, to be handy for the markets. In each of the squares is held a market three days in the week, frequented by 40,000 or 50,000 persons, who bring thither for sale every possible necessary of life, so that there is always an ample supply of every kind of meat and game....

Those markets make a daily display of every kind of vegetables and fruits.... [V]ery good raisins are

_____

°**bezant:** a Byzantine gold coin.

brought from abroad, and wine likewise.... From the Ocean Sea also come daily supplies of fish in great quantity, brought twenty-five miles up the river.... All the ten market places are encompassed by lofty houses, and below these are shops where all sorts of crafts are carried on, and all sorts of wares are on sale, including spices and jewels and pearls. Some of these shops are entirely devoted to the sale of wine made from rice and spices, which is constantly made fresh, and is sold very cheap. Certain of the streets are occupied by the women of the town, who are in such a number that I dare not say what it is. They are found not only in the vicinity of the market places, where usually a quarter is assigned to them, but all over the city. They exhibit themselves splendidly attired and abundantly perfumed, in finely garnished houses, with trains of waiting-women. These women are extremely accomplished in all the arts of allurement, and readily adapt their conversation to all sorts of persons, insomuch that strangers who have once tasted their attractions seem to get bewitched, and are so taken with their blandishments and their fascinating ways that they never can get these out of their heads....

Other streets are occupied by the Physicians, and by the Astrologers, who are also teachers of reading and writing; and an infinity of other professions have their places round about those squares. In each of the squares there are two great palaces facing one another, in which are established the officers appointed by the King to decide differences arising between merchants, or other inhabitants of the quarter....

The crowd of people that you meet here at all hours ... is so vast that no one would believe it possible that victuals enough could be provided for their consumption, unless they should see how, on every market-day, all those squares are thronged and crammed with purchasers, and with the traders who have brought in stores of provisions by land or water; and everything they bring in is disposed of....

The natives of the city are men of peaceful character, both from education and from the example of their kings, whose disposition was the same. They know nothing of handling arms, and keep none in their houses. You hear of no feuds or noisy quarrels or dissensions of any kind among them. Both in their commercial dealings and in their manufactures they are thoroughly honest and truthful, and there is such a degree of good will and neighborly attachment among both men and women that you would take the people who live in the same street to be all one family.

And this familiar intimacy is free from all jealousy or suspicion of the conduct of their women. These they treat with the greatest respect, and a man who should presume to make loose proposals to a married woman would be regarded as an infamous rascal. They also treat the foreigners who visit them for the sake of trade with great cordiality and entertain them in the most winning manner, affording them every help and advice on their business. But on the other hand they hate to see soldiers, and not least those of the Great Kaan's garrisons, regarding them as the cause of their having lost their native kings and lords.

Document 8.3

An Arab Muslim in West Africa

For most of the postclassical millennium, the world of Islam was far more extensive than that of Christendom. Nothing more effectively conveys both the extent and the cultural unity of the Islamic world than the travels of Ibn Battuta (1304–1368). Born in Morocco, this learned Arab scholar traversed nearly 75,000 miles during his extraordinary journeys, which took him to Spain, Anatolia, West and East Africa, Arabia, Iraq, Persia, Central and Southeast Asia, India, and China. He traveled at various times as a pilgrim, as a religious seeker, as a legal scholar, and frequently in the company of Muslim merchants. Remarkably, almost all of his extensive travels occurred within the realm of Islam, where he moved among people who shared his faith and often his Arabic language. Marco Polo, by contrast, had felt himself constantly an outsider, "a stranger in a strange land," for he was traveling almost everywhere beyond the borders of Christendom. But as a visitor from a more-established Islamic society, Ibn Battuta was often highly critical of the quality of Islamic observance in the frontier regions of the faith.

One such frontier region was West Africa, where a new civilization was taking shape, characterized by large empires such as Mali, a deep involvement in trans-Saharan commerce, and the gradual assimilation of Islam (see Map 8.3, p. 350, and pp. 348–51 and 492–94). The new faith had been introduced by North African Muslim traders and had found a growing acceptance, particularly in the urban centers, merchant communities, and ruling classes of West African kingdoms. On the last of his many journeys, Ibn Battuta crossed the Sahara Desert with a traders' caravan to visit Mali in 1352. Upon returning home the following year, he dictated his recollections and experiences to a scribe, producing a valuable account of this West African civilization in the fourteenth century.

- How would you describe Ibn Battuta's impression of Mali? What surprised or shocked him? What did he appreciate?

- What does Ibn Battuta's description of his visit to Mali reveal about his own attitudes and his image of himself?

- What might historians learn from this document about the nature and extent of Islam's penetration in this West African empire? What elements of older and continuing West African cultural traditions are evident in the document?

- What specifically does Ibn Battuta find shocking about the women he encounters on his travels in West Africa?

- What indications of Mali's economic involvement with a wider world are evident in the document?

IBN BATTUTA

Travels in Asia and Africa

1354

Thus we reached the town of Iwalatan° after a journey from Sijilmasa of two months to a day. Iwalatan is the northernmost province of the blacks.... The garments of its inhabitants, most of whom belong to the Massufa tribe, are of fine Egyptian fabrics.

———

°**Iwalatan:** Walata.

———

Source: Ibn Battuta, *Travels in Asia and Africa 1325–1354*, translated and edited by H. A. R. Gibb (London: Broadway House, 1929), 319–34.

Their women are of surpassing beauty, and are shown more respect than the men. The state of affairs amongst these people is indeed extraordinary. Their men show no signs of jealousy whatever; no one claims descent from his father, but on the contrary from his mother's brother. A person's heirs are his sister's sons, not his own sons. This is a thing which I have seen nowhere in the world except among the Indians of Malabar. But those are heathens; these people are Muslims, punctilious in observing the hours of prayer, studying books of law, and memorizing the Koran. Yet their women show no bashfulness before men and do not veil themselves, though they are assiduous in attending the prayers.

The women there have "friends" and "companions" amongst the men outside their own families, and the men in the same way have "companions" amongst the women of other families. A man may go into his house and find his wife entertaining her "companion," but he takes no objection to it. One day at Iwalatan I went into the qadi's° house, after asking his permission to enter, and found with him a young woman of remarkable beauty. When I saw her I was shocked and turned to go out, but she laughed at me, instead of being overcome by shame, and the qadi said to me "Why are you going out? She is my companion." I was amazed at their conduct, for he was a theologian and a pilgrim [to Mecca] to boot....

When I decided to make the journey to Malli,° which is reached in twenty-four days from Iwalatan if the traveler pushes on rapidly, I hired a guide from the Massufa—for there is no necessity to travel in a company on account of the safety of that road—and set out with three of my companions....

A traveler in this country carries no provisions, whether plain food or seasonings, and neither gold nor silver. He takes nothing but pieces of salt and glass ornaments, which the people call beads, and some aromatic goods. When he comes to a village the womenfolk of the blacks bring out millet, milk, chickens, pulped lotus fruit, rice,

"funi" (a grain resembling mustard seed, from which "kuskusu"° and gruel are made), and pounded haricot beans....

Thus I reached the city of Malli, the capital of the king of the blacks. I stopped at the cemetery and went to the quarter occupied by the whites, where I asked for Muhammad ibn al-Faqih. I found that he had hired a house for me and went there.... I met the qadi of Malli, 'Abd ar-Rahman, who came to see me; he is a black, a pilgrim [to Mecca], and a man of fine character. I met also the interpreter Dugha, who is one of the principal men among the blacks. All these persons sent me hospitality gifts of food and treated me with the utmost generosity....

The sultan° of Malli is Mansa Sulayman.... He is a miserly king, not a man from whom one might hope for a rich present. It happened that I spent these two months without seeing him, on account of my illness. Later on he held a banquet... to which the commanders, doctors, qadi, and preacher were invited, and I went along with them. Reading-desks were brought in, and the Koran was read through, then they prayed for our master Abu'l-Hasan° and also for Mansa Sulayman.

When the ceremony was over I went forward and saluted Mansa Sulayman.... When I withdrew, the [sultan's] hospitality gift was sent to me.... I stood up thinking . . . that it consisted of robes of honor and money, and lo!, it was three cakes of bread, and a piece of beef fried in native oil, and a calabash of sour curds. When I saw this I burst out laughing, and thought it a most amazing thing that they could be so foolish and make so much of such a paltry matter.

On certain days the sultan holds audiences in the palace yard, where there is a platform under a tree, with three steps; this they call the "pempi." It is carpeted with silk and has cushions placed on it. [Over it] is raised the umbrella, which is a sort of pavilion made of silk, surmounted by a bird in gold, about the size of a falcon. The sultan comes out of a door in a corner of the palace, carrying a bow in his hand and a quiver on his back. On his head he has a golden

---

°**qadi:** judge.

°**Malli:** the city of Mali.

°**kuskusu:** couscous.

°**sultan:** ruler.

°**Abu'l-Hasan:** the sultan of Morocco.

skullcap, bound with a gold band which has narrow ends shaped like knives, more than a span in length. His usual dress is a velvety red tunic, made of the European fabrics called "mutanfas." The sultan is preceded by his musicians, who carry gold and silver guimbris°, and behind him come three hundred armed slaves. He walks in a leisurely fashion, affecting a very slow movement, and even stops from time to time. On reaching the pempi he stops and looks round the assembly, then ascends it in the sedate manner of a preacher ascending a mosque-pulpit. As he takes his seat the drums, trumpets, and bugles are sounded. Three slaves go out at a run to summon the sovereign's deputy and the military commanders, who enter and sit down. Two saddled and bridled horses are brought, along with two goats, which they hold to serve as a protection against the evil eye....

The blacks are of all people the most submissive to their king and the most abject in their behavior before him.... If he summons any of them while he is holding an audience in his pavilion, the person summoned takes off his clothes and puts on worn garments, removes his turban and dons a dirty skullcap, and enters with his garments and trousers raised knee-high. He goes forward in an attitude of humility and dejection and knocks the ground hard with his elbows, then stands with bowed head and bent back listening to what he says. If anyone addresses the king and receives a reply from him, he uncovers his back and throws dust over his head and back, for all the world like a bather splashing himself with water....

On feast-days..., the poets come in. Each of them is inside a figure resembling a thrush, made of feathers, and provided with a wooden head with a red beak, to look like a thrush's head. They stand in front of the sultan in this ridiculous makeup and recite their poems. I was told that their poetry is a kind of sermonizing in which they say to the sultan: "This pempi which you occupy was that whereon sat this king and that king, and such and such were this one's noble actions and such and such the other's. So do you too do good deeds whose memory will

outlive you.".... I was told that this practice is a very old custom amongst them, prior to the introduction of Islam, and that they have kept it up.

The blacks possess some admirable qualities. They are seldom unjust, and have a greater abhorrence of injustice than any other people. Their sultan shows no mercy to anyone who is guilty of the least act of it. There is complete security in their country. Neither traveler nor inhabitant in it has anything to fear from robbers or men of violence. They do not confiscate the property of any white man who dies in their country, even if it be uncounted wealth. On the contrary, they give it into the charge of some trustworthy person among the whites, until the rightful heir takes possession of it. They are careful to observe the hours of prayer, and assiduous in attending them in congregations, and in bringing up their children to them.

On Fridays, if a man does not go early to the mosque, he cannot find a corner to pray in, on account of the crowd. It is a custom of theirs to send each man his boy [to the mosque] with his prayer-mat; the boy spreads it out for his master in a place befitting him [and remains on it] until he comes to the mosque....

Another of their good qualities is their habit of wearing clean white garments on Fridays. Even if a man has nothing but an old worn shirt, he washes it and cleans it, and wears it to the Friday service. Yet another is their zeal for learning the Koran by heart.... I visited the qadi in his house on the day of the festival. His children were chained up, so I said to him, "Will you not let them loose?" He replied, "I shall not do so until they learn the Koran by heart."

Among their bad qualities are the following. The women servants, slave-girls, and young girls go about in front of everyone naked, without a stitch of clothing on them. Women go into the sultan's presence naked and without coverings, and his daughters also go about naked. Then there is their custom of putting dust and ashes on their heads, as a mark of respect, and the grotesque ceremonies we have described when the poets recite their verses. Another reprehensible practice among many of them is the eating of carrion, dogs, and asses.

°**guimbris:** two-stringed guitars.

I went on…to Gawgaw°, which is a large city on the Nile°, and one of the finest towns in the land of the blacks. It is also one of their biggest and best-provisioned towns, with rice in plenty, milk, and fish.…The buying and selling of its inhabitants is done with cowry shells, and the same is the case at Malli. I stayed there about a month.

°**Gawgaw:** Gogo.

°**Nile:** Niger. The Niger River was long regarded by outsiders as a tributary of The Nile.

Using the Evidence:
Travelers' Tales and Observations

1. **Describing a foreign culture:** Each of these documents was written by an outsider to the people or society he is describing. What different postures toward these foreign cultures are evident in the sources? How did the travelers' various religions shape their perception of places they visited? How did they view the women of their host societies? Were these travelers more impressed by the similarities or by the differences between their home cultures and the ones they visited?

2. **Defining the self-perception of authors:** What can we learn from these documents about the men who wrote them? What motivated them? How did they define themselves in relationship to the societies they observed?

3. **Assessing the credibility of sources:** What information in these sources would be most valuable for historians seeking to understand India, China, and West Africa in the postclassical era? What statements in these sources might be viewed with the most skepticism? You will want to consider the authors' purposes and their intended audiences in evaluating their writings.

4. **Considering outsiders' accounts:** What are the advantages and limitations for historians in drawing on the writings of foreign observers?

Visual Sources

Considering the Evidence:
Art, Religion, and Cultural Exchange
in Central Asia

The huge region between the Caspian Sea and western China is known to scholars as Central Asia, or sometimes as Inner Asia (see Map 8.1, p. 335). Its geography features rugged mountains, vast deserts, extensive grasslands, and a generally arid climate, all of which made settled farming difficult or impossible, except in scattered oases. As a result, most of Central Asia's peoples pursued a pastoral and nomadic way of life, dependent on their horses, camels, sheep, goats, or cattle. Linguistically and culturally, the majority were of Turkic or Mongol background. These features have long given Central Asia a distinctive character, despite the diversity of its many disparate peoples.

In recent centuries, Central Asia gained a reputation as a remote and backward region, far removed from the major centers of global trade and development. During the postclassical millennium, however, that region functioned as a vital Eurasian crossroad. Perhaps most obviously, it was a commercial crossroads, as the Silk Roads traversed its territory, while many of its peoples participated actively in that network of exchange. Central Asia was also a cultural and religious crossroads: Buddhism, Judaism, Christianity, Islam, Manichaeism, elements of Greek and Chinese culture—all of these traditions, born in the outer rim of Eurasian civilizations, found a place among the peoples of Central Asia, frequently carried there by merchants. Finally, Central Asia was an imperial crossroads, for there the empires or military federations periodically established by pastoral societies clashed with the established civilizations and states of China, India, the Middle East, and Europe to the south and west. Thus Central Asia was for many centuries a vast arena of intense cross-cultural interaction. The images that follow provide a brief introduction to a few of its many peoples and to the mingling of their cultures with those of a wider world.

The Kushans were a pastoral nomadic people from the area around Dunhuang at the far western edge of China. In the early centuries B.C.E., they had migrated to the region that now makes up northwestern India, Pakistan, Afghanistan, and Tajikistan, where they established a sizable and prosperous empire linked to the Silk Road trading network. It was a remarkably cosmopolitan place, and it flourished until the third or fourth century C.E. That empire, according to one recent account, "created stable conditions at the heart of Central Asia, allowing for the great flowering of trans-Eurasian mercantile and cultural exchange that occurred along the Silk Roads."[30]

Since parts of this empire had earlier been ruled by Alexander the Great and his Greek successors (see pp. 152–54), classical Mediterranean culture was a prominent element of Kushan culture. The Kushans used the Greek alphabet to write their official language, which was derived from India. The greatest of the Kushan rulers, Kanishka (ruled ca. 127–153 C.E.), styled himself "Great King, King of Kings, Son of God," a title that had both Persian and Chinese precedents. Hindu devotional cults as well as Buddhism flourished, and the Kushan Empire became a launching pad for the spread of Buddhism into Central Asia and ultimately into China and Japan (see pp. 338–40). It was here that the earliest human representations of the Buddha were sculpted, and often with distinctly Greek features. Despite multiple Eurasian influences, Kushan artists depicted their rulers in typical steppe nomadic style: on horseback, wearing loose trousers, heavy boots, and knee-length robes.[31]

In Visual Source 8.1, a Kushan pendant dating to the fourth century C.E. provides an illustration of the cultural blending so characteristic of the region. The medallion features Hariti, originally a fearsome Hindu goddess who abducted and killed children, feeding their flesh to her own offspring. But in an encounter with the Buddha, Hariti repented and was transformed into a compassionate protector of children. Here she is depicted holding in her right hand a lotus blossom, a prominent Buddhist symbol; her left hand holds another lotus flower supporting a flask or cornucopia overflowing with pomegranates (symbolizing food and abundance). According to local mythology, the Buddha had offered Hariti pomegranates (often said to resemble human flesh) as a substitute for the children she was devouring.

While the content of this pendant is thoroughly Indian and Buddhist, scholars believe that this representation of Hariti was probably modeled after the Greek goddess Tyche, also portrayed holding a cornucopia. Furthermore, her short tunic worn with a belt was likewise of Greek or Hellenistic origin. A further cultural influence is found in the decorations that surround the image, for the border of pearls and stylized flowers derives from Persia.

- Why do you think the Kushan artist who created this image chose to weave together so many distinct cultural strands?

- What does the story of Hariti's transformation tell us about the impact of Buddhism in the region?

- Why might the Greek goddess Tyche been used as a model for Hariti? (Hint: you might want to do a little research on Tyche before answering this question.)

Visual Source 8.1 Greek Culture, Buddhism, and the Kushans (V&A Images, Victoria and Albert Museum)

If the Kushan state was a major point of departure for the spread of Buddhism beyond India, that faith soon took hold in many of the Central Asian oasis cities along the Silk Road network, reaching China in the early centuries C.E. (see pp. 335–41). In addition to merchants, Buddhist monks traversed the Silk Roads, some of them headed for India in search of holy texts and sacred relics (see Document 8.1), while others traveled from town to town teaching the message of the Buddha. Thus at least until the rise of Islam (see Chapter 11), Buddhism was a common feature in the experience of many Central Asian peoples and a point of contact with the civilizations of India and China. Visual Source 8.2, a tenth-century Chinese painting, shows a traveling monk on the Silk Road. It derives from the Magao Caves, located near Dunhuang, a major center of Buddhist art and an important stop on the Silk Roads. (See Map 8.1, p. 335, and the photo on p. 339.) Notice that the monk is leading a tiger, long a symbol of protection and courage and a messenger between heaven and the human world (see the photo on p. 91). It also recalls a much-told story of the Buddha, in an earlier life, compassionately offering his blood and body to feed some starving tiger cubs and their mother.

- What function does the small Buddha sitting on a cloud at the upper left play in this painting?

- On his back the monk is carrying a heavy load of Buddhist texts, or *sutras*. Why do you think Buddhist monks were so eager to acquire and to disseminate such texts? (See also Document 8.1, pp. 356–59.)

- At the end of the monk's staff hangs what is probably a container for relics, perhaps a bone or a tuft of hair from the Buddha himself. Why might such relics have had such an appeal for the faithful? Can you identify a similar veneration of relics in other religious traditions?

Visual Source 8.2 Buddhist Monks on the Silk Road (British Museum/The Bridgeman Art Library)

Another central Asian people with extensive involvement in trans-Eurasian commerce were the Uighurs, Turkic-speaking nomads living north of the Gobi Desert (see Map 8.1, p. 335). By the eighth century C.E., they had established a powerful state that endured for about a century (744–840). Controlling a critical passage of the Silk Road network, Uighurs traded extensively with China, exchanging horses, camels, yaks, and hides for enormous quantities of Chinese silk. In fact, Uighur military forces saved the Chinese Tang dynasty from an internal rebellion between 755 and 763 and gained even greater access to Chinese wealth as they looted Chinese cities. A Chinese dynastic history bemoaned the unequal relationship that followed for a time: "The barbarians acquired silk insatiably and we were given useless horses."[32] The Uighur court likewise gained a series of Chinese princesses and considerable Chinese cultural influence.

They also acquired a new religion in China—Manichaeism. This was a faith of Persian origin, whose prophet, Mani (216–274 C.E.), saw himself in a long line of prophets including Zoroaster, the Buddha, and Jesus. Drawing on all of these traditions, Mani fashioned a religion that understood the world as an arena of intense conflict between the forces of Light (the soul) and the Dark (the material world). It spread widely within the Roman Empire and along the Silk Road network into China, where it was soon subject to intense persecution at the hands of Buddhists. From there the invading Uighurs picked it up and made it the official faith of their empire. No one knows precisely why Uighur rulers chose to convert to this Persian-based religion. Perhaps it linked the Uighurs to the larger world of agrarian civilizations, while reducing their cultural dependence on China. In any event, it represents another remarkable example of cultural interchange along the crossroads of Central Asia.

Visual Source 8.3 comes from a page in a Manichaean book dated variously between the eighth and eleventh centuries and found in the Uighur region of Khocho. It shows a number of Manichaean priests, wearing their characteristic tall white hats and writing at their desks. The fragmentary text in the middle, written in a Uighur script, warns against those who "believe in a wrong and contrary law" and "pray false prayers." As if to symbolize the corrupt and inverted world of Darkness, the image presents the priests writing left-handed and the script running from bottom to top instead of the normal top-down fashion.[33]

■ How would you read the overall religious message of the painting? What might suggest the ultimate triumph of the Light? Consider the role of the trees, bearing the flowers and fruits of good deeds.

■ What does the presence of this Persian-based religion among a distant Central Asian people suggest about the postclassical Eurasian world?

Visual Source 8.3 Manichaean Scribes (Bildarchiv Preussischer Kulturbesitz/Art Resource, NY)

Clearly the most well-known of Central Asian peoples were the Mongols, described more fully in Chapter 12. Under the leadership of Chinggis Khan, a number of quite distinct and rival pastoral tribes in what is now Mongolia had been brought together in a powerful military confederation by the early thirteenth century. That newly created Mongol state then embarked on an enormous effort of conquest that gave rise to the world's largest empire. That empire encompassed the civilizations of China, Persia, and Russia as well as many of the other nomadic peoples of Central Asia, and it threatened Japan, Sourtheast Asia, central Europe, and Egypt (see Map 12.1, p. 530.). Its presence loomed all across Eurasia in the thirteenth and fourteenth centuries, generating numerous cross-cultural encounters and interactions.

None of these was of greater significance than the Mongol conquest of China fully accomplished by 1279. While the Mongols ruled China in a largely Chinese fashion, they also sought to preserve much of their own culture. Thus they undertook an annual ritual of scattering mare's milk, employed Mongol shamans at the ruler's court, continued to wear native costumes of leather and fur, and rode to the hunt in traditional Mongol fashion. Mongol women living in China generally gave birth in a traditional felt-covered dwelling rather than in a Chinese-style home.

Visual Source 8.4 illustrates the Mongol effort to maintain their own identity even as they were immersed in the sophisticated culture of China, which had proved so attractive to many neighboring peoples. The painting (ca. 1280) is by the Chinese court artist Liu Guandao and was commissioned by Khubilai Khan, grandson of Chinggis Khan and the Mongol ruler of China from 1264 to 1294. Titled *Khubilai Khan on a Hunt*, it shows the Mongol ruler on a dark horse, wearing a distinctive fur-rimmed white robe that covers his Chinese royal garments, and accompanied by a female consort and a number of servants and officials. The figure in blue in the lower group of hunters carries a hawk, often used by Central Asian peoples during a hunt, while a trained wildcat sits on the horse below.

■ Why do you think Khubilai Khan commissioned such a painting? What impression of himself did he seek to convey?

■ What features of the landscape and depictions of people and animals illustrate the world of pastoral peoples from which the Mongols had come?

■ What elements of Central Asian history are suggested by the camel train in the upper right?

■ How might traditional Chinese officials respond to this painting? How might they react to the inclusion of women in a royal hunt?

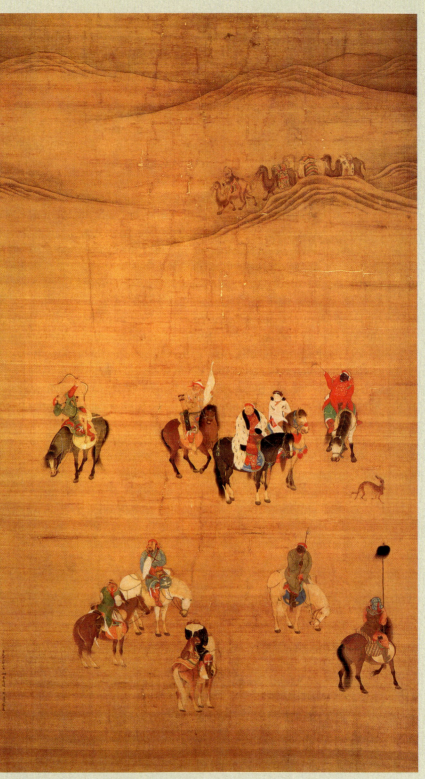

Visual Source 8.4 The Mongols in China (National Palace Museum, Taipei, Taiwan)

Among the peoples of Central Asia, none had a longer-lasting impact on world history than the Turks, a term that refers to a variety of groups speaking related Turkic languages. Originating as pastoral nomads in what is now Mongolia, Turkic peoples gradually migrated westward, occupying much of Central Asia, sometimes creating sizeable empires and settling down as farmers. But the greatest transformation of Turkic culture occurred with the Turkic peoples' conversion to Islam. That process took place between the tenth and fourteenth centuries, as Muslim armies penetrated Central Asia and Muslim merchants became prominent traders on the Silk Road.

Also very important in the Turks' conversion to Islam were Muslim holy men known as dervishes. Operating within the Sufi tradition of Islam, dervishes were spiritual seekers who sought a direct personal experience of the Divine Reality and developed reputations for good works, personal kindness, and sometimes magic or religious powers. A Turkic tale from the fourteenth century tells the story of one such holy man, Baba Tukles, sent by God to convert a ruler named Ozbek Khan. To overcome the opposition of the khan's traditional shamans, Baba Tukles invited one of the shamans to enter a fiery-hot oven pit with him. The shaman was instantly incinerated, while the Muslim holy man emerged unscathed from that test of religious power.[34] Such tales of the supernatural and the conversion of rulers contributed to the attractiveness of Islam among Turkic peoples and have been a common feature in the spread of all of the major world religions.

Visual Source 8.5, a painting dating from the sixteenth century, shows a number of Turkish dervishes performing the turning or whirling dance associated with the Sufi religious order established in the thirteenth century by the great mystical poet Rumi. Intended to bring participants into direct contact with the Divine, the whirling dance itself drew upon the ideas and practices of an ancient Central Asian religious life in which practitioners, known as shamans, entered into an ecstatic state of consciousness and connection to the spirit world. "Especially in Central Asia, the Caucasus and Anatolia," writes one scholar, "the mystical ecstasy [of the whirling dance] was understood in the spirit of the shamanic tradition."[35] This blending of two religious traditions—mystical or Sufi Islam and shamanism—represents yet another example of the cultural interactions that washed across Central Asia in the postclassical millennium.

■ What image of these dervishes was the artist trying to convey?

■ Why might such holy men have been effective missionaries of Islam in Central Asia?

■ Notice the musical instruments that accompany the turning dance—sticks on the left, a flutelike instrument known as a *ney* in the center, and drums on the right. What do you think this music and dance contributed to the religious experience of the participants?

Visual Source 8.5 Islam, Shamanism, and the Turks (Topkapi Library Istanbul/Gianni Dagli Orti/The Art Archive)

Using the Evidence:
Art, Religion, and Cultural Exchange in Central Asia

1. **Considering cross-cultural interactions:** The pastoral peoples of Central Asia and the settled agricultural civilizations adjacent to them did not live in closed or separate worlds. What evidence contained in these visual sources supports or challenges this assertion?

2. **Defining change and continuity:** In what ways do these visual sources indicate that the peoples of Central Asia were changed by their interactions with surrounding civilizations? In what respects did they retain elements of their earlier cultures?

3. **Explaining cultural change:** What aspects of these visual sources indicate that the various peoples of Central Asia were receptive to the religious and cultural traditions of neighboring civilizations?

CHAPTER NINE

China and the World

East Asian Connections

500–1300

"China will be the next superpower."[1] That was the frank assertion of an article in the British newspaper *The Guardian* in June 2006. Nor was it alone in that assessment. As the new millennium dawned, headlines with this message appeared with increasing frequency in public lectures, in newspaper and magazine articles, and in book titles all across the world. China's huge population, its booming economy, its massive trade surplus with the United States, its entry into world oil markets, its military potential, and its growing presence in global political affairs—all of this suggested that China was headed for a major role, perhaps even a dominant role, in the world of the twenty-first century. Few of these authors, however, paused to recall that China's prominence on the world stage was hardly something new or that its nineteenth- and twentieth-century position as a "backward," weak, or dependent country was distinctly out of keeping with its long history. Is China perhaps poised to resume in the twenty-first century a much older and more powerful role in world affairs?

IN THE WORLD OF THIRD-WAVE CIVILIZATIONS, even more than during the classical era that preceded it, China cast a long shadow. Its massive and powerful civilization, widely imitated by adjacent peoples, gave rise to a China-centered "world order" encompassing most of eastern Asia.[2] China extended its borders deep into Central Asia, while its wealthy and cosmopolitan culture attracted visitors from all over Eurasia. None of its many neighbors—whether

Chinese Astronomy: During classical and postclassical times, the impressive achievements of Chinese astronomy included the observation of sunspots, supernovae, and solar and lunar eclipses as well as the construction of elaborate star maps and astronomical devices such as those shown here. The print itself is of Japanese origin and shows a figure wearing the dragon robes of a Chinese official. It illustrates the immense cultural influence of China on its smaller Japanese neighbor. (Courtesy of the Trustees of the British Museum)

nomadic peoples to the north and west or smaller peripheral states such as Tibet, Korea, Japan, and Vietnam—could escape its gravitational pull. All of them had to deal with China. Far beyond these near neighbors, China's booming economy and many technological innovations had ripple effects all across Eurasia.

Even as China so often influenced the world, it too was changed by its many interactions with non-Chinese peoples. Northern nomads—"barbarians" to the Chinese—frequently posed a military threat and on occasion even conquered and ruled parts of China. The country's growing involvement in international trade stimulated important social, cultural, and economic changes within China itself. Buddhism, a religion of Indian origin, took root in China, and, to a lesser extent, so did Christianity and Islam. In short, China's engagement with the wider world became a very significant element in a global era of accelerating connections.

The Reemergence of a Unified China

The collapse of the Han dynasty around 220 C.E. ushered in more than three centuries of political fragmentation in China and signaled the rise of powerful and locally entrenched aristocratic families. It also meant the incursion of northern nomads, many of whom learned Chinese, dressed like Chinese, married into Chinese families, and governed northern regions of the country in a Chinese fashion. Such conditions of disunity, unnatural in the eyes of many thoughtful Chinese, discredited Confucianism and opened the door to a greater acceptance of Buddhism and Daoism among the elite.

Those centuries also witnessed the beginning of Chinese migration southward toward the Yangzi River valley, a movement of people that gave southern China some 60 percent of the country's population by 1000. That movement of Chinese people, accompanied by their intensive agriculture, set in motion a vast environmental transformation, marked by the destruction of the old-growth forests that once covered much of the country and the retreat of the elephants that had inhabited those lands. Around 800 C.E., the Chinese official and writer Liu Zongyuan lamented what was happening.

> A tumbled confusion of lumber as flames on the hillside crackle
> Not even the last remaining shrubs are safeguarded from destruction
> Where once mountain torrents leapt—nothing but rutted gullies.[3]

A "Golden Age" of Chinese Achievement

■ Change
Why are the centuries of the Tang and Song dynasties in China sometimes referred to as a "golden age"?

Unlike the fall of the western Roman Empire, where political fragmentation proved to be a permanent condition, China regained its unity under the Sui dynasty (589–618). Its emperors solidified that unity by a vast extension of the country's canal system, stretching some 1,200 miles in length and described by one scholar as "an engineering feat without parallel in the world of its time."[4] Those canals linked northern and southern China economically and contributed much to the prosperity that followed. But the ruthlessness of Sui emperors and a futile military campaign to conquer Korea exhausted the state's resources, alienated many people, and prompted the overthrow of the dynasty.

This dynastic collapse, however, witnessed no prolonged disintegration of the Chinese state. The two dynasties that followed—the Tang (618–907) and the Song (960–1279)—built on the Sui foundations of renewed unity (see Map 9.1). Together they established patterns of Chinese life that endured into the twentieth century, despite a fifty-year period of disunity between the two dynasties. Culturally, this era

Map 9.1   Tang and Song Dynasty China

During the postclassical millennium, China interacted extensively with its neighbors. The Tang dynasty extended Chinese control deep into Central Asia, while the Song dynasty witnessed incursions by the nomadic Jurchen people, who created the Jin Empire, which ruled parts of northern China.

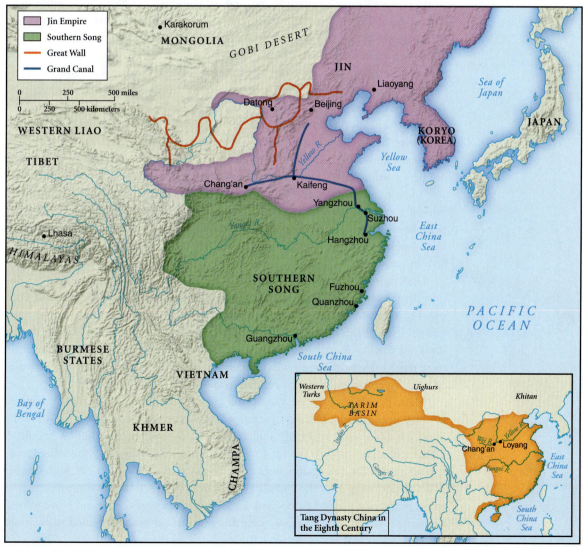

has long been regarded as a "golden age" of arts and literature, setting standards of excellence in poetry, landscape painting, and ceramics. (See Visual Sources: The Leisure Life of Chinese Elites, pp. 417–23, for Chinese painting during this time.) Particularly during the Song dynasty, an explosion of scholarship gave rise to Neo-Confucianism, an effort to revive Confucian thinking while incorporating into it some of the insights of Buddhism and Daoism.

Politically, the Tang and Song dynasties built a state structure that endured for a thousand years. Six major ministries—personnel, finance, rites, army, justice, and public works—were accompanied by the Censorate, an agency that exercised surveillance over the rest of the government, checking on the character and competence of public officials. To staff this bureaucracy, the examination system was revived and made more elaborate, encouraged by the ability to print books for the first time in world history. Efforts to prevent cheating on the exams included searching candidates entering the examination hall and placing numbers rather than names on their papers. Schools and colleges proliferated to prepare candidates for the rigorous exams, which became a central feature of upper-class life. A leading world historian has described Tang dynasty China as "the best ordered state in the world."[5]

Selecting officials on the basis of merit represented a challenge to established aristocratic families' hold on public office. Still, a substantial percentage of official positions went to the sons of the privileged, even if they had not passed the exams. Moreover, because education and the examination system grew far more rapidly than the number of official positions, many who passed lower-level exams could not be accommodated with a bureaucratic appointment. Often, however, they were able to combine landowning and success in the examination system to maintain an immense cultural prestige and prominence in their local areas. Despite the state's periodic efforts to redistribute land in favor of the peasantry, the great families of large landowners continued to encroach on peasant plots. This has been a recurring pattern in rural China from classical times to the present.

Underlying these cultural and political achievements was an "economic revolution" that made Song dynasty China "by far the richest, most skilled, and most populous country on earth."[6] The most obvious sign of China's prosperity was its rapid growth in population, which jumped from about 50 million or 60 million during the Tang dynasty to 120 million by 1200. Behind this doubling of the population were remarkable achievements in agricultural production, particularly the adoption of a fast-ripening and drought-resistant strain of rice from Vietnam.

Many people found their way to the cities, making China the most urbanized country in the world. Dozens of Chinese cities numbered over 100,000, while the Song dynasty capital of Hangzhou was home to more than a million people. A Chinese observer in 1235 provided a vivid description of that city.[7] Specialized markets abounded for meat, herbs, vegetables, books, rice, and much more, with troupes of actors performing for the crowds. Restaurants advertised their unique offerings—sweet bean soup, pickled dates, juicy lungs, meat pies, pigs' feet—and some offered vegetarian fare for religious banquets. Inns of various kinds appealed to different

Kaifeng
This detail comes from a huge watercolor scroll, titled *Upper River during Qing Ming Festival*, originally painted during the Song dynasty. It illustrates the urban sophistication of Kaifeng and other Chinese cities at that time and has been frequently imitated and copied since then. (Palace Museum, Beijing)

groups. Those that served only wine, a practice known as "hitting the cup," were regarded as "unfit for polite company." "Luxuriant inns," marked by red lanterns, featured prostitutes, and "the wine chambers [were] equipped with beds." Specialized agencies managed elaborate dinner parties for the wealthy, complete with a Perfume and Medicine Office to "help sober up the guests." Schools for musicians offered thirteen different courses. Numerous clubs provided companionship for poets, fishermen, Buddhists, physical fitness enthusiasts, antiques collectors, horse lovers, and many other groups. No wonder that the Italian visitor Marco Polo described Hangzhou later in the thirteenth century as "beyond dispute the finest and noblest [city] in the world."[8] (See Document 8.2, pp. 359–62, for a fuller description of Marco Polo's impressions of Hangzhou.)

Supplying these cities with food was made possible by an immense network of internal waterways—canals, rivers, and lakes—stretching perhaps 30,000 miles. They provided a cheap transportation system that bound the country together economically and created the "world's most populous trading area."[9]

Industrial production likewise soared. In both large-scale enterprises employing hundreds of workers and in smaller backyard furnaces, China's iron industry increased its output dramatically. By the eleventh century, it was providing the government with 32,000 suits of armor and 16 million iron arrowheads annually, in addition to supplying metal for coins, tools, construction, and bells in Buddhist monasteries. Technological innovation in other fields also flourished. Inventions in printing, both woodblock and movable type, generated the world's first printed books, and by 1000 relatively cheap books on religious, agricultural, mathematical, and medical topics became widely available in China. Its navigational and shipbuilding technologies led the world. The Chinese invention of gunpowder created within a few centuries a revolution in military affairs that had global dimensions.

Most remarkably, perhaps, all of this occurred within the world's most highly commercialized society, in which producing for the market, rather than for local consumption, became a very widespread phenomenon. Cheap transportation allowed peasants to grow specialized crops for sale, while they bought rice or other staples on the market. In addition, government demands for taxes paid in cash rather than in kind required peasants to sell something in order to meet their obligations. The growing use of paper money as well as financial instruments such as letters of credit and promissory notes further contributed to the commercialization of Chinese society. Two prominent scholars have described the outcome: "Output increased, population grew, skills multiplied, and a burst of inventiveness made Song China far wealthier than ever before—or than any of its contemporaries."[10]

Women in the Song Dynasty

■ Change

In what ways did women's lives change during the Tang and Song dynasties?

The "golden age" of Song dynasty China was perhaps less than "golden" for many of the country's women, for that era marked yet another turning point in the history of Chinese patriarchy. Under the influence of steppe nomads, whose women led less restricted lives, elite Chinese women of the Tang dynasty era, at least in the north, had participated in social life with greater freedom than in classical times. Paintings and statues from that time show aristocratic women riding horses, while the Queen Mother of the West, a Daoist deity, was widely worshipped by female Daoist priests and practitioners (see p. 255 and Visual Sources 9.2 and 9.5, pp. 419 and 422). By the Song dynasty, however, a reviving Confucianism and rapid economic growth seemed to tighten patriarchal restrictions on women and to restore some of the earlier Han dynasty images of female submission and passivity.

Once again Confucian writers highlighted the subordination of women to men and the need to keep males and females separate in every domain of life. The Song dynasty historian and scholar Sima Guang (1019–1086) summed up the prevailing view: "The boy leads the girl, the girl follows the boy; the duty of husbands to be resolute and wives to be docile begins with this."[11] Women were also frequently viewed as a distraction to men's pursuit of a contemplative and introspective life. The remarriage of widows, though legally permissible, was increasingly condemned, for "to walk through two courtyards is a source of shame for a woman."[12]

The most compelling expression of a tightening patriarchy lay in foot binding. Apparently beginning among dancers and courtesans in the tenth or eleventh century C.E., this practice involved the tight wrapping of young girls' feet, usually breaking the bones of the foot and causing intense pain. During the Tang dynasty, foot binding spread widely among elite families and later became even more widespread in Chinese society. It was associated with new images of female beauty and eroticism that emphasized small size, delicacy, and reticence, all of which were necessarily produced by foot binding. It certainly served to keep women restricted to the "inner quarters," where Confucian tradition asserted that they belonged. Many mothers imposed this painful procedure on their daughters, perhaps to enhance their marriage prospects and to assist them in competing with concubines for the attention of their husbands.[13]

Furthermore, a rapidly commercializing economy undermined the position of women in the textile industry. Urban workshops and state factories, run by men, increasingly took over the skilled tasks of weaving textiles, especially silk, which had previously been the work of rural women. But as their economic role in textile production declined, other opportunities beckoned in an increasingly prosperous Song China. In the cities, women operated restaurants, sold fish and vegetables, and worked as maids, cooks, and dressmakers. The growing prosperity of elite families funneled increasing numbers of women into roles as concubines, entertainers, courtesans, and prostitutes. Their ready availability surely reduced the ability of wives to negotiate as equals with their husbands, setting women against one another and creating endless household jealousies.

In other ways, the Song dynasty witnessed more positive trends in the lives of women. Their property rights expanded, in terms of both controlling their own dowries and inheriting property from their families. "Neither in earlier nor in later periods," writes one scholar, "did as much property pass through women's hands" as during the Song dynasty.[14] Furthermore, lower-ranking but ambitious officials strongly urged the education of women, so that they might more effectively raise their sons and increase the family's fortune. Song dynasty China, in short, offered a mixture of tightening restrictions and new opportunities to its women.

Foot Binding
The two young women pictured in this late-nineteenth-century photograph have bound feet, while the boy standing between them does not. A girl of a similar age would likely have begun this painful process already. The practice, dating back to around 1000 C.E., lasted into the twentieth century, when it was largely eliminated by reformist and Communist governments. (Photograph courtesy Peabody Essex Museum; image #A9392)

China and the Northern Nomads: A Chinese World Order in the Making

Chinese history has been subjected to two enduring misconceptions in popular thinking, if not in scholarly writing. First, it was often viewed as the story of an impressive but largely static civilization. In fact, however, China changed substantially over the centuries as its state structures evolved, as its various cultural traditions mixed and blended, as its economy expanded, as its population grew and migrated to the south, and as its patriarchy altered in tone and emphasis. A second misconception has portrayed China as a self-contained civilization. The balance of this chapter challenges this impression by showing how China's many interactions with

Snapshot   **Key Moments in the History of Postclassical China**

Collapse of Han dynasty; end of classical era	220
Political fragmentation of China; incursion of nomads in the north; Buddhism takes root	220–581
Sui dynasty; reunification of China	589–618
Reign of Emperor Wendi; state support for Buddhism	581–604
Tang dynasty; golden age of Chinese culture; expansion into Central Asia; high point of Chinese influence in Japan	618–907
Withdrawal of Chinese military forces from Korea	688
Reign of Empress Wu, China's only female emperor	690–705
State action against Buddhism	9th century
Political breakdown between dynasties	907–960
Vietnam establishes independence from China	939
Song dynasty; China's economic revolution; northern China ruled by peoples of nomadic background (Khitan, Jurchen)	960–1279
Yuan dynasty; Mongol rule of China	1271–1368
Ming dynasty; Chinese rule resumed	1368–1644
Maritime expeditions in the Indian Ocean	1405–1433

a larger Eurasian world shaped both China's own development and that of classical and postclassical world history more generally.

■ **Connection**

How did the Chinese and their nomadic neighbors to the north view each other?

From early times to the nineteenth century, China's most enduring and intense interaction with foreigners lay to the north, involving the many nomadic pastoral or semi-agricultural peoples of the steppes. Living in areas unable to sustain Chinese-style farming, the northern nomads had long focused their economies around the raising of livestock (sheep, cattle, goats) and the mastery of horse riding. Organized locally in small, mobile, kinship-based groups, sometimes called tribes, these peoples also periodically created much larger and powerful states or confederations that could draw upon the impressive horsemanship and military skills of virtually the entire male population of their societies. Such specialized pastoral societies needed grain and other agricultural products from China, and their leaders developed a taste for Chinese manufactured and luxury goods—wine and silk, for example—with which they could attract and reward followers. Thus the nomads were drawn like a magnet toward China, trading, raiding, and extorting in order to obtain the resources so vital to their way of life. For 2,000 years or more, pressure from the steppes and the intrusion of nomadic peoples were constant factors in China's historical development.

From the nomads' point of view, the threat often came from the Chinese, who periodically directed their own military forces deep into the steppes, built the Great Wall to keep the nomads out, and often proved unwilling to allow pastoral peoples easy access to trading opportunities within China.[15] And yet the Chinese needed the nomads. Their lands were the source of horses, so essential for the Chinese military. Other products of the steppes and the forests beyond, such as skins, furs, hides, and amber, were also of value in China. Furthermore, pastoral nomads controlled much of the Silk Road trading network, which funneled goods from the West into China. The continuing interaction between China and the northern nomads brought together peoples occupying different environments, practicing different economies, governing themselves with different institutions, and thinking about the world in quite different ways.

The Tribute System in Theory

An enduring outcome of this cross-cultural encounter was a particular view the Chinese held of themselves and of their neighbors, fully articulated by the time of the Han dynasty (200 B.C.E.–200 C.E.) and lasting for more than two millennia. That understanding cast China as the "middle kingdom," the center of the world, infinitely superior to the "barbarian" peoples beyond its borders. With its long history, great cities, refined tastes, sophisticated intellectual and artistic achievements, bureaucratic state, literate elite, and prosperous economy, China represented "civilization." All of this, in Chinese thinking, was in sharp contrast to the rude cultures and primitive life of the northern nomads, who continually moved about "like beasts and birds," lived in tents, ate mostly meat and milk, and practically lived on their horses, while making war on everyone within reach. Educated Chinese saw their own society as self-sufficient, requiring little from the outside world, while barbarians, quite understandably, sought access to China's wealth and wisdom. Furthermore, China was willing to permit that access under controlled conditions, for its sense of superiority did not preclude the possibility that barbarians could become civilized Chinese. China was a "radiating civilization," graciously shedding its light most fully to nearby barbarians and with diminished intensity to those farther away.[16]

■ **Connection**

What assumptions underlay the tribute system?

Such was the general understanding of literate Chinese about their own civilization in relation to northern nomads and other non-Chinese peoples. That worldview also took shape as a practical system for managing China's relationship with these people. Known to us as the "tribute system," it was a set of practices that required non-Chinese authorities to acknowledge Chinese superiority and their own subordinate place in a Chinese-centered world order. Foreigners seeking access to China had to send a delegation to the Chinese court, where they would perform the kowtow, a series of ritual bowings and prostrations, and present their tribute—produce of value from their countries—to the Chinese emperor. In return for these expressions of submission, he would grant permission for foreigners to trade in China's rich markets and would provide them with gifts or "bestowals," often worth far

The Tribute System
This Qing dynasty painting shows an idealized Chinese version of the tribute system. The Chinese emperor receives barbarian envoys, who perform rituals of subordination and present tribute in the form of a horse. (Réunion des Musées Nationaux/Art Resource, NY)

more than the tribute they had offered. This was the mechanism by which successive Chinese dynasties attempted to regulate their relationships with northern nomads; with neighboring states such as Korea, Vietnam, Tibet, and Japan; and, after 1500, with those European barbarians from across the sea.

Often, this system seemed to work. Over the centuries, countless foreign delegations proved willing to present their tribute, say the required words, and perform the necessary rituals in order to gain access to the material goods of China. Aspiring non-Chinese rulers also gained prestige as they basked in the reflected glory of even this subordinate association with the great Chinese civilization. The official titles, seals of office, and ceremonial robes they received from China proved useful in their local struggles for power.

The Tribute System in Practice

■ **Connection**

How did the tribute system in practice differ from the ideal Chinese understanding of its operation?

But the tribute system also disguised some realities that contradicted its assumptions. Frequently, China was confronting not separate and small-scale barbarian societies, but large and powerful nomadic empires able to deal with China on at least equal terms. An early nomadic confederacy was that of the Xiongnu, established about the same time as the Han dynasty and eventually reaching from Manchuria to Central Asia (see Map 4.5, p. 159). Devastating Xiongnu raids into northern China persuaded the Chinese emperor to negotiate an arrangement that recognized the nomadic state as a political equal, promised its leader a princess in marriage, and, most important, agreed to supply him annually with large quantities of grain, wine, and silk. Although these goods were officially termed "gifts," granted in accord with the tribute system, they were in fact tribute in reverse or even protection money. In return for these goods, so critical for the functioning of the nomadic state, the Xiongnu agreed to refrain from military incursions into China. The basic realities of the situation were summed up in this warning to the Han dynasty in the first century B.C.E.:

> Just make sure that the silks and grain stuffs you bring the Xiongnu are the right measure and quality, that's all. What's the need for talking? If the goods you deliver are up to measure and good quality, all right. But if there is any deficiency or the

quality is no good, then when the autumn harvest comes, we will take our horses and trample all over your crops.[17]

Something similar occurred during the Tang dynasty as a series of Turkic empires arose in Mongolia. Like the Xiongnu, they too extorted large "gifts" from the Chinese. One of these peoples, the Uighurs, actually rescued the Tang dynasty from a serious internal revolt in the 750s. In return, the Uighur leader gained one of the Chinese emperor's daughters as a wife and arranged a highly favorable exchange of poor-quality horses for high-quality silk that brought half a million rolls of the precious fabric annually into the Uighur lands. Despite the rhetoric of the tribute system, the Chinese were clearly not always able to dictate the terms of their relationship with the northern nomads.

Steppe nomads were generally not much interested in actually conquering and ruling China. It was easier and more profitable to extort goods from a functioning Chinese state. On occasion, though, that state broke down, and various nomadic groups moved in to "pick up the pieces," conquering and governing parts of China. Such a process took place following the fall of the Han dynasty and again after the collapse of the Tang dynasty, when the Khitan (907–1125) and then the Jin or Jurchen (1115–1234) peoples established states that encompassed parts of northern China as well as major areas of the steppes to the north. Both of them required the Chinese Song dynasty, located farther south, to deliver annually huge quantities of silk, silver, and tea, some of which found its way into the Silk Road trading network. The practice of "bestowing gifts on barbarians," long a part of the tribute system, allowed the proud Chinese to imagine that they were still in control of the situation even as they were paying heavily for protection from nomadic incursion. Those gifts, in turn, provided vital economic resources to nomadic states.

Cultural Influence across an Ecological Frontier

When nomadic peoples actually ruled parts of China, some of them adopted Chinese ways, employing Chinese advisers, governing according to Chinese practice, and, at least for the elite, immersing themselves in Chinese culture and learning. This process of "becoming Chinese" went furthest among the Jurchen, many of whom lived in northern China and learned to speak Chinese, wore Chinese clothing, married Chinese husbands and wives, and practiced Buddhism or Daoism. On the whole, however, Chinese culture had only a modest impact on the nomadic people of the northern steppes. Unlike the native peoples of southern China, who were gradually absorbed into Chinese culture, the pastoral societies north of the Great Wall generally retained their own cultural patterns. Few of them were incorporated, at least not for long, within a Chinese state, and most lived in areas where Chinese-style agriculture was simply impossible. Under these conditions, there were few incentives for adopting Chinese culture wholesale. But various modes of interaction—peaceful trade, military conflict, political negotiations, economic extortion, some cultural

■ **Connection**
In what ways did China and the nomads influence each other?

influence—continued across the ecological frontier that divided two quite distinct and separate ways of life. Each was necessary for the other. (See Visual Sources 8.2, 8.3, and 8.4, pp. 370–74, for another example of Chinese/nomadic interaction.)

On the Chinese side, elements of steppe culture had some influence in those parts of northern China that were periodically conquered and ruled by nomadic peoples. The founders of the Sui and Tang dynasties were in fact of mixed nomad and Chinese ancestry and came from the borderland region where a blended Chinese/Turkic culture had evolved. High-ranking members of the imperial family personally led their troops in battle in the style of Turkic warriors. Furthermore, Tang dynasty China was awash with foreign visitors from all over Asia—delegations bearing tribute, merchants carrying exotic goods, bands of clerics or religious pilgrims bringing new religions such as Christianity, Islam, Buddhism, and Manichaeism. For a time in the Tang dynasty, almost anything associated with "western barbarians"—Central Asians, Persians, Indians, Arabs—had great appeal among northern Chinese elites. Their music, dancing, clothing, foods, games, and artistic styles found favor among the upper classes. The more traditional southern Chinese, feeling themselves heir to the legacy of the Han dynasty, were sharply critical of their northern counterparts for allowing women too much freedom, for drinking yogurt rather than tea, for listening to "western" music, all of which they attributed to barbarian influence. Around 800 C.E., the poet Yuan Chen gave voice to a growing backlash against this too easy acceptance of things "western":

> Ever since the Western horsemen began raising smut and dust,
> Fur and fleece, rank and rancid, have filled Hsien and Lo [two Chinese cities].
> Women make themselves Western matrons by the study of Western makeup.
> Entertainers present Western tunes, in their devotion to Western music.[18]

Coping with China: Comparing Korea, Vietnam, and Japan

Also involved in tributary relationships with China during the postclassical era were the newly emerging states and civilizations of Korea, Vietnam, and Japan. Unlike the northern nomads, these societies were thoroughly agricultural and sedentary. During the first millennium C.E., they were part of a larger process—the globalization of civilization—which produced new city- and state-based societies in various parts of the world. Proximity to their giant Chinese neighbor decisively shaped the histories of these new East Asian civilizations, for all of them borrowed major elements of Chinese culture. But unlike the native peoples of southern China, who largely became Chinese, the peoples of Korea, Vietnam, and Japan did not. They retained distinctive identities, which have lasted into modern times. While resisting Chinese political domination, they also appreciated Chinese culture and sought the source of Chinese wealth and power. In such ways, these smaller East Asian civilizations resembled the "developing" Afro-Asian societies of the twentieth century, which embraced "modernity" and elements of Western culture, while trying to maintain their political and cultural independence from the European and American centers of that modern way of life. Korea, Vietnam, and Japan, however, encountered China and responded to it in quite different ways.

■ **Comparison**

In what different ways did Korea, Vietnam, and Japan experience and respond to Chinese influence?

Korea and China

Immediately adjacent to northeastern China, the Korean peninsula and its people have long lived in the shadow of their imposing neighbor. Temporary Chinese conquest of northern Korea during the Han dynasty and some colonization by Chinese settlers provided an initial channel for Chinese cultural influence, particularly in the form of Buddhism. Early Korean states, which emerged in the fourth through seventh centuries C.E., all referred to their rulers with the Chinese term *wang* (king). Bitter rivals with one another, these states strenuously resisted Chinese political control, except when they found it advantageous to join with China against a local enemy. In the seventh century, one of these states—the Silla kingdom—allied with Tang dynasty China to bring some political unity to the peninsula for the first time. But Chinese efforts to set up puppet regimes and to assimilate Koreans to Chinese culture provoked sharp military resistance, persuading the Chinese to withdraw their military forces in 688 and to establish a tributary relationship with a largely independent Korea.

Under a succession of dynasties—the Silla (688–900), Koryo (918–1392), and Yi (1392–1910)—Korea generally maintained its political independence while participating in China's tribute system. Its leaders actively embraced the connection with China and, especially during the Silla dynasty, sought to turn their small state into a miniature version of Tang China.

Tribute missions to China provided legitimacy for Korean rulers and knowledge of Chinese court life and administrative techniques, which they sought to replicate back home. A new capital city of Kumsong was modeled directly on the Chinese capital of Chang'an. Tribute missions also enabled both official and private trade, mostly in luxury goods such as ceremonial clothing, silks, fancy teas, Confucian and Buddhist texts, and artwork—all of which enriched the lives of a Korean aristocracy that was becoming increasingly Chinese in culture. Thousands of Korean students were sent to China, where they studied primarily Confucianism but also natural sciences and the arts. Buddhist monks visited centers of learning and pilgrimage in China and brought back popular forms of Chinese Buddhism, which quickly took root in Korea. Schools for the study of Confucianism, using texts in the Chinese language, were established in Korea. In these ways, Korea became a part of the expanding world of Chinese culture, and refugees from the peninsula's many wars carried Chinese culture to Japan as well.

These efforts to plant Confucian values and Chinese culture in Korea had what one scholar has called an "overwhelmingly negative" impact on

Korean Kingdoms about 500 C.E.

Korean women, particularly after 1300.[19] Early Chinese observers noticed, and strongly disapproved of, "free choice" marriages in Korea as well as the practice of women singing and dancing together late at night. With the support of the Korean court, Chinese models of family life and female behavior, especially among the elite, gradually replaced the more flexible Korean patterns. Earlier a Korean woman had generally given birth and raised her young children in her parents' home, where she was often joined by her husband. This was now strongly discouraged, for it was deeply offensive to Confucian orthodoxy, which held that a married woman belonged to her husband's family. Some Korean customs—funeral rites in which a husband was buried in the sacred plot of his wife's family, the remarriage of widowed or divorced women, and female inheritance of property—eroded under the pressure of Confucian orthodoxy. So too did the practice of plural marriages for men. In 1413, a legal distinction between primary and secondary wives required men to identify one of their wives as primary. Because she and her children now had special privileges and status, sharp new tensions emerged within families. Korean restrictions on elite women, especially widows, came to exceed even those in China itself.

Still, Korea remained Korean. After 688, the country's political independence, though periodically threatened, was largely intact. Chinese cultural influence, except for Buddhism, had little impact beyond the aristocracy and certainly did not penetrate the lives of Korea's serf-like peasants. Nor did it register among Korea's many slaves, amounting to about one-third of the country's population by 1100 C.E. A Chinese-style examination system to recruit government officials, though encouraged by some Korean rulers, never assumed the prominence that it gained in Tang and Song dynasty China. Korea's aristocratic class was able to maintain an even stronger monopoly on bureaucratic office than their Chinese counterparts. And in the 1400s, Korea moved toward greater cultural independence by developing a phonetic alphabet, known as *hangul*, for writing the Korean language. Although resisted by male conservative elites, who were long accustomed to using the more prestigious Chinese characters to write Korean, this new form of writing gradually took hold, especially in private correspondence, in popular fiction, and among women. Clearly part of the Chinese world order, Korea nonetheless retained a distinctive culture as well as a separate political existence.

Vietnam and China

At the southern fringe of the Chinese cultural world, the people who eventually came to be called Vietnamese had a broadly similar historical encounter with China. As in Korea, the elite culture of Vietnam borrowed heavily from China—adopting Confucianism, Daoism, Buddhism, administrative techniques, the examination system, artistic and literary styles—even as its popular culture remained distinctive. And, like Korea, Vietnam achieved political independence, while participating fully in the tribute system as a vassal state.

Vietnam

Route of Vietnamese expansion
Present-day boundaries of Vietnam

But there were differences as well. The cultural heartland of Vietnam in the Red River valley was fully incorporated into the Chinese state for more than a thousand years (III B.C.E.–939 C.E.), far longer than corresponding parts of Korea. Regarded by the Chinese as "southern barbarians," the Vietnamese were ruled by Chinese officials who expected to fully assimilate this rich rice-growing region into China culturally as well as politically. To these officials, it was simply a further extension of the southward expansion of Chinese civilization. Thus Chinese-style irrigated agriculture was introduced; Vietnamese elites were brought into the local bureaucracy and educated in Confucian-based schools; Chinese replaced the local language in official business; Chinese clothing and hairstyles became mandatory; and large numbers of Chinese, some fleeing internal conflicts at home, flooded into the relative security of what they referred to as "the pacified south," while often despising the local people.[20]

The heavy pressure of the Chinese presence generated not only a Vietnamese elite thoroughly schooled in Chinese culture but also periodic rebellions. In 39 C.E., a short-lived but long-remembered uprising was launched by two sisters, daughters of a local leader deposed by the Chinese. One of them, Trung Trac, whose husband had been executed, famously addressed some 30,000 soldiers, while dressed in full military regalia:

> Foremost I will avenge my country.
> Second I will restore the Hung lineage.
> Third I will avenge the death of my husband.
> Lastly I vow that these goals will be accomplished.[21]

When the rebellion was crushed several years later, the Trung sisters committed suicide rather than surrender to the Chinese, but in literature, monuments, and public memory, they long remained powerful symbols of Vietnamese resistance to Chinese aggression.

The weakening of the Tang dynasty in the early tenth century C.E. finally enabled a particularly large rebellion to establish Vietnam as a separate state, though one that carefully maintained its tributary role, sending repeated missions to do homage at the Chinese court. Nonetheless, successive Vietnamese dynasties found the Chinese approach to government useful, styling their rulers as emperors, claiming the Mandate of Heaven, and making use of Chinese court rituals, while expanding their state

The Trung Sisters
Although it occurred nearly 2,000 years ago, the revolt of the Trung sisters against Chinese occupation remains a national symbol of Vietnam's independence, as illustrated by this modern Vietnamese painting of the two women, astride war elephants, leading their followers into battle against the Chinese invaders. (From William J. Duiker, *Sacred War: Nationalism and Revolution in a Divided Vietnam* [New York: The McGraw-Hill Companies, 1995])

steadily southward. More so than in Korea, a Chinese-based examination system in Vietnam functioned to undermine an established aristocracy, to provide some measure of social mobility for commoners, and to create a merit-based scholar-gentry class to staff the bureaucracy. Furthermore, the Vietnamese elite class remained deeply committed to Chinese culture, viewing their own country less as a separate nation than as a southern extension of a universal civilization, the only one they knew.[22]

Beyond the elite, however, there remained much that was uniquely Vietnamese, such as a distinctive language, a fondness for cockfighting, the habit of chewing betel nuts, and a greater role for women in social and economic life. Female nature deities and even a "female Buddha" continued to be part of Vietnamese popular religion, even as Confucian-based ideas took root among the elite. These features of Vietnamese life reflected larger patterns of Southeast Asian culture that distinguished it from China. And like Korea, the Vietnamese developed a variation of Chinese writing called *chu nom* ("southern script"), which provided the basis for an independent national literature.

Japan and China

Unlike Korea and Vietnam, the Japanese islands were physically separated from China by 100 miles or more of ocean and were never successfully invaded or conquered by their giant mainland neighbor. Thus Japan's very extensive borrowing from Chinese civilization was wholly voluntary, rather than occurring under conditions of direct military threat or outright occupation. The high point of that borrowing took place during the seventh to the ninth centuries C.E., as the first more or less unified Japanese state began to emerge from dozens of small clan-based aristocratic chiefdoms. That state found much that was useful in Tang dynasty China and set out, deliberately and systematically, to transform Japan into a centralized bureaucratic state on the Chinese model. (See Documents: The Making of Japanese Civilization, pp. 406–16.)

Japan

The initial leader of this effort was Shotoku Taishi (572–622), a prominent aristocrat from one of the major clans. He launched a series of large-scale missions to China, which took hundreds of Japanese monks, scholars, artists, and students to the mainland, and when they returned, they put into practice what they had learned. He issued the Seventeen Article Constitution, proclaiming the Japanese ruler as a Chinese-style emperor and encouraging both Buddhism and Confucianism. In good Confucian fashion, that document emphasized the moral quality of rulers as a foundation for social harmony (see Document 9.1, pp. 406–08). In the decades that followed, Japanese authorities adopted Chinese-style court rituals and a system of court rankings for officials as well as the Chinese calendar. Subsequently, they likewise established Chinese-based taxation systems, law codes, government ministries, and provincial administration, at least on paper. Two capital cities, first Nara and then Heian (Kyoto), arose, both modeled on the Chinese capital of Chang'an.

Chinese culture, no less than its political practices, also found favor in Japan. Various schools of Chinese Buddhism took root, first among the educated and literate classes and later more broadly in Japanese society, affecting, according to one scholar, "nearly every aspect of Japanese life" (see Document 9.2, pp. 408–10). Art, architecture, education, medicine, views of the afterlife, attitudes toward suffering and the impermanence of life—all of this and more reflected the influence of Buddhist culture in Japan.[23] The Chinese writing system—and with it an interest in historical writing, calligraphy, and poetry—likewise proved attractive among the elite.

The absence of any compelling threat from China made it possible for the Japanese to be selective in their borrowing. By the tenth century, deliberate efforts to absorb additional elements of Chinese culture diminished, and formal tribute missions to China stopped, although private traders and Buddhist monks continued to make the difficult journey to the mainland. Over many centuries, the Japanese combined what they had assimilated from China with elements of their own tradition into a distinctive Japanese civilization, which differed from Chinese culture in many ways.

In the political realm, for example, the Japanese never succeeded in creating an effective centralized and bureaucratic state to match that of China. Although the court and the emperor retained an important ceremonial and cultural role, their real political authority over the country gradually diminished in favor of competing aristocratic families, both at court and in the provinces. A Chinese-style university trained officials, but rather than serving as a mechanism for recruiting talented commoners into the political elite, it enrolled students who were largely the sons of court aristocrats.

As political power became increasingly decentralized, local authorities developed their own military forces, the famous *samurai* warrior class of Japanese society. Bearing their exquisite curved swords, the samurai developed a distinctive set of values featuring great skill in martial arts, bravery, loyalty, endurance, honor, and a preference for death over surrender. This was *bushido*, the way of the warrior, illustrated in Document 9.5, pages 414–16. Japan's celebration of the samurai and of military virtues contrasted sharply with China's emphasis on intellectual achievements and political officeholding, which were accorded higher prestige than bearing arms. "The educated men of the land," wrote a Chinese minister in the eleventh century, "regard the carrying of arms as a disgrace."[24] The Japanese, clearly, did not agree.

Religiously as well, Japan remained distinctive. Although Buddhism in many forms took hold in the country, it never completely replaced the native beliefs and practices, which focused attention on numerous *kami*, sacred spirits associated with human ancestors and various natural phenomena. Much later referred to as Shinto, this tradition provided legitimacy to the imperial family, based on claims of descent from the sun goddess, as illustrated in Document 9.3, pages 410–12. Because veneration of the kami lacked an elaborate philosophy or ritual, it conflicted very little with Buddhism. In fact, numerous kami were assimilated into Japanese Buddhism as local expressions of Buddhist deities or principles.

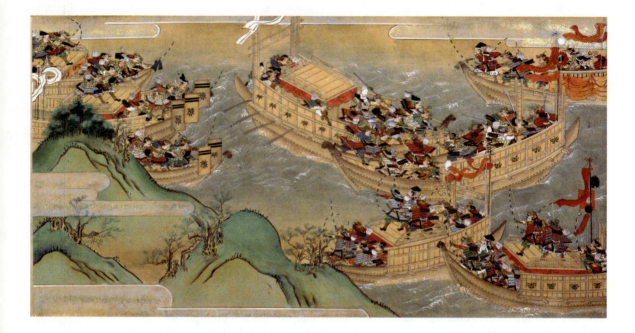

The Samurai of Japan
This twelfth-century painting depicts the famous naval battle of Dan-no-ura (1185), in which the samurai warriors of two rival clans fought to the death. Many of the defeated Taira warriors, along with some of their women, plunged into the sea rather than surrender to their Minamoto rivals. The prominence of martial values in Japanese culture was one of the ways in which Japan differed from its Chinese neighbor, despite much borrowing. (Tokyo National Museum. Image: TNM Images Archives. Source: http://TnmArchives.jp/)

■ **Comparison**

In what different ways did Japanese and Korean women experience the pressures of Confucian orthodoxy?

Japanese literary and artistic culture likewise evolved in distinctive ways, despite much borrowing from China. As in Korea and Vietnam, there emerged a unique writing system that combined Chinese characters with a series of phonetic symbols. A highly stylized Japanese poetic form, known as *tanka*, developed early and has remained a favored means of expression ever since. Particularly during the Heian period of Japanese history (794–1192), a highly refined esthetic culture found expression at the imperial court, even as the court's real political authority melted away. Court aristocrats and their ladies lived in splendor, composed poems, arranged flowers, and conducted their love affairs. "What counted," wrote one scholar, "was the proper costume, the right ceremonial act, the successful turn of phrase in a poem, and the appropriate expression of refined taste."[25] Much of our knowledge of this courtly culture comes from the work of women writers, who composed their diaries and novels in the vernacular Japanese script, rather than in the classical Chinese used by elite men. *The Tale of Genji*, a Japanese novel written by the woman author Murasaki Shikibu around 1000, provides an intimate picture of the intrigues and romances of court life. So too does Sei Shonagon's *Pillow Book*, excerpted in Document 9.4, pages 412–14.

At this level of society, Japan's women, unlike those in Korea, largely escaped the more oppressive features of Chinese Confucian culture, such as the prohibition of remarriage for widows, seclusion within the home, and foot binding. Perhaps this is because the most powerful Chinese influence on Japan occurred during the Tang dynasty, when Chinese elite women enjoyed considerable freedom. Japanese women continued to inherit property; Japanese married couples often lived apart or with the wife's family; and marriages were made and broken easily. None of this corresponded to Confucian values. When Japanese women did begin to lose status in the twelfth century and later, it had less to do with Confucian pressures than with the rise of a warrior culture. As the personal relationships of samurai warriors to their lords replaced marriage alliances as a political strategy, the influence of women in political life was reduced, but this was an internal Japanese phenomenon, not a reflection of Chinese influence.

Japan's ability to borrow extensively from China while developing its own distinctive civilization perhaps provided a model for its encounter with the West in the nineteenth century. Then, as before, Japan borrowed selectively from a foreign culture without losing either its political independence or its cultural uniqueness.

China and the Eurasian World Economy

Beyond China's central role in East Asia was its economic interaction with the wider world of Eurasia generally. On the one hand, China's remarkable economic growth, taking place during the Tang and Song dynasties, could hardly be contained within China's borders and clearly had a major impact throughout Eurasia. On the other hand, China was recipient as well as donor in the economic interactions of the postclassical era, and its own economic achievements owed something to the stimulus of contact with the larger world.

Spillovers: China's Impact on Eurasia

One of the outcomes of China's economic revolution lay in the diffusion of its many technological innovations to peoples and places far from East Asia as the movements of traders, soldiers, slaves, and pilgrims conveyed Chinese achievements abroad. Chinese techniques for producing salt by solar evaporation spread to the Islamic world and later to Christian Europe. Papermaking, known in China since the Han dynasty, spread to Korea and Vietnam by the fourth century C.E., to Japan and India by the seventh, to the Islamic world by the eighth, to Muslim Spain by 1150, to France and Germany in the 1300s, and to England in the 1490s. Printing, likewise a Chinese invention, rapidly reached Korea, where movable type became a highly developed technique, and Japan as well. Both technologies were heavily influenced by Buddhism, which accorded religious merit to the act of reproducing sacred texts. The Islamic world, however, valued handwritten calligraphy highly and generally resisted printing as impious until the nineteenth century. The adoption of printing in Europe was likewise delayed because of the absence of paper until the fourteenth century. Then movable type was reinvented by Johannes Gutenberg in the fifteenth century, although it is unclear whether he was aware of Chinese and Korean precedents. With implications for mass literacy, bureaucracy, scholarship, the spread of

■ **Connection**

In what ways did China participate in the world of Eurasian commerce and exchange, and with what outcomes?

religion, and the exchange of information, papermaking and printing were Chinese innovations of revolutionary and global dimensions.

Chinese technologies were seldom simply transferred from one place to another. More often a particular Chinese technique or product stimulated innovations in more distant lands in accordance with local needs.[26] For example, as the Chinese formula for gunpowder, invented around 1000, became available in Europe, together with some early and simple firearms, these innovations triggered the development of cannons in the early fourteenth century. Soon cannons appeared in the Islamic world and by 1356 in China itself, which first used cast iron rather than bronze in their construction. But the highly competitive European state system drove the "gunpowder revolution" much further and more rapidly than in China's imperial state. Chinese textile, metallurgical, and naval technologies likewise stimulated imitation and innovation all across Eurasia. An example is the magnetic compass, a Chinese invention eagerly embraced by mariners of many cultural backgrounds as they traversed the Indian Ocean.

In addition to its technological influence, China's prosperity during the Song dynasty greatly stimulated commercial life and market-based behavior all across the Eurasian trading world. China's products—silk, porcelain, lacquerware—found eager buyers from Japan to East Africa, and everywhere in between. The immense size and wealth of China's domestic economy also provided a ready market for hundreds of commodities from afar. For example, the lives of many thousands of people in the spice-producing islands of what is now Indonesia were transformed as they came to depend on Chinese consumers' demand for their products. "[O]ne hundred million [Chinese] people," wrote historian William McNeill, "increasingly caught up within a commercial network, buying and selling to supplement every day's livelihood, made a significant difference to the way other human beings made their livings through-out a large part of the civilized world."[27] Such was the ripple effect of China's economic revolution.

On the Receiving End: China as Economic Beneficiary

Chinese economic growth and technological achievements significantly shaped the Eurasian world of the postclassical era, but that pattern of interaction was surely not a one-way street, for China too was changed by its engagement with a wider world. During this period, for example, China had learned about the cultivation and processing of both cotton and sugar from India. From Vietnam, around 1000, China gained access to the new, fast-ripening, and drought-resistant strains of rice that made a highly productive rice-based agriculture possible in the drier and more rugged regions of southern China. This marked a major turning point in Chinese history as the frontier region south of the Yangzi River grew rapidly in population, overtaking the traditional centers of Chinese civilization in the north.

Technologically as well, China's extraordinary burst of creativity owed something to the stimulus of cross-cultural contact. Awareness of Persian windmills, for example, spurred the development of a distinct but related device in China. Printing arose from China's growing involvement with the world of Buddhism, which put a spiritual premium on the reproduction of the Buddha's image and of short religious texts that were carried as charms. It was in Buddhist monasteries during the Tang dynasty that the long-established practice of printing with seals was elaborated by Chinese monks into woodblock printing. The first printed book, in 868 C.E., was a famous Buddhist text, the *Diamond Sutra*. Gunpowder too seems to have had an Indian and Buddhist connection. An Indian Buddhist monk traveling in China in 644 C.E. identified soils that contained saltpeter and showed that they produced a purple flame when put into a fire. This was the beginning of Chinese experiments, which finally led to a reliable recipe for gunpowder.

A further transforming impact of China's involvement with a wider world derived from its growing participation in Indian Ocean trade. By the Tang dynasty, thousands of ships annually visited the ports of southern China, and settled communities of foreign merchants—Arabs, Persians, Indians, Southeast Asians—turned some of these cities into cosmopolitan centers. Buddhist temples, Muslim mosques and cemeteries, and Hindu phallic sculptures graced the skyline of Quanzhou, a coastal city in southern China. Occasionally the tensions of cultural diversity erupted in violence, such as the massacre of tens of thousands of foreigners in Canton during the 870s when Chinese rebel forces sacked the city. Indian Ocean commerce also contributed much to the transformation of southern China from a subsistence economy to one more heavily based on producing for export. In the process, merchants achieved a degree of social acceptance not known before, including their frequent appointment to high-ranking bureaucratic positions. Finally, much-beloved stories of the monkey god, widely popular even in contemporary China, derived from Indian sources transmitted by Indian Ocean commerce.[28]

China and Buddhism

By far the most important gift that China received from India was neither cotton, nor sugar, nor the knowledge of saltpeter, but a religion, Buddhism. The gradual assimilation of this South Asian religious tradition into Chinese culture illustrates the process of cultural encounter and adaptation and invites comparison with the spread of Christianity into Europe. Until the adoption of Marxism in the twentieth century, Buddhism was the only large-scale cultural borrowing in Chinese history. It also made China into a launching pad for Buddhism's dispersion to Korea and from there to Japan as well. Thus, as Buddhism faded in the land of its birth, it became solidly rooted in much of East Asia, providing an element of cultural commonality for a vast region (see Map 9.2).

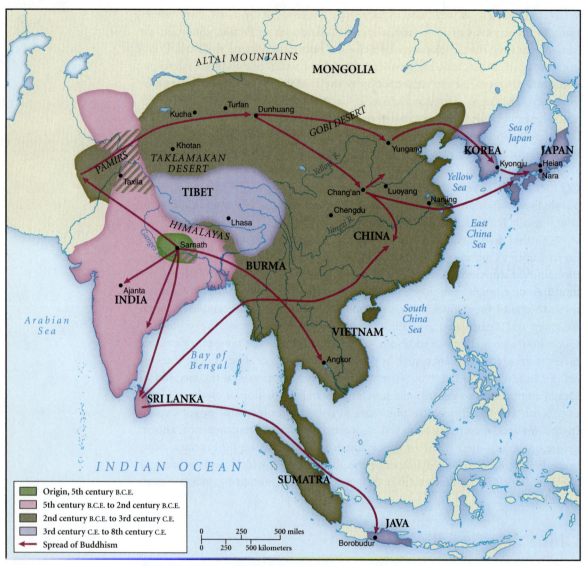

Map 9.2   The World of Asian Buddhism
Born in India, Buddhism later spread widely throughout much of Asia to provide a measure of cultural or religious commonality across this vast region.

Making Buddhism Chinese

■ Change

What facilitated the rooting of Buddhism within China?

Buddhism initially entered China via the Silk Road trading network during the first and second centuries C.E. The stability and prosperity of the Han dynasty, then at its height, ensured that the new "barbarian" religion held little appeal for native Chinese. Furthermore, the Indian culture from which Buddhism sprang was at odds with Chinese understandings of the world in many ways. Buddhism's commitment to a secluded and monastic life for monks and nuns seemed to dishonor Chinese family values, and its concern for individual salvation or enlightenment appeared selfish, contradicting the social orientation of Confucian thinking. Its abstract philosophy ran counter to the more concrete, "this-worldly" concerns of Chinese thinkers; and the Buddhist concept of infinite eons of time, endlessly repeating themselves, was quite a stretch for the Chinese, who normally thought in terms of finite family generations or dynastic cycles. No wonder that for the first several centuries C.E., Buddhism was largely the preserve of foreign merchants and monks living in China.

In the half millennium between roughly 300 and 800 C.E., however, Buddhism took solid root in China within both elite and popular culture, becoming a permanent, though fluctuating, presence in Chinese life. How did this remarkable transformation unfold? It began, arguably, with the collapse of the Han dynasty around 200 C.E. The chaotic, violent, and politically fragmented centuries that followed seriously discredited Confucianism and opened the door to alternative understandings of the world. Nomadic rulers, now governing much of northern China, found Buddhism useful in part because it was foreign. "We were born out of the marches," declared one of them, "and though we are unworthy, we have complied with our appointed destiny and govern the Chinese as their prince.... Buddha being a barbarian god is the very one we should worship."[29] Rulers and elite families provided money and land that enabled the building of many Buddhist monasteries, temples, and works of art. In southern China, where many northern aristocrats had fled following the disastrous decline of the Han dynasty, Buddhism provided some comfort in the face of a collapsing society. Its emphasis on ritual, morality, and contemplation represented an intellectually and esthetically satisfying response to times that were so clearly out of joint.

Meanwhile, Buddhist monasteries increasingly provided an array of social services for ordinary people. In them, travelers found accommodation; those fleeing from China's many upheavals discovered a place of refuge; desperate people received charity; farmers borrowed seed for the next planting; the sick were treated; children learned to read. And for many, Buddhism was associated with access to magical powers as reports of miracles abounded. Battles were won, rain descended on drought-ridden areas, diseases were cured, and guilt was relieved—all through the magical ministrations of charismatic monks.

Accompanying all of this was a serious effort by monks, scholars, and translators to present this Indian religion in terms that Chinese could relate to. Thus the Buddhist term *dharma*, referring to the Buddha's teaching, was translated as *dao*, or "the way," a notion long familiar in both Daoist and Confucian thinking (see Chapter 5). The Buddhist notion of "morality" was translated with the Confucian term that referred to "filial submission and obedience." Some Indian concepts were modified in the process of translation. For example, the idea that "husband supports wife," which reflected a considerable respect for women and mothers in early Indian Buddhism, became in translation "husband controls wife."[30]

As Buddhism took hold in China, it was primarily in its broader Mahayana form—complete with numerous deities, the veneration of relics, many heavens and hells, and bodhisattvas to aid the believer—rather than the more psychological and individualistic Theravada Buddhism (see Chapter 5 and Visual Source 5.4, p. 233). One of the most popular forms of Buddhism in China was the Pure Land School, in which faithfully repeating the name of an earlier Buddha, the Amitabha, was sufficient to ensure rebirth in a beautifully described heavenly realm, the Pure Land. In its emphasis on salvation by faith, without arduous study or intensive meditation, Pure Land Buddhism became a highly popular and authentically Chinese version of the Indian faith (see Visual Source 5.5, p. 234).

China's reunification under the Sui and early Tang dynasties witnessed growing state support for Buddhism. The Sui emperor Wendi (reigned 581–604 C.E.) had monasteries constructed at the base of China's five sacred mountains, further identifying the imported religion with traditional Chinese culture. He even used Buddhism to justify his military campaigns. "With a hundred victories in a hundred battles," he declared, "we promote the practice of the ten Buddhist virtues."[31] With state support and growing popular acceptance, monasteries became centers of great wealth, largely exempt from taxation, owning large estates; running businesses such as oil presses, water mills, and pawn shops; collecting gems, gold, and lavish works of art; and even employing slaves. But Buddhism, while solidly entrenched in Chinese life by the early Tang dynasty, never achieved the independence from state authorities that the Christian church acquired in Europe. The examinations for becoming a monk were supervised by the state, and education in the monasteries included the required study of the Confucian classics. In the mid-ninth century, the state showed quite dramatically just how much control it could exercise over the Buddhist establishment.

Losing State Support: The Crisis of Chinese Buddhism

■ **Change**
What were the major sources of opposition to Buddhism within China?

The impressive growth of Chinese Buddhism was accompanied by a persistent undercurrent of resistance and criticism. Some saw the Buddhist establishment, at least potentially, as a "state within a state" and a challenge to imperial authority. More important was a deepening resentment of its enormous wealth. One fifth-century critic, referring to monks, put the issue squarely: "Why is it that their ideals are noble and far-reaching and their activities still are base and common? [They] become merchants and engage in barter, wrangling with the masses for profit."[32] When state treasuries were short of funds, government officials cast a covetous eye on wealthy and tax-exempt monasteries. Furthermore, Buddhism was clearly of foreign origin and offensive for that reason to some Confucian and Daoist thinkers. The celibacy of the monks and their withdrawal from society, the critics argued, undermined the Confucian-based family system of Chinese tradition.

Such criticisms took on new meaning in the changed environment of China after about 800 C.E. Following centuries of considerable foreign influence in China, a growing resentment against foreign culture, particularly among the literate classes, increasingly took hold. The turning point may well have been the An Lushan rebellion (755–763), in which a general of foreign origin led a major revolt against the Tang dynasty. Whatever its origins, an increasingly xenophobic reaction set in among the upper classes, reflected in a desire to return to an imagined "purity" of earlier times.[33] In this setting, the old criticisms of Buddhism became more sharply focused. In 819, Han Yu, a leading figure in the Confucian counterattack on Buddhism, wrote a scathing memorial to the emperor, criticizing his willingness to honor a relic of the Buddha's finger.

> Now the Buddha was of barbarian origin. His language differed from Chinese speech; his clothes were of a different cut; his mouth did not pronounce the prescribed words of the Former Kings.... He did not recognize the relationship between prince and subject, nor the sentiments of father and son.... I pray that Your Majesty will turn this bone over to the officials that it may be cast into water or fire.[34]

Several decades later, the Chinese state took direct action against the Buddhist establishment as well as against other foreign religions. A series of imperial decrees between 841 and 845 ordered some 260,000 monks and nuns to return to normal life as tax-paying citizens. Thousands of monasteries, temples, and shrines were either destroyed or turned to public use, while the state confiscated the lands, money, metals, and serfs belonging to monasteries. Buddhists were now forbidden to use gold, silver, copper, iron, and gems in constructing their images. These actions dealt a serious blow to Chinese Buddhism. Its scholars and monks were scattered, its creativity diminished, and its institutions came even more firmly under state control.

Despite this persecution, Buddhism did not vanish from China. At the level of elite culture, its philosophical ideas played a role in the reformulation of Confucian thinking that took place during the Song dynasty. At the village level, Buddhism became one element of Chinese popular religion, which also included the veneration of ancestors, the honoring of Confucius, and Daoist shrines and rituals. Temples frequently included statues of Confucius, Laozi, and the Buddha, with little sense of any incompatibility among them. "Every black-haired son of Han," the Chinese have long said, "wears a Confucian thinking cap, a Daoist robe, and Buddhist sandals." Unlike Europe, where an immigrant religion triumphed over and excluded all other faiths, Buddhism in China became assimilated into Chinese culture alongside its other traditions.

Reflections: Why Do Things Change?

The rapidity of change in modern societies is among the most distinctive features of recent history, but change and transformation, though at various rates, have been constants in the human story since the very beginning. Explaining how and why human societies change is perhaps the central issue that historians confront, no matter which societies or periods of time they study. Those who specialize in the history of some particular culture or civilization often emphasize sources of change operating within those societies, although there is intense disagreement as to which are most significant. The ideas of great thinkers, the policies of leaders, struggles for power, the conflict of classes, the impact of new technologies, the growth or decline in population, variations in local climate or weather—all of these and more have their advocates as the primary motor of historical transformation.

Of course, it is not necessary to choose among them. The history of classical and postclassical China illustrates the range of internal factors that have driven change in that civilization. The political conflicts of the "era of warring states" provided the setting and the motivation for the emergence of Confucianism and Daoism, which in turn have certainly shaped the character and texture of Chinese civilization over many centuries. The personal qualities and brutal policies of Shihuangdi surely played a role in China's unification and in the brief duration of the Qin dynasty. The subsequent creation of a widespread network of canals and waterways as well as the country's technological achievements served to maintain that unity over very long periods of time. But the massive inequalities of Chinese society generated the peasant upheavals, which periodically shattered that unity and led to new ruling dynasties. Sometimes natural events, such as droughts and floods, triggered those rebellions.

World historians, more than those who study particular civilizations or nations, have been inclined to find the primary source of change in contact with strangers, in external connections and interactions, whether direct or indirect. The history of China and East Asia provide plenty of examples for this point of view as well. Conceptions of China as the "middle kingdom," infinitely superior to all surrounding societies, grew out of centuries of involvement with its neighbors. Some of those neighbors became Chinese as China's imperial reach grew, especially to the south. Even those that did not, such as Korea, Vietnam, and Japan, were decisively transformed by proximity to the "radiating civilization" of China. China's own cuisine, so distinctive in recent centuries, may well be a quite recent invention, drawing heavily on Indian and Southeast Asian cooking. Buddhism, of course, is an obvious borrowing from abroad, although its incorporation into Chinese civilization and its ups and downs within China owed much to internal cultural and political realities.

In the end, clear distinctions between internal and external sources of change in China's history—or that of any other society—are perhaps misleading. The boundary between "inside" and "outside" is itself a constantly changing line. Should the borderlands of northern China, where Chinese and Turkic peoples met and mingled, be regarded as internal or external to China itself? And, as the histories of Chinese Buddhism and of Japanese culture so clearly indicate, what comes from beyond is always transformed by what it encounters within.

Second Thoughts

What's the Significance?

Sui dynasty

Tang dynasty

Song dynasty economic revolution

Hangzhou

foot binding

tribute system

Xiongnu

Khitan/Jurchen people

Silla dynasty (Korea)

hangul

chu nom

Trung sisters

Shotoku Taishi

bushido

Chinese Buddhism

Emperor Wendi

To assess your mastery of the material in this chapter, visit the **Student Center** at bedfordstmartins.com/strayer.

Big Picture Questions

1. In what ways did Tang and Song dynasty China resemble the classical Han dynasty period, and in what ways had China changed?
2. Based on this chapter, how would you respond to the idea that China was a self-contained or isolated civilization?
3. In what different ways did nearby peoples experience their giant Chinese neighbor, and how did they respond to it?
4. How can you explain the changing fortunes of Buddhism in China?
5. How did China influence the world beyond East Asia? How was China itself transformed by its encounters with a wider world?

Next Steps: For Further Study

Samuel Adshead, *Tang China: The Rise of the East in World History* (2004). Explores the role of China within the larger world.

Patricia Ebrey, *The Inner Quarters* (1993). A balanced account of the gains and losses experienced by Chinese women during the changes of the Song dynasty.

Mark Elvin, *The Pattern of the Chinese Past* (1973). A classic account of the Chinese economic revolution.

Edward Shaffer, *The Golden Peaches of Samarkand* (1985). Examines the interaction between China and Central Asia during the Tang dynasty.

Murasaki Shikibu, *The Tale of Genji,* translated by Royall Tyler (2002). Written around 1000, this saga of Japanese court life is sometimes called the world's first novel.

Arthur F. Wright, *Buddhism in Chinese History* (1959). An older account filled with wonderful stories and anecdotes.

Upper River during the Qing Ming Festival, http://www.ibiblio.org/ulysses/gec/painting/qingming/full.htm. A scrolling reproduction of a huge Chinese painting, showing in detail the Song dynasty city of Kaifeng.

For Web sites and additional documents related to this chapter, see **Make History** at bedfordstmartins.com/strayer.

Documents

Considering the Evidence:
The Making of Japanese Civilization

Japan's historical development during the postclassical era places it among the third-wave civilizations—Russian, Swahili, Srivijaya, west European, Islamic—that took shape between 500 and 1500. Each of them was distinctive in particular ways, but all of them followed the general patterns of earlier civilizations in the creation of cities, states, stratified societies, patriarchies, written languages, and more. Furthermore, many of them borrowed extensively from nearby and older civilizations. In the case of Japan, that borrowing was primarily from China, its towering neighbor to the west. The documents that follow provide glimpses of a distinctive Japanese civilization in the making, even as that civilization selectively incorporated elements of Chinese thinking and practice (see pp. 394–97).

Document 9.1

Japanese Political Ideals

As an early Japanese state gradually took shape in the sixth and seventh centuries, it was confronted by serious internal divisions of clan, faction, and religion. Externally, Japanese forces had been expelled from their footholds in Korea, while Japan also faced the immense power and attractiveness of a reunified China under the Sui and Tang dynasties (see pp. 380–85). In these circumstances, Japanese authorities sought to strengthen their own emerging state by adopting a range of Chinese political values and practices. This Chinese influence in Japanese political thinking was particularly apparent in the so-called Seventeen Article Constitution issued by Shotoku, which was a set of general guidelines for court officials.

- What elements of Buddhist, Confucian, or Legalist thinking are reflected in this document? (Review pp. 192–95 and 199–201 and Documents 4.3, pp. 174–75, and 5.1, pp. 217–19.)

- What can you infer about the internal problems that Japanese rulers faced?

- How might Shotoku define an ideal Japanese state?

- Why do you think Shotoku omitted any mention of traditional Japanese gods or spirits or the Japanese claim that their emperor was descended from the sun goddess Amaterasu?

Despite this apparent embrace of all things Chinese, Shotoku's attitude toward China itself is less clear. In various letters that he sent to the Chinese Sui dynasty ruler, Shotoku inscribed them as follows: "The Son of Heaven of the Land of the Rising Sun to the Son of Heaven of the Land of the Setting Sun." Another read: "The Eastern Emperor Greets the Western Emperor."[35] Considering their country as the Middle Kingdom, greatly superior to all its neighbors, Chinese court officials were incensed at these apparent assertions of equality. It is not clear whether Shotoku was deliberately claiming equivalence with China or if he was simply unaware of how such language might be viewed in China.

SHOTOKU
The Seventeen Article Constitution
604

1. Harmony is to be valued, and an avoidance of wanton opposition to be honored. All men are influenced by class feelings, and there are few who are intelligent. Hence there are some who disobey their lords and fathers, or who maintain feuds with the neighboring villages. But when those above are harmonious and those below are friendly, and there is concord in the discussion of business, right views of things spontaneously gain acceptance....

2. Sincerely reverence the three treasures...the Buddha, the Law [teachings], and the Priesthood [community of monks]....

3. When you receive the Imperial commands, fail not scrupulously to obey them. The lord is Heaven, the vassal is Earth. Heaven overspreads, and Earth upbears.... [W]hen the superior acts, the inferior yields compliance.

4. The Ministers and functionaries should make decorous behavior their leading principle.... If the superiors do not behave with decorum, the inferiors are disorderly....

5. Ceasing from gluttony and abandoning covetous desires, deal impartially with the [legal] suits which are submitted to you....

6. Chastise that which is evil and encourage that which is good. This was the excellent rule of antiquity....

7. Let every man have his own charge, and let not the spheres of duty be confused. When wise men are entrusted with office, the sound of praise arises. If unprincipled men hold office, disasters and tumults are multiplied. In this world, few are born with knowledge: wisdom is the product of earnest meditation. In all things, whether great or small, find the right man, and they will surely be well managed....

Source: W. G. Aston, trans., *Nihongi: Chronicles of Japan from the Earliest Times to A.D. 697* (London: Paul, Trench, Truebner, 1896), 2:129–33.

10. Let us cease from wrath, and refrain from angry looks. Nor let us be resentful when others differ from us. For all men have hearts, and each heart has its own leanings.... [All] of us are simply ordinary men....

11. Give clear appreciation to merit and demerit, and deal out to each its sure reward or punishment. In these days, reward does not attend upon merit, nor punishment upon crime. You high functionaries, who have charge of public affairs, let it be your task to make clear rewards and punishments....

12. Let not the provincial authorities or the [local nobles] levy exactions on the people. In a country, there are not two lords.... The sovereign is the master of the people of the whole country....

15. To turn away from that which is private, and to set our faces toward that which is public—this is the path of a Minister....

16. Let the people be employed [in forced labor] at seasonable times. This is an ancient and excellent rule. Let them be employed, therefore, in the winter months, when they are at leisure. But from spring to autumn, when they are engaged in agriculture or with the mulberry trees, the people should not be so employed. For if they do not attend to agriculture, what will they have to eat? If they do not attend the mulberry trees, what will they do for clothing?

17. Decisions on important matters should not be made by one person alone. They should be discussed with many.

Document 9.2

Buddhism in Japan: The Zen Tradition

Buddhism was perhaps Japan's most significant cultural borrowing. Although the religion had begun in India and entered Japan from Korea in the mid-sixth century, it was widely viewed as a Chinese import, conveying, according to one historian, a "Chinese-style dignity and civilization" for an emerging Japanese state. To the rulers of that new state, Buddhism was politically useful, for it provided a potentially unifying religious tradition for a divided society and support for the imperial regime.[36] Yet Buddhism in Japan was never a single tradition, for a great variety of Buddhist sects, practices, and schools of thought, most of them of Chinese origin, took root in Japan. Frequently they were at odds with one another and with the Japanese state as well.

The Pure Land school of Buddhist practice achieved widespread popularity in Japan beginning in the twelfth century and represented a democratization of a religion that had earlier given special prominence to monks and to elites in aristocratic circles. Its goal was no longer *nirvana*, the enlightenment gained in this life by the strenuous personal effort of a few individuals, but rather rebirth in the Pure Land of the Western Paradise, a heavenly place of beauty and delight where full awakening was virtually guaranteed (see Visual Source 5.5, p. 234). That possibility was now open to many simply by calling repeatedly on the name of Amida, a compassionate Buddha figure from ages past and an earlier incarnation of the historical Buddha. *Nama Amida Butsu* (Praise be to Amida Buddha)—that was the invocation, known as *nembutsu*, that offered divine assistance to all struggling seekers, ordinary people as well as monks, women as well as men, and even outcasts and the impure.

Zen Buddhism, often known as Chan in China, was introduced to Japan about the same time that Pure Land was taking root. Both were concerned with making Buddhism available to the widest possible audience, for all persons possessed a Buddha nature and could potentially achieve awakening. But the Zen tradition decisively rejected the idea of relying on an external divine source, such as the Amida Buddha. Rather, serious practitioners should look within themselves through a highly disciplined form of meditation known as *zazen*. This meant much less emphasis on religious texts and philosophical discussion than in some other expressions of Buddhism. Furthermore, Zen valued very highly the transmission of teachings from master to disciple in an unbroken line of succession from the historical Buddha himself. Document 9.2 presents extracts from the writings of Dogen (1200–1253), among the first and most well-known of those Japanese monks who introduced Zen to their homeland, after extensive study in China.

- What was distinctive about Zen practice?

- Why do you think Zen was particularly attractive for Japan's warlords and its *samurai* warrior class?

- What distinguished Zen from Pure Land Buddhism in Japan?

- What understandings lie behind the strict discipline of Zen? How might Buddhist critics of this approach take issue with Dogen?

DOGEN

Writings on Zen Buddhism
Thirteenth Century

We teach: For all the Buddha dharma—preserving Zen ancestors and Buddhas, sitting upright in the practice of self-actualizing *samādhi* [concentration] is the true path of awakening. Both in India and in China, all who have attained awakening did so in this way. Because in every generation each teacher and each disciple intimately and correctly transmitted this marvelous art, I learned the genuine initiation.

In the correctly transmitted Zen lineage we teach: This directly transmitted, authoritative Buddha dharma is the best of the best. Once you start studying under a good teacher, there is no need for lighting incense, worshipful prostrations, recalling the Buddha (*nembutsu*), repentance, or chanting scripture. Just sit and slough off body-mind....

★ ★ ★

When I stayed at T'ien-t'ung monastery [in China], the venerable Ching used to stay up sitting until the small hours of the morning and then after only a little rest would rise early to start sitting again. In the meditation hall he went on sitting with the other elders, without letting up for even a single night. Meanwhile many of the monks went off to sleep. The elder would go around among them and hit the sleepers with his fist or a slipper, yelling at them to wake up. If their sleepiness persisted, he would go out to the hallway and ring the bell to summon the

Source: William Theodore de Bary et al., *Sources of Japanese Tradition*, 1:321; William Theodore de Bary, *The Buddhist Tradition in India, China and Japan* (New York: Vintage Books, 1969), 372–73.

monks to a room apart, where he would lecture to them by the light of a candle.

"What use is there in your assembling together in the hall only to go to sleep? Is this all that you left the world and joined holy orders for?... Great is the problem of birth and death; fleeting indeed is our transitory existence. Upon these truths both the scriptural and meditation schools agree. What sort of illness awaits us tonight, what sort of death tomorrow? While we have life, not to practice Buddha's Law but to spend the time in sleep is the height of foolishness. Because of such foolishness Buddhism today is in a state of decline....

Upon another occasion his attendants said to him, "The monks are getting overtired or falling ill, and some are thinking of leaving the monastery, all because they are required to sit too long in medita-tion. Shouldn't the length of the sitting period be shortened?" The master became highly indignant. "That would be quite wrong. A monk who is not really devoted to the religious life may very well fall asleep in a half hour or an hour. But one truly devoted to it who has resolved to persevere in his religious discipline will eventually come to enjoy the practice of sitting, no matter how long it lasts. When I was young I used to visit the heads of various mon-asteries, and one of them explained to me, 'Formerly I used to hit sleeping monks so hard that my fist just about broke. Now I am old and weak, so I can't hit them hard enough. Therefore it is difficult to pro-duce good monks. In many monasteries today the superiors do not emphasize sitting strongly enough, and so Buddhism is declining. The more you hit them the better,' he advised me."

Document 9.3

The Uniqueness of Japan

Despite Japan's extensive cultural borrowing from abroad, or perhaps because of that borrowing, Japanese writers often stressed the unique and superior fea-tures of their own country. Nowhere is this theme echoed more clearly than in *The Chronicle of the Direct Descent of Gods and Sovereigns*, written by Kitabatake Chikafusa (1293–1354). A longtime court official and member of one branch of Japan's imperial family, Kitabatake wrote at a time of declining imperial authority in Japan, when two court centers competed in an extended "war of the courts." As an advocate for the southern court, Kitabatake sought to prove that the emperor he served was legitimate because he had descended in unbro-ken line from the Age of the Gods. In making this argument, he was also a spokesman for the revival of Japan's earlier religious tradition of numerous gods and spirits, known later as Shintoism.

- In Kitabatake's view, what was distinctive about Japan in comparison to China and India?

- How might the use of Japan's indigenous religious tradition, especially the Sun Goddess, serve to legitimize the imperial rule of Kitabatake's family?

- How did Kitabatake understand the place of Confucianism and Buddhism in Japan and their relationship to Shinto beliefs?

KITABATAKE CHIKAFUSA

The Chronicle of the Direct Descent of Gods and Sovereigns

1339

Japan is the divine country. The heavenly ancestor it was who first laid its foundations, and the Sun Goddess left her descendants to reign over it forever and ever. This is true only of our country, and nothing similar may be found in foreign lands. That is why it is called the divine country.

In the age of the gods, Japan was known as the "ever-fruitful land of reed-covered plains and luxuriant ricefields." This name has existed since the creation of heaven and earth.... [I]t may thus be considered the prime name of Japan. It is also called the country of the great eight islands. This name was given because eight islands were produced when the Male Deity and the Female Deity begot Japan.... Japan is the land of the Sun Goddess [Amaterasu]. Or it may have thus been called because it is near the place where the sun rises.... Thus, since Japan is a separate continent, distinct from both India and China and lying in a great ocean, it is the country where the divine illustrious imperial line has been transmitted.

The creation of heaven and earth must everywhere have been the same, for it occurred within the same universe, but the Indian, Chinese, and Japanese traditions are each different....

In China, nothing positive is stated concerning the creation of the world, even though China is a country which accords special importance to the keeping of records....

The beginnings of Japan in some ways resemble the Indian descriptions, telling as it does of the world's creation from the seed of the heavenly gods. However, whereas in our country the succession to the throne has followed a single undeviating line since the first divine ancestor, nothing of the kind has existed in India. After their first ruler, King People's

Lord, had been chosen and raised to power by the populace, his dynasty succeeded, but in later times most of his descendants perished, and men of inferior genealogy who had powerful forces became the rulers, some of them even controlling the whole of India. China is also a country of notorious disorders. Even in ancient times, when life was simple and conduct was proper, the throne was offered to wise men, and no single lineage was established. Later, in times of disorder, men fought for control of the country. Thus some of the rulers rose from the ranks of the plebians, and there were even some of barbarian origin who usurped power. Or some families after generations of service as ministers surpassed their princes and eventually supplanted them. There have already been thirty-six changes of dynasty since Fuxi, and unspeakable disorders have occurred.

Only in our country has the succession remained inviolate from the beginning of heaven and earth to the present. It has been maintained within a single lineage, and even when, as inevitably has happened, the succession has been transmitted collaterally, it has returned to the true line. This is due to the ever-renewed Divine Oath and makes Japan unlike all other countries....

Then the Great Sun Goddess...sent her grandchild to the world below. Eighty million deities obeyed the divine decree to accompany and serve him. Among them were thirty-two principal deities.... Two of these deities...received a divine decree specially instructing them to aid and protect the divine grandchild. [The Sun Goddess] uttered these words of command: "Thou, my illustrious grandchild, proceed thither and govern the land. Go, and may prosperity attend thy dynasty, and may it, like Heaven and Earth, endure forever."...

Because our Great Goddess is the spirit of the sun, she illuminates with a bright virtue which is incomprehensible in all its aspects but dependable alike in the realm of the visible and invisible. All

Source: William Theodore de Bary et al., *Sources of Japanese Tradition* (New York: Columbia University Press, 2001), 1:358–63.

sovereigns and ministers have inherited the bright seeds of the divine light, or they are descendants of the deities who received personal instruction from the Great Goddess. Who would not stand in reverence before this fact? The highest object of all teachings, Buddhist and Confucian included, consists in realizing this fact and obeying in perfect consonance its principles. It has been the power of the dissemination of the Buddhist and Confucian texts which has spread these principles.... Since the reign of the Emperor Ōjin, the Confucian writings have been disseminated, and since Prince Shōtoku's time Buddhism has flourished in Japan. Both these men were sages incarnate, and it must have been their intention to spread a knowledge of the way of our country, in accordance with the wishes of the Great Sun Goddess.

Document 9.4

Social Life at Court

For many centuries, high culture in Japan—art, music, poetry, and literature—found a home in the imperial court, where men and women of the royal family and nobility, together with various attendants, mixed and mingled. That aristocratic culture reached its high point between the ninth and twelfth centuries, but, according to one prominent scholar, it "has shaped the aesthetic and emotional life of the entire Japanese people for a millennium."[37] Women played a prominent role in that culture, both creating it and describing it. Among them was Sei Shonagon (966–1017), a lady-in-waiting to the Empress Sadako. In her *Pillow Book*, a series of brief and often witty observations, Sei Shonagon described court life as well as her own likes and dislikes.

- What impression does Sei Shonagon convey about the relationship of men and women at court?

- How would you describe her posture toward men, toward women, and toward ordinary people? What insight can you gain about class differences from her writing?

- In what ways does court life, as Sei Shonagon describes it, reflect Buddhist and Confucian influences, and in what ways does it depart from, and even challenge, those traditions?

SEI SHONAGON

Pillow Book

ca. 1000

That parents should bring up some beloved son of theirs to be a priest is really distressing. No doubt it is an auspicious thing to do; but unfortunately most people are convinced that a priest is as unimportant as a piece of wood, and they treat him accordingly. A priest lives poorly on meager food, and cannot even sleep without being criticized. While he is young, it is only natural that he should be

Source: Ivan Morris, trans. and ed., *The Pillow Book of Sei Shonagon* (New York: Columbia University Press, 1991), 25–26, 39, 44–45, 47, 49–50, 53, 254–55.

curious about all sorts of things, and, if there are women about, he will probably peep in their direction (though, to be sure, with a look of aversion on his face). What is wrong about that? Yet people immediately find fault with him for even so small a lapse....

A preacher ought to be good-looking. For, if we are properly to understand his worthy sentiments, we must keep our eyes on him while he speaks; should we look away, we may forget to listen. Accordingly an ugly preacher may well be the source of sin....

When I make myself imagine what it is like to be one of those women who live at home, faithfully serving their husbands—women who have not a single exciting prospect in life yet who believe that they are perfectly happy—I am filled with scorn....

I cannot bear men who believe that women serving in the Palace are bound to be frivolous and wicked. Yet I suppose their prejudice is understandable. After all, women at Court do not spend their time hiding modestly behind fans and screens, but walk about, looking openly at people they chance to meet. Yes, they see everyone face to face, not only ladies-in-waiting like themselves, but even Their Imperial Majesties (whose august names I hardly dare mention), High Court Nobles, senior courtiers, and other gentlemen of high rank. In the presence of such exalted personages the women in the Palace are all equally brazen, whether they be the maids of ladies-in-waiting, or the relations of Court ladies who have come to visit them, or housekeepers, or latrine-cleaners, or women who are of no more value than a roof-tile or a pebble. Small wonder that the young men regard them as immodest! Yet are the gentlemen themselves any less so? They are not exactly bashful when it comes to looking at the great people in the Palace. No, everyone at Court is much the same in this respect....

Hateful Things

...A man who has nothing in particular to recommend him discusses all sorts of subjects at random as though he knew everything....

An admirer has come on a clandestine visit, but a dog catches sight of him and starts barking. One feels like killing the beast.

One has been foolish enough to invite a man to spend the night in an unsuitable place—and then he starts snoring.

A gentleman has visited one secretly. Though he is wearing a tall, lacquered hat, he nevertheless wants no one to see him. He is so flurried, in fact, that upon leaving he bangs into something with his hat. Most hateful!...

A man with whom one is having an affair keeps singing the praises of some woman he used to know. Even if it is a thing of the past, this can be very annoying. How much more so if he is still seeing the woman!...

A good lover will behave as elegantly at dawn as at any other time. He drags himself out of bed with a look of dismay on his face. The lady urges him on: "Come, my friend, it's getting light. You don't want anyone to find you here." He gives a deep sigh, as if to say that the night has not been nearly long enough and that it is agony to leave. Once up, he does not instantly pull on his trousers. Instead he comes close to the lady and whispers whatever was left unsaid during the night. Even when he is dressed, he still lingers, vaguely pretending to be fastening his sash....

Indeed, one's attachment to a man depends largely on the elegance of his leave-taking. When he jumps out of bed, scurries about the room, tightly fastens his trouser-sash, rolls up the sleeves of his Court cloak, over-robe, or hunting costume, stuffs his belongings into the breast of his robe and then briskly secures the outer sash—one really begins to hate him....

It is very annoying, when one has visited Hase Temple and has retired into one's enclosure, to be disturbed by a herd of common people who come and sit outside in a row, crowded so close together that the tails of their robes fall over each other in utter disarray. I remember that once I was overcome by a great desire to go on a pilgrimage. Having made my way up the log steps, deafened by the fearful roar of the river, I hurried into my enclosure, longing to gaze upon the sacred countenance of Buddha. To my dismay I found that a throng of commoners had settled themselves directly in front of me, where they were incessantly standing up, prostrating themselves, and squatting down again. They looked like so many basket-worms as they crowded together in their hideous clothes, leaving hardly an inch of space between themselves and me. I really felt like pushing them all over sideways.

Document 9.5

The Way of the Warrior

As the Japanese imperial court gradually lost power to military authorities in the countryside, a further distinctive feature of Japanese civilization emerged in the celebration of martial virtues and the warrior class—the *samurai*—that embodied those values. From the twelfth through the mid-nineteenth century, public life and government in Japan was dominated by the samurai, while their culture and values, known as *bushido*, expressed the highest ideals of political leadership and of personal conduct. At least in the West, the samurai are perhaps best known for preferring death over dishonor, a posture expressed in *seppuku* (ritual suicide). But there was much more to bushido than this, for the samurai served not only as warriors but also as bureaucrats—magistrates, land managers, and provincial governors—acting on behalf of their lords (*daimyo*) or in service to military rulers known as *shoguns*. Furthermore, although bushido remained a distinctively Japanese cultural expression, it absorbed both Confucian and Buddhist values as well as those of the indigenous Shinto tradition.

The two selections that follow reflect major themes of an emerging bushido culture, the way of the warrior. The first excerpt comes from the writings of Shiba Yoshimasa (1349–1410), a feudal lord, general, and administrator as well as a noted poet, who wrote a manual of advice for the young warriors of his own lineage. Probably the man who most closely approximated in his own life the emerging ideal of a cultivated warrior was Imagawa Ryoshun (1325–1420), famous as a poet, a military commander, and a devout Buddhist. The second excerpt contains passages from a famous and highly critical letter Imagawa wrote to his adopted son (who was also his younger brother). The letter was published and republished hundreds of times and used for centuries as a primer or school text for the instruction of young samurai.

■ Based on these accounts, how would you define the ideal samurai?

■ What elements of Confucian, Buddhist, or Shinto thinking can you find in these selections? How do these writers reconcile the peaceful emphasis of Confucian and Buddhist teachings with the military dimension of bushido?

■ What does the Imagawa letter suggest about the problems facing the military rulers of Japan in the fourteenth century?

SHIBA YOSIMASA
Advice to Young Samurai
ca. 1400

Wielders of bow and arrow should behave in a manner considerate not only of their own honor, of course, but also of the honor of their descendants. They should not bring on eternal disgrace by solicitude for their limited lives.

That being said, nevertheless to regard your one and only life as like dust or ashes and die when you shouldn't is to acquire a worthless reputation. A genuine motive would be, for example, to give up your life for the sake of the sole sovereign, or serving under the commander of the military in a time of need; these would convey an exalted name to children and descendants. Something like a strategy of the moment, whether good or bad, cannot raise the family reputation much.

Warriors should never be thoughtless or absentminded but handle all things with forethought....

It is said that good warriors and good Buddhists are similarly circumspect. Whatever the matter, it is vexing for the mind not to be calm. Putting others' minds at ease too is something found only in the considerate....

Source: Thomas Cleary, trans. and ed., *Training the Samurai Mind* (Boston: Shambhala, 2008), 18–20.

When you begin to think of yourself, you'll get irritated at your parents' concern and defy their instructions. Even if your parents may be stupid, if you obey their instructions, at least you won't be violating the principle of nature. What is more, eighty to ninety percent of the time what parents say makes sense for their children. It builds up in oneself to become obvious. The words of our parents we defied in irritation long ago are all essential. You should emulate even a bad parent rather than a good stranger; that's how a family culture is transmitted and comes to be known as a person's legacy....

Even if one doesn't perform any religious exercises and never makes a visit to a shrine, neither deities nor buddhas will disregard a person whose mind is honest and compassionate. In particular, the Great Goddess of Ise,° the great bodhisattva Hachiman,° and the deity of Kitano° will dwell in the heads of people whose minds are honest, clean, and good.

°**Great Goddess of Ise:** Amaterasu, the sun goddess.

°**Hachiman:** a Japanese deity who came to be seen as a Buddhist bodhisattva.

°**Kitano:** patron god of learning.

IMAGAWA RYOSHUN
The Imagawa Letter
1412

As you do not understand the Arts of Peace° your skill in the Arts of War° will not, in the end, achieve victory.

°**Arts of Peace:** literary skills including poetry, history, philosophy, and ritual.

°**Arts of War:** horsemanship, archery, swordsmanship.

You like to roam about, hawking and cormorant fishing, relishing the purposelessness of taking life.

You live in luxury by fleecing the people and plundering the shrines.

Source: From Carl Steenstrup, trans., "The Imagawa Letter," *Monumenta Nipponica* 28, no. 3 (Autumn 1973), 295–316.

To build your own dwelling you razed the pagoda and other buildings of the memorial temple of our ancestors.

You do not distinguish between good and bad behavior of your retainers, but reward or punish them without justice.

You permit yourself to forget the kindness that our lord and father showed us; thus you destroy the principles of loyalty and filial piety.

You do not understand the difference in status between yourself and others; sometimes you make too much of other people, sometimes too little.

You disregard other people's viewpoints; you bully them and rely on force.

You excel at drinking bouts, amusements, and gambling, but you forget the business of our clan.

You provide yourself lavishly with clothes and weapons, but your retainers are poorly equipped.

You ought to show utmost respect to Buddhist monks and priests and carry out ceremonies properly.

You impede the flow of travelers by erecting barriers everywhere in your territory.

Whether you are in charge of anything—such as a province or a district—or not, it will be difficult to put your abilities to any use if you have not won the sympathy and respect of ordinary people.

Just as the Buddhist scriptures tell us that the Buddha incessantly strives to save mankind, in the same way you should exert your mind to the utmost in all your activities, be they civil or military, and never fall into negligence.

It should be regarded as dangerous if the ruler of the people in a province is deficient even in a single [one] of the cardinal virtues of human-heartedness, righteousness, propriety, wisdom, and good faith.

You were born to be a warrior, but you mismanage your territory, do not maintain the army, and are not ashamed although people laugh at you. It is, indeed, a mortifying situation for you and our whole clan.

Using the Evidence:
The Making of Japanese Civilization

1. **Considering cultural borrowing and assimilation:** What evidence of cultural borrowing can you identify in these documents? To what extent did those borrowed elements come to be regarded as Japanese?

2. **Looking for continuities:** What older patterns of Japanese thought and practice persisted despite much cultural borrowing from China?

3. **Noticing inconsistencies and change:** No national culture develops as a single set of ideas and practices. What inconsistencies, tensions, or differences in emphasis can you identify in these documents? What changes over time can you identify in these selections?

4. **Considering Japanese Buddhism:** In what different ways did Buddhism play a role in Japan during the postclassical era? How did Buddhism change Japan, and how did Japan change Buddhism?

Visual Sources

Considering the Evidence:
The Leisure Life of China's Elites

From the earliest centuries of Chinese civilization, that country's artists have painted—on pottery, paper, wood, and silk; in tombs, on coffins, and on walls; in albums and on scrolls. Relying largely on ink rather than oils, their brushes depicted human figures, landscapes, religious themes, and images of ordinary life. While Chinese painting evolved over many centuries, both in terms of subject matter and technique, by most accounts it reached a high point of artistic brilliance during the Tang and Song dynasties.

Here, however, we are less interested in the aesthetic achievements of Chinese painting than in what those works can show us about the life of China's elite class—those men who had passed the highest-level examinations and held high office in the state bureaucracy and those women who lived within the circles of the imperial court. While they represented only a tiny fraction of China's huge population, such elite groups established the tone and set the standards of behavior for Chinese civilization. For such people, leisure was a positive value, a time for nurturing relationships and cultivating one's character in good Confucian or Daoist fashion. According to the Tang dynasty writer and scholar Duan Chengshi,

> Leisure is good.
> Dusty affairs don't entangle the mind.
> I sit facing the tree outside the window
> And watch its shadow change direction three times.[38]

Action and work, in the Chinese view of things, need to be balanced by self-reflection and leisure. In the visual sources that follow, we can catch a glimpse of how the Chinese elite lived and interacted with one another, particularly in their leisure time.

Leading court officials and scholar-bureaucrats must have been greatly honored to be invited to an elegant banquet, hosted by the emperor himself, such as that shown in Visual Source 9.1. Usually attributed to the emperor Huizong (1082–1135)—who was himself a noted painter, poet, calligrapher, and collector—the painting shows a refined dinner gathering of high officials drinking tea and wine with the emperor presiding at the left.[39] This emperor's great attention to the arts rather than to affairs of state gained him a reputation as a negligent and dissolute ruler. His reign ended in disgrace as China suffered a humiliating defeat at the hands of northern nomadic Jin people, who took the emperor captive.

■ What features of this painting contribute to the impression of imperial elegance?

■ What mood does this painting evoke?

■ What social distinction among the figures in the painting can you discern?

■ How is the emperor depicted in this painting in comparison to that on page 388? How would you explain the difference?

■ How might you imagine the conversation around this table?

Visual Source 9.1 A Banquet with the Emperor (National Palace Museum, Taipei, Taiwan)

Visual Source 9.2 At Table with the Empress (National Palace Museum, Taipei, Taiwan)

Elite women of the court likewise gathered to eat, drink, and talk, as illustrated in Visual Source 9.2, an anonymous Tang dynasty painting on silk. Hosting the event is the empress, shown seated upright in the middle of the left side of the table, holding a fan and wearing a distinctive headdress. Her guests and paid professional musicians sit around the table.

- How does this gathering of elite women differ from that of the men in Visual Source 9.1? How might their conversation differ from that of the men?

- To what extent are the emperor and empress in Visual Sources 9.1 and 9.2 distinguished from their guests? How do you think the emperor and empress viewed their roles at these functions? Were they acting as private persons among friends or in an official capacity?

- What differences in status among these women can you identify?

- What view of these women does the artist seek to convey?

- What does the posture of the women suggest about the event?

Visual Source 9.3 A Literary Gathering (Palace Museum, Beijing)

Confucian cultural ideals gave great prominence to literature, poetry, and scholarly pursuits as leisure activities appropriate for "gentlemen" (see pp. 193–95). Confucius himself had declared that "gentlemen make friends through literature, and through friendship increase their benevolence." Thus literary gatherings of scholars and officials, often in garden settings, were common themes in Tang and Song dynasty paintings. Visual Source 9.3, by the tenth-century painter Zhou Wenju, provides an illustration of such a gathering.

■ What marks these figures as cultivated men of literary or scholarly inclination?

■ What meaning might you attribute to the outdoor garden setting of this image and that of Visual Source 9.1?

■ Notice the various gazes of the four figures. What do they suggest about the character of this gathering and the interpersonal relationships among its participants?

■ Do you think the artist was seeking to convey an idealized image of what a gathering of officials ought to be or a realistic portrayal of an actual event? What elements of the painting support your answer?

Chinese scholars and bureaucrats are often shown, in their leisure hours, as solitary contemplatives, immersing themselves in nature. The famous Song dynasty painter Ma Yuan (1160–1225) depicted such an image in his masterpiece entitled *On a Mountain Path in Spring*. In Visual Source 9.4, a scholar walks in the countryside watching several birds, while his servant trails behind carrying his master's *qin* (lute). A short poem in the upper right reads:

> Brushed by his sleeves, wild flowers dance in the wind;
> Fleeing from him, the hidden birds cut short their songs.[40]

- How would you define the mood of this painting? What techniques did Ma Yuan use to evoke this mood?

- How might this painting reflect the perspectives of Daoism (see pp. 195–97)? How does it differ from the more Confucian tone of Visual Source 9.3?

- What relationship with nature does this painting convey?

- During Ma Yuan's lifetime, the northern part of China was coming under the control of the feared Mongols. How might an awareness of this situation affect our understanding of this painting?

Visual Source 9.4 Solitary Reflection (National Palace Museum, Taipei, Taiwan)

Visual Source 9.5 An Elite Night Party (Palace Museum, Beijing)

Not all was poetry and contemplation of nature in the leisure-time activities of China's elite. Nor were men and women always so strictly segregated as the preceding visual sources may suggest. Visual Source 9.5 illustrates another side of Chinese elite life. These images are part of a long tenth-century scroll painting entitled *The Night Revels of Han Xizai*. Apparently, the Tang dynasty emperor Li Yu became suspicious that one of his ministers, Han Xizai, was overindulging in suspicious night-long parties in his own home. He therefore commissioned the artist Gu Hongzhong to attend these parties secretly and to record the events in a painting, which he hoped would shame his wayward but talented official into more appropriate and dignified behavior. The entire scroll shows men and women together, sometimes in flirtatious situations, while open sleeping areas suggest sexual activity.

■   What kinds of entertainment were featured at this gathering?

■   What aspects of these parties shown in the scroll paintings might have caused the emperor some concern? Refer back to the "singsong girls," shown on page 253. In what respects might these kinds of gatherings run counter to Confucian values?

■   How are women portrayed in these images? In what ways are they relating to the men in the paintings?

Using the Evidence:
The Leisure Life of China's Elites

1.   **Describing elite society:** Based on these visual sources, write a brief description of the social life of Chinese elites during the Tang and Song dynasties.

2.   **Defining the self-image of an elite:** What do these visual sources suggest about how members of the elite ideally viewed themselves? In what ways do those self-portraits draw upon Confucian, Daoist, or Buddhist teachings?

3. **Noticing differences in the depiction of women:** In what different ways are women represented in these paintings? Keep in mind that all of the artists were men. How might this affect the way women were depicted? How might female artists have portrayed them differently?

4. **Using images to illustrate change:** Reread the sections on Chinese women (pp. 253–55 and 384–85). How might these images be used to illustrate the changes in women's lives that are described in those pages?

5. **Seeking additional sources:** What other kinds of visual sources might provide further insight into the lives of Chinese elites?

CUMSEDEAT KAROLUSMAGNOCORONATUSHONO
ESTIOSIAESIMILIS.   PARQUETHEODOS

CHAPTER TEN

The Worlds of European Christendom

Connected and Divided

500–1300

"We embraced each other once, then again and again. We were like brothers meeting after a long separation."[1] That is how the Eastern Orthodox patriarch Athenagoras described his historic meeting with Roman Catholic Pope Paul VI in early 1964 near the Mount of Olives in Jerusalem, the very site where Jesus had spent the night before his arrest. Not for more than 500 years had the heads of these two ancient branches of Christianity personally met. Now they held each other and exchanged gifts, including a representation of two of Christ's disciples embracing. Then they lifted mutual decrees of excommunication that representatives of their respective churches had imposed almost a thousand years earlier. It was a small step in a still very incomplete process of overcoming this deep rift within Christianity, which had been in the making for well over a millennium. How had the world of Christendom come to be so sharply divided, religiously, politically, and in terms of the larger historical trajectories of its eastern and western halves?

DURING THE POSTCLASSICAL ERA, CHRISTIANITY PROVIDED a measure of cultural commonality for the diverse societies of western Eurasia, much as Chinese civilization and Buddhism did for East Asia. By 1300, almost all of these societies—from Spain and England in the west to Russia in the east—had embraced in some form the teachings of the Jewish carpenter called Jesus, but the world of European Christendom was deeply divided in a way that the Chinese world was not. Its eastern half, known as the Byzantine

Charlemagne: This fifteenth-century manuscript painting depicts Charlemagne, King of the Franks, who was crowned Emperor by the pope in 800 C.E. His reign illustrates the close and sometimes conflicted relationship of political and religious authorities in postclassical Europe. It also represents the futile desire of many in Western Europe to revive the old Roman Empire, even as a substantially new civilization was taking shape in the aftermath of the Roman collapse several centuries earlier. (Victoria & Albert Museum, London, UK/The Bridgeman Art Library)

Empire or Byzantium, encompassed much of the eastern Mediterranean basin while continuing the traditions of the Roman Empire, though on a smaller scale, until its conquest by the Muslim Ottoman Empire in 1453. Centered on the magnificent city of Constantinople, Byzantium gradually evolved a distinctive civilization, all the while claiming to be Roman and seeking to preserve the heritage of the classical Mediterranean. With a particular form of Christianity known as Eastern Orthodoxy, the Byzantine Empire housed one of the major third-wave civilizations.

In Western or Latin Christendom, encompassing what we now know as Western Europe, political and religious leaders also tried to maintain links to the classical world, as illustrated by the spread of Christianity, the use of Latin in elite circles, and various efforts to revive or imitate the Roman Empire. The setting, however, was far different. In the West, the Roman imperial order had largely vanished by 500 C.E., accompanied by the weakening of many features of Roman civilization. Roads fell into disrepair, cities decayed, and long-distance trade shriveled. What replaced the old Roman order was a highly localized society—fragmented, decentralized, and competitive—in sharp contrast to the unified state of Byzantium. Like Byzantium, the Latin West ultimately became thoroughly Christian, but it was a gradual process lasting centuries, and its Roman Catholic Church, increasingly centered on the pope, had an independence from political authorities that the Eastern Orthodox Church did not. Moreover, the western church in particular and its society in general were far more rural than Byzantium and certainly had nothing to compare to the splendor of Constantinople. However, slowly at first and then with increasing speed after 1000, Western Europe emerged as an especially dynamic, expansive, and innovative third-wave civilization, combining elements of its classical past with the culture of Germanic and Celtic peoples to produce a distinctive hybrid, or blended, civilization.

Europe eventually became the global center of Christianity, but that destiny was far from clear in 500 C.E. At that time, only about one-third of the world's Christians lived in Europe, while the rest found their homes in various parts of Africa, the Middle East, and Asia.[2] There they often followed alternate forms of Christianity, such as Nestorianism, which was regarded as heretical in Europe for its distinctive understanding of the nature of Christ. In Egypt, India, and Persia, remnants of these earlier and larger Christian communities have survived as tolerated minorities into the present. By contrast, in early Armenia and Ethiopia (Axum), Christianity became the faith of the majority and has continued to express the national identity of peoples long cut off from contact with other Christian societies. (See Document 7.3, pp. 310–12 for the coming of Christianity to Axum in East Africa.) Finally, the early Christian communities of North Africa, Nubia, Central Asia, and western China largely vanished as these regions subsequently embraced alternative religious traditions, such as Islam, Buddhism, or Confucianism. (See Document 10.6, pp. 462–64, on the brief flourishing of Nestorian Christianity in China.) In this chapter, however, the historical spotlight falls on those regions that became the center of the Christian world—Byzantium and Western Europe.

Eastern Christendom: Building on the Roman Past

Unlike most empires, Byzantium has no clear starting point. Its own leaders, as well as its neighbors and enemies, viewed it as simply a continuation of the Roman Empire. Some historians date its beginning to 330 C.E., when the Roman emperor Constantine, who became a Christian during his reign, established a new capital, Constantinople, on the site of an ancient Greek city called Byzantium. At the end of that century, the Roman Empire was formally divided into eastern and western halves, thus launching a division of Christendom that has lasted into the twenty-first century. Although the western Roman Empire collapsed during the fifth century, the eastern half persisted for another thousand years. Housing the ancient civilizations of Egypt, Greece, Syria, and Anatolia, the eastern Roman Empire (Byzantium) was far wealthier, more urbanized, and more cosmopolitan than its western counterpart; it possessed a much more defensible capital in the heavily walled city of Constantinople; and it had a shorter frontier to guard. Byzantium also enjoyed access to the Black Sea and command of the eastern Mediterranean. With a stronger army, navy, and merchant marine as well as clever diplomacy, its leaders were able to deflect the Germanic and Hun invaders who had overwhelmed the western Roman Empire.

Much that was late Roman—its roads, taxation system, military structures, centralized administration, imperial court, laws, Christian church—persisted in the east for many centuries. Like Tang dynasty China seeking to restore the glory of the Han era, Byzantium consciously sought to preserve the legacy of classical civilization and the Roman Empire. Constantinople was to be a "New Rome," and Byzantines referred to themselves as "Romans." Fearing contamination by "barbarian" customs, emperors forbade the residents of Constantinople from wearing boots, trousers, clothing made from animal skins, and long hairstyles, all of which were associated with

■ **Continuity and Change**

In what respects did Byzantium continue the patterns of the classical Roman Empire? In what ways did it diverge from those patterns?

Snapshot Key Moments in Byzantine History

Founding of Constantinople	330
Final division of Roman Empire into eastern and western halves	ca. 395
Reign of Justinian; attempted reconquest of western empire	527–565
Loss of Syria/Palestine, Egypt, and North Africa to Arab forces	7th century
Iconoclastic controversy	726–843
Conversion of Vladimir, prince of Kiev, to Christianity	988
Mutual excommunication of pope and patriarch	1054
Crusaders sack Constantinople	1204
Ottomans seize Constantinople; end of Byzantine Empire	1453

Germanic peoples, and insisted instead on Roman-style robes and sandals. But much changed as well over the centuries, marking the Byzantine Empire as the home of a distinctive civilization.

The Byzantine State

Perhaps the most obvious change was one of scale, as the Byzantine Empire never approximated the size of its Roman predecessor (see Map 10.1). The western Roman Empire was permanently lost to Byzantium, despite Emperor Justinian's (reigned 527–565) impressive but short-lived attempt to reconquer the Mediterranean basin. The rapid Arab/Islamic expansion in the seventh century resulted in the loss of Syria/Palestine, Egypt, and North Africa. Nonetheless, until roughly 1200, a more compact Byzantine Empire remained a major force in the eastern Mediterranean, controlling Greece, much of the Balkans (southeastern Europe), and Anatolia. A reformed administrative system gave appointed generals civil authority in the empire's

Map 10.1   The Byzantine Empire
The Byzantine Empire reached its greatest extent under Emperor Justinian in the mid-sixth century C.E. It subsequently lost considerable territory to various Christian European powers as well as to Muslim Arab and Turkic invaders.

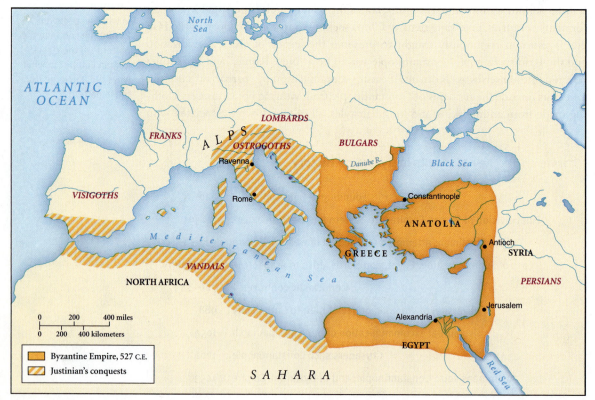

provinces and allowed them to raise armies from the landowning peasants of the region. From that territorial base, the empire's naval and merchant vessels were active in both the Mediterranean and Black seas.

In its heyday, the Byzantine state was an impressive creation. Political authority remained tightly centralized in Constantinople, where the emperor claimed to govern all creation as God's worldly representative, styling himself the "peer of the Apostles" and the "sole ruler of the world." The imperial court tried to imitate the awesome grandeur of what they thought was God's heavenly court, but in fact it resembled ancient Persian imperial splendor. Aristocrats trained in classical Greek rhetoric and literature took jobs in the administration in order to participate in court ceremonies that maintained their elite status. Parades of these silk-clad administrators added splendor to the imperial court, which also included mechanical lions that roared, birds that sang, and an immense throne that quickly elevated the emperor high above his presumably awestruck visitors. Nonetheless, this centralized state touched only lightly on the lives of most people, as it focused primarily on collecting taxes, maintaining order, and suppressing revolts. "Personal freedom in the provinces was constrained more by neighbors and rival households," concluded one historian, "than by the imperial government."[3]

After 1085, Byzantine territory shrank, owing to incursions by aggressive Western European powers, by Catholic Crusaders, and later by Turkic Muslim invaders. The end came in 1453 when the Turkic Ottoman Empire, then known as the "sword of Islam," finally took Constantinople. One eyewitness to the event wrote a moving lament to his fallen city:

> And the entire city was to be seen in the tents of the [Turkish] camp, the city deserted, lying lifeless, naked, soundless, without either form or beauty. O city, head of all cities, center of the four corners of the world, pride of the Romans, civilizer of the barbarians.... Where is your beauty, O paradise...? Where are the bodies of the Apostle of my Lord...? Where are the relics of the saints, those of the martyrs? Where are the remains of Constantine the Great and the other emperors?... Oh, what a loss![4]

The Byzantine Church and Christian Divergence

Intimately tied to the state was the Church, a relationship that became known as caesaropapism. Unlike Western Europe, where the Roman Catholic Church maintained some degree of independence from political authorities, in Byzantium the emperor assumed something of the role of both "caesar," as head of state, and the pope, as head of the Church. Thus he appointed the patriarch, or leader, of the Orthodox Church; sometimes made decisions about doctrine; called church councils into session; and generally treated the Church as a government department. "The [Empire] and the church have a great unity and community," declared a twelfth-century patriarch. "Indeed they cannot be separated."[5] A dense network of bishops and priests brought the message of the Church to every corner of the empire, while numerous

■ **Comparison**
How did Eastern Orthodox Christianity differ from Roman Catholicism?

monasteries accommodated holy men, whose piety, self-denial, and good works made them highly influential among both elite and ordinary people.

Eastern Orthodox Christianity had a pervasive influence on every aspect of Byzantine life. It legitimated the supreme and absolute rule of the emperor, for he was a God-anointed ruler, a reflection of the glory of God on earth. It also provided a cultural identity for the empire's subjects. Even more than being "Roman," they were orthodox, or "right-thinking," Christians for whom the empire and the Church were equally essential to achieving eternal salvation. Constantinople was filled with churches and the relics of numerous saints. And the churches were filled with icons — religious paintings of Jesus, Mary, and the other saints — some of them artistic masterpieces, that many believed conveyed the divine presence to believers. (For more on icons, see Visual Sources: Reading Byzantine Icons, pp. 466–71.) Complex theological issues about the Trinity and especially about the relationship of God and Jesus engaged the attention of ordinary people. One fourth-century bishop complained: "I wish to know the price of bread; one answers 'The Father is greater than the Son.' I inquire whether my bath is ready; one answers 'The Son has been made out of nothing.' "[6] Partisans of competing chariot-racing teams, known as the Greens and the Blues, vigorously debated theological issues as well as the merits of their favorite drivers.

St. Mark's Basilica
Consecrated in 1094, this ornate cathedral, although located in Venice, Italy, is a classic example of Byzantine architecture. Such churches represented perhaps the greatest achievement of Byzantine art and were certainly the most monumental expressions of Byzantine culture. (Erich Lessing/Art Resource, NY)

In its early centuries and beyond, the Christian movement was rent by theological controversy and political division. Followers of Arius, an Egyptian priest, held that Jesus had been created by God the Father rather than living eternally with Him. Nestorius, the fifth-century bishop of Constantinople, argued that Mary had given birth only to the human Jesus, who then became the "temple" of God. This view, defined as heretical in the western Christian world, predominated in a separate Persian church, which spread its views to India, China, and Arabia.

But the most lasting and deepest division within the Christian world occurred as Eastern Orthodoxy came to define itself against an emerging Latin Christianity centered on papal Rome. Both had derived, of course, from the growth of Christianity in the Roman Empire and therefore had much in common — the teachings of Jesus; the Bible; the sacraments; a church hierarchy of patriarchs, bishops, and priests; a missionary impulse; and intolerance toward other religions. Despite these shared features, any sense of a single widespread Christian community was increasingly replaced by an awareness of difference, competition, and outright hostility that even a common fear of Islam could not overcome. In part, this growing religious divergence reflected the political separation and rivalry between the Byzantine Empire and the emerging kingdoms of Western Europe. As the growth of Islam in the seventh century (described more fully in Chapter 11) submerged earlier centers of Christianity in the Middle East and North Africa, Constantinople and Rome alone remained as alternative hubs of the Church. But they were now in different states that competed with each other for territory and for the right to claim the legacy of imperial Rome.

Beyond such political differences were those of language and culture. Although Latin remained the language of the Church and of elite communication in the West, it was abandoned in the Byzantine Empire in favor of Greek, which remained the basis for Byzantine education. More than in the West, Byzantine thinkers sought to formulate Christian doctrine in terms of Greek philosophical concepts.

Differences in theology and church practice likewise widened the gulf between Orthodoxy and Catholicism, despite agreement on fundamental doctrines. Disagreements about the nature of the Trinity, the source of the Holy Spirit, original sin, and the relative importance of faith and reason gave rise to much controversy. So too for a time did the Byzantine efforts to prohibit the use of icons, popular paintings of saints and biblical scenes, usually painted on small wooden panels. (See Visual Sources: Reading Byzantine Icons, pp. 466–71.) Other more modest differences also occasioned mutual misunderstanding and disdain. Priests in the West shaved and, after 1050 or so, were supposed to remain celibate, while those in Byzantium allowed their beards to grow long and were permitted to marry. Orthodox ritual called for using bread leavened with yeast in the Communion, but Catholics used unleavened bread. Far more significant was the question of authority. Eastern Orthodox leaders sharply rejected the growing claims of Roman popes to be the sole and final authority for all Christians everywhere.

The rift in the world of Christendom grew gradually from the seventh century on, punctuated by various efforts to bridge the mounting divide between the western and eastern branches of the Church. A sign of this continuing deterioration occurred in 1054 when representatives of both churches mutually excommunicated each other, declaring in effect that those in the opposing tradition were not true Christians. The Crusades, launched in 1095 by the Catholic pope against the forces of Islam, made things worse. Western Crusaders, passing through the Byzantine Empire on their way to the Middle East, engaged in frequent conflict with local people and thus deepened the distrust between them. From the western viewpoint, Orthodox practices were "blasphemous, even heretical." One western observer of the Second Crusade noted that the Greeks "were judged not to be Christians and the Franks [French] considered killing them a matter of no importance."[7] During the Fourth Crusade in 1204, western forces seized and looted Constantinople and ruled Byzantium for the next half century. Their brutality only confirmed Byzantine views of their Roman Catholic despoilers as nothing more than barbarians. According to one Byzantine account, "they sacked the sacred places and trampled on divine things . . . they tore children from their mothers . . . and they defiled virgins in the holy chapels, fearing neither God's anger nor man's vengeance."[8] After this, the rupture in the world of Christendom proved irreparable.

Byzantium and the World

■ **Connection**

In what ways was the Byzantine Empire linked to a wider world?

Beyond its tense relationship with Western Europe, the Byzantine Empire, located astride Europe and Asia, also interacted intensively with its other neighbors. On a political and military level, Byzantium continued the long-term Roman struggle with the Persian Empire. That persisting conflict weakened both of them and was one factor in the remarkable success of Arab armies as they poured out of Arabia in the seventh century. Although Persia quickly became part of the Islamic world, Byzantium held out, even as it lost considerable territory to the Arabs. A Byzantine military innovation, known as "Greek fire"—a potent and flammable combination of oil, sulfur, and lime that was launched from bronze tubes—helped to hold off the Arabs. It operated something like a flamethrower and subsequently passed into Arab and Chinese arsenals as well. Byzantium's ability to defend its core regions delayed for many centuries the Islamic advance into southeastern Europe, which finally occurred at the hands of the Turkish Ottoman Empire in the fifteenth and sixteenth centuries.

Economically, the Byzantine Empire was a central player in the long-distance trade of Eurasia, with commercial links to Western Europe, Russia, Central Asia, the Islamic world, and China. Its gold coin, the bezant, was a widely used currency in the Mediterranean basin for more than 500 years, and wearing such coins as pendants was a high-status symbol in the less developed kingdoms of Western Europe.[9] The luxurious products of Byzantine craftspeople—jewelry, gemstones, silver and gold work, linen and woolen textiles, purple dyes—were much in demand. Its silk industry, based on Chinese technology, supplied much of the Mediterranean basin with this precious fabric.

The cultural influence of Byzantium was likewise significant. Preserving much of ancient Greek learning, the Byzantine Empire transmitted this classical heritage to the Islamic world as well as to the Christian West. In both places, it had an immensely stimulating impact among scientists, philosophers, theologians, and other intellectuals. Some saw it as an aid to faith and to an understanding of the world, while others feared it as impious and distracting. (See the section "Reason and Faith" later in this chapter.)

Byzantine religious culture also spread widely among Slavic-speaking peoples in the Balkans and Russia. As lands to the south and the east were overtaken by Islam, Byzantium looked to the north. By the early eleventh century, steady military pressure had brought many of the Balkan Slavic peoples, especially the Bulgars, under Byzantine control. Christianity and literacy accompanied this Byzantine offensive. Already in the ninth century, two Byzantine missionaries, Cyril and Methodius, had developed an alphabet, based on Greek letters, with which Slavic languages could be written. This Cyrillic script made it possible to translate the Bible and other religious literature into these languages and greatly aided the process of conversion.

The Conversion of Russia

The most significant expansion of Orthodox Christianity occurred among the Slavic peoples of what is now Ukraine and western Russia. In this culturally diverse region, which also included Finnic and Baltic peoples as well as Viking traders, a modest state known as Kievan Rus—named after the most prominent city, Kiev—emerged in the ninth century C.E. Like many of the new third-wave civilizations, the development of Rus was stimulated by trade, in this case along the Dnieper River, linking Scandinavia and Byzantium. Loosely led by various princes, especially the prince of Kiev, Rus was a society of slaves and freemen, privileged people and commoners, dominant men and subordinate women. This stratification marked it as a third-wave civilization in the making (see Map 10.3 on page 439).

■ **Connection**
How did links to Byzantium transform the new civilization of Kievan Rus?

Religion reflected the region's cultural diversity, with the gods and practices of many peoples much in evidence. Ancestral spirits, household deities, and various gods related to the forces of nature were in evidence with Perun, the god of thunder, perhaps the most prominent. Small numbers of Christians, Muslims, and Jews were likewise part of the mix. Then, in the late tenth century, a decisive turning point occurred. The growing interaction of Rus with the larger world prompted Prince Vladimir of Kiev to affiliate with one of the major religions of the area. He was searching for a faith that would unify the diverse peoples of his region, while linking Rus into wider networks of communication and exchange. According to ancient chronicles, he actively considered Judaism, Islam, Roman Catholicism, and Greek Orthodoxy before finally deciding on the religion of Byzantium. He rejected Islam, the chronicles tell us, because it prohibited alcoholic drink and "drinking is the joy of the Russes." The splendor of Constantinople's Orthodox churches apparently captured the imagination of Rus's envoys, for there, they reported, "[W]e knew not whether we were in heaven or on earth."[10] Political and commercial considerations no doubt also played a role in Vladimir's decision, and he acquired a sister of the Byzantine emperor as his bride, along with numerous Byzantine priests and advisers. Whatever the precise process, it was a freely made decision. Eastern Orthodox Christianity thus came to Rus without the pressure of foreign military defeat or occupation. Eventually, it took deep root among the Russian people.

It was a fateful choice with long-term implications for Russian history, for it brought this fledgling civilization firmly into the world of Orthodox Christianity, separating it from both the realm of Islam and the Roman Catholic West. Like many new civilizations, Rus borrowed extensively from its older and more sophisticated neighbor. Among these borrowings were Byzantine architectural styles, the Cyrillic alphabet, the extensive use of icons, a monastic tradition stressing prayer and service, and political ideals of imperial control of the Church, all of which became part of a transformed Rus. Orthodoxy also provided a more unified identity for this emerging civilization and religious legitimacy for its rulers. Centuries later, when Byzantium had fallen to the Turks, a few Russian church leaders proclaimed the doctrine of a "third Rome." The original Rome had betrayed the faith, and the second Rome, Constantinople, had succumbed to Muslim infidels. Moscow was now the third Rome, the final protector and defender of Orthodox Christianity. Though not widely proclaimed in Russia itself, such a notion reflected the "Russification" of Eastern Orthodoxy and its growing role as an element of Russian national identity. It was also a reminder of the enduring legacy of a thousand years of Byzantine history, long after the empire itself had vanished.

Western Christendom: Rebuilding in the Wake of Roman Collapse

The western half of the Christian world followed a rather different path than that of the Byzantine Empire. For much of the postclassical millennium, it was distinctly on the margins of world history, partly because of its geographic location at the far western end of the Eurasian landmass. Thus it was far removed from the growing routes of world trade—by sea in the Indian Ocean and by land across the Silk Roads to China and the Sand Roads to West Africa. Not until the Eastern and Western hemispheres were joined after 1500 did Western Europe occupy a geographically central position in the global network. Internally, Europe's geography made political unity difficult. It was a region in which population centers were divided by mountain ranges and dense forests as well as by five major peninsulas

Snapshot   Key Moments in the Evolution of Western Civilization

End of the western Roman Empire	476
Papacy of Gregory I	590–604
Muslim conquest of Spain	711
Charlemagne crowned as emperor	800
Otto I crowned as Holy Roman Emperor	962
Viking colony in Newfoundland	1000
Investiture conflict	1059–1152
Crusades begin	1095
Translations of Greek and Arab works available in Europe	12th–13th centuries
Thomas Aquinas	1225–1274
Marco Polo visits China	1271–1295

and two large islands (Britain and Ireland). However, its extensive coastlines and interior river systems facilitated exchange within Europe, while a moderate climate, plentiful rainfall, and fertile soils enabled a productive agriculture that could support a growing population.

Political Life in Western Europe, 500–1000

In the early centuries of the postclassical era, history must have seemed more significant than geography, for the Roman Empire, long a fixture of the western Mediterranean region, had collapsed. The traditional date marking the fall of Rome is 476, when the German general Odoacer overthrew the last Roman emperor in the West. In itself not very important, this event has come to symbolize a major turning point in the West, for much that had characterized Roman civilization also weakened, declined, or disappeared in the several centuries before and after 476. Any semblance of large-scale centralized rule vanished. Disease and warfare reduced Western Europe's population by more than 25 percent. Land under cultivation contracted, while forests, marshland, and wasteland expanded. Urban life too diminished sharply, as Europe reverted to a largely rural existence. Rome at its height was a city of 1 million people, but by the tenth century it numbered perhaps 10,000. Public buildings crumbled from lack of care. Outside Italy, long-distance trade dried up as Roman roads deteriorated, and money exchange gave way to barter in many places. Literacy lost ground as well. Germanic peoples, whom the Romans had viewed as barbarians—Goths, Visigoths, Franks, Lombards, Angles, Saxons—now emerged as the dominant peoples of Western Europe. In the process, Europe's center of gravity moved away from the Mediterranean toward the north and west.

Yet much that was classical or Roman persisted, even as a new order emerged in Europe. On the political front, a series of regional kingdoms—led by Visigoths in Spain, Franks in France, Lombards in Italy, and Angles and Saxons in England—arose to replace Roman authority, but many of these Germanic peoples, originally organized in small kinship-based tribes with strong warrior values, had already been substantially Romanized. Contact with the Roman Empire in the first several centuries C.E. had generated more distinct ethnic identities among them, militarized their societies, and gave greater prominence to Woden, their god of war. As Germanic peoples migrated into or invaded Roman lands, many were deeply influenced by Roman culture, especially if they served in the Roman army. On the funeral monument of one such person was the telling inscription: "I am a Frank by nationality, but a Roman soldier under arms."[11]

The prestige of things Roman remained high, even after the empire itself had collapsed. Now as leaders of their own kingdoms, the Germanic rulers actively embraced written Roman law, using fines and penalties to provide order and justice in their new states in place of feuds and vendettas. One Visigoth ruler named Athaulf (reigned 410–415), who had married a Roman noblewoman, gave voice to the continuing attraction of Roman culture and its empire.

■ **Comparison**

How did the historical development of the European West differ from that of Byzantium in the postclassical era?

■ **Change**

What replaced the Roman order in Western Europe?

At first I wanted to erase the Roman name and convert all Roman territory into a Gothic empire. . . . But long experience has taught me that . . . without law a state is not a state. Therefore I have more prudently chosen the different glory of reviving the Roman name with Gothic vigour, and I hope to be acknowledged by posterity as the initiator of a Roman restoration.[12]

Several of the larger, though relatively short-lived, Germanic kingdoms also had aspirations to re-create something of the unity of the Roman Empire. Charlemagne (reigned 768–814), ruler of the Carolingian Empire, occupying what is now France, Belgium, the Netherlands, and parts of Germany and Italy, erected an embryonic imperial bureaucracy, standardized weights and measures, and began to act like an imperial ruler (see Document 10.3, pp. 458–60). On Christmas Day of the year 800, he was crowned as a new Roman emperor by the pope, although his realm splintered shortly after his death (see Map 10.2). Later Otto I of Saxony (reigned 936–973) gathered much of Germany under his control, saw himself as renewing Roman rule, and was likewise invested with the title of emperor by the pope. Otto's realm, subsequently known as the Holy Roman Empire, was largely limited to Germany and soon proved little more than a collection of quarreling principalities. Though unsuccessful in reviving anything approaching Roman imperial authority, these efforts testify to the continuing appeal of the classical world, even as a new political system of rival kingdoms blended Roman and Germanic elements.

Map 10.2 Western Europe in the Ninth Century Charlemagne's Carolingian Empire brought a temporary unity to parts of Western Europe, but it was subsequently divided among his three sons, who waged war on one another.

Society and the Church, 500–1000

Within these new kingdoms, a highly fragmented and decentralized society widely known as feudalism emerged with great local variation. In thousands of independent, self-sufficient, and largely isolated landed estates or manors, power—political, economic, and social—was exercised by a warrior elite of landowning lords. In the constant competition of these centuries, lesser lords and knights swore allegiance to greater lords or kings and thus became their vassals, frequently receiving lands and plunder in return for military service.

Such reciprocal ties between superior and subordinate were also apparent at the bottom of the social hierarchy, as Roman-style slavery gradually gave way to serfdom. Unlike slaves, serfs were not the personal property of their masters, could not be arbitrarily thrown off their land, and were allowed to live in families. However, they were bound to their masters' estates as peasant laborers and owed various payments and services to the lord of the manor. One family on a manor near Paris in the ninth century owed four silver coins, wine, wood, three hens, and fifteen eggs per year. Women generally were required to weave cloth and make clothing for the lord, while men labored in the lord's fields. In return, the serf family received a small farm and such protection as the lord could provide. In a violent and insecure world adjusting to the absence of Roman authority, the only security available to many individuals or families lay in these communities, where the ties to kin, manor, and lord constituted the primary human loyalties. It was a world apart from the stability of life in imperial Rome or its continuation in Byzantium.

Also filling the vacuum left by the collapse of empire was the Church, later known as Roman Catholic, yet another link to the now defunct Roman world. Its hierarchical organization of popes, bishops, priests, and monasteries was modeled on that of the Roman Empire and took over some of its political, administrative, educational, and welfare functions. Latin continued as the language of the Church even as it gave way to various vernacular languages in common speech. In fact literacy in the classical languages of Greek and Latin remained the hallmark of educated people in the West well into the twentieth century.

Like the Buddhist establishment in China, the Church subsequently became extremely wealthy, with reformers often accusing it of forgetting its central spiritual mission. It also provided a springboard for the conversion of Europe's many "pagan" peoples. Numerous missionaries, commissioned by the pope, monasteries, or already converted rulers, fanned out across Europe, generally pursuing a "top-down" strategy. Frequently it worked, as local kings and warlords found status and legitimacy in association with a literate and "civilized" religion that still bore something of the grandeur of Rome. With "the wealth and protection of the powerful," ordinary people followed their rulers into the fold of the Church.[13] This process was similar to Buddhism's appeal for the nomadic rulers of northern and western China following the collapse of the Han dynasty. Christianity, like Buddhism, also bore the promise of superior supernatural powers, and its spread was frequently associated with reported miracles of healing, rainfall, fertility, and victory in battle.

But it was not an easy sell. Outright coercion was sometimes part of the process, as Document 10.3 (pp. 458–60) clearly shows. More often, however, softer methods prevailed. The Church proved willing to accommodate a considerable range of earlier cultural practices, absorbing them into an emerging Christian tradition. For example, amulets and charms to ward off evil became medals with the image of Jesus or the Virgin Mary, traditionally sacred wells and springs became the sites of churches, and festivals honoring ancient gods became Christian holy days. December 25 was selected as the birthday of Jesus, for it was associated with the winter solstice, the coming of more light, and the birth or rebirth of various deities in pre-Christian European traditions. By 1100, most of Europe had embraced Christianity. Even so, priests and bishops had to warn their congregations against the worship of rivers, trees, and mountains, and for many people, ancient gods, monsters, trolls, and spirits still inhabited the land. The spreading Christian faith, like the new political framework of European civilization, was a blend of many elements. (For more on the rooting of Christianity in Western Europe, see Documents 10.1–10.5, pp. 455–61.)

Church authorities and the nobles/warriors who exercised political influence reinforced each other. Rulers provided protection for the papacy and strong encouragement for the faith. In return, the Church offered religious legitimacy for the powerful and the prosperous. "It is the will of the Creator," declared the teaching of the Church, "that the higher shall always rule over the lower. Each individual and class should stay in its place [and] perform its tasks."[14] But Church and nobility competed as well as cooperated, for they were rival centers of power in post-Roman Europe. Particularly controversial was the right to appoint bishops and the pope himself; this issue, known as the investiture conflict, was especially prominent in the eleventh and twelfth centuries. Was the right to make appointments the responsibility of the Church alone, or did kings and emperors also have a role? In the compromise that ended the conflict, the Church won the right to appoint its own officials, while secular rulers retained an informal and symbolic role in the process.

Accelerating Change in the West, 1000–1300

The pace of change in this emerging civilization picked up considerably in the several centuries after 1000. For the preceding 300 years, Europe had been subject to repeated invasions from every direction. Muslim armies had conquered Spain and threatened the rest of Europe. Magyar (Hungarian) invasions from the east and Viking incursions from the north likewise disrupted and threatened post-Roman Europe (see Map 10.3). But by the year 1000, these invasions had been checked and the invaders absorbed into settled society. The greater security and stability that came with relative peace arguably opened the way to an accelerating tempo of change. The climate also seemed to cooperate. A generally warming trend after 750 reached its peak in the eleventh and twelfth centuries, enhancing agricultural production.

■ **Change**
In what ways was European civilization changing after 1000?

Whatever may have launched this new phase of European civilization, commonly called the High Middle Ages (1000–1300), the signs of expansion and growth were widely evident. The population of Europe grew from perhaps 35 million in 1000 to about 80 million in 1340. With more people, many new lands were opened for cultivation in a process paralleling that of China's expansion to the south at the same time. Great lords, bishops, and religious orders organized new villages on what had recently been forest or wasteland. Marshes were drained; land was reclaimed from the sea in the Netherlands; everywhere trees were felled. By 1300, the forest cover of Europe had been reduced to about 20 percent of the land area. "I believe

Map 10.3   Europe in the High Middle Ages

By the eleventh century, the national monarchies—of France, Spain, England, Poland, and Germany—that would organize European political life had begun to take shape. The earlier external attacks on Europe from Vikings, Magyars, and Muslims had largely ceased, although it was clear that European civilization was developing in the shadow of the Islamic world.

that the forest . . . covers the land to no purpose," declared a German abbot, "and hold this to be an unbearable harm."[15]

The increased production associated with this agricultural expansion stimulated a considerable growth in long-distance trade, much of which had dried up in the aftermath of the Roman collapse. One center of commercial activity lay in Northern

Europe from England to the Baltic coast and involved the exchange of wood, beeswax, furs, rye, wheat, salt, cloth, and wine. The other major trading network centered on northern Italian towns such as Florence, Genoa, and Venice. Their trading partners were the more established civilizations of Islam and Byzantium, and the primary objects of trade included the silks, drugs, precious stones, and spices from Asia. At great trading fairs, particularly those in the Champagne area of France near Paris, merchants from Northern and Southern Europe met to exchange the products of their respective areas, such as northern woolens for Mediterranean spices. Thus the self-sufficient communities of earlier centuries increasingly forged commercial bonds among themselves and with more distant peoples.

The population of towns and cities likewise grew on the sites of older Roman towns, at trading crossroads and fortifications, and around cathedrals all over Europe. Some had only a few hundred people, but others became much larger. In the early 1300s, London had about 40,000 people, Paris had approximately 80,000, and Venice by the end of the fourteenth century could boast perhaps 150,000. To keep these figures in perspective, Constantinople housed some 400,000 people in 1000, Córdoba in Muslim Spain about 500,000, the Song dynasty capital of Hangzhou more than 1 million in the thirteenth century, and the Aztec capital of Tenochtitlán perhaps 200,000 by 1500. Nonetheless, urbanization was proceeding apace in Europe. These towns gave rise to and attracted new groups of people, particularly merchants, bankers, artisans, and university-trained professionals such as lawyers, doctors, and scholars. Many of these groups, including university professors and students, organized themselves into guilds (associations of people pursuing the same line of work) in order to regulate their respective professions. In doing so, they introduced a new and more productive division of labor into European society.

Between the eleventh and thirteenth centuries, economic growth and urbanization offered European women substantial new opportunities. Women were active in a number of urban professions, such as weaving, brewing, milling grain, midwifery, small-scale retailing, laundering, spinning, and prostitution. In twelfth-century Paris, for example, a list of 100 occupations identified 86 as involving women workers, of which 6 were exclusively female. In England, women worked as silk weavers, hatmakers, tailors, brewers, and leather processors and were entitled to train female apprentices in some of these trades. In Frankfurt, about one-third of the crafts and trades were entirely female, another 40 percent were dominated by men, and the rest were open to both. Widows of great merchants sometimes continued their husbands' businesses, and one of them, Rose Burford, lent a large sum of money to the king of England to finance a war against Scotland in 1318.

By the fifteenth century, such opportunities were declining. Most women's guilds were gone, and women were restricted or banned from many others. Even brothels were run by men. Technological progress may have been one reason for this change. Water- and animal-powered grain mills replaced the hand-grinding previously undertaken by women, and larger looms making heavier cloth replaced the

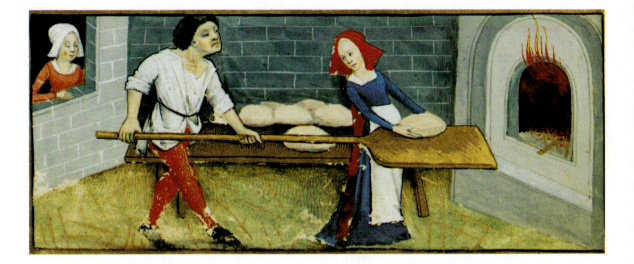

European Women at Work
This manuscript painting from the Middle Ages shows women and men cooperating in the baking of bread, long a staple of European diets. (Bibliothèque nationale de France)

lighter looms that women had worked. Men increasingly took over these professions and trained their sons as apprentices, making it more difficult for women to remain active in these fields.

If urban work roles were diminishing for women, religious life provided other possibilities. As in Buddhist lands, substantial numbers of women, particularly from aristocratic families, were attracted to the secluded life of poverty, chastity, and obedience within a nunnery for the relative freedom from male control that it offered. Here was one of the few places where some women could exercise authority and obtain a measure of education. Operating outside of monastic life, the Beguines were groups of laywomen, often from poorer families in Northern Europe, who lived together, practiced celibacy, and devoted themselves to weaving and to working with the sick, the old, and the poor. Another religious role was that of anchoress, a woman who withdrew to a locked cell, usually attached to a church, where she devoted herself to prayer and fasting. Some of them gained reputations for great holiness and were much sought after for spiritual guidance. For a few women—the nun Hildegard of Bingen and the anchoress Julian of Norwich, for example—religious life brought considerable public prominence and spiritual influence.

A further sign of accelerating change in the West lay in the growth of territorial states with more effective institutions of government commanding the loyalty, or at least the obedience, of their subjects. Since the disintegration of the Roman Empire, Europeans' loyalties had focused on the family, the manor, or the religious community, but seldom on the state. Great lords may have been recognized as kings, but their authority was extremely limited and was exercised through a complex and decentralized network of feudal relationships with earls, counts, barons, and knights, who often felt little obligation to do the king's bidding. But in the eleventh through the thirteenth century, the nominal monarchs of Europe gradually and painfully began to consolidate their authority, and the outlines of French, English, Spanish, Scandinavian, and other states began to appear, each with its own distinct language and culture (see Map 10.3). Royal courts and embryonic bureaucracies were established, and groups of professional administrators appeared. Territorial kingdoms were not universal, however. In Italy, city-states flourished as urban areas grew wealthy and powerful, whereas the Germans remained loyal to a large number of small principalities within the Holy Roman Empire.

Europe Outward Bound: The Crusading Tradition

■ **Change**

What was the impact of the Crusades in world history?

Accompanying the growth of European civilization after 1000 were efforts to engage more actively with both near and more distant neighbors. This "medieval expansion" of Western Christendom took place as the Byzantine world was contracting under pressure from the West, from Arab invasion, and later from Turkish conquest. The western half of Christendom was on the rise, while the eastern part was in decline. It was a sharp reversal of their earlier trajectories.

Expansion, of course, has been characteristic of virtually every civilization and has taken a variety of forms—territorial conquest, empire building, settlement of new lands, vigorous trading initiatives, and missionary activity. European civilization was no exception. As population mounted, settlers cleared new land, much of it on the eastern fringes of Europe. The Vikings of Scandinavia, having raided much of Europe, set off on a maritime transatlantic venture around 1000 that briefly established a colony in Newfoundland in North America, and more durably in Greenland and Iceland. As Western economies grew, merchants, travelers, diplomats, and missionaries brought European society into more intensive contact with more distant peoples and with Eurasian commercial networks. By the thirteenth and fourteenth centuries, Europeans had direct, though limited, contact with India, China, and Mongolia. Europe clearly was outward bound.

Nothing more dramatically revealed European expansiveness and the religious passions that informed it than the Crusades, a series of "holy wars" that captured the imagination of Western Christendom for more than four centuries, beginning in 1095. In European thinking and practice, the Crusades were wars undertaken at God's command and authorized by the pope as the Vicar of Christ on earth. They required participants to swear a vow and in return offered an indulgence, which removed the penalties for any confessed sins, as well as various material benefits, such as immunity from lawsuits and a moratorium on the repayment of debts. Any number of political, economic, and social motives underlay the Crusades, but at their core they were religious wars. Within Europe, the amazing support for the Crusades reflected an understanding of them "as providing security against mortal enemies threatening the spiritual health of all Christendom and all Christians."[16] Crusading drew upon both Christian piety and the warrior values of the elite, with little sense of contradiction between these impulses.

The most famous Crusades were those aimed at wresting Jerusalem and the holy places associated with the life of Jesus from Islamic control and returning them to Christendom (see Map 10.4). Beginning in 1095, wave after wave of Crusaders from all walks of life and many countries flocked to the eastern Mediterranean, where they temporarily carved out four small Christian states, the last of which was recaptured by Muslim forces in 1291. Led or supported by an assortment of kings, popes, bishops, monks, lords, nobles, and merchants, the Crusades demonstrated a growing European capacity for organization, finance, transportation, and recruitment, made all the more impressive by the absence of any centralized direction for the project. They also demonstrated considerable cruelty. The seizure of Jerusalem in 1099 was accompanied by the slaughter of many Muslims and Jews as the Crusaders made their way, according to perhaps exaggerated reports, through streets littered with corpses and ankle deep in blood to the tomb of Christ.

Map 10.4   The Crusades

Western Europe's crusading tradition reflected the expansive energy and religious impulses of an emerging civilization. It was directed against Muslims in the Middle East, Sicily, and Spain as well as the Eastern Orthodox Christians of the Byzantine Empire. The Crusades also involved attacks on Jewish communities, probably the first organized mass pogroms against Jews in Europe's history.

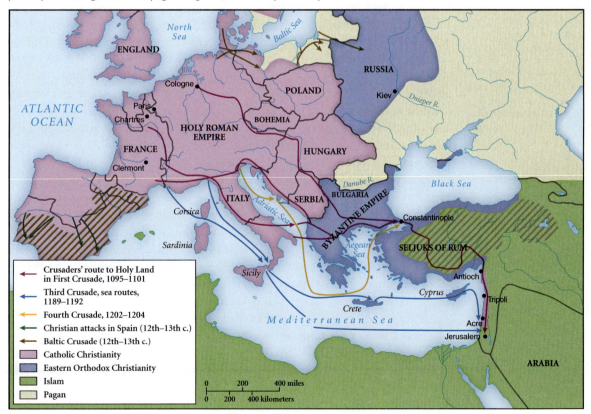

Christians and Muslims
This fourteenth-century painting illustrates the Christian seizure of Jerusalem during the First Crusade in 1099. The crowned figure in the center is Godefroi de Bouillon, a French knight and nobleman who played a prominent role in the attack and was briefly known as the king of Jerusalem. (Snark/Art Resource, NY)

Crusading was not limited to targets in the Islamic Middle East, however. Those Christians who waged war for centuries to reclaim the Iberian Peninsula from Muslim hands were likewise declared "crusaders," with a similar set of spiritual and material benefits. So too were Scandinavian and German warriors who took part in wars to conquer, settle, and convert lands along the Baltic Sea. The Byzantine Empire and Russia, both of which followed Eastern Orthodox Christianity, were also on the receiving end of Western crusading, as were Christian heretics and various enemies of the pope in Europe itself. Crusading, in short, was a pervasive feature of European expansion, which persisted as Europeans began their oceanic voyages in the fifteenth century and beyond.

Surprisingly perhaps, the Crusades had little lasting impact, either politically or religiously, in the Middle East. European power was not sufficiently strong or long-lasting to induce much conversion, and the small European footholds there had come under Muslim control by 1300. The penetration of Turkic-speaking peoples from Central Asia and the devastating Mongol invasions of the thirteenth century were far more significant in Islamic history than were the temporary incursions of European Christians. In fact, Muslims largely forgot about the Crusades until the late nineteenth and early twentieth centuries, when their memory was revived in the context of a growing struggle against European imperialism.

In Europe, however, interaction with the Islamic world had very significant long-term consequences. Spain, Sicily, and the Baltic region were brought permanently into the world of Western Christendom, while a declining Byzantium was further weakened by the Crusader sacking of Constantinople in 1204 and left even more vulnerable to Turkish conquest. In Europe itself, popes strengthened their position, at least for a time, in their continuing struggles with secular authorities. Tens of thousands of Europeans came into personal contact with the Islamic world, from which they picked up a taste for the many luxury goods available there, stimulating a demand for Asian goods. They also learned techniques for producing sugar on large plantations using slave labor, a process that had incalculable consequences in later centuries as Europeans transferred the plantation system to the Americas. Muslim scholarship, together with the Greek learning that it incorporated, also flowed into Europe, largely through Spain and Sicily.

If the cross-cultural contacts born of crusading opened channels of trade, technology transfer, and intellectual exchange, they also hardened cultural barriers between peoples. The rift between Eastern Orthodoxy and Roman Catholicism deepened further and remains to this day a fundamental divide in the Christian world. Christian anti-Semitism was both expressed and exacerbated as Crusaders on their way to Jerusalem found time to massacre Jews in a number of European cities. European empire building, especially in the Americas, continued the crusading notion that "God wills it." And more recently, over the past two centuries, as the world of the Christian West and that of Islam collided, both sides found many occasions in which images of the Crusades, however distorted, proved politically or ideologically useful.[17]

The West in Comparative Perspective

At one level, the making of Western civilization in the postclassical era was unremarkable. Civilizations had risen, fallen, renewed themselves, and evolved at many times and in many places. The European case has received extraordinary scrutiny, not so much because of its special significance at the time, but because of its later role as a globally dominant region. Historians have sometimes sought to account for Western Europe's global influence after 1500 in terms of some unique feature of its earlier history. However we might explain Europe's later rise to prominence on the world stage, its development in the several centuries after 1000 made only modest ripples beyond its own region. In some respects, Europe was surely distinctive, but it was not yet a major player in the global arena. Comparisons, particularly with China, help to place European developments in a world history context.

Catching Up

As the civilization of the West evolved, it was clearly less developed in comparison to Byzantium, China, India, and the Islamic world. European cities were smaller, its political authorities weaker, its economy less commercialized, its technology inferior to the more established civilizations. Muslim observers who encountered Europeans saw them as barbarians. An Arab geographer of the tenth century commented as follows: "Their bodies are large, their manners harsh, their understanding dull, and their tongues heavy. . . . Those of them who are farthest to the north are the most subject to stupidity, grossness and brutishness."[18] Muslim travelers over the next several centuries saw more to be praised in West African kingdoms, where Islam was practiced and gold was plentiful.

Furthermore, thoughtful Europeans who directly encountered other peoples often acknowledged their own comparative backwardness. "In our time," wrote a twelfth-century European scholar, "it is in Toledo [a Spanish city long under Muslim rule] that the teaching of the Arabs . . . is offered to the crowds. I hastened there to listen to the teaching of the wisest philosophers of this world."[19] The Italian traveler Marco Polo in the thirteenth century proclaimed Hangzhou in China "the finest and noblest [city] in the world." In the sixteenth century, Spanish invaders of Mexico were stunned at the size and wealth of the Aztec capital, especially its huge market, claiming that "we had never seen such a thing before."[20]

■ **Change**
In what ways did borrowing from abroad shape European civilization after 1000?

Curious about the rest of the world, Europeans proved quite willing to engage with and borrow from the more advanced civilizations to the east. Growing European economies, especially in the northwest, reconnected with the Eurasian trading system, with which they had lost contact after the fall of Rome. Now European elites eagerly sought spices, silks, porcelain, sugar, and much else that was available on the world market. Despite their belief in Christianity as the "one true religion," Europeans embraced scientific treatises and business practices from the Arabs, philosophical and artistic ideas from the pagan Greeks, and mathematical concepts from India. It was China, however, that was the most significant source of European borrowing, although often indirectly. From that East Asian civilization, Europeans learned about the compass, papermaking, gunpowder, nautical technology, iron casting, a public postal service, and more. When the road to China opened in the thirteenth and fourteenth centuries, many Europeans, including the merchant-traveler Marco Polo, were more than willing to make the long and difficult journey, returning with amazing tales of splendor and abundance far beyond what was available in Europe. When Europeans took to the oceans in the fifteenth and sixteenth centuries, they were seeking out the sources of African and Asian wealth. Thus the accelerating growth of European civilization was accompanied by its reintegration into the larger Afro-Eurasian networks of exchange and communication.

In this willingness to borrow, Europe resembled several other third-wave civilizations of the time. Japan, for example, took much from China; West Africa drew heavily on Islamic civilization; and Russia actively imitated Byzantium. All of them were then developing civilizations, in a position similar to the developing countries of the third world in the twentieth century. The whole process was then rather less deliberate and self-conscious than it became in the last century.

Technological borrowing required adaptation to the unique conditions of Europe and was accompanied by considerable independent invention as well. Together these processes generated a significant tradition of technological innovation that allowed Europe by 1500 to catch up with, and in some areas perhaps to surpass, China and the Islamic world. That achievement bears comparison with the economic revolution of Tang and Song dynasty China, although Europe began at a lower level and depended more on borrowing than did its Chinese counterpart (see Chapter 9). But in the several centuries surrounding 1000 at both ends of Eurasia, major processes of technological innovation were under way.

In Europe, technological breakthroughs first became apparent in agriculture as Europeans adapted to the very different environmental conditions north of the Alps in the several centuries following 500 C.E. They developed a heavy wheeled plow that could handle the dense soils of Northern Europe far better than the light or "scratch" plow used in Mediterranean agriculture. To pull the plow, Europeans began to rely increasingly on horses rather than oxen and to use iron horseshoes and a more efficient collar, which probably originated in China or Central Asia and could support much heavier loads. In addition, Europeans developed a new three-field system of crop rotation, which allowed considerably more land to be planted at any one time. These were the technological foundations for a more productive agriculture that could support the growing population of European civilization, and especially its urban centers, far more securely than before.

Beyond agriculture, Europeans began to tap nonanimal sources of energy in a major way, particularly after 1000. A new type of windmill, very different from an earlier Persian version, was widely used in Europe by the twelfth and thirteenth centuries. The water-driven mill was even more important. The Romans had used such mills largely to grind grain, but their development was limited, given that few streams flowed all year and many slaves were available to do the work. By the ninth century, however, water mills were rapidly becoming more evident in Europe. In the early fourteenth century, a concentration of sixty-eight mills dotted a one-mile stretch of the Seine River near Paris. In addition to grinding grain, these mills provided power for sieving flour, tanning hides, making beer, sawing wood, manufacturing iron, and making paper. Devices such as cranks, flywheels, camshafts, and complex gearing mechanisms, when combined with water or wind power, enabled Europeans of the High Middle Ages to revolutionize production in a number of industries and to break with the ancient tradition of depending almost wholly on animal or human muscle as sources of energy. So intense was the interest of European artisans and engineers in tapping mechanical sources of energy that a number of them experimented with perpetual-motion machines, an idea borrowed from Indian philosophers.

Technological borrowing also was evident in the arts of war. Gunpowder was invented in China, but Europeans were probably the first to use it in cannons, in the early fourteenth century, and by 1500 they had the most advanced arsenals in the world. In 1517, one Chinese official, upon first encountering European ships and weapons, remarked with surprise, "The westerns are extremely dangerous because of their artillery. No weapon ever made since memorable antiquity is superior to their cannon."[21] Advances in shipbuilding and navigational techniques—including the magnetic compass and sternpost rudder from China and adaptations of the Mediterranean or Arab lateen sail, which enabled

European Technology
Europeans' fascination with technology and their religious motivation for investigating the world are apparent in this thirteenth-century portrayal of God as a divine engineer, laying out the world with a huge compass. (Erich Lessing/Art Resource, NY)

vessels to sail against the wind—provided the foundation for European mastery of the seas.

Europe's passion for technology was reflected in its culture and ideas as well as in its machines. About 1260, the English scholar and Franciscan friar Roger Bacon wrote of the possibilities he foresaw, and in doing so, he expressed the confident spirit of the age:

> Machines of navigation can be constructed, without rowers...which are borne under the guidance of one man at a greater speed than if they were full of men. Also a chariot can be constructed, that will move with incalculable speed without any draught animal....Also flying machines may be constructed so that a man may sit in the midst of the machine turning a certain instrument by means of which wings artificially constructed would beat the air after the manner of a bird flying...and there are countless other things that can be constructed.[22]

Pluralism in Politics

■ **Comparison**

Why was Europe unable to achieve the kind of political unity that China experienced? What impact did this have on the subsequent history of Europe?

Unlike the large centralized states of Byzantium, the Islamic world, and China, post-Roman European civilization never regained the unity it had under Roman rule. Rather, political life gradually crystallized into a system of competing states (France, Spain, England, Sweden, Prussia, the Netherlands, and Poland, among others) that has persisted into the twenty-first century and that the European Union still confronts. Geographic barriers, ethnic and linguistic diversity, and the shifting balances of power among its many states prevented the emergence of a single European empire, despite periodic efforts to re-create something resembling the still-remembered unity of the Roman Empire.

This multicentered political system shaped the emerging civilization of the West in many ways. It gave rise to frequent wars, enhanced the role and status of military men, and drove the "gunpowder revolution." Thus European society and values were militarized far more than in China, which gave greater prominence to scholars and bureaucrats. Intense interstate rivalry, combined with a willingness to borrow, also stimulated European technological development. By 1500, Europeans had gone a long way toward catching up with their more advanced Asian counterparts in agriculture, industry, war, and sailing.

But endemic warfare did not halt European economic growth. Capital, labor, and goods found their way around political barriers, while the common assumptions of Christian culture and the use of Latin and later French by the literate elite fostered communication across political borders. Europe's multistate system thus provided enough competition to be stimulating but also sufficient order and unity to allow economic endeavors to prosper.

The states within this emerging European civilization also differed from those to the east. Their rulers generally were weaker and had to contend with competing sources of power. Unlike the Orthodox Church in Byzantium, with its practice of caesaropapism, the Roman Catholic Church in the West maintained a degree of independence from state authority that served to check the power of kings and lords. European vassals had certain rights in return for loyalty to their lords and kings. By the thirteenth century, this meant that high-ranking nobles, acting through formal councils, had the right to advise their rulers and to approve new taxes.

This three-way struggle for power among kings, warrior aristocrats, and church leaders, all of them from the nobility, enabled urban-based merchants in Europe to achieve an unusual independence from political authority. Many cities, where wealthy merchants exercised local power, won the right to make and enforce their own laws and appoint their own officials. Some of them—Venice, Genoa, Pisa, and Milan, for example—became almost completely independent city-states. In the case of other cities, kings granted charters that allowed them to have their own courts, laws, and governments, while paying their own kind of taxes to the king instead of feudal dues. Powerful, independent cities were a distinctive feature of European life after 1100 or so. By contrast, Chinese cities, which were far larger than those of Europe, were simply part of the empire and enjoyed few special privileges. Although commerce was far more extensive in China than in an emerging European civilization, the powerful Chinese state favored the landowners over merchants, monopolized the salt and iron industries, and actively controlled and limited merchant activity far more than the new and weaker royal authorities of Europe were able to do.

The relative weakness of Europe's rulers allowed urban merchants more leeway and, according to some historians, paved the way to a more thorough development of capitalism in later centuries. It also led to the development of representative institutions or parliaments through which the views and interests of these contending forces could be expressed and accommodated. Intended to strengthen royal authority by consulting with major social groups, these embryonic parliaments did not represent the "people" or the "nation" but instead embodied the three great "estates of the realm"—the clergy (the first estate), the landowning nobility (the second estate), and urban merchants (the third estate).

Reason and Faith

A further feature of this emerging European civilization was a distinctive intellectual tension between the claims of human reason and those of faith. Christianity, of course, had developed in a classical world suffused with Greek rationalism. Some early Christian thinkers sought to maintain a clear separation between the new religion and the ideas of Plato and Aristotle. "What indeed has Athens to do with Jerusalem?" asked Tertullian (150–225 C.E.), an early church leader from North Africa. More common, however, was the notion that Greek philosophy could serve as a "handmaiden" to faith, more fully disclosing the truths of Christianity. In the reduced circumstances of Western Europe after the collapse of the Roman Empire,

■ Comparison

In what different ways did classical Greek philosophy and science have an impact in the West, in Byzantium, and in the Islamic world?

European University Life in the Middle Ages
This fourteenth-century manuscript painting shows a classroom scene from the University of Bologna in Italy. Note the sleeping and disruptive students. Some things apparently never change. (Bildarchiv Preussischer Kulturbesitz/Art Resource, NY)

the Church had little direct access to the writings of the Greeks, although some Latin translations and commentaries provided a continuing link to the world of classical thought.

But intellectual life in Europe changed dramatically in the several centuries after 1000, amid a rising population, a quickening commercial life, emerging towns and cities, and the Church's growing independence from royal or noble authorities. Moreover, the West was developing a legal system that guaranteed a measure of independence for a variety of institutions—towns and cities, guilds, professional associations, and especially universities. An outgrowth of earlier cathedral schools, these European universities—in Paris, Bologna, Oxford, Cambridge, Salamanca—became "zones of intellectual autonomy" in which scholars could pursue their studies with some freedom from the dictates of religious or political authorities, although that freedom was never complete and was frequently contested.[23]

This was the setting in which European Christian thinkers, a small group of literate churchmen, began to emphasize, quite self-consciously, the ability of human reason to penetrate divine mysteries and to grasp the operation of the natural order. An early indication of this new emphasis occurred in the late eleventh century when students in a monastic school in France asked their teacher, Anselm, to provide them a proof for the existence of God based solely on reason, without using the Bible or other sources of divine revelation.

The new interest in rational thought was applied first and foremost to theology, the "queen of the sciences" to European thinkers. Here was an effort to provide a rational foundation for faith, not to replace faith or to rebel against it. Logic, philosophy, and rationality would operate in service to Christ. Of course, some people opposed this new emphasis on human reason. Bernard of Clairvaux, a twelfth-century French abbot, declared, "Faith believes. It does not dispute."[24] His contemporary and intellectual opponent, the French scholar William of Conches, lashed out: "You poor fools. God can make a cow out of a tree, but has he ever done so? Therefore show some reason why a thing is so or cease to hold that it is so."[25]

European intellectuals also applied their newly discovered confidence in human reason to law, medicine, and the world of nature, exploring optics, magnetism, astronomy, and alchemy. Slowly and never completely, the scientific study of nature, known as "natural philosophy," began to separate itself from theology. In European universities, natural philosophy was studied in the faculty of arts, which was separate from the faculty of theology, although many scholars contributed to both fields.

This mounting enthusiasm for rational inquiry stimulated European scholars to seek out original Greek texts, particularly those of Aristotle. They found them in the Greek-speaking world of Byzantium and in the Arab world, where they had long ago been translated into Arabic. In the twelfth and thirteenth centuries, an explosion of translations from Greek and Arabic into Latin gave European scholars direct access to the works of ancient Greeks and to the remarkable results of Arab scholarship in astronomy, optics, medicine, pharmacology, and more. Much of this Arab science was now translated into Latin and provided a boost to Europe's changing intellectual life, centered in the new universities. One of these translators, Adelard of Bath (1080–1142), remarked that he had learned, "under the guidance of reason from Arabic teachers," not to trust established authority.[26]

It was the works of the prolific Aristotle, with his logical approach and "scientific temperament," that made the deepest impression. His writings became the basis for university education and largely dominated the thought of Western Europe in the five centuries after 1200. In the work of the thirteenth-century theologian Thomas Aquinas, Aristotle's ideas were thoroughly integrated into a logical and systematic presentation of Christian doctrine. In this growing emphasis on human rationality, at least partially separate from divine revelation, lay one of the foundations of the later Scientific Revolution and the secularization of European intellectual life.

Surprisingly, nothing comparable occurred in the Byzantine Empire, where knowledge of the Greek language was widespread and access to Greek texts was easy. Although Byzantine scholars kept the classical tradition alive, their primary interest lay in the humanities (literature, philosophy, history) and theology rather than in the natural sciences or medicine. Furthermore, both state and church had serious reservations about classical Greek learning. In 529, the emperor Justinian closed Plato's Academy in Athens, claiming that it was an outpost of paganism. Its scholars dispersed into lands that soon became Islamic, carrying Greek learning into the Islamic world. Church authorities as well were suspicious of classical Greek thought, sometimes persecuting scholars who were too enamored with the ancients. Even those who did study the Greek writers did so in a conservative spirit, concerned to preserve and transmit the classical heritage rather than using it as a springboard for creating new knowledge. "The great men of the past," declared the fourteenth-century Byzantine scholar and statesman Theodore Metochites, "have said everything so perfectly that they have left nothing for us to say."[27]

In the Islamic world, classical Greek thought was embraced "with far more enthusiasm and creativity" than in Byzantium.[28] A massive translation project in the ninth and tenth centuries made Aristotle and many other Greek writers available in Arabic. That work contributed to a flowering of Arab scholarship, especially in the sciences and natural philosophy, between roughly 800 and 1200 (see Chapter 11), but it also stimulated a debate about faith and reason among Muslim thinkers, many of whom greatly admired Greek philosophical, scientific, and medical texts. As in the Christian world, the issue was whether secular Greek thought was an aid or a threat to the faith. Western European church authorities after the thirteenth century had come to regard natural philosophy as a wholly legitimate enterprise and had thoroughly incorporated Aristotle into university education, but learned opinion in the Islamic world swung the other way. Though never completely disappearing from Islamic scholarship, the ideas of Plato and Aristotle receded after the thirteenth century in favor of teachings that drew more directly from the Quran or from mystical experience. Nor was natural philosophy a central concern of Islamic higher education as it was in the West. The integration of political and religious life in the Islamic world, as in Byzantium, contrasted with their separation in the West, where there was more space for the independent pursuit of scientific subjects.

Reflections: Remembering and Forgetting: Continuity and Surprise in the Worlds of Christendom

Many of the characteristic features of Christendom, which emerged during the era of third-wave civilizations, have had a long life, extending well into the modern era. The crusading element of European expansion was prominent among the motives of Spanish and Portuguese explorers. Europe's grudging freedom for merchant activity and its eagerness to borrow foreign technology arguably contributed to the growth of capitalism and industrialization in later centuries. The endemic military conflicts of European states, unable to recover the unity of the Roman Empire, found terrible expression in the world wars of the twentieth century. The controversy about reason and faith resonates still, at least in the United States, in debates about the authority of the Bible in secular and scientific matters. The rift between Eastern Orthodoxy and Roman Catholicism remains one of the major divides in the Christian world. Modern universities and the separation of religious and political authority likewise have their origins in the European Middle Ages. Such a perspective, linking the past with what came later, represents one of the great contributions that the study of history makes to human understanding.

Yet that very strength of historical study can be misleading, particularly if it suggests a kind of inevitability, in which the past determines the future. Some historians have argued, looking backward from the present, that Europe's industrial transformation and global domination in the nineteenth century grew inexorably out of its unique character as a changing civilization after 1000. This kind of thinking, however, misses the great surprise of Europe's more recent historical trajectory, and it minimizes the way people at the time understood their world.

Surely in 1000, few people would have predicted the startling reversal of roles between the Eastern and Western wings of Christendom, which the next several centuries witnessed. At that time, the many small, rural, unsophisticated, and endlessly quarreling warrior-based societies of Western Europe would hardly have borne comparison with the powerful Byzantine Empire and its magnificent capital of Constantinople. Even in 1500, when Europe had begun to catch up with China and the Islamic world in various ways, there was little to predict its remarkable transformation over the next several centuries and the dramatic change in the global balance of power that this transformation produced. To recapture the unexpectedness of the historical process and to allow ourselves to be surprised, it may be useful on occasion to forget the future and to see the world as contemporaries viewed it.

Second Thoughts

What's the Significance?

Byzantine Empire

Constantinople

Justinian

caesaropapism

Eastern Orthodox
   Christianity

icons

Kievan Rus

Prince Vladimir of Kiev

Charlemagne

Holy Roman Empire

Roman Catholic Church

Western Christendom

Crusades

European cities

system of competing
   states

Aristotle and classical
   Greek learning

To assess your mastery of the material in this chapter, visit the **Student Center** at bedfordstmartins.com/strayer.

Big Picture Questions

1. How did the histories of the Byzantine Empire and Western Europe differ during the era of third-wave civilizations?
2. What accounts for the different historical trajectories of these two expressions of Christendom?
3. How did Byzantium and Western Europe interact with each other and with the larger world of the postclassical era?
4. Was the civilization of the Latin West distinctive and unique, or was it broadly comparable to other third-wave civilizations?
5. How does the history of the Christian world in the postclassical era compare with that of Tang and Song dynasty China?

Next Steps: For Further Study

Renate Bridenthal et al., eds., *Becoming Visible: Women in European History* (1998). A series of essays that reflects recent scholarship on women.

Edward Grant, *Science and Religion from Aristotle to Copernicus* (2004). Demonstrates the impact of Greek philosophy and science in Europe, with comparisons to Byzantium and the Islamic world.

For Web sites and additional documents related to this chapter, see **Make History** at bedfordstmartins.com/strayer.

Barbara A. Hanawalt, *The Middle Ages: An Illustrated History* (1999). A brief and beautifully illustrated introduction to the Middle Ages in European history.

Rowena Loverance, *Byzantium* (2004). A lavishly illustrated history of the Byzantine Empire, drawing on the rich collection of artifacts in the British Museum.

Christopher Tyerman, *Fighting for Christendom: Holy Wars and the Crusades* (2005). A very well-written, up-to-date history of the Crusades designed for nonspecialists.

Mark Whittow, *The Making of Byzantium, 600–1025* (1996). An engaging account of Byzantium at its height, with an emphasis on its external connections.

"Middle Ages," http://www.learner.org/exhibits/middleages. An interactive Web site with text and images relating to life in Europe after the collapse of the Roman Empire.

Documents

Considering the Evidence:
The Making of Christian Europe . . .
and a Chinese Counterpoint

Like Buddhism, Christianity became a universal religion, taking root well beyond its place of origin. During the classical era, this new faith, born in a Jewish context in Roman Palestine, spread throughout the Roman Empire, where it received state support during the fourth century C.E. In the centuries that followed the collapse of the western Roman Empire, Christianity also took hold among the peoples of Western Europe in what are now England, France, Germany, and Scandinavia. While we often think about this region as solidly Christian, Western Europe in the period between 500 and 1000 C.E. was very much on the frontier of an expanding Christian world. During those centuries, a number of emerging monarchs of post-Roman Europe found the Christian faith and the Church useful in consolidating their new and fragile states by linking them to the legacy of the Roman Empire. Although the religion of Jesus ultimately became widely accepted, the making of Christian Europe was a prolonged and tentative process, filled with setbacks, resistance, and struggles among variant versions of the faith as well as growing acceptance and cultural compromise. An interesting counterpoint to the story of Christianity in Western Europe lies in its spread to China at about the same time. There, however, it did not take root in any permanent fashion, although it briefly generated a fascinating expression of the Christian faith.

Document 10.1

The Conversion of Clovis

Among the Germanic peoples of post-Roman Western Europe, none were of greater significance than the Franks, occupying the region of present-day France (see Map 10.1, p. 428). By the early sixth century, a more or less unified Frankish kingdom had emerged under the leadership of Clovis (reigned 485–511), whose Merovingian dynasty ruled the area until 751. Clovis's conversion to Christianity was described about a century later by a well-known bishop and writer, Gregory of Tours (538–594). It was an important step in the triumph of Christianity over Frankish "paganism." It also marked the victory of what would later become Roman Catholicism, based on the idea of the Trinity, over a rival form of the Christian faith, known as Arianism, which held that Jesus was a created divine being subordinate to God the Father.

- According to Gregory, what led to the conversion of Clovis?

- What issues are evident in the religious discussions of Clovis and his wife, Clotilda?

- Notice how Gregory modeled his picture of Clovis on that of Constantine, the famous Roman emperor whose conversion to Christianity in the fourth century gave official legitimacy and state support to the faith (see Chapter 5). What message did Gregory seek to convey in making this implied comparison?

- How might a modern secular historian use this document to help explain the spread of Christianity among the Franks?

GREGORY OF TOURS

History of the Franks
Late Sixth Century

[Clovis] had a first-born son by queen Clotilda, and as his wife wished to consecrate him in baptism, she tried unceasingly to persuade her husband, saying: "The gods you worship are nothing, and they will be unable to help themselves or any one else. For they are graven out of stone or wood or some metal.... They are endowed rather with the magic arts than with the power of the divine name. But he [God] ought rather to be worshipped who created by his word heaven and earth, the sea and all that in them is out of a state of nothingness... [and] by whose hand mankind was created...."

But though the queen said this, the spirit of the king was by no means moved to belief, and he said: "It was at the command of our gods that all things were created and came forth, and it is plain that your God has no power and, what is more, he is proven

not to belong to the family of the gods." Meantime the faithful queen made her son ready for baptism; she gave command to adorn the church with hangings and curtains, in order that he who could not moved by persuasion might be urged to belief by this mystery. The boy, whom they named Ingomer, died after being baptized, still wearing the white garments in which he became regenerate. At this the king was violently angry, and reproached the queen harshly, saying: "If the boy had been dedicated in the name of my gods he would certainly have lived; but as it is, since he was baptized in the name of your God, he could not live at all." To this the queen said: "I give thanks to the omnipotent God, creator of all, who has judged me not wholly unworthy, that he should deign to take to his kingdom one born from my womb. My soul is not stricken with grief for his sake, because I know that, summoned from this world as he was in his baptismal garments, he will be fed by the vision of God...."

The queen did not cease to urge him to recognize the true God and cease worshipping idols. But he could not be influenced in any way to this belief,

Source: Gregory Bishop of Tours, *History of the Franks*, translated by Ernest Brehaut (New York: Columbia University Press, 1916; copyright renewed 1944), Book 2, selections from Sections 27, 29, 30, 31, 36–41.

until at last a war arose with the Alamanni,° in which he was driven by necessity to confess what before he had of his free will denied. It came about that as the two armies were fighting fiercely, there was much slaughter, and Clovis's army began to be in danger of destruction. He saw it and raised his eyes to heaven, and with remorse in his heart he burst into tears and cried: "Jesus Christ, whom Clotilda asserts to be the son of the living God..., I beseech the glory of thy aid, with the vow that if thou wilt grant me victory over these enemies..., I will believe in thee and be baptized in thy name. For I have invoked my own gods but, as I find, they have withdrawn from aiding me; and therefore I believe that

---

°**Alamanni:** a Germanic people.

they possess no power, since they do not help those who obey them...." And when he said thus, the Alamanni turned their backs, and began to disperse in flight. And when they saw that their king was killed, they submitted to the dominion of Clovis, saying: "Let not the people perish further, we pray; we are yours now." And he stopped the fighting, and after encouraging his men, retired in peace and told the queen how he had had merit to win the victory by calling on the name of Christ. This happened in the fifteenth year of his reign....

And so the king confessed all-powerful God in the Trinity, and was baptized in the name of the Father, Son and Holy Spirit, and was anointed with the holy ointment with the sign of the cross of Christ. And of his army more than 3,000 were baptized.

Document 10.2

Advice on Dealing with "Pagans"

In their dealings with the "pagan," or non-Christian, peoples and kings of Western Europe, church authorities such as missionaries, bishops, and the pope himself sometimes advocated compromise with existing cultural traditions rather than overt hostility to them. Here Pope Gregory (reigned 590–604) urges the bishop of England to adopt a strategy of accommodation with the prevailing religious practices of the Anglo-Saxon peoples of the island. It was contained in a famous work about the early Christian history of England, composed by a Benedictine monk known as The Venerable Bede and completed about 731.

- What can we learn about the religious practices of the Anglo-Saxons from Bede's account?

- In what specific ways did the pope urge toleration? And why did he advocate accommodation or compromise with existing religious practices? Keep in mind that the political authorities in England at the time had not yet become thoroughly Christian.

- What implication might Gregory's policies have for the beliefs and practices of English converts?

POPE GREGORY

Advice to the English Church

601

[T]he temples of the idols in that nation [England] ought not to be destroyed; but let the idols that are in them be destroyed; let holy water be made and sprinkled in the said temples, let altars be erected, and relics placed. For if those temples are well built, it is requisite that they be converted from the worship of devils to the service of the true God; that the nation, seeing that their temples are not destroyed, may remove error from their hearts, and knowing and adoring the true God, may the more familiarly resort to the places to which they have been accustomed.

And because they have been used to slaughter many oxen in the sacrifices to devils, some solemnity must be exchanged for them on this account, as that on the day of the dedication, or the nativities of the holy martyrs, whose relics are there deposited, they may build themselves huts of the boughs of trees, about those churches which have been turned

Source: The Venerable Bede, *The Ecclesiastical History of the English Nation*, edited by Ernest Rhys (London: J. M. Dent and Sons; New York: E. P. Dutton and Co., 1910), 52–53.

to that use from temples, and celebrate the solemnity with religious feasting, and no more offer beasts to the Devil, but kill cattle to the praise of God in their eating, and return thanks to the Giver of all things for their sustenance; to the end that, while some gratifications are outwardly permitted them, they may the more easily consent to the inward consolations of the grace of God. For there is no doubt that it is impossible to efface everything at once from their obdurate minds; because he who endeavors to ascend to the highest place, rises by degrees or steps, and not by leaps.

Thus the Lord made Himself known to the people of Israel in Egypt; and yet He allowed them the use of the sacrifices which they were wont to offer to the Devil, in his own worship; so as to command them in his sacrifice to kill beasts, to the end that, changing their hearts, they might lay aside one part of the sacrifice, while they retained another; that while they offered the same beasts which they were wont to offer, they should offer them to God, and not to idols; and thus they would no longer be the same sacrifices.

Document 10.3

Charlemagne and the Saxons

The policies of peaceful conversion and accommodation described in Document 10.2 did not prevail everywhere, as Charlemagne's dealings with the Saxons reveals. During late eighth and early ninth centuries C.E., Charlemagne (reigned 768–814) was the powerful king of the Franks. He turned his Frankish kingdom into a Christian empire that briefly incorporated much of continental Europe, and he was crowned as a renewed Roman emperor by the pope. In the course of almost constant wars of expansion, Charlemagne struggled for over thirty years (772–804) to subdue the Saxons, a "pagan" Germanic people who inhabited a region on the northeastern frontier of Charlemagne's growing empire (see Map 10.2, p. 436). The document known as the *Capitulary on Saxony* outlines a series of laws, regulations, and punishments (known collectively as a capitulary) regarding religious practice of the Saxons. This document reveals both the coercive policies of Charlemagne and the vigorous resistance of the Saxons to their forcible incorporation into his Christian domain.

- ■ What does this document reveal about the kind of resistance that the Saxons mounted against their enforced conversion?

- ■ How did Charlemagne seek to counteract that resistance?

- ■ What does this document suggest about Charlemagne's views of his duties as ruler?

CHARLEMAGNE

Capitulary on Saxony

785

1. It was pleasing to all that the churches of Christ, which are now being built in Saxony and consecrated to God, should not have less, but greater and more illustrious honor, than the fanes° of the idols had had....

3. If any one shall have entered a church by violence and shall have carried off anything in it by force or theft, or shall have burned the church itself, let him be punished by death.

4. If any one, out of contempt for Christianity, shall have despised the holy Lenten fast and shall have eaten flesh, let him be punished by death. But, nevertheless, let it be taken into consideration by a priest, lest perchance any one from necessity has been led to eat flesh.

5. If any one shall have killed a bishop or priest or deacon, let him likewise be punished capitally.

6. If any one deceived by the devil shall have believed, after the manner of the pagans, that any man or woman is a witch and eats men, and on this account shall have burned the person, or shall have given the person's flesh to others to eat, or shall have

---

°**fanes:** temples.

Source: D. C. Munro, trans., *Translations and Reprints from the Original Sources of European History*, vol. 6, no. 5, *Selections from the Laws of Charles the Great* (Philadelphia: University of Pennsylvania Press, 1900), 2–4.

eaten it himself, let him be punished by a capital sentence.

7. If any one, in accordance with pagan rites, shall have caused the body of a dead man to be burned and shall have reduced his bones to ashes, let him be punished capitally....

9. If any one shall have sacrificed a man to the devil, and after the manner of the pagans shall have presented him as a victim to the demons, let him be punished by death.

10. If any one shall have formed a conspiracy with the pagans against the Christians, or shall have wished to join with them in opposition to the Christians, let him be punished by death; and whoever shall have consented to this same fraudulently against the king and the Christian people, let him be punished by death....

17. Likewise, in accordance with the mandate of God, we command that all shall give a tithe of their property and labor to the churches and priests;

18. That on the Lord's day no meetings and public judicial assemblages shall be held, unless perchance in a case of great necessity or when war compels it, but all shall go to the church to hear the word of God, and shall be free for prayers or good works. Likewise, also, on the especial festivals they shall devote themselves to God and to the services of the church, and shall refrain from secular assemblies.

19. Likewise,... all infants shall be baptized within a year....

21. If any one shall have made a vow at springs or trees or groves, or shall have made any offerings after the manner of the heathen and shall have partaken of a repast in honor of the demons, if he shall

be a noble, [he must pay a fine of] 60 solidi,° if a freeman 30, if a litus° 15.

——————————

°**solidi:** gold coins.

°**litus:** neither a slave nor a free person.

Documents 10.4 and 10.5

The Persistence of Tradition

Conversion to Christianity in Western Europe was neither easy nor simple. Peoples thought to have been solidly converted to the new faith continued to engage in earlier practices. Others blended older traditions with Christian rituals. The two documents that follow illustrate both patterns. Document 10.4 describes the encounter between Saint Boniface (672–754), a leading missionary to the Germans, and the Hessians during the eighth century. It was written by one of Boniface's devoted followers, Willibald, who subsequently composed a biography of the missionary. Document 10.5 comes from a tenth-century Anglo-Saxon manuscript known as the *Leechbook*, a medical text that describes cures for various problems caused by "elves and nightgoers."

- What practices of the Hessians conflicted with Boniface's understanding of Christianity? How did he confront the persistence of these practices?

- What do these documents reveal about the process of conversion to Christianity?

- How might Pope Gregory (Document 10.2), Charlemagne (Document 10.3), and Boniface (Document 10.4) have responded to the cures and preventions described in the *Leechbook*?

WILLIBALD

Life of Boniface

ca. 760 C.E.

Now many of the Hessians who at that time had acknowledged the Catholic faith were confirmed by the grace of the Holy Spirit and received the laying-on of hands. But others, not yet strong in the spirit, refused to accept the pure teachings of the church in their entirety. Moreover, some continued secretly, others openly, to offer sacrifices to trees and springs, to inspect the entrails of victims; some practiced divination, legerdemain, and incantations; some turned their attention to auguries, auspices, and other sacrificial rites; while others, of a more

——————————

Source: Willibald, "Life of Boniface," in *The Anglo-Saxon Missionaries in Germany*, translated by C. H. Talbot (London: Sheed and Ward, 1954), 45–46.

reasonable character, forsook all the profane practices of the [heathens] and committed none of these crimes.

With the counsel and advice of the latter persons, Boniface in their presence attempted to cut down...a certain oak of extraordinary size, called in the old tongue of the pagans the Oak of Jupiter. Taking his courage in his hands (for a great crowd of pagans stood by watching and bitterly cursing in their hearts the enemy of the gods), he cut the first notch. But when he had made a superficial cut, suddenly, the oak's vast bulk, shaken by a mighty blast of wind from above crashed to the ground shivering its topmost branches into fragments in its fall. As if by the express will of God (for the brethren present had done nothing to cause it) the oak burst asunder into four parts, each part having a trunk of equal length.

At the sight of this extraordinary spectacle the heathens who had been cursing ceased to revile and began, on the contrary, to believe and bless the Lord. Thereupon the holy bishop took counsel with the brethren, built an oratory° from the timber of the oak and dedicated it to Saint Peter the Apostle. He then set out on a journey to Thuringia.... Arrived there, he addressed the elders and the chiefs of the people, calling on them to put aside their blind ignorance and to return to the Christian religion that they had formerly embraced.

°**oratory:** a place of prayer.

The Leechbook
Tenth Century

Work a salve against elfkind and nightgoers,... and the people with whom the Devil has intercourse. Take eowohumelan, wormwood, bishopwort, lupin, ashthroat, henbane, harewort, haransprecel, heathberry plants, cropleek, garlic, hedgerife grains, githrife, fennel. Put these herbs into one cup, set under the altar, sing over them nine masses; boil in butter and in sheep's grease, add much holy salt, strain through a cloth; throw the herbs in running water. If any evil temptation, or an elf or nightgoers, happen to a man, smear his forehead with this salve, and put on his eyes, and where his body is sore, and cense him [with incense], and sign [the cross] often. His condition will soon be better.

...Against elf disease...Take bishopwort, fennel, lupin, the lower part of *ælfthone*, and lichen from the holy sign of Christ [cross], and incense; a handful of each. Bind all the herbs in a cloth, dip in hallowed font water thrice. Let three masses be sung over it, one "Omnibus sanctis [For all the saints]," a second "Contra tribulationem [Against tribulation]," a third "Pro infirmis [For the sick]." Put then coals in a coal pan, and lay the herbs on it. Smoke the man with the herbs before...[9 A.M.] and at night; and sing a litany, the Creed [Nicene], and the Pater noster [Our Father]; and write on him Christ's mark on each limb. And take a little handful of the same kind of herbs, similarly sanctified, and boil in milk; drip holy water in it thrice. And let him sip it before his meal. It will soon be well with him.

Against the Devil and against madness,...a strong drink. Put in ale hassock, lupin roots, fennel, ontre, betony, hind heolothe, marche, rue, wormwood, nepeta (catmint), helenium, *ælfthone*, wolfs comb. Sing twelve masses over the drink; and let him drink. It will soon be well with him.

A drink against the Devil's temptations: thefanthorn, cropleek, lupin, ontre, bishopwort, fennel, hassock, betony. Sanctify these herbs; put into ale holy water. And let the drink be there in where the sick man is. And continually before he drinks sing thrice over the drink,..."God, in your name make me whole (save me)."

Source: Karen Louise Jolly, *Popular Religion in Late Saxon England: Elf Charms in Context* (Chapel Hill: University of North Carolina Press, 1996), 159–67.

Document 10.6

The Jesus Sutras in China

In 635 C.E. the Tang dynasty emperor Taizon welcomed a Persian Christian monk named Alopen and some two dozen of his associates to the Chinese capital of Chang'an (now Xian, see Map 5.1, p. 213). The Chinese court at this time was unusually open to a variety of foreign cultural traditions, including Buddhism, Islam, and Zoroastrianism in addition to Christianity. The version of Christianity that Alopen brought to China was known as Nestorianism (see p. 426). Regarded as heretics in the West and much persecuted, Nestorians had found refuge in Persia and from there introduced the faith into India, Mongolia, and China.

In sharp contrast to its success in Europe, Christianity did not establish a widespread or lasting presence in China. Isolation from the Persian heartland of Nestorian Christianity, opposition from Buddhists, and state persecution of all foreign religions in the ninth century reduced the Nestorian presence to near extinction. But for several centuries, under more favorable political conditions, a number of small Christian communities had flourished, generating a remarkable set of writings known as the "Jesus sutras." (A sutra is a Buddhist religious text.)

Some were carved on large stone slabs, while others were written on scrolls discovered early in the twentieth century in the caves of Dunhuang in northwestern China. What has fascinated scholars about these writings is the extent to which they cast the Christian message in distinctively Chinese terms, making use particularly of Buddhist and Daoist concepts long familiar in China. For example, at the top of a large stone tablet known as the Nestorian Monument is a Christian cross arising out of a white cloud (a characteristic Daoist symbol) and a lotus flower (an enduring Buddhist image). The written texts themselves, which refer to Christianity as the "Religion of Light from the West" or the "Luminous Religion," describe its arrival in China and outline its message within the framework of Chinese culture.

- What was the role of the emperor in establishing Christianity in China? How does this compare with the religious role of European monarchs such as Clovis or Charlemagne in Europe?

- How do the sutras depict the life, death, and teachings of Jesus?

- In what ways are Daoist or Buddhist concepts used to express the Christian message? (See pp. 195–97 and 199–201.)

- How does this Persian/Chinese version of Christianity differ from that of Catholic Europe?

The Jesus Sutras
635–1005

On the Coming of Christianity to China

The Emperor Taizong was a champion of culture. He created prosperity and encouraged illustrious sages to bestow their wisdom on the people....

In...638 C.E.,...the Emperor issued a proclamation saying:

"There is no single name for the Way.

Sages do not come in a single form.

These Teachings embrace everyone and can be adopted in any land.

A Sage of great virtue, Aleben, has brought these scriptures...and offered them to us in the Capital.

We have studied these scriptures and found them otherwordly, profound and full of mystery....

These teachings will save all creatures and benefit mankind, and it is only proper that they be practiced throughout the world."

Following the Emperor's orders, the Greater Qin Monastery was built....Twenty-one ordained monks of the Luminous Religion were allowed to live there....

Imperial officers were ordered to paint a portrait of the Emperor on the wall of the monastery....This auspicious symbol of the imperial presence added brilliance and bestowed favor upon the religion....

The Luminous Religion spread throughout all ten provinces, the Empire prospered and peace prevailed. Temples were built in 100 cities and countless families received the blessings of the Luminous Religion.

On the Story of Jesus

The Lord of Heaven sent the Cool Wind to a girl named Mo Yen. It entered her womb and at that moment she conceived....

Source: Martin Palmer, *The Jesus Sutras* (New York: Random House, 2001), 62–65, 68–69, 80–83, 90, 91, 103, 106, 107, 115–19.

Mo Yen became pregnant and gave birth to a son named Jesus, whose father is the Cool Wind....

When Jesus Messiah was born, the world saw clear signs in heaven and earth. A new star that could be seen everywhere appeared in heaven above....

From the time the Messiah was 12 until he was 32 years old, he sought out people with bad karma and directed them to turn around and create good karma by following a wholesome path. After the Messiah had gathered 12 disciples, he concerned himself with the suffering of others. Those who had died were made to live. The blind were made to see. The deformed were healed and the sick were cured. The possessed were freed of their demons and the crippled were made to walk. People with all kinds of illnesses drew near to the Messiah to touch his ragged robe and be healed....

The scribes who drank liquor and ate meat and served other gods brought false testimony against him. They waited for an opportunity to kill him. But many people had come to have faith in his teaching and so the scribes could not kill the Messiah. Eventually these people, whose karma was unwholesome, formed a conspiracy against him....

When the Messiah was 32 years old, his enemies came before the Great King Pilate and accused him by saying, The Messiah has committed a capital offense. The Great King should condemn him....

For the sake of all living beings and to show us that a human life is as frail as a candle flame, the Messiah gave his body to these people of unwholesome karma. For the sake of the living in this world, he gave up his life....

On the Four Laws of Dharma

The first law is no desire. Your heart seeks one thing after another, creating a multitude of problems. You must not allow them to flare up.... Desire can sap wholesome energy from the four limbs and the body's openings, turning it into unwholesome activity. This cuts us off from the roots of Peace and Joy. That is why you must practice the law of no desire.

The second law is no action. Doing things for mundane reasons is not part of your true being. You have to cast aside vain endeavors and avoid shallow experiences. Otherwise you are deceiving yourself.... We live our lives veering this way and that: We do things for the sake of progress and material gain, neglecting what is truly important and losing sight of the Way. That is why you must distance yourself from the material world and practice the law of no action.

The third law is no virtue. Don't try to find pleasure by making a name for yourself through good deeds. Practice instead universal loving kindness that is directed toward everyone. Never seek praise for what you do.... But do it without acclaim. This is the law of no virtue.

The fourth law is no truth. Don't be concerned with facts, forget about right and wrong, sinking or rising, winning or losing. Be like a mirror.... It reflects everything as it is, without judging. Those who have awakened to the Way, who have attained the mind of Peace and Joy, who can see all karmic conditions and who share their enlightenment with others, reflect the world like a mirror, leaving no trace of themselves.

On God, Humankind and the Sutras

Heaven and earth are the creation of the One God. The power and will of God pass like the wind over everything. His is not a body of flesh, but a divine consciousness, completely unseen to human eyes....

People can live only by dwelling in the living breath of God. Only in this way can they be at peace and realize their aspirations. From sunrise to sunset, they dwell in the living breath of God; every sight and thought is part of that breath. God provides a place for them filled with clarity and bliss and stillness. All the Buddhas are moved by this wind, which blows everywhere in the world. God resides permanently in this still, blissful place; no karma is done without God....

Do what you have to do here on earth and your actions will determine your place in the next world. We are not born to live forever in the world, but are here to plant wholesome seeds that will produce good fruit in the world beyond this one. Everyone who seeks the other world will attain it if they plant good seeds before departing....

Anyone who crosses the ocean must have a boat before taking on the wind and waves. But a broken boat won't reach the far shore. It is the Sutras of the Luminous Religion that enable us to cross the sea of birth and death to the other shore, a land fragrant with the treasured aroma of Peace and Joy.

Using the Evidence:
The Making of Christian Europe . . .
and a Chinese Counterpoint

1. **Describing cultural encounters:** Consider the spread of Christianity in Europe and China from the viewpoint of those seeking to introduce the new religion. What obstacles did they encounter? What strategies did they employ? What successes and failures did they experience?

2. **Describing cultural encounters . . . from another point of view:** Consider the same process from the viewpoint of new adherents to Christianity. What were the motives for or the advantages of conversion for both political elites and ordinary people? To what extent was it possible to combine prevailing practices and beliefs with the teachings of the new religion?

3. **Making comparisons:** How did the spread of Christianity to China differ from its introduction to Western Europe? How might you describe and explain the very different outcomes of those two processes?

4. **Defining a concept:** The notion of "conversion" often suggests a quite rapid and complete transformation of religious commitments based on sincere inner conviction. In what ways do these documents support or challenge this understanding of religious change?

5. **Noticing point of view and assessing credibility:** From what point of view is each of the documents written? Which statements in each document might historians find unreliable and which would they find most useful?

Visual Sources

Considering the Evidence: Reading Byzantine Icons

Within the world of Byzantine or Eastern Orthodox Christianity, the icon—a Greek word meaning image, likeness, or picture—came to have a prominent role in both public worship and private devotion. Since Christianity had emerged in a Roman world filled with images—statues of the emperor, busts of ancestors and famous authors, frescoes, and murals—it is hardly surprising that Christians felt a need to represent their faith in some concrete fashion. Icons fulfilled that need.

The creation of icons took off in earnest as Christianity became the official religion of the Roman Empire in the fourth century C.E. Usually painted by monks, icons depicted Jesus, the Virgin Mary, saints, scenes from biblical stories, church feasts, and more. To Byzantine believers, such images were "windows on heaven," an aid to worship that conveyed the very presence of God, bestowing divine grace on the world. They were also frequently associated with miracles, and on occasion people scraped paint off an icon, mixing it with water to produce a "holy medicine" that could remedy a variety of ailments. Icons also served a teaching function for a largely illiterate audience. As Pope Gregory II in the eighth century explained:

> What books are to those who can read, that is a picture to the ignorant who look at it; in a picture even the unlearned may see what example they should follow; in a picture they who know no letters may yet read. Hence, for Barbarians especially a picture takes the place of a book.[29]

Icons were deliberately created—or "written"—as flat, two-dimensional images, lacking the perspective of depth. This nonrepresentational, nonrealistic portrayal of human figures was intended to suggest another world and to evoke the mysteries of faith that believers would encounter as they knelt before the image, crossed themselves, and kissed it. The images themselves were full of religious symbolism. The posture of the body, the position of the hand, and the fold of the clothing were all rich with meaning: a saint touching his hand to his cheek conveyed sorrow; a halo surrounding the head of a human figure reflected divinity or sacredness. Likewise, colors were symbolic: red stood for either love or the blood of martyrs; blue suggested faith, humility, or heaven; and purple indicated royalty. Those who painted icons were bound by strict traditions derived from the distant past. Lacking what we might consider "artistic freedom," they sought to faithfully replicate earlier models.

In Judaism, Christianity, and Islam alike, the artistic representation of God occasioned heated debates. After all, the Ten Commandments declared, "You shall not make for yourselves a graven image or any likeness of anything that is in heaven above." Almost since the beginning of Christian art, an undercurrent of opposition had criticized efforts to represent the divine in artistic form. Between 726 and 843, Byzantine emperors took the offensive against the use of icons in worship, arguing that they too easily became "idols," distracting believers from the adoration of God himself. Some scholars suggest that this effort, known as iconoclasm (icon breaking), also reflected a concern of religious and political authorities in Byzantium about the growing power of monks, who both created icons and ardently supported their use in worship. It may also have owed something to a desire to avoid offending a rapidly expanding Islamic world, which itself largely prohibited the representation of the human form.[30] Icons were collected from both homes and churches and burned in public square. Thousands of monks fled, and active supporters of icon use were subject to severe punishment. Some critics accused the emperor of sympathy with Islam. But by 843 this controversy was resolved in favor of icon use, an event still commemorated every year in Orthodox churches as the Triumph of Orthodoxy. Thereafter, the creation and use of icons flourished in the Byzantine Empire and subsequently in Russia, where Eastern Christianity began to take root in the late tenth century.

The three icons reproduced here provide an opportunity for you to "read" these visual sources and to imagine what religious meaning they may have conveyed to the faithful of Byzantine Christianity.

Visual Source 10.1, among the oldest icons in existence, dates from the sixth century and survived the destruction of icons during the century of iconoclasm. In contrast to many images of the suffering Jesus on the cross, this icon belongs to a tradition of icon painting that depicts Jesus as Christ Pantokrator. *Pantokrator* derives from a Greek term translated as "Almighty," "Ruler of All," or "Sustainer of the World." Wearing a dark purple robe and surrounded by a halo of light, Jesus holds a copy of the gospels in his left hand. Notice that Jesus' right hand is raised in blessing with the three fingers together representing the trinity and the two remaining fingers symbolizing the dual nature of Christ, both human and divine. Many observers have suggested that this important theological statement of Christ's divine and human nature is also conveyed in the asymmetrical character of the image.

Visual Source 10.1 Christ Pantokrator
(Ancient Art & Architecture Collection)

■ What differences can you notice in the
two sides of Christ's face? (Pay attention
to the eyebrows, the irises and pupils,
the hair, the mustache, and the cheeks.
Notice also the difference in color
between the face and the hands.)

■ How does this image portray Jesus as
an all-powerful ruler?

■ How does this depiction of Jesus differ
from others you may have seen?

■ Which features of this image suggest
Christ's humanity and which might
portray his divinity?

Icons frequently portrayed important stories from the Bible, none of which was more
significant than that of the nativity. Visual
Source 10.2, from fifteenth-century Russia,
graphically depicts the story of Jesus' birth
for the faithful. The central person in the image is not Jesus but his mother,
Mary, who in Orthodox theology was known as the God-bearer.

■ Why do you think Mary is pictured as facing outward toward the
viewer rather than focusing on her child?

■ Notice the three rays from heaven, symbolizing the trinity—God the
Father, the Son, and the Holy Spirit—represented by the three figures
at the top. What other elements of the biblical story of Jesus' birth can
you identify in the image?

■ The figure in the bottom left is that of a contemplative and perhaps
troubled Joseph, Mary's husband-to-be. What do you imagine that
Joseph is thinking? Why might he be troubled?

■ Facing Joseph is an elderly person, said by some to represent Satan and
by others to be a shepherd comforting Joseph. What thinking might lie
behind each of these interpretations?

Visual Source 10.2 The Nativity (Private Collection/The Bridgeman Art Library)

Visual Source 10.3 Ladder of Divine Ascent (Roger Wood/Corbis)

Visual Source 10.3 is a twelfth-century Byzantine painting intended to illustrate an instructional book for monks, written in the sixth century by Saint John Climacus. Both the book and the icon are known as the *Ladder of Divine Ascent*. Written by an ascetic monk with a reputation for great piety and wisdom, the book advised monks to renounce the world with its many temptations and vices and to ascend step by step toward union with God in heaven. The icon served as a visual illustration of that process. The monks are climbing the ladder of the spiritual journey toward God but are beset by winged demons representing various sins—lust, anger, and pride, for example—which are described in Climacus's book. Some have fallen off the ladder into the mouth of a dragon, which represents hell.

- How does this icon portray the spiritual journey?

- What sources of help are available for the monks on the ladder? Notice the figures in the upper left and lower right.

- What message might beginning monks have taken from this image?

Using the Evidence: Reading Byzantine Icons

1. **Viewing icons from opposing perspectives:** How might supporters and opponents of icons have responded to these visual sources?

2. **Identifying religious ideas in art:** What elements of religious thought or practice can you identify in these icons? In what ways were these religious ideas represented artistically?

3. **Comparing images of Jesus:** In what different ways is Jesus portrayed in the three icons? What similarities can you identify?

4. **Comparing religious art cross-culturally:** How might you compare these icons to the Buddha images in Chapter 5? Consider their purposes, their religious content, and their modes of artistic representation.

ما الحج سير ك تأوبباً وادلاجا ولا لعينيك أجمالاً واجدالا

CHAPTER ELEVEN

The Worlds of Islam

Afro-Eurasian Connections

600–1500

"There were tens of thousands of pilgrims, from all over the world. They were of all colors, from blue-eyed blondes to black-skinned Africans. But we were all participating in the same ritual, display-ing a spirit of unity and brotherhood that my experiences in America had led me to believe never could exist between the white and non-white. . . . I have never before seen sincere and true brotherhood practiced by all colors together, irrespective of their color."[1] So said Malcolm X, the American black radical leader and convert to Islam, following his participation in 1964 in the hajj, or pilgrimage, to Mecca. That experience persuaded him to abandon his earlier com-mitment to militant black separatism, for he was now convinced that racial barriers could indeed be overcome within the context of Islam.

As the twenty-first century dawned, Islam had acquired a notice-able presence in the United States, with more than 1,200 mosques and an estimated 8 million Muslims, of whom some 2 million were African Americans. Here was but one sign of the growing interna-tional influence of the Islamic world. Independence from colonial rule, the Iranian Revolution of 1979, repeated wars between Israel and its Arab neighbors, the rising price of oil—all of this focused global attention on the Islamic world in the second half of the twen-tieth century. Osama bin Laden and the September 11, 2001, attacks on the United States, U.S. military action in Afghanistan and Iraq, and the increasing assertiveness of Muslims in Europe likewise signaled the growing role of Islam in world affairs in the first decade of the new millennium.

The Hajj: The pilgrimage to Mecca, known as the *hajj*, has long been a central religious ritual in Islamic practice. It also embodies the cosmopolitan character of Islam as pilgrims from all over the vast Islamic realm assemble in the city where the faith was born. This painting shows a group of joyful pilgrims, led by a band, on their way to Mecca.
(Bibliothèque nationale de France)

PROMINENCE ON THE WORLD STAGE, OF COURSE, was nothing new for Muslim societies. For a thousand years (roughly 600–1600), peoples claiming allegiance to Islam represented a highly successful, prosperous, and expansive civilization, encompassing parts of Africa, Europe, the Middle East, and Asia. While Chinese culture and Buddhism provided the cultural anchor for East Asia during the postclassical millennium and Christianity did the same for western Eurasia, the realm of Islam touched on both of them and decisively shaped the history of the entire Afro-Eurasian world.

The significance of a burgeoning Islamic world was enormous. It thrust the previously marginal and largely nomadic Arabs into a central role in world history, for it was among them and in their language that the newest of the world's major religions was born. The sudden emergence and rapid spread of that religion in the seventh century C.E. was accompanied by the creation of a huge empire that stretched from Spain to India. Both within that empire and beyond it, a new and innovative civilization took shape, drawing on Arab, Persian, Turkish, Greco-Roman, South Asian, and African cultures. It was clearly the largest and most influential of the new third-wave civilizations. Finally, the broad reach of Islam generated many of the great cultural encounters of this age of accelerating connections, as Islamic civilization challenged and provoked Christendom, penetrated and was transformed by African cultures, and also took root in India, Central Asia, and Southeast Asia. The spread of Islam continued in the modern era so that by the beginning of the twenty-first century, perhaps 1.2 billion people, or 22 percent of the world's population, identified as Muslims. It was second only to Christianity as the world's most widely practiced religion, and it extended far beyond the Arab lands where it had originated.

The Birth of a New Religion

Most of the major religious or cultural traditions of the classical era had emerged from the core of established civilizations—Confucianism and Daoism from China, Hinduism and Buddhism from India, Greek philosophy from the Mediterranean world, and Zoroastrianism from Persia. Christianity and Islam, by contrast, emerged more from the margins of Mediterranean and Middle Eastern civilizations. The former, of course, appeared among a small Middle Eastern people, the Jews, in a remote province of the Roman Empire, while Islam took hold in the cities and deserts of the Arabian Peninsula.

The Homeland of Islam

■ Description
In what ways did the early history of Islam reflect its Arabian origins?

The central region of the Arabian Peninsula had long been inhabited by nomadic Arabs, known as Bedouins, who herded their sheep and camels in seasonal migrations. These peoples lived in fiercely independent clans and tribes, which often engaged in bitter blood feuds with one another. They recognized a variety of gods, ancestors, and nature spirits; valued personal bravery, group loyalty, and hospitality; and greatly treasured their highly expressive oral poetry. But there was more to Arabia than camel-herding nomads. Scattered oases, the highlands of Yemen, and interior mountains supported sedentary village-based agriculture, and in the north-ern and southern regions of Arabia, small kingdoms had flourished in ear-lier times. Arabia also sat astride increasingly important trade routes that connected the Indian Ocean world with that of the Mediterranean Sea and gave rise to more cosmopolitan commercial cities, whose values and prac-tices were often in conflict with those of traditional Arab tribes.

One of those cities, Mecca, came to occupy a distinctive role in Arabia. Though somewhat off the major long-distance trade routes, Mecca was the site of the Kaaba, the most prominent religious shrine in Arabia, which housed representations of some 360 deities and was the destination for many pilgrims. Mecca's dominant tribe, the Quraysh, had come to control access to the Kaaba and grew wealthy by taxing the local trade that accompanied the annual pilgrimage season. By the sixth century C.E., Mecca was home to

Arabia at the Time of Muhammad

people from various tribes and clans as well as an assortment of individual outlaws, exiles, refugees, and foreign merchants, but much of its growing wealth was concentrated in the hands of a few ruling Quraysh families.

Furthermore, Arabia was located on the periphery of two established and rival civilizations of that time—the Byzantine Empire, heir to the Roman world, and the Sassanid Empire, heir to the imperial traditions of old Persia. This location, coupled with long-distance trade, ensured some familiarity with the larger world, particularly in the cities and settled farming regions of the peninsula. Many Jews and Christians as well as some Zoroastrians lived among the Arabs, and their monotheistic ideas became widely known. By the time of Muhammad, most of the settled Arabs had acknowl-edged the preeminent position of Allah, the supreme god of the Arab pantheon, although they usually found the lesser gods, including the three daughters of Allah, far more accessible. Moreover, they increasingly identified Allah with Yahweh, the Jewish High God, and regarded themselves too as "children of Abraham." A few Arabs were beginning to explore the possibility that Allah/Yahweh was the only God and that the many others, residing in the Kaaba and in shrines across the peninsula, were nothing more than "helpless and harmless idols."[2]

To an outside observer around 600, it might well have seemed that Arabs were moving toward Judaism religiously or that Christianity, the most rapidly growing reli-gion in western Asia, would encompass Arabia as well. Any such expectations, how-ever, were thoroughly confounded by the dramatic events of the seventh century.

The Messenger and the Message

The catalyst for those events and for the birth of this new religion was a single indi-vidual, Muhammad Ibn Abdullah (570–632 C.E.), who was born in Mecca to a Quraysh family. As a young boy, Muhammad lost his parents, came under the care of an uncle, and worked as a shepherd to pay his keep. Later he became a trader and traveled as far north as Syria. At the age of twenty-five, he married a wealthy widow, Khadija, herself a prosperous merchant, with whom he fathered six children. A highly

■ **Comparison**

How does the core message of Islam compare with that of Judaism and Christianity?

$\mathcal{S}$napshot   **Key Moments in the Early History of Islam**

Birth of Muhammad	570
Beginning of Muhammad's revelations	610
Hijra (the emigration from Mecca to Medina)	622
Muhammad returns to Mecca in triumph	630
Death of Muhammad	632
Rightly Guided Caliphs	632–661
Arab victories against Byzantine and Persian forces	636–637
Conquest of Egypt	640
Compilation of the Quran	650s
Umayyad caliphate	661–750
Conquest of Spain	711–718
Abbasid caliphate	750–1258
Battle of Talas River	751

reflective man deeply troubled by the religious corruption and social inequalities of Mecca, he often undertook periods of withdrawal and meditation in the arid mountains outside the city. There, like the Buddha and Jesus, Muhammad had a powerful, overwhelming religious experience that left him convinced, albeit reluctantly, that he was Allah's messenger to the Arabs, commissioned to bring to them a scripture in their own language.

According to Muslim tradition, the revelations began in 610 and continued periodically over the next twenty-two years. Those revelations, recorded in the Quran, became the sacred scriptures of Islam, which to this day Muslims everywhere regard as the very words of God and the core of their faith. Intended to be recited rather than simply read for information, the Quran, Muslims claim, when heard in its original Arabic, conveys nothing less than the very presence of the divine. Its unmatched poetic beauty, miraculous to Muslims, convinced many that it was indeed a revelation from God. One of the earliest converts testified to its power: "When I heard the Quran, my heart was softened and I wept and Islam entered into me."[3] (See Document 11.1, pp. 502–04 for selections from the Quran.)

In its Arabian setting, the Quran's message, delivered through Muhammad, was revolutionary. Religiously, it was radically monotheistic, presenting Allah as the only God, the all-powerful Creator, good, just, and merciful. It rejected as utterly false and useless the many gods housed in the Kaaba and scorned the Christian notion of the Trinity. Allah was the "Lord sustainer of the worlds, the Compassionate, the Caring, master of the day of reckoning."[4] Here was an exalted conception of the Deity that drew heavily on traditions of Jewish and Christian monotheism. As "the Messenger of

God," Muhammad presented himself in the line of earlier prophets—Abraham, Moses, Jesus, and many others. He was the last, "the seal of the prophets," bearing God's final revelation to humankind. It was not so much a call to a new faith as an invitation to return to the old and pure religion of Abraham from which Arabs, Jews, and Christians alike had deviated.

Submission to Allah ("Muslim" means "one who submits") was the primary obligation of believers and the means of achieving a place in paradise

Muslims, Jews, and Christians
The close relationship of three Middle Eastern monotheistic traditions is illustrated in this fifteenth-century Persian painting, which portrays Muhammad leading Moses, Abraham, and Jesus in prayer. The fire surrounding the prophet's head represents his religious fervor. The painting reflects the Islamic belief that the revelations granted to Muhammad built upon and completed those given earlier to Jews and Christians. (Bibliothèque nationale de France)

after death. According to the Quran, however, submission was not merely an individual or spiritual act, for it involved the creation of a whole new society. Over and again, the Quran denounced the prevailing social practices of an increasingly prosperous Mecca: the hoarding of wealth, the exploitation of the poor, the charging of high rates of interest on loans, corrupt business deals, the abuse of women, and the neglect of the widows and orphans. Like the Jewish prophets of the Old Testament, the Quran demanded social justice and laid out a prescription for its implementation. It sought a return to the older values of Arab tribal life—solidarity, equality, concern for the poor—which had been undermined, particularly in Mecca, by growing wealth and commercialism.

The message of the Quran challenged not only the ancient polytheism of Arab religion and the social injustices of Mecca but also the entire tribal and clan structure of Arab society, which was so prone to war, feuding, and violence. The just and moral society of Islam was the *umma*, the community of all believers, replacing tribal, ethnic, or racial identities. Such a society would be a "witness over the nations," for according to the Quran, "You are the best community evolved for mankind, enjoining what is right and forbidding what is wrong."[5] In this community, women too had an honored and spiritually equal place. "The believers, men and women, are protectors of one another," declared the Quran.[6] The umma, then, was to be a new and just community, bound by a common belief, rather than by territory, language, or tribe.

The core message of the Quran—surrendering to the divine—was effectively summarized as a set of five requirements for believers, known as the Pillars of Islam. The first pillar expressed the heart of the Islamic message: "There is no god but Allah, and Muhammad is the messenger of God." The second pillar was prayer, to be performed five times a day while facing in the direction of Mecca. The accompanying rituals, including cleansing, bowing, kneeling, and prostration, expressed believers' submission to Allah and provided a frequent reminder, amid the busyness of daily life, that they were living in the presence of the divine. The third pillar, almsgiving, reflected the Quran's repeated demands for social justice by requiring believers to give generously to support the poor and needy of the community. The fourth pillar established a month of fasting during Ramadan, which meant abstaining from food, drink, and sexual relations from the first light of dawn to sundown. It provided an occasion for self-purification and a reminder of the needs of the hungry. The fifth pillar encouraged a pilgrimage to Mecca, known as the *hajj*, where believers from all over the Islamic world assembled once a year and put on identical simple white clothing as they performed together rituals reminding them of key events in Islamic history. For at least the few days of the hajj, the many worlds of Islam must surely have seemed a single realm.

A further requirement for believers, sometimes called the sixth pillar, was "struggle," or *jihad* in Arabic. Its more general meaning, which Muhammad referred to as the "greater jihad," was an interior personal effort of each Muslim against greed and selfishness, a spiritual striving toward living a God-conscious life. In its "lesser" form, the "jihad of the sword," the Quran authorized armed struggle against the forces of unbelief and evil as a means of establishing Muslim rule and of defending the umma from the threats of infidel aggressors. The understanding and use of the jihad concept has varied widely over the many centuries of Islamic history and remains a matter of controversy among Muslims in the twenty-first century.

The Transformation of Arabia

■ **Change**

In what ways was the rise of Islam revolutionary, both in theory and in practice?

As the revelations granted to Muhammad became known in Mecca, they attracted a small following of some close relatives, a few prominent Meccan leaders, and an assortment of lower-class dependents, freed slaves, and members of poorer clans. Those teachings also soon attracted the vociferous opposition of Mecca's elite families, particularly those of Muhammad's own tribe, the Quraysh. Muhammad's claim to be a "messenger of Allah," his unyielding monotheism, his call for social reform, his condemnation of Mecca's business practices, and his apparent disloyalty to his own tribe enraged the wealthy and ruling families of Mecca. So great had this opposition become that in 622 Muhammad and his small band of followers emigrated to the more welcoming town of Yathrib, soon to be called Medina, the city of the Prophet. This agricultural settlement of mixed Arab and Jewish population had invited Muhammad to serve as an arbitrator of their intractable conflicts. The emigration to Yathrib, known in Arabic as the *hijra*, was a momentous turning point in the early history of Islam and thereafter marked the beginning of a new Islamic calendar.

The Islamic community, or umma, that took shape in Medina was a kind of "supertribe," but very different from the traditional tribes of Arab society. Membership was a matter of belief rather than birth, allowing the community to expand rapidly. Furthermore, all authority, both political and religious, was concentrated in the hands of Muhammad, who proceeded to introduce radical changes. Usury was outlawed, tax-free marketplaces were established, and a mandatory payment to support the poor was imposed.

In Medina, Muhammad not only began to create a new society but also declared Islam's independence from its earlier affiliation with Judaism. In the early years, he had anticipated a warm response from Jews and Christians, based on a common mono-theism and prophetic tradition, and had directed his followers to pray facing Jerusalem. But when some Jewish groups allied with his enemies, Muhammad acted harshly to suppress them, exiling some and enslaving or killing others. This was not, however, a general suppression of Jews, since others among them remained loyal to Muhammad's new state. But the prophet now redirected Muslims' prayer toward Mecca, essentially declaring Islam an Arab religion, though one with a universal message.

From its base in Medina, the Islamic community rapidly extended its reach throughout Arabia. Early military successes against Muhammad's Meccan opponents convinced other Arab tribes that the Muslims and their God were on the rise, and they sought to negotiate alliances with the new power. Growing numbers, though not all, converted. The religious appeal of the new faith, its promise of material gain, the end of incessant warfare among feuding tribes, periodic military actions skillfully led by Muhammad, and the Prophet's willingness to enter into marriage alliances with leading tribes—all of this contributed to the consolidation of Islamic control through-out Arabia. In 630, Muhammad triumphantly and peacefully entered Mecca itself, purging the Kaaba of its idols and declaring it a shrine to the one God, Allah. By the time Muhammad died in 632, most of Arabia had come under the control of this new Islamic state, and many had embraced the new faith.

Thus the birth of Islam differed sharply from that of Christianity. Jesus' teach-ing about "giving to Caesar what is Caesar's and to God what is God's" reflected the minority and subordinate status of the Jews within the Roman Empire. Early Christians found themselves periodically persecuted by Roman authorities for more than three centuries, requiring them to work out some means of dealing with an often hostile state. The answer lay in the development of a separate church hierar-chy and the concept of two coexisting authorities, one religious and one political, an arrangement that persisted even after the state became Christian.

The young Islamic community, by contrast, found itself constituted as a state, and soon a huge empire, at the very beginning of its history. Muhammad was not only a religious figure but also, unlike Jesus or the Buddha, a political and military leader able to implement his vision of an ideal Islamic society. Nor did Islam give rise to a separate religious organization, although tension between religious and polit-ical goals frequently generated conflict. No professional clergy mediating between God and humankind emerged within Islam. Teachers, religious scholars, prayer lead-ers, and judges within an Islamic legal system did not have the religious role that priests held within Christianity. No distinction between religious law and civil law, so important in the Christian world, existed within the realm of Islam. One law, known as the *sharia*, regulated every aspect of life. The sharia (literally, a path to water, which is the source of life) evolved over the several centuries following the birth of this new religion and found expression in a number of separate schools of Islamic legal practice.

In little more than twenty years (610–632), a profound transformation had occurred in the Arabian Peninsula. A new religion had been born, though one that had roots in earlier Jewish, Christian, and Zoroastrian traditions. A new and vigorous state had emerged, bringing peace to the warring tribes of Arabia. Within that state, a distinctive society had begun to take shape, one that served ever after as a model for Islamic communities everywhere. In his farewell sermon, Muhammad described the outlines of this community:

> All mankind is from Adam and Eve, an Arab has no superiority over a non-Arab nor a non-Arab has any superiority over an Arab; also a white has no superiority over a black nor a black has any superiority over a white—except by piety and good action. Learn that every Muslim is a brother to every Muslim and that the Muslims constitute one brotherhood.[7]

The Making of an Arab Empire

It did not take long for the immense transformations occurring in Arabia to have an impact beyond the peninsula. In the centuries that followed, the energies born of those vast changes profoundly transformed much of the Afro-Eurasian world. The new Arab state became a huge empire, encompassing all or part of Egyptian, Roman/Byzantine, Persian, Mesopotamian, and Indian civilizations. The Islamic faith spread widely within and outside that empire. So too did the culture and language of Arabia, as many Arabs migrated far beyond their original homeland and many others found it advantageous to learn Arabic. From the mixing and blending of these many peoples emerged the new and distinctive third-wave civilization of Islam, bound by the ties of a common faith but divided by differences of culture, class, politics, gender, and religious understanding. These enormously consequential processes—the making of a new religion, a new empire, and a new civilization—were central to world history during the postclassical millennium.

War and Conquest

■ Change

Why were Arabs able to construct such a huge empire so quickly?

Within a few years of Muhammad's death in 632, Arab armies engaged the Byzantine and Persian Sassanid empires, the great powers of the region. It was the beginning of a process that rapidly gave rise to an Islamic/Arab empire that stretched from Spain to India, penetrating both Europe and China and governing most of the lands between them (see Map 11.1). In creating that empire, Arabs were continuing a long pattern of tribal raids into surrounding civilizations, but now the Arabs were newly organized in a state of their own with a central command able to mobilize the military potential of the entire Arab population. The Byzantine and Persian empires, weakened by decades of war with each other and by internal revolts, continued to view the Arabs as a mere nuisance rather than a serious threat. But the Sassanid Empire was defeated by Arab forces during the 650s, while Byzantium soon lost the southern half of its territories. Beyond these victories, Arab forces, operating on both land and sea, swept westward across North Africa, conquered Spain in the early 700s, and attacked southern France. To the east, Arab

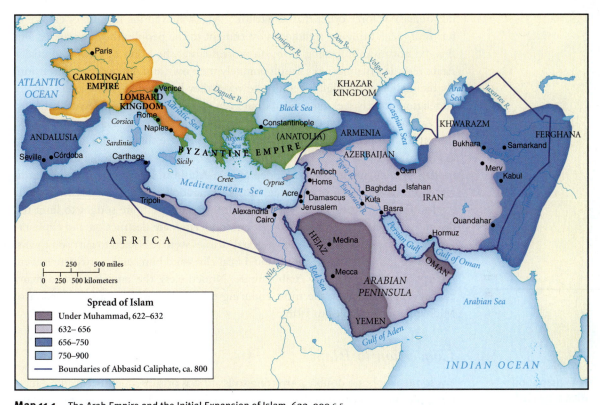

Map 11.1   The Arab Empire and the Initial Expansion of Islam, 622–900 c.e.
Far more so than with Buddhism or Christianity, the initial spread of Islam was both rapid and extensive.
And unlike the other two world religions, Islam gave rise to a huge empire, ruled by Muslim Arabs, which
encompassed many of the older civilizations of the region.

forces reached the Indus River and seized some of the major oases towns of Central
Asia. In 751, Arab armies inflicted a crushing defeat on Chinese forces in the Battle
of Talas River, which had lasting consequences for the cultural evolution of Asia,
for it checked the further expansion of China to the west and made possible the
conversion to Islam of Central Asia's Turkic-speaking people.

The motives driving the creation of the Arab Empire were in many ways similar to those of other empires. The merchant leaders of the new Islamic community
wanted to capture profitable trade routes and wealthy agricultural regions. Individual
Arabs found in military expansion a route to wealth and social promotion. The need
to harness the immense energies of the Arabian transformation was also important.
The fragile unity of the umma threatened to come apart after Muhammad's death,
and external expansion provided a common task for the community.

Also apparent in the making of the Arab Empire was a distinctly religious dimension. To the Arabs themselves, the only possible explanation for their amazing, indeed
miraculous, success was that "God gave us the victory over them, allowing us to take
their countries and to settle in their lands, their homes, and their property, we having

no strength or force other than the truth."[8] Many viewed the mission of empire in terms of jihad, bringing righteous government to the peoples they conquered, but this did not mean imposing Islam on individuals at the point of a sword. Initially, Arabs regarded Islam as a revelation uniquely their own and discouraged conversion. By the middle of the eighth century, however, they had come to view it as a universal religion actively seeking converts, but even then they recognized Jews, Christians, and Zoroastrians as "people of the book," giving them the status of *dhimmis* (protected subjects). Such people were permitted to freely practice their own religion, so long as they paid a special tax known as the *jizya*. Theoretically the tax was a substitute for military service, supposedly forbidden to non-Muslims. In practice, many dhimmis served in the highest offices within Muslim kingdoms and in their armies as well.

In other ways too, the Arab rulers of an expanding empire sought to limit the disruptive impact of conquest. To prevent indiscriminate destruction and exploitation of conquered peoples, occupying Arab armies were restricted to garrison towns, segregated from the native population. Local elites and bureaucratic structures were incorporated into the new Arab Empire. Nonetheless, the empire worked many changes on its subjects, the most enduring of which was the mass conversion of Middle Eastern peoples to Islam.

Conversion to Islam

■ Explanation
What accounts for the widespread conversion to Islam?

For some people, no doubt, converting to Islam was or subsequently became a matter of profound spiritual or psychological transformation, but far more often, at least initially, it was "social conversion," defined as "movement from one religiously defined social community to another."[9] It happened at various rates and in different ways, but in the four centuries or so after the death of Muhammad, millions of individuals and many whole societies within the Arab Empire found their cultural identity bound up with a belief in Allah and the message of his prophet. They had become Muslims. How had this immense cultural change occurred?

In some ways, perhaps, the change was not so dramatic, as major elements of Islam—monotheism; ritual prayer and cleansing ceremonies; fasting; divine revelation; the ideas of heaven, hell, and final judgment—were quite familiar to Jews, Christians, and Zoroastrians. Furthermore, Islam was from the beginning associated with the sponsorship of a powerful state, quite unlike the experience of early Buddhism or Christianity. Conquest called into question the power of old gods, while the growing prestige of the Arab Empire attracted many to Allah. Although deliberately forced conversion was rare, living in an Islamic-governed state provided a variety of incentives for claiming Muslim identity.[10] Slaves and prisoners of war were among the early converts, particularly in Persia. Converts could also avoid the jizya, the tax imposed on non-Muslims. In Islam, merchants found a religion friendly to commerce, and in the Arab Empire they enjoyed a huge and secure arena for trade. People aspiring to official positions found conversion to Islam an aid to social mobility.

Conversion was not an automatic or easy process. Vigorous resistance delayed conversion for centuries among the Berbers of North Africa; a small group of zealous Spanish Christians in the ninth century provoked their own martyrdom by publicly insulting the Prophet; and some Persian Zoroastrians fled to avoid Muslim rule. More generally, though, a remarkable and lasting religious transformation occurred throughout the Arab Empire. In Persia, for example, between 750 and 900, about 80 percent of the population had made the transition to a Muslim religious identity, while retaining their own ancient language.[11] In places where large-scale Arab migration had occurred, such as Egypt, North Africa, and Iraq, Arabic culture and language, as well as the religion of Islam, took hold. Such areas are today both Muslim and Arab, while Iran, Turkey, and Pakistan, for example, have "Islamized" without "Arabizing."

Divisions and Controversies

The ideal of a unified Muslim community, so important to Muhammad, proved difficult to realize as conquest and conversion vastly enlarged the Islamic umma. A central problem was that of leadership and authority in the absence of Muhammad's towering presence. Who should hold the role of caliph, the successor to Muhammad as the political leader of the umma, the protector and defender of the faith? That issue crystallized a variety of emerging conflicts within the Islamic world—between early and later converts, among various Arab tribes and factions, between Arabs and non-Arabs, between privileged and wealthy rulers and their far less fortunate subjects. Many of these political and social conflicts found expression in religious terms as various understandings of the Quran and of Muhammad's life and teachings took shape within the growing Islamic community.

The first four caliphs, known among most Muslims as the Rightly Guided Caliphs (632–661), were close "companions of the Prophet," selected by the Muslim elders of Medina. Division surfaced almost immediately as a series of Arab tribal rebellions and new "prophets" persuaded the first caliph, Abu Bakr, to suppress them forcibly. The third and fourth caliphs, Uthman and Ali, were both assassinated, and by 656, less than twenty-five years after Muhammad's death, civil war pitted Muslim against Muslim.

■ Comparison
What is the difference between Sunni and Shia Islam?

Out of that conflict emerged one of the deepest and most enduring rifts within the Islamic world. On one side were the Sunni Muslims, who held that the caliphs were rightful political and military leaders, selected by the Islamic community. On the other side of this sharp divide was the Shia (an Arabic word meaning "party" or "faction") branch of Islam. Its adherents felt strongly that leadership in the Islamic world should derive from the line of Ali and his son Husayn, blood relatives of Muhammad, both of whom died at the hands of their political or religious enemies.

In the beginning, therefore, this divide was simply a political conflict without serious theological or religious meaning, but over time the Sunni/Shia split acquired deeper significance. For Sunni Muslims, religious authority in general emerged

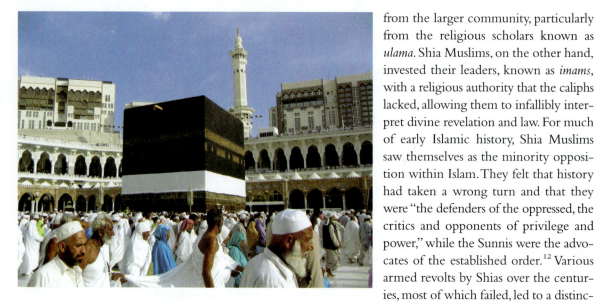

The Kaaba
Located in Mecca, this stone structure covered with a black cloth and known as the Kaaba was originally home to the numerous deities of pre-Islamic Arabia. Cleansed by Muhammad, it became the sacred shrine of Islam and the destination of countless pilgrims undertaking the hajj. Part of that ritual involves circling the Kaaba seven times, as shown here in a photograph from 2004. (Dan Mohiuddin, photographer)

from the larger community, particularly from the religious scholars known as *ulama*. Shia Muslims, on the other hand, invested their leaders, known as *imams*, with a religious authority that the caliphs lacked, allowing them to infallibly interpret divine revelation and law. For much of early Islamic history, Shia Muslims saw themselves as the minority opposition within Islam. They felt that history had taken a wrong turn and that they were "the defenders of the oppressed, the critics and opponents of privilege and power," while the Sunnis were the advocates of the established order.[12] Various armed revolts by Shias over the centuries, most of which failed, led to a distinctive conception of martyrdom and to the expectation that their defeated leaders were merely in hiding and not really dead and that they would return in the fullness of time. Thus a messianic element entered Shia Islam. The Sunni/Shia schism was a lasting division in the Islamic world, reflected in conflicts among various Islamic states, and was exacerbated by further splits among the Shia. Those divisions echo still in the twenty-first century.

As the Arab Empire grew, its caliphs were transformed from modest Arab chiefs into absolute monarchs of the Byzantine or Persian variety, complete with elaborate court rituals, a complex bureaucracy, a standing army, and centralized systems of taxation and coinage. They were also subject to the dynastic rivalries and succession disputes common to other empires. The first dynasty, following the era of the Rightly Guided Caliphs, came from the Umayyad family (ruled 661–750). Under its rule, the Arab Empire expanded greatly, caliphs became hereditary rulers, and the capital moved from Medina to the cosmopolitan Roman/Byzantine city of Damascus in Syria. Its ruling class was an Arab military aristocracy, drawn from various tribes. But Umayyad rule provoked growing criticism and unrest. The Shia viewed the Umayyad caliphs as illegitimate usurpers, and non-Arab Muslims resented their second-class citizenship in the empire. Many Arabs protested the luxurious living and impiety of their rulers. The Umayyads, they charged, "made God's servants slaves, God's property something to be taken by turns among the rich, and God's religion a cause of corruption."[13]

Such grievances lay behind the overthrow of the Umayyads in 750 and their replacement by a new Arab dynasty, the Abbasids. With a splendid new capital in Baghdad, the Abbasid caliphs presided over a flourishing and prosperous Islamic civilization in which non-Arabs, especially Persians, now played a prominent role. Persian influence was reflected in a new title for the caliph, "the shadow of God on earth." Persian became the language of elite culture in the eastern Islamic lands; Persian poetry, painting, architecture, and court rituals were widely imitated. (See Visual Sources: Islamic Civilization in Persian Miniature Paintings, pp. 512–19, for examples of Persian miniature painting.) But the political unity of the Abbasid Empire did not last long. Beginning in the mid-ninth century, many local governors or military commanders effectively asserted the autonomy of their regions, while still giving formal allegiance to the caliph in Baghdad. Long before Mongol conquest put an official end to the Abbasid Empire in 1258, the Islamic world had fractured politically into a series of "sultanates," many ruled by Persian or Turkish military dynasties.

A further tension within the world of Islam, though seldom a violent conflict, lay in different answers to the central question: What does it mean to be a Muslim, to submit wholly to Allah? That question took on added urgency as the expanding Arab Empire incorporated various peoples and cultures that had been unknown during Muhammad's lifetime. One answer lay in the development of the sharia (see Document 11.3, pp. 506–09), the body of Islamic law developed by religious scholars, the ulama, primarily in the eighth and ninth centuries.

■ **Comparison**

In what ways were Sufi Muslims critical of mainstream Islam?

Based on the Quran, the life and teachings of Muhammad, deductive reasoning, and the consensus of scholars, the emerging sharia addressed in great detail practically every aspect of religious and social life. It was a blueprint for an authentic Islamic society, providing detailed guidance for prayer and ritual cleansing; marriage, divorce, and inheritance; business and commercial relationships; the treatment of slaves; political life; and much more. Debates among the ulama led to the creation of four schools of law among Sunni Muslims and still others in the lands of Shia Islam. To the ulama and their followers, living as a Muslim meant following the sharia and thus participating in the creation of an Islamic society.

A second and quite different understanding of the faith emerged among those who saw the worldly success of Islamic civilization as a distraction and deviation from the purer spirituality of Muhammad's time. Known as Sufis, they represented Islam's mystical dimension, in that they sought a direct and personal experience of the divine. Through renunciation of the material world, meditation on the words of the Quran, chanting the names of God, the use of music and dance, the veneration of Muhammad and various "saints," Sufis pursued the taming of the ego and spiritual union with Allah. To describe that inexpressible experience, they often resorted to metaphors of drunkenness or the embrace of lovers. "Stain your prayer rug with wine," urged the famous Sufi poet Hafiz, referring to the intoxication of the believer with the divine presence. Rabia, an eighth-century woman and Sufi master, conveyed something of the fervor of early Sufi devotion in her famous prayer:

> O my Lord, if I worship Thee from fear of Hell, burn me in Hell; and if I worship Thee from hope of Paradise, exclude me thence; but if I worship Thee for Thine own sake, then withhold not from me Thine Eternal Beauty.[14]

(See Document 11.4, pp. 509–10, for another expression of Sufi religious sensibility from the thirteenth-century poet Rumi.)

This mystical tendency in Islamic practice, which became widely popular by the ninth and tenth centuries, was sharply critical of the more scholarly and legalistic practitioners of the sharia. To Sufis, establishment teachings about the law and correct behavior, while useful for daily living, did little to bring the believer into the presence of God. For some, even the Quran had its limits. Why spend time reading a love letter (the Quran), asked one Sufi master, when one might be in the very presence of the Beloved who wrote it?[15] Furthermore, they felt that many of the ulama had been compromised by their association with worldly and corrupt governments. Sufis therefore often charted their own course to God, implicitly challenging the religious authority of the ulama. For these orthodox religious scholars, Sufi ideas and practice verged on heresy, as Sufis claimed to be one with God, to receive new revelations, or to incorporate religious practices from outside the Islamic world.

Despite their differences, the legalistic emphasis of the ulama and Sufi spirituality never became irreconcilable versions of Islam. A major Islamic thinker, al-Ghazali (1058–1111), himself both a legal scholar and a Sufi practitioner, in fact worked out an intellectual accommodation among different strands of Islamic thought. Rational philosophy alone could never enable believers to know Allah, he argued. Nor were revelation and the law sufficient, for Muslims must know God in their hearts, through direct personal encounter with Allah. Thus al-Ghazali incorporated Sufism into mainstream Islamic thinking. Nonetheless, differences in emphasis remained an element of tension and sometimes discord within the world of Islam.

Women and Men in Early Islam

■ **Change**

How did the rise of Islam change the lives of women?

What did the rise of Islam and the making of the Arab Empire mean for the daily lives of women and their relationship with men? Virtually every aspect of this question has been and remains highly controversial. The debates begin with the Quran itself. Did its teachings release women from earlier restrictions, or did they impose new limitations? At the level of spiritual life, the Quran was quite clear and explicit: men and women were equal.

> Those who surrender themselves to Allah and accept the true faith; who are devout, sincere, patient, humble, charitable, and chaste; who fast and are ever mindful of Allah—on these, both men and women, Allah will bestow forgiveness and rich reward.[16]

But in social terms, and especially within marriage, the Quran, like the written texts of almost all civilizations, viewed women as inferior and subordinate:

> Men have authority over women because Allah has made the one superior to the other, and because they spend their wealth to maintain them. Good women are obedient. They guard their unseen parts because Allah has guarded them. As for those from whom you fear disobedience, admonish them and send them to beds apart and beat them. Then if they obey you, take no further action against them.[17]

More specifically, the Quran provided a mix of rights, restrictions, and protections for women. The earlier Arab practice of female infanticide, for example, was forbidden. Women were given control over their own property, particularly their dowries, and were granted rights of inheritance, but at half the rate of their male counterparts. Marriage was considered a contract between consenting parties, thus making marriage by capture illegitimate. Within marriage, women were expected to enjoy sexual satisfaction and could sue for divorce if they had not had sexual relations for more than four months. Divorce was thus possible for both parties, although it was far more readily available for men. The practice of taking multiple husbands, which operated in some pre-Islamic Arab tribes, was prohibited, while polygyny (the practice of having multiple wives) was permitted, though more clearly regulated than before. Men were limited to four wives and required to treat each of them equally. The difficulty of doing so has been interpreted by some as virtually requiring monogamy. Men were, however, permitted to have sexual relations with female slaves, but any children born of those unions were free, as was the mother once her owner died. Furthermore, men were strongly encouraged to marry orphans, widows, and slaves.

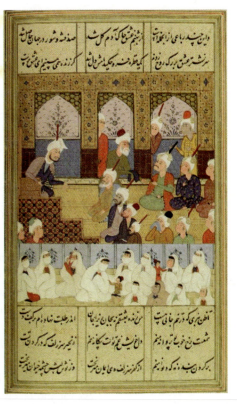

Men and Women at Worship
This sixteenth-century Persian painting of a mosque service shows older men with beards toward the front, younger men behind them, and veiled women and children in a separate area. (Bodleian Library, University of Oxford, Ms. Ouseley. Add 24, fol. 55v)

Such Quranic prescriptions were but one factor shaping the lives of women and men. At least as important were the long-established practices of the societies into which Islam spread and the growing sophistication, prosperity, and urbanization of Islamic civilization. As had been the case in Athens and China during their "golden ages," women, particularly in the upper classes, experienced growing restrictions as Islamic civilization flourished culturally and economically in the Abbasid era. In early Islamic times, a number of women played visible public roles, particularly Muhammad's youngest wife, Aisha. Women prayed in the mosques, although separately, standing beside the men. Nor were women generally veiled or secluded. As the Arab empire grew in size and splendor, however, the position of women became more limited. The second caliph, Umar, asked women to offer prayers at home. Now veiling and the seclusion of women became standard practice among the upper and ruling classes, removing them from public life. Separate quarters within the homes of the wealthy were the domain of women, from which they could emerge only completely veiled. The caliph Mansur (ruled 754–775) carried this separation of the sexes even further when he ordered a separate bridge for women to be built over the Euphrates in the new capital of Baghdad. Such seclusion was less possible for lower-class women, who lacked the servants of the rich and had to leave the home for shopping or work.

Such practices derived far more from established traditions of Middle Eastern cultures than from the Quran itself, but they soon gained an Islamic rationale in the writings of Muslim thinkers. The famous philosopher and religious scholar al-Ghazali clearly saw a relationship between Muslim piety and the separation of the sexes:

> It is not permissible for a stranger to hear the sound of a pestle being pounded by a woman he does not know. If he knocks at the door, it is not proper for the woman to answer him softly and easily because men's hearts can be drawn to [women] for the most trifling [reason].... However, if the woman has to answer the knock, she should stick her finger in her mouth so that her voice sounds like that of an old woman.[18]

Other signs of a tightening patriarchy—such as "honor killing" of women by their male relatives for violating sexual taboos and, in some places, clitorectomy (female genital cutting)—likewise derived from local cultures, with no sanction in the Quran or Islamic law. Where they were practiced, such customs often came to be seen as Islamic, but they were certainly not limited to the Islamic world. In many cultures, concern with family honor, linked to women's sexuality, dictated harsh punishments for women who violated sexual taboos.

Negative views of women, presenting them variously as weak, deficient, and a sexually charged threat to men and social stability, emerged in the *hadiths*, traditions about the sayings or actions of Muhammad, which became an important source of Islamic law. (See Document 11.2, pp. 505–06, for examples of hadiths.) A changing interpretation of the Adam and Eve story illustrates the point. In the Quran, equal blame attaches to both of them for yielding to the temptation of Satan, and both alike ask for and receive God's forgiveness. Nothing suggests that Eve tempted or seduced Adam into sin. In later centuries, however, several hadiths and other writings took up Judeo-Christian versions of the story that blamed Eve, and thus women in general, for Adam's sin and for the punishment that followed, including expulsion from the garden and pain in childbirth.[19]

Even as women faced growing restrictions in society generally, Islam, like Buddhism and Christianity, also offered new outlets for them in religious life. The Sufi practice of mystical union with Allah allowed a greater role for women than did mainstream Islam. Some Sufi orders had parallel groups for women, and a few welcomed women as equal members. Within the world of Shia Islam, women teachers of the faith were termed *mullahs*, the same as their male counterparts. Islamic education, either in the home or in Quranic schools, allowed some to become literate and a few to achieve higher levels of learning. Visits to the tombs of major Islamic figures as well as the ritual of the public bath provided some opportunity for women to interact with other women beyond their own family circle.

Islam and Cultural Encounter: A Four-Way Comparison

In its earliest centuries, the rapid spread of Islam had been accompanied by the creation of an immense Arab Empire, very much in the tradition of earlier Mediterranean and Middle Eastern empires. By the tenth century, however, little political unity

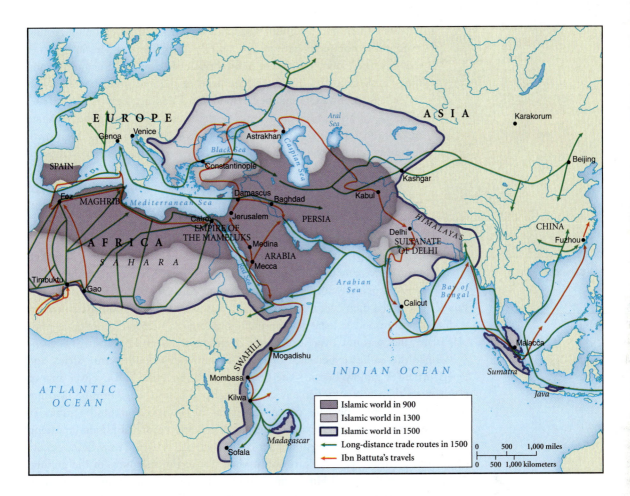

Map 11.2 The Growing World of Islam (900–1500) Islam as a religion, a civilization, and an arena of commerce continued to grow even as the Arab Empire fragmented.

remained, and in 1258 even the powerless symbol of that earlier unity vanished as Mongol forces sacked Baghdad and killed the last Abbasid caliph. But even as the empire disintegrated, the civilization that was born within it grew and flourished. Perhaps the most significant sign of a flourishing Islamic civilization was the continued spread of the religion both within and beyond the boundaries of a vanishing Arab Empire (see Map 11.2), although that process differed considerably from place to place. The examples of India, Anatolia, West Africa, and Spain illustrate the various ways that Islam penetrated these societies as well as the rather different outcomes of these epic cultural encounters.

The Case of India

In South Asia, Islam found a permanent place in a long-established civilization as invasions by Turkic-speaking warrior groups from Central Asia, recently converted to Islam, brought the faith to India. Thus the Turks became the third major carrier of Islam, after the Arabs and Persians, as their conquests initiated an enduring encounter

■ **Comparison**

What similarities and differences can you identify in the spread of Islam to India, Anatolia, West Africa, and Spain?

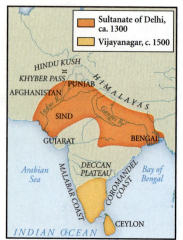

The Sultanate of Delhi

between Islam and a Hindu-based Indian civilization. Beginning around 1000, those conquests gave rise to a series of Turkic and Muslim regimes that governed much of India until the British takeover in the eighteenth and nineteenth centuries. The early centuries of this encounter were violent indeed, as the invaders smashed Hindu and Buddhist temples and carried off vast quantities of Indian treasure. With the establishment of the Sultanate of Delhi in 1206, Turkic rule became more systematic, although their small numbers and internal conflicts allowed only a very modest penetration of Indian society.

In the centuries that followed, substantial Muslim communities emerged in India, particularly in regions less tightly integrated into the dominant Hindu culture. Disillusioned Buddhists as well as low-caste Hindus and untouchables found the more egalitarian Islam attractive. So did peoples just beginning to make the transition to settled agriculture. Others benefited from converting to Islam by avoiding the tax imposed on non-Muslims. Sufis were particularly important in facilitating conversion, for India had always valued "god-filled men" who were detached from worldly affairs. Sufi missionaries, willing to accommodate local gods and religious festivals, helped to develop a "popular Islam" that was not always so sharply distinguished from Hinduism.

Unlike the earlier experience of Islam in the Middle East, North Africa, and Persia, where it rapidly became the dominant faith, in India it was never able to claim more than 20 to 25 percent of the total population. Furthermore, Muslim communities were especially concentrated in the Punjab and Sind regions of northwestern India and in Bengal to the east. The core regions of Hindu culture in the northern Indian plain were not seriously challenged by the new faith, despite centuries of Muslim rule. One reason perhaps lay in the sharpness of the cultural divide between Islam and Hinduism. Islam was the most radically monotheistic of the world's religions, forbidding any representation of Allah, while Hinduism was surely among the most prolifically polytheistic, generating endless statues and images of the divine in many forms. The Muslim notion of the equality of all believers contrasted sharply with the hierarchical assumptions of the caste system. The sexual modesty of Muslims was deeply offended by the open eroticism of some Hindu religious art.

Although such differences may have limited the appeal of Islam in India, they also may have prevented it from being absorbed into the tolerant and inclusive embrace of Hinduism as had so many other religious ideas, practices, and communities. The religious exclusivity of Islam, born of its firm monotheistic belief and the idea of a unique revelation, set a boundary that the great sponge of Hinduism could not completely absorb.

Certainly not all was conflict across that boundary. Many prominent Hindus willingly served in the political and military structures of a Muslim-ruled India. Mystical seekers after the divine blurred the distinction between Hindu and Muslim, suggesting that God was to be found "neither in temple nor in mosque." "Look within your heart," wrote the great fifteenth-century mystic poet Kabir, "for there you will find both [Allah] and Ram [a famous Hindu deity]."[20] In fact, during the early sixteenth century, a new and distinct religious tradition emerged in India, known as Sikhism, which blended elements of Islam, such as devotion to one universal God, with Hindu concepts, such as karma and rebirth. "There is no Hindu and no Muslim. All are children of God," declared Guru Nanak (1469–1539), the founder of Sikhism.

Nonetheless, Muslims usually lived quite separately, remaining a distinctive minority within an ancient Indian civilization, which they now largely governed but which they proved unable to completely transform.

The Case of Anatolia

At the same time that India was being subjected to Turkic invasion, so too was Anatolia (now modern Turkey), where the largely Christian and Greek-speaking population was then governed by the Byzantine Empire (see Maps 11.1 and 11.3). Here, as in India, the invaders initially wreaked havoc as Byzantine authority melted away in the eleventh century. Sufi missionaries likewise played a major role in the process of conversion. The outcome, however, was a far more profound cultural transformation than in India. By 1500, the population was 90 percent Muslim and largely Turkic-speaking, and Anatolia was the heartland of the powerful Turkish Ottoman Empire that had overrun Christian Byzantium. Why did the Turkic intrusion into Anatolia generate a much more thorough Islamization than in India?

One factor clearly lies in a very different demographic balance. The population of Anatolia—perhaps 8 million—was far smaller than India's roughly 48 million people, but far more Turkic-speaking peoples settled in Anatolia, giving them a much greater cultural weight than the smaller colonizing force in India. Furthermore, the disruption of Anatolian society was much more extensive. Massacres, enslavement, famine, and flight led to a sharp drop in the native population. The Byzantine state had been fatally weakened. Church properties were confiscated, and monasteries were destroyed or deserted. Priests and bishops were sometimes unable to serve their congregations. Christians, though seldom forced to convert, suffered many discriminations. They had to wear special clothing and pay special taxes, and they were forbidden to ride saddled horses or carry swords. Not a few Christians came to believe that these disasters represented proof that Islam was the true religion.[21] Thus Byzantine civilization in Anatolia, focused on the centralized institutions of church and state, was rendered leaderless and dispirited, whereas India's decentralized civilization, lacking a unified political or religious establishment, was better able to absorb the shock of external invasion while retaining its core values and identity.

The Turkish rulers of Anatolia built a new society that welcomed converts and granted them material rewards and opportunity for high office. Moreover, the cultural barriers to conversion were arguably less severe than in India. The common monotheism of Islam and Christianity, and Muslim respect for Jesus and the Christian

■ **Comparison**
Why was Anatolia so much more thoroughly Islamized than India?

Legend:
- Ottoman Empire in 1359
- Ottoman Empire in 1451

Venice

WALLACHIA
Danube R.
BOSNIA
Black Sea
Ragusa
SERBIA
Maritsa R.
BULGARIA
Thessalonika
Constantinople
Bursa
GREECE
ANATOLIA

Mediterranean Sea

0   250   500 miles
0   250   500 kilometers

Map 11.3   The Ottoman Empire by the Mid-Fifteenth Century
As Turkic-speaking migrants bearing the religion of Islam penetrated Anatolia, the Ottoman Empire took shape, reaching into southeastern Europe and finally displacing the Christian Byzantine Empire. Subsequently, it came to control much of the Middle East and North Africa as well.

scriptures, made conversion easier than crossing the great gulf between Islam and Hinduism. Such similarities lent support to the suggestion of some Sufi teachers that the two religions were but different versions of the same faith. Sufis also established schools, mills, orchards, hospices, and rest places for travelers and thus replaced the destroyed or decaying institutions of Christian Anatolia.[22] All of this contributed to the thorough religious transformation of Anatolia and laid a foundation for the Ottoman Empire, which by 1500 became the most impressive and powerful state within the Islamic world (see Map 11.3).

But the Islamization of Anatolia occurred within a distinctly Turkish context. A Turkish language, not Arabic, predominated. Some Sufi religious practices, such as ecstatic turning dances, derived from Central Asian Turkic shamanism (see Visual Source 8.5, p. 376). And Turkic traditions offering a freer, more gender-equal life for women, common among pastoral people, persisted well after conversion to Islam, much to the distress of the Arab Moroccan visitor Ibn Battuta during his travels among them in the fourteenth century: "A remarkable thing that I saw... was the respect shown to women by the Turks, for they hold a more dignified position than the men.... The windows of the tent are open and her face is visible, for the Turkish women do not veil themselves."[23] He was not pleased.

The Case of West Africa

Still another pattern prevailed in West Africa. Here Islam accompanied Muslim traders across the Sahara rather than being brought by invading Arab or Turkic armies. Its acceptance in the emerging civilization of West African states in the centuries after 1000 was largely peaceful and voluntary, lacking the incentives associated elsewhere with foreign conquest. Introduced by Muslim merchants from an already Islamized North Africa, the new faith was accepted primarily in the urban centers of the West African empires—Ghana, Mali, Songhay, Kanem-Bornu, and others (see Map 11.4). For African merchant communities, Islam provided an important link to Muslim trading partners, much as Buddhism had done in Southeast Asia. For the monarchs and their courts, it offered a source of literate officials to assist in state administration as well as religious legitimacy, particularly for those who gained the prestige conferred by a pilgrimage to Mecca. Islam was a world religion with a single Creator-God, able to comfort and protect people whose political and

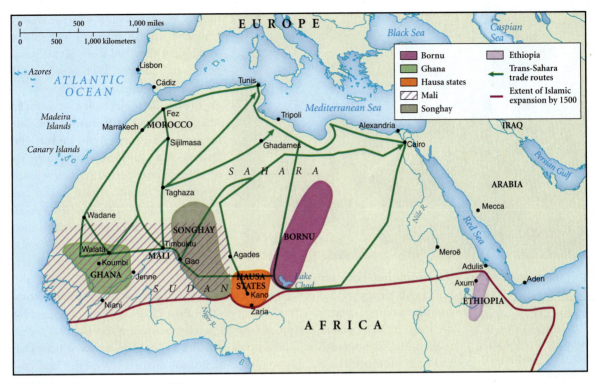

Map 11.4   West Africa and the World of Islam

Both trans-Saharan commerce and Islam linked the civilization of West Africa to the larger Muslim world.

economic horizons had expanded well beyond the local realm where ancestral spirits and traditional deities might be effective. It had a religious appeal for societies that were now participating in a wider world.

By the sixteenth century, a number of West African cities had become major centers of Islamic religious and intellectual life, attracting scholars from throughout the Muslim world. Timbuktu boasted more than 150 lower-level Quranic schools and several major centers of higher education with thousands of students from all over West Africa and beyond. Libraries held tens of thousands of books and scholarly manuscripts. Monarchs subsidized the construction of mosques as West Africa became an integral part of a larger Islamic world. Arabic became an important language of religion, education, administration, and trade, but it did not become the dominant language of daily life. Nor did West Africa experience the massive migration of Arab peoples that had promoted the Arabization of North Africa and the Middle East. Moreover, in contrast to India and Anatolia, Sufi holy men played little role until at least the eighteenth century. Scholars, merchants, and rulers, rather than mystic preachers, initially established Islam in West Africa.

Islam remained the culture of urban elites and spread little into the rural areas of West Africa until the nineteenth century. No thorough religious transformation occurred in West Africa as it had in Anatolia. Although many rulers adopted Islam,

The Great Mosque at Jenne
This mosque in the city of Jenne, initially constructed in the thirteenth century, illustrates the assimilation of Islam into West African civilization. (Bildagentur/TIPS Images)

they governed people who steadfastly practiced African religions and whose sensibilities they had to respect if social peace were to prevail. Thus they made few efforts to impose the new religion on their rural subjects or to govern in strict accordance with Islamic law. The fourteenth-century Arab visitor Ibn Battuta was appalled that practicing Muslims in Mali permitted their women to appear in public almost naked and to mingle freely with unrelated men. "The association of women with men is agreeable to us," he was told, "and a part of good conduct to which no suspicion attaches. They are not like the women of your country."[24] Ibn Battuta also noted with disapproval a "dance of the masks" on the occasion of an Islamic festival and the traditional practice of sprinkling dust on their heads as a sign of respect for the king. (See Document 8.3, pp. 362–65, for a fuller account if Ibn Battuta's travels in West Africa.) Sonni Ali, a fifteenth-century ruler of Songhay, observed Ramadan and built mosques, but he also consulted traditional diviners and performed customary sacrifices. In such ways, Islam became Africanized even as parts of Africa became Islamized.

The Case of Spain

The chief site of Islamic encounter with Catholic Europe occurred in Spain (called al-Andalus by Muslims), which was conquered by Arab and Berber forces in the early eighth century during the first wave of Islamic expansion. But there, Islam did not overwhelm Christianity as it did later in Anatolia. In fact, Muslim Spain in the several centuries that followed conquest has often been portrayed as a vibrant civilization characterized by harmony and tolerance between its Muslim rulers and its Christian and Jewish subjects.

Certainly Spain's agricultural economy was the most prosperous in Europe during the ninth and tenth centuries, and at that time its capital of Córdoba was among the largest and most splendid cities in the world. Muslims, Christians, and Jews alike contributed to a brilliant high culture in which astronomy, medicine, the arts, architecture, and literature flourished. It was largely from Spain that the rich heritage of Islamic learning became available to Christian Europe.

Furthermore, social relationships among upper-class members of different faiths were easy and frequent. More than a few Christians converted to Islam, and many others, known as Mozarabs (would-be Arabs), learned Arabic, veiled their women, stopped eating pork, appreciated Arabic music and poetry, and sometimes married

Muslims. One Christian bishop complained that Spanish Christians knew the rules of Arabic grammar better than those of Latin. During the reign of Abd al-Rahman III (912–961), freedom of worship was declared as well as the opportunity for all to rise in the bureaucracy of the state.

Even assimilated or Arabized Christians, however, remained infidels in the eyes of their Muslim counterparts, and by the late tenth century the era of toleration began to erode. Warfare with the remaining Christian states in northern Spain picked up in the tenth and eleventh centuries, and more puritanical and rigid forms of Islam entered Spain from North Africa. In these circumstances, the golden age of religious harmony faded. Under the rule of Abu Amir al-Mansur (981–1002), an official policy of tolerance turned to one of overt persecution against Christians, which now included the plundering of churches. Social life also changed. Devout Muslims avoided contact with Christians; Christian homes had to be built lower than those of Muslims; priests were forbidden to carry a cross or a Bible, lest they offend Muslim sensibilities; and Mozarabs were permitted to live only in particular places. Thus, writes one scholar, "the era of harmonious interaction between Muslim and Christian in Spain came to an end, replaced by intolerance, prejudice, and mutual suspicion."[25]

That intolerance was perpetuated as the Christian reconquest of Spain gained ground after 1200. Many Muslims were then forced out of Spain, while those who remained could no longer give the call to prayer, go on pilgrimage, or publicly practice their faith. When the reconquest was completed in 1492, all Jews, some 200,000 of them, were likewise expelled from the country. Thus, as Christianity was displaced by Islam in Anatolia, the opposite process was taking place in Spain, though with far less tolerance for other religions.

The World of Islam as a New Civilization

As the religion spread and the Abbasid dynasty declined, the civilization of Islam, like Western Christendom and the Hindu world, operated without a single political center, bound more by a shared religious culture than by a shared state. Unlike the other civilizations, however, the Islamic world by 1500 embraced at least parts of virtually every other civilization in the Afro-Eurasian hemisphere. It was in that sense "history's first truly global civilization," although the Americas, of course, were not involved.[26] What held the Islamic world together? What enabled many people to feel themselves part of a single civilization despite its political fragmentation, religious controversies, and cultural and regional diversity?

Networks of Faith

At the core of that vast civilization was a common commitment to Islam. No group was more important in the transmission of those beliefs and practices than the ulama. These learned scholars were not "priests" in the Christian sense, for in Islam, at least theoretically, no person could stand between the believer and Allah. Rather

■ Description
What makes it possible to speak of the Islamic world as a distinct and coherent civilization?

they served as judges, interpreters, administrators, prayer leaders, and reciters of the Quran, but especially as preservers and teachers of the sharia. Supported mostly by their local communities, some also received the patronage of *sultans*, or rulers, and were therefore subject to criticism for corruption and undue submission to state authority. In their homes, mosques, shrines, and Quranic schools, the ulama passed on the core teachings of the faith. Beginning in the eleventh century, formal colleges called *madrassas* offered more advanced instruction in the Quran and the sayings of Muhammad; grammar and rhetoric; sometimes philosophy, theology, mathematics, and medicine; and, above all else, law. Teaching was informal, mostly oral, and involved much memorization of texts. It was also largely conservative, seeking to preserve an established body of Islamic learning.

The ulama were an "international elite," and the system of education they created served to bind together an immense and diverse civilization. Common texts were shared widely across the world of Islam. Students and teachers alike traveled great distances in search of the most learned scholars. From Indonesia to West Africa, educated Muslims inhabited a "shared world of debate and reference."[27]

Paralleling the educational network of the ulama were the emerging religious orders of the Sufis. By the tenth century, particular Sufi *shaykhs*, or teachers, began to attract groups of disciples who were eager to learn their unique devotional practices and ways of achieving union with Allah. The disciples usually swore eternal allegiance to their teacher and valued highly the chain of transmission by which those teachings and practices had come down from earlier masters. In the twelfth and thirteenth centuries, Sufis began to organize in a variety of larger associations, some limited to particular regions and others with chapters throughout the Islamic world. The Qadiriya order, for example, began in Baghdad but spread widely throughout the Arab world and into sub-Saharan Africa. Sufi orders were especially significant in the frontier regions of Islam because they followed conquering armies or traders into Central and Southeast Asia, India, Anatolia, West Africa, and elsewhere. Their devotional teachings, modest ways of living, and reputation for supernatural powers gained a hearing for the new faith. Their emphasis on personal experience of the divine, rather than on the law, allowed the Sufis to accommodate elements of local belief and practice and encouraged the growth of a popular or blended Islam. But that flexibility also often earned them the enmity of the ulama, who were sharply critical of such deviations from the sharia.

Like the madrassas and the sharia, Sufi religious ideas and institutions spanned the Islamic world and were yet another thread in the cosmopolitan web of Islamic civilization. Particular devotional teachings and practices spread widely, as did the writings of such famous Sufi poets as Hafiz and Rumi. (For the poetry of Rumi, see Document 11.4, pp. 509–10.) Devotees made pilgrimages to the distant tombs of famous teachers, who, they often believed, might intercede with God on their behalf. Wandering Sufis, in search of the wisdom of renowned shaykhs, found fellow seekers and welcome shelter in the compounds of these religious orders.

In addition to the networks of the Sufis and the ulama, many thousands of people, from kings to peasants, made the grand pilgrimage to Mecca—the hajj— each year, no doubt gaining some sense of the umma. There men and women together, hailing from all over the Islamic world, joined as one people to rehearse the central elements of their faith. The claims of local identities based on family, clan, tribe, ethnicity, or state never disappeared, but now overarching them all was the inclusive unity of the Muslim community.

Networks of Exchange

The world of Islamic civilization cohered not only as a network of faith but also as an immense arena of exchange in which goods, technologies, food products, and ideas circulated widely. It rapidly became a vast trading zone of hemispheric dimensions. In part, this was due to its central location in the Afro-Eurasian world and the breaking down of earlier political barriers between the Byzantine and Persian empires. Furthermore, commerce was valued positively within Islamic teaching, for Muhammad himself had been a trader, and the pilgrimage to Mecca likewise fostered commerce. The extraordinary spurt of urbanization that accompanied the growth of Islamic civilization also promoted trade. (See Visual Source 11.2, p. 516, for a sixteenth-century image of an Islamic city.) Baghdad, established in 756 as the capital of the Abbasid Empire, soon grew into a magnificent city of half a million people. The appetite of urban elites for luxury goods stimulated both craft production and the desire for foreign products.

> ■ **Connection**
>
> In what ways was the world of Islam a "cosmopolitan civilization"?

Thus Muslim merchants, Arabs and Persians in particular, quickly became prominent and sometimes dominant players in all of the major Afro-Eurasian trade routes of the postclassical era—in the Mediterranean Sea, along the revived Silk Roads, across the Sahara, and throughout the Indian Ocean basin (see Chapter 8). By the eighth century, Arab and Persian traders had established a commercial colony in Canton in southern China, thus linking the Islamic heartland with Asia's other giant and flourishing economy. Various forms of banking, partnerships, business contracts, and instruments for granting credit facilitated these long-distance economic relationships and generated a prosperous, sophisticated, and highly commercialized economy that spanned the Old World.[28]

The vast expanses of Islamic civilization also contributed to the diffusion of agricultural products and practices from one region to another, a process already under way in the earlier Roman and Persian empires. The Muslim conquest of northwestern India opened the Middle East to a veritable treasure trove of crops that had been domesticated long before in South and Southeast Asia, including rice, sugarcane, new strains of sorghum, hard wheat, bananas, lemons, limes, watermelons, coconut palms, spinach, artichokes, and cotton. Some of these subsequently found their way into the Middle East and Africa and by the thirteenth century to Europe as well.[29] Both cotton and sugarcane, associated with complex production processes and slave labor, came to play central roles in the formation of the modern global system after 1500. These new crops and the development of the intensified agricultural techniques that often accompanied them contributed to increased food production, population growth, urbanization, and industrial development characteristic of the Muslim Middle East in early Abbasid times.

Technology too diffused widely within the Islamic world. Ancient Persian techniques for obtaining water by drilling into the sides of hills now spread across North Africa as far west as Morocco. Muslim technicians made improvements on rockets, first developed in China, by developing one that carried a small warhead and another used to attack ships.[30] Papermaking techniques entered the Abbasid Empire from China in the eighth century, with paper mills soon operating in Persia, Iraq, and Egypt. This revolutionary technology, which everywhere served to strengthen bureaucratic governments, spread from the Middle East into India and Europe over the following centuries.

Ideas likewise circulated across the Islamic world. The religion itself drew heavily and quite openly on Jewish and Christian precedents. Persia also contributed much in the way of bureaucratic practice, court ritual, and poetry, with Persian becoming a major literary language in elite circles. Scientific, medical, and philosophical texts, especially from ancient Greece, the Hellenistic world, and India, were systematically translated into Arabic, for several centuries providing an enormous boost to Islamic scholarship and science. In 830, the Abbasid caliph al-Mamun, himself a poet and scholar with a passion for foreign learning, established the House of Wisdom in Baghdad as an academic center for this research and translation. Stimulated by Greek texts, a school of Islamic thinkers known as Mutazalites ("those who stand apart") argued that reason, rather than revelation, was the "surest way to truth."[31] In the long run, however, the philosophers' emphasis on logic, rationality, and the laws of nature was subject to increasing criticism by those who held that only the Quran, the sayings of the Prophet, or mystical experience represented a genuine path to God.

But the realm of Islam was much more than a museum of ancient achievements from the civilizations that it encompassed. Those traditions mixed and blended to generate a distinctive Islamic civilization with many new contributions to the world of learning.[32] (See the Snapshot on p. 499.) Using Indian numerical notation, for example, Arab scholars developed algebra as a novel mathematical discipline. They also undertook much original work in astronomy and optics. They built upon earlier Greek and Indian practice to create a remarkable tradition in medicine and pharmacology. Arab physicians such as al-Razi and Ibn Sina accurately

A Muslim Astronomical Observatory

Drawing initially on Greek, Indian, and Persian astronomy, the Islamic world after 1000 developed its own distinctive tradition of astronomical observation and prediction, reflected in this Turkish observatory constructed in 1557. Muslim astronomy subsequently exercised considerable influence in both China and Europe. (University Library, Istanbul, Turkey/The Bridgeman Art Library)

Snapshot   **Key Achievements in Islamic Science and Scholarship**

Person/Dates	Achievement
al-Khwarazim (790–840)	Mathematician; spread use of Arabic numerals in Islamic world; wrote first book on algebra
al-Razi (865–925)	Discovered sulfuric acid; wrote a vast encyclopedia of medicine drawing on Greek, Syrian, Indian, and Persian work and his own clinical observation
al-Biruni (973–1048)	Mathematician, astronomer, cartographer; calculated the radius of the earth with great accuracy; worked out numerous mathematical innovations; developed a technique for displaying a hemisphere on a plane
Ibn Sina (Avicenna) (980–1037)	Prolific writer in almost all fields of science and philosophy; especially known for *Canon of Medicine*, a fourteen-volume work that set standards for medical practice in Islamic and Christian worlds for centuries
Omar Khayyam (1048–1131)	Mathematician; critic of Euclid's geometry; measured the solar year with great accuracy; Sufi poet; author of *The Rubaiyat*
Ibn Rushd (Averroës) (1126–1198)	Translated and commented widely on Aristotle; rationalist philosopher; made major contributions in law, mathematics, and medicine
Nasir al-Din Tusi (1201–1274)	Founder of the famous Maragha observatory in Persia (data from Maragha probably influenced Copernicus); mapped the motion of stars and planets
Ibn Khaldun (1332–1406)	Greatest Arab historian; identified trends and structures in world history over long periods of time

diagnosed many diseases, such as hay fever, measles, smallpox, diphtheria, rabies, and diabetes. In addition, treatments such as using a mercury ointment for scabies, cataract and hernia operations, and filling teeth with gold emerged from Arab doctors. The first hospitals, traveling clinics, and examinations for physicians and pharmacologists also were developed within the Islamic world. In the eleventh and twelfth centuries, this enormous body of Arab medical scholarship entered Europe via Spain, and it remained at the core of European medical practice for many centuries.[33]

Reflections: Past and Present: Choosing Our History

Prominent among the many uses of history is the perspective it provides on the present. Although historians sometimes worry that an excessive "present-mindedness" may distort our perception of the past, all of us look to history, almost instinctively, to comprehend the world we now inhabit. Given the obvious importance of the Islamic world in the international arena of the twenty-first century, how might some grasp of the early development of Islamic civilization assist us in understanding our present circumstances?

First, that history reminds us of the central role that Islam played in the Afro-Eurasian world for a thousand years or more. From 600 to 1600 or later, it was a proud, cosmopolitan, often prosperous, and frequently powerful civilization that spanned Africa, Europe, the Middle East, and Asia. What followed were several centuries of European or Western imperialism that many Muslims found humiliating, even if some were attracted by elements of modern Western culture. In their recent efforts to overcome those centuries of subordination and exploitation, Muslims have found encouragement and inspiration in reflecting on the more distant and perhaps more glorious past. But they have not all chosen to emphasize the same past. Those labeled as "fundamentalists" have often viewed the early Islamic community associated with Medina, Mecca, and Muhammad as a model for Islamic renewal in the present. Others, often known as Islamic modernizers, have looked to the somewhat later achievements of Islamic science and scholarship as a foundation for a more open engagement with the West and the modern world.

The history of Islam also reveals to us a world of great diversity and debate. Sharp religious differences between Sunni and Shia understandings of the faith; differences in emphasis between advocates of the sharia and of Sufi spirituality; political conflicts among various groups and regions within the larger Islamic world; different postures toward women in Arab lands and in West Africa—all of this and more divided the umma and divide it still. Recalling that diversity is a useful reminder for any who would tag all Muslims with a single label.

A further dimension of that diversity lies in the many cultural encounters that the spread of Islam has spawned. Sometimes great conflict and violence have accompanied those encounters as in the Crusades and in Turkic invasions of India and Anatolia. At other times and places, Muslims and non-Muslims have lived together in relative tranquillity and tolerance—in Spain, in West Africa, in India, and in the Ottoman Empire. Some commentaries on the current interaction of Islam and the West seem to assume an eternal hostility or an inevitable clash of civilizations. The record of the past, however, shows considerable variation in the interaction of Muslims and others. While the past certainly shapes and conditions what happens next, the future, as always, remains open. Within limits, we can choose the history on which we seek to build.

Second Thoughts

What's the Significance?

Quran	ulama	Ibn Battuta
umma	Umayyad caliphate	Timbuktu
Pillars of Islam	Abbasid caliphate	al-Andalus
hijra	al-Ghazali	madrassas
sharia	Sikhism	House of Wisdom
jizya	Anatolia	Ibn Sina

To assess your mastery of the material in this chapter, visit the **Student Center** at bedfordstmartins.com/strayer.

Big Picture Questions

1. What distinguished the first centuries of Islamic history from the early history of Christianity and Buddhism? What similarities and differences characterized their religious outlooks?
2. How might you account for the immense religious and political/military success of Islam in its early centuries?
3. In what ways might Islamic civilization be described as cosmopolitan, international, or global?
4. "Islam was simultaneously both a single world of shared meaning and interaction and a series of separate and distinct communities, often in conflict with one another." What evidence could you provide to support both sides of this argument?
5. What changes did Islamic expansion generate in those societies that encountered it, and how was Islam itself transformed by those encounters?

Next Steps: For Further Study

Reza Aslan, *No God but God* (2005). A well-written and popular history of Islam by an Iranian immigrant to the United States.

Richard Bulliet, *Conversion to Islam in the Medieval Period* (1979). A scholarly study of the meaning and process of conversion in the early history of Islam and in several distinct places.

Richard Eaton, *Islamic History as Global History* (1990). A short account by a major scholar that examines Islam in a global framework.

John Esposito, ed., *The Oxford History of Islam* (1999). Up-to-date essays on various periods and themes in Islamic history. Beautifully illustrated.

Francis Robinson, ed., *Cambridge Illustrated History of the Islamic World* (1996). A series of essays by major scholars, with lovely pictures and maps.

Judith Tucker, *Gender and Islamic History* (1994). A brief overview of the changing lives of Islamic women.

"The Travels of Ibn Battuta: A Virtual Tour with the Fourteenth Century Traveler," http://www.sfusd.k12.ca.us/schwww/sch618/Ibn_Battuta/Battuta's_Trip_Twelve.html. A beautifully illustrated journey across the Islamic world in the early 1300s.

For Web sites and additional documents related to this chapter, see **Make History** at bedfordstmartins.com/strayer.

Documents

Considering the Evidence:
Voices of Islam

Like every other great religious tradition, Islam found expression in various forms. Its primary text, the Quran, claimed to represent the voice of the divine, God's final revelation to humankind. Other early Islamic writings, known as *hadith*, recorded the sayings and deeds of the Prophet Muhammad. Still others reflected the growing body of Islamic law, the *sharia*, which sought to construct a social order aligned with basic religious teachings. Devotional practices and expressions of adoration for Allah represented yet another body of Islamic literature. All of this gave rise to differing interpretations and contending views, generating for Islam a rich and complex literary tradition that has been the source of inspiration and debate for almost 1,400 years. From this immense body of work, we present just a few samples of the voices of Islam.

Document 11.1

The Voice of Allah

To Muslims, the Quran contains the very words of God. The term *quran* itself means "recitation" in Arabic, and the faithful believe that the angel Gabriel spoke God's words to Muhammad, who then recited them. Often called "noble" or "glorious," the Quran, compiled into an established text within thirty years of the Prophet's death, was regarded as a book without equal, written in the most sublime Arabic. Copying it was an act of piety, memorizing it was the starting point for Muslim education, and reciting it was both an art form and a high honor. Organized in 114 Surahs (chapters), the Quran was revealed to Muhammad over a period of some twenty-two years. Often the revelations came in response to particular problems that the young Islamic community and the Prophet were facing. The selections that follow convey something of the Quran's understanding of God, of humankind, of the social life prescribed for believers, of relations with non-Muslims, and much more.

■ What are the chief characteristics of Allah, to Muslims the single source of all life and being?

■ What religious practices are prescribed for Muslims in these passages? What are their purposes in the life of believers?

■ What specific prescriptions for social life do these selections contain? Notice in particular those directed toward the weakest members of society. How would you describe the Quran's view of a good society?

■ What attitude toward Jews, Christians, and other non-Muslim peoples do these passages suggest?

■ What circumstances surrounding the birth of Islam might help to explain the references in the Quran to fighting and warfare?

■ The sacred texts of all religious traditions provide ample room for conflicting understandings and interpretations. What debates or controversies might arise from these passages? Consider in particular views of women, of religious practice, of warfare, and of relationships with Jews and Christians.

The Quran
Seventh Century C.E.

Surah 1

In the name of God, the Most Gracious and the Dispenser of Grace. All praise is due to God alone, the sustainer of all the worlds... Lord of the Day of Judgment. Thee alone do we worship; and unto Thee alone do we turn for aid. Guide us in the straight way, the way of those upon whom Thou hast bestowed Thy blessing, not of those who have been condemned, nor those who go astray.

Surah 2

This divine writ [the Quran]—let there be no doubt about it—is [meant to be] a guidance for all the God-conscious who believe in [the existence of] that which is beyond the reach of human perception, and are constant in prayer, and spend on others out of what We provide for them as sustenance; and who believe in that which has been bestowed from on high upon thee, [O Prophet,] as well as in that which was bestowed before thy time....

Verily, those who have attained to faith, as well as those who follow the Jewish faith, and the Christians...—all who believe in God and the Last Day and do righteous deeds—shall have their reward with their Sustainer; and no fear need they have, and neither shall they grieve....

And they say, "Be Jews"—or, "Christians"—"and you shall be on the right path." Say: "Nay, but [ours is] the creed of Abraham, who turned away from all that is false, and was not of those who ascribe divinity to aught beside God." Say: "We believe in God, and in that which has been bestowed from on high upon us, and that which has been bestowed upon Abraham and Ishmael and Isaac and Jacob, and their descendants, and that which has been vouchsafed to Moses and Jesus; and that which has been vouchsafed to all the [other] prophets by their Sustainer: we make no distinction between any of them...."

Verily, in the creation of the heavens and of the earth, and the succession of night and day: and in the ships that speed through the sea with what is useful to man: and in the waters which God sends down from the sky, giving life thereby to the earth after it had been lifeless, and causing all manner of living creatures to multiply thereon: and in the change of the winds, and the clouds that run their appointed courses between sky and earth: [in all this] there are messages indeed for people who use their reason....

Source: Muhammad Asad, *The Message of the Qur'ān* (Bristol: The Book Foundation, 2003), Surahs 1, 2, 4, 5.

True piety does not consist in turning your faces toward the east or the west, but truly pious is he who believes in God, and the Last Day; and the angels, and revelation, and the prophets; and spends his substance — however much he himself may cherish it — upon his near of kin, and the orphans, and the needy, and the wayfarer, and the beggars, and for the freeing of human beings from bondage....

Fasting is ordained for you as it was ordained for those before you, so that you might remain conscious of God....

And fight in God's cause against those who wage war against you, but do not commit aggression, for verily, God does not love aggressors. And slay them wherever you may come upon them, and drive them away from wherever they drove you away, for oppression is even worse than killing. And fight not against them near the Inviolable House of Worship° unless they fight against you there first; but if they fight against you, slay them: such shall be the recompense of those who deny the truth. But if they desist, behold, God is much-forgiving, a dispenser of grace. Hence, fight against them until there is no more oppression and all worship is devoted to God alone; but if they desist, then all hostility shall cease, save against those who [willfully] do wrong....

And perform the pilgrimage... [to Mecca] in honor of God; and if you are held back, give instead whatever offering you can easily afford....

There shall be no coercion in matters of faith....

Do not deprive your charitable deeds of all worth by stressing your own benevolence and hurting [the feelings of the needy], as does he who spends his wealth only to be seen and praised by men....

God has made buying and selling lawful and usury° unlawful. Hence, whoever... desists [from

---

°**Inviolable House of Worship:** a mosque.

°**usury:** the lending of money to be paid back with interest.

usury], may keep his past gains, and it will be for God to judge him; but as for those who return to it they are destined for the fire.... God deprives usurious gains of all blessing, whereas He blesses charitable deeds with manifold increase.

Surah 4

[R]ender unto the orphans their possessions... and do not consume their possessions together with your own: this, verily, is a great crime....

Men shall have a share in what parents and kinsfolk leave behind, and women shall have a share in what parents and kinsfolk leave behind, whether it be little or much....

And as for those of your women who become guilty of immoral conduct, call upon four from among you who have witnessed their guilt; and if these bear witness thereto, confine the guilty women to their houses until death takes them away or God opens for them a way [through repentance]. And punish [thus] both of the guilty parties; but if they both repent and mend their ways, leave them alone: for, behold, God is an acceptor of repentance, a dispenser of grace....

And it will not be within your power to treat your wives with equal fairness, however much you may desire it; and so, do not allow yourselves to incline toward one to the exclusion of the other, leaving her in a state, as it were, of having and not having a husband.

Surah 5

Do not take the Jews and Christians for your allies: they are but allies of one another — and whoever of you allies himself with them becomes, verily, one of them.

Document II.2

The Voice of the Prophet Muhammad

As an expression of Islam, the sayings and deeds of Muhammad, known as the *hadiths*, are second in importance only to the Quran. In various collections of hadiths, Muslims hear the voice and witness the actions of their prophet. While they do not have the authority of divine revelation, these statements have served to guide and inspire Muslims to this day.

In the several centuries following his death, an enormous number of stories about Muhammad circulated within the Islamic community. Scholars gradually developed methods of authentication designed to discover which of these stories most reliably represented the Prophet's words and actions. Considerable controversy accompanied this process, and no single collection of hadiths has ever achieved universal acceptance. One of the earliest and most highly respected of these collections was the work the Persian scholar al-Bukhari (810–870). Traveling extensively throughout the Islamic world, al-Bukhari is said to have collected some 600,000 stories, memorized 200,000 of them, and finally authenticated and published 7,275. The selections that follow suggest something of the range and variety of the hadiths.

- What portrait of Muhammad emerges from this record of his sayings and actions?

- How do these hadiths reflect or build on the teaching of the Quran in Document II.1?

- What religious and social values do these hadiths highlight?

- In what ways do these hadiths reflect common themes in many of the world's "wisdom traditions," and in what respects are they distinctly Islamic?

The Hadith
Eighth and Ninth Centuries

The Apostle of Allah... was asked which [good] work was the most excellent, and he answered: "Belief in Allah and in His Apostle." He was asked: "And then which?" He replied: "Jihād in the way of Allah." He was again asked: "And then what?" and he replied: "An acceptable pilgrimage."...

Source: Arthur Jeffery, ed. and trans., *A Reader on Islam* (The Hague: Mouton, 1962), 81–86.

If a slave serves honestly his [earthly] master and worships earnestly his [heavenly] Lord, he will have a double recompense.

He who shows concern for the widows and the unfortunate [ranks as high] as one who goes on Jihād in the way of Allah, or one who fasts by day and who rises at night [for prayer].

A [true] believer views his sins as though he were sitting beneath a mountain which he fears may fall on him, but as evil-doer views his sins as a fly that moves across his nose.

In this world be as a stranger, or as one who is just passing along the road.

In two things an old man's heart never ceases to be that of a youth, in love of this world and in hoping long....

To look at a woman is forbidden, even if it is a look without desire, so how much the more is touching her.

Said he—upon whom be Allah's blessing and peace—"Avoid seven pernicious things." [His Companions] said: "And what are they, O Apostle of Allah?" He answered: "Associating anything with Allah, sorcery, depriving anyone of life where Allah has forbidden that save for just cause, taking usury, devouring the property of orphans, turning the back on the day of battle, and slandering chaste believing women even though they may be acting carelessly."

No one who enters Paradise will ever want to return to this world, even could he possess the earth and all that is on it, save the martyrs who desire to return to this world and be killed ten times so great is the regard in which they find themselves held.

To be stationed on the frontier for one day during Holy War is better than (to possess) this world and all that is on it. A place in Paradise the size of one of your whip-lashes is better than this world and all that is on it....

If a man sees something in [the conduct of] his ruler which he dislikes let him put up with it patiently, for there is no one who separates himself even a span from the community and dies [in that separation], but dies a pagan death....

Said the Prophet...: "I had a look into Paradise and I saw that the poor made up most of its inhabitants, and I had a look into Hell and saw that most of its inhabitants were women....

Treat women-folk kindly for woman was created of a rib. The crookedest part of a rib is its upper part. If you go to straighten it out you will break it, and if you leave it alone it will continue crooked. So treat women in kindly fashion....

Said the Apostle of Allah...: "O band of youths, let him among you who is able to make a home get married, and let him who is not able betake himself to fasting for he will find in that a quencher [of his passions]."

The worst of foods is that of a feast to which the rich have been invited and the poor overlooked....

Said the Apostle of Allah—upon whom be Allah's blessing and peace—: "Do not wear silks and satins, and do not drink from gold and silver vessels nor eat from dishes made thereof, for these things are theirs in this world but ours in the world to come."...

Said the Prophet—upon whom be Allah's blessing and peace—: "He who drinks wine in this world and repents not of it will be forbidden it in the world to come."...

Al-Aqra' said: "I have ten sons but never have I kissed any one of them." The Apostle of Allah—upon whom be Allah's blessing and peace—looked at him, and then said: "He who does not show tenderness will not have tenderness shown him."

Document 11.3

The Voice of the Law

While Christian scholarship emphasized theology and correct belief, learned Muslims gave more attention to law and correct behavior. That law was known as the sharia, an Arabic term that referred to a path toward water, which is the source of life. To many Muslims, that was the role of law—to construct the good society within which an authentic religious life could find expression.

The sharia emerged as the early Islamic community confronted the practical problems of an expanding empire with a very diverse population. But no single legal framework developed. Rather, four major schools of Islamic law crystallized, agreeing on fundamentals but differing in emphasis. How much weight should be given to the hadiths and which of them were most reliably authentic? What scope should reason and judgment have in applying religious principles to particular circumstances? Despite disagreement on such questions, each of the four approaches to legal interpretation sought to be all-embracing, providing highly detailed guidance on ritual performance, personal behavior, marriage and family matters, crime and punishment, economic transactions, and political action. The selections that follow, drawn from various legal traditions, illustrate this comprehensive nature of Islamic law and its centrality in an evolving Islamic civilization.

■ What do you find most striking about the legal prescriptions in these passages?

■ In what ways do these selections draw on and apply the teachings of the Quran and the hadiths?

■ How does the role of law in early Islamic civilization differ from that of modern Western society?

■ Why do you think the role of law was so central, so highly detailed, and so comprehensive in Islamic civilization?

■ What do this document and Document 11.2 suggest about the problems that the early Islamic community confronted?

The Sharia
Ninth Century

On Prayer

The five prayers are obligatory for every Muslim who has reached the age of puberty and has the use of reason, except for women who are menstruating or recovering from childbirth.

If Muslims deny the necessity of prayer through ignorance, one must instruct them; if they deny it willfully, they have apostatized....

If Muslims abstain from saying the prayers from negligence, one should ask them three times to repent; if they repent, it is well, and if they refuse, it is lawful to put them to death.

Source: John Alden Williams, trans. and ed., *The Word of Islam* (Austin: University of Texas Press, 1994), 71, 80–82, 88–89, 94–95, 98–101, 104–5.

On *Zakat*°

The obligation pertains only to a free Muslim who has complete ownership of the property on which it is due.... *Zakat* is due only on animals, agricultural products, precious metals, objects intended for sale, the products of mines, and treasure troves.

Whoever has the obligation to pay *zakat* and is able must pay it; if not, they commit a fault for which they must answer. If anyone refuses to pay it and denies its obligatory character they have committed apostasy and may be put to death. If they refuse it from avarice, they shall have the amount taken from them and be given a sentence at the judge's discretion.

°*Zakat*: alms for the poor.

On Marriage

[Marriage] is contracted by means of declaration and consent. When both parties are Muslims, it must be contracted in the presence of two male or one male and two female Muslim witnesses who are free, sane, and adult....

It is not lawful for a man to marry two women who are sisters or to cohabit with two sisters who are his slaves....

A man may not marry his slave-girl unless he sets her free first, and a woman may not marry her slave, since marriage has as its object that the children belong equally to both parents, and ownership and slavery are not equal states.

Similarly, marriage with an idolatress is forbidden, until she accepts Islam or a religion of the Book.

It is not lawful for a man already married to a free woman to marry a slave.... However, a man may lawfully marry a free woman after a slave.

A free man may marry four women, free or slave, but no more. It is unlawful for a slave to marry more than two women....

On Government

There are ten things a Caliph° must do in public affairs:

1) Maintain religion according to its established principles.
2) Apply legal judgments for litigants so that equity reigns without aiding the oppressor or weakening the oppressed.
3) Protect the flock...so that people may gain their living and move from place to place securely.
4) Apply the *hudud*, or punishments of the Law, so as to secure God's prohibitions from violation.
5) Fortify the marches so that the enemy will not appear due to neglect, shedding the blood of any Muslim or protected person.
6) Wage *jihad* against those who reject Islam so that they become either Muslims or protected people.
7) Collect the *zakat* and taxes on conquered territory...without fear or oppression.
8) Administer treasury expenditures.
9) Delegate loyal and trustworthy people.
10) Directly oversee matters and not delegate his authority seeking to occupy himself with either pleasure or devotion....

It is necessary therefore to cause the masses to act in accord with divine laws in all the affairs, both in this world and in the world to come. The authority to do so was possessed by the prophets and after them by their successors.

On Things Disliked in the Law

It is not permitted to men or women to eat or drink or keep unguents° in vessels of gold or silver....

It is not permitted for a man to wear silk, but it is permitted for a woman....

It is not permitted for a man to wear gold or silver, except for silver on a ring, or on a weapon.

It is not permitted for a man to look at a strange woman.°...A woman frequently needs to bare her hands and face in transactions with men. Abu Hanifa said it was also permitted to look at her feet and Abu Yusuf said it was permitted to look at her forearms as well.... However, if a man is not secure from feeling lust, he should not look needlessly even at the face or hands, to avoid sin. He is not allowed to touch her face or hands even if he is free from lust, whether he be young or old.

On the Economy

It is disliked to corner the market in food for humans or animals if it occurs in a town where this may prove harmful to the people. It is disliked to sell weapons in a time of trouble.

°**Caliph:** successor to Muhammad as political leader of the Islamic community.

°**unguents:** ointments.

°**strange woman:** a woman from outside one's immediate family.

There is no harm in selling fruit juice to someone who will make wine of it, since the transgression is not in the juice but in the wine after it has been changed....

Earning a living by changing money is a great danger to the religion of the one who practices it.... It is the duty of the *muhtasib*° to search out the money changers' places of business and spy on them,

---

°**Muhtasib:** an inspector of the markets.

and if he finds one of them practicing usury or doing something illegal...he must punish that person....

Owners of ships and boats must be prevented from loading their vessels above the usual load, for fear of sinking.... If they carry women on the same boat with men, there must be a partition between them.

Sellers of [pottery] are not to overlay any that are pierced or cracked with gypsum...and then sell them as sound.

Document 11.4

The Voice of the Sufis

Alongside the law, there ran a very different current of Islamic thinking and expression known as Sufism. The Sufis, sometimes called the "friends of God," were the mystics of Islam, those for whom the direct, personal, and intoxicating experience of the divine source was of far greater importance than the laws, regulations, and judgments of the sharia (see pp. 485–86, 496). Organized in hundreds of separate orders, or "brotherhoods," the Sufis constituted one of the transregional networks that linked the far-flung domains of the Islamic world. Often they were the missionaries of Islam, introducing the faith to Anatolia, India, Central Asia, and elsewhere.

Among the most prominent exemplars of Sufi sensibility was Rumi (1207–1273), born in what is now Afghanistan and raised in a Persian cultural tradition. Rumi's family later migrated to Anatolia, and Rumi lived most of his adult life in the city of Konya, where he is buried. There he wrote extensively, including a six-volume work of rhymed couplets known as the *Mathnawi*. Following Rumi's death, his son established the Mevlevi Sufi order, based on Rumi's teachings and known in the West as the "whirling dervishes," on account of the turning dances that became a part of their practice (see Visual Source 8.5 on p. 376).

Rumi's poetry has remained a sublime expression of the mystical dimension of Islamic spiritual seeking and has provided inspiration and direction for millions, both within and beyond the Islamic world. In the early twenty–first century, Rumi was the best-selling poet in the United States. The selections that follow provide a brief sample of the Sufi approach to religious life.

■ How would you define the religious sensibility of Rumi's poetry?

■ How does it differ from the approach to Islam reflected in the sharia?

■ What criticisms might the orthodox legal scholars (ulama) have made regarding the Sufi understanding of Islam?

Inscription in Rumi's Tomb
Thirteenth Century

Come, come, whoever you are,
Wanderer, worshipper, lover of leaving.

It doesn't matter.
Ours is not a caravan of despair.
Come, even if you have broken your vow a
    thousand times,
Come, yet again, come, come.

Source: A frequently quoted inscription hanging inside the tomb of Rumi and generally, though not universally, attributed to him; translator unknown.

RUMI

Poem
Thirteenth Century

I searched for God among the Christians and on
    the Cross and therein I found Him not.
I went into the ancient temples of idolatry; no
    trace of Him was there.

I entered the mountain cave of Hira and then went
    as far as Qandhar but God I found not....
Then I directed my search to the Kaaba, the resort
    of old and young; God was not there even.
Turning to philosophy I inquired about him from
    ibn Sina but found Him not within his range....
Finally, I looked into my own heart and there I
    saw Him; He was nowhere else.

Source: M. M. Sharif, *A History of Muslim Philosophy*, (Wiesbaden: Harrassowitz, 1966), 2:838.

RUMI

"Drowned in God," Mathnawi
Thirteenth Century

I am the torrent of ecstasy when it runs in
    flood,
So that it won't bring shame and ruin.
But why should I fear ruin?
Under the ruin waits a treasure.
He that is drowned in God wishes to be more
    drowned.
While his spirit is tossed up and down by the
    waves of the sea,

He asks, "Is the bottom of the sea more delightful
    or the top?"
Is the Beloved's arrow more fascinating, or the
    shield?
O heart, if you recognize any difference between
    joy and sorrow,
These lies will tear you apart.
Although your desire tastes sweet,
Doesn't the Beloved desire you to be desireless?
The life of lovers is in death:
You will not win the Beloved's heart unless you
    lose your own.

Source: From Kabir Helminski, ed., *The Pocket Rumi Reader* (Boston: Shambhala, 2001), 89.

Using the Evidence:
Voices of Islam

1. **Defining differences within Islam:** In what different ways do the various voices of Islam represented in these documents understand and express the common religious tradition of which they are all a part? What grounds for debate or controversy can you identify within or among them?

2. **Comparing religious traditions:** How would you compare Islamic religious ideas and practices with those of other traditions such as Hinduism, Buddhism, and Christianity?

3. **Considering gender and Islam:** How do these documents represent the roles of men and women in Islamic society? Pay particular attention to differences in emphasis.

4. **Seeking additional sources:** Notice that all of these documents derive from literate elites, and each of them suggests or prescribes appropriate behavior. What additional documents would you need if you were to assess the impact of these prescriptions on the lives of ordinary people? What specific questions might you want to pose to such documents?

Visual Sources

Considering the Evidence: Islamic Civilization in Persian Miniature Paintings

Iran, homeland of the ancient Persian Empire and its successors, entered the world of Islam rather differently than did Iraq, Syria, Egypt, and North Africa. In the latter regions, converts to Islam gradually abandoned their native languages, adopted Arabic, and came to be seen as Arabs. In Iran or Persia, by contrast, Arab conquest did not involve the cultural Arabization of the region, despite some initial efforts to impose the Arabic language (see Map 11.1, p. 481). By the tenth century, the vast majority of Persians were Muslims, but the Persian language, Farsi (still spoken in modern Iran), flourished, enriched now by a number of Arabic loan words and written in an Arabic script. In 1010, that language received its classic literary expression when the Persian poet Ferdowsi completed his epic work, the *Shahnama* (*The Book of Kings*). A huge text of some 60,000 rhyming couplets, it recorded the mythical and pre-Islamic history of Iran and gave an enduring expression to a distinctly Persian cultural identity.

That culture had an enormous influence within the world of Islam. Many religious ideas of Persian Zoroastrianism—an evil satanic power, final judgment, heaven and hell, paradise—found their way into Islam, often indirectly via Jewish or Christian precedents. In Iran, Central Asia, India, and later in the Ottoman Empire, Persian influences were pervasive. Persian administrative and bureaucratic techniques; Persian court practices with their palaces, gardens, and splendid garments; Persian architecture, poetry, music, and painting—all of this decisively shaped the high culture of these eastern Islamic lands. One of the Abbasid caliphs, himself an Arab, observed: "The Persians ruled for a thousand years and did not need us Arabs even for a day. We have been ruling them for one or two centuries and cannot do without them for an hour."[34]

Prominent among the artistic achievements of Persian culture were miniature paintings—small, colorful, and exquisitely detailed works often used to illustrate books or manuscripts. One art historian described them as "little festivals of color in images separated from each other by pages of text."[35] This artistic style flourished especially from the thirteenth through the sixteenth centuries, when Persia was invaded and ruled by a succession of Mongol or Turkic dynasties. These invasions, especially that of the Mongols in the thirteenth century, were highly destructive. Great cities were devastated, libraries burned, and artists forced to flee. But the new rulers also proved to be generous patrons of the arts and served as carriers of Buddhist and Chinese artistic forms that enriched Persian painting.

During these centuries, the artists who created these Persian miniatures drew heavily on Persian mythology, poetry, and history as subjects for their paintings. Landscapes, influenced by Chinese techniques, also appeared in Persian miniatures. Scenes from the life of the Prophet Muhammad were likewise among the themes explored by Persian artists, although explicitly Islamic subject matter was represented in only a small proportion of these paintings. Particularly helpful to historians, images of daily life also found a place in Persian miniature painting, providing glimpses into social life in the Arab or Persian centers of Islamic civilization.

Visual Sources 11.1 and 11.2, dating from the early to mid-sixteenth century and measuring about eight by eleven inches, illustrate this focus within Persian miniature painting. Visual sources such as these are often most revealing in their detail, as artists depicted elements of daily life not often recorded elsewhere. Both of them, however, are idealized images that reflect enduring values within the Islamic world rather than referring to specific times or places.

Visual Source 11.1 offers a window on the life of desert pastoral nomads of Arabia.[36] The style of both clothing and tents indicate that this is an Arab nomadic encampment. The image focuses the viewer's attention on the two older men seated inside the elaborately decorated blue tent in the lower left. Seven cups are lined up in front of the men at the bottom, together with their lids, perhaps to keep the beverage warm or the bugs out. The red tent at the left is decorated with a *simurgh*, a legendary Persian winged creature with the head of a dog and the claws of a lion, said to have lived so long that it had acquired universal knowledge. Outside the tent of the woman at the right of the painting are her slippers, and above her another woman tenderly feeds her child. In perhaps the only directly Islamic reference in the painting, the old man approaching the washerwoman holds prayer beads in his right hand. Notice also some apparent Chinese influence in the painting. The presentation of rocks, clouds, and twisted trees reflects features of Chinese landscape painting, while the blue-and-white ceramic bowl near the woman washing clothes suggests some trade with China.

According to some art historians, this image has yet another level of meaning, for it may have served to illustrate the well-known and ancient Arab love story of Layla and Majnun, tragic star-crossed lovers prevented (like Romeo and Juliet) from marrying by a family feud and united only in death. The young man tending the fire at the upper right may represent Majnun, driven mad and into the wilderness by his unfulfilled love. The woman in the beautiful green

Visual Source 11.1 An Arab Camp Scene (Harvard Art Museum, Arthur M. Sackler Museum, Gift of John Goelet)

gown sitting in the doorway of the red tent on the left side of the painting may be Layla. In this interpretation of the image, the meeting of the two older men represents an incident in the story in which Majnun's father, together with his relatives, asks for Layla's hand in marriage from her father.

■ What specific features and activities of nomadic life does the painting portray? What marks this image as an idealized version of an Arab camp? What features of nomadic life may have been omitted?

■ Do the writing implements at the very bottom left of the painting— books, a pencase, an inkwell—offer a clue to the discussion that the two men may be having?

■ What social distinctions are revealed in this painting?

■ What differences in the lives of men and women are suggested in this image?

■ What other details do you notice as you study this miniature painting?

Unlike the rural scene of Visual Source 11.1, the urban landscape of Visual Source 11.2 corresponds to no identifiable story or narrative. Also a sixteenth-century painting, it reflects the urban bustle and commercial sophistication of Islamic civilization. Here buildings replace tents as the major structures in the painting. Nine separate sources of light—lamps, candles, and torches—mark this as a nighttime scene, but in Persian painting, unlike in European art, light does not reflect on people or objects and does not cast shadows.

Three distinct sections of the painting illustrate various elements of city life. On the left and bottom of the image, a young prince holds court in his court pavilion attended by various turbaned courtiers. Above and to the right of the court scene, characteristic urban activities unfold along a city street. Finally, in the upper left a woman lounges on the balcony of an urban dwelling, while another woman speaks to an older turbaned man. Notice also the mosque in the upper right corner, inscribed with a well-known saying of Muhammad: "He who builds a mosque for God, God will build for him a dwelling in Paradise." There is also an inscription above the building in the lower right from the fourteenth-century Persian Sufi poet Hafiz: "The pupil of my eye is your nesting place; be kind, alight, for it is your home." As in Visual Source 11.1, intriguing details abound: the garden seen through the window in the arched pavilion; various types of musical instruments; the headscarves on women and the henna decorations on their hands; the elaborate geometric designs on buildings; the prayer beads in the hand of the young boy in front of the mosque.

Visual Source 11.2 City Life in Islamic Persia (Harvard Art Museum, Arthur M. Sackler Museum, Gift of John Goelet)

■ What might a historian interested in daily urban life in the Islamic world notice in this painting? What different social groups can you identify?

■ What in particular seems to be going on in the court scene? What products and transactions can you find in or around the several shops that line the street?

■ How would you define the roles of women as depicted here? Notice in particular the three young women above the court pavilion, seeking to observe the excitement below, from which they were presumably excluded.

■ In what ways are the activities shown in the painting idealized?

■ How might you understand the inscriptions of Muhammad and Hafiz in the context of this painting?

■ What details do you find most striking in Visual Source 11.2?

The Persian miniature painting in Visual Source 11.3 moves from ordinary life to religious imagination. While explicitly religious themes appear only infrequently in these paintings, the most common religious subject by far was that of the Prophet Muhammad's Night Journey, said to have taken place in 619 or 620. The Quran refers briefly to God taking the prophet "from the sacred place of worship to the far distant place of worship." This passage became the basis for a story, much embellished over the centuries, of rich and deep meaning for Muslims. In this religious narrative, Muhammad was led one night by the angel Gabriel from Mecca to Jerusalem. For the journey he was given a *buraq*, a mythical winged creature with the body of a mule or donkey and the face of a woman. Upon arriving in Jerusalem, he led prayers for an assembly of earlier prophets including Abraham, Moses, and Jesus. (See p. 477 for another illustration of Muhammad's relationship with earlier Jewish and Christian prophets.) Then, accompanied by many angels, Muhammad made his way through seven heavens into the presence of God, where, according to the Quran, "he did see some of the most profound of his Sustainer's symbols." There too Allah spoke to Muhammad about the importance of regular prayer, commanding fifty prayers a day, a figure later reduced to five on the advice of Moses.

From the beginning, Muslims have been divided on how to interpret this journey of the Prophet. For most, perhaps, it was taken quite literally as a miraculous event. Some, however, viewed it as a dream or a vision, while others understood it as the journey of Muhammad's soul but not his body. The Prophet's youngest wife, Aisha, for example, reported that "his body did not leave its place." Visual Source 11.3, dating from the early sixteenth century, is one of many representations of the Night Journey that emerged within Persian miniature painting.

Visual Source 11.3 The Night Journey of Muhammad (© British Library Board)

- How do you understand the halo of fire that surrounds the Prophet's image in the center of the painting? Notice also that a similar halo envelops the head of the angel Gabriel (in blue dress), who is leading Muhammad heavenward.

- What significance might attach to the female head of the buraq?

- What are the accompanying angels offering to the Prophet during his journey?

- What meaning might the artist seek to convey by the image of the world below and slightly to the right of the buraq?

- The willingness of Persian artists to represent Muhammad bodily contrasts sharply with a general Arab unwillingness to do so. Nonetheless, the Prophet's face is not shown. Why do you think Muslim artists have often been reluctant to represent the Prophet in human form? How might veiling his face address these concerns? Do you see any similarity with the controversy over icons in the Christian tradition? (See pp. 466–71.)

- Consider finally the larger meaning of the Night Journey within Islam. What is the significance of Muhammad's encounter with earlier prophets such as Abraham, Moses, and Jesus? How does the story explain the second of the five pillars of Islam, the requirement to pray five times a day?

- Review the discussion of the Sufi tradition of Islam on pages 485–86. How might Sufis have understood the Night Journey? How might it serve as a metaphor for the spiritual journey?

Using the Evidence:
Islamic Civilization in Persian Miniature Paintings

1. **Noticing point of view:** Consider these three visual sources together with the six other photos within the chapter (pp. 475, 477, 484, 487, 494, and 498). What general impression of the Islamic world emerges? What point of view, if any, is reflected in the selection of visual sources? Do they convey a positive, negative, or neutral impression of Islamic civilization? Explain your answer with specific references to the various images.

2. **Making comparisons:** Compare these visual sources to the icons in the Visual Sources section in Chapter 10 (pp. 466–71) in terms of purpose, artistic style, and themes. In particular, how does Visual Source 11.3 and the story of the Night Journey compare to the *Ladder of Divine Ascent* (Visual Source 10.3, p. 470) as artistic representations of the spiritual quest?

3. **Using images as evidence:** In what ways can historians use these visual sources? What insights about Islamic civilization can we derive from them? How should consideration of artist/author, audience, and purpose affect historians' assessment of these paintings?

CHAPTER TWELVE

Pastoral Peoples on the Global Stage

The Mongol Moment

1200–1500

In 1937, the great Mongol warrior Chinggis Khan lost his soul, some seven centuries after his death. According to Mongol tradition, a warrior's soul was contained in his spirit banner, consisting of strands of hair from his best horses attached to a spear. For many centuries, Chinggis Khan's spirit banner had been housed in a Buddhist monastery in central Mongolia, where lamas (religious teachers) had tended it.[1] But in the 1930s, Mongolia, then under communist control and heavily dominated by Stalin's Soviet Union, launched a brutal antireligious campaign that destroyed many monasteries and executed some 2,000 monks. In the confusion that ensued, Chinggis Khan's spirit banner, and thus his soul, disappeared.

By the end of the twentieth century, as communism faded away, the memory of Chinggis Khan, if not his spirit banner, made a remarkable comeback in the land of his birth. Vodka, cigarettes, a chocolate bar, two brands of beer, the country's best rock band, and the central square of the capital city all bore his name, while his picture appeared on Mongolia's stamps and money. Rural young people on horseback sang songs in his honor, and their counterparts in urban Internet cafés constructed Web sites to celebrate his achievements. The country organized elaborate celebrations in 2006 to mark the 800th anniversary of his founding of the Mongol Empire.

ALL OF THIS IS A REMINDER OF THE ENORMOUS AND SURPRISING role that the Mongols played in the Eurasian world of the thirteenth and fourteenth centuries and of the continuing echoes of that long-vanished empire. More generally, the story of the Mongols serves as

Chinggis Khan at Prayer: This sixteenth-century Indian painting shows Chinggis Khan at prayer in the midst of battle. He is perhaps praying to Tengri, the great sky god, on whom the Mongol conqueror based his power. (Werner Forman/Art Resource, NY)

a useful corrective to the almost exclusive focus that historians often devote to agricultural peoples and their civilizations, for the Mongols, and many other such peoples, were pastoral nomads who disdained farming while centering their economic lives around their herds of animals. Normally they did not construct elaborate cities, enduring empires, or monumental works of art, architecture, and written literature. Nonetheless, they left an indelible mark on the historical development of the entire Afro-Eurasian hemisphere, and particularly on the agricultural civilizations with which they so often interacted.

Looking Back and Looking Around: The Long History of Pastoral Nomads

The "revolution of domestication," beginning around 11,500 years ago, involved both plants and animals. People living in more favored environments were able to combine farming with animal husbandry and on this economic foundation generated powerful and impressive civilizations with substantial populations. But on the arid margins of agricultural lands, where productive farming was difficult or impossible, an alternative kind of food-producing economy emerged around 4000 B.C.E., focused on the raising of livestock. Peoples practicing such an economy learned to use the milk, blood, wool, hides, and meat of their animals to occupy lands that could not support agricultural societies. Some of those animals also provided new baggage and transportation possibilities. Horses, camels, goats, sheep, cattle, yaks, and reindeer were the primary animals that separately, or in some combination, enabled the construction of pastoral or herding societies. Such societies took shape in the vast grasslands of inner Eurasia and sub-Saharan Africa, in the Arabian and Saharan deserts, in the subarctic regions of the Northern Hemisphere, and in the high plateau of Tibet. Pastoralism emerged only in the Afro-Eurasian world, for in the Americas the absence of large animals that could be domesticated precluded a herding economy. But where such animals existed, their domestication shaped unique societies adapted to diverse environments.

The World of Pastoral Societies

■ Comparison

In what ways did pastoral societies differ from their agricultural counterparts?

Despite their many differences, pastoral societies shared several important features that distinguished them from settled agricultural communities and civilizations. Pastoral societies' generally less productive economies and their need for large grazing areas meant that they supported far smaller populations than did agricultural societies. People generally lived in small and widely scattered encampments of related kinfolk rather than in the villages, towns, and cities characteristic of agrarian civilizations. Beyond the family unit, pastoral peoples organized themselves in kinship-based groups or clans that claimed a common ancestry, usually through the male line. Related clans might on occasion come together as a tribe, which could also absorb unrelated people into the community. Although their values stressed equality and individual achievement, in some pastoral societies clans were ranked as noble or commoner,

Snapshot   **Varieties of Pastoral Societies²**

Region and Peoples	Primary Animals	Features
Inner Eurasian steppes (Xiongnu, Yuezhi, Turks, Uighurs, Mongols, Huns, Kipchaks)	Horses; also sheep, goats, cattle, Bactrian (two-humped) camel	Domestication of horse by 4000 B.C.E.; horseback riding by 1000 B.C.E.; site of largest nomadic empires
Southwestern and Central Asia (Seljuks, Ghaznavids, Mongol Il-khans, Uzbeks, Ottomans)	Sheep and goats; used horses, camels, and donkeys for transport	Close economic relationship with neighboring towns; provided meat, wool, milk products, and hides in exchange for grain and manufactured goods
Arabian and Saharan deserts (Bedouin Arabs, Berbers, Tuareg)	Dromedary (one-humped) camel; sometimes sheep	Camel caravans made possible long-distance trade; camel-mounted warriors central to early Arab/Islamic expansion
Grasslands of sub-Saharan Africa (Fulbe, Nuer, Turkana, Masai)	Cattle; also sheep and goats	Cattle were a chief form of wealth and central to ritual life; little interaction with wider world until nineteenth century
Subarctic Eurasia (Lapps)	Reindeer	Reindeer domesticated only since 1500 C.E.; little impact on world history
Tibetan plateau (Tibetans)	Yaks; also sheep, cashmere goats, some cattle	Tibetans supplied yaks as baggage animal for overland caravan trade; exchanged wool, skins, and milk with valley villagers and received barley in return

and considerable differences emerged between wealthy aristocrats owning large flocks of animals and poor herders. Many pastoral societies held slaves as well.

Furthermore, nomadic societies generally offered women a higher status, fewer restrictions, and a greater role in public life than their sisters in agricultural civilizations enjoyed. Everywhere women were involved in productive labor as well as having domestic responsibility for food and children. The care of smaller animals such as sheep and goats usually fell to women, although only rarely did women own or control their own livestock. Among the Mongols, the remarriage of widows carried none of the negative connotations that it did among the Chinese, and women could initiate divorce. Mongol women frequently served as political advisers and were active in military affairs as well. A thirteenth-century European visitor, the Franciscan friar Giovanni DiPlano Carpini, recorded his impressions of Mongol women:

> Girls and women ride and gallop as skillfully as men. We even saw them carrying quivers and bows, and the women can ride horses for as long as the men; they have shorter stirrups, handle horses very well, and mind all the property. [Mongol] women make everything: skin clothes, shoes, leggings, and everything made of leather. They drive carts and repair them, they load camels, and are quick and vigorous in all their tasks. They all wear trousers, and some of them shoot just like men.[3]

(See Document 12.5, pp. 557–59, for more on Mongol women.)

■ **Connection**
In what ways did pastoral societies interact with their agricultural neighbors?

Certainly literate observers from adjacent civilizations noticed and clearly disapproved of the freedom granted to pastoral women. Ancient Greek writers thought that the pastoralists with whom they were familiar were "women governed." To Han Kuan, a Chinese Confucian scholar in the first century B.C.E., China's northern nomadic neighbors "[made] no distinction between men and women."[4]

The most characteristic feature of pastoral societies was their mobility. As people frequently on the move, they are often referred to as nomads because they shifted their herds in regular patterns. These movements were far from aimless wanderings, as popular images often portray them, but rather sought to systematically follow the seasonal changes in vegetation and water supply. It was a life largely dictated by local environmental conditions and based on turning grass, which people cannot eat, into usable food and energy. Nor were nomads homeless; they took their homes, often elaborate felt tents, with them. According to a prominent scholar of pastoral life, "They know where they are going and why."[5]

Even though nomadic pastoralists represented an alternative to the agricultural way of life that they disdained, they were almost always deeply connected to, and often dependent on, their agricultural neighbors. Few nomadic peoples could live solely from the products of their animals, and most of them actively sought access to

The Scythians
An ancient horse-riding nomadic people during the classical era, the Scythians occupied a region in present-day Kazakhstan and southern Russia. Their pastoral way of life is apparent in this detail from an exquisite gold necklace from the fourth century B.C.E. (Private Collection/Photo Boltin Picture Library/The Bridgeman Art Library)

the foodstuffs, manufactured goods, and luxury items available from the urban workshops and farming communities of nearby civilizations. Particularly among the nomadic peoples of inner Eurasia, this desire for the fruits of civilization periodically stimulated the creation of tribal confederations or nomadic states that could more effectively deal with the powerful agricultural societies on their borders. The Mongol Empire of the thirteenth century was but the most recent and largest in a long line of such efforts, dating back to the first millennium B.C.E.

Constructing a large state among nomadic pastoralists was no easy task. Such societies generally lacked the wealth needed to pay for the professional armies and bureaucracies that everywhere sustained the states and empires of agricultural civilizations. And the fierce independence of widely dispersed pastoral clans and tribes as well as their internal rivalries made any enduring political unity difficult to achieve. Nonetheless, charismatic leaders, such as Chinggis Khan, were periodically able to weld together a series of tribal alliances that for a time became powerful states. In doing so, they often employed the device of "fictive kinship," designating allies as blood relatives and treating them with a corresponding respect.

Despite their limited populations, such states had certain military advantages in confronting larger and more densely populated civilizations. They could draw upon the horseback-riding and hunting skills of virtually the entire male population and some women as well. Easily transferred to the role of warrior, these skills, which were practiced from early childhood, were an integral part of pastoral life. But what sustained nomadic states was their ability to extract wealth, through raiding, trading, or extortion, from agricultural civilizations such as China, Persia, and Byzantium. As long as that wealth flowed into pastoral states, rulers could maintain the fragile alliances among fractious clans and tribes. When it was interrupted, however, those states often fragmented.

Pastoral nomads interacted with their agricultural neighbors not only economically and militarily but also culturally as they "became acquainted with and tried on for size all the world and universal religions."[6] At one time or another, Judaism, Buddhism, Islam, and several forms of Christianity all found a home somewhere among the nomadic peoples of inner Eurasia. So did Manichaeism, a religious tradition born in third-century Persia and combining elements of Zoroastrian, Christian, and Buddhist practice. (See Visual Sources: Art, Religion, and Cultural Exchange in Central Asia, pp. 367–77 in Chapter 8, for cultural exchanges involving Central Asian nomadic peoples.) Usually conversion was a top-down process as nomadic elites and rulers adopted a foreign religion for political purposes, sometimes changing religious allegiance as circumstances altered. Nomadic peoples, in short, did not inhabit a world totally apart from their agricultural and civilized neighbors.

Surely the most fundamental contribution of pastoralists to the larger human story was their mastery of environments unsuitable for agriculture. Through the creative use of their animals, they brought a version of the food-producing revolution and a substantial human presence to the arid grasslands and desert regions of Afro-Eurasia. As the pastoral peoples of the Inner Asian steppes learned the art of horseback riding, by roughly 1000 B.C.E., their societies changed dramatically. Now they could accumulate and tend larger herds of horses, sheep, and goats and move more rapidly over a much wider territory. New technologies, invented or adapted by pastoral societies, added to the mastery of their environment and spread widely across the Eurasian steppes, creating something of a common culture in this vast region. These innovations included complex horse harnesses, saddles with iron stirrups, a small compound bow that could be fired from horseback, various forms of armor, and new kinds of swords. Agricultural peoples were amazed at the centrality of the

The Xiongnu Confederacy

■ **Significance**

In what ways did the Xiongnu, Arabs, and Turks make an impact on world history?

horse in pastoral life. As one observer noted, "From their horses, by day and night every one of that [nomadic] nation buys and sells, eats and drinks, and bowed over the narrow neck of the animal relaxes in a sleep so deep as to be accompanied by many dreams."[7]

The Xiongnu: An Early Nomadic Empire

What enabled pastoral peoples to make their most visible entry onto the stage of world history was the military potential of horse-back riding, and of camel riding somewhat later. Their mastery of mounted warfare made possible a long but intermittent series of nomadic empires across the steppes of inner Eurasia and elsewhere. For 2,000 years, those states played a major role in Eurasian history and represented a standing challenge to and influence upon the agrarian civilizations on their borders.

During the classical era, one such large-scale nomadic empire was associated with the people known as the Xiongnu, who lived in the Mongolian steppes north of China (see Chapter 9). Provoked by Chinese penetration of their territory, the Xiongnu in the third and second centuries B.C.E. created a huge military confederacy that stretched from Manchuria deep into Central Asia. Under the charismatic leadership of Modun (reigned 210–174 B.C.E.), the Xiongnu Empire effected a revolution in nomadic life. Earlier fragmented and egalitarian societies were now transformed into a far more centralized and hierarchical political system in which power was concentrated in a divinely sanctioned ruler and differences between "junior" and "senior" clans became more prominent. "All the people who draw the bow have now become one family," declared Modun. Tribute, exacted from other nomadic peoples and from China itself, sustained the Xiongnu Empire and forced the Han dynasty emperor Wen to acknowledge, unhappily, the equality of people he regarded as barbarians. "Our two great nations," he declared, no doubt reluctantly, "the Han and the Xiongnu, stand side by side."[8]

Although it subsequently disintegrated under sustained Chinese counterattacks, the Xiongnu Empire created a model that later Turkic and Mongol empires emulated. Even without a powerful state, various nomadic or seminomadic peoples played a role in the collapse of already weakened classical Chinese and Roman empires and the subsequent rebuilding of those civilizations (see Chapter 4).

The Arabs and the Turks

It was during the era of third-wave civilizations (500–1500 C.E.) that nomadic peoples made their most significant mark on the larger canvas of world history. Arabs, Berbers, Turks, and Mongols—all of them of nomadic origin—created the largest and most influential empires of that postclassical millennium. The most expansive religious tradition of the era, Islam, derived from a largely nomadic people, the Arabs, and was carried to new regions by another nomadic people, the Turks. In that millennium, most of the great civilizations of outer Eurasia—Byzantium, Persia, India, and China—had come under the control of previously nomadic people, at least for a time. But as pastoral nomads entered and shaped the arena of world history, they too were transformed by the experience.

The first and most dramatic of these nomadic incursions came from Arabs. In the Arabian Peninsula, the development of a reliable camel saddle somewhere between 500 and 100 B.C.E. enabled nomadic Bedouin (desert-dwelling) Arabs to fight effectively from atop their enormous beasts. With this new military advantage, they came to control the rich trade routes in incense running through Arabia. Even more important, these camel nomads served as the shock troops of Islamic expansion, providing many of the new religion's earliest followers and much of the military force that carved out the Arab Empire. Although intellectual and political leadership came from urban merchants and settled farming communities, the Arab Empire was in some respects a nomadic creation that subsequently became the foundation of a new and distinctive civilization.

Even as the pastoral Arabs encroached on the world of Eurasian civilizations from the south, Turkic-speaking nomads were making inroads from the north. Never a single people, various Turkic-speaking clans and tribes migrated from their homeland in Mongolia and southern Siberia generally westward and entered the historical record as creators of a series of nomadic empires between 552 and 965 C.E., most of them lasting little more than a century. Like the Xiongnu Empire, they were fragile alliances of various tribes headed by a supreme ruler known as a *kaghan*, who was supported by a faithful corps of soldiers called "wolves," for the wolf was the mythical ancestor of Turkic peoples. From their base in the steppes, these Turkic states confronted the great civilizations to their south—China, Persia, Byzantium— alternately raiding them, allying with them against common enemies, trading with them, and extorting tribute payments from them. Turkic language and culture spread widely over much of Inner Asia, and elements of that culture entered the agrarian civilizations. In the courts of northern China, for example, yogurt thinned with water, a drink derived from the Turks, replaced for a time the traditional beverage of tea, and at least one Chinese poet wrote joyfully about the delights of snowy evenings in a felt tent.[9]

A major turning point in the history of the Turks occurred with their conversion to Islam between the tenth and fourteenth centuries. This extended process represented a major expansion of the faith and launched the Turks into a new role as the third major carrier of Islam, following the Arabs and the Persians. It also brought the Turks into an increasingly important position within the heartland of an established Islamic civilization as they migrated southward into the Middle East. There they served first as slave soldiers within the Abbasid caliphate, and then, as the caliphate declined, they increasingly took political and military power themselves. In the Seljuk Turkic Empire of the eleventh and twelfth centuries, centered in Persia and present-day Iraq, Turkic rulers began to claim the Muslim title of *sultan* (ruler) rather than the Turkic *kaghan*. Although the Abbasid caliph remained the formal ruler, real power was exercised by Turkic sultans.

Not only did Turkic peoples become Muslims themselves, but they carried Islam to new areas as well. Their invasions of northern India solidly planted Islam in that ancient civilization. In Anatolia, formerly ruled by Christian Byzantium, they brought both Islam and a massive infusion of Turkic culture, language, and people, even as they created the Ottoman Empire, which by 1500 became one of the great powers of Eurasia (see pp. 584–86). In both places, Turkic dynasties governed and would continue to do so well into the modern era. Thus Turkic people, many of them at least, had transformed themselves from pastoral nomads to sedentary farmers, from creators of steppe empires to rulers of agrarian civilizations, and from polytheistic worshippers of their ancestors and various gods to followers and carriers of a monotheistic Islam.

The Masai of East Africa

■ Comparison

Did the history and society of the East African Masai people parallel that of Asian nomads?

In East African history as well, the relationship between nomads and settled farmers worked itself out over many centuries, although solid historical information in this case largely dates to after 1500. Unlike Inner Asia, no large states or chiefdoms developed among either agricultural or pastoral peoples in present-day Kenya and Tanzania. Instead the nomadic cattle-keeping Masai and their settled agricultural neighbors found another way to bind their people together beyond the ties of village and clan. Adolescent boys from a variety of villages or lineages were initiated together in a ritual that often included circumcision, an experience that produced a profound bond among them. This ceremony created an "age-set," which then moved through a series of "age-grades" or ranks, from warrior through elder, during their lives. Such a system provided an alternative to the state as a means of mobilizing young men for military purposes, for integrating outsiders into the community, and for establishing a larger social identity. (See Document 2.2, pp. 71–73).

Sharp distinctions and strong views separated people practicing agricultural and pastoral ways of living. From the viewpoint of the Masai, who composed songs and poems in honor of their cattle, pastoralism was a vastly superior way of life, whereas farming was seen as demeaning and as destroying land that could be much better used for grazing. Farmers were fit only to provide beer, wives, and occasionally food for herding peoples. Conversely, agricultural peoples often saw the Masai as arrogant, aggressive, and lazy, stubbornly unwilling to engage in the hard work of cultivation or even to eat the products of the land.[10] Such views paralleled those that the Chinese and Xiongnu held of one another.

But ways of life were hardly static in East Africa. Earlier in their history, the proudly pastoral Masai had in fact raised sorghum and millet, fully abandoning cultivation only in the eighteenth and nineteenth centuries as they

The Masai of East Africa

Present area of Masai habitation

Lake Turkana

UGANDA   KENYA

GIKUYU

Lake Victoria   • Nairobi

RWANDA   Mt. Kilimanjaro

BURUNDI

TANZANIA   Pemba

Lake Tanganyika   Zanzibar

Dar es Salaam

INDIAN OCEAN

migrated southward from the upper Nile Valley into the more arid regions of central Kenya. Later several Masai groups returned to agriculture after bitter conflicts in the mid-nineteenth century drove them to the periphery of Masai territory. Furthermore, the Masai, while trumpeting the superiority of their culture, were altogether willing to admit others into its charmed circle, much like the Chinese in relation to surrounding barbarians. Outsiders could become Masai, and many did so by obtaining a herd of cattle, by joining a Masai age-set, by learning the language, or by giving a woman in marriage to a Masai man and receiving "bride-wealth" in cattle in return.

The Masai
This contemporary Masai woman from Tanzania is milking goats while carrying a child on her back, in much the same fashion as her ancestors have done for centuries. (The Africa Image Library, photographersdirect .com. Photographer: Ariadne Van Zandbergen)

The Masai were also dependent on those practicing other ways of life. Although they despised hunters as "poor people without cattle," the Masai relied on them for animal skins, bows and arrows, shields, and, most of all, honey, which was required in their ritual ceremonies. They were even more involved with neighboring agricultural peoples. Despite a great deal of mutual raiding and warfare, that relationship also involved substantial economic exchange as women conducted frequent trade to supplement the diet of milk, meat, and blood derived from their cattle. Elaborate peace negotiations after periods of conflict, frequent intermarriage, and occasional military alliances against a common enemy also brought the Masai into close contact with nearby farmers, such as the Gikuyu. And in times of desperation owing to drought or disease, the Masai might find refuge with hunters or farmers with whom they had long-established relationships.[11]

The prestige and the military success of the Masai encouraged those agricultural societies to borrow elements of Masai culture, such as hairstyles, shield decorations, terms referring to cattle, and the name for their high god. Farming societies also adopted elements of Masai military organization, the long Masai spear, and the practice of drinking cow's milk before battle.[12] Peaceful interaction and mutual dependence as well as conflict and hostility characterized the relationship of nomadic herders and settled farmers in East Africa, much as it did in Eurasia.

Breakout: The Mongol Empire

Of all the pastoral peoples who took a turn on the stage of world history, the Mongols made the most stunning entry. Their thirteenth-century breakout from Mongolia gave rise to the largest land-based empire in all of human history, stretching from the Pacific coast of Asia to Eastern Europe (see Map 12.1). This empire joined

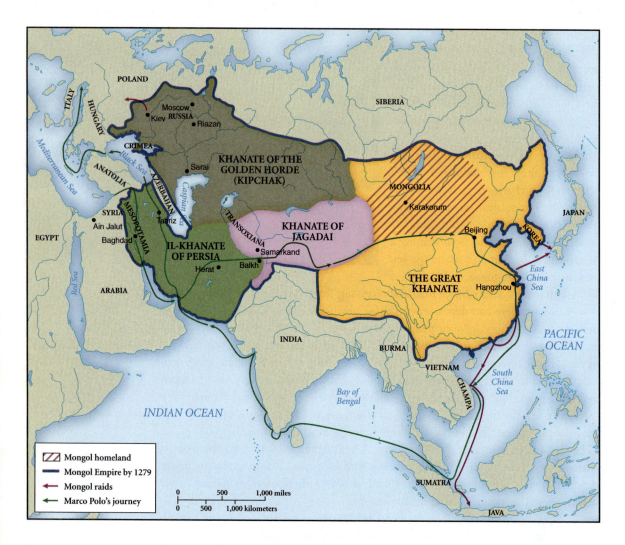

Map 12.1   The Mongol Empire
Encompassing much of Eurasia, the Mongol Empire was divided into four khanates after the death of Chinggis Khan.

the nomadic peoples of the inner Eurasian steppes with the settled agricultural civilizations of outer Eurasia more extensively and more intimately than ever before. It also brought the major civilizations of Eurasia—Europe, China, and the Islamic world—into far more direct contact than in earlier times. Both the enormous destructiveness of the process and the networks of exchange and communication that it spawned were the work of the Mongols, numbering only about 700,000 people. It was another of history's unlikely twists.

For all of its size and fearsome reputation, the Mongol Empire left a surprisingly modest cultural imprint on the world it had briefly governed. Unlike the Arabs, the Mongols bequeathed to the world no new religion or civilization. Whereas the Islamic community offered a common religious home for all converts—conquerors and conquered alike—the Mongols never tried to spread their own faith among subject peoples. At the level of family life, that religion centered on rituals invoking the ancestors, which were performed around the hearth. Rulers sometimes consulted religious specialists, known as *shamans*, who might predict the future, offer sacrifices, and communicate with the spirit world, and particularly with Tengri, the supreme sky god of the Mongols. There was little in this tradition to attract outsiders, and in any event the Mongols proved uninterested in religious imperialism.

The Mongols offered the majority of those they conquered little more than the status of defeated, subordinate, and exploited people, although people with skills were put to work in ways useful to Mongol authorities. Unlike the Turks, whose languages and culture flourish today in many places far from the Turkic homeland, Mongol culture remains confined largely to Mongolia. Furthermore, the Mongol Empire, following in the tradition of Xiongnu and Turkic state building, proved to be "the last, spectacular bloom of pastoral power in Inner Eurasia."[13] Some Mongols themselves became absorbed into the settled societies they conquered. After the decline and disintegration of the Mongol Empire, the tide turned against the pastoralists of inner Eurasia, who were increasingly swallowed up in the expanding Russian or Chinese empires. Nonetheless, while it lasted and for a few centuries thereafter, the Mongol Empire exercised an enormous impact throughout the entire Eurasian world.

Snapshot   Key Moments in Mongol History

Birth of Temujin	1162
Temujin gains title of Chinggis Khan ("universal ruler")	1206
Reign of Chinggis Khan	1206–1227
Beginning of Mongol conquests	1209
Conquest of China	1209–1279
Initial assault on Persia	1219–1221
Conquest of Russia	1237–1240
Attacks in Eastern Europe; then withdrawal	1241–1242
Mongol seizure of Baghdad	1258
Khubilai Khan as ruler of China	1271–1294
Failed Mongol attacks on Japan	1274, 1281
Conversion of Il-khan Ghazan to Islam	1295
High point of plague in Europe	1348–1350
Ming dynasty established; end of Mongol rule in China	1368
End of "Mongol yoke" in Russia; Moscow emerges as center of a Russian state	1480

From Temujin to Chinggis Khan: The Rise of the Mongol Empire

■ **Description**

Identify the major steps in the rise of the Mongol Empire.

World historians are prone to focus attention on large-scale and long-term processes of change in explaining "what happened in history," but in understanding the rise of the Mongol Empire, most scholars have found themselves forced to look closely at the role of a single individual—Temujin (1162–1227), later known as Chinggis Khan (universal ruler). The twelfth-century world into which he was born found the Mongols an unstable and fractious collection of tribes and clans, much reduced from a somewhat earlier and more powerful position in the shifting nomadic alliances in what is now Mongolia. "Everyone was feuding," declared a leading Mongol shaman. "Rather than sleep, they robbed each other of their possessions.... There was no respite, only battle. There was no affection, only mutual slaughter."[14]

The early life of Temujin showed few signs of a prominent future. The boy's father had been a minor chieftain of a noble clan, but he was murdered by tribal rivals before Temujin turned ten, and the family was soon deserted by other members of the clan. As social outcasts, Temujin's small family, headed by his resourceful mother, was forced to live by hunting, fishing, and gathering wild foods. Without livestock, they had fallen to the lowest level of nomadic life. In these desperate circumstances, Temujin's remarkable character came into play. His personal magnetism and courage and his inclination to rely on trusted friends rather than ties of kinship allowed him to build up a small following and to ally with a more powerful tribal leader. This alliance received a boost from Chinese patrons, who were always eager to keep the nomads divided. Military victory over a rival tribe resulted in Temujin's recognition as a chief in his own right with a growing band of followers.

Temujin's rise to power amid the complex tribal politics of Mongolia was a surprise to everyone. It took place among shifting alliances and betrayals, a mounting string of military victories, the indecisiveness of his enemies, a reputation as a leader generous to friends and ruthless to enemies, and the incorporation of warriors from defeated tribes into his own forces. In 1206, a Mongol tribal assembly recognized Temujin as Chinggis Khan, supreme leader of a now unified Great Mongol Nation (see Document 12.1, pp. 550–52). It was a remarkable achievement, but one little noticed beyond the highland steppes of Mongolia. That would soon change.

The unification of the Mongol tribes raised an obvious question: What was Chinggis Khan to do with the powerful army he had assembled? Without a common task, the new and fragile unity of the Mongols would surely dissolve into quarrels and chaos; and without external resources to reward his followers, Chinggis Khan would be hard-pressed to maintain his supreme position. Both considerations pointed in a single direction—expansion, particularly toward China, long a source of great wealth for nomadic peoples.[15]

In 1209, the first major attack on the settled agricultural societies south of Mongolia set in motion half a century of a Mongol world war, a series of military campaigns, massive killing, and empire building without precedent in world history. In the process, Chinggis Khan, followed by his sons and grandsons (Ogodei, Mongke, and Khubilai), constructed an empire that contained China, Korea, Central Asia, Russia, much of the Islamic Middle East, and parts of Eastern Europe (see Map 12.1). "In a flash," wrote a recent scholar, "the Mongol warriors would defeat every army, capture every fort, and bring down the walls of every city they encountered. Christians, Muslims, Buddhists, and Hindus would soon kneel before the dusty boots of illiterate young Mongol horsemen."[16]

Various setbacks—the Mongols' withdrawal from Eastern Europe (1242), their defeat at Ain Jalut in Palestine at the hands of Egyptian forces (1260), the failure of their invasion of Japan owing to two typhoons (1274, 1281), and the difficulty of penetrating the tropical jungles of Southeast Asia—marked the outer limits of the Mongol Empire. But what an empire it was! How could a Mongol confederation, with a total population of less than 1 million people and few resources beyond their livestock, assemble an imperial structure of such staggering transcontinental dimensions?

Explaining the Mongol Moment

Like the Roman Empire but far more rapidly, the Mongol Empire grew of its own momentum without any grand scheme or blueprint for world conquest. Each fresh victory brought new resources for making war and new threats or insecurities that seemed to require further expansion. As the empire took shape and certainly by the end of his life, Chinggis Khan had come to see his career in terms of a universal mission. "I have accomplished a great work," he declared, "uniting the whole world in one empire."[17] Thus the Mongol Empire acquired an ideology in the course of its construction.

What made this "great work" possible? The odds seemed overwhelming, for China alone, after all, outnumbered the Mongols 100 to 1 and possessed incomparably greater resources. Nor did the Mongols enjoy any technological superiority over their many adversaries. They did, however, enjoy the luck of good timing, for China was divided, having already lost control of its northern territory to the nomadic Jurchen people, while the decrepit Abbasid caliphate, once the center of the Islamic world, had shrunk to a fraction of its earlier size. But clearly, the key to the Mongols' success lay in their army. According to one scholar, "Mongol armies were simply better led, organized, and disciplined than those of their opponents."[18] In an effort to diminish a divisive tribalism, Chinggis Khan reorganized the entire social structure of the Mongols into military units of 10, 100, 1,000, and 10,000 warriors, an arrangement that allowed for effective command and control. Conquered tribes especially were broken up and their members scattered among these new units, which enrolled virtually all nomadic men and supplied the cavalry forces of Mongol armies. A highly prestigious imperial guard, also recruited across tribal lines, marked the further decline of the old tribalism as a social revolution, imposed from above by Chinggis Khan, reshaped Mongol society.

An impressive discipline and loyalty to their leaders characterized Mongol military forces, and discpline was reinforced by the provision that should any members of a unit desert in battle, all were subject to the death penalty. More positively, loyalty

■ **Explanation**
What accounts for the political and military success of the Mongols?

was cemented by the leaders' willingness to share the hardships of their men. "I eat the same food and am dressed in the same rags as my humble herdsmen," wrote Chinggis Khan. "I am always in the forefront, and in battle I am never at the rear."[19] (See Document 12.2, pp. 553–54.) Such discipline and loyalty made possible the elaborate tactics of encirclement, retreat, and deception that proved decisive in many a battle. Furthermore, the enormous flow of wealth from conquered civilizations benefited all Mongols, though not equally. Even ordinary Mongols could now dress in linens and silks rather than hides and felt, could own slaves derived from the many prisoners of war, and had far greater opportunities to improve their social position in a constantly expanding empire.

To compensate for their own small population, the Mongols incorporated huge numbers of conquered peoples into their military forces. "People who lived in felt tents"—mostly Mongol and Turkic nomads—were conscripted en masse into the cavalry units of the Mongol army, while settled agricultural peoples supplied the infantry and artillery forces. As the Mongols penetrated major civilizations, with their walled cities and elaborate fortifications, they quickly acquired Chinese techniques and technology of siege warfare. Some 1,000 Chinese artillery crews, for example, took part in the Mongol invasion of distant Persia. Beyond military recruitment, Mongols demanded that their conquered people serve as laborers, building roads and bridges and ferrying supplies over long distances. Artisans, craftsmen, and skilled people generally were carefully identified, spared from massacre, and often sent to distant regions of the empire where their services were required.

A Mongol Warrior
Horseback-riding skills, honed in herding animals and adapted to military purposes, were central to Mongol conquests, as illustrated in this Ming-dynasty Chinese painting of a mounted Mongol archer. (Victoria and Albert Museum, London/V&A Images)

A French goldsmith, captured by Mongol forces in Hungary, wound up as a slave in the Mongol capital of Karakorum, where he constructed an elaborate silver fountain that dispensed wine and other intoxicating drinks.

A further element in the military effectiveness of Mongol forces lay in a growing reputation for a ruthless brutality and utter destructiveness. Chinggis Khan's policy was clear: "whoever submits shall be spared, but those who resist, they shall be destroyed with their wives, children and dependents . . . so that the others who hear and see should fear and not act the same."[20] The Central Asian kingdom of Khwarizm, whose ruler had greatly offended Chinggis Khan by murdering and mutilating Mongol envoys and merchants, was among the first, but by no means the last, to feel the full effects of Mongol terror. City after city was utterly destroyed, and enemy soldiers were passed out in lots to Mongol troops for execution, while women and skilled craftsmen were enslaved. Unskilled civilians served as human shields for attacks on the next city or were used as human fill in the moats surrounding those cities.

One scholar explained such policies in this way: "Extremely conscious of their small numbers and fearful of rebellion, Chinggis often chose to annihilate a region's entire population, if it appeared too troublesome to govern."[21] These policies also served as a form of psychological warfare, a practical inducement to surrender for those who knew of the Mongol terror. Historians continue to debate the extent and uniqueness of the Mongols' brutality, but their reputation for unwavering harshness proved a military asset.

Underlying the purely military dimensions of the Mongols' success was an impressive ability to mobilize both the human and material resources of their growing empire. Elaborate census taking allowed Mongol leaders to know what was available to them and made possible the systematic taxation of conquered people. An effective system of relay stations, about a day's ride apart, provided rapid communication across the empire and fostered trade as well. Marco Polo, the Venetian trader who traveled through Mongol domains in the thirteenth century, claimed that the Mongols maintained some 10,000 such stations, together with 200,000 horses available to authorized users. The beginnings of a centralized bureaucracy with various specialized offices took shape in the new capital of Karakorum. There scribes translated official decrees into the various languages of the empire, such as Persian, Uighur, Chinese, and Tibetan.

Other policies appealed to various groups among the conquered peoples of the empire. Interested in fostering commerce, Mongol rulers often offered merchants 10 percent or more above their asking price and allowed them the free use of the relay stations for transporting their goods. In administering the conquered regions, Mongols held the highest decision-making posts, but Chinese and Muslim officials held many advisory and lower-level positions in China and Persia respectively. In religious matters, the Mongols welcomed and supported many religious traditions—Buddhist, Christian, Muslim, Daoist—as long as they did not become the focus of political opposition. This policy of religious toleration allowed Muslims to seek converts among Mongol troops and afforded Christians much greater freedom than they had enjoyed under Muslim rule.[22] Toward the end of his life and apparently feeling his approaching death, Chinggis Khan himself summoned a famous Daoist master from China and begged him to "communicate to me the means of preserving life." One of his successors, Mongke, arranged a debate among representatives of several religious faiths, after which he concluded: "Just as God gave different fingers to the hand, so has He given different ways to men."[23] Such economic, administrative, and religious policies provided some benefits and a place within the empire—albeit subordinate—for many of its conquered peoples.

Encountering the Mongols: Comparing Three Cases

The Mongol moment in world history represented an enormous cultural encounter between nomadic pastoralists and the settled civilizations of Eurasia. Differences among those civilizations—Confucian China, Muslim Persia, Christian Russia—ensured considerable diversity as this encounter unfolded across a vast realm. The process of conquest, the length and nature of Mongol rule, the impact on local people, and the extent of Mongol assimilation into the cultures of the conquered—all this and more varied considerably across the Eurasian domains of the empire. The experiences of China, Persia, and Russia provide brief glimpses into several expressions of this massive clash of cultures.

China and the Mongols

■ **Change**

How did Mongol rule change China? In what ways were the Mongols changed by China?

Long the primary target for nomadic steppe-dwellers in search of agrarian wealth, China proved the most difficult and extended of the Mongols' many conquests, lasting some seventy years, from 1209 to 1279. The invasion began in northern China, which had been ruled for several centuries by various dynasties of nomadic origin, and was characterized by destruction and plunder on a massive scale. Southern China, under the control of the native Song dynasty, was a different story, for there the Mongols were far less violent and more concerned to accommodate the local population. Landowners, for example, were guaranteed their estates in exchange for their support or at least their neutrality. By whatever methods, the outcome was the unification of a divided China, a treasured ideal among educated Chinese. This achievement persuaded many of them that the Mongols had indeed been granted the Mandate of Heaven and, despite their foreign origins, were legitimate rulers. (See Document 12.4, pp. 555–57, for a positive Chinese view of their Mongol rulers.)

Having acquired China, what were the Mongols to do with it? One possibility, apparently considered by the Great Khan Ogodei in the 1230s, was to exterminate everyone in northern China and turn the country into pastureland for Mongol herds. That suggestion, fortunately, was rejected in favor of extracting as much wealth as possible from the country's advanced civilization. Doing so meant some accommodation to Chinese culture and ways of governing, for the Mongols had no experience with the operation of a complex agrarian society.

That accommodation took many forms. The Mongols made use of Chinese administrative practices, techniques of taxation, and their postal system. They gave themselves a Chinese dynastic title, the Yuan, suggesting a new beginning in Chinese history. They transferred their capital from Karakorum in Mongolia to what is now Beijing, building a wholly new capital city there known as Khanbalik, the "city of the khan." Thus the Mongols were now rooting themselves solidly on the soil of a highly sophisticated civilization, well removed from their homeland on the steppes.

Khubilai Khan, the grandson of Chinggis Khan and China's Mongol ruler from 1271 to 1294, ordered a set of Chinese-style ancestral tablets to honor his ancestors and posthumously awarded them Chinese names. Many of his policies evoked the values of a benevolent Chinese emperor as he improved roads, built canals, lowered some taxes, patronized scholars and artists, limited the death penalty and torture, supported peasant agriculture, and prohibited Mongols from grazing their animals on peasants' farmland. Mongol khans also made use of traditional Confucian rituals, supported the building of some Daoist temples, and were particularly attracted to a Tibetan form of Buddhism, which returned the favor with strong political support for the invaders.

Despite these accommodations, Mongol rule was still harsh, exploitative, foreign, and resented. The Mongols did not become Chinese, nor did they accommodate every aspect of Chinese culture. Deep inside the new capital, the royal family and court could continue to experience something of steppe life. There, animals roamed freely in large open areas, planted with steppe grass. Many of the Mongol elite much preferred to live, eat, sleep, and give birth in the traditional tents that sprouted everywhere. In administering the country, the Mongols largely ignored the traditional Chinese examination system and relied heavily on foreigners, particularly Muslims from Central Asia and the Middle East, to serve as officials, while keeping the top decision-making posts for themselves. Few Mongols learned Chinese, and Mongol

Marco Polo and Khubilai Khan

In ruling China, the Mongols employed in high positions a number of Muslims and a few Europeans, such as Marco Polo, shown here kneeling before Khubilai Khan in a painting from the fifteenth century. (Ms 2810 f.5. Nicolo and Marco Polo before the Great Khan [vellum], Boucicaut Master, [fl. 1390–1430, and workshop]/Bibliothèque nationale de France, Paris, France/The Bridgeman Art Library) law discriminated against the Chinese, reserving for them the most severe punishments. In social life, the Mongols forbade intermarriage and prohibited Chinese scholars from learning the Mongol script. Mongol women never adopted foot binding and scandalized the Chinese by mixing freely with men at official gatherings and riding to the hunt with their husbands. Furthermore, the Mongols honored and supported merchants and artisans far more than Confucian bureaucrats had been inclined to do.

However one assesses Mongol rule in China, it was brief, lasting little more than a century. By the mid-fourteenth century, intense factionalism among the Mongols, rapidly rising prices, furious epidemics of the plague, and growing peasant rebellions combined to force the Mongols out of China. By 1368, rebel forces had triumphed, and thousands of Mongols returned to their homeland in the steppes. For several centuries, they remained a periodic threat to China, but during the Ming dynasty that followed, the memory of their often brutal and alien rule stimulated a renewed commitment to Confucian values and practices and an effort to wipe out all traces of the Mongols' impact.

Persia and the Mongols

■ Comparison
How was Mongol rule in
Persia different from that
in China?

A second great civilization conquered by the Mongols was that of an Islamic Persia. There the Mongol takeover was far more abrupt than the extended process of conquest in China. A first invasion (1219–1221), led by Chinggis Khan himself, was followed thirty years later by a second assault (1251–1258) under his grandson Hulegu, who became the first il-khan (subordinate khan) of Persia. More destructive than the conquest of Song dynasty China, the Mongol offensive against Persia and Iraq had no precedent in their history, although Persia had been repeatedly attacked, from the invasion of Alexander the Great to that of the Arabs. The most recent incursion had featured Turkic peoples, but they had been Muslims, recently converted, small in number, and seeking only acceptance within the Islamic world. The Mongols, however, were infidels in Muslim eyes, and their stunning victory was a profound shock to people accustomed to viewing history as the progressive expansion of Islamic rule. Furthermore, Mongol military victory brought in its wake a degree of ferocity and slaughter that simply had no parallel in Persian experience. The Persian historian Juwayni described it in fearful terms:

> Every town and every village has been several times subjected to pillage and massacre and has suffered this confusion for years so that even though there be generation and increase until the Resurrection the population will not attain to a tenth part of what it was before.[24]

The sacking of Baghdad in 1258, which put an end to the Abbasid caliphate, was accompanied by the massacre of more than 200,000 people, according to Hulegu himself.

Beyond this human catastrophe lay the damage to Persian and Iraqi agriculture and to those who tilled the soil. Heavy taxes, sometimes collected twenty or thirty times a year and often under torture or whipping, pushed large numbers of peasants off their land. Furthermore, the in-migration of nomadic Mongols, together with their immense herds of sheep and goats, turned much agricultural land into pasture and sometimes into desert. In both cases, a fragile system of underground water channels that provided irrigation to the fields was neglected, and much good agricultural land was reduced to waste. Some sectors of the Persian economy gained, however. Wine production increased because the Mongols were fond of alcohol, and the Persian silk industry benefited from close contact with a Mongol-ruled China. In general, though, even more so than in China, Mongol rule in Persia represented "disaster on a grand and unparalleled scale."[25]

Nonetheless, the Mongols in Persia were themselves transformed far more than their counterparts in China. They made extensive use of the sophisticated Persian bureaucracy, leaving the greater part of government operations in Persian hands. During the reign of Ghazan (1295–1304), they made some efforts to repair the damage caused by earlier policies of ruthless exploitation, by rebuilding damaged cities and repairing neglected irrigation works. Most important, the Mongols who conquered Persia became Muslims, following the lead of Ghazan, who converted to Islam in 1295. No such widespread conversion to the culture of the conquered occurred in China or in Christian Russia. Members of the court and Mongol elites learned at least some Persian, unlike most of their counterparts in China. A number of Mongols also turned to farming, abandoning their nomadic ways, while some married local people. When the Mongol dynasty of Hulegu's descendants collapsed in the 1330s for lack of a suitable heir, the Mongols were not driven out of Persia as they had been from China. Rather they and their Turkic allies simply disappeared, assimilated into Persian society. From a Persian point of view, the barbarians had been civilized.

Russia and the Mongols

When the Mongol military machine rolled over Russia between 1237 and 1240, it encountered a relatively new third-wave civilization, located on the far eastern fringe of Christendom (see Chapter 10). Whatever political unity this new civilization of Kievan Rus had earlier enjoyed was now gone, and various independent princes proved unable to unite even in the face of the Mongol onslaught. Although they had interacted extensively with nomadic people of the steppes north of the Black Sea, nothing had prepared them for the Mongols.

The devastation wrought by the Mongol assault matched or exceeded anything experienced by the Persians or the Chinese. City after city fell to Mongol forces, which were now armed with the catapults and battering rams adopted from Chinese or Muslim sources. The slaughter that sometimes followed was described in horrific terms by Russian chroniclers, although twentieth-century historians often regard such

■ **Comparison**
What was distinctive about the Russian experience of Mongol rule?

Mongol Russia
This sixteenth-century painting depicts the Mongol burning of the Russian city of Ryazan in 1237. Similar destruction awaited many Russian towns that resisted the invaders. (Sovfoto/Eastfoto)

accounts as exaggerated. (See Document 12.3, pp. 554–55, for one such account.) From the survivors and the cities that surrendered early, laborers and skilled craftsmen were deported to other Mongol lands or sold into slavery. A number of Russian crafts were so depleted of their workers that they did not recover for a century or more.

If the ferocity of initial conquest bore similarities to the experiences of Persia, Russia's incorporation into the Mongol Empire was very different. To the Mongols, it was the Kipchak Khanate, named after the Kipchak Turkic-speaking peoples north of the Caspian and Black seas, among whom the Mongols had settled. To the Russians, it was the "Khanate of the Golden Horde." By whatever name, the Mongols had conquered Russia, but they did not occupy it as they had China and Persia. Because there were no garrisoned cities, permanently stationed administrators, or Mongol settlement, the Russian experience of Mongol rule was quite different than elsewhere. From the Mongol point of view, Russia had little to offer. Its economy was not nearly as developed as that of more established civilizations; nor was it located on major international trade routes. It was simply not worth the expense of occupying. Furthermore, the availability of extensive steppe lands for pasturing their flocks north of the Black and Caspian seas meant that the Mongols could maintain their preferred nomadic way of life, while remaining in easy reach of Russian cities when the need arose to send further military expeditions. They could dominate and exploit Russia from the steppes.

And exploit they certainly did. Russian princes received appointment from the khan and were required to send substantial tribute to the Mongol capital at Sarai, located on the lower Volga River. A variety of additional taxes created a heavy burden, especially on the peasantry, while continuing border raids sent tens of thousands of Russians into slavery. The Mongol impact was highly uneven, however. Some Russian princes benefited considerably because they were able to manipulate their role as tribute collectors to grow wealthy. The Russian Orthodox Church likewise flourished under the Mongol policy of religious toleration, for it received exemption from many taxes. Nobles who participated in Mongol raids earned a share of the loot. Some cities, such as Kiev, resisted the Mongols and were devastated, while others collaborated and were left undamaged. Moscow in particular emerged as the primary collector of tribute for the Mongols, and its princes parlayed this position into a leading role as the nucleus of a renewed Russian state when Mongol domination receded in the fifteenth century.

The absence of direct Mongol rule had implications for the Mongols themselves, for they were far less influenced by or assimilated within Russian cultures than their counterparts in China and Persia had been. The Mongols in China had turned themselves into a Chinese dynasty, with the khan as a Chinese emperor. Some learned calligraphy, and a few came to appreciate Chinese poetry. In Persia, the Mongols had converted to Islam, with some becoming farmers. Not so in Russia. There "the Mongols of the Golden Horde were still spending their days in the saddle and their nights in tents."[26] They could dominate Russia from the adjacent steppes without in any way adopting Russian culture. Even though they remained culturally separate from Russia, eventually the Mongols assimilated to the culture and the Islamic faith of the Kipchak people of the steppes, and in the process they lost their distinct identity and became Kipchaks.

Despite this domination from a distance, "the impact of the Mongols on Russia was, if anything, greater than on China and Iran [Persia]," according to a leading scholar.[27] Russian princes, who were more or less left alone if they paid the required tribute and taxes, found it useful to adopt the Mongols' weapons, diplomatic rituals, court practices, taxation system, and military draft. Mongol policies facilitated, although not intentionally, the rise of Moscow as the core of a new Russian state, and that state made good use of the famous Mongol mounted courier service, which Marco Polo had praised so highly. Mongol policies also strengthened the hold of the Russian Orthodox Church and enabled it to penetrate the rural areas more fully than before. Some Russians, seeking to explain their country's economic backwardness and political autocracy in modern times, have held the Mongols responsible for both conditions, though most historians consider such views vastly exaggerated.

Divisions among the Mongols and the growing strength of the Russian state, centered now on the city of Moscow, enabled the Russians to break the Mongols' hold by the end of the fifteenth century. With the earlier demise of Mongol rule in China and Persia, and now in Russia, the Mongols had retreated from their brief but spectacular incursion into the civilizations of outer Eurasia. Nonetheless, they continued to periodically threaten these civilizations for several centuries, until their homelands were absorbed into the expanding Russian and Chinese empires. But the Mongol moment in world history was over.

The Mongol Empire as a Eurasian Network

During the postclassical millennium, Chinese culture and Buddhism provided a measure of integration among the peoples of East Asia; Christianity did the same for Europe, while the realm of Islam connected most of the lands in between. But it was the Mongol Empire, during the thirteenth and fourteenth centuries, that brought all of these regions into a single interacting network. It was a unique moment in world history and an important step toward the global integration of the modern era.

Toward a World Economy

■ **Connection**

In what ways did the Mongol Empire contribute to the globalization of the Eurasian world?

The Mongols themselves produced little of value for distant markets, nor were they active traders. Nonetheless, they consistently promoted international commerce, largely so that they could tax it and thus extract wealth from more developed civilizations. The Great Khan Ogodei, for example, often paid well over the asking price in order to attract merchants to his capital of Karakorum. The Mongols also provided financial backing for caravans, introduced standardized weights and measures, and gave tax breaks to merchants.

In providing a relatively secure environment for merchants making the long and arduous journey across Central Asia between Europe and China, the Mongol Empire brought the two ends of the Eurasian world into closer contact than ever before and launched a new phase in the history of the Silk Roads. Marco Polo was only the most famous of many European merchants, mostly from Italian cities, who made their way to China through the Mongol Empire. So many traders attempted the journey that guidebooks were published with much useful advice about the trip. Merchants returned with tales of rich lands and prosperous commercial opportunities, but what they described were long-established trading networks of which Europeans had been largely ignorant.

The Mongol trading circuit was a central element in an even larger commercial network that linked much of the Afro-Eurasian world in the thirteenth century (see Map 12.2). Mongol-ruled China was the fulcrum of this vast system, connecting the overland route through the Mongol Empire with the oceanic routes through the South China Sea and Indian Ocean. Here, some historians have argued, lay the beginnings of those international economic relationships that have played such a major role in the making of the modern world.

Diplomacy on a Eurasian Scale

Not only did the Mongol Empire facilitate long-distance commerce, but it also prompted diplomatic relationships from one end of Eurasia to the other. As their invasion of Russia spilled over into Eastern Europe, Mongol armies destroyed Polish, German, and Hungarian forces in 1241–1242 and seemed poised to march on Central and Western Europe. But the death of the Great Khan Ogodei required Mongol leaders to return to Mongolia, and Western Europe lacked adequate pasture for Mongol herds. Thus Western Europe was spared the trauma of conquest, but fearing the possible return of the Mongols, both the pope and European rulers dispatched delegations to the Mongol capital, mostly led by Franciscan friars. They hoped to

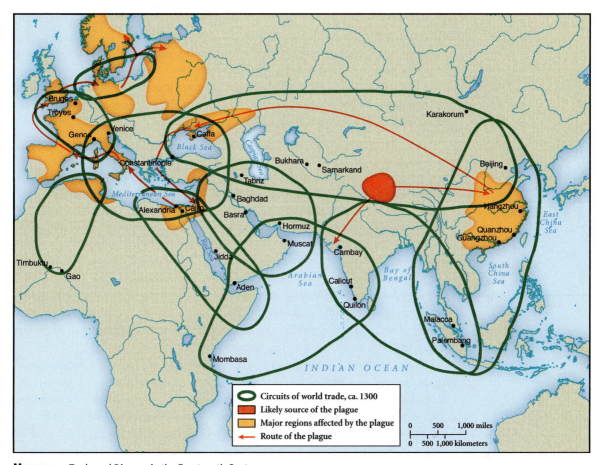

Map 12.2   Trade and Disease in the Fourteenth Century
The Mongol Empire played a major role in the commercial integration of the Eurasian world as well as in the spread of the plague across this vast area.

learn something about Mongol intentions, to secure Mongol aid in the Christian crusade against Islam, and, if possible, to convert Mongols to Christianity.

These efforts were largely in vain, for no alliance or widespread conversion occurred. In fact, one of these missions came back with a letter for the pope from the Great Khan Guyuk, demanding that Europeans submit to him. "But if you should not believe our letters and the command of God nor hearken to our counsel," he warned, "then we shall know for certain that you wish to have war. After that we do not know what will happen."[28] Perhaps the most important outcome of these diplomatic probings was the useful information about lands to the east that European missions brought back. Those reports contributed to a dawning European awareness of a wider world, and they have certainly provided later historians with much useful information about the Mongols (see Document 12.5, pp. 557–59). Somewhat later, in 1287, the il-khanate of Persia sought an alliance with European powers to take Jerusalem and crush the forces of Islam, but the Persian Mongols' conversion to Islam soon put an end to any such anti-Muslim coalition.

Within the Mongol Empire itself, close relationships developed between the courts of Persia and China. They regularly exchanged ambassadors, shared intelligence information, fostered trade between their regions, and sent skilled workers back and forth. Thus political authorities all across Eurasia engaged in diplomatic relationships with one another to an unprecedented degree.

Cultural Exchange in the Mongol Realm

Accompanying these transcontinental economic and diplomatic relationships was a substantial exchange of peoples and cultures. Mongol policy forcibly transferred many thousands of skilled craftsmen and educated people from their homelands to distant parts of the empire, while the Mongols' religious tolerance and support of merchants drew missionaries and traders from afar. The Mongol capital at Karakorum was a cosmopolitan city with places of worship for Buddhists, Daoists, Muslims, and Christians. Actors and musicians from China, wrestlers from Persia, and a jester from Byzantium provided entertainment for the Mongol court. Persian and Arab doctors and administrators were sent to China, while Chinese physicians and engineers found their skills in demand in the Islamic world.

This movement of people facilitated the exchange of ideas and techniques, a process actively encouraged by Mongol authorities. A great deal of Chinese technology and artistic conventions — such as painting, printing, gunpowder weapons, compass navigation, high-temperature furnaces, and medical techniques — flowed westward. Acupuncture, for example, was poorly received in the Middle East because it required too much bodily contact for Muslim taste, but Chinese techniques for diagnosing illness by taking the pulse of patients proved quite popular, as they involved minimal body contact. Muslim astronomers brought their skills and knowledge to China because Mongol authorities wanted "second opinions on the reading of heavenly signs and portents" and assistance in constructing accurate calendars, so necessary for ritual purposes.[29] Plants and crops likewise circulated within the Mongol domain. Lemons and carrots from the Middle East found a welcome reception in China, while the Persian Il-Khan Ghazan sent envoys to India, China, and elsewhere to seek "seeds of things which are unique in that land."[30]

Europeans arguably gained more than most from these exchanges, for they had long been cut off from the fruitful interchange with Asia, and in comparison to the Islamic and Chinese worlds, they were less technologically developed. Now they could reap the benefits of much new technology, new crops, and new knowledge of a wider world. And almost alone among the peoples of Eurasia, they could do so without having suffered the devastating consequences of Mongol conquest. In these circumstances, some historians have argued, lay the roots of Europe's remarkable rise to global prominence in the centuries that followed.

The Plague: A Eurasian Pandemic

Any benefits derived from participation in Mongol networks of communication and exchange must be measured alongside the Eurasian catastrophe known as the "plague" or the "pestilence" and later called the Black Death. Originating most likely in Central Asia, the bacteria responsible for the disease spread across the trade routes of the vast Mongol Empire in the early fourteenth century (see Map 12.2). Carried by rodents and transmitted by fleas to humans, the plague erupted initially in 1331 in northeastern China and had reached the Middle East and Western Europe by 1347. One lurid but quite uncertain story has the Mongols using catapults to hurl corpses infected with the plague into the Genoese city of Caffa in the Crimea.

■ Change
Disease changes societies. How might this argument apply to the plague?

The disease itself was associated with swelling of the lymph nodes, most often in the groin; terrible headaches; high fever; and internal bleeding just below the skin. Infected people generally died within a few days. In the densely populated civilizations of China, the Islamic world, and Europe as well as in the steppe lands of the nomads, the plague claimed enormous numbers of human victims, causing a sharp contraction in Eurasian population for a century or more. Chroniclers reported rates of death that ranged from 50 to 90 percent of the affected population, depending on the time and place. A recent study suggests that about half of Europe's people perished during the initial outbreak of 1348–1350.[31] A fifteenth-century Egyptian historian wrote that within a month of the plague's arrival in 1349, "Cairo had become an abandoned desert.... Everywhere one heard lamentations and one could not pass by any house without being overwhelmed by the howling."[32] The Middle East generally had lost perhaps one-third of its population by the early fifteenth century.[33] The intense first wave of the plague was followed by periodic visitations over the next several centuries, although India and sub-Saharan Africa were much less affected than other regions of the eastern hemisphere.

The Plague

This illustration depicts a European doctor visiting a patient with the plague. Notice that the doctor and others around the bedside cover their noses to prevent infection. During the Black Death, doctors were often criticized for refusing to treat dying patients, as they feared for their own lives. (The Granger Collection, New York)

But in those places where it struck, the plague left thoughtful people grasping for language with which to describe a horror of such unprecedented dimensions. One Italian man, who had buried all five of his children with his own hands, wrote in 1348 that "so many have died that everyone believes it is the end of the world."[34] Another Italian, the Renaissance scholar Francesco Petrarch, was equally stunned by the impact of the Black Death; he wrote to a friend in 1349:

> When at any time has such a thing been seen or spoken of? Has what happened in these years ever been read about: empty houses, derelict cities, ruined estates, fields strewn with cadavers, a horrible and vast solitude encompassing the whole world? Consult historians, they are silent; ask physicians, they are stupefied; seek the answers from philosophers, they shrug their shoulders, furrow their brows, and with fingers pressed against their lips, bid you be silent. Will posterity believe these things, when we who have seen it can scarcely believe it…?[35]

In the Islamic world, the famous historian Ibn Khaldun, who had lost both of his parents to the plague, also wrote about it in apocalyptic terms:

> Civilization in both the East and the West was visited by a destructive plague which devastated nations and caused populations to vanish. It swallowed up many of the good things of civilization and wiped them out.… It was as if the voice of existence had called out for oblivion and restriction, and the world responded to its call.[36]

(See Visual Sources: The Black Death and Religion in Western Europe, pp. 560–67, for more on religious response to the plague in Europe.)

Beyond its immediate devastation, the Black Death worked longer-term changes in European society, the region where the plague's impact has been most thoroughly studied. Labor shortages following the initial outburst provoked sharp conflict between scarce workers, who sought higher wages or better conditions, and the rich, who resisted those demands. A series of peasant revolts in the fourteenth century reflected this tension, which also undermined the practice of serfdom. That labor shortage also may have fostered a greater interest in technological innovation and created, at least for a time, more employment opportunities for women. Thus a resilient European civilization survived a cataclysm that had the power to destroy it. In a strange way, that catastrophe may have actually fostered its future growth.

Whatever its impact in particular places, the plague also had larger consequences. Ironically, that human disaster, born of the Mongol network, was a primary reason for the demise of that network in the fourteenth and fifteenth centuries. Population contracted, cities declined, and the volume of trade diminished all across the Mongol world. By 1350, the Mongol Empire itself was in disarray, and within a century the Mongols had lost control of Chinese, Persian, and Russian civilizations. The Central Asian trade route, so critical to the entire Afro-Eurasian world economy, largely closed.

This disruption of the Mongol-based land routes to the east, coupled with a desire to avoid Muslim intermediaries, provided incentives for Europeans to take to the sea in their continuing efforts to reach the riches of Asia. Their naval technology gave them military advantages on the seas, much as the Mongols' skill with the bow and their mobility on horseback gave these nomads a decisive edge in land battles.

As Europeans penetrated Asian waters in the sixteenth century, they took on, in some ways, the role of the Mongols in organizing and fostering world trade and in creating a network of communication and exchange over an even larger area. Like the Mongols, Europeans were people on the periphery of the major established civilizations: they too were economically less developed in comparison to Chinese and Islamic civilizations, and both were prone to forcibly plundering the wealthier civilizations they encountered.[37] Europeans, of course, brought far more of their own culture and many more of their own people to the societies they conquered, as Christianity, European languages, settler societies, and western science and technology took root within their empires. Although their imperial presence lasted far longer and operated on a much larger scale, European actions at the beginning of their global expansion bore some resemblance to those of their Mongol predecessors. They were, as one historian put it, "the Mongols of the seas."[38]

Reflections: Changing Images of Nomadic Peoples

Until recently, nomads generally received bad press in history books. Normally they entered the story only when they were threatening or destroying established civilizations. In presenting a largely negative image of pastoral peoples, historians were reflecting the long-held attitudes of literate elites in the civilizations of Eurasia. Fearing and usually despising nomadic peoples, educated observers in China, the Middle East, and Europe often described them as bloodthirsty savages or barbarians, bringing only chaos and destruction in their wake. Han Kuan, a Chinese scholar of the first century B.C.E., described the Xiongnu people as "abandoned by Heaven . . . in foodless desert wastes, without proper houses, clothed in animal hides, eating their meat uncooked and drinking blood."[39] To the Christian Saint Jerome (340–420 C.E.), the nomadic Huns "filled the whole earth with slaughter and panic alike as they flitted hither and thither on their swift horses."[40] Almost a thousand years later, the famous Arab historian Ibn Khaldun described nomads in a very similar fashion: "It is their nature to plunder whatever other people possess."[41]

Because nomadic peoples generally did not have written languages, the sources available to historians came from less-than-unbiased observers in adjacent agricultural civilizations. Furthermore, in the long-running conflict across the farming/pastoral frontier, agricultural civilizations ultimately triumphed. Over the centuries, some nomadic or barbarian peoples, such as the Germanic tribes of Europe and the Arabs, created new civilizations. Others, such as the Turkic and Mongol peoples, took over existing civilizations or were encompassed within established agrarian empires. By the early twentieth century, and in most places much earlier, nomadic peoples everywhere had lost their former independence and had often shed their nomadic life as well. Since "winners" usually write history, the negative views of nomads held by agrarian civilizations normally prevailed.

Reflecting more inclusive contemporary values, historians in recent decades have sought to present a more balanced picture of nomads' role in world history, emphasizing what they created as well as what they destroyed. These historians have highlighted the achievements of nomadic peoples, such as their adaptation to inhospitable environments; their technological innovations; their development of horse-, camel-, or cattle-based cultures; their role in fostering cross-cultural exchange; and their state-building efforts.

A less critical or judgmental posture toward the Mongols may also owe something to the "total wars" and genocides of the twentieth century, in which the mass slaughter of civilians became a strategy to induce enemy surrender. During the cold war, the United States and the Soviet Union were prepared, apparently, to obliterate each other's entire population with nuclear weapons in response to an attack. In light of this recent history, Mongol massacres may appear a little less unique. Historians living in the glass houses of contemporary societies are perhaps more reluctant to cast stones at the Mongols. In understanding the Mongols, as in so much else, historians are shaped by the times and circumstances of their own lives as much as by "what really happened" in the past.

Second Thoughts

What's the Significance?

To assess your mastery of the material in this chapter, visit the **Student Center** at bedfordstmartins.com/strayer.

pastoralism
Xiongnu
Modun
Turks
Masai

Temujin/Chinggis Khan
the Mongol world war
Yuan dynasty China
Khubilai Khan
Hulegu

Kipchak Khanate/Golden Horde
Black Death/plague

Big Picture Questions

1. Prior to the rise of the Mongols, in what ways had pastoral peoples been significant in world history?
2. What accounts for the often negative attitudes of settled societies toward the pastoral peoples living on their borders? Why have historians often neglected pastoral peoples' role in world history?
3. In what ways did the Mongol Empire resemble other empires, and in what ways did it differ from them? Why did it last a relatively short time?
4. In what different ways did Mongol rule affect the Islamic world, Russia, China, and Europe?
5. How would you define both the immediate and the long-term significance of the Mongols in world history?
6. How would you assess the perspective of this chapter toward the Mongols? Does it strike you as negative and critical of the Mongols, as bending over backward to portray them in a positive light, or as a balanced presentation?

Next Steps: For Further Study

John Aberth, *The First Horseman: Disease in Human History* (2007). A global study of the history of disease, with a fine chapter on the Black Death.

Thomas Allsen, *Culture and Conquest in Mongol Eurasia* (2001). A history of cultural exchange within the Mongol realm, particularly between China and the Islamic world.

Thomas J. Barfield, *The Nomadic Alternative* (1993). An anthropological and historical survey of pastoral peoples on a global basis.

Carter Finley, *The Turks in World History* (2005). The evolution of Turkic-speaking people, from their nomadic origins to the twentieth century.

Jack Weatherford, *Genghis Khan and the Making of the Modern World* (2004). A lively, well-written, and balanced account of the world the Mongols made and the legacy they left for the future.

"The Mongols in World History," http://afe.easia.columbia.edu/mongols. A wonderful resource on the Mongols generally, with a particular focus on their impact in China.

For Web sites and additional documents related to this chapter, see **Make History** at bedfordstmartins.com/strayer.

Documents

Considering the Evidence:
Perspectives on the Mongols

How did the Mongols understand themselves and the enormous empire they had created? How did the peoples who were forcibly incorporated within that empire or threatened by it view the Mongols? In studying the Mongol phenomenon, historians use documents that reflect both the Mongols' perception of themselves and the perspectives of outsiders. The first two documents derive from Mongol sources, while the final three represent views from Russian, Chinese, and Western European observers (see Map 12.1, p. 530).

Sorting through these various perceptions of the Mongols raises questions about the kinds of understandings—or misunderstandings—that arise as culturally different peoples meet, especially under conditions of conquest. These documents also require reflection on the relative usefulness of sources that come from the Mongols themselves as well as those that derive from the victims of Mongol aggression.

Document 12.1

Mongol History from a Mongol Source

The major literary work to emerge from the Mongols themselves, widely known as *The Secret History of the Mongols*, was written a decade or two after the death in 1227 of Chinggis Khan. The unknown author of this work was clearly a contemporary of the Great Khan and likely a member of the royal household. The first selection discusses the Mongol practice of *anda*, a very close relationship between two unrelated men. Although they later broke with one another, the anda relationship of Temujin, the future Chinggis Khan, and his friend Jamugha was important in Temujin's rise to power. The second selection from the *Secret History* describes the process by which Temujin was elevated to the rank of Chinggis Khan, the ruler of a united Mongol nation, while the third recounts the reflections of Ogodei, Chinggis Khan's son and successor, probably toward the end of his reign, which lasted from 1229 to 1241.

- How would you describe the anda relationship?

- What does the *Secret History* suggest about the nature of political authority and political relationships among the Mongols?

- What did Ogodei regard as his greatest achievements and his most notable mistakes?

- What evidence do the selections from the *Secret History* provide that the author was an insider?

The Secret History of the Mongols
ca. 1240

Anda: Temujin and Jamugha

Temujin and Jamugha pitched their tents in the
   Khorkonagh Valley.
With their people united in one great camp,
the two leaders decided they should renew their
   friendship,
their pledge of anda.
They remembered when they'd first made that
   pledge,
and said, "We should love one another again."
That first time they'd met Temujin was eleven
   years old. . . .
So Temujin and Jamugha said to each other:
"We've heard the elders say,
'When two men become anda their lives
   become one.
One will never desert the other and will always
   defend him.'
This is the way we'll act from now on.
We'll renew our old pledge and love each other
   forever."
Temujin took the golden belt he'd received
in the spoils from Toghtoga's defeat
and placed it around Anda Jamugha's waist.
Then he led out the Merkid chief's warhorse,
a light yellow mare with black mane and tail,
and gave it to Anda Jamugha to ride.
Jamugha took the golden belt he'd received
in the spoils from Dayir Usun's defeat
and placed it around the waist of Anda Temujin.
Then he led out the whitish-tan warhorse of
   Dayir Usun

and had Anda Temujin ride on it.
Before the cliffs of Khuldaghar
in the Khorkhonagh Valley,
beneath the Great Branching Tree of the Mongol,
they pledged their friendship and promised to
   love one another.
They held a feast on the spot
and there was great celebration.
Temujin and Jamugha spent that night alone,
sharing one blanket to cover them both.

Temujin and Jamugha loved each other for
   one year,
and when half of the second year had passed
they agreed it was time to move camp. . . .

Temujin Becomes Chinggis Khan

Then they moved the whole camp
to the shores of Blue Lake in the Gurelgu
   Mountains.
Altan, Khuchar, and Sacha Beki conferred with
   each other there,
and then said to Temujin:
"We want you to be khan.
Temujin, if you'll be our khan
we'll search through the spoils
for the beautiful women and virgins,
for the great palace tents,
for the young virgins and loveliest women,
for the finest geldings and mares.
We'll gather all these and bring them to you.
When we go off to hunt for wild game
we'll go out first to drive them together for you
   to kill.
We'll drive the wild animals of the steppe together
so that their bellies are touching.

Source: Paul Kahn, *The Secret History of the Mongols: The Origin of Chingis Khan* (San Francisco: North Point Press, 1984), 44–45, 48–49, 192–93.

We'll drive the wild game of the mountains together
   so that they stand leg to leg.
If we disobey your command during battle
take away our possessions, our children, and wives.
Leave us behind in the dust,
cutting off our heads where we stand and letting
   them fall to the ground.
If we disobey your counsel in peacetime
take away our tents and our goods, our wives, and
   our children.
Leave us behind when you move,
abandoned in the desert without a protector."
Having given their word,
having taken this oath,
they proclaimed Temujin khan of the Mongol
and gave him the name Chingis Khan....

Reflections of Ogodei

Then Ogodei Khan spoke these words:
"Since my father the Khan passed away
and I came to sit on his great throne,
what have I done?
I went to war against the people of Cathay° and I
   destroyed them.
For my second accomplishment
I established a network of post stations
so that my words are carried across the land with
   great speed.
Another of my accomplishments has been
to have my commanders dig wells in the desert
so that there would be pasture and water for the
   people there.
Lastly I placed spies and agents among all the
   people of the cities.
In all directions I've brought peace to the Nation
   and the people,
making them place their feet on the ground;
making them place their hands on the earth.
Since the time of my father the Khan
I added these four accomplishments to all that
   he did.

°**Cathay:** China.

But also since my father passed away
and I came to sit on his great throne
with the burden of all the numerous people on
   my shoulders
I allowed myself to be conquered by wine.
This was one of my mistakes.
Another of my mistakes was to listen to a woman
   with no principles
and because of her
take away the daughters who belonged to my
   Uncle Odchigin.
Even though I'm the Khan,
the Lord of the Nation,
I have no right to go against established principle,
so this was my mistake.
Another mistake was to secretly harm Dokholkhu.
If you ask, 'Why was this wrong?'
I would say that to secretly harm Dokholkhu,
a man who had served his proper lord, my father
   the Khan,
performing heroic deeds in his service, was a
   mistake.
Now that I've done this
who'll perform heroic deeds in my service?
So now I admit that I was wrong and didn't
   understand.
I secretly harmed a man who had served my
   father the Khan,
someone who deserved my protection.
Then my last mistake was to desire too much,
to say to myself,
'I'm afraid that all the wild game born under
   Heaven
will run off toward the land of my brothers.'
So I ordered earthen walls to be built
to keep the wild game from running away,
but even as these walls were being built
I heard my brothers speaking badly of me.
I admit that I was wrong to do this.
Since the time of my father the Khan
I've added four accomplishments to all that
   he'd done
and I've done four things which I admit were
   wrong."

Document 12.2

A Letter from Chingghis Khan

Document 12.2 comes from a remarkable letter that Chinggis Khan sent to an elderly Chinese Daoist master named Changchun in 1219, requesting a personal meeting with the teacher. Changchun in fact made the arduous journey to the camp of Chinggis Khan, then located in Afghanistan, where he stayed with the Mongol ruler for almost a year, before returning to China.

- ■ Why did Chinggis Khan seek a meeting with Changchun?

- ■ How does Chinggis Khan define his life's work? What is his image of himself?

- ■ How would you describe the tone of Chinggis Khan's letter to Changchun? What does the letter suggest about Mongol attitudes toward the belief systems of conquered peoples?

- ■ How do Documents 12.1 and 12.2 help explain the success of the Mongols' empire-building efforts?

- ■ What core Mongol values do these documents suggest?

CHINGGIS KHAN

Letter to Changchun

1219

Heaven has abandoned China owing to its haughtiness and extravagant luxury. But I, living in the northern wilderness, have not inordinate passions. I hate luxury and exercise moderation. I have only one coat and one food. I eat the same food and am dressed in the same tatters as my humble herdsmen. I consider the people my children, and take an interest in talented men as if they were my brothers.... At military exercises I am always in the front, and in time of battle am never behind. In the space of seven years I have succeeded in accomplishing a great work, and uniting the whole world into one empire. I have not myself distinguished qualities. But the government of the [Chinese] is inconstant, and therefore Heaven assists me to obtain the throne.... All together have acknowledged my supremacy. It seems to me that since the remote time...such an empire has not been seen.... Since the time I came to the throne I have always taken to heart the ruling of my people; but I could not find worthy men to occupy [high offices]....With respect to these circumstances I inquired, and heard that thou, master, hast penetrated the truth.... For a long time thou has lived in the caverns of the rocks, and hast retired from the world; but to thee the people who have acquired sanctity repair, like clouds on the paths of the immortals, in innumerable multitudes....But what shall I do? We are separated by mountains and plains of great extent, and I cannot meet thee. I can only descend from the throne and stand by the side. I have fasted and washed. I have ordered my adjutant...to prepare an escort and a cart for thee.

Source: E. Bretschneider, *Mediaeval Researches from Eastern Asiatic Sources* (London, 1875), 37–39.

Do not be afraid of the thousand *li*.° I implore thee to move thy sainted steps. Do not think of the extent of the sandy desert. Commiserate the people

---

°*li*: a great distance.

in the present situation of affairs, or have pity upon me, and communicate to me the means of preserving life. I shall serve thee myself. I hope that at least thou wilt leave me a trifle of thy wisdom. Say only one word to me and I shall be happy.

Document 12.3

A Russian View of the Mongols

The initial impression of the Mongol impact in many places was one of utter devastation, destruction, and brutality. Document 12.3 offers a Russian commentary from that perspective drawn from the *Chronicle of Novgorod*, one of the major sources for the history of early Russia.

- How did the Russian writer of the *Chronicle* account for what he saw as the disaster of the Mongol invasion?

- Can you infer from the document any additional reasons for the Mongol success?

- Beyond the conquest itself, what other aspects of Mongol rule offended the Russians?

- To what extent was the Mongol conquest of Russia also a clash of cultures?

The Chronicle of Novgorod
1238

That same year [1238] foreigners called Tartars° came in countless numbers, like locusts, into the land of Ryazan, and on first coming they halted at the river Nukhla, and took it, and halted in camp there. And thence they sent their emissaries to the *Knyazes*° of Ryazan, a sorceress and two men with her, demanding from them one-tenth of everything: of men and *Knyazes* and horses—of everything

---

°**Tartars:** Mongols.

°***Knyazes***: Princes.

Source: Robert Mitchell and Nevill Forbes, trans., *The Chronicle of Novgorod, 1016–1471* (New York: AMS Press, 1970; repr. from the edition of 1914, London), 81–83, 88.

one-tenth. And the *Knyazes* of Ryazan, Gyurgi, Ingvor's brother, Oleg, Roman Ingvorevich, and those of Murom and Pronsk, without letting them into their towns, went out to meet them to Voronazh. And the *Knyazes* said to them: "Only when none of us remain then all will be yours.".... And the *Knyazes* of Ryazan sent to Yuri of Volodimir asking for help, or himself to come. But Yuri neither went himself nor listened to the request of the *Knyazes* of Ryazan, but he himself wished to make war separately. But it was too late to oppose the wrath of God....Thus also did God before these men take from us our strength and put into us perplexity and thunder and dread and trembling for our sins. And then the pagan foreigners surrounded Ryazan and fenced it in with a stockade....And the Tartars took the town on

December 21, and they had advanced against it on the 16th of the same month. They likewise killed the *Knyaz* and *Knyaginya*, and men, women, and children, monks, nuns and priests, some by fire, some by the sword, and violated nuns, priests' wives, good women and girls in the presence of their mothers and sisters. But God saved the Bishop, for he had departed the same moment when the troops invested the town. And who, brethren, would not lament over this, among those of us left alive when they suffered this bitter and violent death? And we, indeed, having seen it, were terrified and wept with sighing day and night over our sins, while we sigh every day and night, taking thought for our possessions and for the hatred of brothers.

. . . The pagan and godless Tartars, then, having taken Ryazan, went to Volodimir. . . . And when the lawless ones had already come near and set up battering rams, and took the town and fired it on Friday before Sexagesima Sunday, the *Knyaz* and *Knyaginya* and *Vladyka*, seeing that the town was on fire and that the people were already perishing, some by fire

and others by the sword, took refuge in the Church of the Holy Mother of God and shut themselves in the Sacristy. The pagans breaking down the doors, piled up wood and set fire to the sacred church; and slew all, thus they perished, giving up their souls to God. . . . And Rostov and Suzdal went each its own way. And the accursed ones having come thence took Moscow, Pereyaslavi, Yurev, Dmitrov, *Volok*, and Tver; there also they killed the son of Yaroslav. And thence the lawless ones came and invested Torzhok on the festival of the first Sunday in Lent. They fenced it all round with a fence as they had taken other towns, and here the accursed ones fought with battering rams for two weeks. And the people in the town were exhausted and from Novgorod there was no help for them; but already every man began to be in perplexity and terror. And so the pagans took the town, and slew all from the male sex even to the female, all the priests and the monks, and all stripped and reviled gave up their souls to the Lord in a bitter and a wretched death, on March 5 . . . Wednesday in Easter week.

Document 12.4

Chinese Perceptions of the Mongols

Chinese responses to Mongol rule varied considerably. To some, of course, the Mongols were simply foreign conquerors and therefore illegitimate as Chinese rulers. Marco Polo, who was in China at the time, reported that some Mongol officials or their Muslim intermediaries treated Chinese "just like slaves," demanding bribes for services, ordering arbitrary executions, and seizing women at will—all of which generated outrage and hostility. Document 12.4 illustrates another side to Chinese perception of the Mongols. It comes from a short biography of a Mongol official named Menggu, which was written by a well-educated Chinese scholar on the occasion of Menggu's death. Intended to be inscribed on stone and buried with the Mongol officer, it emphasizes the ways in which Menggu conformed to Chinese ways of governing. Such obituaries were an established form of Chinese historical writing, usually commissioned by the children of the deceased.

■ Why might Menggu's children have requested such a document and asked a Chinese scholar to compose it? What does this suggest about Mongol attitudes to Chinese culture?

- What features of Menggu's governship did this Chinese author appreciate? In what ways did Menggu's actions and behavior reflect Confucian values? What might the writer have omitted from his account?

- What might inspire a highly educated Chinese scholar to compose such a flattering public tribute to a Mongol official?

- Why might historians be a bit skeptical about this document? Which statements might be most suspect?

Epitaph for the Honorable Menggu

1274

Emperor Taizu [Chinggis Khan] received the mandate of Heaven and subjugated all regions. When Emperor Taizong [Ogodei Khan] succeeded, he revitalized the bureaucratic system and made it more efficient and organized. At court, one minister supervised all the officials and helped the emperor rule. In the provinces, commanderies and counties received instructions from above and saw that they got carried out. Prefects and magistrates were as a rule appointed only after submitting [to the Mongols]. Still one Mongol, called the governor, was selected to supervise them. The prefects and magistrates all had to obey his orders....

In the fourth month of 1236, the court deemed Menggu capable of handling Zhangde, so promoted him...to be its governor.... Because regulations were lax, the soldiers took advantage of their victory to plunder. Even in cities and marketplaces, some people kept their doors closed in the daytime. As soon as Menggu arrived, he took charge. Knowing the people's grievances, he issued an order, "Those who oppress the people will be dealt with according to the law. Craftsmen, merchants, and shopkeepers, you must each go about your work with your doors open, peaceably attending to your business without fear. Farmers, you must be content with your lands and exert yourselves diligently according to the seasons. I will instruct or punish those who mistreat

you." After this order was issued, the violent became obedient and no one any longer dared violate the laws. Farmers in the fields and travelers on the roads felt safe, and people began to enjoy life.

In the second month of 1238, Wang Rong, prefect of Huaizhou, rebelled. The grand preceptor and prince ordered Menggu to put down this rebellion, telling him to slaughter everyone. Menggu responded, "When the royal army suppresses rebels, those who were coerced into joining them ought to be pardoned, not to mention those who are entirely innocent." The prince approved his advice and followed it. When Wang Rong surrendered, he was executed but the region was spared. The residents, with jugs of wine and burning incense, saw Menggu off tearfully, unable to bear his leaving. Forty years later when he was put in charge of Henei, the common people were delighted with the news, saying, "We will all survive—our parents and relatives through marriage all served him before."

In 1239 locusts destroyed all the vegetation in Xiang and Wei, so the people were short of food. Menggu reported this to the great minister Quduqu, who issued five thousand piculs of army rations to save the starving. As a consequence no one had to flee or starve....

At that time [1247] the harvest failed for several years in a row, yet taxes and labor services were still exacted. Consequently, three or four of every ten houses was vacant. Menggu ordered the officials to travel around announcing that those who returned to their property would be exempt from

Source: Patricia Buckley Ebrey, ed. and trans., *Chinese Civilization: A Sourcebook* (New York: Free Press, 1991), 192–94.

taxes and services for three years. That year seventeen thousand households returned in response to his summons....

When there was a drought in 1263, Menggu prayed for rain and it rained. That year he was given the title Brilliant and August General and made governor of Zhongshan prefecture. In 1270 he was transferred and became governor of Hezhong prefecture. In the spring of 1274 he was allowed to wear the golden tiger tablet in recognition of his long and excellent service, his incorruptibility, and the repute in which he was held where he had served....

The house where Menggu lived when he governed Zhangde nearly forty years ago, and the fields from which he obtained food then, were just adequate to keep out the wind and rain and supply enough to eat. When he died there were no estates or leftover wealth to leave his sons or grandsons. Therefore they had to model themselves on him and concentrate on governing in a way that would bring peace and safety, show love for the people, and benefit all. They have no need to be ashamed even if compared to the model officials of the Han and Tang dynasties.

Document 12.5

Mongol Women through European Eyes

Document 12.5 provides some insight into the roles of Mongol women and men through the eyes of a European observer, William of Rubruck (1220–1293). A Flemish Franciscan friar, William was one of several emissaries sent to the Mongol court by the pope and the king of France. They hoped that these diplomatic missions might lead to the conversion of the Mongols to Christianity, perhaps an alliance with the Mongols against Islam, or at least some useful intelligence about Mongol intentions. While no agreements with the Mongols came from these missions, William of Rubruck left a detailed account of Mongol life in the mid-thirteenth century, which included observations about the domestic roles of men and women.

■ How does William of Rubruck portray the lives of Mongol women? What was the class background of the Mongol women he describes?

■ What do you think he would have found most upsetting about the position of women in Mongol society?

■ Based on this account, how might you compare the life of Mongol women to that of women in more established civilizations, such as China, Europe, or the Islamic world?

WILLIAM OF RUBRUCK
Journey to the Land of the Mongols
ca. 1255

The matrons° make for themselves most beautiful (luggage) carts.... A single rich Mo'al or Tartar° has quite one hundred or two hundred such carts with coffers. Baatu° has twenty-six wives, each of whom has a large dwelling, exclusive of the other little ones which they set up after the big one, and which are like closets, in which the sewing girls live, and to each of these (large) dwellings are attached quite two hundred carts. And when they set up their houses, the first wife places her dwelling on the extreme west side, and after her the others according to their rank, so that the last wife will be in the extreme east; and there will be the distance of a stone's throw between the yurt of one wife and that of another. The *ordu*° of a rich Mo'al seems like a large town, though there will be very few men in it.

When they have fixed their dwelling, the door turned to the south, they set up the couch of the master on the north side. The side for the women is always the east side... on the left of the house of the master, he sitting on his couch his face turned to the south. The side for the men is the west side... on the right. Men coming into the house would never hang up their bows on the side of the woman.

It is the duty of the women to drive the carts, get the dwellings on and off them, milk the cows, make butter and *gruit*,° and to dress and sew skins, which they do with a thread made of tendons. They divide the tendons into fine shreds, and then twist them into one long thread. They also sew the boots, the socks, and the clothing. They never wash clothes, for they say that God would be angered, and that it would thunder if they hung them up to dry. They will even beat those they find washing [their clothes]. Thunder they fear extraordinarily; and when it thunders they will turn out of their dwellings all strangers, wrap themselves in black felt, and thus hide themselves till it has passed away. Furthermore, they never wash their bowls, but when the meat is cooked they rinse out the dish in which they are about to put it with some of the boiling broth from the kettle, which they pour back into it. They [the women] also make the felt and cover the houses.

The men make bows and arrows, manufacture stirrups and bits, make saddles, do the carpentering on their dwellings and the carts; they take care of the horses, milk the mares, churn the *cosmos* or mare's milk, make the skins in which it is put; they also look after the camels and load them. Both sexes look after the sheep and goats, sometimes the men, other times the women, milking them.

They dress skins with a thick mixture of sour ewe's milk and salt. When they want to wash their hands or head, they fill their mouths with water, which they let trickle onto their hands, and in this way they also wet their hair and wash their heads.

As to their marriages, you must know that no one among them has a wife unless he buys her; so it sometimes happens that girls are well past marriageable age before they marry, for their parents always keep them until they sell them.... Among them no widow marries, for the following reason: they believe that all who serve them in this life shall serve them in the next, so as regards a widow they believe that she will always return to her first husband after death. Hence this shameful custom prevails among them, that sometimes a son takes to wife all his father's wives, except his own mother; for the *ordu* of the father and mother always belongs to the youngest son, so it is he who must provide for all his

---

°**matrons:** married women.

°**Mo'al or Tartar:** Mongol.

°**Baatu:** grandson of Chinggis Khan.

°*ordu*: residence.

°*gruit*: sour curd.

Source: *The Journey of William of Rubruck...*, translated from the Latin and edited, with an introductory notice, by William Woodville Rockhill (London: Hakluyt Society, 1900), chaps 2, 7.

father's wives... and if he wishes it, he uses them as wives, for he esteems not himself injured if they return to his father after death. When then anyone has made a bargain with another to take his daughter, the father of the girl gives a feast, and the girl flees to her relatives and hides there. Then the father says: "Here, my daughter is yours: take her wheresoever you find her." Then he searches for her with his friends till he finds her, and he must take her by force and carry her off with a semblance of violence to his house.

Using the Evidence:
Perspectives on the Mongols

1. **Assessing sources:** What are the strengths and limitations of these documents for understanding the Mongols? Taking the position of their authors into account, what exaggerations, biases, or misunderstandings can you identify in these sources? What information seems credible and what should be viewed more skeptically?

2. **Characterizing the Mongols:** Based on these documents and on the text of Chapter 12, write an essay assessing the Mongol moment in world history. How might you counteract the view of many that the Mongols were simply destructive barbarians? How do your own values affect your understanding of the Mongol moment?

3. **Considering self-perception and practice:** How would you describe the core values of Mongol culture? (Consider their leaders' goals, attitudes toward conquered peoples, duties of rulers, views of political authority, role of women.) To what extent were these values put into practice in acquiring and ruling their huge empire? And in what ways were those values undermined or eroded as that empire took shape?

Visual Sources

Considering the Evidence:
The Black Death and Religion
in Western Europe

Among the most far-reaching outcomes of the Mongol moment in world history was the spread all across Eurasia and North Africa of that deadly disease known as the plague or the Black Death. While the Mongols certainly did not cause the plague, their empire facilitated the movement not only of goods and people but also of the microorganisms responsible for this pestilence (see Map 12.2, p. 543 and pp. 545–47). The impact of the Black Death was catastrophic almost everywhere it struck, but it is from Western Europe that our most detailed accounts and illustrations have survived about how people responded to that calamity.

Religion permeated the cultural world of Western Europe in the fourteenth century. The rituals of the Roman Catholic Church attended the great passages of life such as birth, marriage, and death, while the major themes of Christian teaching—sin and repentance, salvation and heaven, the comfort available through Jesus, Mary, and the saints—shaped most people's outlook on life and the world. It is hardly surprising, then, that many people would turn to religion in their efforts to understand and cope with a catastrophe of such immense proportions.

Seeking the aid of parish priests, invoking the intercession of the Virgin Mary, participating in religious processions and pilgrimages, attending mass regularly, increasing attention to private devotion—these were among the ways that beleaguered people sought to tap the resources of faith to alleviate the devastating impact of the plague. From Church leaders, the faithful heard a message of the plague as God's punishment for sins. An Italian layman reflected this understanding when he wrote *A History of the Plague* in 1348. There he pictured God witnessing the world "sinking and sliding into all kinds of wickedness." In response, "the quivering spear of the Almighty, in the form of the plague, was sent down to infect the whole human race."[42]

Accompanying such ideas were religiously based attacks on prostitutes, homosexuals, and Jews, people whose allegedly immoral behavior or alien beliefs had invited God's retribution. In Florence alone, some 17,000 men were accused of sodomy during the fifteenth century. Jews, who were sometimes held responsible for deliberately spreading the disease, were subject to terrible persecution, including the destruction of synagogues, massacres, burnings, expulsion, and seizure of property. Although several popes and kings defended them, many Jews fled to Poland, where authorities welcomed their urban and commercial skills, leading to a flourishing Jewish culture there in the several centuries that followed.

The most well-known movement reflecting an understanding of the plague as God's judgment on a sinful world was that of the flagellants, whose name derived from the Latin word *flagella*, "whips." The practice of flagellation, whipping oneself or allowing oneself to be whipped, had a long tradition within the Christian world and elsewhere as well. Flagellation served as a penance for sin and as a means of identifying with Christ, who was himself whipped prior to his crucifixion. It reemerged as a fairly widespread practice, especially in Germany, between 1348 and 1350 in response to the initial outbreak of the plague. Its adherents believed that perhaps the terrible wrath of God could be averted by performing this extraordinary act of atonement or penance. Groups of flagellants moved from city to city, where they called for repentance, confessed their sins, sang hymns, and participated in ritual dances, which climaxed in whipping themselves with knotted cords sometimes embedded with iron points. Visual Source 12.1 is a contemporary representation of the flagellants in the town of Doornik in the Netherlands in 1349. The text at the bottom reads in part:

> In [1349] it came to pass that on the day of the Assumption of the Blessed Virgin (Aug. 15) some 200 persons came here from Bruges about noon.... [I]mmediately the whole town was filled with curiosity as to why these folk had come.... Meantime the folk from Bruges prepared to perform their ceremonies which they called "penance." The inhabitants of both sexes, who had never before seen any such thing, began to imitate the actions of the strangers, to torment themselves also by the penitential exercises and to thank God for this means of penance which seemed to them most effectual.

■ Flagellation was but one form of penance. What other forms of self-inflicted punishment for sin are suggested in the image?

■ What is the significance of the Christ on the cross that precedes the flagellants?

■ Does the procession seem spontaneous or organized? Do Church authorities appear to have instigated or approved this procession?

■ How might the flagellants have understood their own actions?

■ Church authorities generally opposed the flagellant movement. Why do you think they did so?

Visual Source 12.1 The Flagellants (Private Collection/The Bridgeman Art Library)

While many people certainly turned to religion for solace in the face of the unimaginable disaster of the Black Death, others found traditional Christian rituals and teachings of little use or difficult to reconcile with the overwhelming realities of the disease. For some the plague prompted an orgy of hedonism, perhaps to affirm life in the face of endless death or simply to live to the full in what time remained to them. A contemporary Italian observer noted, "As they wallowed in idleness, their dissolution led them into the sin of gluttony, into banquets, taverns, delicate foods, and gambling. The rushed headlong into lust."[43] In 1394 a representative of the pope threatened excommunication for those who practiced debauchery in the graveyards.

Among the deepest traumas inflicted by the plague was its interference with proper Christian rituals surrounding death and dying, practices that were believed to assist the dead to achieve eternal rest and the living to accept their loss and find hope for reunion in heaven. Priests were scarce and sometimes refused to administer last rites, fearing contact with the dying. The sheer numbers of dead were overwhelming. City authorities at times ordered quick burials in mass graves to avoid the spread of the disease. A French observer in 1348 wrote, "No relatives, no friends showed concern for what might be happening. No priest came to hear the confessions of the dying, or to administer the sacraments

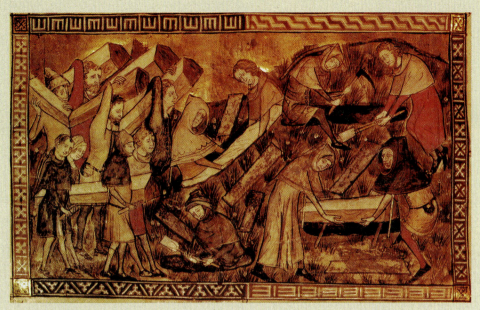

Visual Source 12.2 Burying the Dead (Bibliothèque Royale de Belgique, Brussels, Belgium/The Bridgeman Art Library)

to them."[44] The fourteenth-century Italian poet Boccaccio echoed those sentiments: "[T]here were no tears or candles or mourners to honor the dead; in fact no more respect was accorded to dead people than would nowadays be shown toward dead goats."[45] Visual Source 12.2, published in 1352, illustrates a burial of plague victims of 1349 in the city of Tournai in what is now Belgium.

- How does this visual source support or contradict the written accounts excerpted above?

- How would you characterize the burial scene in this visual source?

- How does it differ from what an image of a proper Christian burial might contain? How might survivors of the plague have regarded such a burial?

The initial and subsequent outbreaks of the plague in Western Europe generated an understandable preoccupation with death, which was reflected in the art of the time. A stained-glass window in a church in Norwich, England, from about 1500 personified Death as a chess player contesting with a high Church official. A type of tomb called a cadaver tomb included a sculpture of the deceased as a rotting cadaver, sometimes with flesh-eating worms emerging from the body. An inscription on one such tomb in the Canterbury Cathedral in England explained the purpose of the image:

Whoever you be who will pass by, I ask you to remember,
You will be like me after you die,
For all [to see]: horrible, dust, worms, vile flesh.[46]

Visual Source 12.3 A Culture of Death (St. Nicolair's Church, Tallinn, now the Niguliste Museum. Photo: Visual Connection Archive)

This intense awareness of the inevitability of death and its apparent indiscriminate occurrence was also expressed in the Dance of Death, which began in France in 1348 as a ritual intended to prevent the plague or to cure the afflicted. During the performance people would periodically fall to the ground, allowing others to trample on them. By 1400 such performances took place in a number of parish churches and subsequently in more secular settings. The Dance of Death also received artistic expression in a variety of poems, paintings, and sketches. The earliest of the paintings dates from 1425 and depicts dozens of people—from an emperor, king, pope, and bishop to a merchant, peasant, and an infant—each dancing with skeletal figures enticing them toward death. Visual Source 12.3 reproduces a portion of one of these Dance of Death paintings, originally created by the German artist Berndt Notke in 1463 and subsequently restored and reproduced many times.

In the inscriptions at the bottom of the painting, each living character addresses a skeletal figure, who in turn makes a reply. Here is the exchange between the empress (shown in a red dress at the far right of the image) and Death. First, the empress speaks:

> I know, Death means me!
> I was never terrified so greatly!
> I thought he was not in his right mind,
> after all, I am young and also an empress.
> I thought I had a lot of power,
> I had not thought of him
> or that anybody could do something against me.
> Oh, let me live on, this I implore you!

And then Death replies:

> Empress, highly presumptuous,
> I think, you have forgotten me.
> Fall in! It is now time.
> You thought I should let you off?
> No way! And were you ever so much,
> You must participate in this play,
> And you others, everybody—
> Hold on! Follow me, Mr Cardinal![47]

■ How is the status of each of the various living figures—from left to right: the pope, the emperor, the empress—depicted?

■ What does the white sheet around each of the death images represent? What do their expressions suggest about their attitude toward the living?

■ Notice that the living figures face outward toward the viewer rather than toward the entreating death figures on either side of them. What might this mean?

■ Does the portrayal of death pictured here reflect Christian views of death or does it challenge them?

■ How is the exchange between the empress and Death reflected in the painting?

The horrific experience of the Black Death also caused some people to question fundamental Christian teachings about the mercy and benevolence of God or even of his power to affect the outcome of the plague. A late-fourteenth-century clergyman in England expressed the dismay that many must have felt:

> For God is deaf nowadays and will not hear us
> And for our guilt, he grinds good men to dust.[48]

In a similar vein, the fourteenth-century Italian Renaissance scholar Francesco Petrarch questioned why God's vengeance had fallen so hard on the people of his own time: "While all have sinned alike, we alone bear the lash." He asked whether it was possible "that God does not care for mortal men." In the end, Petrarch dismissed that idea but still found God's judgments "inscrutable and inaccessible to human senses."[49] Thus the Black Death eroded more optimistic thirteenth-century Christian views, based on the ideas of the ancient Greek philosopher Aristotle, that human rationality could penetrate the mind of God.

Efforts to interpret Visual Source 12.4, a fifteenth-century English painting, raise similar issues to those expressed by Petrarch.

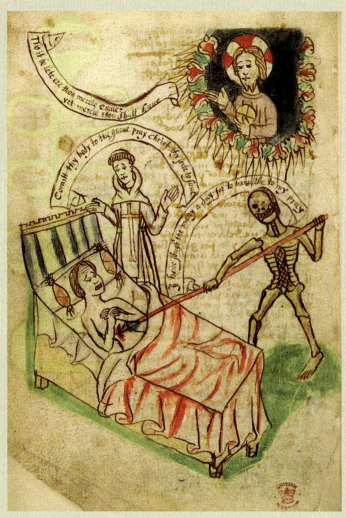

Visual Source 12.4 In the Face of Catastrophe—Questioning or Affirming the Faith (HIP/Art Resource, New York)

- Why is the death figure smiling?

- How does this skeletal figure differ from the ones in Visual Source 12.3?

- How are the priest and the Christ figure depicted? What possible interpretations of their gestures can you imagine?

- Notice that the death figure spears the dying person in the side, an action that evokes the biblical account of Jesus being speared in his side during his crucifixion. What might the artist have sought to convey by such a reference?

- The captions, from top to bottom, read: Christ figure: "Tho it be late ere thou mercie came: yet mercie thou shalt have." Priest figure: "Commit thy body to the grave: pray Christ thy soul to save." Death figure: "I have sought thee many a day: for to have thee to my pray." How do these captions influence your understanding of the painting?

- Would you characterize the overall message of this painting as one of hopefulness, despair, or something else? What elements in the painting might support each of these conclusions?

Using the Evidence:
The Black Death and Religion
in Western Europe

1. **Assessing motives:** Do you think the artists who created these visual sources sought to reinforce traditional Christian teachings or to challenge them?

2. **Using art as evidence:** What do these visual sources tell you about the impact of and responses to the plague in fourteenth- and fifteenth-century Western Europe?

3. **Connecting past and present:** Considering the various ways that people sought to avert, cope with, or explain the plague in these visual sources, what parallels to the human responses to crises or catastrophes in more recent centuries or in our own time can you identify?

CHAPTER THIRTEEN

The Worlds of the Fifteenth Century

During 2005, Chinese authorities marked the 600th anniversary of the initial launching of their country's massive maritime expeditions in 1405. Some eighty-seven years before Columbus sailed across the Atlantic with three small ships and a crew of about ninety men, the Chinese admiral Zheng He had captained a fleet of more than 300 ships and a crew numbering some 27,000 people, which brought a Chinese naval presence into the South China Sea and the Indian Ocean as far as the East African coast. Now in 2005, China was celebrating. Public ceremonies, books, magazine articles, two television documentaries, an international symposium, a stamp in honor of Zheng He—all of this and more was part of a yearlong remembrance of these remarkable voyages.

Given China's recent engagement with the larger world, Chinese authorities sought to use Zheng He as a symbol of their country's expanding, but peaceful, role on the international stage. Until recently, however, his achievement was barely noticed in China's collective memory, and for six centuries Zheng He had been largely forgotten or ignored. Columbus, on the other hand, had long been highly visible in the West, celebrated as a cultural hero and more recently harshly criticized as an imperialist, but certainly remembered. The voyages of both of these fifteenth-century mariners were pregnant with meaning for world history. Why were they remembered so differently in the countries of their origin?

THE FIFTEENTH CENTURY, DURING WHICH BOTH ZHENG HE and Columbus undertook their momentous expeditions, proved in

The Meeting of Two Worlds: This famous sixteenth-century engraving by the Flemish artist Theodore de Bry shows Columbus landing in Hispaniola (Haiti), where the Taino people bring him presents, while the Europeans claim the island for God and queen. In light of its long-range consequences, this voyage was arguably the most important single event of the fifteenth century. (Bildarchiv Preussischer Kulturbesitz/Art Resource, NY)

Snapshot   **Major Developments around the World in the Fifteenth Century**

Region	Major Developments
Central, East, and Southeast Asia	Ming dynasty China, 1368–1644 Conquests of Timur, 1370–1406 Zheng He's maritime voyages, 1405–1433 Spread of Islam into Southeast Asia Rise of Malacca Civil war among competing warlords in Japan
South Asia/India	Timur's invasion of India, 1398 Various Muslim sultanates in northern India Rise of Hindu state of Vijayanagar in southern India Founding of Mughal Empire, 1526
Middle East	Expansion of Ottoman Empire Ottoman seizure of Constantinople, 1453 Founding of Safavid Empire in Persia, 1501 Ottoman siege of Vienna, 1529
Christendom/Europe	European Renaissance Portuguese voyages of exploration along West African coast Completion of reconquest of Spain, ending Muslim control End of the Byzantine Empire, 1453 End of Mongol rule in Russia; reign of Ivan the Great, 1462–1505
Africa	Songhay Empire in West Africa, 1464–1591 Kingdom of the Kongo in West Central Africa Expansion of Ethiopian state in East Africa Kingdom of Zimbabwe/Mwene Mutapa in southern Africa
The Americas/Western Hemisphere	Aztec Empire in Mesoamerica, 1345–1521 Inca Empire along the Andes, 1438–1533 Iroquois confederacy (New York State) "Complex" Paleolithic societies along west coast of North America
Pacific Oceania	Paleolithic persistence in Australia Chiefdoms and stratified societies on Pacific islands Yap as center of oceanic trading network with Guam and Palau

retrospect to mark a major turning point in the human story. At the time, of course, no one was aware of it. No one knew in 1405 that the huge armada under Zheng He's command would be recalled in 1433, never to sail again. And no one knew in 1492 that Columbus's minuscule fleet of three ships would utterly transform the world, bringing the people of two "old worlds" and two hemispheres permanently together, with enduring consequences for them all. The outcome of the processes set in motion by those three small ships included the Atlantic slave trade, the decimation of the native population of the Americas, the massive growth of world population, the Industrial Revolution, and the growing prominence of Europeans on the world stage. But none of these developments were even remotely foreseeable in 1492.

Thus the fifteenth century, as a hinge of major historical change, provides an occasion for a bird's-eye view of the world through a kind of global tour. This excursion around the world will serve to briefly review the human saga thus far and to establish a baseline from which the transformations of the modern era might be measured. How then might we describe the world, and the worlds, of the fifteenth century?

The Shapes of Human Communities

One way to describe the world of the fifteenth century is to identify the various types of societies that it contained. Bands of hunters and gatherers, villages of agricultural peoples, newly emerging chiefdoms or small states, nomadic/pastoral communities, established civilizations and empires—all of these social or political forms would have been apparent to a widely traveled visitor in the fifteenth century. They represented alternative ways of organizing human communities and responded to differences in the environment, in the historical development of various regions, and in the choices made by particular peoples. All of them were long established by the fifteenth century, but the balance among these distinctive kinds of societies at the end of the post-classical millennium (1500) was quite different than it had been at the beginning (500).

Paleolithic Persistence

Despite millennia of agricultural advance, substantial areas of the world still hosted gathering and hunting societies, known to scholars as Paleolithic (old stone-age) peoples. All of Australia, much of Siberia, the arctic coastlands, and parts of Africa and the Americas fell into this category. These peoples were not simply relics of a bygone age, however. They too had changed over time, though more slowly than their agricultural counterparts, and they too interacted with their neighbors. In short, they had a history, although most history books largely ignore them after the age of agriculture arrived. Nonetheless, this most ancient way of life still had a sizable and variable presence in the world of the fifteenth century.

Consider, for example, Australia. That continent's many separate groups, some 250 of them, still practiced a gathering and hunting way of life in the fifteenth century, a pattern that continued well after Europeans arrived in the late eighteenth century.

■ **Comparison**

In what ways did the gathering and hunting people of Australia differ from those of the northwest coast of North America?

Over many thousands of years, these people had assimilated various material items or cultural practices from outsiders—outrigger canoes, fish hooks, complex netting techniques, artistic styles, rituals, and mythological ideas—but despite the presence of farmers in nearby New Guinea, no agricultural practices penetrated the Australian mainland. Was it because large areas of Australia were unsuited for the kind of agriculture practiced in New Guinea? Or did the peoples of Australia, enjoying an environment of sufficient resources, simply see no need to change their way of life?

Despite the absence of agriculture, Australia's peoples had mastered and manipulated their environment, in part through the practice of "firestick farming," a pattern of deliberately set fires, which they described as "cleaning up the country." These controlled burns served to clear the underbrush, thus making hunting easier and encouraging the growth of certain plant and animal species. In addition, native Australians exchanged goods among themselves over distances of hundreds of miles, created elaborate mythologies and ritual practices, and developed sophisticated traditions of sculpture and rock painting. They accomplished all of this on the basis of an economy and technology rooted in the distant Paleolithic past.

A very different kind of gathering and hunting society flourished in the fifteenth century along the northwest coast of North America among the Chinookan, Tulalip, Skagit, and other peoples. With some 300 edible animal species and an abundance of salmon and other fish, this extraordinarily bounteous environment provided the foundation for what scholars sometimes call "complex" or "affluent" gathering and hunting cultures. What distinguished the northwest coast peoples from those of Australia were permanent village settlements with large and sturdy houses, considerable economic specialization, ranked societies that sometimes included slavery, chiefdoms dominated by powerful clan leaders or "big men," and extensive storage of food.

Although these and other gathering and hunting peoples persisted still in the fifteenth century, both their numbers and the area they inhabited had contracted greatly as the Agricultural Revolution unfolded across the planet. That relentless advance of the farming frontier continued in the centuries ahead as the Russian, Chinese, and European empires encompassed the lands of the remaining Paleolithic peoples. By the early twenty-first century, what was once the only human way of life had been reduced to minuscule pockets of people whose cultures seemed doomed to a final extinction.

Agricultural Village Societies

■ Change
What kinds of changes were transforming West African agricultural village societies and those of the Iroquois as the fifteenth century dawned?

Far more numerous than hunters and gatherers were those many peoples who, though fully agricultural, had avoided incorporation into larger empires or civilizations and had not developed their own city- or state-based societies. Living usually in small village-based communities and organized in terms of kinship relations, such people predominated during the fifteenth century in much of North America and in parts of the Amazon River basin, Southeast Asia, and Africa south of the equator. They had created societies largely without the oppressive political authority, class inequalities, and seclusion of women that were so common in civilizations. Historians have largely relegated such societies to the periphery of world history, marginal to their overwhelming focus on large-scale civilizations. Viewed from within their own circles, though, these societies were of course at the center of things, each with its own history of migration, cultural transformation, social conflict, incorporation of new people, political rise and fall, and interaction with strangers. In short, they too changed as their histories unfolded.

In the forested region of what is now southern Nigeria in West Africa, for example, three quite different patterns of change emerged in the centuries between 1000 and 1500 (see Map 13.3, p. 582). Each of them began from a base of farming village societies whose productivity was generating larger populations.

Among the Yoruba-speaking people, a series of rival city-states emerged, each within a walled town and ruled by an *oba*, or "king" (some of whom were women), who performed both religious and political functions. As in ancient Mesopotamia or classical Greece, no single state or empire encompassed all of Yorubaland. Nearby lay the kingdom of Benin, a small, highly centralized territorial state that emerged by the fifteenth century and was ruled by a warrior king named Ewuare, said to have conquered 201 towns and villages in the process of founding the new state. His administrative chiefs replaced the heads of kinship groups as major political authorities, while the ruler sponsored extensive trading missions and patronized artists who created the remarkable brass sculptures for which Benin is so famous.

East of the Niger River lay the lands of the Igbo peoples, where dense population and extensive trading networks might well have given rise to states, but the deliberate Igbo preference was to reject the kingship and state-building efforts of their neighbors, boasting on occasion that "the Igbo have no kings." Instead they relied on other institutions—title societies in which wealthy men received a series of prestigious ranks, women's associations, hereditary ritual experts serving as mediators, a balance of power among kinship groups—to maintain social cohesion beyond the level of the village. It was a "stateless society," famously described in Chinua Achebe's *Things Fall Apart*, the most widely read novel to emerge from twentieth-century Africa.

The Yoruba, Bini, and Igbo peoples did not live in isolated, self-contained societies, however. They traded actively among themselves and with more distant peoples, such as the large African kingdom of Songhay far to the north. Cotton cloth, fish, copper and iron goods, decorative objects, and more drew neighboring peoples into networks of exchange. Common artistic traditions reflected a measure of cultural unity in a politically fragmented region, and all of these peoples seem to have changed from a matrilineal to a patrilineal system of tracing their descent. Little of this registered in the larger civilizations of the Afro-Eurasian world, but to the peoples of the West African forest during the fifteenth century, these processes were central to their history and their daily lives. Soon, however, all of them would be caught up in the transatlantic slave trade and would be changed substantially in the process.

Benin Bronzes
With the patronage of the royal court, Benin's artists produced an array of wood, ivory, and most famously exquisite brass or bronze sculptures, most of which celebrated the royal family and decorated their palaces. Here is a sixteenth-century representation of the Queen Mother of Benin. (National Museum, Lagos, Nigeria/The Bridgeman Art Library)

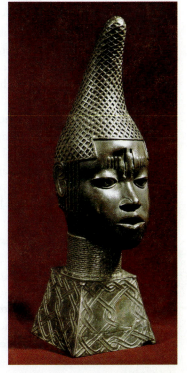

Across the Atlantic in what is now central New York State, other agricultural village societies were also in the process of substantial change during the several centuries preceding their incorporation into European trading networks and empires. The Iroquois-speaking peoples of that region had only recently become fully agricultural, adopting maize- and bean-farming techniques that had originated long ago in Mesoamerica. As this productive agriculture took hold by 1300 or so, the population grew, the size of settlements increased, and distinct peoples emerged, such as the Onondaga, Seneca, Cayuga, Oneida, and Mohawk. Frequent warfare also erupted among them. Some scholars have speculated that as agriculture, largely seen as women's work, became the primary economic activity, "warfare replaced successful food getting as the avenue to male prestige."[1]

Whatever caused it, this increased level of conflict among Iroquois peoples triggered a remarkable political innovation—a loose alliance or confederation among five Iroquois peoples based on an agreement known as the Great Law of Peace (see Map 13.5, p. 589). It was an agreement to settle their differences peacefully through a confederation council of clan leaders, some fifty of them altogether, who had the authority to adjudicate disputes and set reparation payments. Operating by consensus, the Iroquois League of Five Nations effectively suppressed the blood feuds and tribal conflicts that had only recently been so widespread. It also coordinated their peoples' relationship with outsiders, including the Europeans, who arrived in growing numbers in the centuries after 1500.

The Iroquois League also gave expression to values of limited government, social equality, and personal freedom, concepts that some European colonists found highly attractive. One British colonial administrator declared in 1749 that the Iroquois had "such absolute Notions of Liberty that they allow no Kind of Superiority of one over another, and banish all Servitude from their Territories."[2] Such equality extended to gender relationships, for among the Iroquois, descent was matrilineal (reckoned through the woman's line), married couples lived with the wife's family, and women controlled agriculture. While men were hunters, warriors, and the primary political officeholders, women selected and could depose those leaders.

Wherever they lived in 1500, over the next several centuries independent agricultural peoples such as the Iroquois, Yoruba, and Igbo were increasingly encompassed in expanding economic networks and conquest empires based in Western Europe, Russia, China, or India. In this respect, they repeated the experience of many other village-based farming communities that had much earlier found themselves forcibly included in the powerful embrace of Egyptian, Mesopotamian, Roman, Indian, Chinese, and other civilizations.

■ **Significance**

What role did Central Asian and West African pastoralists play in their respective regions?

Herding Peoples

Nomadic pastoral peoples impinged more directly and dramatically on civilizations than did hunting and gathering or agricultural village societies. The Mongol incursion, along with the enormous empire to which it gave rise, was one in a long series of challenges from the steppes, but it was not the last. As the Mongol Empire disintegrated, a brief attempt to restore it occurred in the late fourteenth and early fifteenth centuries under the leadership of a Turkic warrior named Timur, born in what is now Uzbekistan and known in the West as Tamerlane (see Map 13.1, p. 576).

With a ferocity that matched or exceeded that of his model, Chinggis Khan, Timur's army of nomads brought immense devastation yet again to Russia, Persia, and India. Timur himself died in 1405, while preparing for an invasion of China. Conflicts among his successors prevented any lasting empire, although his descendants retained control of the area between Persia and Afghanistan for the rest of the fifteenth century. That state hosted a sophisticated elite culture, combining Turkic and Persian elements, particularly at its splendid capital of Samarkand, as its rulers patronized artists, poets, traders, and craftsmen. Timur's conquest proved to be the last great military success of nomadic peoples from Central Asia. In the centuries that followed, their homelands were swallowed up in the expanding Russian and Chinese empires, as the balance of power between steppe nomads of inner Eurasia and the civilizations of outer Eurasia turned decisively in favor of the latter.

In Africa, pastoral peoples stayed independent of established empires several centuries longer than the nomads of Inner Asia, for not until the late nineteenth century were they incorporated into European colonial states. The experience of the Fulbe, West Africa's largest pastoral society, provides a useful example of an African herding people with a highly significant role in the fifteenth century and beyond. From their homeland in the western fringe of the Sahara along the upper Senegal River, the Fulbe migrated gradually eastward in the centuries after 1000 C.E. (see Map 13.3, p. 582). Unlike the pastoral peoples of Inner Asia, they generally lived in small communities among agricultural peoples and paid various grazing fees and taxes for the privilege of pasturing their cattle. Relations with their farming hosts often were tense because the Fulbe resented their subordination to agricultural peoples, whose way of life they despised. That sense of cultural superiority became even more pronounced as the Fulbe, in the course of their eastward movement, slowly adopted Islam. Some of them in fact dropped out of a pastoral life and settled in towns, where they became highly respected religious leaders. In the eighteenth and nineteenth centuries, the Fulbe were at the center of a wave of religiously based uprisings, or jihads, that greatly expanded the practice of Islam and gave rise to a series of new states, ruled by the Fulbe themselves.

Civilizations of the Fifteenth Century: Comparing China and Europe

Beyond the foraging, farming, and herding societies of the fifteenth-century world were its civilizations, those city-centered and state-based societies that were far larger and more densely populated, more powerful and innovative, and much more unequal in terms of class and gender than other forms of human community. Since the First Civilizations had emerged between 3500 and 1000 B.C.E., both the geographic space they encompassed and the number of people they embraced had grown substantially. By the fifteenth century, a considerable majority of the world's population lived within one or another of these civilizations, although most of these people no doubt identified more with local communities than with a larger civilization. What might an imaginary global traveler notice about the world's major civilizations in the fifteenth century?

Ming Dynasty China

■ **Description**

How would you define the major achievements of Ming dynasty China?

Such a traveler might well begin his or her journey in China, heir to a long tradition of effective governance, Confucian and Daoist philosophy, a major Buddhist presence, sophisticated artistic achievements, and a highly productive economy. That civilization, however, had been greatly disrupted by a century of Mongol rule, and its population had been sharply reduced by the plague. During the Ming dynasty (1368–1644), however, China recovered (see Map 13.1). The early decades of that dynasty witnessed an effort to eliminate all signs of foreign rule, discouraging the use

Map 13.1   Asia in the Fifteenth Century

The fifteenth century in Asia witnessed the massive Ming dynasty voyages into the Indian Ocean, the last major eruption of nomadic power in Timur's empire, and the flourishing of the maritime city of Malacca.

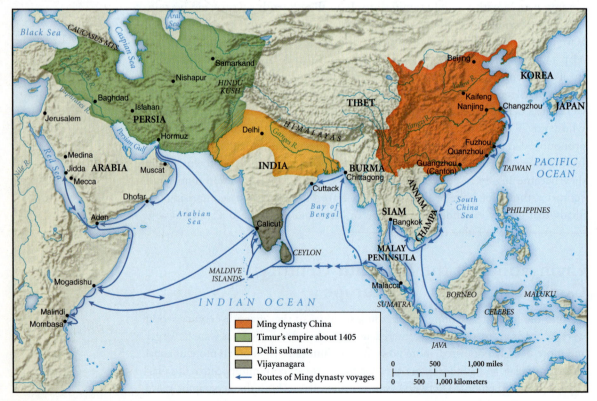

of Mongol names and dress, while promoting Confucian learning based on earlier models from the Han, Tang, and Song dynasties. Emperor Yongle (reigned 1402–1422) sponsored an enormous *Encyclopedia* of some 11,000 volumes. With contributions from more than 2,000 scholars, this work sought to summarize or compile all previous writing on history, geography, ethics, government, and more. Yongle also relocated the capital to Beijing, ordered the building of a magnificent imperial residence known as the Forbidden City, and constructed the Temple of Heaven, where subsequent rulers performed Confucian-based rituals to ensure the well-being of Chinese society (see Visual Source 13.1, p. 610). Culturally speaking, China was looking to its past.

Politically, the Ming dynasty reestablished the civil service examination system that had been neglected under Mongol rule and went on to create a highly centralized government. Power was concentrated in the hands of the emperor himself, while a cadre of eunuchs (castrated men) personally loyal to the emperor exercised great authority, much to the dismay of the official bureaucrats. The state acted vigorously to repair the damage of the Mongol years by restoring millions of acres to cultivation; rebuilding canals, reservoirs, and irrigation works; and planting, according to some estimates, a billion trees in an effort to reforest China. As a result, the economy rebounded, both international and domestic trade flourished, and the population grew. During the fifteenth century, China had recovered and was perhaps the best-governed and most prosperous of the world's major civilizations.

China also undertook the largest and most impressive maritime expeditions the world had ever seen. Since the eleventh century, Chinese sailors and traders had been a major presence in the South China Sea and in Southeast Asian port cities, with much of this activity in private hands. But now, after decades of preparation, an enormous fleet, commissioned by Emperor Yongle himself, was launched in 1405, followed over the next twenty-eight years by six more such expeditions. On board more than 300 ships of the first voyage was a crew of some 27,000, including 180 physicians, hundreds of government officials, 5 astrologers, 7 high-ranking or grand eunuchs, carpenters, tailors, accountants, merchants, translators, cooks, and thousands of soldiers and sailors. Visiting many ports in Southeast Asia, Indonesia, India, Arabia, and East Africa, these fleets, captained by the Muslim eunuch Zheng He, sought to enroll distant peoples and states in the Chinese tribute system (see Map 13.1). Dozens of rulers accompanied the fleets back to China, where they presented tribute, performed the required rituals of submission, and received in return abundant gifts, titles, and trading opportunities. Chinese officials were amused by some of the exotic products to be found abroad—ostriches, zebras, and giraffes, for

Comparing Chinese and European Ships
Among the largest vessels in Zheng He's early-fifteenth-century fleet were "treasure ships" such as this vessel measuring more than 400 feet long and carrying a crew of perhaps 1,000 men. The figure at the bottom right represents one of Columbus's ships. (© Dugald Stermer)

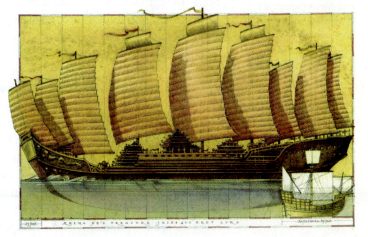

example. Officially described as "bringing order to the world," Zheng He's expeditions served to establish Chinese power and prestige in the Indian Ocean and to exert Chinese control over foreign trade in the region. The Chinese, however, did not seek to conquer new territories, establish Chinese settlements, or spread their culture, though they did intervene in a number of local disputes. On one of the voyages, Zheng He erected on the island of Ceylon (Sri Lanka) a tablet honoring alike the Buddha, Allah, and a Hindu deity.

The most surprising feature of these voyages was how abruptly and deliberately they were ended. After 1433, Chinese authorities simply stopped such expeditions and allowed this enormous and expensive fleet to deteriorate in port. "In less than a hundred years," wrote a recent historian of these voyages, "the greatest navy the world had ever known had ordered itself into extinction."[3] Part of the reason involved the death of the emperor Yongle, who had been the chief patron of the enterprise. Many high-ranking officials had long seen the expeditions as a waste of resources because China, they believed, was the self-sufficient "middle kingdom," requiring little from the outside world. In their eyes, the real danger to China came from the north, where nomadic barbarians constantly threatened. Finally, they viewed the voyages as the project of the court eunuchs, whom these officials despised. Even as these voices of Chinese officialdom prevailed, private Chinese merchants and craftsmen continued to settle and trade in Japan, the Philippines, Taiwan, and Southeast Asia, but they did so without the support of their government. The Chinese state quite deliberately turned its back on what was surely within its reach—a large-scale maritime empire in the Indian Ocean basin.

European Comparisons: State Building and Cultural Renewal

■ **Comparison**

What political and cultural differences stand out in the histories of fifteenth-century China and Western Europe? What similarities are apparent?

At the other end of the Eurasian continent, similar processes of demographic recovery, political consolidation, cultural flowering, and overseas expansion were under way. Western Europe, having escaped Mongol conquest but devastated by the plague, began to regrow its population during the second half of the fifteenth century. As in China, the infrastructure of civilization proved a durable foundation for demographic and economic revival.

Politically too Europe joined China in continuing earlier patterns of state building. In China, however, this meant a unitary and centralized government that encompassed almost the whole of its civilization, while in Europe a decidedly fragmented system of many separate, independent, and highly competitive states made for a sharply divided Christendom (see Map 13.2). Many of these states—Spain, Portugal, France, England, the city-states of Italy (Milan, Venice, and Florence), various German principalities—learned to tax their citizens more efficiently, to create more effective administrative structures, and to raise standing armies. A small Russian state centered on the city of Moscow also emerged in the fifteenth century as Mongol rule faded away. Much of this state building was driven by the needs of war, a frequent occurrence in such a fragmented and competitive political environment. England and

Map 13.2   Europe in 1500
By the end of the fifteenth century, Christian Europe had assumed its early modern political shape as a system of competing states threatened by an expanding Muslim Ottoman Empire.

France, for example, fought intermittently for more than a century in the Hundred Years' War (1337–1453) over rival claims to territory in France. Nothing remotely similar disturbed the internal life of Ming dynasty China.

A renewed cultural blossoming, known in European history as the Renaissance, likewise paralleled the revival of all things Confucian in Ming dynasty China. In Europe, however, that blossoming celebrated and reclaimed a classical Greek tradition that earlier had been obscured or viewed through the lens of Arabic or Latin translations. Beginning in the vibrant commercial cities of Italy between roughly 1350 and 1500, the Renaissance reflected the belief of the wealthy elite that they were living in a wholly new era, far removed from the confined religious world of feudal Europe. Educated citizens of these cities sought inspiration in the art and literature of ancient Greece and Rome; they were "returning to the sources," as they put it. Their purpose was not so much to reconcile these works with the ideas of Christianity, as the twelfth- and thirteenth-century university scholars had done, but to use them as a cultural standard to imitate and then to surpass. The elite patronized great Renaissance artists such as Leonardo da Vinci, Michelangelo, and Raphael, whose paintings and sculptures were far more naturalistic, particularly in portraying the human body, than those of their medieval counterparts.

Although religious themes remained prominent, Renaissance artists now included portraits and busts of well-known contemporary figures and scenes from ancient mythology. In the work of scholars, known as "humanists," reflections on secular topics such as grammar, history, politics, poetry, rhetoric, and ethics complemented more religious matters. For example, Niccolò Machiavelli's (1469-1527) famous work *The Prince* was a prescription for political success based on the way politics actually operated in a highly competitive Italy of rival city-states rather than on idealistic and religiously based principles. To the question of whether a prince should be feared or loved, Machiavelli replied:

> One ought to be both feared and loved, but as it is difficult for the two to go together, it is much safer to be feared than loved. . . . For it may be said of men in general that they are ungrateful, voluble, dissemblers, anxious to avoid danger, and covetous of gain. . . . Fear is maintained by dread of punishment which never fails. . . . In the actions of men, and especially of princes, from which there is no appeal, the end justifies the means.[4]

Heavily influenced by classical models, Renaissance figures were more interested in capturing the unique qualities of particular individuals and in describing the world as it was than in portraying or exploring eternal religious truths. In its focus on the affairs of this world, Renaissance culture reflected the urban bustle and commercial preoccupations of the Italian cities. Its secular elements challenged the otherworldliness of Christian culture, and its individualism signaled the dawning of a more capitalist economy of private entrepreneurs. A new Europe was in the making, rather more different from its own recent past than Ming dynasty China was from its pre-Mongol glory.

European Comparisons: Maritime Voyaging

■ Comparison

In what ways did European maritime voyaging in the fifteenth century differ from that of China? What accounts for these differences?

A global traveler during the fifteenth century might be surprised to find that Europeans, like the Chinese, were also launching outward-bound maritime expeditions. Initiated in 1415 by the small country of Portugal, those voyages sailed ever farther down the west coast of Africa, supported by the state and blessed by the pope (see Map 13.3). As the century ended, two expeditions marked major breakthroughs, although few suspected it at the time. In 1492, Christopher Columbus, funded by Spain, Portugal's neighbor and rival, made his way west across the Atlantic hoping to arrive in the East and, in one of history's most consequential mistakes, ran into the Americas. Five years later, in 1497, Vasco da Gama launched a voyage that took him

Snapshot   **Key Moments in European Maritime Voyaging**

Portuguese seize Ceuta in Morocco	1415
Prince Henry the Navigator launches Portuguese exploration of the West African coast	1420
Portuguese settle the Azores	1430s
Chinese fleets withdrawn from Indian Ocean	1433
Portuguese reach the Senegal River; beginning of Atlantic slave trade	1440s
Portuguese contact with Kongo; royal family converts to Christianity	1480s
Sugar production begins in Atlantic islands (Canaries, São Tomé)	1480s
Establishment of trading station at Elmina (in present-day Ghana)	1480s
First transatlantic voyage of Columbus	1492
John Cabot sails across North Atlantic to North America	1496
Vasco da Gama enters Indian Ocean and reaches India	1497–1498
Portuguese attacks on various Swahili cities; establishment of Fort Jesus at Mombasa; Portuguese contacts with Christian Ethiopia	1497–1520s
Magellan's voyage to Asia via the Americas; first circumnavigation of the globe	1520–1523

around the tip of South Africa, along the East African coast, and, with the help of a Muslim pilot, across the Indian Ocean to Calicut in southern India.

The differences between the Chinese and European oceangoing ventures were striking, most notably perhaps in terms of size. Columbus captained three ships and a crew of about 90, while da Gama had four ships, manned by perhaps 170 sailors. These were minuscule fleets compared to Zheng He's hundreds of ships and a crew in the many thousands. "All the ships of Columbus and da Gama combined," according to a recent account, "could have been stored on a single deck of a single vessel in the fleet that set sail under Zheng He."[5]

Motivation as well as size differentiated the two ventures. Europeans were seeking the wealth of Africa and Asia—gold, spices, silk, and more. They also were in search of Christian converts and of possible Christian allies with whom to continue their long crusading struggle against threatening Muslim powers. China, by contrast, faced no equivalent power, needed no military allies in the Indian Ocean basin, and required little that these regions produced. Nor did China possess an impulse to convert foreigners to Chinese culture or religion as the Europeans surely did. Furthermore, the confident and overwhelmingly powerful Chinese fleet sought neither conquests nor colonies, while the Europeans soon tried to monopolize by force the commerce of the Indian Ocean and violently carved out huge empires in the Americas.

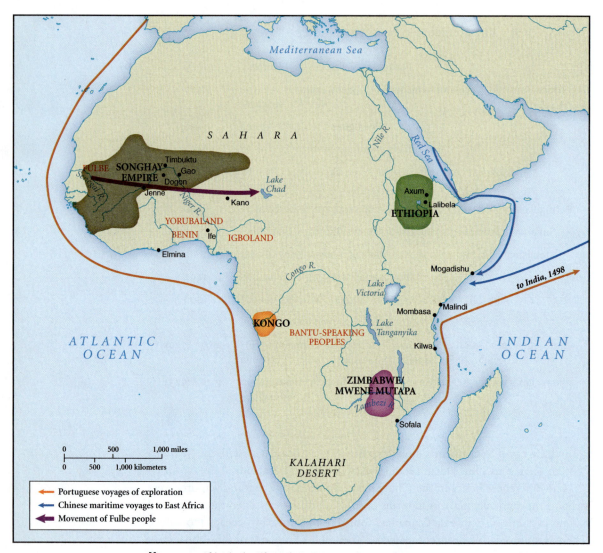

Map 13.3   Africa in the Fifteenth Century

By the 1400s, Africa was a virtual museum of political and cultural diversity, encompassing large empires, such as Songhay; smaller kingdoms, such as Kongo; city-states among the Yoruba, Hausa, and Swahili peoples; village-based societies without states at all, as among the Igbo; and nomadic pastoral peoples, such as the Fulbe. Both European and Chinese maritime expeditions touched on Africa during that century, even as Islam continued to find acceptance in the northern half of the continent.

The most striking difference in these two cases lay in the sharp contrast between China's decisive ending of its voyages and the continuing, indeed escalating, European effort, which soon brought the world's oceans and growing numbers of the world's people under its control. This is the reason that Zheng He's voyages were so long neglected in China's historical memory. They led nowhere, whereas the initial European expeditions, so much smaller and less promising, were but the first steps on a journey to world power. But why did the Europeans continue a process that the Chinese had deliberately abandoned?

In the first place, of course, Europe had no unified political authority with the power to order an end to its maritime outreach. Its system of competing states, so unlike China's single unified empire, ensured that once begun, rivalry alone would drive the Europeans to the ends of the earth. Beyond this, much of Europe's elite had an interest in overseas expansion. Its budding merchant communities saw opportunity for profit; its competing monarchs eyed the revenue that could come from taxing overseas trade or from seizing overseas resources; the Church foresaw the possibility of widespread conversion; impoverished nobles might imagine fame and fortune abroad. In China, by contrast, support for Zheng He's voyages was very shallow in official circles, and when the emperor Yongle passed from the scene, those opposed to the voyages prevailed within the politics of the court.

Finally, the Chinese were very much aware of their own antiquity, believed strongly in the absolute superiority of their culture, and felt with good reason that, should they desire something from abroad, others would bring it to them. Europeans too believed themselves unique, particularly in religious terms as the possessors of Christianity, the "one true religion." In material terms, though, they were seeking out the greater riches of the East, and they were highly conscious that Muslim power blocked easy access to these treasures and posed a military and religious threat to Europe itself. All of this propelled continuing European expansion in the centuries that followed.

The Waldseemüller Map of 1507
Just fifteen years after Columbus landed in the Western Hemisphere, this map, which was created by the German cartographer Martin Waldseemüller, reflected a dawning European awareness of the planet's global dimensions and location of the world's major landmasses. (Bildarchiv Preussischer Kulturbesitz/Art Resource, NY)

The Chinese withdrawal from the Indian Ocean actually facilitated the European entry. It cleared the way for the Portuguese to enter the region, where they faced only the eventual naval power of the Ottomans. Had Vasco da Gama encountered Zheng He's massive fleet as his four small ships sailed into Asian waters in 1498, world history may well have taken quite a different turn. As it was, however, China's abandonment of oceanic voyaging and Europe's embrace of the seas marked different responses to a common problem that both civilizations shared—growing populations and land shortage. In the centuries that followed, China's rice-based agriculture was able to expand production internally by more intensive use of the land, while the country's territorial expansion was inland toward Central Asia. By contrast, Europe's agriculture, based on wheat and livestock, expanded primarily by acquiring new lands in overseas possessions, which were gained as a consequence of a commitment to oceanic expansion.

Civilizations of the Fifteenth Century: The Islamic World

■ Comparison
What differences can you identify among the four major empires in the Islamic world of the fifteenth and sixteenth centuries?

Beyond the domains of Chinese and European civilization, our fifteenth-century global traveler would surely have been impressed with the transformations of the Islamic world. Stretching across much of Afro-Eurasia, the enormous realm of Islam experienced a set of remarkable changes during the fifteenth and early sixteenth centuries, as well as the continuation of earlier patterns. The most notable change lay in the political realm, for an Islamic civilization that had been severely fragmented since at least 900 now crystallized into four major states or empires (see Map 13.4). At the same time, a long-term process of conversion to Islam continued the cultural transformation of Afro-Eurasian societies both within and beyond these new states.

In the Islamic Heartland: The Ottoman and Safavid Empires

The most impressive and enduring of the new Islamic states was the Ottoman Empire, which lasted in one form or another from the fourteenth to the early twentieth century. It was the creation of one of the many Turkic warrior groups that had earlier migrated into Anatolia. By the mid-fifteenth century, these Ottoman Turks had already carved out a state that encompassed much of the Anatolian peninsula and had pushed deep into southeastern Europe (the Balkans), acquiring in the process a substantial Christian population. In the two centuries that followed, the Ottoman Empire extended its control to much of the Middle East, coastal North Africa, the lands surrounding the Black Sea, and even farther into Eastern Europe.

The Ottoman Empire was a state of enormous significance in the world of the fifteenth century and beyond. In its huge territory, long duration, incorporation of many diverse peoples, and economic and cultural sophistication, it was

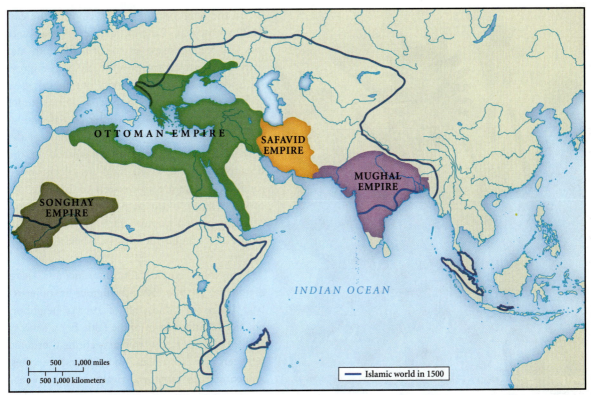

Map 13.4   Empires of the Islamic World
The most prominent political features of the vast Islamic world in the fifteenth and sixteenth centuries were four large states: the Songhay, Ottoman, Safavid, and Mughal empires.

one of the great empires of world history. In the fifteenth century, only Ming dynasty China and the Incas matched it in terms of wealth, power, and splendor. The empire represented the emergence of the Turks as the dominant people of the Islamic world, ruling now over many Arabs, who had initiated this new faith more than 800 years before. In adding "caliph" (successor to the Prophet) to their other titles, Ottoman sultans claimed the legacy of the earlier Abbasid Empire. They sought to bring a renewed unity to the Islamic world, while also serving as protector of the faith, the "strong sword of Islam."

The Ottoman Empire also represented a new phase in the long encounter between Christendom and the world of Islam. In the Crusades, Europeans had taken the aggressive initiative in that encounter, but the rise of the Ottoman Empire reversed their roles. The seizure of Constantinople in 1453 marked the final demise of Christian Byzantium and allowed Ottoman rulers to see themselves as successors to the Roman Empire. In 1529, a rapidly expanding Ottoman Empire laid siege to Vienna in the heart of Central Europe. The political and military expansion of Islam, at the expense of Christendom, seemed clearly under way. Many Europeans spoke fearfully of the "terror of the Turk."

Ottoman Janissaries
Originating in the fourteenth century, the Janissaries became the elite infantry force of the Ottoman Empire. Complete with uniforms, cash salaries, and marching music, they were the first standing army in the region since the days of the Roman Empire. When gunpowder technology became available, Janissary forces soon were armed with muskets, grenades, and handheld cannon. This image dates from the seventeenth century. (Austrian National Library, picture archive, Vienna: Cod. 8626, fol. 15r)

Des obristen Kamerling Vnd Trüchses

In the neighboring Persian lands to the east of the Ottoman Empire, another Islamic state was also taking shape in the late fifteenth and early sixteenth centuries — the Safavid Empire. Its leadership was also Turkic, but in this case it had emerged from a Sufi religious order founded several centuries earlier by Safi al-Din (1252–1334). The long-term significance of the Safavid Empire, which was established in the decade following 1500, was its decision to forcibly impose a Shia version of Islam as the official religion of the state. Over time, this form of Islam gained popular support and came to define the unique identity of Persian (Iranian) culture.

This Shia empire also introduced a sharp divide into the political and religious life of heartland Islam, for almost all of Persia's neighbors practiced a Sunni form of the faith. For a century (1534–1639), periodic military conflict erupted between the Ottoman and Safavid empires, reflecting both territorial rivalry and sharp religious differences. In 1514, the Ottoman sultan wrote to the Safavid ruler in the most bitter of terms:

You have denied the sanctity of divine law… you have deserted the path of salvation and the sacred commandments… you have opened to Muslims the gates of tyranny and oppression… you have raised the standard of irreligion and heresy…. [Therefore] the *ulama* and our doctors have pronounced a sentence of death against you, perjurer and blasphemer.[6]

This Sunni/Shia hostility has continued to divide the Islamic world into the twenty-first century.

On the Frontiers of Islam: The Songhay and Mughal Empires

While the Ottoman and Safavid empires brought both a new political unity and a sharp division to the heartland of Islam, two other states performed a similar role on the expanding African and Asian frontiers of the faith. In the West African savannas, the Songhay Empire rose in the second half of the fifteenth century. It was the most recent and the largest in a series of impressive states that operated at a crucial intersection of the trans-Saharan trade routes and that derived much of their revenue from taxing that commerce. Islam was a growing faith in Songhay but was limited largely to urban elites. This cultural divide within Songhay largely accounts for the religious behavior of its fifteenth-century monarch Sonni Ali (reigned 1465–1492), who gave alms and fasted during Ramadan in proper Islamic style but also enjoyed a reputation as a magician and possessed a charm thought to render his soldiers invisible to their enemies. Nonetheless, Songhay had become a major center of Islamic learning and commerce by the early sixteenth century. A North African traveler known as Leo Africanus remarked on the city of Timbuktu:

> Here are great numbers of [Muslim] religious teachers, judges, scholars, and other learned persons who are bountifully maintained at the king's expense. Here too are brought various manuscripts or written books from Barbary [North Africa] which are sold for more money than any other merchandise....Here are very rich merchants and to here journey continually large numbers of negroes who purchase here cloth from Barbary and Europe....It is a wonder to see the quality of merchandise that is daily brought here and how costly and sumptuous everything is.[7]

Sonni Ali's successor made the pilgrimage to Mecca and asked to be given the title "Caliph of the Land of the Blacks." Songhay then represented a substantial Islamic state on the African frontier of a still-expanding Muslim world.

The Mughal Empire in India bore similarities to Songhay, for both governed largely non-Muslim populations. Much as the Ottoman Empire initiated a new phase in the interaction of Islam and Christendom, so too did the Mughal Empire continue an ongoing encounter between Islamic and Hindu civilizations. Established in the early sixteenth century, the Mughal Empire was the creation of yet another Islamized Turkic group, which invaded India in 1526. Over the next century, the Mughals (a Persian term for Mongols) established unified control over most of the Indian peninsula, giving it a rare period of political unity and laying the foundation for subsequent British colonial rule. During its first several centuries, the Mughal Empire, a land of great wealth and imperial splendor, was the location of a remarkable effort to blend many Hindu groups and a variety of Muslims into an effective partnership. The inclusive policies of the early Mughal emperors showed that Muslim rulers could accommodate their overwhelmingly Hindu subjects in somewhat the same fashion as Ottoman authorities provided religious autonomy for their Christian peoples. In southernmost India, however, the distinctly Hindu kingdom of Vijayanagara flourished in the fifteenth century, even as it borrowed architectural styles from the Muslim states of northern India and sometimes employed Muslim mercenaries in its military forces.

Together these four Muslim empires—Ottoman, Safavid, Songhay, and Mughal—brought to the Islamic world a greater measure of political coherence, military power, economic prosperity, and cultural brilliance than it had known since the early centuries of Islam. This new energy, sometimes called a "second flowering of Islam," impelled the continuing spread of the faith to yet new regions. The most prominent of these was oceanic Southeast Asia, which for centuries had been intimately bound up in the world of Indian Ocean commerce. By the fifteenth century, that trading network was largely in Muslim hands, and the demand for Southeast Asian spices was mounting as the Eurasian world recovered from the devastation of Mongol conquest and the plague. Growing numbers of Muslim traders, many of them from India, settled in Java and Sumatra, bringing their faith with them. Thus, unlike the Middle East and India, where Islam was established in the wake of Arab or Turkic conquest, in Southeast Asia, as in West Africa, it was introduced by traveling merchants and solidified through the activities of Sufi holy men.

The rise of Malacca, strategically located on the waterway between Sumatra and Malaya, was a sign of the times (see Map 13.1, p. 576). During the fifteenth century, it was transformed from a small fishing village to a major Muslim port city. A Portuguese visitor in 1512 observed that Malacca had "no equal in the world.... Commerce between different nations for a thousand leagues on every hand must come to Malacca."[8] That city also became a springboard for the spread of Islam throughout the region. The Islam of Malacca, however, demonstrated much blending with local and Hindu/Buddhist traditions, while the city itself, like many port towns, had a reputation for "rough behavior." An Arab Muslim pilot in the 1480s commented critically:

> They have no culture at all.... You do not know whether they are Muslim or not.... They are thieves, for theft is rife among them and they do not mind.... They appear liars and deceivers in trade and labor.[9]

Nonetheless, Malacca, like Timbuktu, became a center for Islamic learning, and students from elsewhere in Southeast Asia were studying there in the fifteenth century. As the more central regions of Islam were consolidating politically, the frontier of the faith continued to move steadily outward.

Civilizations of the Fifteenth Century: The Americas

■ **Comparison**

What distinguished the Aztec and Inca empires from each other?

Across the Atlantic, centers of civilization had long flourished in Mesoamerica and in the Andes. The fifteenth century witnessed new, larger, and more politically unified expressions of those civilizations in the Aztec and Inca empires. Both were the work of previously marginal peoples who had forcibly taken over and absorbed older cultures, giving them new energy, and both were decimated in the sixteenth century at the hands of Spanish conquistadores and their diseases. To conclude this global tour of world civilizations, we will send our weary traveler to the Western Hemisphere for a brief look at these American civilizations (see Map 13.5).

The Aztec Empire

The empire known to history as the Aztec state was largely the work of the Mexica people, a seminomadic group from northern Mexico who had migrated southward and by 1325 had established themselves on a small island in Lake Texcoco. Over the

Inuit seal hunters

forest hunter-gatherers

West coast foraging, hunting
and fishing peoples

Plateau fishers and
hunter-gatherers

Plains bison hunters

Plains farmers

Iroquois
Confederation

Desert hunter-gatherers

Mississippian
Mound Builders

Gulf of
Mexico

Chichén
Itzá
Maya

Tenochtitlán • Aztec
Empire

MESO-AMERICAN
CIVILIZATION

Caribbean Sea

ATLANTIC
OCEAN

North Andean
chiefdoms

Amazonian
chiefdoms

PACIFIC
OCEAN

Rain-forest farmers

ANDEAN
CIVILIZATION

Inca
Empire

Machu Picchu •
Cuzco •

Savanna and highland farmers

Savanna hunter-gatherers

Pampas hunter-gatherers

Shellfish gatherers and seal hunters

0   500   1,000 miles
0   500 1,000 kilometers

Hunting/gathering peoples
Village farming peoples
Chiefdoms
State-based civilizations

Map 13.5   The Americas in the Fifteenth Century
The Americas before Columbus represented a world almost completely separate from Afro-Eurasia. It featured similar kinds of societies, though with a different balance among them, but it completely lacked the pastoral economies that were so important in the Eastern Hemisphere.

next century, the Mexica developed their military capacity, served as mercenaries for more powerful people, negotiated elite marriage alliances with them, and built up their own capital city of Tenochtitlán. In 1428, a Triple Alliance between the Mexica and two other nearby city-states launched a highly aggressive program of military conquest, which in less than 100 years brought more of Mesoamerica within a single political framework than ever before. Aztec authorities, eager to shed their rather undistinguished past, now claimed descent from earlier Mesoamerican peoples such as the Toltecs and Teotihuacán.

With a core population recently estimated at 5 to 6 million people, the Aztec Empire was a loosely structured and unstable conquest state that witnessed frequent rebellions by its subject peoples. Conquered peoples and cities were required to regularly deliver to their Aztec rulers impressive quantities of textiles and clothing, military supplies, jewelry and other luxuries, various foodstuffs, animal products, building materials, rubber balls, paper, and more. The process was overseen by local imperial tribute collectors, who sent the required goods on to Tenochtitlán, a metropolis of 150,000 to 200,000 people, where they were meticulously recorded.

That city featured numerous canals, dikes, causeways, and bridges. A central walled area of palaces and temples included a pyramid almost 200 feet high. Surrounding the city were "floating gardens," artificial islands created from swamplands that supported a highly productive agriculture. Vast marketplaces reflected the commercialization of the economy. A young Spanish soldier who beheld the city in 1519 described his reaction:

> Gazing on such wonderful sights, we did not know what to say, or whether what appeared before us was real, for on one side, on the land there were great cities, and in the lake ever so many more, and the lake was crowded with canoes, and in the causeway were many bridges at intervals, and in front of us stood the great city of Mexico.[10]

Beyond tribute from conquered peoples, ordinary trade, both local and long-distance, permeated Aztec domains. The extent of empire and rapid population growth stimulated the development of markets and the production of craft goods, particularly in the fifteenth century. Virtually every settlement, from the capital city to the smallest village, had a marketplace that hummed with activity during weekly market days. The largest was that of Tlatelolco, near the capital city, which stunned the Spanish with its huge size, its good order, and the immense range of goods available. Hernán Cortés, the Spanish conquistador who defeated the Aztecs, wrote that "every kind of merchandise such as can be met with in every land is for sale there, whether of food and victuals, or ornaments of gold and silver, or lead, brass, copper, tin, precious stones, bones, shells, snails and feathers."[11] Professional merchants, known as *pochteca*, were legally commoners, but their wealth, often exceeding that of the nobility, allowed them to rise in society and become "magnates of the land." (See Document 13.1, pp. 601–04, for another Spanish view of the Aztec realm.)

■ **Description**
How did Aztec religious thinking support the empire?

Among the "goods" that the pochteca obtained were slaves, many of whom were destined for sacrifice in the bloody rituals so central to Aztec religious life. Long a part of Mesoamerican and many other world cultures, human sacrifice assumed an unusually prominent role in Aztec public life and thought during the fifteenth century. Tlacaelel (1398–1480), who was for more than half a century a prominent official of the Aztec Empire, is often credited with crystallizing the ideology of state that gave human sacrifice such great importance.

In that cyclical understanding of the world, the sun, central to all of life and identified with the Aztec patron deity Huitzilopochtli, tended to lose its energy in a constant battle against encroaching darkness. Thus the Aztec world hovered always on the edge of catastrophe. To replenish its energy and thus postpone the descent into endless darkness, the sun required the life-giving force found in human blood. Because the gods had shed their blood ages ago in creating humankind, it was wholly proper for people to offer their own blood to nourish the gods in the present. The high calling of the Aztec state was to supply this blood, largely through its wars of expansion and

Aztec Women
Within the home, Aztec women cooked, cleaned, spun and wove cloth, raised their children, and undertook ritual activities. Outside the home, they served as officials in palaces, priestesses in temples, traders in markets, teachers in schools, and members of craft workers' organizations. This domestic image comes from the sixteenth-century Florentine Codex, which was compiled by the Spanish but illustrated by Aztec artists. (Templo Mayor Library Mexico/Gianni Dagli Orti/The Art Archive)

from prisoners of war, who were destined for sacrifice. The victims were "those who have died for the god." The growth of the Aztec Empire therefore became the means for maintaining cosmic order and avoiding utter catastrophe. This ideology also shaped the techniques of Aztec warfare, which put a premium on capturing prisoners rather than on killing the enemy. As the empire grew, priests and rulers became mutually dependent, and "human sacrifices were carried out in the service of politics."[12] Massive sacrificial rituals, together with a display of great wealth, served to impress enemies, allies, and subjects alike with the immense power of the Aztecs and their gods.

Alongside these sacrificial rituals was a philosophical and poetic tradition of great beauty, much of which mused on the fragility and brevity of human life. Such an outlook characterized the work of Nezahualcoyotl (1402–1472), a poet and king of the city-state of Texcoco, which was part of the Aztec Empire:

Truly do we live on Earth?
Not forever on earth; only a little while here.
Be it jade, it shatters.
Be it gold, it breaks.
Be it a quetzal feather, it tears apart.
Not forever on earth; only a little while here.

Like a painting, we will be erased.
Like a flower, we will dry up here on earth.
Like plumed vestments of the precious bird,
That precious bird with an agile neck,
We will come to an end.[13]

The Inca Empire

While the Mexica were constructing an empire in Mesoamerica, a relatively small community of Quechua-speaking people, known to us as the Inca, was building the Western Hemisphere's largest imperial state along the spine of the Andes Mountains, which run almost the entire length of the west coast of South America. Much as the Aztecs drew upon the traditions of the Toltecs and Teotihuacán, the Incas incorporated the lands and cultures of earlier Andean civilizations: the Chavín, Moche, Nazca, and Chimu. The Inca Empire, however, was much larger than the Aztec state; it stretched some 2,500 miles along the Andes and contained perhaps 10 million subjects. Although the Aztec Empire controlled only part of the Mesoamerican cultural region, the Inca state encompassed practically the whole of Andean civilization during its short life in the fifteenth and early sixteenth centuries.

Both the Aztec and Inca empires represent rags-to-riches stories in which quite modest and remotely located people very quickly created by military conquest the largest states ever witnessed in their respective regions, but the empires themselves were quite different. In the Aztec realm, the Mexica rulers largely left their conquered people alone, if the required tribute was forthcoming. No elaborate administrative system arose to integrate the conquered territories or to assimilate their people to Aztec culture.

The Incas, on the other hand, erected a rather more bureaucratic empire, though with many accommodations for local circumstances. At the top reigned the emperor, an absolute ruler regarded as divine, a descendant of the creator god Viracocha and the son of the sun god Inti. In theory, the state owned all land and resources, and each of the some eighty provinces in the empire had an Inca governor. At least in the central regions of the empire, subjects were grouped into hierarchical units of 10, 50, 100, 500, 1,000, 5,000, and 10,000 people, each headed by local officials, who were appointed and supervised by an Inca governor or the emperor. A separate set of "inspectors" provided the imperial center with an independent check on provincial

■ **Description**

In what ways did Inca authorities seek to integrate their vast domains?

officials. Births, deaths, marriages, and other population data were carefully recorded on *quipus*, the knotted cords that served as an accounting device. A resettlement program moved one-quarter or more of the population to new locations, in part to disperse conquered and no doubt resentful people.

Efforts at cultural integration required the leaders of conquered peoples to learn Quechua. Their sons were removed to the capital of Cuzco for instruction in Inca culture and language. Even now, millions of people from Ecuador to Chile still speak Quechua, and it is the official second language of Peru after Spanish. While the Incas required their subject peoples to acknowledge major Inca deities, these peoples were then largely free to carry on their own religious traditions. Human sacrifice took place on great public occasions or at times of special difficulty, but nothing remotely on the scale of the Aztec practice.

Like the Aztec Empire, the Inca state represented an especially dense and extended network of economic relationships within the "American web," but these relationships took shape in quite a different fashion. Inca demands on their conquered people were expressed, not so much in terms of tribute, but as labor service, known as *mita*, which was required periodically of every household.[14] What people produced at home usually stayed at home, but almost everyone also had to work for the state. Some labored on large state farms or on "sun farms," which supported temples and religious institutions; others herded, mined, served in the military, or toiled on state-directed construction projects. Those with particular skills were put to work manufacturing textiles, metal goods, ceramics, and stonework. The most well known of these specialists were the "chosen women," who were removed from their homes as young girls, trained in Inca ideology, and set to producing corn beer and cloth at state centers. Later they were given as wives to men of distinction or sent to serve as priestesses in various temples, where they were known as "wives of the Sun." In return for such labor services, Inca ideology, expressed in terms of family relationships, required the state to provide elaborate feasts at which large quantities of food and drink were consumed. Thus the authority of the state penetrated and directed the Incas' society and economy far more than did that of the Aztecs. (See Document 13.2, pp. 605–07, for an early Spanish account of Inca governing practices.)

If the Inca and Aztec civilizations differed sharply in their political and economic arrangements, they resembled each other more closely in their gender

Machu Picchu
Machu Picchu, high in the Andes Mountains, was constructed by the Incas in the 1400s on a spot long held sacred by local people. Its 200 buildings stand at some 8,000 feet above sea level, making it truly a "city in the sky." According to scholars, it was probably a royal retreat or religious center, rather than serving administrative, commercial, or military purposes. The outside world became aware of Machu Picchu only in 1911, when it was discovered by a Yale University archeologist. (Crispin Rodwell/Alamy)

systems. Both societies practiced what scholars call "gender parallelism," in which "women and men operate in two separate but equivalent spheres, each gender enjoying autonomy in its own sphere."[15]

In both Mesoamerican and Andean societies, such systems had emerged long before their incorporation into the Aztec and Inca empires. In the Andes, men reckoned their descent from their fathers and women from their mothers, while Mesoamericans had long viewed children as belonging equally to their mothers and fathers. Parallel religious cults for women and men likewise flourished in both societies. Inca men venerated the sun, while women worshipped the moon, with matching religious officials. In Aztec temples, both male and female priests presided over rituals dedicated to deities of both sexes. Particularly among the Incas, parallel hierarchies of male and female political officials governed the empire, while in Aztec society, women officials exercised local authority under a title that meant "female person in charge of people." Social roles were clearly defined and different for men and women, but the domestic concerns of women—childbirth, cooking, weaving, cleaning—were not regarded as inferior to the activities of men. Among the Aztec, for example, sweeping was a powerful and sacred act with symbolic significance as "an act of purification and a preventative against evil elements penetrating the center of the Aztec universe, the home."[16] In the Andes, men broke the ground, women sowed, and both took part in the harvest.

None of this meant gender equality. Men occupied the top positions in both political and religious life, and male infidelity was treated more lightly than was women's unfaithfulness. As the Inca and Aztec empires expanded, military life, limited to men, grew in prestige, perhaps skewing an earlier gender parallelism. In other ways, the new Aztec and Inca rulers adapted to the gender systems of the people they had conquered. Among the Aztecs, the tools of women's work, the broom and the weaving spindle, were ritualized as weapons; sweeping the home was believed to assist men at war; and childbirth for women was regarded as "our kind of war."[17] Inca rulers did not challenge the gender parallelism of their subjects but instead replicated it at a higher level, as the *sapay Inca* (the Inca ruler) and the *coya* (his female consort) governed jointly, claiming descent respectively from the sun and the moon.

Webs of Connection

■ **Connection**

In what different ways did the peoples of the fifteenth century interact with one another?

Few people in the fifteenth century lived in entirely separate and self-contained communities. Almost all were caught up, to one degree or another, in various and overlapping webs of influence, communication, and exchange. Such interactions represent, of course, one of the major concerns of world history. What kinds of webs or networks linked the various societies and civilizations of the fifteenth century?[18]

Perhaps most obvious were the webs of empire, large-scale political systems that brought together a variety of culturally different people. Christians and Muslims encountered each other directly in the Ottoman Empire, as did Hindus and Muslims in the Mughal Empire. No empire tried more diligently to integrate its diverse peoples than the fifteenth-century Incas.

Religion too linked far-flung peoples, and divided them as well. Christianity provided a common religious culture for peoples from England to Russia, although the great divide between Roman Catholicism and Eastern Orthodoxy endured, and in the sixteenth century the Protestant Reformation would shatter permanently the Christian unity of the Latin West. Although Buddhism had largely vanished from its South Asian homeland, it remained a link among China, Korea, Tibet, Japan, and parts of Southeast Asia, even as it splintered into a variety of sects and practices. More than either of these, Islam actively brought together its many peoples. In the hajj, the pilgrimage to Mecca, Africans, Arabs, Persians, Turks, Indians, and many others joined as one people as they rehearsed together the events that gave birth to their common faith. And yet divisions and conflicts persisted within the vast realm of Islam, as the violent hostility between the Sunni Ottoman Empire and the Shia Safavid Empire so vividly illustrates.

Long-established patterns of trade among peoples occupying different environments and producing different goods were certainly much in evidence during the fifteenth century, as they had been for millennia. Hunting societies of Siberia funneled furs and other products of the forest into the Silk Road trading network traversing the civilizations of Eurasia. In the fifteenth century, some of the agricultural peoples in southern Nigeria were receiving horses brought overland from the drier regions to the north, where those animals flourished better. The Mississippi River in North America and the Orinoco and Amazon rivers in South America facilitated a canoe-borne commerce along those waterways. Coastal shipping in large seagoing canoes operated in the Caribbean and along the Pacific coast between Mexico and Peru. In the Pacific, the Micronesian island of Yap by the fifteenth century was the center of an oceanic trading network, which included the distant islands of Guam and Palau and used large stone disks as money. Likewise the people of Tonga, Samoa, and Fiji intermarried and exchanged a range of goods, including mats and canoes.

The great long-distance trading patterns of the Afro-Eurasian world, in operation for a thousand years or more, likewise continued in the fifteenth century, although the balance among them was changing (see Map 13.6). The Silk Road overland network, which had flourished under Mongol control in the thirteenth and fourteenth centuries, contracted in the fifteenth century as the Mongol Empire broke up and the devastation of the plague reduced demand for its products. The rise of the Ottoman Empire also blocked direct commercial contact between Europe and China, but oceanic trade from Japan, Korea, and China through the islands of Southeast Asia and across the Indian Ocean picked up considerably. Larger ships made it possible to trade in bulk goods such as grain as well as luxury products, while more sophisticated partnerships and credit mechanisms greased the wheels of commerce. A common Islamic culture over much of this vast region likewise smoothed the passage of goods among very different peoples, as it also did for the trans-Saharan trade.

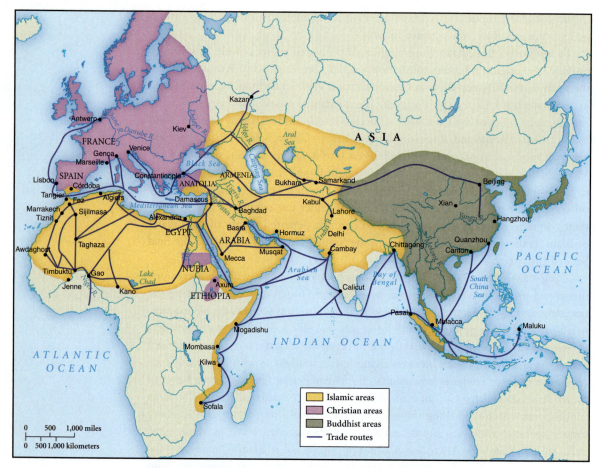

Map 13.6   Religion and Commerce in the Afro-Eurasian World
By the fifteenth century, the many distinct peoples and societies of the Eastern Hemisphere were linked
to one another by ties of religion and commerce. Of course, not everyone was involved in long-distance
trade, and many people in areas shown as Buddhist or Islamic on the map practiced other religions.

A Preview of Coming Attractions: Looking Ahead to the Modern Era, 1500–2010

While ties of empire, culture, and commerce surely linked many of the peoples in the
world of the fifteenth century, none of those connections operated on a genuinely
global scale. Although the densest webs of connection had been woven within the
Afro-Eurasian zone of interaction, this huge region had no sustained ties with the
Americas, and neither of them had meaningful contact with the peoples of Pacific
Oceania. That situation was about to change as Europeans in the sixteenth century
and beyond forged a set of genuinely global relationships that generated sustained
interaction among all of these regions. That huge process and the many outcomes
that flowed from it marked the beginning of what historians commonly call the

modern age—the more than five centuries that followed the voyages of Columbus starting in 1492.

Over those five centuries, the previously separate worlds of Afro-Eurasia, the Americas, and Pacific Oceania became inextricably linked, with enormous consequences for everyone involved. Global empires, a global economy, global cultural exchanges, global migrations, global disease, global wars, and global environmental changes have made the past 500 years a unique phase in the human journey. Those webs of communication and exchange have progressively deepened, so much so that by the end of the twentieth century few people in the world lived beyond the cultural influences, economic ties, or political relationships of a globalized world.

A second distinctive feature of the past five centuries involves the emergence of a radically new kind of human society, also called "modern," which took shape first in Europe during the nineteenth century and then in various forms elsewhere in the world. The core feature of such societies was industrialization, rooted in a sustained growth of technological innovation. The human ability to create wealth made an enormous leap forward in a very short period of time, at least by world history standards. Accompanying this economic or industrial revolution was an equally distinctive and unprecedented jump in human numbers, a phenomenon that has affected not only human beings but also many other living species and the earth itself (see the Snapshot).

Moreover, these modern societies were far more urbanized and much more commercialized than ever before, as more and more people began to work for wages, to produce for the market, and to buy the requirements of daily life rather than

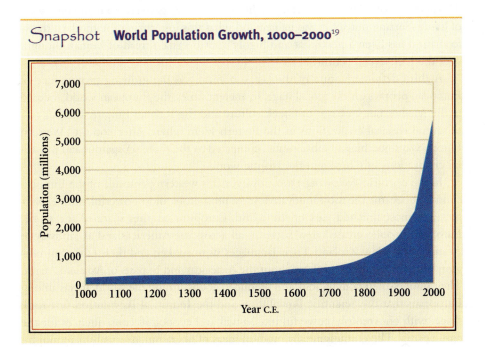

Snapshot **World Population Growth, 1000–2000**[19]

growing or making those products for their own use. These societies gave prominence and power to holders of urban wealth—merchants, bankers, industrialists, educated professionals—at the expense of rural landowning elites, while simultaneously generating a substantial factory working class and diminishing the role of peasants and handicraft artisans.

Modern societies were generally governed by states that were more powerful and intrusive than earlier states and empires had been, and they offered more of their people an opportunity to play an active role in public and political life. Literacy in modern societies was far more widespread than ever before, while new national identities became increasingly prominent, competing with more local loyalties. To the mix of established religious ideas and folk traditions were now added the challenging outlook and values of modern science, with its secular emphasis on the ability of human rationality to know and manipulate the world. Modernity has usually meant a self-conscious awareness of living and thinking in new ways that deliberately departed from tradition.

This revolution of modernity, comparable in its pervasive consequences only to the Agricultural Revolution of some 10,000 years ago, introduced new divisions and new conflicts into the experience of humankind. The ancient tensions between rich and poor within particular societies were now paralleled by new economic inequalities among entire regions and civilizations and a much-altered global balance of power. The first societies to experience the modern transformation—those in Western Europe and North America—became both a threat and a source of envy to much of the rest of the world. As modern societies emerged and spread, they were enormously destructive of older patterns of human life, even as they gave rise to many new ways of living. Sorting out what was gained and what was lost during the modern transformation has been a persistent and highly controversial thread of human thought over the past several centuries.

A third defining feature of the last 500 years was the growing prominence of European peoples on the global stage. In ancient times, the European world, focused in the Mediterranean basin of Greek culture and the Roman Empire, was but one of several classical civilizations in the Eastern Hemisphere. After 500 c.e., Western Europe was something of a backwater, compared to the more prosperous and powerful civilizations of China and the Islamic world.

In the centuries following 1500, however, this western peninsula of the Eurasian continent became the most innovative, most prosperous, most powerful, most expansive, and most imitated part of the world. European empires spanned the globe. European peoples created new societies all across the Americas and as far away as Australia and New Zealand. Their languages were spoken and their Christian religion was widely practiced throughout the Americas and in parts of Asia and Africa. Their businessmen bought, sold, and produced goods around the world. It was among Europeans that the Scientific Revolution and the Industrial Revolution first took shape, with enormously powerful intellectual and economic consequences for the entire planet. The quintessentially modern ideas of liberalism, nationalism, feminism, and socialism all bore the imprint of their European origin. By the beginning of the twentieth century, Europeans or peoples of European descent exercised unprecedented influence and control over the earth's many other peoples, a wholly novel experience in human history.

For the rest of the world, growing European dominance posed a common task. Despite their many differences, the peoples of Asia, Africa, the Middle East, the Americas, and Pacific Oceania all found themselves confronted by powerful and intrusive Europeans. The impact of this intrusion and how various peoples responded to it—resistance, submission, acceptance, imitation, adaptation—represent critically important threads in the world history of the past five centuries.

Reflections: What If? Chance and Contingency in World History

Seeking meaning in the stories they tell, historians are inclined to look for deeply rooted or underlying causes for the events they recount. And yet, is it possible that, at least on occasion, history turns less on profound and long-term causes than on coincidence, chance, or the decisions of a few that might well have gone another way?

Consider, for example, the problem of explaining the rise of Europe to a position of global power in the modern era. What if the Great Khan Ogodei had not died in 1241, requiring the forces then poised for an assault on Germany to return to Mongolia? It is surely possible that Central and Western Europe might have been overrun by Mongol armies as so many other civilizations had been, a prospect that could have drastically altered the trajectory of European history. Or what if the Chinese had decided in 1433 to continue their huge maritime expeditions, creating an empire in the Indian Ocean basin and perhaps moving on to "discover" the Americas and Europe? Such a scenario suggests a wholly different future for world history than the one that in fact occurred. Or what if the forces of the Ottoman Empire had taken the besieged city of Vienna in 1529? Might they then have incorporated even larger parts of Europe into their expanding domain, requiring a halt to Europe's overseas empire-building enterprise?

None of this necessarily means that the rise of Europe was merely a fluke or an accident of history, but it does raise the issue of "contingency," the role of unforeseen or small events in the unfolding of the human story. An occasional "what if" approach to history reminds us that alternative possibilities existed in the past and that the only certainty about the future is that we will be surprised.

Second Thoughts

What's the Significance?

Paleolithic persistence	Iroquois	Ming dynasty China
Benin	Timur	Zheng He
Igbo	Fulbe	European Renaissance

To assess your mastery of the material in this chapter, visit the **Student Center** at bedfordstmartins.com/strayer.

Ottoman Empire	Songhay Empire	Aztec Empire
seizure of Constantinople	Timbuktu	Inca Empire
(1453)	Mughal Empire	
Safavid Empire	Malacca	

Big Picture Questions

1. Assume for the moment that the Chinese had *not* ended their maritime voyages in 1433. How might the subsequent development of world history have been different? What value is there in asking this kind of "what if" or counterfactual question?

2. How does this chapter distinguish among the various kinds of societies that comprised the world of the fifteenth century? What other ways of categorizing the world's peoples might work as well or better?

3. What would surprise a knowledgeable observer from 500 C.E., were he or she to make a global tour in the fifteenth century? What features of that earlier world might still be recognizable?

4. What predictions about the future might a global traveler of the fifteenth century reasonably have made? To what extent would it depend on precisely when and where those predictions were made?

Next Steps: For Further Study

For Web sites and additional documents related to this chapter, see **Make History** at bedfordstmartins.com/strayer.

Terence N. D'Altroy, *The Incas* (2002). A history of the Inca Empire that draws on recent archeological and historical research.

Edward L. Dreyer, *Zheng He: China and the Oceans in the Early Ming Dynasty* (2006). The most recent scholarly account of the Ming dynasty voyages.

Halil Inalcik and Donald Quataert, *An Economic and Social History of the Ottoman Empire, 1300–1914* (1994). A classic study of the Ottoman Empire.

Robin Kirkpatrick, *The European Renaissance, 1400–1600* (2002). A beautifully illustrated history of Renaissance culture as well as the social and economic life of the period.

Charles Mann, *1491: New Revelations of the Americas before Columbus* (2005). A review of Western Hemisphere societies and academic debates about their pre-Columbian history.

J. R. McNeill and William H. McNeill, *The Human Web* (2003). A succinct account of the evolving webs or relationships among human societies in world history.

Michael Smith, *The Aztecs* (2003). A history of the Aztec Empire, with an emphasis on the lives of ordinary people.

"Ming Dynasty," http://www.metmuseum.org/toah/hd/ming/hd_ming.htm. A sample of Chinese art from the Ming dynasty from the collection of the Metropolitan Museum of Art.

"Renaissance Art in Italy," http://witcombe.sbc.edu/ARTHrenaissanceitaly.html. An extensive collection of painting and sculpture from the Italian Renaissance.

Documents

Considering the Evidence:
The Aztecs and the Incas
through Spanish Eyes

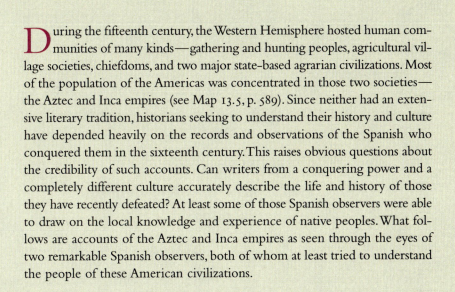

During the fifteenth century, the Western Hemisphere hosted human communities of many kinds—gathering and hunting peoples, agricultural village societies, chiefdoms, and two major state-based agrarian civilizations. Most of the population of the Americas was concentrated in those two societies—the Aztec and Inca empires (see Map 13.5, p. 589). Since neither had an extensive literary tradition, historians seeking to understand their history and culture have depended heavily on the records and observations of the Spanish who conquered them in the sixteenth century. This raises obvious questions about the credibility of such accounts. Can writers from a conquering power and a completely different culture accurately describe the life and history of those they have recently defeated? At least some of those Spanish observers were able to draw on the local knowledge and experience of native peoples. What follows are accounts of the Aztec and Inca empires as seen through the eyes of two remarkable Spanish observers, both of whom at least tried to understand the people of these American civilizations.

Document 13.1

Diego Duran on the Aztecs

Coming to Mexico with his family as a young boy, Diego Duran (1537–1588) subsequently became a Dominican friar, learned to speak fluently the native Nahuatl language of the Aztecs, and began a lifelong enterprise of studying their history and culture. His research often involved extensive interviewing of local people in the rural areas where he worked and resulted in three books published between 1574 and 1581. The first excerpt records a series of laws or decrees, which Duran attributes to the Aztec ruler Moctezuma I, who governed the empire between 1440 and 1469. They reveal something of the court practices and social hierarchy of the Aztec realm as the empire was establishing itself in the middle decades of the fifteenth century. The second excerpt touches on various aspects of Aztec culture—religion, human sacrifice, social mobility, commercial markets, and slavery.

- What do Moctezuma's laws tell us about the social and moral values of the Aztecs?

- Based on these two excerpts, how would you describe Aztec society? What distinct social groups or classes can you identify? How were they distinguished from one another? What opportunities for social mobility were available? How might people fall into slavery?

- What impressed Duran about the markets operating within the Aztec Empire?

- How was human sacrifice related to war, to market activity, to slavery, and to religious belief and practice?

- Duran's accounts of Aztec life and history were written more than fifty years after the Spanish conquest of the Aztec Empire. To what extent do you think this compromises his efforts to describe preconquest Aztec society?

KING MOCTEZUMA I

Laws, Ordinances, and Regulations

ca. 1450

The following laws were decreed:

1. The king must never appear in public except when the occasion is extremely important and unavoidable.

2. Only the king may wear a golden diadem in the city, though in war all the great lords and brave captains may wear this (but on no other occasion)....

3. Only the king and the prime minister Tlacaelel may wear sandals within the palace.... [N]oblemen are the only ones to be allowed to wear sandals in the city and no one else, also under pain of death, with the exception of men who have performed some great feat in war....

4. Only the king is to wear the final mantles of cotton brocaded with designs and threads of different colors and adorned with featherwork....

5. The great lords, who are twelve, may wear special mantles of certain make and design, and the minor lords, according to their valor and accomplishments, may wear others.

6. The common soldiers are permitted to wear only the simplest type of mantle. They are prohibited from using any special designs that might set them off from the rest....

7. The commoners will not be allowed to wear cotton clothing, under pain of death, but can use only garments of maguey fiber....

8. Only the great noblemen and valiant warriors are given license to build a house with a second story; for disobeying this law a person receives the death penalty....

9. Only the great lords are to wear labrets, ear plugs, and nose plugs of gold and precious stones, except for commoners who are strong men, brave captains, and soldiers, but their labrets, ear plugs, and nose plugs must be of bone, wood, or other inferior material of little value....

Source: Fray Diego Duran, *The History of the Indies of New Spain*, translated by Doris Heyden (Norman: University of Oklahoma Press, 1994), 208–10.

11. In the royal palace there are to be diverse rooms where different classes of people are to be received, and under pain of death no one is to enter that of the great lords or to mix with those men [unless of that class himself]....

12. An order of judges is to be established, beginning with the judges of the supreme council. After these would come regular court judges, municipal judges, district officials, constables, and councilmen, although none of them may give the death sentence without notifying the king. Only the sovereign can sentence someone to death or pardon him....

13. All the barrios will possess schools or monasteries for young men where they will learn religion and correct comportment. They are to do penance, lead hard lives, live with strict morality, practice for warfare, do physical work, fast, endure disciplinary

measures, draw blood from different parts of the body, and keep watch at night. There are to be teachers and old men to correct them and chastise them and lead them in their exercises and take care that they are not idle, do not lose their time. All of these youth must observe chastity in the strictest way, under pain of death.

14. There is to be a rigorous law regarding adulterers. They are to be stoned and thrown into the rivers or to the buzzards.

15. Thieves will be sold for the price of their theft, unless the theft be grave, having been committed many times. Such thieves will be punished by death.

16. Great privileges and exemptions are to be given those who dedicate themselves to religion, to the temples and the gods. Priests will be awarded great distinction, reverence, and authority.

DIEGO DURAN

Book of the Gods and Rites
1574–1576

I wish to tell of the way in which the natives sacrificed....

So ended the ceremony of the blessing of the pieces of dough in the form of the bones and the flesh of the god. They were revered and honored in the name of Huitzilopochtli with all the respectful veneration that we ourselves hold for the Divine Sacrament of the Altar. To exalt the occasion further, the sacrificers of men were also present....

Smeared with black, the six sacrificers appeared.... Seeing them come out with their ghastly aspect filled all the people with dread and terrible fear! The high priest carried in one hand a large stone knife, sharp and wide. Another carried a wooden yoke carved in the form of a snake. They humbled themselves before the idol and then stood

in order next to a pointed stone, which stood in front of the door of the idol's chamber....

All the prisoners of war who were to be sacrificed upon this feast were then brought forth.... They seized the victims one by one, one by one foot, another by the other, one priest by one hand, another by the other hand. The victim was thrown on his back, upon the pointed stone, where the wretch was grabbed by the fifth priest, who placed the yoke upon his throat. The high priest then opened the chest and with amazing swiftness tore out the heart, ripping it out with his own hands. Thus steaming, the heart was lifted toward the sun, and the fumes were offered up to the sun. The priest then turned toward the idol and cast the heart in its face. After the heart had been extracted, the body was allowed to roll down the steps of the pyramid....

All the prisoners and captives of war brought from the towns we have mentioned were sacrificed in this manner, until none were left. After they had been slain and cast down, their owners—those who

Source: Fray Diego Duran, *Book of the Gods and Rites and the Ancient Calendar*, translated by Fernando Horcasitas and Doris Heyden (Norman: University of Oklahoma Press, 1971), 90–92, 137–38, 273–76, 279, 281–82.

had captured them—retrieved the bodies. They were carried away, distributed, and eaten, in order to celebrate the feast. There were at least forty or fifty captives, depending upon the skill which the men had shown in seizing and capturing men in war. . . .

[M]any strove, in every possible way, to lift their names on high, to obtain glory, to procure greater honors, to found lineages and titles, and [to gain] good fame for their persons. There were three established and honored ways in all the nations [for obtaining these rewards]. The first and principal path which the kings designated was soldiery—to make oneself known in war through valiant feats, to be outstanding in killing, taking prisoners, to destroy armies and squadrons, to have directed these things. These [warriors] were given great honors, rewards, weapons, and insignia which were proof of their splendid deeds and valor. . . .

The second way in which men rose was through religion, entering the priesthood. After having served in the temples in a virtuous, penitential, and cloistered way of life, in their old age they were sent out to high and honorable posts. . . . They were present when the government councils were held, their opinions and advice were listened to, and they were part of the ruling boards and juntas. Without their council and opinion kings did not dare act. . . .

The third and least glorious manner of [rising in the world] was that of becoming a merchant or trader, that of buying and selling, going forth to all the markets of the land, bartering cloth for jewels, jewels for feathers, feathers for stones, and stones for slaves, always dealing in things of importance, of renown, and of high value. These [men] strengthened their social position with their wealth. . . . They acquired wealth and obtained slaves to sacrifice to this their god [Quetzalcoatl]. And so they were considered among the magnates of the land, just as the valorious soldier brought sacrificial captives from war, gaining fame as a brave. . . .

[I]n olden times there was a god of markets and fairs. . . .

The gods of these market places threatened terrible ills and made evil omens and auguries to the neighboring villages which did not attend their market places. . . .

The markets were so inviting, pleasurable, appealing, and gratifying to these people that great crowds attended, and still attend, them, especially during the big fairs, as is well known to all. . . .

The markets in this land were all enclosed by walls and stood either in front of the temples of the gods or to one side. Market day in each town was considered a main feast in that town or city. And thus in that small shrine where the idol of the market stood were offered ears of corn, chili, tomatoes, fruit, and other vegetables, seeds, and breads—in sum, everything sold in the *tianguiz*. . . .

Furthermore, a law was established by the republic prohibiting the selling of goods outside the market place. Not only were there laws and penalties connected with this, but there was a fear of the supernatural, of misfortune, and of the ire and wrath of the god of the market. No one ventured, therefore, to trade outside [the market limits]. . . .

There were many ways of becoming a slave within the law of the Indian nations. . . .

First, he who stole the number of pieces of cloth or ears of corn, jewels, or turkeys which the laws of the republic had determined and set a penalty for was himself sold for the same amount in order to satisfy the owner of the purloined goods. . . .

Second, another way in which a native could become a slave was that of the gambler who risked all his possessions on the dice or in any other game which the natives played. . . .

Third, if the father of a family had many sons and daughters and among them was one [who was] incorrigible, disobedient, shameless, dissolute, incapable of receiving counsel or advice, the law . . . permitted [the father] to sell him in the public market place as an example and lesson to bad sons and daughters. . . .

Fourth, one became a slave if he borrowed valuable things, such as cloth, jewels, featherwork, and did not return them on the appointed date. . . .

In times of famine a man and wife could agree to a way of satisfying their needs and rise from their wretched state. They could sell one another, and thus husband sold wife and wife sold husband, or they sold one of their children.

Document 13.2

Pedro de Cieza de Léon on the Incas

Like Duran, Pedro de Cieza de Léon (1520–1554), a Spanish chronicler of the Inca Empire, came to the Americas as a boy. But unlike Duran, he came alone at the age of thirteen, and he followed a very different career. For the next seventeen years Cieza took part as a soldier in a number of expeditions that established Spanish rule in various parts of South America. Along the way, he collected a great deal of information, especially about the Inca Empire, which he began to publish upon his return to Spain in 1550. Despite a very limited education, Cieza wrote a series of works that have become a major source for historians about the workings of the Inca Empire and about the Spanish conquest of that land. The selection that follows focuses on the techniques that the Inca used to govern their huge empire.

■ How would you describe Cieza's posture toward the Inca Empire? What in particular did he seem to appreciate about it?

■ Based on this account, what difficulties did the Inca rulers face in governing their large and diverse realm?

■ What policies or practices did the Inca authorities follow in seeking to integrate their empire? How do these compare with other empires that you have studied?

■ Some modern observers have described the Inca Empire as "totalitarian" or "socialist." Do such terms seem appropriate? How else might you describe the Inca state?

PEDRO DE CIEZA DE LÉON

Chronicles of the Incas

ca. 1550

The Incas had the seat of their empire in the city of Cuzco, where the laws were given and the captains set out to make war.... As soon as one of these large provinces was conquered, ten or twelve thousand of the men and their wives, or six thousand, or the number decided upon, were ordered to leave and remove themselves from it. These were transfered to another town or province of the same climate and nature as that which they left.... And they had another device to keep the natives from hating them, and this was that they never divested the natural chieftains of their power. If it so happened that one of them committed a crime or in some way deserved to be stripped of his power, it was vested in his sons or brothers, and all were ordered to obey them....

★ ★ ★

Source: *The Incas of Pedro de Cieza de Leon*, translated by Harriet de Onis (Norman: University of Oklahoma Press, 1959), 56–57, 158–60, 165–73, 177–78.

One of the things most to be envied these rulers is how well they knew to conquer such vast lands....

[T]hey entered many lands without war, and the soldiers who accompanied the Inca were ordered to do no damage or harm, robbery or violence. If there was a shortage of food in the province, he ordered supplies brought in from other regions so that those newly won to his service would not find his rule and acquaintance irksome....

In many others, where they entered by war and force of arms, they ordered that the crops and houses of the enemy be spared.... But in the end the Incas always came out victorious, and when they had vanquished the others, they did not do them further harm, but released those they had taken prisoner, if there were any, and restored the booty, and put them back in possession of their property and rule, exhorting them not to be foolish and try to compete with his royal majesty nor abandon his friendship, but to be his friends as their neighbors were. And saying this, he gave them a number of beautiful women and fine pieces of wool or gold....

They never deprived the native chieftains of their rule. They were all ordered to worship the sun as God, but they were not prohibited from observing their own religions and customs....

It is told for a fact of the rulers of this kingdom that in the days of their rule they had their representatives in the capitals of all the provinces.... They served as head of the provinces or regions, and from every so many leagues around the tributes were brought to one of these capitals, and from so many others, to another. This was so well organized that there was not a village that did not know where it was to send its tribute. In all these capitals the Incas had temples of the sun, mints, and many silversmiths who did nothing but work rich pieces of gold or fair vessels of silver.... The tribute paid by each of these districts where the capital was situated, and that turned over by the natives, whether gold, silver, clothing, arms, and all else they gave, was entered in the accounts of the [quipu-] camayocs, who kept the quipus and did everything ordered by the governor in the matter of finding the soldiers or supplying whomever the Inca ordered, or making delivery to Cuzco; but when they came from the city of Cuzco to go over the accounts, or they were ordered to go to Cuzco to give an accounting, the accountants themselves gave it by the quipus, or went to give it where there could be no fraud, but everything had to come out right. Few years went by in which an accounting of all these things was not made....

When the Incas set out to visit their kingdom, it is told that they traveled with great pomp, riding in rich litters set upon smooth, long poles of the finest wood and adorned with gold and silver....

So many people came to see his passing that all the hills and slopes seemed covered with them, and all called down blessings upon him....

He [the Inca] traveled four leagues each day, or as much as he wished; he stopped wherever he liked to inquire into the state of his kingdom; he willingly listened to those who came to him with complaints, righting wrongs and punishing those who had committed an injustice....

[T]hese rulers, as the best measure, ordered and decreed, with severe punishment for failure to obey, that all the natives of their empire should know and understand the language of Cuzco, both they and their women.... This was carried out so faithfully that in the space of a very few years a single tongue was known and used in an extension of more than 1,200 leagues; yet, even though this language was employed, they all spoke their own [languages], which were so numerous that if I were to list them it would not be credited....

[The Inca] appointed those whose duty it was to punish wrongdoers, and to this end they were always traveling about the country. The Incas took such care to see that justice was meted out that nobody ventured to commit a felony or theft. This was to deal with thieves, ravishers of women, or conspirators against the Inca; however, there were many provinces that warred on one another, and the Incas were not wholly able to prevent this.

By the river [Huatanay] that runs through Cuzco justice was executed on those who were caught or brought in as prisoners from some other place.

There they had their heads cut off, or were put to death in some other manner which they chose. Mutiny and conspiracy were severely punished, and, above all, those who were thieves and known as such; even their wives and chidren were despised and considered to be tarred with the same brush....

[I]n each of the many provinces there were many storehouses filled with supplies and other needful things; thus, in times of war, wherever the armies went they draw upon the contents of these store-houses, without ever touching the supplies of their confederates or laying a finger on what they had in their settlements. And when there was no war, all this stock of supplies and food was divided up among the poor and the widows. These poor were the aged, or the lame, crippled, or paralyzed, or those afflicted with some other diseases.... If there came a lean year, the storehouses were opened and the provinces were lent what they needed in the way of supplies; then, in a year of abundance, they paid back all they had received.

Using the Evidence:
The Aztecs and the Incas
through Spanish Eyes

1. **Assessing documents:** Both Duran and Cieza were outsiders to the societies they described, and they were part of the conquering Spanish forces. In what ways did these conditions affect their descriptions of the Aztec and Inca empires?

2. **Considering the subtext of documents:** In what ways might these authors have been using their observation of Aztec or Inca society to praise or to criticize their own European homeland?

3. **Evaluating the credibility of documents:** Which statements in these documents do you find most credible and which ones might you be inclined to question or challenge? What criteria might you use to assess the evidence in these documents?

4. **Relating primary documents and text narrative:** How might you use the information in these documents to support the descriptions of the Aztec and Inca empires that are contained in this chapter? Are there ways the documents might challenge statements in the text?

5. **Making comparisons:** What similarities and differences between Aztec and Inca societies can you glean from these documents?

6. **Seeking more data:** What additional primary sources about the Aztec and Inca empires of the fifteenth century would you like to have? What other perspectives on those states would be useful for historians?

Visual Sources

Considering the Evidence:
Sacred Places in the World
of the Fifteenth Century

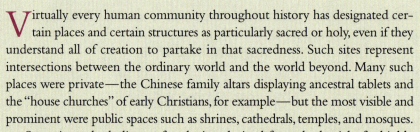

Virtually every human community throughout history has designated certain places and certain structures as particularly sacred or holy, even if they understand all of creation to partake in that sacredness. Such sites represent intersections between the ordinary world and the world beyond. Many such places were private—the Chinese family altars displaying ancestral tablets and the "house churches" of early Christians, for example—but the most visible and prominent were public spaces such as shrines, cathedrals, temples, and mosques.

Sometimes the holiness of such sites derived from the burial of a highly respected figure, such as the tomb of Abraham in Israel, sacred to Jews and Muslims alike, or Lenin's tomb in Moscow, virtually a shrine to faithful communists. Particular historical or religious events, such as the birth of Jesus or the enlightenment of the Buddha, have contributed to the sacred status of structures erected in those places. Formal rites of consecration, the presence of relics, and rituals of devotion such as the Muslim pilgrimage to Mecca add to the extraordinary character of particular buildings. So too did distinctive architectural styles as well as the sensory stimulus of bells, calls to prayer, and the burning of incense or candles.[20] Still other buildings acquired a sacred character because they were gathering places for prayer or worship.

Such sacred sites, however, did not function exclusively in the spiritual realm; they often operated as well in the more secular domains of commerce and politics. The New Testament records that Jesus angrily drove the money changers from the temple in Jerusalem, while Buddhist monasteries on the Silk Road and elsewhere often became wealthy centers of trade. Furthermore, sacred places played important political roles as rulers sought the blessing and support of religious leaders and the aura of legitimacy that derived from some association with the realm of the holy. State authorities and wealthy elites often patronized the construction of sacred buildings and contributed to their upkeep. Sacred sites have sometimes spawned violence as rivalries erupted among competing sects or between political and religious authorities.

The four sacred sites shown in this section might well have been on the itinerary of an imaginary global traveler in the fifteenth century. Together they illustrate something of the diversity of such places in terms of their physical setting and architectural styles, the sources of their sacredness, their intended function, and their relationship to those who exercised political power. Yet they also bore similarities to one another. All of them were deliberately set apart from the profane or ordinary world, were linked to a wider sacred geography, and were commissioned and funded by a ruler.

Perhaps not surprisingly, the largest sacred site in the world of the fifteenth century lay in China. Known as the Temple of Heaven, it was constructed during the early fifteenth century in the Ming dynasty capital of Beijing by the ambitious emperor Yongle (reigned 1402–1424), who likewise ordered the building of the magnificent imperial residence of the Forbidden City. (He also sent Zheng He on his immense maritime voyages in the Indian Ocean; see pp. 577–78.)

Set in a forest of more than 650 acres, the Temple of Heaven was, in Chinese thinking, the primary place where Heaven and earth met. From his residence in the Forbidden City, the Chinese emperor led a procession of thousands twice a year to this sacred site, where he offered sacrifices, implored the gods for a good harvest, and performed those rituals that maintained the cosmic balance. These sacred ceremonies, from which commoners were barred even from watching, demonstrated the emperor's respect for the age-old source of his imperial authority, the Mandate of Heaven, from which Chinese emperors derived their legitimate right to rule. As the emperor bowed to Heaven, he was modeling in good Confucian fashion the respect required of all subordinates to their social superiors and especially to the emperor himself.

The temple complex was laced with ancient symbolism. The southern part of the wall that enclosed the complex was square, symbolizing the earth, while the northern wall was rounded or semicircular, suggesting Heaven in Daoist thinking. Major buildings were likewise built in the round while being situated within a square enclosure, also symbolizing the intersection of Heaven and earth. The most prominent building was the Hall of Prayer for Good Harvest (Visual Source 13.1), constructed by 1420. There the emperor prayed and conducted rituals to ensure a successful agricultural season on which the country's well-being and his own legitimacy depended. The emperor and others approached the hall from the south on a gradually ascending 360-meter walkway symbolizing progression from earth to Heaven. The walkway divides into three parallel paths: the center one for the gods; the left for the emperor; and the right for the empress and court officials. Originally the three roofs of the structure were of different colors: the top was blue, suggesting Heaven; the middle was yellow, the color of the emperor; and the lowest was green, indicating commoners or the earth. Later all three roofs were painted blue.

■ Which symbolic features can you identify in Visual Source 13.1?

■ What did the original color scheme of the roofs suggest?

■ What was the role of the emperor within the Temple of Heaven and in the larger religious or cosmological framework of Chinese thinking?

■ What impressions or understandings might those who observed the ceremonies or learned about them take away from that experience?

About the same time as the Temple of Heaven was taking shape in China, another sacred site was under construction in Kyoto, Japan: a Buddhist temple known as Kinkakuji, or the "Temple of the Golden Pavilion" (Visual Source 13.2). Like the Chinese structure, Kinkakuji was a project of the Japanese ruler of the time, the *shogun* (military leader) Yoshimitsu Ashikaga (1358–1408), rather than the emperor. Unlike his Chinese counterpart, the Japanese emperor functioned more as a symbol of Japan's historical tradition rather than its effective ruler. Initially, Kinkakuji was constructed as part of a villa to which Yoshimitsu retired when he gave up his formal political role in 1394 to devote himself to Buddhist practice and the arts. After his death it was converted into a Zen Buddhist temple, as he had wished.

The building itself reflects the strong influence of Chinese culture on Japan. Yoshimitsu, well known as a lover of all things Chinese, modeled Kinkakuji on the lakeside villas of earlier Chinese emperors and collected in the Golden Pavilion thousands of Chinese paintings. He also accepted the title "King of Japan" from a Ming dynasty emperor and reopened trade relations with China.

As a Buddhist temple, Kinkakuji is situated in a garden setting at the edge of a "mirror lake," suggesting, some have said, a position between heaven and earth. The lake contained a series of rocks and small islands representing the eight oceans and nine mountains of the Buddhist creation story. Inside were statues of the Amida Buddha, the benevolent bodhisattva of compassion known as Kannon, and dozens of other sacred figures. It also became known as one of the few Buddhist temples housing relics of the historical Buddha himself.

While Buddhism has a reputation as a religion of peace and tranquillity, in Japan from the tenth century on, various Buddhist sects organized private armies, fought among themselves, and contested both imperial and samurai authorities. Kinkakuji itself was burned several times in the fifteenth century amid the wars that racked Japan and left Kyoto in ruins.

■ How might you compare the purposes that Kinkakuji served with those of the Temple of Heaven?

Visual Source 13.2 Kinkakuji: A Buddhist Temple in Japan (© Craig Lovell/Corbis)

- What elements of Kinkakuji and its surroundings contribute to its sacredness?

- What emotions do you think Kinkakuji was intended to evoke?

- In what ways did Kinkakuji have a political as well as a religious significance?

In the Islamic world of the fifteenth century, the structure known as the Dome of the Rock in Jerusalem (Visual Source 13.3) was second only to Mecca as a pilgrimage site for Muslims. When expanding Muslim forces took control of Jerusalem in 638 and subsequently constructed the Dome of the Rock (687–691), that precise location had long been regarded as sacred. To Jews, it contained the rock on which Abraham prepared to offer his son Isaac as a sacrifice to God, and it was the site of the first two Jewish temples. To Christians, it was a place that Jesus had visited as a youngster to converse with learned teachers and later to drive out the moneychangers.

Thus, when the Umayyad caliph (successor to the prophet) Abd al-Malik ordered the construction of the Dome of the Rock on that site, he was appropriating for Islam both Jewish and Christian legacies. But he was also demonstrating the victorious arrival of a new faith and announcing to Christians that "the Islamic state was here to stay."[21] The architecture and decoration of the Dome of the Rock drew heavily on Roman, Byzantine, and Persian precedents as if to show that "'unbelievers' had been defeated and brought into the fold of the true faith."[22] The domed rotunda had long been used in the Christian Byzantine Empire to denote holy sites, often the burial place of a martyr, saint, or prophet. The Muslim structure, designed and built by Christian architects and artisans, closely resembled the nearby Church of the Holy Sepulcher. Interior decorations featured crowns, jewels, breastplates, and flowers of Persian origins.

Nonetheless, the Dome of the Rock was distinctly Islamic, as its many mosaics lacked any representations of animals or humans, while multiple inscriptions from the Quran emphasized Islamic monotheism, presenting Jesus as an honored prophet but not as the divine son of God. Furthermore, the Dome of the Rock was soon thought to cover the stone from which Muhammad had made his famous Night Journey into the presence of God as suggested

Visual Source 13.3 The Dome of the Rock, Jerusalem (© Aaron Horowitz/Corbis)

in the Quran and embellished in popular mythology. Some claimed to see an indentation in that stone, which lies uncovered in the center of the dome, as the footprint of the prophet himself.

Over many centuries, and even to the present, the Dome of the Rock has been an enormously contested site. When Christian crusaders seized Jerusalem in 1099, they did not destroy the Muslim shrine but converted it into a Christian sacred place—the Temple of the Lord—and erected a huge golden cross on its dome. Likewise, when Muslim forces retook Jerusalem in 1187, they removed that cross, replaced it with a Muslim crescent, and then cleansed the Dome of the Rock three times with rose water. In the fifteenth century, the Dome was under the control and protection of a Turkic dynasty, known as Mamluks, based in Egypt. In 1517 it fell within the domains of the Ottoman Empire.

■ The Dome of the Rock was never intended as a mosque for regular worship but rather as a pilgrimage site. How might you imagine the reaction of a Muslim pilgrim encountering it for the first time during the fifteenth century? How would that pilgrim's place of origin (Arabia, Africa, India, or Europe, for example) have made a difference in how he or she responded to it?

■ What contributed to the sacred character of the Dome of the Rock?

■ How might you compare the intended purpose of the Dome of the Rock to that of the Temple of Heaven in China?

■ You might do a little research on the current disputes about the Dome of the Rock. What role does it play in the contemporary Israeli/Palestinian conflict?

In seeking sacred sites within the Christian world of the fifteenth century, our imaginary global traveler would have had a wide range of choices. He or she might well have visited one of the many Renaissance cathedrals of Italy or chosen from among the dozens of impressive Christian churches scattered across Europe. The newly reconstructed Kremlin in Moscow might also have been of interest, for in that fortified enclosure lay an elaborate palace for Grand Prince Ivan III as well as a number of churches, demonstrating the close relationship of religious and political authority in the emerging Russian state. But in the highlands of Ethiopia, amid some of the most remarkable Christian architecture of the time, the rock churches of Lalibela provide a useful reminder that the Christian world of the fifteenth century was not limited to Europe.

With its origins in the ancient civilization of Axum well before the birth of Christ, Ethiopia by the fifteenth century had hosted a Christian culture for more than a thousand years. By then, the center of that civilization had moved southward to the region later known as Lalibela. There, in the twelfth

Visual Source 13.4 The Church of St. George, Lalibela, Ethiopia (Heltler/Robert Harding World Imagery/Corbis)

century, a local prince had seized the throne and initiated the Zagwe dynasty. Zagwe rulers, in particular King Lalibela (ruled early thirteenth century), for whom the region was subsequently named, sponsored the creation of eleven remarkable underground churches, carved from the soft volcanic rock of the region. This enormous and sacred project served to legitimate the rule of these upstart Zagwe monarchs over this ancient Christian kingdom and provided an alternative to the older political and religious center of Ethiopian civilization in Axum to the north.

A further motivation for the construction of these churches lay perhaps in Ethiopia's long relationship with Jerusalem. Ancient stories linked its monarchy to the union of King Solomon and the Queen of Sheba, said to be an Ethiopian monarch. Local legends held that King Lalibela had been mysteriously transported to Jerusalem, where he received divine instructions about building the churches. Certainly, Ethiopian Christians had long made pilgrimages to the Holy City. When Muslim forces reconquered Jerusalem from the Christian crusaders in 1187, Ethiopia's Zagwe monarchs apparently determined to create a New Jerusalem in their kingdom. The churches of Lalibela, many of them named for famous sites in Jerusalem, were the outcome of that project.

Thus, while the Dome of the Rock physically occupied an already sacred site in Jerusalem, the rock churches of Lalibela sought to symbolically re-create the Holy City in the highlands of Ethiopia. They have been both a monastic site and a pilgrimage destination ever since.

These belowground churches represent an enormously impressive architectural achievement, said by local people to have been assisted by angels. But well before the coming of Christianity, the local Agaw-speaking people had long incorporated rock shrines into their religious practice. And the architecture of the churches shows a clear connection to earlier Axumite styles.

While this sacred site clearly had indigenous roots, these churches were certainly distinctive as Christian structures. Unlike almost all other religious architecture—Christian or otherwise—they were virtually invisible from a distance, becoming apparent only when the observer was looking down on them from ground level. In fact these eleven churches were not really constructed at all, but rather excavated, using only hammers and chisels. Underground, they were connected to one another by a series of "hidden tunnels, dark twisting passages, and secret chambers," while the whole complex abounded with "columns and arches, shafts and galleries, courts and terraces."[23] The first European observer to see them, the Portuguese priest Francisco Alvarez in the 1520s, was stunned. "I weary of writing more about these buildings," he declared, "because it seems to me that I shall not be believed if I write more."[24] Visual Source 13.4 shows one of these structures, the Church of St. George, the patron saint of Ethiopia.

- How might our imaginary traveler, a pilgrim who had toured the grand Christian cathedrals of Europe, have responded to these Ethiopian churches? How might he or she understand their belowground construction? What might strike such a traveler as distinctive about Lalibela as a sacred site in comparison to the others presented here?

- What do these churches disclose about the outlook of the Zagwe monarchs who ordered their creation?

- What might you infer about the labor and social organization required to create these churches?

Using the Evidence:
Sacred Places in the World of the Fifteenth Century

1. **Comparing experiences of the sacred:** What do these visual sources and the documents for this chapter (see pp. 601–07) suggest about the experience of the sacred? What common features and what differences

characterize that experience? In particular, how might our global traveler have responded to sacred places among the Aztecs after visiting the various sites shown here?

2. **Considering the construction of the sacred:** What historical circumstances and what motivations contributed to the creation of each site? What factors rendered them holy in the eyes of believers? What evidence of cultural borrowing can you see in these sites?

3. **Defining purpose:** How would you compare the purposes for which each of these sacred places was intended?

4. **Thinking about religion and politics:** In what ways were these sacred sites embedded in the political circumstances of their societies? How might people of the fifteenth century have understood the connection between the religious and the political as evidenced in these images? To what extent did those understandings differ from more modern views?

Notes

Prologue

1. Adapted from Carl Sagan, *The Dragons of Eden* (New York: Random House, 1977), 13–17.
2. See David Christian, *Maps of Time* (Berkeley: University of California Press, 2004).
3. Voltaire, *Treatise on Toleration*, chap. 22.
4. See David Christian, "World History in Context," *Journal of World History* 14, no. 4 (December 2003), 437–58.

Part One

Chapter 1

1. Richard Rainsford, "What Chance, the Survival Prospects of East Africa's Last Hunting and Gathering Tribe," 1997, http://www.ntz.info/gen/n00757.html.
2. What follows comes from Sally McBreatry and Alison S. Brooks, "The Revolution That Wasn't: A New Interpretation of the Origin of Modern Human Behavior," *Journal of Human Evolution* 39 (2000): 453–563.
3. Peter Bogucki, *The Origins of Human Society* (Oxford: Blackwell, 1999), 94–95.
4. Paul G. Bahn and Jean Vertut, *Images of the Ice Age* (New York: Facts on File, 1988), chap. 7.
5. John Mulvaney and Johan Kaminga, *Prehistory of Australia* (Washington, D.C.: Smithsonian Institution Press, 1999), 93–102.
6. For a recent summary of this debate, see Charles C. Mann, *1491: New Revelations of the Americas before Columbus* (New York: Alfred Knopf, 2005), chap. 5.
7. Brian M. Fagan, *Ancient North America* (London: Thames and Hudson, 1995), 77–87.
8. Ben Finney, "The Other One-Third of the Globe," *Journal of World History* 5, no. 2 (Fall 1994): 273–85.
9. David Christian, *Maps of Time* (Berkeley: University of California Press, 2004), 143.
10. Richard B. Lee, *The Dobe Ju/'hoansi* (New York: Harcourt Brace, 1993), 58.
11. J. C. Beaglehole, *The Journals of Captain James Cook* (Cambridge: Hakluyt Society, 1968), 1:399.
12. Inga Clendinnen, *Dancing with Strangers* (Cambridge: Cambridge University Press, 2005), 159–67.
13. Marshall Sahlins, *Stone Age Economics* (London: Tavistock, 1972), 1–39.
14. Christopher Ehret, *The Civilizations of Africa* (Charlottesville: University of Virginia Press, 2002), chap. 2.
15. Marija Gimbutas, *The Language of the Goddess* (San Francisco: HarperCollins, 1989), 316–18.
16. Derived from Christian, *Maps of Time*, 208.
17. D. Bruce Dickson, *The Dawn of Belief* (Tucson: University of Arizona Press, 1990), 210.
18. Brian Fagan, *People of the Earth* (New York: HarperCollins, 1992), 200–201.
19. Jan Platvoet, "At War with God: Ju/'hoan Curing Dances," *Journal of Religion in Africa* 29, no. 1 (1999): 5.
20. J. David Lewis-Williams, *Believing and Seeing: Symbolic Meaning in Southern San Rock Paintings* (London: Academic Press, 1981).
21. Lee, *The Dobe Ju/'hoansi*. Unless otherwise noted, all information and quotes about the Ju/'hoansi come from this book.
22. Elizabeth Marshall Thomas, *The Harmless People* (New York: Vintage Books, 1989), 180.
23. For a contemporary account of a curing dance, see Bradford Keeney, "Ropes to God: Experiencing the Bushman Spiritual Universe," *Parabola* 27, no. 3 (2002): S1–S16.
24. Platvoet, "At War with God."
25. Brian Fagan, *Before California* (New York: Rowman and Littlefield, 2003), 153–55, 341–44.
26. Jeanne E. Arnold, *The Origins of a Pacific Coast Chiefdom* (Salt Lake City: University of Utah Press, 2001), 14.
27. Chester King, "Chumash Inter-Village Economic Exchange," in *Native Californians*, edited by Lowell John Bean and Thomas C. Blackburn (Menlo Park: Ballena Press, 1976), 289–318. The quote is on p. 297.
28. http://www.lonker.net/art_aboriginal_1.htm (accessed April 1, 2009).
29. Elaine Godden and Jutta Malnic, *Rock Paintings of Aboriginal Australia* (London: New Holland Publishers, 2001), preface.

Chapter 2

1. "Population 1: The Town That's Been Reclaimed by the Prairie," *International Observer*, November 20, 2005, http://observer.guardian.co.uk/international/story/0,6903,1646659,00.html?gusrc=rss.
2. Peter Bellwood, *First Farmers* (London: Blackwood, 2005), 7.

3. Mark Nathan Cohen, *The Food Crisis in Prehistory* (New Haven: Yale University Press, 1977).

4. Bruce Smith, *The Emergence of Agriculture* (New York: Scientific American Library, 1995), 206–14.

5. Jared Diamond, *Guns, Germs, and Steel* (New York: Vintage, 1997), 132, 157–75.

6. Bellwood, *First Farmers*, 54–55.

7. Steven Mithen, *After the Ice: A Global Human History, 20,000–50,000 B.C.* (Cambridge, Mass.: Harvard University Press, 2004), 87.

8. Neil Roberts, *The Holocene: An Environmental History* (Oxford: Blackwell, 1998), 116.

9. Nina V. Federoff, "Prehistoric GM Corn," *Science* 302 (November 2003): 1158.

10. Diamond, *Gun, Germs, and Steel*, 367.

11. The most recent summary of an immense literature on the spread of languages is found in Bellwood, *First Farmers*.

12. Many of these dates are much debated. See John Staller et al., *Histories of Maize* (Boston: Academic Press, 2006).

13. John A. Mears, "Agricultural Origins in Global Perspective," in *Agricultural and Pastoral Societies in Ancient and Classical History*, edited by Michael Adas (Philadelphia: Temple University Press, 2001), 63–64.

14. Elizabeth Wayland Barber, *Women's Work: The First 20,000 Years* (New York: W. W. Norton, 1994), chap. 3.

15. Andrew Sherrat, "The Secondary Exploitation of Animals in the Old World," *World Archeology* 15, no. 1 (June 1983): 90–104.

16. Clive Ponting, *A Green History of the World* (New York: St. Martin's Press, 1991), 69.

17. Anatoly M. Khazanov, *Nomads and the Outside World* (Madison: University of Wisconsin Press, 1994), 15.

18. Ian Hodder, "Women and Men at Catalhoyuk," *Scientific American* 15, no. 1 (2005): 35–41.

19. Allen W. Johnson and Timothy Earle, *The Evolution of Human Societies* (Stanford, Calif.: Stanford University Press, 2000), 281–94.

20. Ian Hodder, "Discussions with the Goddess Community," Catalhöyük: Excavations of a Neolithic Anatolian Höyük, http://www.catalhoyuk.com/library/goddess.html (accessed April 1, 2009).

21. Ian Hodder, "A Journey to 9,000 Years Ago," January 17, 2008, http://sci.tech-archive.net/Archive/sci.archaeology/2008-01/msg00519.html (accessed April 1, 2009).

22. http://www.reuters.com/article/scienceNews/idUSLM62397220080922 (accessed April 15, 2009).

23. Reuters, "Stonehenge May Have Been Pilgrimage Site for Sick," September 22, 2008, http://uk.reuters.com/article/scienceNews/idUKTRE48M0R320080923 (accessed April 15, 2009).

Chapter 3

1. Utah Outventures, http://www.utahoutventures.com/multiactivity/raftoffroadtours.htm (accessed April 1, 2009).

2. Charles C. Mann, 1491: *New Revelations of the Americas before Columbus* (New York: Alfred A. Knopf, 2005), 174–91; Proyecto Arqueológico Norte Chico, Project Description, 2005, http://www.fieldmuseum.org/research_collections/anthropology/anthro_sites/PANC/proj_desc.htm.

3. Jonathan Mark Kenoyer, *Ancient Cities of the Indus Valley Civilization* (Oxford: Oxford University Press, 1998), 83–84.

4. For a summary of many theories, see Stephen K. Sanderson, *Social Transformations* (Oxford: Blackwell, 1995), chap. 3.

5. Robert Carneiro, "A Theory of the Origin of the State," *Science* 169 (1970): 733–38.

6. Susan Pollock, *Ancient Mesopotamia* (Cambridge: Cambridge University Press, 1999), 48.

7. *The Epic of Gilgamesh*, translated and edited by Benjamin R. Foster (New York: W. W. Norton, 2001), 10, Tablet 1:226–32.

8. Samuel Noah Kramer, *History Begins at Sumer* (Philadelphia: University of Pennsylvania Press, 1981), 3–4.

9. James Legge, trans., *The Chinese Classics* (London: Henry Frowde, 1893), 4:171–72.

10. Marija Gimbutas, *The Living Goddess* (Berkeley: University of California Press, 1999).

11. Margaret Ehrenberg, *Women in Prehistory* (London: British Museum Publications, 1989), 107.

12. David Christian, *Maps of Time* (Berkeley: University of California Press, 2004), 256–57, 263–64.

13. Sherry Ortner, "Is Female to Male as Nature Is to Culture?" in *Women, Culture, and Society*, edited by Michelle Rosaldo and Louise Lamphere (Stanford, Calif.: Stanford University Press, 1974), 67–88.

14. Gerda Lerner, *The Creation of Patriarchy* (New York: Oxford University Press, 1986), 70.

15. Miriam Lichtheim, *Ancient Egyptian Literature* (Berkeley: University of California Press, 1975), 2:184–85.

16. Ibid., 2:168–75.

17. Prologue to *The Code of Hammurabi*, http://www.wsu.edu/~dee/MESO/CODE.HTM.

18. Gary Urton, "From Knots to Narratives: Reconstructing the Art of Historical Record-Keeping in the Andes from Spanish Transcriptions of Inka Khipus," *Ethnohistory* 45, no. 3 (1998): 409–38.

19. Adolf Erman, *The Literature of the Ancient Egyptians*, translated by Aylward M. Blackman (London: Methuen, 1927), 136–37.

20. Henri Frankfort, H. A. Frankfort, John A. Wilson, and Thorkild Jacobsen *Before Philosophy: The Intellectual Adventure of Ancient Man* (Baltimore: Penguin Books, 1963), 39, 138.

21. Quoted in Peter Stearns et al., *World Civilizations* (New York: Longman, 1996), 1:30.

22. See Clive Ponting, *A Green History of the World* (New York: St. Martin's Press, 1991), chap. 5.

23. Samuel Kramer, *The Sumerians* (Chicago: University of Chicago Press, 1963), 142.

24. Cyril Aldred, *The Egyptians* (London: Thames and Hudson, 1998), 138.

25. For a recent summary of a long debate about the relationship of Egypt and Africa, see David O'Connor and Andrew Reid, eds., *Ancient Egypt in Africa* (London: UCL Press, 2003).

26. James B. Pritchard, ed., *Ancient Near Eastern Texts Relating to the Old Testament* (Princeton: Princeton University Press, 1969), 647–48.

27. Lichtheim, *Ancient Egyptian Literature*, 1:25–27.

28. Joan Oates, *Babylon* (London: Thames and Hudson, 1986), 91.

29. Marvin Harris, ed., *Cannibals and Kings* (New York: Vintage, 1978), 102.

30. Lichtheim, *Ancient Egyptian Literature*, 2:177.

31. Jonathan M. Kenoyer, *Ancient Cities of the Indus Valley Civilization* (Karachi: Oxford University Press, 1998), 84.

32. Ibid., 100.

33. Gregory L. Possehl, *The Indus Civilization: A Contemporary Perspective* (Walnut Creek, Calif.: AltaMira Press, 2002), 114.

Part Two

1. Stephen K. Sanderson, *Social Transformation* (Oxford: Blackwell, 1995), chap. 4.

2. From ibid., 103.

3. Colin Ronan and Joseph Needham, *The Shorter Science and Civilization in China* (Cambridge: Cambridge University Press, 1978), 58.

4. Sidney W. Mintz, *Sweetness and Power* (New York: Penguin Books, 1985), chap. 2.

5. William H. McNeill, *Plagues and Peoples* (New York: Doubleday, 1977), 94.

6. See world population estimates by region in Paul Adams et al., *Experiencing World History* (New York: New York University Press, 2000), 334.

Chapter 4

1. Cullen Murphy, *Are We Rome? The Fall of an Empire and the Fate of America* (Boston: Houghton Mifflin, 2007).

2. J. M. Cook, *The Persian Empire* (London: J. M. Dent & Sons, 1983), 76.

3. George Rawlinson, trans., *The Histories of Herodotus* (London: Dent, 1910), 1:131–40.

4. Erich F. Schmidt, *Persepolis I: Structures, Reliefs, Inscriptions*, OIP 68 (Chicago: University of Chicago Press, 1953), 63.

5. Quoted in Thomas R. Martin, *Ancient Greece from Prehistoric to Hellenistic Times* (New Haven: Yale University Press, 1996), 86.

6. Christian Meier, *Athens* (New York: Metropolitan Books, 1993), 93.

7. Arrian, *The Campaigns of Alexander*, translated by Aubrey de Selincourt, revised by J. R. Hamilton (London: Penguin, 1971), 395–96.

8. Stanley Burstein, *The Hellenistic Period in World History* (Washington, D.C.: American Historical Association, 1996), 12.

9. Norman F. Cantor, *Antiquity* (New York: HarperCollins, 2003), 25.

10. Greg Woolf, "Inventing Empire in Ancient Rome," in *Empires: Perspectives from Archeology and History*, edited by Susan Alcock et al. (Cambridge: Cambridge University Press, 2001), 314.

11. S. A. M. Adshead, *China in World History* (London: McMillan Press, 1988), 4–21.

12. See Padma Manian, "Harappans and Aryans: Old and New Perspectives on Ancient Indian History," *The History Teacher* 32, no. 1 (November 1998): 17–32.

13. Roger Boesche, *The First Great Political Realist: Kautilya and His Arthashastra* (Lanham, Md.: Lexington Books, 2002), 17.

14. Stanley Wolpert, *A New History of India* (New York: Oxford University Press, 1993), chap. 5.

15. Zhengyuan Fu, *Autocratic Tradition and Chinese Politics* (New York: Cambridge University Press, 1993), 188.

16. Jane Portal, ed., *The First Emperor: China's Terracotta Army* (London: The British Museum Press, 2007), 110.

17. Quoted in Anders Blixt, "Qin Shi Huang Di, 'The Tiger Emperor': The First Emperor of China," http://biphome.spray.se/coif/history/qin/shie09.html (accessed Feb. 1, 2009).

18. Portal, *First Emperor*, 21.

Chapter 5

1. S. N. Eisenstadt, ed., *The Origins and Diversity of Axial Age Civilizations* (Albany: SUNY Press, 1986), 1–4; Karen Armstrong, *The Great Transformation* (New York: Alfred A. Knopf, 2006).

2. Quoted in Arthur Waley, *Three Ways of Thought in Ancient China* (Garden City, N.Y.: Doubleday, 1956), 159–60.

3. Nancy Lee Swann, trans., *Pan Chao: Foremost Woman Scholar of China* (New York: Century, 1932), 111–14.

4. Quoted in Huston Smith, *The Illustrated World's Religions* (San Francisco: HarperCollins, 1994), 123.

5. Lao Tsu, *Tao Te Ching*, translated by Gia-Fu Feng and Jane English (New York: Vintage Books, 1972), 80.

6. George Bühler, trans., *The Laws of Manu*, 5:148, http://www.sacred-texts.com/hin/manu/manu05.htm (accessed Feb. 1, 2009).

7. Quoted in Karen Andrews, "Women in Theravada Buddhism," http://www.enabling.org/ia/vipassana/ Archive/A/Andrews/womenTheraBudAndrews.html (accessed Feb. 1, 2009).

8. A. L. Basham, *The Wonder That Was India* (London: Sidgwick and Jackson, 1967), 309.

9. S. A. Nigosian, *The Zoroastrian Faith: Tradition and Modern Research* (Montreal: McGill–Queen's University Press, 1993), 95–97.

10. Isaiah 1:11–17.

11. Plato, *Apologia*.

12. Hippocrates, *On the Sacred Disease*, http://classics.mit.edu/ Hippocrates/sacred.html.

13. Thanissaro Bhikkhu, trans., "Karaniya Metta Sutta, 2004," http://www.accesstoinsight.org/tipitaka/kn/snp/snp.1.08 .than.html (accessed Feb. 1, 2009).

14. Matthew 5:43–44.

15. See Marcus Borg, ed., *Jesus and Buddha: The Parallel Sayings* (Berkeley, Calif.: Ulysses Press, 1997).

16. For a popular summary of the voluminous scholarship on Jesus, see Stephen Patterson et al., *The Search for Jesus: Modern Scholarship Looks at the Gospels* (Washington, D.C.: Biblical Archeological Society, 1994).

17. Galatians 3:28.

18. Ephesians 5:22; 1 Corinthians 14:35.

19. Ekkehard W. Stegemann and Wolfgang Stegemann, *The Jesus Movement: A History of Its First Century* (Minneapolis: Fortress Press, 1999), 291–96.

20. Ramsay MacMullen, *Christianizing the Roman Empire* (New Haven: Yale University Press, 1984), chap. 4.

21. Peter Brown, *The Rise of Western Christendom* (London: Blackwell, 2003), 69–71.

22. Mary Ann Rossi, "Priesthood, Precedent, and Prejudice: On Recovering the Women Priests of Early Christianity," *Journal of Feminist Studies* 7, no. 1 (1991): 73–94.

23. Chai-Shin Yu, *Early Buddhism and Christianity* (Delhi: Motilal Banarsidass, 1981), 211.

24. "Footprints of the Buddha," http://www.sacred-texts.com/ shi/igj/igj09.htm.

Chapter 6

1. Po Chu-I, "After Passing the Examination," in Arthur Waley, *More Translations from the Chinese* (New York: Alfred A. Knopf, 1919), 37.

2. Quoted in Michael Lowe, *Everyday Life in Early Imperial China* (New York: Dorset, 1968), 38.

3. Selected Poems from Tang Dynasty: http://shixuewang.com/ xlib/lingshidao/hanshi/tang1.htm.

4. A. L. Basham, *The Wonder That Was India* (London: Sidgwick and Jackson, 1967), 138.

5. Karl Jacoby, "Slaves by Nature: Animals and Human Slaves," *Slavery and Abolition* 15 (1994): 89–97.

6. Orlando Patterson, *Slavery and Social Death* (Cambridge, Mass.: Harvard University Press, 1982).

7. Basham, *The Wonder That Was India*, 152.

8. Sarah Pomeroy et al., *Ancient Greece* (New York: Oxford University Press, 1999), 63, 239.

9. R. Zelnick-Abramovitz, *Not Wholly Free* (Leiden: Brill, 2005), 337, 343.

10. Keith Bradley, *Slavery and Society at Rome* (Cambridge: Cambridge University Press, 1994), 30.

11. 1 Peter 2:18.

12. Milton Meltzer, *Slavery: A World History* (New York: Da Capo Press, 1993), 189.

13. Quoted in Bret Hinsch, *Women in Early Imperial China* (Oxford: Rowman and Littlefield, 2002), 155.

14. Nancy Lee Swann, trans., *Pan Chao: Foremost Woman Scholar of China* (New York: Century, 1932), 111–14.

15. Lisa Raphals, *Sharing the Light: Representations of Women and Virtue in Early China* (Albany: SUNY Press, 1998).

16. Valerie Hansen, *The Open Empire* (New York: Norton, 2000), 183–84; Thomas Barfield, *The Perilous Frontier* (Cambridge: Blackwell, 1989), 140.

17. Vivian-Lee Nyitray, "Confucian Complexities," in *A Companion to Gender History* edited by Teresa A. Meade and Merry E. Weisner-Hanks (Oxford: Blackwell, 2004), 278.

18. Aristotle, *Politica*, ed. Loeb Classical Library, 1254b10–14.

19. Quoted in Pomeroy et al., *Ancient Greece*, 146.

20. "The Destruction of Pompeii, 79 AD," EyeWitness to History, www.eyewitnesstohistory.com/pompeii.htm (accessed April 1, 2009).

21. August Mau, *Pompeii: Its Life and Art* (New Rochelle: Caratzas Brothers, 1982), 16.

22. "Graffiti from Pompeii," http://www.pompeiana.org/ Resources/Ancient/Graffiti%20from%20Pompeii.htm (accessed April 1, 2009).

Chapter 7

1. Rethinking Schools *Online*, Fall 1999, http://www.rethinkingschools.org/archive/14_01/ poor141.shtml.

2. Thomas Benjamin, "A Time of Reconquest: History, the Maya Revival, and the Zapatista Rebellion in Chiapas," *American Historical Review* 105, no. 2 (April 2000): 417.

3. Population figures are taken from Paul Adams et al., *Experiencing World History* (New York: New York University Press, 2000), 334.

4. Roderick J. McIntosh, *Ancient Middle Niger* (Cambridge: Cambridge University Press, 2005), 10.

5. Roderick J. McIntosh, *The Peoples of the Middle Niger* (Oxford: Blackwell, 1998), 177.

6. Kairn A. Klieman, *"The Pygmies Were Our Compass": Bantu and Batwa in the History of West Central Africa, Early Times to c. 1900 C.E.* (Portsmouth, N.H.: Heinemann, 2003), chaps. 4, 5.

7. Christopher Ehret, *The Civilizations of Africa* (Charlottesville: University of Virginia Press, 2002), 175.

8. See Jan Vansina, *Paths in the Rainforest* (Madison: University of Wisconsin Press, 1990), 95–99.

9. Richard E. W. Adams, *Prehistoric Mesoamerica* (Norman: University of Oklahoma Press, 2005), 16.

10. Richard E. W. Adams, *Ancient Civilizations of the New World* (Boulder, Colo.: Westview Press, 1997), 53–56; T. Patrick Culbert, "The New Maya," Archeology 51, no. 5 (September–October 1998): 47–51.

11. William Haviland, "State and Power in Classic Maya Society," *American Anthropologist* 94, no. 4 (1992):937.

12. Jared Diamond, *Collapse: How Societies Choose to Fail or Succeed* (New York: Viking, 2005), chap. 5.

13. Esther Pasztory, *Teotihuacan: An Experiment in Living* (Norman: University of Oklahoma Press, 1997), 193.

14. George L. Cowgill, "The Central Mexican Highlands . . . ," in *The Cambridge History of the Native Peoples of the Americas*, vol. 2, part 1, Mesoamerica, edited by Richard E. W. Adams and Murdo J. MacLeod (Cambridge: Cambridge University Press, 2000), 289.

15. Karen Olsen Bruhns, *Ancient South America* (Cambridge: Cambridge University Press, 1994), 126–41; Sylvia R. Kembel and John W. Rick, "Building Authority at Chavín de Huántar," in *Andean Archeology*, edited by Helaine Silverman (Oxford: Blackwell, 2004), 59–76.

16. Garth Bawden, *The Moche* (Oxford: Blackwell, 1996), chaps. 9, 10.

17. John E. Kicza, *The Peoples and Civilizations of the Americas before Contact* (Washington, D.C.: American Historical Association, 1998), 43–44.

18. Much of this section draws on Brian M. Fagan, *Ancient North America* (London: Thames and Hudson, 2005), chaps. 14, 15. The quote is on p. 345.

19. George R. Milner, *The Moundbuilders: Ancient Peoples of Eastern North America* (London: Thames and Hudson, 2004).

20. David Hurst Thomas, *Exploring Ancient Native America* (New York: Routledge, 1999), 137–42.

21. Stephen H. Lekson and Peter N. Peregrine, "A Continental Perspective for North American Archeology," *The SAA Archeological Record* 4, no. 1 (January 2004): 15–19.

22. Fagan, *Ancient North America*, 475.

23. Quoted in Lynda Norene Shaffer, *Native Americans before 1492* (Armonk, N.Y.: M. E. Sharpe, 1992), 70.

24. See Stanley Burstein, *Ancient African Civilizations: Kush and Axum* (Princeton: Markus Weiner Publishers, 1998), 14–20. I am grateful to Professor Burstein and this book for references to many of the documents in this section.

25. Mary Ellen Miller, *Maya Art and Architecture* (London: Thames & Hudson, 1999), 8–11.

26. Linda Schele and Mary Ellen Miller, *The Blood of Kings* (London: Thames & Hudson, 1992), 176.

27. Mary Miller and Simon Martin, *Courtly Art of the Ancient Maya* (New York: Thames & Hudson, 2004), 63.

Part Three

1. Marshall G. S. Hodgson, *The Venture of Islam* (Chicago: University of Chicago Press, 1974), 1:71.

2. Lynda Shaffer, "Southernization," *Journal of World History* 5, no. 1 (Spring 1994): 7.

Chapter 8

1. Somini Sengupta, "Sahara Journal," *New York Times*, November 25, 2003.

2. Seneca the Younger, *Declamations*, vol. 1.

3. Liu Xinru, "Silks and Religion in Eurasia, A.D. 600–1200," *Journal of World History* 6, no. 1 (Spring 1995): 25–48.

4. Jerry Bentley, "Hemispheric Integration, 500–1500 C.E.," *Journal of World History* 9, no. 2 (Fall 1998): 241–44.

5. See Jerry Bentley, *Old World Encounters* (New York: Oxford University Press, 1993), 42–53, 69–84.

6. Liu Xinru, *The Silk Road* (Washington, D.C.: American Historical Association, 1998), 10.

7. See William H. McNeill, *Plagues and Peoples* (New York: Doubleday, 1977), chaps. 3, 4.

8. Boccaccio, *The Decameron*, translated by M. Rigg (London: David Campbell, 1921), 1:5–11.

9. Kenneth McPherson, *The Indian Ocean* (Oxford: Oxford University Press, 1993), 15.

10. Janet L. Abu-Lughod, *Before European Hegemony* (Oxford: Oxford University Press, 1989), 269.

11. Nigel D. Furlonge, "Revisiting the Zanj and Revisioning Revolt," *Negro History Bulletin* 62 (December 1999).

12. Patricia Risso, *Merchants and Faith: Muslim Commerce and Culture in the Indian Ocean* (Boulder, Colo.: Westview, 1995), 54.

13. McPherson, *The Indian Ocean*, 97.

14. Kenneth R. Hall, *Maritime Trade and State Development in Early Southeast Asia* (Honolulu: University of Hawaii Press, 1985), 101.

15. Lynda Norene Shaffer, *Maritime Southeast Asia to 1500* (Armonk, N.Y.: M. E. Sharpe, 1996), 37, 46.

16. M. C. Horton and T. R. Burton, "Indian Metalwork in East Africa: The Bronze Lion Statuette from Shanga," *Antiquities* 62 (1988): 22.

17. Ross Dunn, *The Adventures of Ibn Battuta* (Berkeley: University of California Press, 1986), 124.

18. Christopher Ehret, *The Civilizations of Africa* (Charlottesville: University of Virginia Press, 2002), 255.

19. Ibid., 227–32.

20. Nehemia Levtzion and Jay Spaulding, eds., *Medieval West Africa: Views from Arab Scholars and Merchants* (Princeton, N.J.: Marcus Wiener, 2003), 5.

21. Quoted in John Iliffe, *Africans: The History of a Continent* (Cambridge: Cambridge University Press, 1995), 75–76.

22. J. R. McNeill and William McNeill, *The Human Web* (New York: W. W. Norton, 2003), 160.

23. Lauren Ristvet, *In the Beginning* (New York: McGraw-Hill, 2007), 165.

24. Maria Rostworowski de Diez Canseco, *History of the Inca Realm* (Cambridge: Cambridge University Press, 1999), 209–12.

25. Michael Haederle, "Mystery of Ancient Pueblo Jars Is Solved," *New York Times*, February 4, 2009.

26. Anthony Andrews, "America's Ancient Mariners," *Natural History*, October 1991, 72–75.

27. Richard Blanton and Gary Feinman, "The Mesoamerican World System," *American Anthropologist* 86, no. 3 (September 1984): 677.

28. Li Rongxi (trans.), *A Biography of the Tripitaka Master of the Great Ci'en Monastery of the Great Tang Dynasty* (Berkeley: Numata Center for Buddhist Translation, 1995), 31.

29. For a brief account of Xuanzang's life and travels, see Stephen S. Gosch and Peter N. Stearns, *Premodern Travel in World History* (New York: Routledge, 2008), 75–101.

30. Craig Benjamin, "The Kushans in World History," *World History Bulletin*, XXV:1 (Spring 2009), 30.

31. Xinru Liu and Lynda N. Shaffer, *Connections across Eurasia* (Boston: McGraw-Hill, 2007), 56–63.

32. Quoted in David Christian, *Inner Eurasia from Prehistory to the Mongol Empire* (Oxford: Blackwell Publishers, 1998), 267.

33. Hans-Joachim Klimkeit, *Manichaean Art and Calligraphy* (Leiden: E. J. Brill, 1982), 38

34. Carter Findley, *The Turks in World History* (Oxford: Oxford University Press, 2005), 61–64.

35. Bahodir Sidikov, "Sufism and Shamanism" in Eva Fridman and Mariko Walter (eds), *Shamanism* (ABC-Clio, 2004), 241.

Chapter 9

1. *The Guardian*, June 15, 2006.

2. John K. Fairbank, ed., *The Chinese World Order* (Cambridge, Mass.: Harvard University Press, 1968).

3. Quoted in Mark Elvin, *The Retreat of the Elephants* (New Haven: Yale University Press, 2004), chap. 1. The quote is on p. 19.

4. Mark Elvin, *The Pattern of the Chinese Past* (London: Eyre Methuen, 1973), 55.

5. Samuel Adshead, *T'ang China: The Rise of the East in World History* (New York: Palgrave, 2004), 30.

6. Elvin, *The Pattern of the Chinese Past*, part 2; William McNeill, *The Pursuit of Power* (Chicago: University of Chicago Press, 1984), 50.

7. See "The Attractions of the Capital," in *Chinese Civilization: A Sourcebook* edited by Patricia B. Ebrey (New York: Free Press, 1993), 178–85.

8. Marco Polo, "The Glories of Kinsay," *Medieval Sourcebook*, http://www.fordham.edu/halsall/source/polo-kinsay.html.

9. John K. Fairbank, *China: A New History* (Cambridge, Mass.: Harvard University Press, 1992), 89.

10. J. R. McNeill and William H. McNeill, *The Human Web* (New York: W. W. Norton, 2003), 123.

11. Francesca Bray, *Technology and Gender: Fabrics of Power in Late Imperial China* (Berkeley: University of California Press, 1997), 116.

12. Patricia Ebrey, *The Inner Quarters* (Berkeley: University of California Press, 1993), 207.

13. Ibid., 37–43.

14. Ibid., 6.

15. See Nicolas DiCosmo, *Ancient China and Its Enemies* (Cambridge: Cambridge University Press, 2002), chap. 6.

16. Ibid., 94.

17. Quoted in Thomas J. Barfield, "Steppe Empires, China, and the Silk Route," in *Nomads in the Sedentary World*, edited by Anatoly M. Khazanov and Andre Wink (Richmond: Kurzon Press, 2001), 237.

18. Quoted in Edward H. Shafer, *The Golden Peaches of Samarkand* (Berkeley: University of California Press, 1963), 28.

19. Susan Mann, "Women in East Asia," in *Women's History in Global Perspective*, edited by Bonnie Smith (Urbana: University of Illinois Press, 2005), 2:53–56.

20. Joseph Buttinger, *A Dragon Defiant: A Short History of Vietnam* (New York: Praeger, 1972), 32–34; Jerry Bentley, *Old World Encounters* (New York: Oxford University Press, 1993), 85–86.

21. Cited in "Trung Trac and Trung Nhi," http://www.viettouch .com/trungsis.

22. Liam C. Kelley, *Beyond the Bronze Pillars: Envoy Poetry and the Sino-Vietnamese Relationship* (Honolulu: University of Hawai'i Press, 2005).

23. H. Paul Varley, "Japan, 550–838," in *Asia in Western and World History*, edited by Ainslee T. Embrey and Carol Gluck (Armonk, N.Y.: M. E. Sharpe, 1997), 353.

24. Quoted in McNeill, *The Pursuit of Power*, 40.

25. John K. Fairbank et al., *East Asia: Tradition and Transformation* (Boston: Houghton Mifflin, 1978), 353.

26. Arnold Pacey, *Technology in World Civilization* (Cambridge, Mass.: MIT Press, 1991), 50–53.

27. McNeill, *The Pursuit of Power*, 24–25.

28. Hugh Clark, "Muslims and Hindus in the Culture and Morphology of Quanzhou from the Tenth to the Thirteenth Century," *Journal of World History* 6, no. 1 (Spring 1995): 49–74.

29. Quoted in Arthur F. Wright, *Studies in Chinese Buddhism* (New Haven: Yale University Press, 1990), 16.

30. Arthur F. Wright, *Buddhism in Chinese History* (Stanford, Calif.: Stanford University Press, 1959), 36–39.

31. Quoted in Wright, *Buddhism in Chinese History*, 67.

32. Quoted in Eric Zurcher, *The Buddhist Conquest of China* (Leiden: E. J. Brill, 1959), 1:262.

33. Jacquet Gernet, *A History of Chinese Civilization* (Cambridge: Cambridge University Press, 1996), 291–96.

34. Edwin O. Reischauer, *Ennin's Travels in T'ang China* (New York: Ronald Press, 1955), 221–24.

35. William Theodore de Bary et al., *Sources of Japanese Tradition* (New York: Columbia University Press, 2001), 1:42.

36. Kenneth Henshall, *A History of Japan* (New York: Palgrave Macmillan, 2004), 17.

37. Donald Keene, *Seeds in the Heart* (New York: Henry Holt, 1993), 477–78.

38. Quoted in China History Forum, http://www.chinahistoryforum.com/index.php ?showtopic=17789&st=30&start=30.

39. I Lo-fen, "Dialogue Between the 'Fatuous Emperor' and the 'Treacherous Minister': Song Hui Zong's 'Literary Gathering' Painting (Wen-Hui Tu) and Its Poetic Inscriptions," *Literature and Philosophy* 8 (June 2006): 253–78.

40. Quoted at Charles Hartman's site for SUNY–Albany students in his Chinese Painting course, http://www.albany .edu/faculty/hartman/eac280/25.html.

Chapter 10

1. "East and West Churches Reconcile," http://chi.gospelcom .net/DAILYF/2002/12/daily-12-07-2002.shtml.

2. Paul R. Spickard and Kevin M. Cragg, *A Global History of Christians* (Grand Rapids, Mich.: Baker Academic, 1994), chap. 6.

3. Leonora Neville, *Authority in Byzantine Provincial Society, 950–1100* (Cambridge: Cambridge University Press, 2004), 2.

4. Quoted in Deno John Geanakoplos, *Byzantium: Church, Society, and Civilization Seen through Contemporary Eyes* (Chicago: University of Chicago Press, 1984), 389.

5. Quoted in ibid., 143.

6. Quoted in A. A. Vasiliev, *History of the Byzantine Empire* (Madison: University of Wisconsin Press, 1978), 79–80.

7. Quoted in Geanakoplos, *Byzantium*, 362.

8. Quoted in ibid., 369.

9. Rowena Loverance, *Byzantium* (Cambridge, Mass.: Harvard University Press, 2004), 43.

10. Daniel H. Kaiser and Gary Marker, *Reinterpreting Russian History* (Oxford: Oxford University Press, 1994), 63–67.

11. Quoted in Patrick J. Geary, *Before France and Germany* (New York: Oxford University Press, 1988), 79.

12. Quoted in Stephen Williams, *Diocletian and the Roman Recovery* (London: Routledge, 1996), 218.

13. Peter Brown, *The Rise of Western Christendom* (London: Blackwell, 1996), 305.

14. Quoted in John M. Hobson, *The Eastern Origins of Western Civilization* (New York: Cambridge University Press, 2004), 113.

15. Clive Ponting, *A Green History of the World* (New York: St. Martin's, 1991), 121–23.

16. Christopher Tyerman, *Fighting for Christendom: Holy Wars and the Crusades* (Oxford: Oxford University Press, 2004), 16.

17. Edward Peters, "The Firanj Are Coming—Again," *Orbis* 48, no. 1 (Winter 2004), 3–17.

18. Quoted in Peter Stearns, *Western Civilization in World History* (New York: Routledge, 2003), 52.

19. Quoted in Jean Gimple, *The Medieval Machine* (New York: Holt, 1976), 178.

20. Quoted in Stuart B. Schwartz, ed., *Victors and Vanquished* (Boston: Bedford/St. Martins, 2000), 147.

21. Quoted in Carlo Cipolla, *Before the Industrial Revolution* (New York: Norton, 1976), 207.

22. Quoted in S. Lilley, *Men, Machines, and History* (New York: International, 1965), 62.

23. See Toby Huff, *The Rise of Early Modern Science* (Cambridge: Cambridge University Press, 1993).

24. Quoted in Edward Grant, *Science and Religion from Aristotle to Copernicus* (Westport, Conn.: Greenwood Press, 2004), 158.

25. Quoted in L. Thorndike, *A History of Magic and Experimental Science* (New York: Columbia University Press, 1923), 2:58.

26. Quoted in Edward Grant, *God and Reason in the Middle Ages* (Cambridge: Cambridge University Press, 2001), 70.

27. Grant, *Science and Religion*, 228–29.

28. Marcia L. Colish, *Medieval Foundations of the Western Intellectual Tradition* (New Haven: Yale University Press, 1997), 128.

29. Charles G. Herbermann, ed., *The Catholic Encyclopedia* (New York: The Encyclopedia Press, 1913), 7:668.

30. Simon Morsink, *The Power of Icons* (Ghent: Snoek, 2006), 12; Robin Cormack, *Icons* (London: The British Museum Press, 2007), 29.

Chapter 11

1. Al-Hajj Malik El-Shabazz (Malcolm X), "The Pilgrimage to Mecca," Islam Online, http://www.islamonline.net/English/hajj/2002/01/Experience/article2.shtml.

2. Reza Aslan, *No God but God* (New York: Random House, 2005), 14.

3. Quoted in Karen Armstrong, *A History of God* (New York: Ballantine Books, 1993), 146.

4. Quran 1:5.

5. Quran 3:110.

6. Quran 9:71.

7. "The Prophet's Farewell Sermon," Islam Online, http://www.islamonline.net/English/In_Depth/mohamed/1424/kharitah/article02.shtml.

8. Quoted in Patricia Crone, "The Rise of Islam in the World," in *Cambridge Illustrated History of the Islamic World*, edited by Francis Robinson (Cambridge: Cambridge University Press, 1996), 11.

9. Richard Bulliet, *Conversion to Islam in the Medieval Period* (Cambridge, Mass.: Harvard University Press, 1979), 33.

10. Nehemiah Levtzion, ed., *Conversion to Islam* (New York: Holmes and Meier, 1979), chap. 1.

11. Jerry Bentley, *Old World Encounters* (New York: Oxford University Press, 1993), 93.

12. Bernard Lewis, *Islam and the West* (New York: Oxford University Press, 1993), 157.

13. Quoted in Crone, "The Rise of Islam in the World," 14.

14. Quoted in Margaret Smith, *Readings from the Mystics of Islam* (London: Luzac, 1972), 11.

15. Aslan, *No God but God*, 201.

16. Quran 33:35.

17. Quran 4:34.

18. Quoted in Judith Tucker, "Gender and Islamic History," in *Islamic and European Expansion*, edited by Michael Adas (Philadelphia: Temple University Press, 1993), 46.

19. Nikki R. Keddie, "Women in the Middle East since the Rise of Islam," in *Women's History in Global Perspective*, edited by Bonnie G. Smith (Urbana: University of Illinois Press, 2005), 74–75.

20. Quoted in William T. de Bary, ed., *Sources of Indian Tradition* (New York: Columbia University Press, 1958), 2:355–57.

21. V. L. Menage, "The Islamization of Anatolia," in *Conversion to Islam*, edited by Nemehia Levtzion (New York: Holmes and Meier, 1979), chap. 4.

22. Ira M. Lapidus, *A History of Islamic Societies* (Cambridge: Cambridge University Press, 1988), 304–6.

23. Quoted in Keddie, "Women in the Middle East," 81.

24. Ross Dunn, *The Adventures of Ibn Battuta* (Berkeley: University of California Press, 1986), 300.

25. Jane I. Smith, "Islam and Christendom," in *The Oxford History of Islam*, edited by John L. Esposito (Oxford: Oxford University Press, 1999), 317–21.

26. Richard Eaton, "Islamic History as Global History," in *Islamic and European Expansion*, edited by Michael Adas (Philadelphia: Temple University Press, 1993), 12.

27. Francis Robinson, "Knowledge, Its Transmission and the Making of Muslim Societies," in *Cambridge Illustrated History of the Islamic World*, edited by Francis Robinson (Cambridge: Cambridge University Press, 1996), 230.

28. Janet L. Abu-Lughod, *Before European Hegemony* (Oxford: Oxford University Press, 1989), 216–24.

29. Andrew Watson, *Agricultural Innovation in the Early Islamic World* (Cambridge: Cambridge University Press, 1983); Michael Decker, "Plants and Progress: Rethinking the Islamic Agricultural Revolution," *Journal of World History* 20; no. 2 (June 2009): 187–206.

30. Arnold Pacey, *Technology in World History* (Cambridge, Mass.: MIT Press, 1991), 8, 74.

31. Robinson, "Knowledge, Its Transmission," 215.

32. Ahmad Dallal, "Science, Medicine, and Technology: The Making of a Scientific Culture," in *The Oxford History of Islam*, edited by John Esposito (Oxford: Oxford University Press, 1999), chap. 4.

33. David W. Tschanz, "The Arab Roots of European Medicine," *Aramco World*, May–June 1997, 20–31.

34. Bertold Spuler. *The Muslim World*, vol. 1, *The Age of the Caliph* (Leiden: E. J. Brill, 1960), 29.

35. Oleg Grabar, *Mostly Miniatures: An Introduction to Persian Painting* (Princeton: Princeton University Press, 2000), 2.

36. The commentary on both Visual Sources 11.1 and 11.2 draws on Oleg Grabar and Mika Natif, "Two Safavid

Paintings: An Essay in Interpretation," *Muqarnas* 18 (2001): 173–202.

Chapter 12

1. Jack Weatherford, *Genghis Khan and the Making of the Modern World* (New York: Crown, 2004), xv.

2. Data derived from Thomas J. Barfield, "Pastoral Nomadic Societies," in *Berkshire Encyclopedia of World History* (Great Barrington: Berkshire, 2005), 4:1432–37.

3. Giovanni Carpini, *The Story of the Mongols*, translated by Erik Hildinger (Boston: Braden, 1996), 54.

4. Quoted in Peter B. Golden, "Nomads and Sedentary Societies in Eurasia," in *Agricultural and Pastoral Societies in Ancient and Classical History*, edited by Michael Adas (Philadelphia: Temple University Press, 2001), 73.

5. Thomas J. Barfield, *The Nomadic Alternative* (Englewood Cliffs, N.J.: Prentice Hall, 1993), 12.

6. Anatoly Khazanov, "The Spread of World Religions in Medieval Nomadic Societies of the Eurasian Steppes," in *Nomadic Diplomacy, Destruction and Religion from the Pacific to the Adriatic*, edited by Michael Gervers and Wayne Schlepp (Toronto: Joint Center for Asia Pacific Studies, 1994), 11.

7. Quoted in Gregory Guzman, "Were the Barbarians a Negative or Positive Factor in Ancient and Medieval History?" *The Historian* 50 (August 1988): 558–72.

8. Carter Finley, *The Turks in World History* (Oxford: Oxford University Press, 2005), 28–37.

9. Ibid., 40.

10. Thomas Spear and Richard Waller, eds., *Being Maasai* (London: James Curry, 1993), 6, 12.

11. Richard Waller, ""Ecology, Migration, and Expansion in East Africa," *African Affairs* 84 (1985): 347–70; Thomas Spear, *Kenya's Past* (London: Longman, 1981), 107.

12. Godfrey Muriuki, *A History of the Kikuyu* (Nairobi: Oxford University Press, 1974), chap. 4.

13. David Christian, *A History of Russia, Central Asia, and Mongolia* (London: Blackwell, 1998), 1:385.

14. Quoted in ibid., 389.

15. David Morgan, *The Mongols* (Oxford: Blackwell, 1986), 63–67.

16. Weatherford, *Genghis Khan*, 86.

17. Chinggis Khan, "Letter to Changchun" in E. Bretschneider, *Mediaeval Researches from Eastern Asiatic Sources* (London: Kegan, Paul, Trench, Trübner, 1875), 37–39.

18. Thomas T. Allsen, *Mongol Imperialism* (Berkeley: University of California Press, 1987), 6.

19. Chinggis Khan, "Letter to Changchun."

20. Quoted in Weatherford, *Genghis Khan*, 111.

21. Barfield, *The Nomadic Alternative*, 166.

22. Peter Jackson, "The Mongols and the Faith of the Conquered," in *Mongols, Turks, and Others*, edited by Reuven Amitai and Michael Biran (Leiden: Brill, 2005), 262.

23. Quoted in Christian, *A History of Russia*, 425.

24. Quoted in David Morgan, *Medieval Persia* (London: Longman, 1988), 79.

25. Morgan, *Medieval Persia*, 82.

26. Charles J. Halperin, *Russia and the Golden Horde* (Bloomington: Indiana University Press, 1985), 126.

27. Charles H. Halperin, "Russia in the Mongol Empire in Comparative Perspective," *Harvard Journal of Asiatic Studies* 43, no. 1 (June 1983): 261.

28. Quoted in Kevin Reilly, ed., *Worlds of History* (Boston: Bedford, 2004), 1:420.

29. Thomas Allsen, *Culture and Conquest in Mongol Eurasia* (Cambridge: Cambridge University Press, 2001), 211.

30. Quoted in ibid., 121.

31. John Aberth, *From the Brink of the Apocalypse* (New York: Routledge, 2000), 122–131.

32. Quoted in John Aberth, *The Black Death: The Great Mortality of 1348–1350* (Boston: Bedford/St. Martin's, 2005), 84–85.

33. Michael Dols, *The Black Death in the Middle East* (Princeton: Princeton University Press, 1977), 212, 223.

34. Quoted in John Aberth, *A Knight at the Movies: Medieval History on Film* (New York: Routledge, 2003), 225.

35. Aberth, *The Black Death*, 72.

36. Quoted in Dols, *The Black Death in the Middle East*, 67.

37. Andre Gunder Frank, *ReOrient* (Berkeley: University of California Press, 1998), 256.

38. Arnold Pacey, *Technology in World Civilization* (Cambridge, Mass.: MIT Press, 1990), 62.

39. Quoted in Golden, "Nomads and Sedentary Societies," 72–73.

40. Quoted in Guzman, "Were the Barbarians a Negative or Positive Factor?" 558–72.

41. Quoted in Barfield, *The Nomadic Alternative*, 3.

42. Quoted in Aberth, *The Black Death*, 99

43. Quoted in David Herlihy, *The Black Death and the Transformation of the West* (Cambridge: Harvard University Press, 1997), 65.

44. Quoted in ibid., 62.

45. Quoted in Aberth, *The Black Death*, 79.

46. Quoted in ibid., 174.

47. "Lübeck's Dance of Death," http://www.dodedans.com/Etext2.htm.

48. Quoted in Norman Cantor, *In the Wake of the Plague* (New York: The Free Press, 2001), 6.

49. Quoted in Aberth, *The Black Death*, 73–74.

Chapter 13

1. Brian Fagan, *Ancient North America* (London: Thames and Hudson, 2005), 503.

2. Quoted in Charles C. Mann, *1491: New Revelations of the Americas before Columbus* (New York: Alfred A. Knopf, 2005), 334.

3. Louise Levanthes, *When China Ruled the Seas* (New York: Simon and Schuster, 1994), 175.

4. Niccolò Machiavelli, *The Prince* (New York: New American Library, 1952), 90, 94.

5. Frank Viviano, "China's Great Armada," *National Geographic*, July 2005, 34.

6. Quoted in John J. Saunders, ed., *The Muslim World on the Eve of Europe's Expansion* (Englewood Cliffs, N.J.: Prentice Hall, 1966), 41–43.

7. Leo Africanus, *History and Description of Africa* (London: Hakluyt Society, 1896), 824–25.

8. Quoted in Craig A. Lockhard, *Southeast Asia in World History* (Oxford: Oxford University Press, 2009), 67.

9. Quoted in Patricia Risso, *Merchants and Faith* (Boulder, Colo.: Westview Press, 1995), 49.

10. Quoted in Stuart B. Schwartz, ed., *Victors and Vanquished* (Boston: Bedford/St. Martin's, 2000), 8.

11. Quoted in Michael E. Smith, *The Aztecs* (London: Blackwell, 2003), 108.

12. Smith, *The Aztecs*, 220.

13. Miguel Leon-Portilla, *Aztec Thought and Culture*, translated from the Spanish by Jack Emory Davis (Norman: University of Oklahoma Press, 1963), 7; Miguel Leon-Portilla, *Fifteen Poets of the Aztec World* (Norman: University of Oklahoma Press, 1992), 80–81.

14. Terence N. D'Altroy, *The Incas* (London: Blackwell, 2002), chaps. 11, 12.

15. For a summary of this practice among the Aztecs and Incas, see Karen Vieira Powers, *Women in the Crucible of Conquest* (Albuquerque: University of New Mexico Press, 2005), chap. 1.

16. Ibid., 25.

17. Louise Burkhart, "Mexica Women on the Home Front," in *Indian Women of Early Mexico*, edited by Susan Schroeder et al. (Norman: University of Oklahoma Press, 1997), 25–54.

18. The "web" metaphor is derived from J. R. McNeill and William H. McNeill, *The Human Web* (New York: W. W. Norton, 2003).

19. Graph from David Christian, *Map of Time* (Berkeley: University of California Press, 2004), 343.

20. Andrew Spicer and Sarah Hamilton, eds., *Defining the Holy: Sacred Space in Medieval and Early Modern Europe* (Farnham, U.K.: Ashgate Publishing, 2006), Chap. 1.

21. Oleg Grabar, "The Umayyad Dome of the Rock in Jerusalem," in Eva R. Hoffman, ed., *Late Antique and Medieval Art of the Mediterranean World* (London: John Wiley and Sons, 2007), 166.

22. Ibid., 161.

23. Trudy Ring, ed., *International Dictionary of Historic Places*, vol. 4, *Middle East and Africa* (Chicago: Fitzroy Dearborn, 1994–96), 444.

24. Francisco Alvarez, *The Prester John of the Indies* (Cambridge: Hakluyt Society, 1961), 226.

Acknowledgments

Chapter 3

Benjamin R. Foster. "Come then, Enkidu, to ramparted Uruk." Excerpt (7 lines) from *The Epic of Gilgamesh*, translated by Benjamin R. Foster, p. 10. Tablet 1: 226–232. Copyright © 2001 by W.W. Norton & Company. Used by permission of W.W. Norton & Company, Inc.

Miriam Lichtheim. "Seven days to yesterday, I have not seen the 'sister.'" As appears in *Ancient Egyptian Literature*, volume 2, pp. 184–185 by Miriam Lichtheim, translator. Copyright © 1976 by University of California Press. Reproduced with permission of University of California Press, in the format Textbook via Copyright Clearance Center.

Miriam Lichtheim. "Now the scribe lands on the shore." From *Ancient Egyptian Literature*, volume 2, translated by Miriam Lichtheim, pp. 168–175. As appears in *A Book of Readings: the New Kingdom* by Miriam Lichtheim, translator. Copyright © 1976 by University of California Press. Reproduced with permission of University of California Press, in the format textbook via Copyright Clearance Center.

N. K. Sandars. "You will never find that life for which you are looking…." Excerpts from *The Epic of Gilgamesh*, translated with an introduction by N. K. Sandars (Penguin Classics 1960, Third Edition 1972). Copyright © N.K. Sandars, 1960, 1964, 1972. Reproduced by permission of Penguin Books, Ltd.

Miriam Lichtheim. "The gatekeeper comes out to you." From *Ancient Egyptian Literature*, volume 2, translated by Miriam Lichtheim, pp. 124–126. As appears in *A Book of Readings: the New Kingdom* by Miriam Lichtheim, translator. Copyright © 1976 by University of California Press. Reproduced with permission of University of California Press, in the format textbook via Copyright Clearance Center.

Samuel Kramer. "After your city had been destroyed, how now can you exist!" From *The Sumerians*, translated by Samuel Kramer, p. 142. Copyright © 1963 by University of Chicago Press. Used by permission of University of Chicago Press.

Samuel Kramer. "In those days the dwellings of Agade were filled with gold." Translated by Samuel Kramer. As appears in *Ancient Near Eastern Texts Relating to the Old Testament* by James Pritchard, ed., pp. 647–648. Copyright © 1969 Princeton University Press. Used by permission of Princeton University Press.

Chapter 5

Lao Tsu. "A small country has few people." From *Tao Te Ching* by Lau Tsu, translated by Gia-Fu Feng and Jane English, p. 80. Copyright © 1972 by Gia-Fu Feng and Jane English. Translation copyright © 1997 by Jane English. Used by permission of Alfred A. Knopf, a division of Random House, Inc.

Sappho. "If you will come, I shall put out new pillows for you to rest on." From *Sappho: A New Translation* by Mary Bernard, translator. Copyright © 1958 by University of California Press. Reproduced with permission of University of California Press, in the format Textbook via Copyright Clearance Center.

Ovid. "Add gifts of mind to bodily language…." From *The Art of Love and Other Poems*, translated by H. H. Mozley. Published by William Heinemann, 1929, pp. 73, 75.

Chapter 9

Yuan Chen. "Ever since the Western horsemen began raising smut and dust." Quoted in *The Golden Peaches of Samarkand: A Study of T'ang Exotics*, by Edward H. Shafer, translator. Copyright © 1963 by University of California Press. Reproduced by permission of University of California Press in the format Textbook via Copyright Clearance Center.

Chapter 11

Visual Source 11.1. Attributed to Mir Sayyid 'Ali, *Nomadic Encampment*, folio from a manuscript of the *Khamsa* (quintet) of Nizami, mid-16th century. Opaque watercolor, gold, and silver on paper, 28.4 x 20 cm. Harvard Art Museum, Arthur M. Sackler Museum, Gift of John Goelet, formerly in the collection of Louis J. Cartier, 1958.75. Photo: Katya Kallsen. © President and Fellows of Harvard College.

Visual Source 11.2. Attributed to Mir Sayyid 'Ali, *Nighttime in a Palace*, folio from a manuscript, c. 1539–1543. Opaque watercolor, gold, and silver on paper; 28.6 x 20 cm. Harvard Art Museum, Arthur M. Sackler Museum, Gift of John Goelet, formerly in the collection of Louis J. Cartier, 1958.76. Photo: Katya Kallsen. © President and Fellows of Harvard College.

Chapter 13

Miguel Leon-Portilla. "Like a painting, we will be erased." From *Fifteen Poets of the Aztec World* by Miguel Leon-Portilla, editor and translator. Copyright © 1992 by the University of Oklahoma Press, Norman. Reprinted by permission.

Index

Note: Names of individuals are in **boldface** and: (f) figures, including charts and graphs; (i) illustrations, including photographs and artifacts in the narrative portion of the book only, not in the docutext sections; (m) maps; (t) tables; (v) visual sources, including all illustrations in the docutext portion of the book; (d) documents in the docutext portion of the book

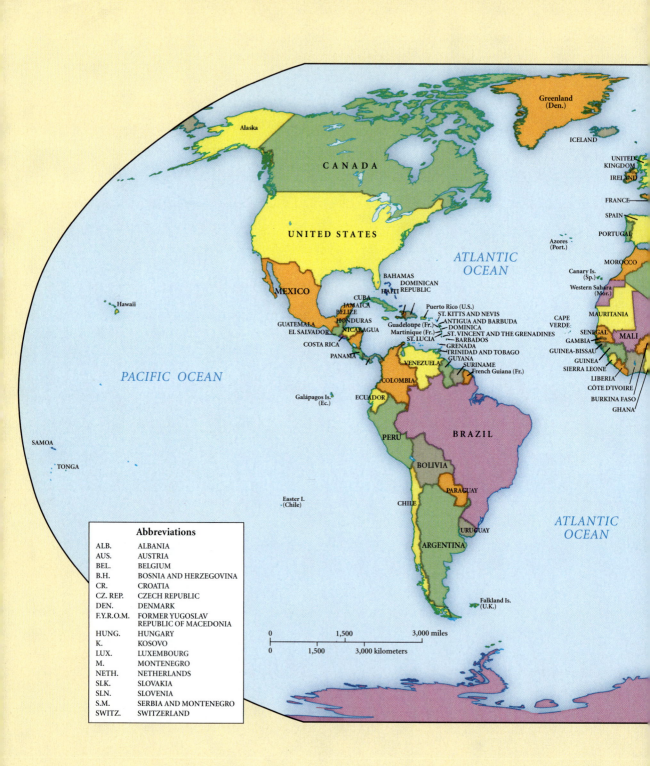

Alaska

Greenland
(Den.)

ICELAND

C A N A D A

UNITED
KINGDOM

IRELAND

FRANCE

SPAIN

Hawaii

UNITED STATES

ATLANTIC
OCEAN

PORTUGAL

Azores
(Port.)

MOROCCO

Canary Is.
(Sp.)

Western Sahara
(Mor.)

CAPE
VERDE

MAURITANIA

BAHAMAS
DOMINICAN
REPUBLIC

MEXICO

CUBA
JAMAICA
BELIZE
HONDURAS
GUATEMALA
EL SALVADOR   NICARAGUA

HAITI

Puerto Rico (U.S.)
ST. KITTS AND NEVIS
ANTIGUA AND BARBUDA
Guadeloupe (Fr.)   DOMINICA
Martinique (Fr.)   ST. VINCENT AND THE GRENADINES
ST. LUCIA   BARBADOS
GRENADA
TRINIDAD AND TOBAGO
GUYANA

SENEGAL
GAMBIA
GUINEA-BISSAU

MALI

GUINEA
SIERRA LEONE
LIBERIA
CÔTE D'IVOIRE
BURKINA FASO
GHANA

PACIFIC OCEAN

COSTA RICA

PANAMA

VENEZUELA

SURINAME
French Guiana (Fr.)

COLOMBIA

Galápagos Is.
(Ec.)

ECUADOR

PERU

SAMOA

TONGA

BRAZIL

BOLIVIA

PARAGUAY

Easter I.
(Chile)

CHILE

ATLANTIC
OCEAN

URUGUAY

ARGENTINA

Falkland Is.
(U.K.)

Abbreviations

ALB.	ALBANIA
AUS.	AUSTRIA
BEL.	BELGIUM
B.H.	BOSNIA AND HERZEGOVINA
CR.	CROATIA
CZ. REP.	CZECH REPUBLIC
DEN.	DENMARK
F.Y.R.O.M.	FORMER YUGOSLAV REPUBLIC OF MACEDONIA
HUNG.	HUNGARY
K.	KOSOVO
LUX.	LUXEMBOURG
M.	MONTENEGRO
NETH.	NETHERLANDS
SLK.	SLOVAKIA
SLN.	SLOVENIA
S.M.	SERBIA AND MONTENEGRO
SWITZ.	SWITZERLAND

0   1,500   3,000 miles

0   1,500   3,000 kilometers

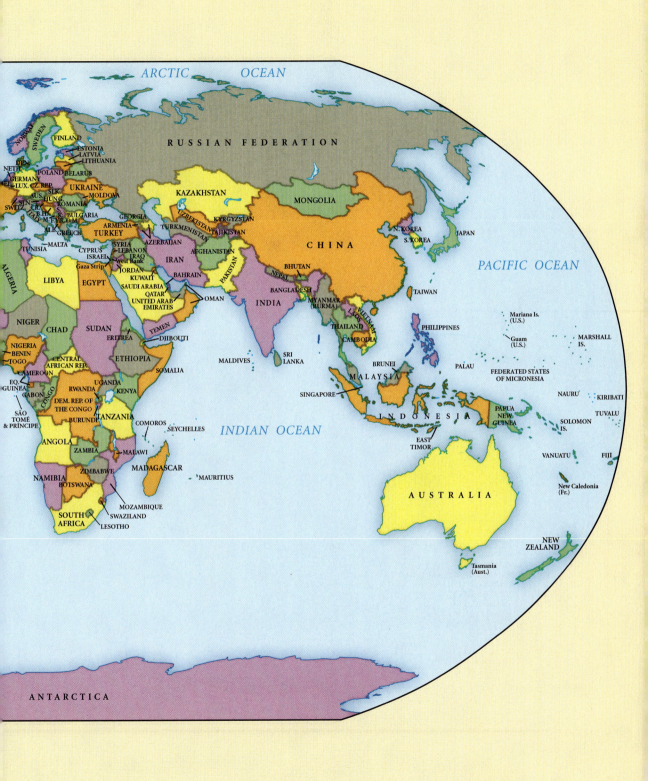

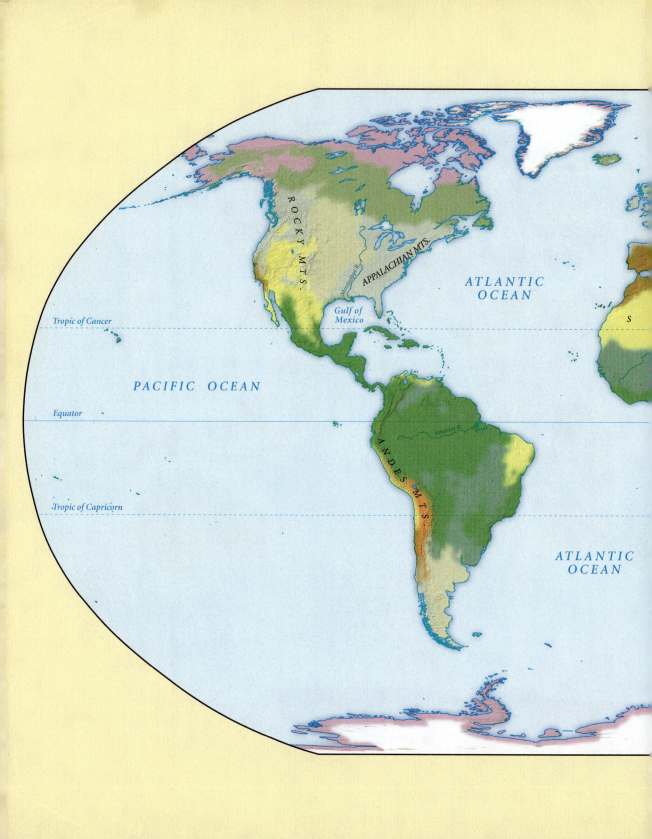

ROCKY MTS.

Mississippi R.

APPALACHIAN MTS.

ATLANTIC
OCEAN

Tropic of Cancer

Gulf of
Mexico

S

PACIFIC   OCEAN

Equator

Amazon R.

A N D E S   M T S.

Tropic of Capricorn

ATLANTIC
OCEAN

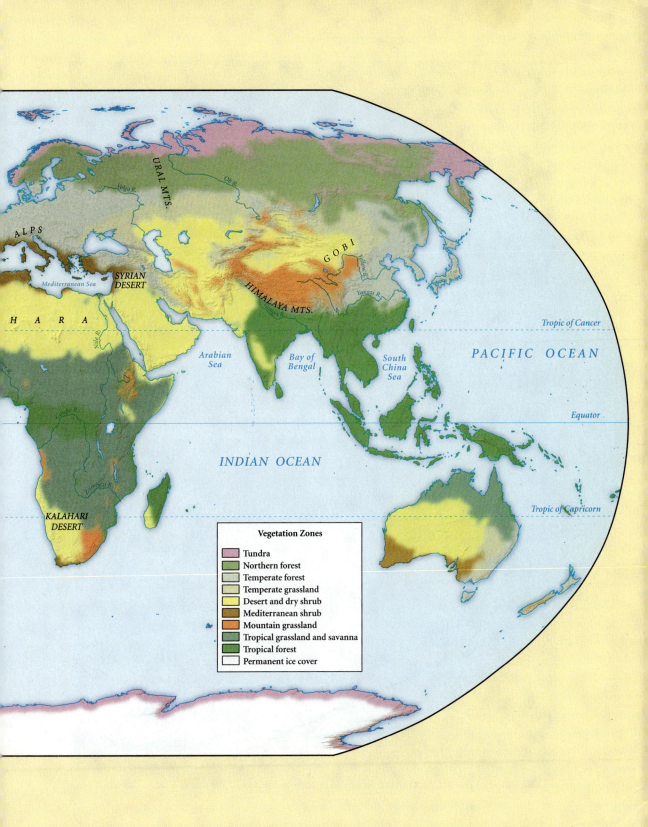

URAL MTS.

Ob R.

Volga R.

ALPS

Mediterranean Sea

SYRIAN
DESERT

G O B I

Yellow R.

HIMALAYA MTS.

Yangzi R.

H A R A

Nile R.

Tropic of Cancer

PACIFIC OCEAN

Arabian
Sea

Bay of
Bengal

South
China
Sea

Congo R.

Equator

INDIAN OCEAN

Zambezi R.

KALAHARI
DESERT

Tropic of Capricorn

Vegetation Zones

- Tundra
- Northern forest
- Temperate forest
- Temperate grassland
- Desert and dry shrub
- Mediterranean shrub
- Mountain grassland
- Tropical grassland and savanna
- Tropical forest
- Permanent ice cover

About the Author

Robert W. Strayer (Ph.D., University of Wisconsin) brings wide experience in world history to the writing of this text. His teaching career began with two years of high school instruction in Ethiopia as part of the Peace Corps. At the university level, he taught African, Soviet, and world history for many years at SUNY College at Brockport, where he received Chancellor's Awards for Excellence in Teaching and for Excellence in Scholarship. In 1998 he was visiting professor of world and Soviet history at the University of Canterbury in Christchurch, New Zealand. Since moving to California in 2002, he has taught world history at the University of California, Santa Cruz; California State University, Monterey Bay; and Cabrillo College. He is a long-time member of the World History Association and served on its Executive Committee.

His publications include *Kenya: Focus on Nationalism* (1975), *The Making of Mission Communities in East Africa* (1978), *The Making of the Modern World* (1988, 1995), *Why Did the Soviet Union Collapse?* (1998), and *The Communist Experiment* (2007). He has also published in a number of academic journals, including the *Journal of World History*.

"Strayer writes beautifully and clearly about complicated issues."

–Deborah Gerish, *Emporia State University*